엠브이피 보카

편입 VOCA 대표 수험서

MVP

Vol.1 워크북

김영편입 컨텐츠평가연구소 편저

김영편입

PREFACE

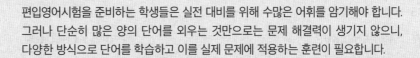

a smart and wise way to Memorize your Vocabulary Powerfully!

편입영어시험을 준비하는 학생들은 실전 대비를 위해 수많은 어휘를 암기해야 합니다. 그러나 단순히 많은 양의 단어를 외우는 것만으로는 문제 해결력이 생기지 않으니, 다양한 방식으로 단어를 학습하고 이를 실제 문제에 적용하는 훈련이 필요합니다.

"MVP 워크북"은 이러한 학생들의 고민을 덜어주기 위해 기획된 책으로, "MVP"의 DAY별 표제어를 바탕으로하여 DAILY CHECKUP을 제공합니다. "MVP"에서 외운 표제어의 뜻을 써보고, 20지 선택형 논리완성 문제를 통해 문장의 빈칸을 유추하고 단어의 쓰임을 확인할 수 있도록 했습니다. 그리고 각 표제어에 대한 동의어 암기를 빠르게 확인할 수 있도록 뜻이 다른 어휘 찾기 문제를 수록했습니다. 또한, 편입영어시험의 가장 대표적 유형인 동의어 문제를 수록하여 암기한 어휘를 실전문제에 적용하는 연습을 할 수 있도록 했으며, APPENDIX에는 관용어구의 쓰임을 응용한 생활영어 기출문제를 수록했습니다.

단순한 동의어 문제에서 벗어나 다양한 문제 유형을 통해 단어를 암기하는 학습법은 어휘 공부를 하는 학생들에게 큰 도움이 될 것입니다. 이제 "MVP 워크북"을 통해 자신의 어휘력을 한 단계 업그레이드 해보세요!

김영편입 단행본팀

CONTENTS

🔍 HOW TO STUDY

STEP 01

MVP 표제어와 관련된 동의어, 반의어, 파생어의 통합적 어휘 암기

0001 ★★★	vt. 몹시 싫어하다, 혐오하다 = abominate, detest, hate, loathe
abhor [æbhɔːr]	Most feminists **abhor** the thought of a woman being judged on her physical appearance. 대부분의 여권주의자들은 외모를 바탕으로 여성을 판단한다는 생각을 혐오한다. **MVP** abhorrence n. 몹시 싫어함, 혐오(= aversion, loathing) abhorrent a. 몹시 싫은, 혐오스러운

0002 ★★★	a. 불법의, 부정한; 불의의 = illegal, illegitimate, unlawful
illicit [ilísit]	The police are trying to stop the **illicit** sale of drugs. 경찰은 마약의 불법판매를 막는 데 노력하고 있다.

각 DAY별 표제어 50개와 동의어,
반의어, 파생어를 암기합니다.

각 DAY의 어휘 수준은 초급부터
고급까지 다양하므로, 빠른 학습을
위해 이미 알고 있는 단어는 건너뛰고
모르는 단어들을 중점적으로 외웁
니다.

STEP 02

MVP 표제어 뜻 쓰기

문제 풀이에 앞서 표제어 50개를 가볍게 확인할 수 있도록
구성했습니다.

표제어의 뜻을 빈칸에 써봄으로써 학습한 어휘의 암기
여부를 확인할 수 있습니다.

STEP

03 20지 선택형 논리완성

다시 한번 표제어를 학습하는 효과를 얻을 수 있도록 각 DAY별 표제어로 구성했습니다.

기출문제와의 연계성을 높이기 위해 이화여대 20지 선택형 논리완성과 같은 문제로 구성했습니다.

각 문제는 문맥상 빈칸에 들어갈 단어를 추론할 수 있는 문장들로 출제되었습니다.

STEP

04 뜻이 다른 어휘 찾기 문제

각 DAY별 10개의 문제가 있으며, MVP 표제어와 함께 제시된 동의어의 암기 여부를 빠르게 확인할 수 있는 문제들로 구성했습니다.

* STEP 01-04가 끝난 후 체크박스에 표시한 단어 및 틀린 문제의 단어를 개인 단어장에 정리하면서 다시 한 번 어휘를 암기합니다.

🔍 HOW TO STUDY

STEP
05
ACTUAL TEST & 정답

ACTUAL TEST는 5일 간의 표제어를 바탕으로 출제된 기출문제와 예상 문제로 구성됐습니다.

100문항에 제한시간 60분을 두어 빠른 속도로 문제를 풀 수 있도록 했습니다.

선택지의 단어 또한 주요 기출어휘로 구성되어 있으므로, 정답을 확인하며 암기가 미진한 단어의 경우 어휘 옆에 있는 체크박스에 표시를 해두고 다시 한번 단어장에 정리를 합니다.

STEP
06
APPENDIX 문제 & 정답

2012~2023학년도 중앙대에서 출제 됐던 관용어구의 쓰임을 응용한 생활 영어 유형 총 25문제를 수록했습니다.

각 대화문은 관용어의 쓰임을 응용한 생활영어 문제입니다.

학습플랜 체크 및 복습

학습 계획을 세우고 관리할 수 있는 기능을 제공합니다.

학습 진도를 체크하면서 빠진 부분이 없는지 꼼꼼히 확인하고, 틀렸던 단어나 어려웠던 단어를 주기적으로 반복 학습하여 영단어를 효율적으로 외울 수 있도록 합니다.

학습이 완료되면 좌측 체크박스(□)에 표기를 하여 진도를 확인합니다.

📋 학습플랜 다양한 문제를 통한 집중 반복 학습으로 영단어 암기 효과 극대화

	1일	2일	3일	4일	5일	주간 Review
1주	☐ MVP DAY 01 ☐ MVP 01 DAILY CHECKUP	☐ MVP DAY 02 ☐ MVP 02 DAILY CHECKUP	☐ MVP DAY 03 ☐ MVP 03 DAILY CHECKUP	☐ MVP DAY 04 ☐ MVP 04 DAILY CHECKUP	☐ MVP DAY 05 ☐ MVP 05 DAILY CHECKUP	☐ MVP DAY 01-05 ☐ MVP 01-05 ACTUAL TEST
2주	☐ MVP DAY 06 ☐ MVP 06 DAILY CHECKUP	☐ MVP DAY 07 ☐ MVP 07 DAILY CHECKUP	☐ MVP DAY 08 ☐ MVP 08 DAILY CHECKUP	☐ MVP DAY 09 ☐ MVP 09 DAILY CHECKUP	☐ MVP DAY 10 ☐ MVP 10 DAILY CHECKUP	☐ MVP DAY 06-10 ☐ MVP 06-10 ACTUAL TEST
3주	☐ MVP DAY 11 ☐ MVP 11 DAILY CHECKUP	☐ MVP DAY 12 ☐ MVP 12 DAILY CHECKUP	☐ MVP DAY 13 ☐ MVP 13 DAILY CHECKUP	☐ MVP DAY 14 ☐ MVP 14 DAILY CHECKUP	☐ MVP DAY 15 ☐ MVP 15 DAILY CHECKUP	☐ MVP DAY 11-15 ☐ MVP 11-15 ACTUAL TEST
4주	☐ MVP DAY 16 ☐ MVP 16 DAILY CHECKUP	☐ MVP DAY 17 ☐ MVP 17 DAILY CHECKUP	☐ MVP DAY 18 ☐ MVP 18 DAILY CHECKUP	☐ MVP DAY 19 ☐ MVP 19 DAILY CHECKUP	☐ MVP DAY 20 ☐ MVP 20 DAILY CHECKUP	☐ MVP DAY 16-20 ☐ MVP 16-20 ACTUAL TEST
5주	☐ MVP DAY 21 ☐ MVP 21 DAILY CHECKUP	☐ MVP DAY 22 ☐ MVP 22 DAILY CHECKUP	☐ MVP DAY 23 ☐ MVP 23 DAILY CHECKUP	☐ MVP DAY 24 ☐ MVP 24 DAILY CHECKUP	☐ MVP DAY 25 ☐ MVP 25 DAILY CHECKUP	☐ MVP DAY 21-25 ☐ MVP 21-25 ACTUAL TEST
6주	☐ MVP DAY 26 ☐ MVP 26 DAILY CHECKUP	☐ MVP DAY 27 ☐ MVP 27 DAILY CHECKUP	☐ MVP DAY 28 ☐ MVP 28 DAILY CHECKUP	☐ MVP DAY 29 ☐ MVP 29 DAILY CHECKUP	☐ MVP DAY 30 ☐ MVP 30 DAILY CHECKUP	☐ MVP DAY 26-30 ☐ MVP 26-30 ACTUAL TEST

어휘 암기와 문제 풀이를 통해 기본 어휘 실력을 높이는 **MVP 60일 완성 Study Planner**

	1일	2일	3일	4일	5일	주간 Review
7주	☐ MVP DAY **31** ☐ MVP **31** DAILY CHECKUP	☐ MVP DAY **32** ☐ MVP **32** DAILY CHECKUP	☐ MVP DAY **33** ☐ MVP **33** DAILY CHECKUP	☐ MVP DAY **34** ☐ MVP **34** DAILY CHECKUP	☐ MVP DAY **35** ☐ MVP **35** DAILY CHECKUP	☐ MVP DAY **31-35** ☐ MVP **31-35** ACTUAL TEST
8주	☐ MVP DAY **36** ☐ MVP **36** DAILY CHECKUP	☐ MVP DAY **37** ☐ MVP **37** DAILY CHECKUP	☐ MVP DAY **38** ☐ MVP **38** DAILY CHECKUP	☐ MVP DAY **39** ☐ MVP **39** DAILY CHECKUP	☐ MVP DAY **40** ☐ MVP **40** DAILY CHECKUP	☐ MVP DAY **36-40** ☐ MVP **36-40** ACTUAL TEST
9주	☐ MVP DAY **41** ☐ MVP **41** DAILY CHECKUP	☐ MVP DAY **42** ☐ MVP **42** DAILY CHECKUP	☐ MVP DAY **43** ☐ MVP **43** DAILY CHECKUP	☐ MVP DAY **44** ☐ MVP **44** DAILY CHECKUP	☐ MVP DAY **45** ☐ MVP **45** DAILY CHECKUP	☐ MVP DAY **41-45** ☐ MVP **41-45** ACTUAL TEST
10주	☐ MVP DAY **46** ☐ MVP **46** DAILY CHECKUP	☐ MVP DAY **47** ☐ MVP **47** DAILY CHECKUP	☐ MVP DAY **48** ☐ MVP **48** DAILY CHECKUP	☐ MVP DAY **49** ☐ MVP **49** DAILY CHECKUP	☐ MVP DAY **50** ☐ MVP **50** DAILY CHECKUP	☐ MVP DAY **46-50** ☐ MVP **46-50** ACTUAL TEST
11주	☐ MVP DAY **51** ☐ MVP **51** DAILY CHECKUP	☐ MVP DAY **52** ☐ MVP **52** DAILY CHECKUP	☐ MVP DAY **53** ☐ MVP **53** DAILY CHECKUP	☐ MVP DAY **54** ☐ MVP **54** DAILY CHECKUP	☐ MVP DAY **55** ☐ MVP **55** DAILY CHECKUP	☐ MVP DAY **51-55** ☐ MVP **51-55** ACTUAL TEST
12주	☐ MVP DAY **56** ☐ MVP **56** DAILY CHECKUP	☐ MVP DAY **57** ☐ MVP **57** DAILY CHECKUP	☐ MVP DAY **58** ☐ MVP **58** DAILY CHECKUP	☐ MVP DAY **59** ☐ MVP **59** DAILY CHECKUP	☐ MVP DAY **60** ☐ MVP **60** DAILY CHECKUP	☐ MVP DAY **56-60** ☐ MVP **56-60** ACTUAL TEST

MVP

Vol.1 워크북

01 ~ 60

DAILY CHECKUP
&
ACTUAL TEST

[1] Write the meaning of the following words.

☐ abhor	☐ insist
☐ illicit	☐ dogmatic
☐ plausible	☐ polemic
☐ differ	☐ exceed
☐ request	☐ amenable
☐ shallow	☐ nihilism
☐ pact	☐ homely
☐ adequate	☐ commit
☐ zeal	☐ bogus
☐ tacit	☐ transcribe
☐ settle	☐ lawsuit
☐ macabre	☐ endear
☐ hail	☐ deadlock
☐ ominous	☐ secede
☐ churlish	☐ elaborate
☐ react	☐ vanity
☐ similarity	☐ minimize
☐ imminent	☐ crestfallen
☐ memoir	☐ fabricate
☐ wander	☐ attitude
☐ pecuniary	☐ participate
☐ sacred	☐ brutal
☐ guile	☐ eclat
☐ famous	☐ admire
☐ calamity	☐ dialect

[2] Select <u>the most</u> appropriate word from the box below. Each word should be used only once.

① illicit	② sacred	③ crestfallen	④ dogmatic
⑤ shallow	⑥ fabricate	⑦ bogus	⑧ deadlock
⑨ minimize	⑩ pecuniary	⑪ homely	⑫ polemic
⑬ tacit	⑭ brutal	⑮ eclat	⑯ secede
⑰ amenable	⑱ dialect	⑲ guile	⑳ plausible

1 It's prohibited to kill endangered elephants, but many poachers still engage in the _____ ivory trade.

2 For humans to survive in the _____ winters of Siberia, one may think thorough preparations are necessary, but the Chukchi survive with only tents and blankets.

3 Acting like you have a job on Wall Street when you're actually unemployed would take a lot of _____.

4 While his pedigree is unquestionable, he is considered less _____ than his famously stubborn father.

5 The worst offense that can be committed by a(n) _____ is to stigmatize those who hold a contrary opinion as bad and immoral men.

6 Retail stores usually make a(n) _____ collusion with each other to keep prices high, but that silent agreement could break down in peak shopping demand periods.

7 "Comely" is the opposite of the similar-looking, "_____", which means "plain-looking, almost ugly."

8 The company hit a(n) _____ with the union's warning of full-swing strikes.

9 Russia's claim that they've destroyed more than 400 Ukrainian planes doesn't seem _____, given independent estimates of the Ukrainian fleet's size are at least half that number.

10 A(n) _____ personality is open to influence or control and is willing to agree or yield.

[3] Choose the one which is different from the others.

11 ① pact   ② deal   ③ treaty   ④ resolution

12 ① enough   ② adequate   ③ partial   ④ sufficient

13 ① rush   ② wander   ③ roam   ④ saunter

14 ① elaborate   ② docile   ③ delicate   ④ exquisite

15 ① vanity   ② conceit   ③ arrogance   ④ apathy

16 ① hate   ② detest   ③ abhor   ④ assimilate

17 ① sinister   ② eccentric   ③ portentous   ④ ominous

18 ① boorish   ② churlish   ③ rude   ④ attentive

19 ① wrath   ② zeal   ③ ardor   ④ enthusiasm

20 ① imminent   ② impending   ③ consecutive   ④ forthcoming

✓ Answers

1 ① | 멸종 위기에 처한 코끼리를 죽이는 것은 금지되어 있지만, 많은 밀렵꾼들은 여전히 불법 상아 거래를 하고 있다.

2 ⑭ | 인간이 혹독한 시베리아의 겨울에 살아남으려면 철저한 준비가 필요하다고 생각할 수도 있지만, 추크치(Chukchi)족은 오로지 천막과 담요만으로 살아간다.

3 ⑲ | 실제로는 실직 상태인데도 월스트리트에 직장이 있는 것처럼 행동하는 것은 많은 속임수가 필요할 것이다.

4 ④ | 그의 혈통은 의심의 여지가 없지만, 완고하기로 유명한 그의 아버지보다 덜 독단적으로 여겨진다.

5 ⑫ | 논객에 의해 저질러지는 최악의 모욕은 반대 의견을 가진 사람들을 나쁘고 부도덕한 사람으로 오명을 씌우는 것이다.

6 ⑬ | 소매점들은 보통 가격을 높게 유지하기 위해 암묵적인 담합을 하지만, 이러한 암묵적 합의는 판매 수요가 가장 높은 기간에는 깨질 수 있다.

7 ⑪ | comely(용모가 아름다운)는 비슷한 형태의 homely의 반대말로, homely는 '평범해 보이는', 대체로 '못생긴' 것을 의미한다.

8 ⑧ | 그 회사는 노조의 전면 파업 선언으로 교착상태에 봉착했다.

9 ⑳ | 400여 대의 우크라이나 전투기를 파괴했다는 러시아의 주장은 독자적인 우크라이나 함대 규모의 추정치가 적어도 그 수의 절반이라는 점을 고려할 때 타당해 보이지 않는다.

10 ⑰ | 순응하는 성격은 영향이나 통제에 개방적이며 기꺼이 찬성하거나 양보한다.

11 ④   **12** ③   **13** ①   **14** ②   **15** ④   **16** ④   **17** ②   **18** ④   **19** ①   **20** ③

[1] Write the meaning of the following words.

☐ yell	☐ measure
☐ laconic	☐ rhyme
☐ narrow	☐ shorten
☐ gracious	☐ iconoclastic
☐ pale	☐ probation
☐ telling	☐ bewitch
☐ machination	☐ competition
☐ dainty	☐ dignity
☐ scold	☐ miscellaneous
☐ boredom	☐ accidental
☐ earnest	☐ peruse
☐ theology	☐ cache
☐ vacillate	☐ abase
☐ piety	☐ efface
☐ climactic	☐ float
☐ savior	☐ ponderous
☐ rebellious	☐ aspiration
☐ hallucination	☐ certify
☐ aggravate	☐ hygienic
☐ unctuous	☐ spank
☐ intuition	☐ facade
☐ sagacious	☐ inquire
☐ denounce	☐ dolorous
☐ simultaneous	☐ offense
☐ adjustment	☐ embryo

[2] Select the most appropriate word from the box below. Each word should be used only once.

① rebellious	② gracious	③ dignity	④ boredom
⑤ laconic	⑥ inquire	⑦ denounce	⑧ peruse
⑨ float	⑩ narrow	⑪ earnest	⑫ measure
⑬ hygienic	⑭ bewitch	⑮ piety	⑯ probation
⑰ ponderous	⑱ iconoclastic	⑲ miscellaneous	⑳ unctuous

1   She was a(n) _____ poet who built her reputation on using words as sparingly as possible.

2   Politicians love to _____ the shady behavior of their opponents.

3   Sanitary products are often unaffordable or simply not available for many, so many rely on homemade alternatives that are not always _____.

4   He had a(n) _____ escape when a bus swerved past him on Oxford Street.

5   Some criminals are released from jail early and put on _____.

6   Nuns who pray all day long are famous for their _____.

7   A(n) _____ approach to art and music has given rise to the development of new genres and styles through breaking the rules.

8   The high level of buoyancy in the Dead Sea makes people _____.

9   Human Rights activists believe that everyone has the right to live with _____.

10   Sebastian was a(n) _____ child who often got into trouble and hung out with juvenile delinquents.

[3] Choose the one which is different from the others.

11 ① pallid ② pale ③ cruel ④ wan

12 ① aggravate ② worsen ③ exacerbate ④ alleviate

13 ① replace ② efface ③ erase ④ obliterate

14 ① appearance ② gist ③ facade ④ exterior

15 ① scold ② exonerate ③ reprimand ④ chide

16 ① judicious ② sagacious ③ discerning ④ ignorant

17 ① sanguine ② dolorous ③ grievous ④ sorrowful

18 ① oscillate ② waver ③ bicker ④ vacillate

19 ① resentment ② anger ③ offense ④ obedience

20 ① cache ② divulge ③ hide ④ conceal

✔ Answers

1 ⑤ │ 그녀는 가능한 한 단어를 아껴서 사용하여 명성을 쌓은 (문제가) 간결한 시인이었다.

2 ⑦ │ 정치인들은 상대편의 부정한 행동을 비난하는 것을 좋아한다.

3 ⑬ │ 위생용품은 종종 가격이 비싸거나 많은 사람들이 쉽게 구입할 수 없기 때문에, 많은 사람들은 항상 위생적이지 않은 손수 만든 대체품에 의존한다.

4 ⑩ │ 옥스퍼드 가에서 버스 한 대가 급커브를 틀며 그를 지나쳐 가서 그는 가까스로 위기를 모면했다.

5 ⑯ │ 일부 범죄자들은 조기 석방되어 보호관찰을 받는다.

6 ⑮ │ 하루 종일 기도하는 수녀들은 신앙심이 깊기로 유명하다.

7 ⑱ │ 예술과 음악에 대한 인습 타파적인 접근 방식은 규칙을 깨뜨리는 것을 통해 새로운 장르와 스타일의 발전을 가져왔다.

8 ⑨ │ 사해의 높은 부력은 사람들을 뜨게 한다.

9 ③ │ 인권 운동가들은 모든 사람이 존엄하게 살 권리가 있다고 믿는다.

10 ① │ 세바스찬(Sebastian)은 종종 문제를 일으키고 비행 청소년들과 어울리는 반항적인 아이였다.

- -

11 ③   **12** ④   **13** ①   **14** ②   **15** ②   **16** ④   **17** ①   **18** ③   **19** ④   **20** ②

[1] Write the meaning of the following words.

☐ cogent	☐ shabby
☐ earmark	☐ ennui
☐ pacific	☐ boorish
☐ sack	☐ adversary
☐ tactile	☐ damp
☐ jealous	☐ complain
☐ abandon	☐ sinecure
☐ factotum	☐ imperative
☐ mediate	☐ magnanimous
☐ wayward	☐ legerdemain
☐ thrift	☐ solidify
☐ diffuse	☐ ambivalent
☐ effeminate	☐ flagrant
☐ vane	☐ architect
☐ peep	☐ detail
☐ negotiation	☐ poignant
☐ scandalous	☐ decadence
☐ hype	☐ belie
☐ perspective	☐ respite
☐ realize	☐ hefty
☐ acerbic	☐ minority
☐ cease	☐ cabal
☐ sect	☐ inflict
☐ itinerary	☐ doctrine
☐ predicate	☐ outdistance

[2] Select <u>the most</u> appropriate word from the box below. Each word should be used only once.

① poignant	② diffused	③ magnanimous	④ wayward
⑤ earmark	⑥ sacked	⑦ adversary	⑧ sinecure
⑨ ambivalent	⑩ legerdemain	⑪ hype	⑫ inflict
⑬ peep	⑭ solidified	⑮ cease	⑯ complain
⑰ effeminate	⑱ hefty	⑲ decadence	⑳ abandon

1   The labor union decided to _____ the slowdown and return to normal work.

2   Conscription officials accused of taking bribes and smuggling people out of the country have been _____ in an anti-corruption purge.

3   Movie critics might describe a touching portrayal as _____ if there isn't a dry eye in the house.

4   The play is similarly _____: its path sometimes random, its chronology scrambled for no reason.

5   In response to the public backlash from Sweden's traditionally _____ immigration policies, the country implemented tighter asylum laws.

6   Regular exposure to loud music and noise can _____ permanent hearing damage.

7   Loving her parents one moment and hating them the next, Judy was confused by her _____ feelings toward them.

8   The death of a young Chinese man who said he was bullied for being too _____ has sparked discussions in the country about gender norms.

9   His status as a leading actor was _____ with subsequent hits.

10   Because he was the brother of the CEO, he was offered a(n) _____ in the company: he showed up each day and collected a paycheck, but others actually did his work.

[3] Choose the one which is different from the others.

11 ① austerity ② thrift ③ bounty ④ frugality

12 ① tidy ② shabby ③ ragged ④ worn-out

13 ① flagrant ② assiduous ③ atrocious ④ heinous

14 ① persuasive ② convincing ③ coincidental ④ cogent

15 ① plot ② intrigue ③ cacophony ④ cabal

16 ① deliberate ② mediate ③ arbitrate ④ intercede

17 ① doctrine ② creed ③ heterodoxy ④ tenet

18 ① tedium ② languor ③ ennui ④ pique

19 ① deceive ② mislead ③ belie ④ deploy

20 ① acrid ② bitter ③ tepid ④ acerbic

✓Answers

1 ⑮ | 노조는 태업을 중단하고 정상업무로 복귀하기로 결정했다.

2 ⑥ | 뇌물을 받고 사람들을 국외로 밀출국시킨 혐의로 기소된 징집 관리들이 반부패 척결로 해고되었다.

3 ① | 영화 평론가들은 감동적인 묘사도 극장 안에 있던 모든 사람들이 울었다면 가슴 아픈 묘사라고 설명할지도 모른다.

4 ④ | 그 연극도 비슷하게 제멋대로이다. 그 줄거리는 때때로 무작위적이고, 시간의 배열이 아무 이유 없이 뒤섞여 있다.

5 ③ | 전통적으로 관대한 스웨덴의 이민 정책에 대한 대중의 반발에 응하여, 그 나라는 더 엄격한 망명법을 시행했다.

6 ⑫ | 시끄러운 음악이나 소음에 정기적으로 노출되면 영구적인 청각 손상을 입을 수 있다.

7 ⑨ | 한 순간은 부모님을 사랑하고 다음 순간에는 미워하면서 주디(Judy)는 부모님에 대한 상반된 감정이 교차하는 것에 혼란스러워졌다.

8 ⑰ | 너무 여성스럽다는 이유로 괴롭힘을 당했다고 말한 젊은 중국 남성의 죽음은 중국에서 성 규범에 대한 논의를 촉발시켰다.

9 ⑭ | 주연 남자 배우로서 그의 위상은 연이은 후속작의 흥행성공으로 확고해졌다.

10 ⑧ | 그는 CEO의 동생이었기 때문에 회사에서 한직을 제공받았다. 그는 매일 출근해 월급을 받았지만, 다른 사람들이 실제로 그의 일을 했다.

11 ③ **12** ① **13** ② **14** ③ **15** ③ **16** ① **17** ③ **18** ④ **19** ④ **20** ③

☑ **DAILY CHECKUP**

[1] Write the meaning of the following words.

☐ facilitate		☐ camouflage
☐ salubrious		☐ illuminate
☐ quack		☐ abnegate
☐ hackneyed		☐ foliage
☐ thorough		☐ corpulent
☐ pant		☐ slacken
☐ veracious		☐ adolescence
☐ bilateral		☐ destruction
☐ emaciated		☐ agitate
☐ mushroom		☐ entity
☐ penchant		☐ generate
☐ scowl		☐ homonym
☐ ignoble		☐ procure
☐ undo		☐ discernible
☐ mellow		☐ impose
☐ sediment		☐ spontaneous
☐ consecutive		☐ anthropomorphic
☐ pitfall		☐ celebrate
☐ obdurate		☐ ramshackle
☐ elevate		☐ dominion
☐ accountable		☐ tamper
☐ shorthand		☐ lackadaisical
☐ dabble		☐ backbite
☐ plebeian		☐ magnitude
☐ nascent		☐ refuse

[2] Select <u>the most</u> appropriate word from the box below. Each word should be used only once.

① camouflage	② veracious	③ imposing	④ ramshackle
⑤ emaciated	⑥ refuse	⑦ plebeians	⑧ salubrious
⑨ pitfalls	⑩ slackening	⑪ obdurate	⑫ abnegate
⑬ hackneyed	⑭ entities	⑮ undo	⑯ elevated
⑰ dabble	⑱ illuminated	⑲ corpulent	⑳ tamper

1   The success of anti-pollution measures means that demand for thermal coal, as used in power stations, is _____.

2   The vaccine phobics _____ to have his or her kids vaccinated.

3   If you want to major in English, but your parents are _____ that you should go premed, they might go so far as to threaten not to pay your tuition.

4   Some wing colors help a moth _____ itself more effectively, be eaten less often by predators, and survive longer than moths of other colors.

5   Since the actor who played the lead was somewhat _____, the property manager had to let out the costumes and have the furniture used in the production reinforced.

6   Manatee rehabilitation centers have been overloaded with _____ animals, and officials are struggling to find new places to care for sick animals.

7   Saudi Arabia wants oil prices to stay _____ to make sure it has a steady stream of income while it tries to diversify its economy.

8   A drunken driver paid off the police to _____ with his traffic accident records.

9   After the Conflict of the Orders, many _____ became wealthy and powerful, while certain patrician families saw their fortunes decline and disappeared from history.

10   If a person keeps his words even in small things, if he can do what he says he will do, and lastly, if he can admit mistakes and apologize, then we can call him a(n) _____ person.

[3] Choose the one which is different from the others.

11 ① accountable   ② potential   ③ responsible   ④ liable

12 ① functional   ② discernible   ③ apparent   ④ recognizable

13 ① bilateral   ② mutual   ③ reciprocal   ④ intermittent

14 ① languid   ② lackadaisical   ③ lively   ④ lethargic

15 ① facilitate   ② expedite   ③ promote   ④ impede

16 ① disposition   ② qualm   ③ penchant   ④ liking

17 ① forthright   ② ignoble   ③ despicable   ④ mean

18 ① nascent   ② embryonic   ③ solitary   ④ incipient

19 ① amiable   ② mellow   ③ callow   ④ clement

20 ① cherish   ② defame   ③ slander   ④ backbite

☑ DAILY CHECKUP

[1] Write the meaning of the following words.

☐ definite	☐ fumble
☐ timid	☐ improvement
☐ malefactor	☐ egalitarian
☐ sapid	☐ sovereign
☐ vacuum	☐ pilgrim
☐ abbreviate	☐ chew
☐ capacious	☐ dastard
☐ racism	☐ plummet
☐ parch	☐ ingenuous
☐ nemesis	☐ mourn
☐ scoff	☐ porous
☐ impassive	☐ tendency
☐ analyze	☐ adjacent
☐ semblance	☐ obligatory
☐ fastidious	☐ languish
☐ weary	☐ gadget
☐ recuperate	☐ cripple
☐ perennial	☐ euphony
☐ shrewd	☐ diligent
☐ bounty	☐ befall
☐ utter	☐ habitual
☐ siesta	☐ coincidence
☐ mendacious	☐ tear
☐ karma	☐ doom
☐ given	☐ hideous

[2] Select <u>the most</u> appropriate word from the box below. Each word should be used only once.

① shrewd	② mourn	③ malefactor	④ cripple
⑤ mendacious	⑥ weary	⑦ euphony	⑧ befall
⑨ pilgrim	⑩ habitual	⑪ fumble	⑫ timid
⑬ recuperate	⑭ doom	⑮ plummet	⑯ nemesis
⑰ scoff	⑱ egalitarian	⑲ capacious	⑳ porous

1   The salacious tabloid press routinely publishes the most malignantly _____ stories about celebrities.

2   The police spent seven months working on the case but were never able to determine the identity of the _____.

3   Despite her dull and sluggish style, she is a(n) _____ businesswoman who knows how to market her brand: herself.

4   If temperatures are high even at night, the body doesn't get a chance to _____, increasing the possibility of illnesses and higher medical bills.

5   The opposite of a(n) _____ system could be a fascist society or dictatorship.

6   The heroine of a popular novel is described as so _____ that she would faint at the sight of a mouse.

7   His long struggle with illness has left him _____ in both body and mind.

8   Granting clemency to offenders on national festivities is a universal phenomenon, but it is getting so frequent and _____ that it is hurting the law-abiding spirit of the people.

9   Safety questions arose about an experimental drug used to treat a deadly disease, causing stock of the drug's maker to _____.

10   North Koreans who flee to South Korea — an estimated 30,000 since the end of the 1950-53 Korean War — have mostly used the more _____ border between North Korea and China.

[3] Choose the one which is different from the others.

11	① fussy	② meticulous	③ submissive	④ fastidious
12	① impassive	② susceptible	③ stolid	④ callous
13	① despise	② languish	③ weaken	④ wither
14	① obligatory	② compulsory	③ mandatory	④ voluntary
15	① shorten	② abbreviate	③ abridge	④ amplify
16	① sluggish	② diligent	③ assiduous	④ industrious
17	① appearance	② component	③ guise	④ semblance
18	① ephemeral	② continual	③ perennial	④ lasting
19	① sapid	② bland	③ savory	④ palatable
20	① hideous	② dreadful	③ frightful	④ acquiescent

✓ Answers

1 ⑤ | 그 선정적인 타블로이드 신문은 유명인사들에 대한 가장 심술궂은 거짓 이야기들을 정기적으로 게재한다.

2 ③ | 경찰은 그 사건을 수사하는 데 7개월을 보냈지만 범인의 신원을 밝혀낼 수 없었다.

3 ① | 둔하고 느린 스타일에도 불구하고, 그녀는 그녀의 브랜드인 자기 자신을 선전하는 법을 알고 있는 영리한 사업가이다.

4 ⑬ | 밤에도 기온이 높으면 몸이 회복할 기회를 얻지 못해 질병의 가능성이 높아지고 의료비도 증가한다.

5 ⑱ | 평등주의 체제의 반대는 파시스트 사회나 독재 정부가 될 수 있다.

6 ⑫ | 대중 소설의 여주인공은 너무 겁이 많은 것으로 묘사되어 그녀는 쥐를 보아도 기절할 것이다.

7 ⑥ | 그는 오랜 투병생활로 몸과 마음이 지쳤다.

8 ⑩ | 국가의 축제일에 범법자들을 사면해 주는 것은 보편적인 현상이지만, 이것이 너무 자주 습관적으로 이루어져서 국민들의 법 준수 정신을 해치고 있다.

9 ⑮ | 치명적인 질병을 치료하는 데 쓰이는 시약에 대한 안전 문제가 제기되면서 그 제약 회사의 주가가 폭락했다.

10 ⑳ | 1950-53년 한국전쟁이 끝난 이후 약 3만 명으로 추정되는 한국으로 피신한 북한 사람들은 주로 북한과 중국 사이의 더 구멍이 많은(허술한) 국경을 이용해왔다.

11 ③ **12** ② **13** ① **14** ④ **15** ④ **16** ① **17** ② **18** ① **19** ② **20** ④

[01-100] Choose the one that is closest in meaning to the underlined part.

01 He was slow and <u>fastidious</u> in composition, and the poem suffered from overelaboration.
① meticulous ② perfect
③ tenacious ④ fractious

02 No single sentence, however <u>cogent</u>, however full of meaning it may be, can do more than illustrate one aspect of a great central truth.
① concise ② convincing
③ confounding ④ controversial

03 In the study, the birds were allowed to <u>cache</u> two kinds of food: peanuts and wax-moth larvae, which they much prefer.
① hide ② taste
③ take ④ choose

04 It takes a long time to <u>efface</u> memories.
① erase ② convulse
③ edify ④ elude

05 Ms. Thomas was quoted as the most <u>sagacious</u> member of the committee.
① wise ② timid
③ attractive ④ flamboyant

06 This choice is particularly <u>poignant</u> because the film racializes the world of the matrix and the real world.
① sharp ② preposterous
③ significant ④ blended

07 This employee has no <u>discernible</u> skills in computer work now, but we may be able to teach her quickly.
① obvious ② diagnostic
③ careful ④ competent

08 The matches were <u>damp</u> and he couldn't make them strike.
① dank ② hot
③ cold ④ warm

09 Interest among new college freshmen in pursuing business careers continued to decline for the fourth <u>consecutive</u> year.
① straight ② leap
③ preceding ④ descending

10 Since 1830, suspended <u>sediment</u> in the river has risen continuously.
① ensilage ② deposition
③ embayment ④ dolmen

11 People sometimes tend to <u>backbite</u>, saying unkind things about others.
① reign ② writhe
③ dissemble ④ defame

12 Carl and Martin may inherit their grandmother's possessions when she dies. The thought <u>agitates</u> her.
① irritates ② scares
③ disturbs ④ confuses

13 Early in life children <u>spontaneously</u> acquire language, excluding exceptional circumstances.

① with great pleasure

② with much difficulty

③ without being forced

④ at an unbelievable speed

14 Although always genial and fair, he never attempted to make the students like him. He did not act as if he were a <u>perennial</u> contestant in a popularity contest.

① industrious

② willing

③ lasting

④ indulgent

15 The police working on the kidnapping case failed to identify the <u>malefactor</u>.

① insurgent

② dilettante

③ culprit

④ agitator

16 Writers of color and women increasingly responded to the <u>imperative</u> to speak for themselves and for others like themselves who had been silenced in history.

① purpose

② impact

③ comment

④ demand

17 The newspaper hasn't printed his letter, either because it is too <u>acerbic</u> or because it was submitted too soon after his previous one was printed.

① slovenly

② pungent

③ verbose

④ irrelevant

18 Chinua Achebe twice refused to accept Nigeria's National Honors on the grounds that the country's many problems still remain unsolved. This has only <u>solidified</u> his reputation as a man of ultimate principle.

① dissolved

② strengthened

③ embraced

④ paralyzed

19 Negotiators were called in to <u>mediate</u> between the two sides.

① interpose

② intercept

③ immediate

④ impose

20 Mohammadi Ashtiani told reporters that the Bild am Sonntag(BAS) journalists had "embarrassed" her, but refused to <u>elaborate</u>.

① explain

② give up

③ sue

④ criticize

21 His speeches were aimed at the <u>plebeian</u> minds and emotions.

① patrician

② common

③ lugubrious

④ cordial

22 In popular culture, <u>emaciated</u> fashion models are considered as standards of female beauty.

① corpulent

② lean

③ lucrative

④ charming

23 There is a certain knack or <u>legerdemain</u> in argument.

① trickery

② trend

③ glibness

④ logic

24 The discovery suggested that strong political action to halt production of chlorofluorocarbons might be <u>imminent</u>, and fortunately, the chemical industry no longer felt compelled to oppose such action.
① impending ② distant
③ delayed ④ avoidable

25 The notion that our lives should have some <u>semblance</u> of serenity seems to be taking hold.
① enmity ② assembly
③ ensemble ④ appearance

26 By the year 2000, that figure is likely to <u>exceed</u> 1.5 billion.
① be more than ② be less than
③ equal ④ approach

27 Training is the key to ensure that an individual has a good <u>perspective</u> of what is going on around him.
① conviction ② overview
③ interpretation ④ appreciation

28 His telling of the discovery of PAS reads more like a spiritual vision based on scientific <u>intuition</u>, rather than a methodical piece of inference.
① falsification ② hunch
③ reason ④ calculation

29 The look on her face was <u>a definite</u> sign that something was wrong.
① a careful ② an obvious
③ a minor ④ a vague

30 The news from the National Assembly may signal a kind of political <u>deadlock</u>.
① majority ② standstill
③ turning point ④ upgrade

31 The president publicly <u>denounced</u>, but privately celebrated, the illegal activities of the director of the Central Intelligence Agency.
① condemned ② depicted
③ acknowledged ④ humiliated

32 While the economy <u>plummeted</u> around him, business was booming for the company.
① established ② resumed
③ grew ④ declined

33 It's obvious that the cat has a <u>penchant</u> for sunny windows and tuna tidbits. He always leaps from the kitchen windowsill and runs into his dish when he smells fish.
① discipline
② definite liking
③ lack of appreciation
④ abhorrence

34 Writers often have as many concerns about expressing <u>ambivalence</u> as they do about expressing disagreement or agreement.
① indecision ② atrophy
③ apathy ④ cynicism

35 They have <u>languished</u> in filthy jails, suffering the abuse and brutality of the policemen.
① flourished ② declined
③ ameliorated ④ degraded

36 You'd have to be completely <u>ingenuous</u> to believe such a stupid story like that.
① guileless ② intrepid
③ unscientific ④ fanciful

37 People have adopted veganism for virtuous reasons, but <u>vanity</u> plays an undeniable role as well.
① conceit ② obesity
③ impulse ④ circumstance

38 If history is a guide, the worse Obama fares as commander in chief, the better he might shine as ex-commander in chief. "It may sound whimsical, but it's true," says historian Richard Norton Smith. An administration that ends badly creates an equal and opposite <u>zeal</u> for rehabilitating a legacy, says Smith.
① direction ② passion
③ requirement ④ tendency

39 Don't try to <u>impose</u> your wish on us.
① lift ② imply
③ change ④ force

40 Effective analysis and recognized techniques can <u>generate</u> a great improvement.
① carry on ② count on
③ come across ④ bring about

41 As for all those time-saving <u>gadgets</u>, many people grumble that these bits of wizardry chew up far too much of their days, whether they are moldering in traffic, navigating robotic voice-messaging systems or scything away at email.

① commodities ② gizmos
③ techniques ④ ganoids

42 What am I, a man who strives to embody healing, doing smoking cigarettes? This is <u>flagrant</u> hypocrisy!
① blatant ② contradictory
③ flaming ④ unethical

43 In criminal law, a fine is a <u>pecuniary</u> penalty imposed on an offender by a court.
① strict ② civil
③ monetary ④ discretionary

44 There is a well stocked CD library with audio-visual study courses in 22 languages at various levels and a very large collection of <u>miscellaneous</u> recordings in several languages, which includes literary, historical, political, and cultural material.
① rare ② sound
③ diverse ④ interesting

45 They may want to secure that this important document is not lightly <u>tampered</u> with, but solemnly, with due notice and deliberation, consciously amended.
① upgraded ② implied
③ interfered ④ guaranteed

46 Each of these subsystems has two <u>nascent</u> technologies in common.
① dawning ② confidential
③ expensive ④ dangerous

47 It is seldom acceptable to <u>abbreviate</u> words in formal writing.
① omit   ② explain
③ forge   ④ shorten

48 Lauren had a way of raising and turning her head which suggested not so much caution as a kind of <u>ceaseless</u>, nervous tension.
① serious   ② anxious
③ continuous   ④ emotional

49 His <u>wayward</u> behavior often confuses people when they are judging him.
① discursive   ② inquisitive
③ erratic   ④ prosaic

50 Unless we hold our elected representatives <u>accountable</u> for their actions, corruption in politics will continue.
① predictable   ② appropriate
③ responsible   ④ grateful

51 The museum for children was filled with <u>tactile</u> art: statues to climb and mobiles to twirl.
① sensible   ② touchable
③ flexible   ④ valuable

52 The night was made <u>hideous</u> by the sound of wolves howling at the door of the lodge.
① dreadful   ② painful
③ exciting   ④ amazing

53 Gallup polling in India reveals Indians are more <u>amenable</u> than hostile to closer ties with China, and see the country's growing influence as beneficial to India.

① visible   ② agreeable
③ feasible   ④ audible

54 The unanimous ruling was <u>hailed</u> by civil libertarians as a signal moment in the struggle for free speech.
① applauded   ② forestalled
③ repulsed   ④ overturned

55 The shy child's natural <u>timidity</u> had made her afraid to try out for the team.
① fearfulness   ② reverence
③ inclination   ④ impulse

56 The delegates hammered out an agreement — actually a bundle of <u>shrewd</u> compromises.
① practical   ② unfair
③ important   ④ clever

57 The opposition party argues the new measure will <u>aggravate</u> the already unstable national labor market and threaten the livelihood of workers.
① impede   ② prevent
③ destroy   ④ worsen

58 One reviewer wrote of her incomparable <u>calamity</u>: "You will find it hard to forget this material of human erosion."
① acuity   ② discernment
③ mishap   ④ prospect

59 A central <u>tenet</u> of our strategy is turning security responsibilities over to the Iraqi army.
① traitor   ② doctrine
③ figure   ④ core

60 Since the days of Vietnam and Watergate, journalists have become adversaries of the government.
① enemies   ② speakers
③ partners   ④ observers

61 The company's traditional reluctance to offer promotions has been turning away thrifty customers.
① prospective   ② frugal
③ scrupulous   ④ demanding

62 The artist's paintings often depicted scenes with a macabre tone, featuring eerie and unsettling imagery.
① stodgy   ② paranormal
③ riveting   ④ grisly

63 The Nobel Peace Prize he won the following year elevated his cause to the world, but it brought him no respite from Chinese authorities.
① respect   ② recognition
③ reprieve   ④ rejection

64 News on the internet is not so much fact but rather a flood of meaningless celebrity gossip and mendacious political propaganda.
① provocative   ② reasonable
③ aggressive   ④ deceitful

65 After the match, the coach reprimanded the players for their lackadaisical state of mind.
① tranquil   ② languid
③ vigilant   ④ attentive

66 The subject is far too important for us to engage in polemic.
① contention   ② chatter
③ scrutiny   ④ escapade

67 For some people at least, Brexit is now a pretext for simply standing back and smugly scoffing at the fate of the places where a majority of people voted for it.
① contemplating ② sneering at
③ noticing   ④ denouncing

68 We decided to negotiate with the taxi drivers to get a cheap ride to the town.
① discuss   ② nibble
③ inform   ④ agree

69 As a scholar, she had written many ponderous articles about English morals and manners, but she made her fortune as a best-selling novelist writing lightweight mysteries.
① intricate   ② dull
③ meticulous   ④ critical

70 The location was especially salubrious during the winter months.
① pleasant   ② frigid
③ variable   ④ inhospitable

71 By the time the receiving line had ended, the bride and groom's thanks sounded trite and tired.
① hackneyed   ② exhausted
③ vacant   ④ tepid

72 Most feminists abhor the thought of a woman being judged on her physical appearance.
① prefer   ② reconcile
③ hate   ④ imagine

73 His boorish behavior at the formal dinner made it clear that he lacked the proper etiquette for such occasions.
① unrefined   ② retentive
③ susceptible   ④ unilateral

74 The demand for the vote by American women was first formulated in earnest at the Seneca Falls Convention.
① seriously   ② originally
③ theoretically ④ primarily

75 Teachers tended to scold girls for shouting out answers, especially in math and science classes.
① corrugate   ② consort
③ chide   ④ cinch

76 The Southern states seceded from the Union in 1860.
① benefited from
② withdrew from
③ terminated
④ discriminated against

77 Because the rest of the snake is well camouflaged in dead leaves, the frog or lizard becomes prey when focusing its attention on the tail and mistaking it for something to eat.

① captivated by   ② cared for in
③ confident in   ④ concealed by

78 Two children answered the teacher's question simultaneously.
① respectively   ② in turn
③ immediately   ④ concurrently

79 A new civilization is always being made: the state of affairs that we enjoy today illustrates what happens to the aspirations of each age for a better one.
① suspicions   ② inspirations
③ articulations   ④ desires

80 There was a tacit agreement among survivors not to mention their traumatic experiences.
① expressed   ② implied
③ outspoken   ④ unanimous

81 The results may facilitate the optimum design and fabrication of the sensors needed for safe autonomous driving.
① go along with
② make easy
③ put into action
④ put in jeopardy

82 The tension between outer facade and inner conflicts is a central theme in literature and psychology.
① calmness   ② dimension
③ beauty   ④ appearance

83 A corpulent person is generally more susceptible to heart disease.

① A hazardous   ② A misguided

③ A boring   ④ An obese

84 Success can sometimes seem a distant dream, but he envisions himself dodging all pitfalls.

① queries   ② qualms

③ restraints   ④ perils

85 Huawei has long been accused of leaving secret vulnerabilities or "back doors" in its software and hardware that would permit illicit access to private data.

① illegal   ② imminent

③ irresponsible   ④ immediate

86 After signing the peace treaty, the two adjacent countries demilitarized their shared border.

① warring   ② neighboring

③ affiliated   ④ protracted

87 To achieve spiritual liberation, the hermit abandons earthly pleasures.

① postpones   ② curses

③ anticipates   ④ gives up

88 The island of Delos, sacred to the old Greeks, became a great slave-market.

① based on moral obligation

② treated with great reverence

③ very distinguished

④ introspected

89 The details of the dispute illuminate major hurdles that countries around the globe will face in eliminating coal from their energy mix.

① exclude   ② elucidate

③ disguise   ④ obfuscate

90 I sat in a small and not very sanitary cafe in Kwangju.

① quiet   ② bright

③ hygienic   ④ reasonable

91 All good parents should teach their children to chew properly before swallowing food.

① masticate   ② abacinate

③ fornicate   ④ impennate

92 The extent of capacity was to be negotiated in the bilateral agreement.

① active   ② multilateral

③ concentrated   ④ mutual

93 We are once again face to face with an obdurate opponent who has proved himself ready to sacrifice the lives of combatants and innocents alike to realize his odious goals.

① obsequious   ② unyielding

③ insidious   ④ uncanny

94 His car broke down, so he has a plausible explanation as to why he is late.

① urgent   ② modest

③ impolite   ④ reasonable

95 He sings the praises of his people, damns their indolence, and <u>mourns</u> their sorrows.

① expresses   ② accepts

③ laments   ④ glorifies

96 In Hemingway's novels which have been highly acclaimed for his simple and artless style, the idea of nature as a place in which men could <u>recuperate</u> things is a recurring motif.

① revere   ② revolve

③ retract   ④ recover

97 Snow White's decision to barge into the Seven Dwarfs' home without invitation <u>belied</u> her gentle nature.

① degraded   ② contradicted

③ manifested   ④ presaged

98 The American Indians have been depicted as <u>impassive</u> people, undemonstrative and stoical.

① disruptive   ② reserved

③ ruthless   ④ belligerent

99 The waste ground next to the theater has been <u>earmarked</u> for office development.

① embarked   ② pinpointed

③ allocated   ④ replaced

100 Not many groups became universally recognizable during the twentieth century, and those that did often had <u>ominous</u> overtones, such as the Mafia.

① threatening   ② enhancing

③ restraining   ④ disturbing

☑ DAILY CHECKUP

[1] Write the meaning of the following words.

☐ vacant	☐ discordant
☐ acme	☐ prospect
☐ indicate	☐ champion
☐ palatable	☐ altar
☐ jam	☐ slender
☐ radical	☐ engage
☐ ban	☐ illustrious
☐ eccentric	☐ label
☐ salvation	☐ beforehand
☐ reprieve	☐ odious
☐ prevalent	☐ necessity
☐ monograph	☐ tarnish
☐ sensual	☐ clairvoyant
☐ debacle	☐ irrigate
☐ organization	☐ mercenary
☐ undulate	☐ torpor
☐ adept	☐ lure
☐ equality	☐ abate
☐ disapprove	☐ gaffe
☐ maintain	☐ sweep
☐ cadence	☐ haggard
☐ factitious	☐ dowry
☐ pique	☐ allege
☐ hierarchy	☐ foible
☐ shortchange	☐ commandeer

[2] Select <u>the most</u> appropriate word from the box below. Each word should be used only once.

① vacant	② swept	③ illustrious	④ palatable
⑤ alleged	⑥ gaffes	⑦ reprieve	⑧ haggard
⑨ odious	⑩ sensual	⑪ radicals	⑫ prospects
⑬ debacle	⑭ clairvoyant	⑮ equality	⑯ undulate
⑰ commandeer	⑱ cadence	⑲ ban	⑳ tarnished

1   Additives like sugar and caramel are added to give the drink a more _____ flavour.

2   He is so _____ that he can literally see into the years ahead.

3   He won a brief _____ from prison life last spring when he was furloughed because of the coronavirus pandemic.

4   Reports of excess amounts of pesticide on some of its vegetables _____ the otherwise outstanding reputation of the produce company.

5   The collapse of the financial conglomerate was described as the greatest financial _____ in US history.

6   His eyes were sunken and his unshaved face was covered with the _____ beginnings of a beard.

7   Throughout history, there have been individuals known as _____ who have actively advocated for extreme changes in societal and political structures.

8   The underground parking space in my apartment complex is so limited that I can't find a(n) _____ parking space.

9   Nadal's achievement in reaching a 29th Grand Slam final comes only a few months after he thought a foot injury could end his _____ career.

10   The sanctions _____ the sale of any products excepting medical supplies and food.

[3] Choose the one which is different from the others.

11 ① pique   ② anger   ③ vexation   ④ contentment

12 ① lanky   ② slender   ③ sturdy   ④ lean

13 ① fault   ② defect   ③ foible   ④ allure

14 ① lucrative   ② widespread   ③ rampant   ④ prevalent

15 ① salvation   ② confinement   ③ deliverance   ④ redemption

16 ① inertia   ② levity   ③ torpor   ④ lethargy

17 ① acme   ② apex   ③ cluster   ④ zenith

18 ① esoteric   ② dissonant   ③ cacophonous   ④ discordant

19 ① abate   ② dwindle   ③ slacken   ④ detest

20 ① artificial   ② cautionary   ③ unnatural   ④ factitious

✔ Answers

1 ④ | 설탕과 캐러멜과 같은 첨가물은 음료에 더 맛있는 풍미를 주기 위해 첨가된다.

2 ⑭ | 그는 예지력이 뛰어나 말 그대로 여러 해 앞을 내다볼 수 있다.

3 ⑦ | 그는 코로나바이러스 팬데믹으로 인해 일시 출소를 허가받았던 지난봄 감옥 생활을 잠시 유예받았다.

4 ⑳ | 일부 채소들에 과도한 양의 살충제가 사용되었다는 보고는 보고되지 않았다면 훌륭했을 그 농산물 회사의 명성을 손상시켰다.

5 ⑬ | 그 복합금융기업의 파산은 미국 역사상 가장 큰 재정적 재난으로 묘사되었다.

6 ⑧ | 그의 눈은 움푹 들어가 있었고 면도하지 않은 얼굴은 갓 자란 초췌한 턱수염으로 덮여 있었다.

7 ⑪ | 역사적으로 사회와 정치 구조의 극단적 변화를 적극적으로 주장해 온 급진주의자들이 있었다.

8 ① | 우리 아파트 단지 내의 지하 주차장은 너무 협소해서 빈 주차 공간을 찾을 수가 없다.

9 ③ | 29번째 그랜드 슬램 결승전에 진출한 나달(Nadal)의 위업은 그가 발 부상으로 그의 화려한 경력이 끝날 수도 있다고 생각한 지 불과 몇 달 만에 이루어졌다.

10 ⑲ | 그 제재는 의약품과 식품을 제외하고는 어떤 물품의 판매도 금한다.

11 ④   **12** ③   **13** ④   **14** ①   **15** ②   **16** ②   **17** ③   **18** ①   **19** ④   **20** ②

☑ DAILY CHECKUP

[1] Write the meaning of the following words.

generous	implore
rampant	feature
accentuate	thorny
elegy	border
magnificent	specify
henceforth	debris
taboo	endue
saline	lethargic
palliative	obesity
cajole	incandescent
edible	fundamental
scrutinize	solecism
anecdote	abash
sloppy	charity
witness	discreet
identity	vitiate
bigoted	utility
sentient	ascetic
renovate	drawback
memento	lodge
negligible	coherent
dazzle	placebo
quadruple	mulct
plead	bliss
cronyism	prompt

[2] Select <u>the most</u> appropriate word from the box below. Each word should be used only once.

① ascetic	② vitiate	③ memento	④ palliative
⑤ taboo	⑥ coherent	⑦ incandescent	⑧ plead
⑨ cronyism	⑩ endue	⑪ mulct	⑫ lethargic
⑬ anecdote	⑭ bigoted	⑮ rampant	⑯ feature
⑰ edible	⑱ scrutinize	⑲ magnificent	⑳ dazzle

1   Her sister is extrovert and fun-loving, while she is _____ and strict.

2   A governor appointing his inexperienced daughter to an important staff position is one example of _____.

3   Thinking about philosophical questions can help us clarify our concepts and categories and make our worldview more _____.

4   Since no cure for the disease has yet been discovered, treatment is _____ at best.

5   After countless bribery scandals involving politicians, the public came to believe that corruption was _____ in their country's politics.

6   When you conduct scientific experiment, it's essential to carefully _____ the data to draw meaningful conclusions.

7   Being depressed makes him _____ and unable to get out of bed in the mornings.

8   The environmental law required new light bulbs to use 28% less power than existing _____ lights, essentially ending the sale of some older bulbs.

9   Certain insects are _____, which just means that you can consume them without getting sick.

10   As Chinese army incursions continue to recur, India has cautioned China that any disturbance of peace and tranquility in the border areas can _____ the overall atmosphere of bilateral ties.

[3] Choose the one which is different from the others.

11 ① discreet   ② defunct   ③ prudent   ④ considerate

12 ① sneer   ② implore   ③ beseech   ④ entreat

13 ① underscore   ② emphasize   ③ accentuate   ④ contradict

14 ① coax   ② galvanize   ③ wheedle   ④ cajole

15 ① imperative   ② insignificant   ③ negligible   ④ trivial

16 ① solecism   ② gaffe   ③ propriety   ④ faux pas

17 ① flaw   ② impetus   ③ drawback   ④ defect

18 ① prickly   ② thorny   ③ spiny   ④ hoary

19 ① sloppy   ② slipshod   ③ sullen   ④ slovenly

20 ① pliable   ② prompt   ③ expeditious   ④ immediate

✔ Answers

1 ① | 그녀의 여동생은 외향적이고 쾌락을 즐기지만, 그녀는 금욕적이고 엄격하다.

2 ⑨ | 주지사가 경험이 부족한 자기 딸을 중요한 참모직에 임명하는 것은 정실인사의 한 예이다.

3 ⑥ | 철학적 질문에 대해 생각하는 것은 우리의 개념과 범주를 명확히 하고 우리의 세계관을 더 일관되게 만드는 데 도움을 줄 수 있다.

4 ④ | 그 질병에 대한 치료법이 아직 발견되지 않았기 때문에, 현재의 치료는 기껏해야 병을 완화하는 정도이다.

5 ⑮ | 정치인들이 연루된 셀 수 없이 많은 뇌물 스캔들 이후에 대중은 부패행위가 나라의 정치에 만연해있다고 믿게 되었다.

6 ⑱ | 과학 실험을 할 때는 의미 있는 결론을 도출하기 위해 데이터를 면밀히 검사하는 것이 필수적이다.

7 ⑫ | 우울해지면 그는 무기력감에 빠져 아침에 일어날 수가 없다.

8 ⑦ | 그 환경법은 새로운 전구들이 기존의 백열등보다 28% 적은 전력을 사용하도록 요구했고, 본질적으로 오래된 전구의 판매를 중단하게 했다.

9 ⑰ | 어떤 곤충들은 먹을 수 있는데, 이것은 당신이 몸에 탈이 나지 않고 곤충을 먹을 수 있다는 것을 의미한다.

10 ② | 중국군의 침공이 계속 되풀이되자, 인도는 국경 지역에서의 그 어떤 평화와 평온의 교란도 양국 간의 전반적인 유대 관계를 해칠 수 있다고 중국에 경고했다.

11 ②   **12** ①   **13** ④   **14** ②   **15** ①   **16** ③   **17** ②   **18** ④   **19** ③   **20** ①

[1] Write the meaning of the following words.

☐ harmful	☐ coerce
☐ sanctuary	☐ retinue
☐ ebullient	☐ undaunted
☐ peccadillo	☐ bleach
☐ abut	☐ quest
☐ dilettante	☐ infest
☐ ransack	☐ satisfaction
☐ palpable	☐ appellation
☐ callow	☐ officiate
☐ embrace	☐ ingredient
☐ nadir	☐ snowball
☐ martinet	☐ commodity
☐ pinpoint	☐ abruptly
☐ bare	☐ plethora
☐ skim	☐ specious
☐ efficient	☐ fragrant
☐ lack	☐ genocide
☐ tentative	☐ vehement
☐ mitigate	☐ ordeal
☐ sensible	☐ confidential
☐ drizzle	☐ morale
☐ impeccable	☐ topple
☐ equation	☐ hiatus
☐ debilitate	☐ laboratory
☐ ambience	☐ blur

[2] Select <u>the most</u> appropriate word from the box below. Each word should be used only once.

① impeccable	② sanctuary	③ officiated	④ genocide
⑤ infest	⑥ confidential	⑦ coerce	⑧ hiatus
⑨ ransacked	⑩ toppled	⑪ bare	⑫ undaunted
⑬ harmful	⑭ nadir	⑮ embrace	⑯ quest
⑰ pinpoint	⑱ mitigate	⑲ blur	⑳ specious

1 The forbidding jungle can offer _____ to the guerrilla rebels.

2 Improved hygiene practices among wastewater users will _____ the risk of dermatological problems.

3 Some protesters raided military buildings and even _____ the home of the most senior military commander.

4 Government officials remain _____ at trying to encourage electric vehicle use, saying that even if only a small fraction of drivers switch to a plug-in car, the reduction in carbon emissions could be significant.

5 People can be taught to banish the unhelpful thoughts that lead to negative feelings and behaviour and to _____ positive, helpful thoughts.

6 The reasoning in this editorial is so _____ that we cannot see how anyone can be deceived by it.

7 Luxury is now defined by _____ craftsmanship and use of the best materials.

8 In the Rwandan _____ of 1994, members of one ethnic group, the Hutus, killed some 850,000 Tutsis in an attempt to wipe them out completely.

9 Since the Taliban _____ the Western-backed government nearly two years ago, the group has erased most obvious vestiges of the western-led nation building.

10 Alcoholics Anonymous takes its name from the fact that it's a(n) _____ group — people use only their first names and do not identify one another as members of the group.

[3] Choose the one which is different from the others.

11 ① ebullient   ② exuberant   ③ ephemeral   ④ enthusiastic

12 ① misdeed   ② ramification   ③ peccadillo   ④ slip

13 ① respite   ② hardship   ③ suffering   ④ ordeal

14 ① enfeeble   ② renounce   ③ debilitate   ④ enervate

15 ① palpable   ② obvious   ③ conspicuous   ④ copious

16 ① temporary   ② tentative   ③ versatile   ④ provisional

17 ① excess   ② plethora   ③ glut   ④ optimum

18 ① hilarious   ② vehement   ③ fervent   ④ fierce

19 ① odorous   ② fragrant   ③ redolent   ④ tranquil

20 ① suddenly   ② intricately   ③ abruptly   ④ unexpectedly

✓Answers

1 ② | 들어가기 어려운 정글은 게릴라 반군에게 은신처를 제공할 수 있다.

2 ⑱ | 폐수를 사용하는 사람들의 개선된 위생 습관은 피부 문제의 위험을 경감시켜 줄 것이다.

3 ⑨ | 일부 시위대는 군 건물을 습격하고 최고위 군사령관의 집을 약탈하기까지 했다.

4 ⑫ | 정부 관리들은 소수의 운전자들만이라도 플러그인 자동차로 전환한다면, 탄소배출량이 상당히 감소할 수 있다고 말하면서 전기차 사용을 장려하는 데 주저하지 않고 있다.

5 ⑮ | 사람들은 부정적 감정과 행동을 낳는 무용한 생각을 떨쳐 버리고, 긍정적이고 유용한 생각을 받아들이도록 가르쳐질 수 있다.

6 ⑳ | 이 사설 속의 추론은 너무 허울만 그럴듯해서 도대체 누가 여기에 속을 수 있을지 알 수가 없다.

7 ① | 명품은 이제 흠잡을 데 없는 장인 정신과 최고 재료의 사용으로 정의된다.

8 ④ | 1994년 르완다 대량 학살에서 후투족이라는 한 민족은 투치족을 완전히 말살하기 위해 85만여 명의 투치족을 죽였다.

9 ⑩ | 거의 2년 전 탈레반이 서방의 지원을 받는 정부를 무너뜨린 이후, 이 단체는 서방이 이끄는 국가 건설의 가장 명백한 흔적들을 지웠다.

10 ⑥ | 알코올 중독자 갱생회는 그것이 비밀 그룹이라는 사실, 즉 사람들이 성을 빼고 이름만 사용하고 그룹의 일원으로서 서로 신원을 확인하지 않는다는 사실에서 그 명칭을 따왔다.

11 ③   **12** ②   **13** ①   **14** ②   **15** ④   **16** ③   **17** ④   **18** ①   **19** ④   **20** ②

☑ DAILY CHECKUP

[1] Write the meaning of the following words.

☐ bizarre	☐ sangfroid
☐ trailblazer	☐ undercover
☐ messy	☐ physiognomy
☐ calibrate	☐ demote
☐ pandemonium	☐ heave
☐ rancid	☐ gaiety
☐ sequester	☐ colloquial
☐ opponent	☐ withhold
☐ expenditure	☐ allowance
☐ impart	☐ immense
☐ furious	☐ snap
☐ bode	☐ brim
☐ plastic	☐ dilatory
☐ motley	☐ cozy
☐ taciturn	☐ investigation
☐ embellish	☐ verbal
☐ sculpture	☐ jargon
☐ distraught	☐ arrogate
☐ reside	☐ manufacture
☐ laity	☐ duel
☐ sluggish	☐ vengeful
☐ pensive	☐ fidelity
☐ activate	☐ linger
☐ chivalry	☐ austerity
☐ everlasting	☐ spare

[2] Select <u>the most</u> appropriate word from the box below. Each word should be used only once.

① trailblazer	② opponent	③ chivalry	④ duel
⑤ bode	⑥ bizarre	⑦ heave	⑧ laity
⑨ taciturn	⑩ dilatory	⑪ embellishing	⑫ rancid
⑬ everlasting	⑭ demoted	⑮ withholding	⑯ messy
⑰ fidelity	⑱ motley	⑲ activate	⑳ colloquial

1 The chairman was so _____ that we often discovered that we had absolutely no idea what he was thinking.

2 Statistically, what happens on this superstitious day, Friday the 13th, is no more _____ than what goes on during any other day of the year.

3 Ending the regular season with a bitter 0-12 (0 wins and 12 losses) record, the head coach was _____ back to an assistant.

4 Known for their devotion, the dogs were often used as symbols of _____ in Medieval and Renaissance painting.

5 A Florida mother was arrested for child neglect last week after investigators found cockroaches, soiled mattresses and _____ food in her home.

6 If you are always late to appointments, people may accuse you of being _____.

7 The information found in the newspaper is expressed in a(n) _____ combination of colloquial, literary, technical, and scientific words.

8 The reduction of sales and increase of costs do not _____ well for the company's future.

9 He has admitted to _____ his résumé and to the fact that he did not graduate from any institution of higher education.

10 James DePreis, longtime music director of the Oregon Symphony, was a(n) _____; it would have been pioneering enough for him to be one of the few black conductors to lead major orchestras.

[3] Choose the one which is different from the others.

11	① pensive	② meditative	③ thoughtful	④ sensuous
12	① aplomb	② sangfroid	③ agitation	④ composure
13	① comfortable	② elegant	③ cozy	④ homely
14	① solitude	② vivacity	③ glee	④ gaiety
15	① covert	② winsome	③ undercover	④ clandestine
16	① furious	② enraged	③ angry	④ curious
17	① tantalize	② isolate	③ sequester	④ insulate
18	① gauge	② calibrate	③ fabricate	④ measure
19	① seize	② arrogate	③ usurp	④ abstain
20	① soothed	② distracted	③ agitated	④ distraught

✔ Answers

1 ⑨ ｜ 그 회장은 너무 말이 없어서 우리는 그가 무슨 생각을 하고 있는지 전혀 모르고 있다는 것을 종종 발견했다.

2 ⑥ ｜ 통계적으로 보면, 13일의 금요일이라는 이 미신적인 날에 일어나는 일도 연중 다른 그 어떤 날에 일어나는 일과 마찬가지로 기이하지 않다.

3 ⑭ ｜ 0승 12패라는 지독하게 나쁜 성적으로 정규시즌을 마감했기 때문에 감독은 다시 코치로 강등됐다.

4 ⑰ ｜ (주인에 대한) 헌신으로 잘 알려져 있었기 때문에, 개는 종종 중세와 르네상스 회화에서 충성의 상징으로 사용되었다.

5 ⑫ ｜ 플로리다주의 한 어머니는 지난주 조사관들이 그녀의 집에서 바퀴벌레, 더러워진 매트리스, 상한 음식을 발견한 후 아동 방임죄로 체포되었다.

6 ⑩ ｜ 당신이 항상 약속 시간에 늦는다면, 사람들은 당신이 꾸물거린다고 비난할지도 모른다.

7 ⑱ ｜ 신문에 나오는 정보는 구어체, 문학적, 기술적 그리고 과학적인 단어가 잡다하게 조합되어 표현된다.

8 ⑤ ｜ 판매 감소와 비용 증가는 회사 장래에 좋은 징조가 못 된다.

9 ⑪ ｜ 그는 자신의 이력서를 과장했다는 것과 자신이 어떤 고등 교육기관도 졸업하지 않았다는 사실을 인정했다.

10 ① ｜ 오랫동안 오리건 심포니의 음악 감독이었던 제임스 드프라이스(James DePreis)는 선구자였다. 그는 주요 오케스트라들을 이끄는 몇 안 되는 흑인 지휘자 중 한 명일 만큼 충분히 선구적이었을 것이다.

- -

11 ④   12 ③   13 ②   14 ①   15 ②   16 ④   17 ①   18 ③   19 ④   20 ①

[1] Write the meaning of the following words.

☐ temporary	☐ neologism
☐ abode	☐ social
☐ recalcitrant	☐ translate
☐ counterfeit	☐ wirepuller
☐ galvanize	☐ inspect
☐ onslaught	☐ slipshod
☐ impending	☐ heckle
☐ delinquent	☐ vacuous
☐ majesty	☐ mutiny
☐ adjourn	☐ debar
☐ emissary	☐ keen
☐ merciless	☐ shudder
☐ utmost	☐ carnage
☐ panacea	☐ poise
☐ channel	☐ intermingle
☐ raft	☐ annoyance
☐ eligible	☐ drowsy
☐ sacrilege	☐ freeze
☐ facetious	☐ lecherous
☐ pediatrician	☐ sprawl
☐ boost	☐ backbone
☐ analogous	☐ haphazard
☐ scare	☐ complicit
☐ excoriate	☐ disquisition
☐ phenomenal	☐ applaud

[2] Select <u>the most</u> appropriate word from the box below. Each word should be used only once.

① counterfeit	② majesty	③ recalcitrant	④ merciless
⑤ galvanize	⑥ delinquent	⑦ phenomenal	⑧ utmost
⑨ temporary	⑩ adjourned	⑪ excoriated	⑫ immense
⑬ complicity	⑭ heckle	⑮ backbone	⑯ carnage
⑰ boost	⑱ slipshod	⑲ applaud	⑳ keen

1 Writers are frequently referring to _____ Democrats and Republicans, since many people are stubbornly loyal to their political parties and unwilling to change.

2 When we visited Washington, D.C., Congress was not in session; it had _____ for the Thanksgiving weekend.

3 Government launched a major campaign to stamp out the production and distribution of _____ software.

4 Despite a plethora of Asian employees, the entire technology industry was roundly _____ for its stunning deficiency in racial diversity.

5 African heart-nosed bats can have such a(n) _____ sense of sound that they can hear the footsteps of a beetle walking on sand from six feet away.

6 Keith was guilty of _____ when he purposely left the computer store open so his friends could steal laptops.

7 Officials were fined or sentenced to short prison terms for allowing illegal design changes and _____ construction of the building.

8 Your impassioned speech might _____ the other members of the Ecology Club to start a school-wide recycling initiative.

9 The city defines a juvenile _____ as a child between the ages of 7 and 18 who committed an act that would qualify as a crime if committed by an adult.

10 "Oh my goodness! That's a tattoo," your mother might shriek. You might tell her not to worry, since it's only _____, and will wear off in a few days.

[3] Choose the one which is different from the others.

11	① impending	② forthcoming	③ imminent	④ remote
12	① blasphemy	② sacrilege	③ reverence	④ profanity
13	① loquacious	② lustful	③ lascivious	④ lecherous
14	① sleepy	② vigilant	③ drowsy	④ soporific
15	① mutiny	② insurrection	③ revolt	④ subservience
16	① onslaught	② assault	③ incursion	④ liaison
17	① scare	② assuage	③ frighten	④ startle
18	① solemn	② facetious	③ jocular	④ humorous
19	① vacuous	② empty	③ void	④ laden
20	① debar	② empower	③ forbid	④ prohibit

✓ Answers

1 ③ | 많은 사람들이 자신들이 소속된 정당에 완고하게 충성하고 변화를 꺼리기 때문에 작가들이 고집 센 민주당원과 공화당원을 언급하고 있을 때가 자주 있다.

2 ⑩ | 우리가 워싱턴DC를 방문했을 때, 의회는 개회 중이 아니었다. 의회는 추수감사절 주말을 위해 휴회를 했었다.

3 ① | 정부는 가짜 소프트웨어의 생산과 유통을 근절시키기 위해 대대적인 캠페인을 시작했다.

4 ⑪ | 수많은 아시아계 직원들이 있음에도 불구하고, 전체 기술 산업은 인종의 다양성이 놀라울 정도로 부족하다는 이유로 호되게 맹비난을 받았다.

5 ⑳ | 아프리카 하트코박쥐는 아주 예민한 청각을 가지고 있어서, 이 박쥐들은 6피트 떨어진 곳에서 모래 위를 걷는 딱정벌레의 발자국 소리를 들을 수 있다.

6 ⑬ | 키스(Keith)는 컴퓨터 가게의 문을 일부러 열어두어 그의 친구들이 노트북을 훔칠 수 있도록 한 공모의 죄를 범했다.

7 ⑱ | 공무원들은 불법적인 설계 변경과 건물의 날림 공사를 허용한 혐의로 벌금이나 단기 징역형을 선고받았다.

8 ⑤ | 당신의 열정적인 연설은 생태학 클럽의 다른 회원들이 학교 전체의 재활용 계획을 시작하도록 격려할지도 모른다.

9 ⑥ | 그 도시는 성인이 범하면 범죄에 해당할 행동을 저지른 7~18세 사이의 아동을 비행 청소년으로 정의한다.

10 ⑨ | "오 세상에! 그거 문신이구나"라고 어머니가 소리를 지르며 말할 수 있는데, 당신은 그 문신은 일시적일 뿐이고 며칠 안에 없어질 것이니까 걱정하지 말라고 말할 것이다.

11 ④   12 ③   13 ①   14 ②   15 ④   16 ④   17 ②   18 ①   19 ④   20 ②

[01-100] Choose the one that is closest in meaning to the underlined part.

01 So much time has passed. So many firsts. Yet the question lingers in my mind: I will always wonder if he would love me more if I had carried her. Would our bond be even tighter?
① strikes   ② remains
③ hides   ④ fades

02 At the COP24 climate talks, nations must agree to a rulebook palatable to all 183 states who have ratified the Paris deal.
① acceptable   ② sustainable
③ recoverable   ④ irrevocable

03 These should be understood if they are to be properly mitigated.
① alleviated   ② clarified
③ imposed   ④ discussed

04 We have no time to discuss such specious arguments.
① professional   ② diverse
③ aggressive   ④ misleading

05 They were a motley crowd of youths who flocked about him and helped him to create European philosophy.
① bloated   ② minuscule
③ variegated   ④ destitute

06 Insecurity, worry, and nervous breakdown are rampant among white-collar workers.
① gossiped   ② obstinate
③ prevalent   ④ troublesome

07 The governor has championed the movement to ratify the Equal Rights Amendment since taking office.
① patronized   ② repealed
③ monopolized   ④ defeated

08 She had impeccable taste in clothes.
① naive   ② horrible
③ peculiar   ④ excellent

09 One of the world's great wildlife sanctuaries is located near Chiang Mai.
① shelters   ② inhabitants
③ wastelands   ④ institutions

10 In modern writing, the distinction between literary expression and colloquial expression is often blurred.
① exaggerated   ② reversed
③ indistinct   ④ unintentional

11 If you allow them to transfer the money into your bank account, you will be eligible for ten percent of the fortune.
① responsible   ② entitled
③ guilty   ④ sufficient

12 My father was very <u>furious</u> when I told him that I had got fired from my school again.
① drowsy   ② sympathetic
③ surprised ④ angry

13 Her <u>ebullient</u> nature could not be repressed. She was always laughing and gay.
① exuberant   ② quixotic
③ placid   ④ incandescent

14 The late Chinese leader Deng Xiaoping ordered the violent 1989 Tiananmen Square crackdown out of fear that demonstrators could <u>topple</u> the communist party.
① overturn   ② defile
③ slander   ④ vilify

15 In 2009, an American toy company opened a huge store on the main shopping street in a major city in China, and the store <u>featured</u> the company's famous doll.
① created   ② liquidated
③ highlighted ④ distributed

16 In large part, Japan's lead in green-car technology is an outgrowth of its old <u>austerity</u>.
① ingenuity   ② convention
③ abstention   ④ tenacity

17 The strange men turned out to be <u>merciless</u> killers.
① compassionate ② lenient
③ relenting   ④ pitiless

18 He was pale and a bit <u>haggard</u> when he glanced around at the angry faces watching him.
① bold   ② gaunt
③ vigorous ④ daring

19 I think he is a pianist of absolutely <u>phenomenal</u> talent.
① secular   ② great
③ superficial ④ terrible

20 The second step was the legislation <u>promptly</u> and patriotically passed by Congress.
① quickly   ② unanimously
③ ideally   ④ definitely

21 If Blair's credibility is <u>tarnished</u>, it will lessen his influence in Europe.
① blemished   ② enhanced
③ questioned ④ shattered

22 Certain colors when incorporated into the decor of a room can produce a <u>cozy</u> atmosphere.
① light   ② roomy
③ cluttered ④ comfortable

23 By decorating their house with plastic beach balls and Popsicle sticks, the Flemmings created a playful <u>ambience</u> that delighted young children.
① oblivion   ② extravaganza
③ atmosphere ④ audacity

24 Language is only attending to its proper business when it comprehends a multitude of like things under the same appellation.
① label   ② view
③ apparatus   ④ condition

25 Students post ample contact information on their Facebook pages, which has me contemplate other uses, such as tracking down recalcitrant advisees and frequent absentees from my classes.
① contrite   ② frantic
③ grateful   ④ stubborn

26 Never eat wild mushrooms, even though they look edible. They may be poisonous.
① eatable   ② ripen
③ delicious   ④ blazing

27 The alcoholic singer's management team sequestered him in a rehab center while telling the public he was busy creating new songs.
① facilitated ② evicted
③ confined   ④ vested

28 The three-page letter to the editor excoriated the publication for printing the rumor without verifying the source.
① complimented ② denounced
③ accommodated ④ ratified

29 Many city dwellers are turning vacant lots into thriving gardens.
① small   ② shady
③ empty   ④ costly

30 Molly was so anxious not to be thought ascetic that she told the Hell's Angels she would love to spend the week with them in Las Vegas.
① prurient   ② preposterous
③ profligate   ④ puritanical

31 For decades, progress for civil rights groups was painfully slow. It took the words and actions of Dr. Martin Luther King Jr. to renew and galvanize the movement.
① relegate   ② energize
③ emancipate   ④ sanction

32 Dali's paintings can inspire a pensive mood.
① cheerful   ② depressed
③ thoughtful   ④ fresh

33 The phrase "Gangnam Style" is a Korean neologism that refers to a lifestyle associated with the Gangnam District of Seoul.
① simile   ② coinage
③ epigram   ④ shibboleth

34 Any pronouncement about educational technology needs to be scrutinized with great care to ascertain what part of the process is involved — the machinery, the software, or the methodology.
① utilized   ② selected
③ systemized   ④ examined

35 Sun Tzu told warriors over 2,000 years ago that "All warfare is deception," and "To subdue the enemy without fighting is the acme of skill."
① culmination   ② subjugation
③ qualification   ④ protestation

36 Several of the dunes in the desert are obviously factitious; if I were to dig for buried treasure, that is where I would start.
① clean   ② truthful
③ artificial ④ attractive

37 The project entailed a great expenditure of energy.
① expense   ② expertise
③ rationale   ④ exposure

38 All revolutions are at the same time expressions of sharp class contradictions and radical attempts to resolve those contradictions.
① practical   ② fundamental
③ conventional   ④ occasional

39 The court had to adjourn after rain started dripping from the ceiling.
① submerge   ② hasten
③ suspend   ④ renovate

40 Fair trade is certainly not a panacea, but it can facilitate regulated global exchanges and integration.
① challenge   ② implementation
③ mechanism   ④ solution

41 Their bizarre attitude ultimately prompted unexpected reactions.
① cruel   ② suspicious
③ crazy   ④ asserted

42 Labor is bought and sold like any other commodity.
① foundry   ② goods
③ subsidy   ④ embargo

43 He has spoken out against officials seeking to embellish their credentials through cooking up statistics.
① decorate   ② destroy
③ compile   ④ install

44 Colleges that pay for celebrity speakers say they can impress donors and pique the interest of potential students.
① tailor   ② fudge
③ smother   ④ incite

45 The 34-year-old midfielder, a World Cup winner in 1998, was playing in the final match of his illustrious career.
① insignificant   ② nasty
③ notorious   ④ remarkable

46 People expected Winston Churchill to take his painting lightly, but Churchill, no dilettante, regarded his artistic efforts most serious indeed.
① zealot   ② altruist
③ tyro   ④ renegade

47 Science probably has never demanded a more sweeping change in a traditional way of thinking about a subject, nor has there ever been a more important subject.
① overall   ② regional
③ smooth   ④ impressive

48 They showed themselves adept at many tricks for obtaining what they wanted.
① immature   ② impatient
③ earnest   ④ skillful

49 More than once he had hoped the fury of the blizzard might abate.
① adjourn   ② assent
③ loiter   ④ lessen

50 The package of butter we used to bake the cake must have been rancid.
① discolored   ② fresh
③ spoiled   ④ organic

51 While the woman enjoyed talking freely, her husband was a taciturn man who preferred to listen.
① disconcerted   ② undaunted
③ astounded   ④ reserved

52 Any bookkeeping system has certain drawbacks.
① features   ② disadvantages
③ versions   ④ withdrawals

53 He then repeated the solecism at his inauguration balls on Tuesday night, when the eyes of billions around the world were upon him.

① gaffe   ② harangue
③ disdain   ④ stalemate

54 Offices have been ransacked, company cars stolen, and communications systems destroyed.
① abandoned   ② repaired
③ painted   ④ robbed

55 Despite various state-law bans and nationwide campaigns to prevent texting from behind the wheel, the number of people texting while driving is actually on the rise, a new study suggests.
① offer   ② permit
③ restriction   ④ institution

56 She has the kind of generous mind that seems to hold endless information and ideas on any subject.
① cadaverous   ② careless
③ captive   ④ capacious

57 Her next remark abruptly terminated the conversation.
① sadly   ② shortly
③ gradually   ④ unexpectedly

58 The report said that primary responsibility for the debacle lies with the government and called on the current minister, on behalf of the government, to take responsibility.
① disruption   ② opulence
③ lowness   ④ squalidness

59 A confidential report of a highly sensitive nature was submitted to the board.
① A vociferous   ② An undisclosed
③ A reproachful   ④ An agitative

60 To lure more caring individuals to the field, schools are seeking older students as well as non-science majors.
① refer   ② employ
③ entice   ④ transform

61 After a long and monotonous workday, many people find themselves in a state of mental torpor.
① pabulum   ② disorder
③ lethargy   ④ acuity

62 The president exerted his influence to cajole other leaders at the summit into supporting his agenda.
① yank   ② dodge
③ tout   ④ coax

63 Death threats from angry Trump supporters forced Georgia election worker Ruby Freeman to flee her home of 20 years. Offering the first detailed account of her ordeal, the woman told Reuters about threats of lynching and racial slurs, along with alarming visits by strangers to the homes of Freeman and her mother.
① experience   ② challenge
③ action   ④ trial

64 The atmosphere also protects us by absorbing and scattering harmful radiation from the sun and space.
① perpetual   ② addictive
③ benevolent   ④ pernicious

65 The books had been piled on the shelves in a haphazard fashion.
① random   ② neat
③ ordered   ④ scattered

66 Jane alleged that Evangeline devoted her life to the search for her son.
① declared   ② admonished
③ accentuated   ④ allotted

67 Citizens who fail to vote out of indifference or laziness are delinquent in their civic duties.
① remiss   ② puzzling
③ callow   ④ submissive

68 My aging immune system is without doubt more sluggish than it used to be.
① slow   ② weak
③ quick   ④ swift

69 We were here to see the untitled kinetic sculpture, which undulated in the current of air we initiated as we entered the building.
① surged   ② induced
③ smothered   ④ sneaked

70 Undergoing the huge loss of lives due to the savage storms, the exploration team remained undaunted.
① fearless   ② wavering
③ disoriented   ④ intimidated

71 I can remember very vividly the first time I become aware of my existence; how for the first time I realized that I was a <u>sentient</u> human being in a perceptible world.

① senile   ② melancholy

③ vulnerable   ④ conscious

72 *Lovejoy*, the hero of Jonathan Gash's mystery novels, is an antique dealer who gives the reader advice on how to tell <u>counterfeit</u> antiques from the authentic ones.

① spurious   ② genuine

③ precarious   ④ enigmatic

73 They insisted upon taking an oath of <u>fidelity</u> to the country.

① protection   ② loyalty

③ diligence   ④ hostility

74 We know that the human brain is highly <u>plastic</u>; neurons and synapses change as circumstances change. When we adapt to a new cultural phenomenon, including the use of a new medium, we end up with a different brain.

① original   ② vulnerable

③ transparent   ④ malleable

75 I grew convinced that truth, sincerity, and integrity were of the utmost importance to the <u>felicity</u> of life.

① quality   ② bliss

③ pursuit   ④ cradle

76 The ability to manage one's emotions is an essential <u>ingredient</u> of effective leadership.

① tenet   ② element

③ disposition   ④ antecedent

77 We had expected his presentation speech to be brilliant, but it turned out to be not even <u>coherent</u>.

① confusing   ② logical

③ irritating   ④ tedious

78 Most of the population of Namirov was lost in the <u>holocaust</u>.

① operation   ② carnival

③ suicide   ④ genocide

79 The temperamental tennis player was known for his <u>vehement</u> dislike of linesmen.

① concealed   ② disarmed

③ displeased   ④ passionate

80 Artists, craftsmen and entrepreneurs offer a <u>plethora</u> of handmade items and services.

① lot   ② bit

③ set   ④ bundle

81 Laws such as these simply serve to <u>accentuate</u> inequality.

① weaken   ② appease

③ mitigate   ④ emphasize

82 He is very thoughtful, <u>discreet</u>, and cooperative, and coworkers have found it a great pleasure to work with him.

① intelligent   ② violent

③ wealthy   ④ prudent

83 Analysts point to several culprits: the proportional delegate system, his <u>gaffes</u>, his flip-flops, his message, even his faith.
① advantages ② costumes
③ manners ④ mistakes

84 Neglect is the most <u>prevalent</u> form of child maltreatment.
① preferred ② widespread
③ unfavourable ④ suitable

85 Patti's <u>foibles</u> included a tendency to prefer dogs to people.
① defects ② assets
③ riddles ④ hardships

86 The flood of undiscriminating investment capital that flows toward art these days may yet produce a crisis <u>analogous to</u> the one that nearly sank the Bordeaux wine industry in the early 1970s.
① similar to ② due to
③ related to ④ superior to

87 The loss of trust between the U.S. and Europe was especially <u>palpable</u> at this year's summit, a traditional show of mutual reassurance among NATO allies.
① negligible ② fuzzy
③ discernible ④ damaging

88 Verena Owen's four sons eat fish from the pristine waters that <u>abut</u> their Lake County home two miles north of Zion.
① adjoin ② abolish
③ bestow ④ render

89 Jane <u>implored</u> Miller to get there in 10 days.
① insisted ② suggested
③ shouted ④ begged

90 The essay has a long history, but there is something else more striking than this — it has power. By "power" I mean precisely the capacity to do what force always does: <u>coerce</u> assent.
① bring about by persuasion
② compel by pressure
③ coax
④ restrain by force

91 No one likes to work with a <u>lethargic</u> partner.
① hypersensitive ② apathetic
③ arrogant ④ rigid

92 Our proposal about shipping our town's garbage to the moon was <u>facetious</u>, but the first selectman took it seriously.
① petulant ② lugubrious
③ illogical ④ humorous

93 A whodunnit is <u>a colloquial</u> expression for a detective story.
① an appealing ② a literal
③ a mythological ④ a conversational

94 The research lab was run by an <u>eccentric</u> but brilliant scientist named John Baek.
① unfair ② conventional
③ peculiar ④ sociable

95 Professional bicyclists made their final preparations for the <u>impending</u> start of the day's segment of the grueling Tour de France race.

① seminal   ② resilient

③ imminent   ④ exemplary

96 Despite his <u>callow</u> appearance, Germany's teen tycoon was remarkably composed and confident last week.

① ugly   ② tough

③ handsome   ④ immature

97 The Chicago Post's Christopher Herbert documented research showing how Republicans were far more likely than Democrats to <u>embrace</u> "democratic backsliding" — a "retreat from upholding democratic norms," as one expert put it.

① petrify   ② circumscribe

③ obviate   ④ espouse

98 The boxer has beaten <u>an opponent</u> even at a disadvantage.

① an amateur   ② a professional

③ a descendant   ④ an adversary

99 Although the detailed program of the conference is <u>tentative</u> at this point, it has been announced, for sure, that there will be three keynote speeches.

① tenable   ② conclusive

③ putative   ④ temporary

100 You ought to <u>make allowance for</u> his recent misfortune.

① give way to

② put up with

③ take into account

④ take care of

☑ **DAILY CHECKUP**

[1] Write the meaning of the following words.

☐ aboriginal	☐ segment
☐ recourse	☐ estate
☐ ubiquitous	☐ quake
☐ taint	☐ nebulous
☐ lassitude	☐ dull
☐ perpendicular	☐ censure
☐ serpentine	☐ immutable
☐ enact	☐ ferment
☐ middle-of-the-road	☐ spew
☐ outcast	☐ opportune
☐ barren	☐ tenement
☐ pragmatism	☐ liquidate
☐ scarce	☐ dynasty
☐ rubicund	☐ gild
☐ decipher	☐ collision
☐ comparison	☐ via
☐ eclectic	☐ shield
☐ paralyze	☐ intermission
☐ monopoly	☐ assume
☐ somber	☐ filibuster
☐ aggrandize	☐ blot
☐ diametric	☐ contiguous
☐ howl	☐ indict
☐ alert	☐ apothecary
☐ puny	☐ stash

[2] Select the most appropriate word from the box below. Each word should be used only once.

① rubicund	② barren	③ nebulous	④ serpentine
⑤ paralyze	⑥ recourse	⑦ aboriginal	⑧ immutable
⑨ ubiquitous	⑩ indict	⑪ eclectic	⑫ stash
⑬ diametric	⑭ alert	⑮ middle-of-the-road	⑯ decipher
⑰ shield	⑱ perpendicular	⑲ assume	⑳ liquidate

1　Rivers, soil and grassland are drying up, resulting in a(n) _____ and deadly environment.

2　To reach Pleasantville, the traveller should drive with extreme caution along the _____ curves of the mountain road.

3　Although sugar was one of the world's most valuable commodities for millennia, modern geology, technology, and food processing have made it cheap and _____.

4　His own musical tastes are _____: lately, in addition to opera he's been listening to Lukas Graham, the Danish pop band, and nineties hip-hop groups.

5　Your _____ face might possibly give away your embarrassment at being unprepared for the speech you're about to give.

6　Drinking coffee helps people remain _____ even if they have not had enough sleep.

7　Synthetic biology is a(n) _____ term and it is difficult to say how, if at all, it differs from genetic engineering.

8　When two people get married, it is with the assumption that their feelings for each other are _____ and will never alter.

9　The firm has already paid half the fine, but it will have to _____ additional assets in order to pay the rest.

10　The police investigated him without physical detention, and the prosecution did not _____ him because the case against him was weak.

[3] Choose the one which is different from the others.

11 ① lassitude   ② languor   ③ lavish   ④ lethargy

12 ① mend   ② taint   ③ contaminate   ④ pollute

13 ① pariah   ② vagabond   ③ novice   ④ outcast

14 ① amplify   ② ameliorate   ③ aggrandize   ④ magnify

15 ① puny   ② trivial   ③ insignificant   ④ punctilious

16 ① reprimand   ② implore   ③ condemn   ④ censure

17 ① timely   ② opportune   ③ indolent   ④ propitious

18 ① contiguous   ② adjacent   ③ neighboring   ④ copious

19 ① somber   ② capricious   ③ dismal   ④ gloomy

20 ① dull   ② monotonous   ③ tedious   ④ judicious

✓ Answers

1 ② | 강, 토양, 초원이 말라붙어가고 있어, 척박하고 치명적인 환경이 되고 있다.

2 ④ | 플레전트빌(Pleasantville)에 이르기 위해서는, 여행자는 산악도로의 구불구불한 커브 길을 따라 매우 조심스럽게 운전해야 한다.

3 ⑨ | 비록 설탕은 수천 년 동안 세계에서 가장 귀중한 상품들 가운데 하나였지만, 현대 지질학, 기술, 그리고 식품가공 등은 설탕을 값싸고 어디에나 있는 흔한 물건으로 만들었다.

4 ⑪ | 그의 음악적 취향은 폭넓다. 그는 최근 오페라 이외에도 덴마크 팝 밴드인 루카스 그레이엄(Lukas Graham)의 노래와 90년대 힙합 그룹의 노래를 듣고 있다.

5 ① | 당신의 불그레한 얼굴은 아마도 당신이 곧 행할 연설에 준비가 되어있지 않은 것에 대한 당신의 당혹감을 보여줄지도 모른다.

6 ⑭ | 커피를 마시는 것은 사람들이 잠을 충분히 자지 않았는데도 여전히 정신을 차리고 있도록 도움을 준다.

7 ③ | 합성 생물학은 모호한 용어이고, 그것이 유전 공학과 다른 점이 혹 있다고 해도 어떻게 다른지 말하기가 어렵다.

8 ⑧ | 두 사람이 결혼할 때, 그것은 서로에 대한 그들의 감정이 불변하며 앞으로도 절대 변하지 않을 것이라는 가정하에 이루어지는 것이다.

9 ⑳ | 그 회사는 이미 벌금의 반을 냈지만, 그 나머지를 갚으려면 추가로 자산을 정리해야 할 것이다.

10 ⑩ | 경찰은 그를 불구속 수사했고, 검찰은 그에 대한 공소사실이 근거가 약하다는 이유로 불기소 처분했다.

- -

11 ③   12 ①   13 ③   14 ②   15 ④   16 ②   17 ③   18 ④   19 ②   20 ④

☑ DAILY CHECKUP

[1] Write the meaning of the following words.

☐ complacent	☐ sober
☐ abduct	☐ tickle
☐ metaphysics	☐ niche
☐ excessive	☐ annihilate
☐ satiate	☐ standstill
☐ yen	☐ redoubtable
☐ plague	☐ mobile
☐ deciduous	☐ pacify
☐ impugn	☐ cacophony
☐ optimistic	☐ disguise
☐ spleen	☐ seismic
☐ elongate	☐ favorable
☐ inchoate	☐ herculean
☐ charlatan	☐ ventilate
☐ whine	☐ fortress
☐ terse	☐ pharisaic
☐ comment	☐ sphere
☐ maladroit	☐ brag
☐ deform	☐ dole
☐ hub	☐ appraise
☐ garrulous	☐ urgent
☐ prose	☐ local
☐ idyllic	☐ benefactor
☐ ravage	☐ abundant
☐ embargo	☐ decoy

[2] Select <u>the most</u> appropriate word from the box below. Each word should be used only once.

① terse	② standstill	③ disguise	④ idyllic
⑤ complacent	⑥ fortress	⑦ dole	⑧ herculean
⑨ appraise	⑩ pacify	⑪ garrulous	⑫ urgent
⑬ sober	⑭ deciduous	⑮ impugn	⑯ inchoate
⑰ sphere	⑱ cacophony	⑲ abduct	⑳ whine

1   Someone who is _____ talks a great deal, especially about things that are not important.

2   In the heated debate, he attempted to _____ his opponent's credibility by casting doubts on their past actions and statements.

3   A(n) _____ paradise of palm trees and pineapples, sun, sand and serenity is what comes to mind when you think of Bali.

4   The police asked the diplomat to take a breathalyzer test in order to confirm that he was _____.

5   De Niro has a reputation as a man of few words, notorious for responding to journalists' questions with _____ monosyllables.

6   Airlines, retailers and many other industries are in dire shape after lockdowns that brought much of the global economy to a(n) _____.

7   The passenger must gain entry to the cockpit, which, since the 9/11 terrorist attacks, has become a(n) _____ against intruders.

8   Bankers _____ all applicants' financial circumstances before issuing them credit cards.

9   You can make a(n) _____ effort to accomplish a daunting task.

10   When the orchestra tunes up before a show, it sounds like a(n) _____ because each musician is playing a completely different tune, at different times, and at different volumes.

[3] Choose the one which is different from the others.

11 ① inept   ② maladroit   ③ dexterous   ④ awkward

12 ① decoy   ② bait   ③ lure   ④ disposal

13 ① austere   ② insincere   ③ hypocritical   ④ pharisaic

14 ① optimistic   ② roseate   ③ sanguine   ④ morose

15 ① swindler   ② proselyte   ③ charlatan   ④ imposter

16 ① inchoate   ② incipient   ③ nascent   ④ moribund

17 ① eradicate   ② saturate   ③ annihilate   ④ exterminate

18 ① abundant   ② bountiful   ③ ample   ④ acquisitive

19 ① formidable   ② prosaic   ③ redoubtable   ④ strong

20 ① immense   ② celestial   ③ seismic   ④ tremendous

✔ Answers

1 ⑪ | 수다스러운 사람은 특히 중요하지 않은 것들에 관해 말을 많이 한다.

2 ⑮ | 열띤 논쟁 속에서 그는 상대의 과거 행동과 진술에 의문을 제기함으로써 상대의 신빙성에 의문을 제기하려고 했다.

3 ④ | 당신이 발리를 생각하면 떠오르는 것은 야자수와 파인애플, 태양, 모래 그리고 평온함이 있는 목가적인 천국이다.

4 ⑬ | 경찰은 그 외교관이 술에 취하지 않았다는 것을 확인하기 위해 그에게 음주측정기 검사를 받을 것을 요구했다.

5 ① | 드 니로(De Niro)는 기자들의 질문에 간결한 단음절어로 답변을 하는 것으로 유명한 과묵한 사람이라는 평판을 가지고 있다.

6 ② | 전 세계 경제의 많은 부분을 정체에 빠지게 한 봉쇄 조치 이후 항공사, 소매업체, 그리고 다른 많은 산업들이 심각한 상태에 있다.

7 ⑥ | 9/11 테러 공격 이후 승객이 조종실에 들어가기 위해서는 입장허가를 받아야하는데, 조종실은 침입자에 대한 요새가 되어왔다.

8 ⑨ | 은행은 신용카드를 발급하기 전에 모든 신청자의 재무 상태를 평가한다.

9 ⑧ | 당신은 힘든 일을 완수하기 위해 엄청난 노력을 할 수 있다.

10 ⑱ | 오케스트라가 공연 전 악기를 조율할 때, 그 음은 불협화음처럼 들린다. 왜냐하면 각 음악가들이 완전히 다른 곡을, 서로 다른 시간에, 그리고 다른 음량으로 연주하기 때문이다.

---

11 ③   **12** ④   **13** ①   **14** ④   **15** ②   **16** ④   **17** ②   **18** ④   **19** ②   **20** ②

[1] Write the meaning of the following words.

☐ periodic	☐ slay
☐ dank	☐ career
☐ obey	☐ incipient
☐ lopsided	☐ mammal
☐ jaunty	☐ disingenuous
☐ abnormal	☐ preserve
☐ sanctity	☐ specimen
☐ miserly	☐ annotate
☐ electrify	☐ ensemble
☐ noblesse oblige	☐ torture
☐ shrink	☐ bulk
☐ circumscribe	☐ reciprocal
☐ whimsical	☐ deity
☐ tactless	☐ furnish
☐ confide	☐ vintage
☐ plutocracy	☐ humble
☐ blanch	☐ dominate
☐ seamless	☐ libertine
☐ egregious	☐ despot
☐ glitch	☐ feeble
☐ mete	☐ imperil
☐ internal	☐ backwater
☐ aim	☐ adapt
☐ creed	☐ script
☐ oppressive	☐ ramble

[2] Select the most appropriate word from the box below. Each word should be used only once.

① lopsided	② confide	③ feeble	④ imperil
⑤ furnish	⑥ mete	⑦ incipient	⑧ reciprocal
⑨ whimsical	⑩ preserved	⑪ dominate	⑫ electrify
⑬ ramble	⑭ periodic	⑮ circumscribed	⑯ tactless
⑰ annotate	⑱ adapt	⑲ internal	⑳ seamless

1   During the four decades of the one-child policy, parents often preferred sons, resulting in a(n) _____ gender ratio that has intensified competition for wives.

2   Women's lives remain _____ by moral codes that hinder their ability to live, dress and behave freely.

3   Ray's family, aware of his _____ nature, was always ready for a sudden change of plan.

4   In literature classes, students are often encouraged to _____ passages in their books to better grasp the author's intent and literary devices used.

5   The two colleges have a(n) _____ arrangement whereby students from one college can attend classes at the other.

6   When we want to talk about something sensitive, we look for someone to _____ in.

7   Though they cried out for help, their voice was so _____ that it could not be heard by neighbours.

8   An employee who constantly botches his job and never understands why is _____.

9   An emerging energy crisis, which has raised prices and triggered blackouts, could _____ efforts to get developing economies to phase out polluting fuels.

10   The ruling party came to _____ the National Assembly following its landslide victory in the election.

[3] Choose the one which is different from the others.

11 ① jaunty   ② jocund   ③ brusque   ④ vivacious

12 ① aptness   ② sanctity   ③ divinity   ④ holiness

13 ① shrink   ② dwindle   ③ diminish   ④ retreat

14 ① dank   ② scorching   ③ humid   ④ damp

15 ① ridiculous   ② congenial   ③ absurd   ④ egregious

16 ① brevity   ② glitch   ③ malfunction   ④ defect

17 ① oppressive   ② harsh   ③ gaunt   ④ tyrannical

18 ① doctrine   ② dogma   ③ creed   ④ atheism

19 ① distress   ② assassinate   ③ slaughter   ④ slay

20 ① libertine   ② puritanical   ③ dissolute   ④ licentious

✔Answers

1 ① | 한 자녀 정책이 시행된 40년 동안 부모들은 아들을 선호하는 경우가 많았고, 이로 인해 한쪽으로 기운 성(性) 비율이 생겨 아내를 두고 경쟁이 심화되었다.

2 ⑮ | 여성의 삶은 자유롭게 살고, 옷을 입고, 행동할 수 있는 여성의 능력을 방해하는 도덕적 규범에 여전히 제한되어 있다.

3 ⑨ | 레이(Ray)의 가족은 그의 변덕스러운 성격을 알아서 갑작스러운 계획 변경에 언제나 준비가 되어있었다.

4 ⑰ | 문학 수업에서 학생들은 저자의 의도와 사용된 문학적 장치를 더 잘 이해하기 위해 책의 구절에 주석을 달도록 종종 권장된다.

5 ⑧ | 그 두 대학은 상호 협정을 맺고 있어서 한 대학에 다니는 학생들은 다른 대학의 수업을 들을 수 있다.

6 ② | 민감한 이야기를 하고 싶을 때 우리는 속마음을 털어놓을 사람을 찾는다.

7 ③ | 그들은 도와달라고 외쳤지만, 그들의 목소리가 너무 희미해서 이웃집 사람들에게 들리지 않았다.

8 ⑯ | 끊임없이 일을 망치고 그 이유를 전혀 이해하지 못하는 직원은 요령이 없다.

9 ④ | 가격을 인상시키고 정전을 촉발할 새로운 에너지 위기는 개발도상국이 환경을 오염시키는 연료를 단계적으로 없애도록 하는 노력을 위태롭게 할 수 있다.

10 ⑪ | 여당이 선거에서 압승을 거둬 국회를 장악하게 되었다.

11 ③   **12** ①   **13** ④   **14** ②   **15** ②   **16** ①   **17** ③   **18** ④   **19** ①   **20** ②

[1] Write the meaning of the following words.

☐ harness	☐ posthumous
☐ impetuous	☐ shed
☐ manifesto	☐ hirsute
☐ rehearse	☐ instinct
☐ commotion	☐ condescend
☐ numerous	☐ apathetic
☐ sequel	☐ perjury
☐ distinguish	☐ stealthy
☐ partisan	☐ excel
☐ additive	☐ depredation
☐ qualify	☐ contemn
☐ generic	☐ vendor
☐ sanguine	☐ faithful
☐ elixir	☐ asseverate
☐ abound	☐ candid
☐ underdog	☐ sophist
☐ tedious	☐ rally
☐ bequeath	☐ bout
☐ entry	☐ ogle
☐ laudatory	☐ legend
☐ soil	☐ inculcate
☐ pittance	☐ dejected
☐ venerate	☐ marvel
☐ thesis	☐ advert
☐ discipline	☐ miserable

[2] Select <u>the most</u> appropriate word from the box below. Each word should be used only once.

① perjury	② pittance	③ underdog	④ sanguine
⑤ condescend	⑥ dejected	⑦ posthumous	⑧ faithful
⑨ distinguished	⑩ instinct	⑪ stealthy	⑫ elixir
⑬ inculcate	⑭ commotion	⑮ manifesto	⑯ ogle
⑰ asseverate	⑱ candid	⑲ generic	⑳ bequeath

1   Her normally _____ complexion lost its usual glow when she heard the news of her brother's accident.

2   He was eventually tried and cleared of the espionage charges, but he was convicted of _____ by deliberately lying about facts related to the case under oath.

3   The sad little boy sat quietly in the corner of the room with a(n) _____ look on his face.

4   Guerilla art is a fun and _____ way of sharing your vision with the world. It is a method of art making which entails leaving anonymous art pieces in public places.

5   The whole unit was thrown into _____ when one of the soldiers ran away.

6   In a rapidly industrializing nation, in which there were many perils of poverty and violence, as well as opportunity, schools needed to _____ thrift, civility, and self-control in the young.

7   When a professional basketball player faces off against a high school student who's a foot shorter, the high schooler is the _____.

8   Musk said the subsidies for Tesla and SolarCity are a(n) _____ compared with government substantial support of the oil and gas industry.

9   The actor died right before the Academy Awards ceremony, receiving a(n) _____ Oscar.

10   My grandparents were very _____ about their past and never indicated that they were hiding a secret.

[3] Choose the one which is different from the others.

11 ① miserable ② pathetic ③ wretched ④ meddlesome

12 ① hasty ② innocuous ③ impetuous ④ impulsive

13 ① odd ② boring ③ irksome ④ tedious

14 ① despise ② contemn ③ concede ④ scorn

15 ① callous ② exuberant ③ apathetic ④ indifferent

16 ① venerate ② revere ③ worship ④ vacillate

17 ① partisan ② one-sided ③ even-handed ④ biased

18 ① panegyrical ② laudatory ③ complimentary ④ apprehensive

19 ① excel ② surrender ③ exceed ④ surpass

20 ① demise ② depredation ③ pillage ④ plunder

✔ Answers

1 ④ | 그녀가 오빠의 사고 소식을 들었을 때, 보통 때 혈색이 좋던 그녀의 얼굴빛은 평상시의 홍조를 잃었다.

2 ① | 그는 결국 재판을 받아 간첩 혐의를 벗었지만, 법정에서 선서를 하고 그 사건과 관련된 사실에 대해서 고의로 허위 진술을 함으로써 위증죄로 유죄 판결을 받았다.

3 ⑥ | 슬픔에 빠진 그 어린 소년은 낙담한 표정을 한 채 방구석에 조용히 앉아 있었다.

4 ⑪ | 게릴라 예술은 당신의 생각을 세계와 공유하는 재밌고 비밀스러운 방식이다. 그 예술은 공공장소에 익명의 예술품을 남기는 작품 창작의 한 방식이다.

5 ⑭ | 부대원 한 명이 탈영하자 온 부대가 발칵 뒤집혔다.

6 ⑬ | 빠르게 산업화되고 있는 국가에는 기회뿐 아니라 가난과 폭력의 위험도 많이 있었는데, 그곳의 학교들은 젊은이들에게 검약, 공손함, 자제력을 가르칠 필요가 있었다.

7 ③ | 프로농구 선수가 키가 1피트 작은 고등학생과 대결한다면, 그 고등학생은 약자이다.

8 ② | 머스크는 테슬라와 솔라시티에 대한 보조금이 석유 및 가스 산업에 대한 정부의 엄청난 지원에 비해 아주 적다고 말했다.

9 ⑦ | 아카데미상 시상식 직전에 죽은 영화배우가 사후에 오스카상을 수상했다.

10 ⑱ | 나의 조부모님은 자신들의 과거에 대해 매우 솔직했고, 비밀을 숨기고 있는 모습을 결코 보이지 않았다.

11 ④   **12** ②   **13** ①   **14** ③   **15** ②   **16** ④   **17** ③   **18** ④   **19** ②   **20** ①

☑ DAILY CHECKUP

[1] Write the meaning of the following words.

☐ weird	☐ haul
☐ impede	☐ courteous
☐ deleterious	☐ emanate
☐ rate	☐ ken
☐ sardonic	☐ maudlin
☐ throe	☐ loosen
☐ moral	☐ solstice
☐ gnaw	☐ authentic
☐ regimen	☐ behemoth
☐ slack	☐ abstract
☐ complicated	☐ germane
☐ neophyte	☐ vaccination
☐ old-fashioned	☐ tantalize
☐ dirge	☐ default
☐ permeate	☐ alienate
☐ identical	☐ megalomania
☐ spate	☐ compliment
☐ bother	☐ lackluster
☐ fiesta	☐ fallacy
☐ effete	☐ cavernous
☐ possess	☐ essential
☐ indignation	☐ shrill
☐ acquaint	☐ anthem
☐ pliant	☐ dispense
☐ stiff	☐ pantry

[2] Select <u>the most</u> appropriate word from the box below. Each word should be used only once.

① lackluster	② impede	③ fallacy	④ dispense
⑤ acquaint	⑥ courteous	⑦ neophyte	⑧ moral
⑨ pliant	⑩ maudlin	⑪ old-fashioned	⑫ compliment
⑬ dirge	⑭ behemoth	⑮ alienate	⑯ default
⑰ permeable	⑱ abstract	⑲ identical	⑳ possess

1 Travel is so important in the global market place that aerophobia can greatly _____ someone's ability to do international business.

2 He is a political _____ who for years delivered caustic commentary from the sidelines but has never run for office.

3 In order to survive the recession, the company had to be _____ and adjust to the new economic conditions.

4 Google is the world's dominant search engine, owns the biggest mobile operating system in Android and runs the _____ video site YouTube.

5 The _____ on the loan led to the collapse of the company in the end.

6 Some retailers have experienced a decline in revenue due to _____ consumer spending in the United States.

7 The illusion that when we reach a goal we will finally attain happiness is called the arrival _____.

8 In science class, you might have learned about a(n) _____ membrane — a thin material that is porous enough to let liquids or gases to pass through.

9 About 99.8 percent of human DNA is _____ among all people. However, the remaining 0.2 percent contains enough differences to give each person a unique genetic signature.

10 U.S. and other Western oil companies have long shied away from Israel, in part because they do not want to _____ Arab countries.

[3] Choose the one which is different from the others.

11 ① sardonic ② cynical ③ sarcastic ④ terse

12 ① rage ② zeal ③ indignation ④ fury

13 ① weird ② strange ③ genuine ④ bizarre

14 ① fertile ② effete ③ exhausted ④ feeble

15 ① emanate ② emit ③ exude ④ embrace

16 ① poignant ② noxious ③ detrimental ④ deleterious

17 ① complicated ② intricate ③ contrite ④ convoluted

18 ① germane ② trivial ③ pertinent ④ relevant

19 ① arbitrary ② authentic ③ genuine ④ bona fide

20 ① stiff ② inflexible ③ rigid ④ pliable

✓ Answers

1 ② ┃ 여행은 세계 시장에서 아주 중요하기 때문에 비행공포증은 국제 사업 능력을 크게 저하시킬 수 있다.

2 ⑦ ┃ 그는 방관자적 입장에서 수년 동안 신랄한 논평을 했지만 공직에 출마한 적이 없는 정치 초보자이다.

3 ⑨ ┃ 불황에서 살아남기 위해 그 회사는 유연성을 갖고 새로운 경제 상황에 적응해야 했다.

4 ⑭ ┃ 구글은 세계에서 지배적인 검색 엔진이며 가장 큰 안드로이드 모바일 운영 체제를 소유하고 있으며 거대한 비디오 사이트인 유튜브를 운영하고 있다.

5 ⑯ ┃ 대출 불이행으로 인해 결국 회사는 파산하게 됐다.

6 ① ┃ 미국 내 소비자 지출 부진으로 인해 일부 소매업체는 매출이 감소했다.

7 ③ ┃ 우리가 목표에 도달했을 때 마침내 행복을 얻을 것이라는 착각을 도착오류라고 한다.

8 ⑰ ┃ 과학 시간에 당신은 투과성 막, 즉 액체나 기체가 통과할 수 있을 정도로 투과성이 있는 얇은 물질에 대해 배웠을지도 모른다.

9 ⑲ ┃ 인간 DNA의 약 99.8퍼센트는 모든 사람들 간에 동일하다. 그러나 나머지 0.2퍼센트의 DNA에는 각각의 사람들에게 독특한 유전적 특징을 부여할 만큼 충분한 차이들이 포함되어 있다.

10 ⑮ ┃ 미국과 다른 서방 석유회사들은 오랫동안 이스라엘을 꺼려왔는데, 부분적으로 아랍 국가들을 소외시키기를 원하지 않기 때문이다.

. . . .

11 ④ **12** ② **13** ③ **14** ① **15** ④ **16** ① **17** ③ **18** ② **19** ① **20** ④

ACTUAL TEST

[01-100] Choose the one that is closest in meaning to the underlined part.

01 Despite his outgoing demeanor, Milne gets humble when talking about his 40-plus years donating time.
① modest
② attentive
③ patient
④ devout

02 In a terse statement yesterday, the company announced that it was closing three of its factories.
① concise
② authentic
③ expedient
④ logical

03 If a reference is deemed suitable for an experimental program, the researcher must then be extremely alert to the manner in which the material is treated once it is received at the laboratory.
① watchful
② opportunistic
③ selective
④ adventurous

04 The judge had a very sober expression on his face.
① serious
② painful
③ mysterious
④ ambiguous

05 Little Rock is the hub of the federal interstate highways that cross Arkansas.
① high point
② summit
③ path
④ center

06 The processes to which a dead body may be subjected are after all to some extent circumscribed by law.
① diverted
② upheld
③ bypassed
④ restricted

07 I picked an opportune moment to ask a favor of her.
① a wrong
② a right
③ a miserable
④ a happy

08 Scientists are gradually deciphering the genetic structure found in the cells of organisms.
① declaring
② devising
③ deciding
④ decoding

09 Despite incipient signs of recovery, the economy fell into a deeper recession.
① initial
② final
③ ultimate
④ insufficient

10 If the grand jury indicts the suspect, he will go to trial.
① charges
② acquits
③ condones
④ sentences

11 How <u>maladroit</u> it was of me to mention seeing you out partying last night! From the look on his face, I take it that your boyfriend thought you were otherwise occupied.
① smart
② clumsy
③ generous
④ sympathetic

12 Taekwondo is one of the <u>indigenous</u> sports which has been developed in Korea.
① invincible
② cardinal
③ aboriginal
④ congenial

13 All his supporters were expelled, exiled, or <u>liquidated</u>.
① killed
② freed
③ punished
④ prisoned

14 Time was, national crises stimulated saving. But thrift today has a negative, <u>miserly</u> connotation.
① misfiring
② stingy
③ ominous
④ generous

15 Nine years later he gave up public appearances to spend the rest of his working life in a record studio, usually at night, working obsessively over an <u>eclectic</u> range of music.
① occult
② selective
③ imaginative
④ vivacious

16 All I can hope is that the good name of the bank will not be <u>impugned</u> in some way.
① perished
② disconcerted
③ challenged
④ implemented

17 The man <u>ogled</u> the woman so hard that she became angry.
① grilled
② doffed
③ leered
④ pretermitted

18 The picture is often one that presents an image of beauty, wealth, and <u>idyllic</u> location or lifestyle, romance or popularity, things that we as the audience are assumed to desire or to want to be associated with.
① lucrative
② exasperating
③ arcadian
④ occidental

19 The national writing contest was created in order to <u>inculcate</u> the analytical writing skills the students would need.
① improvise
② impart
③ implicate
④ immunize

20 Over time, creative virtuosity became increasingly a male <u>preserve</u>. With painting, for example, women became confined within particular genres such as portraiture, landscapes and still-lives and usually exhibited as amateurs rather than as artists.
① dispersion
② propriety
③ association
④ domain

21 In the course of evolution, venomous animals have produced peptide toxins, <u>redoubtable</u> weapons of defense against predators.
① efficacious
② implicit
③ reproducible
④ formidable

22 That is an interesting point, but it is not germane to our discussion.
① incompatible ② extraneous
③ incongruous ④ pertinent

23 As citizens grew complacent and temperatures dropped, the pandemic has returned with a vengeance.
① condescending ② exasperated
③ self-satisfied ④ nonchalant

24 It's far easier, and cheaper, to protect the health and habitat of an abundant species than one whose numbers have already been reduced to single digits.
① pitiful ② plentiful
③ ponderous ④ punctual

25 I didn't know that he has a habit of getting maudlin when he is drunk.
① violent ② taciturn
③ boisterous ④ mawkish

26 He was a tall man with a craggy, rubbery face which twisted and turned, often into a sardonic grin.
① lustful ② glamorous
③ sneering ④ annoying

27 She often painted desert landscapes, often with the blanched skull of a longhorn in the foreground.
① shattered ② prominent
③ whitened ④ inexplicable

28 Under the new regulation, companies will also be required to disclose now ubiquitous data breaches within 72 hours.
① common ② famous
③ notorious ④ powerful

29 One can think of the vacuum fluctuations as pairs of particles that appear together at some time, move apart, come together, and annihilate each other.
① decimate ② condone
③ castigate ④ prevaricate

30 Perjury in a serious court case can result in life imprisonment.
① Lying under oath
② Aiding a criminal
③ Destroying
④ Threatening the jury

31 Publications from the institute denounced Laplace as a modern charlatan and a "Newtonian idolater."
① receiver ② celebrity
③ deceiver ④ offender

32 As part of the review, employees will be asked to appraise their own performance.
① evaluate ② commend
③ underrate ④ publicize

33 I found it at the identical place where I left it.
① hidden ② dark
③ same ④ unknown

34 A <u>qualified</u> number of students are allowed in Professor Martin's Classics class.
① belittled   ② limited
③ completed   ④ reproved

35 Hong Kong: East or West, Chinese or British, traditional or modern, colonial or postcolonial? Issues of identity continue to <u>plague</u> the territory.
① deter   ② flourish
③ change   ④ disturb

36 We can't <u>dispense with</u> sleep for too many days.
① do away with   ② do for
③ do without   ④ do with

37 Printed textbooks are rapidly being replaced by ebooks, which <u>harness</u> the interactive capabilities of handheld devices and take pupils beyond the static page with a simple swipe and tap of the finger.
① exploit   ② restrict
③ contract   ④ welcome

38 Taxi drivers <u>paralyzed</u> public services.
① despised   ② disabled
③ displaced   ④ degraded

39 I found his most recent movie to be extremely <u>tedious</u>.
① disorganized   ② instructive
③ prosaic   ④ exhilarating

40 One stack of mail is <u>urgent</u> and should be acted upon before I make any phone calls.
① important   ② confidential
③ unpredictable   ④ dangerous

41 He continues to <u>impede</u> their progress, even after he was cautioned.
① utilize   ② render
③ infuse   ④ hinder

42 By <u>feeble</u> contractions, the jellyfish propels itself along, buoyed up by the surrounding water.
① weak   ② rhythmic
③ deliberate   ④ automatic

43 A sanguine attitude at a critical time such as this is not justified by the <u>somber</u> news reaching us from the war front.
① gloomy   ② optimistic
③ wholesome   ④ ignoble

44 Just as uncompleted projects line the arteries of Nigeria, <u>inchoate</u> probes and investigations afflict the system.
① threatening   ② haphazard
③ incipient   ④ tricky

45 If God has an idea of Caesar's acting otherwise, then Caesar has access to it, though he probably will not take advantage of that access owing to <u>lassitude</u>, or lack of time, or attachment to his senses.
① reaction   ② ecstasy
③ conviction   ④ lethargy

46 According to socialists, inequality is the worst blasphemy against the <u>sanctity</u> of humanity, because it privileges peripheral qualities of humans over their universal essence.
① spirit   ② divinity
③ vanity   ④ modesty

47 The target audience became familiar with <u>disingenuous</u> car sales ads that make grand promises such as huge discount or less interest rate for car loan.
① bellicose   ② deliberate
③ deceitful   ④ distinguished

48 He was deposed and replaced by a more <u>pliant</u> successor.
① biddable   ② dexterous
③ brawny   ④ cerebral

49 For some users, Cyberse is a positive way to stay connected with friends, but others who use it to size themselves up by comparing accomplishments can suffer <u>deleterious</u> effects.
① everlasting   ② irreversible
③ pernicious   ④ vigilant

50 In colonial times the influence of religion <u>permeated</u> the entire way of life.
① held sway over
② shed light on
③ spread into
④ shaped up

51 She was unable to find a boat to sleep in. "There's not one boat here," she said <u>dejectedly</u>.
① cheerfully   ② sadly
③ hopefully   ④ inquiringly

52 The student was <u>censured</u> for his indiscreet act.
① praised   ② blamed
③ realized   ④ welcomed

53 One out of five bridges in the United States is <u>outmoded</u>.
① narrow   ② reinforced concrete
③ illegal   ④ old-fashioned

54 Many artists and writers have been ignored during their lifetimes only to achieve <u>posthumous</u> fame.
① prim   ② postmortem
③ primal   ④ posthaste

55 High-school success is not determined by a set of <u>immutable</u> characteristics but rather by the conditions of schooling that educators create and control.
① indefinable   ② intangible
③ unalterable   ④ uncountable

56 Owners would modify emission controls to under-aspirate an engine, resulting in huge belches of sooty exhaust and increased power. These <u>egregious</u> driving offences must stop.
① heinous   ② assiduous
③ salacious   ④ crustaceous

57 She was filled with indignation at the conditions under which miners were forced to work.
① pity   ② anger
③ disappointment ④ sympathy

58 Heading into the tunnel, he mumbles a prayer to the deity who rules the mountain and all the gold within.
① nature   ② king
③ god   ④ ghost

59 It is impossible for a parent to shield his children from every danger.
① make free   ② protect
③ conserve   ④ involve

60 When the Erie Canal was built, it was the engineering marvel of its time.
① wonder   ② dispute
③ frustration   ④ model

61 Despite various well-meaning plans to pacify the Delta, the government has failed to stop the region's unrest.
① calm   ② give up
③ develop   ④ patrol

62 The dullness of the work caused her to be overcome by fatigue within a mere two hours.
① dossil   ② drudgery
③ duarchy   ④ drollness

63 Three thousand years ago, in one small area of the Mediterranean world, there came a break with the earlier traditions of state building which were all despotic.
① gentile   ② democratic
③ tribal   ④ tyrannical

64 Kim's political career was also tainted by the imprisonment of two of his sons for fraud.
① upgraded   ② affected
③ stained   ④ ended

65 Rumors abound as to the reasons for her death.
① die out   ② occur
③ bounce back   ④ proliferate

66 You are a very attractive person, and you have an inner beauty you try to disguise.
① obtain   ② include
③ show   ④ hide

67 This lady is very whimsical even when there is presumably little or no reason.
① amicable   ② enthusiastic
③ capricious   ④ hilarious

68 The tactless preaching of the Anglican priest and dean of St. Paul's Cathedral in London brought him into disfavor with Queen Elizabeth I.
① thoughtless   ② delicate
③ diplomatic   ④ ruthless

69 In writing a book of this kind, my main aim has been to <u>acquaint</u> the reader with what is the generally accepted view of the authors and periods under discussion.
① familiarize ② explain
③ classify ④ acquire

70 It is so easy to become <u>apathetic</u> about the environment when we are busy with day-to-day life.
① lame ② futile
③ shrewd ④ indifferent

71 Congress considered placing an <u>embargo</u> on foreign cars.
① diction ② ban
③ emblem ④ compass

72 John was so <u>impetuous</u> that he never took more than a few seconds to make up his mind.
① illustrious ② impolite
③ immune ④ impulsive

73 The play received mostly <u>laudatory</u> reviews.
① conclusive ② impartial
③ complimentary ④ disparaging

74 This ring has been <u>handed down</u> from generation to generation.
① rebuked ② bequeathed
③ preserved ④ collected

75 Seeking refuge in graduate schools in a <u>lackluster</u> labor market is a time-tested strategy.
① external ② competitive
③ intrinsic ④ dull

76 People who work at night have to <u>adapt</u> themselves to sleeping in the daytime.
① adjust ② admonish
③ advocate ④ attribute

77 My dog has <u>stealthy</u> ways of eating table scraps when my attention is elsewhere.
① surreptitious ② baleful
③ raucous ④ benevolent

78 The <u>ravaged</u> rural economies in many countries would be boosted by the creation of tens of thousands of new jobs in forestry, transportation, and power plant operation.
① reduced ② changed
③ increased ④ destroyed

79 A nation in the <u>throes</u> of revolution will not welcome outside interference.
① wars ② agonies
③ fights ④ enmities

80 Far from a bolt from the blue, the commission has demonstrated over the last 19 months that the Sept. 11 attacks were foreseen, at least in general terms, and might well have been prevented, had it not been for misjudgments, mistakes and <u>glitches</u>, some within the White House.
① problems ② stitches
③ signals ④ glossaries

81 The philosopher introduced the falsification principle as a way to distinguish scientific theories from non-scientific ones.
① differentiate ② persuade
③ exempt ④ prevent

82 It suddenly began to rain. The birds had increased commotion, and were wheeling about overhead in a confused, indecisive way.
① agitation ② grimace
③ petulance ④ sonority

83 Since then, the virus has emerged periodically and infected people in several African countries.
① suddenly ② widely
③ regularly ④ eternally

84 The writer's arrogance alienated him from everyone including the publishers.
① complimented ② perished
③ distanced ④ endeared

85 Having made an error, she was candid in her explanation.
① austere ② forthright
③ nonpareil ④ rhetorical

86 The democratic party took a middle-of-the-road stance on educational issues.
① a backward ② an extreme
③ a futuristic ④ a moderate

87 As we entered the farmyard, we were met with a cacophony of animal sound.
① a harmonious relation
② an agreeable sound
③ a discordant sound
④ an unpleasant behaviour

88 She was hesitant to confide in her best friend.
① believe ② affront
③ protract ④ upbraid

89 In the paintings of Dix and Lea, the meaning of war does not emanate from tactical movements or divine proclamations.
① dwindle ② eulogize
③ emerge ④ deteriorate

90 Our new, modern Tribeca office was beautifully airy and yet remarkably oppressive.
① relieving ② cramped
③ burdensome ④ balmy

91 These new rules have complicated the tax system even further.
① straightened out
② disentangled
③ entangled
④ simplified

92 The legislation was enacted in the aftermath of two high-profile child abuse cases last year.
① waived ② dramatized
③ carried out ④ legislated

93 Tax collection agencies should be nonpartisan.
① economical ② party-spirited
③ just ④ prejudiced

94 As she watched the waves crash on the shore, a sense of yen for adventure and exploration overcame her.
① futility ② relief
③ outrage ④ longing

95 John brags about his beautiful wife.
① lies ② criticizes
③ boasts ④ is secretive

96 Banks and investors prefer the structure of a corporation to the often more nebulous organization of a sole proprietorship.
① pliable ② ambiguous
③ invincible ④ swift

97 In a trade agreement, nations generally make reciprocal concessions when setting tariffs.
① functional ② enthusiastic
③ mutual ④ graduated

98 Some abnormal human behavior may be caused by eating substances that upset delicate chemical balances in the brain.
① flawless ② unusual
③ typical ④ symbolic

99 Software is a generic term for the sets of programs which control a computer.
① specific ② technical
③ scientific ④ general

100 He has a sanguine personality.
① buoyant ② pessimistic
③ improvising ④ stressful

[1] Write the meaning of the following words.

☐ clarify	☐ argument
☐ metaphor	☐ bigotry
☐ irate	☐ lament
☐ vague	☐ connotation
☐ recount	☐ insert
☐ stud	☐ fecund
☐ pollutant	☐ demonstrate
☐ ensnare	☐ necrology
☐ skimp	☐ arbitrary
☐ heathen	☐ gear
☐ factor	☐ unanimous
☐ salient	☐ telepathy
☐ malicious	☐ condense
☐ pose	☐ dementia
☐ referendum	☐ scrupulous
☐ diction	☐ behoove
☐ acquit	☐ latitude
☐ subsidy	☐ tranquil
☐ empirical	☐ omniscient
☐ oblation	☐ avenge
☐ decimate	☐ eerie
☐ implicit	☐ paradigm
☐ misprision	☐ cantankerous
☐ jaundiced	☐ painstaking
☐ rob	☐ hedonism

[2] Select the most appropriate word from the box below. Each word should be used only once.

① jaundiced	② subsidy	③ ensnared	④ omniscient
⑤ decimated	⑥ unanimous	⑦ condense	⑧ recounted
⑨ heathen	⑩ implicit	⑪ arbitrary	⑫ bigotry
⑬ acquit	⑭ demonstrate	⑮ eerie	⑯ hedonism
⑰ oblation	⑱ telepathy	⑲ skimp	⑳ behoove

1   Nearly _____ by disease and the destruction of their habitat, koalas are now found only in isolated parts of eucalyptus forests.

2   In the end, we had a declaration that garnered _____ support from all G20 member nations without a single dissenting note.

3   The conductor's choice of tempo seemed entirely _____, so that each successive movement of the piece seemed to have no necessary connection to what had come before.

4   You may love every word of your 1000-page novel, but you'll have to _____ the plot into a 2-page summary for your editor.

5   The court must _____ the accused if there is enough evidence of innocence.

6   No doctor is _____; guidelines keep changing and it's impossible to keep abreast of the mountain of knowledge.

7   In Ancient Greece, _____ really did have an ethical component, and its adherents really believed that society would be best served if you as an individual cultivated those things that gave you the greatest pleasure.

8   Many school districts offer a(n) _____ to low-income families for lunch costs.

9   Boris Johnson stepped down less than three years after a landslide election victory, following a series of scandals that have _____ his government.

10   When tomato prices are high, a cost-conscious restaurant might _____ on the amount of chopped tomatoes it puts on salads.

[3] Choose the one which is different from the others.

11 ① irate ② furious ③ intrepid ④ enraged

12 ① prosaic ② salient ③ conspicuous ④ noticeable

13 ① esoteric ② practical ③ pragmatic ④ empirical

14 ① knavery ② misprision ③ delinquency ④ penury

15 ① fecund ② sterile ③ fertile ④ prolific

16 ① calm ② mundane ③ serene ④ tranquil

17 ① diligent ② earnest ③ painstaking ④ frivolous

18 ① cantankerous ② grumpy ③ timorous ④ irascible

19 ① obfuscate ② clarify ③ elucidate ④ explicate

20 ① vague ② definite ③ ambiguous ④ nebulous

✓Answers

1 ⑤ ┃ 질병과 서식지의 파괴로 인해 거의 멸종되었기 때문에, 오늘날 코알라는 유칼립투스 숲의 외딴 지역에서만 발견된다.

2 ⑥ ┃ 결국 우리는 한 표의 반대도 없이 G20 회원국 모두의 만장일치 지지를 얻은 선언문을 채택했다.

3 ⑪ ┃ 그 지휘자의 박자 선택이 완전히 임의적인 것 같았고, 그래서 곡의 연속으로 이어지는 악장은 앞서 나온 악장과 필연적 인 관련성을 전혀 가지고 있지 않은 것처럼 보였다.

4 ⑦ ┃ 당신은 당신이 쓴 천 페이지에 달하는 소설의 한 단어 한 단어를 좋아할 수도 있지만, 당신의 편집자를 위해 그 줄거리 를 두 페이지 요약본으로 간추려야 한다.

5 ⑬ ┃ 무죄의 증거가 충분하다면 법원은 피고에게 무죄를 선고해야 한다.

6 ④ ┃ 어떤 의사도 모든 것을 다 알고 있지는 않다. 지침은 계속 바뀌고 방대한 양의 지식에 뒤지지 않고 따라가는 것은 불가 능하다.

7 ⑯ ┃ 고대 그리스에서 쾌락주의는 실제로 윤리적 요소를 갖고 있었고, 그 지지자들은 개인에게 가장 큰 즐거움을 주는 것들을 길러낸다면 사회에 가장 도움이 될 것이라고 정말로 믿었다.

8 ② ┃ 많은 학군들은 저소득층 가정에 점심 비용에 대한 보조금을 제공한다.

9 ③ ┃ 보리스 존슨(Boris Johnson)은 자신의 행정부를 곤경에 빠뜨린 일련의 스캔들로 인해 압도적인 선거 승리 후 3년도 채 안 되어 사임했다.

10 ⑲ ┃ 토마토 가격이 높을 때, 비용에 민감한 식당은 샐러드에 넣는 잘게 썬 토마토의 양을 줄일 수 있다.

....

11 ③ **12** ① **13** ① **14** ④ **15** ② **16** ② **17** ④ **18** ③ **19** ① **20** ②

[1] Write the meaning of the following words.

☐ quaint	☐ spillover
☐ epicure	☐ gainsay
☐ autocratic	☐ barrack
☐ proponent	☐ sapient
☐ obtain	☐ pillage
☐ concave	☐ desolate
☐ sibling	☐ various
☐ rapacious	☐ flatter
☐ intervene	☐ economical
☐ bombastic	☐ tavern
☐ decline	☐ assure
☐ impertinent	☐ colossal
☐ scatter	☐ nepotism
☐ vertex	☐ weld
☐ aberrant	☐ adversity
☐ interact	☐ mandatory
☐ sly	☐ high-end
☐ casuistry	☐ emulate
☐ torment	☐ logomachy
☐ legitimate	☐ cheat
☐ second-hand	☐ parochial
☐ percussion	☐ determination
☐ relapse	☐ accumulate
☐ manumit	☐ mien
☐ diabolical	☐ far-fetched

[2] Select the most appropriate word from the box below. Each word should be used only once.

① far-fetched	② desolate	③ parochial	④ pillaged
⑤ nepotism	⑥ second-hand	⑦ assured	⑧ welded
⑨ concave	⑩ gainsay	⑪ adversity	⑫ manumit
⑬ epicure	⑭ legitimate	⑮ mandatory	⑯ flatter
⑰ mien	⑱ proponent	⑲ spillover	⑳ high-end

1   Many Koreans still have the _____ idea that they unconditionally support candidates from their hometown while hating candidates from outside.

2   He was widely accused of corruption and _____, and the economic boom he presided over benefited mainly his family and a coterie of advisers.

3   Critics of the smoking ban cannot _____ the very positive impact it has had, according to the impressive figures released at the weekend.

4   Children are especially good at coming up with _____ notions because of their powerful imaginations.

5   Attendance at the workshop is _____ for all faculty members except those scheduled to teach while it is in session.

6   Most fine restaurants these days will charge you an arm and a leg for a meal good enough to satisfy a real _____.

7   During slavery in the United States, it was rare for a slave owner to _____ his slaves.

8   The U.S. and U.K. financial market crises had a(n) _____ effect on the rest of the world, which explains the synchronized global slowdown.

9   Looters _____, burned and vandalized shops in Haiti's capital after two days of violent protests over the government's attempt to raise fuel prices.

10   Refugees from war-torn countries encounter terrible _____.

[3] Choose the one which is different from the others.

11 ① prudent ② unerring ③ sapient ④ sage

12 ① nadir ② apex ③ pinnacle ④ vertex

13 ① despotic ② autocratic ③ tyrannical ④ autonomous

14 ① avaricious ② insatiable ③ grisly ④ rapacious

15 ① grandiloquent ② provocative ③ bombastic ④ pompous

16 ① aberrant ② abnormal ③ deviant ④ definitive

17 ① tricky ② sly ③ vigilant ④ wily

18 ① biddable ② diabolical ③ fiendish ④ devilish

19 ① desolate ② barren ③ dreary ④ gregarious

20 ① logomachy ② edification ③ bicker ④ quarrel

✔ Answers

1 ③ | 아직도 많은 한국인들은 자신의 고향 출신 후보를 맹목적으로 지지하지만, 외부에서 온 후보를 싫어하는 편협한 생각을 가지고 있다.

2 ⑤ | 그는 부패와 족벌주의로 매우 비난받았고, 그가 주도한 경제 호황은 주로 자신의 가족과 조언자들의 집단에게 이로웠다.

3 ⑩ | 주말에 공개된 인상 깊은 수치에 따르면 금연정책을 비판하는 사람들은 금연정책이 미치는 긍정적인 영향을 부인할 수 없다.

4 ① | 아이들은 특히 상상력이 풍부하기 때문에 억지스러운 생각을 잘 떠올린다.

5 ⑮ | 워크숍 기간 중에 수업을 진행하기로 예정되어 있는 교수들을 제외하고는 워크숍 참가는 모든 교수들에게 의무사항이다.

6 ⑬ | 요즘 대부분의 고급 레스토랑은 진정한 미식가를 만족시킬 만큼 훌륭한 식사에 대해 많은 비용을 청구한다.

7 ⑫ | 미국에서 노예 제도가 있던 기간 동안 노예를 소유했던 사람이 자신의 노예를 풀어주는 경우는 거의 없었다.

8 ⑲ | 미국과 영국의 금융시장 위기가 전 세계에 파급효과를 미쳤고, 이는 동시다발적인 세계적 경기 침체를 설명한다.

9 ④ | 정부의 유류 가격 인상 시도에 대한 이틀간의 폭력 시위가 있은 후 아이티 수도에서 약탈자들이 상점들을 약탈하고, 불태우고, 파손했다.

10 ⑪ | 전쟁으로 짓밟힌 나라의 난민들은 끔찍한 역경을 겪는다.

- -

11 ② **12** ① **13** ④ **14** ③ **15** ② **16** ④ **17** ③ **18** ① **19** ④ **20** ②

[1] Write the meaning of the following words.

☐ clumsy	☐ meditate
☐ decry	☐ ransom
☐ introduction	☐ tantamount
☐ viable	☐ load
☐ backfire	☐ concoct
☐ underpinning	☐ skeptical
☐ tender	☐ formula
☐ scapegoat	☐ hazardous
☐ doublespeak	☐ saunter
☐ quantify	☐ monotheism
☐ perigee	☐ elucidate
☐ squeeze	☐ passionate
☐ aisle	☐ choreography
☐ naive	☐ atone
☐ detached	☐ global
☐ incite	☐ falsify
☐ plaintive	☐ bivouac
☐ hemorrhage	☐ odd
☐ snatch	☐ somersault
☐ affable	☐ ethos
☐ massacre	☐ immediate
☐ poll	☐ thread
☐ effulgent	☐ accommodate
☐ recapitulate	☐ coffin
☐ opium	☐ dissension

[2] Select <u>the most</u> appropriate word from the box below. Each word should be used only once.

① atoned	② naive	③ tantamount	④ decry
⑤ accommodated	⑥ concoct	⑦ quantify	⑧ somersault
⑨ skeptical	⑩ saunter	⑪ scapegoated	⑫ tender
⑬ detached	⑭ backfire	⑮ recapitulate	⑯ immediate
⑰ viable	⑱ falsifying	⑲ bivouac	⑳ squeezing

1 Because without fins a shark can not survive, shark defenders _____ practice of finning.

2 A.I. systems based on large language models can _____ false information. That is because the models are engineered to predict the next word in a sequence. They do not stick to facts.

3 South Koreans say Japan never properly apologized or _____ for its brutal colonial rule of the Korean Peninsula from 1910 to 1945.

4 He saw racism becoming more "obvious" in recent years as some politicians _____ immigrants to cover "for their poor administration."

5 Any aggressive act on their part now would be _____ to war.

6 She thought that spreading those rumors about her rival would work in her favor, but little did she know it would eventually _____.

7 That scientific communities regard _____ data as such a serious crime is meant to reduce that temptation.

8 Israelis see their politicians as self-absorbed, totally _____ from the everyday life of their constituency, as if they live on another planet.

9 Penny stocks are notoriously volatile and often manipulated, frequently causing _____ investors to lose most or all of their money.

10 During the presentation, the speaker was asked to summarize the main points and key takeaways. In response, the speaker proceeded to _____.

[3] Choose the one which is different from the others.

11 ① clumsy ② awkward ③ gauche ④ suave

12 ① doleful ② plaintive ③ raucous ④ mournful

13 ① enthusiastic ② apathetic ③ ardent ④ passionate

14 ① ponder ② contemplate ③ meditate ④ overlook

15 ① rectify ② clarify ③ elucidate ④ explicate

16 ① incandescent ② effulgent ③ spatial ④ radiant

17 ① underpinning ② conciliation ③ brace ④ buttress

18 ① provoke ② instigate ③ incite ④ mutilate

19 ① affable ② adroit ③ amiable ④ congenial

20 ① typical ② bizarre ③ strange ④ odd

✔ Answers

1 ④ | 지느러미가 없이 상어는 살 수 없기 때문에 상어보호주의자들은 지느러미를 자르는 행위를 비난한다.

2 ⑥ | 대규모 언어 모델을 기반으로 한 인공지능 시스템은 잘못된 정보를 만들어낼 수 있다. 즉 그 모델들은 순서대로 다음 단어를 예측하도록 설계되었기 때문인데, 이 모델들은 사실을 고수하지 않는다.

3 ① | 한국인들은 일본이 1910년부터 1945년까지 한반도를 잔혹하게 식민 통치한 것에 대해 제대로 사과하거나 속죄하지 않았다고 말한다.

4 ⑪ | 그는 일부 정치인들이 "그들의 부실한 행정"을 감추기 위해 이민자들을 희생양으로 삼으면서 인종차별이 최근 몇 년간 더 악화되어 가는 것을 보았다.

5 ③ | 그들 편에서 하는 그 어떤 침략행위도 이제 전쟁과 다를 바 없는 게 될 것이다.

6 ⑭ | 그녀는 경쟁자에 대한 소문을 퍼뜨리는 것이 그녀에게 유리할 것이라고 생각했지만, 그것이 결국 역효과를 가져올 것이라는 것은 알지 못했다.

7 ⑱ | 과학계가 데이터를 위조하는 것을 심각한 범죄로 간주하는 것은 그러한 유혹을 줄이기 위한 것이다.

8 ⑬ | 이스라엘 사람들은 정치인들을 마치 또 다른 행성에 사는 것처럼 자기 선거구의 일상적인 삶에서 완전히 분리된 자기중심적인 사람으로 여긴다.

9 ② | 페니스톡(투기적 저가주(低價株): 1주의 가격이 1달러 미만의 주식)은 변동성이 심하기로 악명 높고 종종 조작되어 순진한 투자자들이 그들의 돈의 대부분 또는 전부를 잃게 만든다.

10 ⑮ | 발표가 진행되는 동안 발표자는 주요 내용과 핵심 요점을 요약해 달라는 요청을 받았다. 이에 응하여 발표자는 요점을 되풀이해서 말했다.

11 ④ **12** ③ **13** ② **14** ④ **15** ① **16** ③ **17** ② **18** ④ **19** ② **20** ①

☑ **DAILY CHECKUP**

[1] Write the meaning of the following words.

☐ rebuke	☐ warrant
☐ genuine	☐ passive
☐ chunk	☐ javelin
☐ inadvertent	☐ smuggle
☐ brood	☐ exact
☐ stenography	☐ afflict
☐ malignant	☐ out-of-date
☐ plenary	☐ vomit
☐ slim	☐ circumstance
☐ taunt	☐ lesion
☐ embark	☐ merger
☐ daring	☐ bestial
☐ nod	☐ deficiency
☐ disposition	☐ apologize
☐ shoal	☐ illusion
☐ inherit	☐ cognitive
☐ far-reaching	☐ velocity
☐ charge	☐ flabbergast
☐ effrontery	☐ deft
☐ solid	☐ appendix
☐ long-winded	☐ boundary
☐ acquired	☐ pallid
☐ haven	☐ responsible
☐ percolate	☐ muzzle
☐ terrific	☐ scrap

[2] Select <u>the most</u> appropriate word from the box below. Each word should be used only once.

① lesion	② flabbergasted	③ daring	④ responsible
⑤ appendix	⑥ effrontery	⑦ acquired	⑧ passive
⑨ haven	⑩ cognitive	⑪ malignant	⑫ smuggled
⑬ afflicted	⑭ pallid	⑮ percolated	⑯ merger
⑰ bestial	⑱ javelin	⑲ inadvertent	⑳ muzzle

1   Despite the potential risks and uncertainties, she embarked on a(n) _____ adventure to climb the treacherous mountain peaks.

2   The politician had the _____ to ask the people he had insulted to vote for him.

3   Ecuador has long been a relatively safe _____ in the region, but in recent years it has seen rising violence and a skyrocketing homicide rate.

4   Illegal immigrants may be _____ into the country for a fee, but if caught they can be deported.

5   Some of the same problems that seemed to have always _____ humanity — hunger, disease, violence and war — continue to weigh heavily on the lives of millions of people.

6   She was _____ when she came to wrap a laptop she bought on Amazon and found the shipping box stuffed with two cartons of cereal.

7   A reclusive author was _____ from spending too much time indoors.

8   Domain names such as "Amazom.com" had been registered to take advantage of _____ misspellings of online users of Amazon.

9   He is widely regarded as a(n) _____ narcissist; twisting the truth, gaslighting and bullying.

10   While human beings learn to rise above their _____ nature, animals are simply animals.

[3] Choose the one which is different from the others.

11	① disposition	② bent	③ animosity	④ propensity
12	① recondite	② adroit	③ deft	④ skillful
13	① veritable	② genuine	③ sincere	④ spurious
14	① absolute	② partial	③ plenary	④ complete
15	① rebuke	② reprimand	③ reproach	④ refrain
16	① confide	② mull	③ brood	④ contemplate
17	① core	② border	③ boundary	④ perimeter
18	① long-winded	② prolix	③ terse	④ verbose
19	① solid	② hard	③ sturdy	④ flimsy
20	① widespread	② provincial	③ broad	④ far-reaching

✓ Answers

1 ③ | 잠재적인 위험과 불확실성에도 불구하고, 그녀는 위험한 산봉우리를 오르는 대담한 모험을 시작했다.

2 ⑥ | 그 정치가는 뻔뻔스럽게도 그가 모욕한 사람들에게 자신을 위해 투표해 달라고 부탁했다.

3 ⑨ | 에콰도르는 오랫동안 이 지역에서 비교적 안전한 안식처였지만, 최근 몇 년 동안 폭력이 증가하고 살인율이 치솟고 있다.

4 ⑫ | 불법 이민자들은 수수료를 내고 밀입국할 수 있지만, 적발되면 추방될 수 있다.

5 ⑬ | 배고픔, 질병, 폭력, 그리고 전쟁과 같이, 인류를 항상 괴롭혀 온 것처럼 보이는 똑같은 문제들 중 일부는 수백만 명의 삶을 지금도 계속해서 짓누르고 있다.

6 ② | 그녀는 아마존에서 산 노트북을 포장하러 왔다가 시리얼 두 상자가 들어있는 배송 상자를 발견했을 때 깜짝 놀랐다.

7 ⑭ | 은둔한 작가는 실내에서 너무 많은 시간을 보내서 창백했다.

8 ⑲ | "아마좀 닷컴(Amazom.com)"과 같은 도메인 이름은 아마존의 온라인 사용자들의 부주의한 스펠링 실수를 이용하기 위해서 등록되었다.

9 ⑪ | 그는 진실을 왜곡하고 가스라이팅을 하며 괴롭힘을 가하는 악의적인 나르시시스트로 널리 여겨진다.

10 ⑰ | 인간은 짐승의 본성을 초월하는 법을 배우지만, 동물은 그저 동물일 뿐이다.

11 ③ **12** ① **13** ④ **14** ② **15** ④ **16** ② **17** ① **18** ③ **19** ④ **20** ②

☑ **DAILY CHECKUP**

[1] Write the meaning of the following words.

☐ accelerate	☐ askew
☐ tenuous	☐ impel
☐ mayhem	☐ hangover
☐ deceit	☐ exponential
☐ commodious	☐ gauge
☐ reconcile	☐ conglomerate
☐ kernel	☐ include
☐ sedulous	☐ encyclopedia
☐ chance	☐ sift
☐ bulge	☐ perfunctory
☐ misconception	☐ fidgety
☐ defy	☐ emerge
☐ persistent	☐ taper
☐ liable	☐ severe
☐ specialize	☐ vanguard
☐ frolic	☐ obliterate
☐ desirable	☐ tempest
☐ belated	☐ marginal
☐ aggressive	☐ stillborn
☐ parliament	☐ clutter
☐ obstreperous	☐ premium
☐ statistics	☐ heinous
☐ inactive	☐ deluge
☐ uproot	☐ extenuate
☐ nasty	☐ tropic

[2] Select <u>the most</u> appropriate word from the box below. Each word should be used only once.

① mayhem	② vanguard	③ belated	④ tenuous
⑤ defy	⑥ heinous	⑦ fidgety	⑧ desirable
⑨ frolic	⑩ reconcile	⑪ gauge	⑫ extenuate
⑬ exponential	⑭ sift	⑮ uprooted	⑯ impel
⑰ obliterate	⑱ deluge	⑲ stillborn	⑳ bulge

1   Mars receives only about half as much of the sun's warming radiance as Earth, and the Red Planet's atmosphere is too _____ to hold on to much heat.

2   Terrorists will continue to rely on the tactics of the past: attacks on aviation and the use of conventional explosives to spread _____.

3   A mediator is an impartial person who helps _____ a dispute between two or more parties.

4   A New World lizard, the basilisk, occasionally does something that seems to _____ physics: it runs across the surface of water for distances of up to thirty feet.

5   The pandemic has exacerbated the struggles of local economies and _____ many people from their communities.

6   Despite his efforts to remain calm, the patient became increasingly _____ as the wait for the doctor grew longer.

7   The group of innovators who are at the forefront of a movement or change are often referred to as the _____.

8   Japanese imperialists instituted a policy to _____ Korean language and customs by forcing Korea to use their own system and culture.

9   Since the judge feels that defendant's offence is _____, he will probably give him a hefty sentence.

10   The lawyer worked hard to present evidence that would help _____ the defendant's role in the crime.

[3] Choose the one which is different from the others.

11 ① sedulous   ② unilateral   ③ assiduous   ④ diligent

12 ① core   ② gist   ③ kernel   ④ sequence

13 ① boisterous   ② obstreperous   ③ coarse   ④ loud

14 ① nimble   ② dormant   ③ inactive   ④ inert

15 ① perfunctory   ② cursory   ③ superficial   ④ meticulous

16 ① tempest   ② trepidation   ③ commotion   ④ tumult

17 ① accelerate   ② expedite   ③ retard   ④ hasten

18 ① deceit   ② fraud   ③ trickery   ④ fidelity

19 ① preposterous ② aggressive   ③ belligerent   ④ hostile

20 ① ample   ② extravagant   ③ spacious   ④ commodious

✓ Answers

1 ④ ┃ 화성은 지구에 비해 태양의 따뜻한 빛을 절반 정도만 받고, 화성의 대기는 너무 희박해서 많은 열을 지킬 수 없다.

2 ① ┃ 테러리스트들은 무차별 폭력을 확산시키기 위해 항공기에 대한 공격과 재래식 폭발물을 사용하는 등 과거의 전술에 계속 의존할 것이다.

3 ⑩ ┃ 중재자는 둘 이상의 당사자 간의 분쟁을 조정하는 데 도움이 되는 공정한 사람이다.

4 ⑤ ┃ 신세계의 도마뱀인 바실리스크는 때때로 물리학을 거스르는 것처럼 보이는 일을 해낸다. 물 위를 최대 30피트의 거리만 큼 뛰어서 건너는 것이다.

5 ⑮ ┃ 팬데믹은 지역 경제의 어려움을 악화시켰고, 많은 사람들을 그들의 공동체에서 몰아내었다.

6 ⑦ ┃ 침착하려고 노력했음에도 불구하고 의사를 기다리는 시간이 길어지면서 그 환자는 점점 안절부절못하게 되었다.

7 ② ┃ 운동이나 변화의 최전선에 있는 혁신가 집단을 종종 선봉장이라고 부른다.

8 ⑰ ┃ 일본 제국주의자들은 한국인들에게 자국의 제도와 문화를 사용하도록 강요함으로써 한국의 언어와 관습을 말살하는 정책을 폈다.

9 ⑥ ┃ 판사는 피고의 범죄가 극악하다고 생각하기 때문에, 그는 아마도 그에게 무거운 형을 내릴 것이다.

10 ⑫ ┃ 변호사는 범죄에서 피고인의 역할을 경감시키는 데 도움이 될 증거를 제시하기 위해 열심히 노력했다.

11 ②   **12** ④   **13** ③   **14** ①   **15** ④   **16** ②   **17** ③   **18** ④   **19** ①   **20** ②

ACTUAL TEST

[01-100] Choose the one that is closest in meaning to the underlined part.

01 The judge convicted some, while others were <u>acquitted</u>.
① disregarded   ② absolved
③ upbraided   ④ condemned

02 Pollutants introduced into a lake can rapidly <u>accelerate</u> its natural aging process.
① facilitate   ② devastate
③ decelerate   ④ fluctuate

03 The trailer became <u>detached</u> from the truck that was pulling it.
① damaged   ② fixed
③ fastened   ④ loose

04 Bellow's characters have selves and <u>interact</u> with society.
① agree   ② identify
③ compete   ④ mingle

05 They <u>frolicked</u> for half an hour.
① played   ② practiced
③ walked   ④ rode

06 Zidane had suffered <u>taunts</u> throughout his career because of his Algerian heritage.
① compliment   ② indifference
③ mockery   ④ prejudice

07 According to <u>proponents</u> of code-based approaches to reading, reading should be taught by presenting the basic skills that underlie reading.
① initiators   ② commentators
③ advocates   ④ specialists

08 Illustrations of this sort could be multiplied by reference to the <u>belated</u> identification of uranium fission.
① beloved   ② tardy
③ related   ④ premature

09 Democrats suggested the tweet was <u>tantamount</u> to a criminal act, and could be added to possible articles of impeachment.
① equivalent   ② tenable
③ revealing   ④ generous

10 Every citizen has a stake in the <u>emergence</u> of the United States as a leader in a free world.
① acceptance   ② joining
③ status   ④ appearance

11 Bureaucracies, by the very nature of their structure and function, are <u>geared to</u> stability or slow change.
① provided with   ② resistant to
③ oriented to   ④ equipped with

12 In polytheisms, the divinities are universally represented as male or female, virile and **fecund**.
① benedictory ② sacred
③ reciprocal ④ prolific

13 Many priceless artworks would have been lost forever, had it not been for their **painstaking** efforts.
① exuberant ② thorough
③ vivacious ④ impeccable

14 The situation has improved somewhat with **mandatory** hearing tests and the Internet, but can be grim sometimes.
① modified ② compulsory
③ exemplary ④ mundane

15 Current business conditions call for **aggressive** cost containment measures on our part.
① minimal ② prompt
③ active ④ severe

16 After Duke Ellington had been afflicted by cancer, his strength was **decimated**.
① recovered slowly
② was greatly decreased
③ was reduced little by little
④ made up for the loss

17 On the **skeptical** side, psychologist Shawn Bryant observes that some reports of alien encounters have been linked to strong electromagnetic fields.
① doubtful ② authentic
③ universal ④ psychological

18 She **embarked on** her career by working as a newspaper reporter in Wisconsin.
① took a trip to
② started out on
③ improved upon
④ had an opinion about

19 He is a stoic. He bears his pain or sorrow without complaint, and meets **adversity** with unflinching fortitude.
① chance ② failure
③ opposition ④ difficulties

20 A 'phantom,' in the sense that neurologists use, is a **persistent** image or memory of part of the body, usually a limb, for months or years after its loss.
① enduring ② pernicious
③ perplexed ④ perilous

21 She had been bed-ridden for half a year, and when she finally appeared in public, her **pallid** face gave her a ghost-like appearance.
① pale ② grotesque
③ distorted ④ paltry

22 Tom had planned to go to the beach, but a typhoon **intervened**.
① intertwined ② intruded
③ disappeared ④ percolated

23 It was Daniel Chester French who created the **colossal** figure of Abraham Lincoln in the Lincoln Memorials in Washington, D.C.
① gigantic ② somber
③ dignified ④ inspiring

24 What has drawn the most <u>ire</u> is the first exhibit at the museum, which does not reflect the reality to the people's mind.
① discomfort   ② praise
③ disappointment   ④ anger

25 Johnson's statement included <u>an implicit</u> threat of U. S. intervention.
① a tacit   ② a definite
③ a concrete   ④ an inevitable

26 In a world ruled by photographic images, all framing borders seem <u>arbitrary</u>: anything can be separated and made discontinuous, from anything else.
① whimsical   ② tyrannical
③ random   ④ absolute

27 When he <u>sauntered</u> onto the scene at 12:50, there was really no harm done.
① came together   ② strolled
③ entered   ④ retired

28 "Economy" is the title of the first chapter of *Walden*, and Thoreau's definition of that term <u>recapitulates</u> the lesson he learned from his life in the woods.
① reveals   ② summarizes
③ exemplifies   ④ augments

29 The students enjoyed the professor's <u>sapient</u> digressions more than his formal lectures.
① pious   ② smart
③ noisy   ④ assured

30 I never understand his intention; he speaks so <u>vaguely</u>.
① equivocally   ② demonstrably
③ loudly   ④ contentedly

31 The newcomer, though highly paid, was sadly dissatisfied with the <u>parochial</u> attitudes of the people in the workplace.
① hostile   ② naive
③ unenergetic   ④ narrow-minded

32 We notice that alcohol and drugs are a major factor influencing <u>aberrant</u> behavior.
① fastidious   ② deviant
③ impulsive   ④ rebellious

33 The government has agreed to allow the mines to stay in operation, as long as they can show that they can become <u>viable</u>.
① credible   ② decisive
③ forcible   ④ practicable

34 The main tendency of modern economics is to leave uninvestigated its own method and the historical, empirical and social <u>underpinnings</u> of the subject unchallenged.
① foundation   ② probabilities
③ understanding   ④ contemplation

35 No year in our history has ever been free of tumult and trauma; the belief that there was a time when our nation enjoyed <u>tranquility</u> and prosperity is sheer illusion.
① equity   ② quietude
③ maturity   ④ sincerity

36 The snow was so heavy that it obliterated the highway.
① distorted   ② blocked
③ froze   ④ effaced

37 European farmers are planning a massive demonstration against farm subsidy cuts.
① incentive   ② financial aid
③ graft   ④ settlement

38 The dealer confirmed that the sapphire was genuine.
① imitations   ② inexpensive
③ artificial   ④ real

39 Mr. John Bath elucidated that this problem can be solved without further survey.
① contended   ② clarified
③ condensed   ④ implied

40 Be sure to do your homework. Keep track of names, faces, connections and important dates — people are flattered when you remember things about them.
① get angry
② feel betrayed
③ get frightened
④ feel pleased

41 Many criticize the idea of universal basic income as a naive, utopian ideal that will never be realized.
① enviable   ② inevitable
③ ingenuous   ④ versatile

42 In a total eclipse, the moon covers the entire surface of the sun, bringing an eerie twilight to observers in the path of totality and revealing the sun's ghostly corona.
① awesome   ② spooky
③ cloudy   ④ elusive

43 Electricity would rob the cottage of its quaint charm and romance.
① old-fashioned ② elegant
③ outstanding   ④ rural

44 The ex-convict devoted himself to community service in an attempt to atone for his past misdeeds.
① cover up
② make amends
③ have concern
④ show consideration

45 Do not attempt to increase your stature by decrying the efforts of your opponents.
① deleting   ② deceiving
③ disparaging   ④ deluding

46 I never expected my proposal to create such dissension among the new members of our organization.
① wild applaud
② great curiosity
③ shared fear
④ strong disagreement

47 Neon is an element which does not combine readily with any other element. Because of this property, it is referred to as an <u>inactive</u> element.
① obsolete   ② inert
③ acute   ④ effective

48 Anyone who is forced to do this must stop because it would be better for their salvation. There is no crime more <u>heinous</u> than this.
① hazardous   ② heedless
③ atrocious   ④ hindmost

49 John's behaviour caused <u>affliction</u> to Jane as she did not expect such a wild behaviour.
① utility   ② anguish
③ feature   ④ capability

50 The teacher continually <u>rebuked</u> the pupil for the missing assignments.
① regarded   ② admonished
③ complimented   ④ refined

51 The <u>scrupulous</u> care he put into his work helped him advance at the company.
① unrelenting   ② obsessive
③ escalating   ④ meticulous

52 The newspaper's error was <u>inadvertent</u>; the editor did not mean to include the victim's name.
① tolerant   ② negligible
③ inevitable   ④ unintended

53 I shall now therefore humbly propose my own thoughts, which I hope will not be <u>liable</u> to the least objection.
① answerable   ② understandable
③ inevitable   ④ consentable

54 To avoid being penalized for missing practice, the footballer <u>concocted</u> a story about getting a flat tire.
① made up   ② showed off
③ picked on   ④ came by

55 The <u>kernel</u> of that message was that peace must not be a source of advantage or disadvantage for anyone.
① core   ② format
③ channel   ④ hospitality

56 Members of the Committee reached <u>unanimous</u> agreement on certain points.
① wanton   ② effective
③ accordant   ④ tenable

57 I have to <u>decline</u> your invitation to the party, for I have a prearrangement.
① accept   ② refuse
③ consider   ④ apply

58 People often <u>charge</u> that a knowledge of mathematics leads to the illusion of certainty and a consequent arrogance.
① claim   ② propose
③ demand   ④ blame

59 Amid the elegant decor, there was an <u>odd</u> painting on the wall that seemed to clash with the overall aesthetic of the room.
① splendid   ② peculiar
③ paltry   ④ sketchy

60 The summit meeting will bring about a reconciliation between groups which were formerly antagonistic to one another.
① modesty　② competition
③ frugality　④ pacification

61 We have to uproot the sexual caste system that is the most pervasive power structure in society.
① eradicate　② entangle
③ adorn　④ nourish

62 Mickey Mouse's close association with children required that he always remain upstanding and moral, leaving the cantankerous Donald Duck to get into all the trouble.
① greedy　② reckless
③ grumpy　④ self-indulgent

63 Primitive peoples do devote certain types of goods to facilitating production, and from time to time accumulate them in advance for this specific purpose.
① exhaust　② scatter
③ hoard　④ disperse

64 As for the two countries' leaders, even a perfunctory handshake in Beijing would be something, while a substantive meeting would be best of all.
① superficial　② hostile
③ spontaneous　④ calculated

65 At times you are extroverted, affable, and sociable, but at other times you are wary and reserved.
① mean　② aggressive
③ prudent　④ friendly

66 California politicians are patting themselves on the back for enacting the nation's first comprehensive overhaul of home-mortgage laws that will protect struggling homeowners from rapacious bankers.
① giving unwillingly
② ready to give
③ greedy for money
④ difficult to deal with

67 The music has a very plaintive air about it.
① healthy　② noisy
③ melancholy　④ pleasant

68 Your mood seems very meditative this evening.
① gleeful　② thoughtful
③ desperate　④ stern

69 Some legislators made a rather tenuous argument against the bill.
① spurious　② flimsy
③ recalcitrant　④ gauche

70 What is lamentable is that beauty is the only form of power that most women are encouraged to seek.
① respectable　② accountable
③ surprising　④ sad

71 Rhetoric is the art of using language persuasively. That is not to say that rhetoric is always used with <u>malicious</u> motives.

① spiteful   ② irritable

③ contrived   ④ assiduous

72 The speaker was asked to <u>condense</u> his presentation in order to allow his audience to ask questions.

① abbreviate   ② expand

③ continue   ④ postpone

73 Mr. Mayfield was reluctant to <u>tender</u> an apology to me.

① soft   ② regret

③ offer   ④ deny

74 Storytelling has been used by Palestinians to <u>recount</u> the suffering that they have incurred since they were dispossessed of their land over the years.

① describe   ② remember

③ record   ④ relieve

75 The <u>deluge</u> of information generated in recent years placed a burden on the government.

① chaos   ② dagger

③ oasis   ④ flood

76 Many colleges seem to distill the free-floating <u>bigotry</u> of American society into a lethal brew.

① exertion   ② volition

③ perspective   ④ intolerance

77 Chinese efforts were <u>assuredly</u> part of a larger plan to spread its influence across the world.

① allegedly   ② particularly

③ certainly   ④ ultimately

78 Starbucks isn't the only <u>upscale</u> company facing pressure from cheaper alternatives.

① high-end   ② tacky

③ reasonable   ④ upbeat

79 I do not pretend to be <u>omniscient</u>, but I am positive about this fact.

① optimistic   ② credulous

③ all-knowing   ④ philosophical

80 China is preparing strong policies to support locally based semi-conductor companies, following an agreement with the U.S. to <u>scrap</u> its preferential tax regime.

① discard   ② collectivize

③ implement   ④ modify

81 For miles around, there was nothing but the lonely and <u>desolate</u> forest.

① noisy   ② busy

③ empty   ④ queer

82 Intellectual curiosity acts as <u>an impelling</u> force in science.

① a deterrent   ② an organizing

③ a motivating   ④ an encroaching

83 Novelist Ernest Hemingway <u>deftly</u> depicted the human misery that lay beneath the superficial gaiety of the 1920's.
① skillfully   ② prudently
③ occasionally   ④ humorously

84 Why do you always take such a <u>jaundiced</u> view of everything?
① pessimistic   ② cynical
③ prejudiced   ④ optimistic

85 Many people believe that Tom's <u>disposition</u> is responsible for this great result.
① affluence   ② temperament
③ dominance   ④ background

86 The flamingo eats in a peculiar manner: It plunges its head underwater and <u>sifts</u> the mud with a fine hairlike "comb" along the edge of its bent bill.
① pull something out sharply
② change in position or direction
③ move suddenly forwards or downwards
④ put something through a sieve

87 Young children definitely <u>emulate</u> older brothers or sisters, so siblings must pay attention to who is watching them.
① quarrel with   ② imitate
③ admire   ④ entertain

88 The owner seemed determined to <u>defy</u> his guests, not to mention his employees.
① flutter   ② disobey
③ manipulate   ④ solicit

89 She messed everything up but had the <u>effrontery</u> to act as if nothing had happened.
① allegiance   ② audacity
③ discretion   ④ vacillation

90 They are attempting to <u>gauge</u> his general ability by asking questions about every kind of topic.
① demonstrate   ② measure
③ distort   ④ imitate

91 The court handed down prison sentences to affluent parents who illegally sent their children to international schools by <u>falsifying</u> documents.
① forging   ② attesting
③ allocating   ④ shredding

92 He was willing to change his views when the <u>empirical</u> evidence led him to believe that his original perceptions were wrong.
① inventive   ② experimental
③ absolute   ④ convertible

93 The population of Seattle is a <u>conglomerate</u> of people from different ethnic and cultural backgrounds.
① company   ② fluctuation
③ coalition   ④ matching

94 The novel addresses the <u>bestial</u> nature of man once civilization is broken down.
① ostentatious   ② prosaic
③ furtive   ④ brutal

95 Their quarters are a ramshackle tenement called the Ark, where the walls are green with mold and the stair rails have been pillaged for firewood.

① waived   ② harried

③ pummeled   ④ minced

96 Among Joe's salient features is his square jaw.

① noticeable   ② ugly

③ strange   ④ attractive

97 I assert that legislative power gainsays prerogative power.

① fritters   ② bolsters

③ opposes   ④ intrudes

98 They were forced to skimp on necessities in order to make their limited supplies last the winter.

① bluff   ② consume

③ squander   ④ economize

99 Many users of personal computers have rarely thought twice about making copies of their favorite software programs for friends. Now a growing number of corporations and schools are doing the same thing. They are permitting, even encouraging, their employees to duplicate software rather than buy a program for each computer in the organization. Four pirated versions are made for every legitimate package sold, according to some industry estimates.

① licensed   ② fancy

③ up-to-date   ④ equivalent

100 Almost 150 years after photovoltaic cells and wind turbines were invented, they still generate only 7% of the world's electricity. Yet something remarkable is happening. From being peripheral to the energy system just over a decade ago, they are now growing faster than any other energy source and their falling costs are making them competitive with fossil fuels. Researchers expect renewables to account for half of the growth in global energy supply over the next 20 years. It is no longer far-fetched to think that the world is entering an era of clean, unlimited, and cheap power. About time, too.

① logical   ② misleading

③ premature   ④ unrealistic

[1] Write the meaning of the following words.

☐ wane		☐ deplore
☐ individuality		☐ tonic
☐ exhilarating		☐ preferable
☐ detergent		☐ veto
☐ recipient		☐ agile
☐ compatible		☐ fealty
☐ squat		☐ threaten
☐ horizon		☐ aphorism
☐ incessant		☐ concentration
☐ mastermind		☐ ungainly
☐ garish		☐ shortcoming
☐ impoverish		☐ remark
☐ seasoned		☐ mountebank
☐ penal		☐ debunk
☐ deputy		☐ quality
☐ persuade		☐ affiance
☐ onlooker		☐ testy
☐ amend		☐ encounter
☐ sojourn		☐ vendetta
☐ philanthropy		☐ classify
☐ lissome		☐ fatuous
☐ marital		☐ palliate
☐ bolster		☐ extemporaneous
☐ stale		☐ bastard
☐ cosmic		☐ sponsor

[2] Select <u>the most</u> appropriate word from the box below. Each word should be used only once.

① waning	② exhilarating	③ amend	④ agile
⑤ threaten	⑥ debunk	⑦ philanthropy	⑧ palliate
⑨ compatible	⑩ fealty	⑪ preferable	⑫ penal
⑬ persuade	⑭ bolster	⑮ shortcoming	⑯ affiance
⑰ ungainly	⑱ extemporaneous	⑲ classify	⑳ encounter

1 The vaccines still do a decent job of preventing serious illness and death from these emerging strains of COVID, but their ability to protect against infection is _____.

2 I tried to distinguish between the *feeling* that science and religion sometimes conflict and the *belief* that they were ultimately _____.

3 An overcrowded, corrupt and poorly financed _____ system has become a breeding ground for prison gangs.

4 He sees his businesses as a form of _____, because they are focused on helping people in need.

5 During the financial meltdown, the region poured tens of billions of dollars into their economies to _____ activity and shore up employment.

6 In the water, polar bears are good swimmers but not nearly _____ enough to catch a fleeing seal, so they rely on sea ice as a platform from which to hunt.

7 Though graceful and fluid while swimming, ducks are somehow _____ on land.

8 Cynical about every existing theory, Mariella attempts to _____ the status quo every chance she gets.

9 Your dentist might give you pain-killing drugs to _____ the discomfort caused by an impacted molar.

10 _____ debate is judged on style and nimble argumentation, as the participants receive the resolution minutes before debating begins.

[3] Choose the one which is different from the others.

11	① seasoned	② fastidious	③ adroit	④ experienced
12	① tawdry	② lissome	③ slender	④ svelte
13	① bemoan	② deplore	③ commend	④ lament
14	① foolish	② inane	③ fatuous	④ egregious
15	① intermittent	② constant	③ incessant	④ perpetual
16	① garish	② austere	③ gaudy	④ showy
17	① stale	② flat	③ culinary	④ vapid
18	① marital	② conjugal	③ nuptial	④ pedantic
19	① irascible	② chimerical	③ petulant	④ testy
20	① pardon	② vendetta	③ retaliation	④ vengeance

✔Answers

1 ① | 백신은 여전히 이러한 신종 코로나바이러스로 인한 심각한 질병과 사망을 예방하는 데 효과적이지만, 감염으로부터 보호하는 능력은 약화되고 있다.

2 ⑨ | 나는 과학과 종교가 때때로 충돌한다는 '느낌'과 과학과 종교는 궁극적으로 양립할 수 있다는 '믿음'을 구분하려고 노력했다.

3 ⑫ | 혼잡하고 부패하며 자금이 부족한 형벌 시스템은 교도소 갱단의 온상이 되었다.

4 ⑦ | 그는 자신의 사업이 도움이 필요한 사람들을 돕는 것에 중점을 두고 있기 때문에 자선사업의 한 형태로 생각한다.

5 ⑭ | 금융위기 동안 그 지역은 경기를 부양하고 고용을 강화하기 위해 지역 경제에 수백억 달러의 돈을 쏟아부었다.

6 ④ | 물속에서 북극곰은 수영을 잘하지만 도망가는 물개를 잡을 만큼 민첩하지는 않기 때문에 사냥을 위한 발판으로 해빙에 의존한다.

7 ⑰ | 오리는 물속에서는 우아하고 유연하게 헤엄치는지 몰라도 땅 위에서는 볼품없다.

8 ⑥ | 모든 기존의 이론에 대해 냉소적인 마리엘라(Mariella)는 기회가 있을 때마다 현상(現狀)이 잘못되었음을 밝히려고 한다.

9 ⑧ | 당신의 치과의사는 턱뼈 속에 매복해 있는 어금니로 인한 통증을 완화하기 위해 진통제를 줄 수 있다.

10 ⑱ | 즉석 토론은 참가자들이 토론이 시작되기 몇 분 전에 해결 방법을 받기 때문에, 표현법과 민첩한 토론으로 판단된다.

| 11 ② | 12 ① | 13 ③ | 14 ④ | 15 ① | 16 ② | 17 ③ | 18 ④ | 19 ② | 20 ① |

[1] Write the meaning of the following words.

☐ obsolete	☐ dreary
☐ perspicacious	☐ titanic
☐ enamor	☐ affect
☐ heretic	☐ felicity
☐ impatient	☐ construct
☐ salute	☐ envy
☐ mawkish	☐ anadromous
☐ pamphlet	☐ devout
☐ deflect	☐ uncharted
☐ outdated	☐ commission
☐ tally	☐ bibliophile
☐ inflate	☐ awake
☐ commensurate	☐ defamation
☐ smut	☐ elastic
☐ baffle	☐ petrify
☐ transparent	☐ sophisticated
☐ sob	☐ inertia
☐ maelstrom	☐ whip
☐ larceny	☐ vigorous
☐ recur	☐ outgrow
☐ yearn	☐ firmament
☐ pastoral	☐ capitalize
☐ gateway	☐ shrine
☐ hasten	☐ abiding
☐ ailment	☐ modest

[2] Select <u>the most</u> appropriate word from the box below. Each word should be used only once.

① perspicacious	② larceny	③ mawkish	④ salute
⑤ bibliophile	⑥ obsolete	⑦ ailment	⑧ defamation
⑨ abiding	⑩ commensurate	⑪ transparent	⑫ elastic
⑬ felicity	⑭ inertia	⑮ smut	⑯ petrify
⑰ anadromous	⑱ devout	⑲ envy	⑳ maelstrom

1 Computers aren't going away anytime soon, but that doesn't mean paper notebooks need to become _____. On the contrary, it's best to start using them at an early age.

2 Many _____ investors sold their tech stocks long before the market crashed.

3 The obituary to evoke emotions through overly sentimental language felt forced and _____.

4 After the enforcement of the real-name financial transaction system, the market has become more _____.

5 If you illegally download music or plagiarize a text, that may be theft, but it is not _____ because there was no physical property involved.

6 As a preacher, he was one whom all appreciated, and whose words of wise counsel, expressed with _____, and often with the charm of poetry, sank deep into the heart of the hearer.

7 Ramadan is a month of physical sacrifice and spiritual repentance, where _____ Muslims refrain from eating and drinking between sunrise to sunset.

8 The movie star filed a lawsuit against the tabloid for spreading false information about her, accusing the publication of engaging in _____.

9 The community's _____ respect for its traditions and customs has helped preserve its unique cultural identity over generations.

10 The boat flipped and hurled its passengers into the _____.

[3] Choose the one which is different from the others.

11 ① heretic   ② heathen   ③ pagan   ④ orthodoxy

12 ① vulgar   ② pastoral   ③ arcadian   ④ bucolic

13 ① fretful   ② deliberate   ③ impatient   ④ restless

14 ① outdated   ② obsolete   ③ contemporary   ④ antiquated

15 ① perplex   ② taunt   ③ bewilder   ④ baffle

16 ① indulge   ② yearn   ③ crave   ④ long

17 ① bleak   ② intimate   ③ dreary   ④ dismal

18 ① cultivated   ② sophisticated   ③ rustic   ④ urbane

19 ① vigorous   ② strenuous   ③ active   ④ placid

20 ① assuming   ② modest   ③ humble   ④ unpretending

✔ Answers

1 ⑥ ┃ 컴퓨터가 어느 때고 곧 사라지지는 않겠지만(앞으로 오랫동안 있겠지만), 그렇다고 해서 종이 공책이 쓸모없어졌다는 말은 아니다. 그렇기는커녕 오히려 어려서부터 공책을 사용하는 것이 좋다.

2 ① ┃ 선견지명이 있는 많은 투자자들은 시장이 폭락하기 훨씬 전에 기술주를 팔았다.

3 ③ ┃ 지나치게 감상적인 언어를 통해 감정을 불러일으키려는 부고는 억지스럽고 역겹게 느껴졌다.

4 ⑪ ┃ 금융실명제 시행 이후 시장은 더욱 투명해졌다.

5 ② ┃ 불법적으로 음악을 다운로드하거나 텍스트를 표절하는 경우 절도일 수 있지만, 물리적 재산이 관련되지 않았으므로 절도죄는 아니다.

6 ⑬ ┃ 설교자로서, 그는 모두가 높이 평가하는 사람이었고, 적절하게 그리고 또 때로는 시적으로 매력 있게 표현된 그의 지혜로운 조언들은 듣는 사람의 가슴에 깊이 스며들었다.

7 ⑱ ┃ 라마단은 육체적 희생과 영적 회개를 기리는 달로, 독실한 무슬림 교도들은 해가 뜰 때부터 해가 질 때까지 먹고 마시는 것을 삼간다.

8 ⑧ ┃ 그 영화배우는 자신에 대한 허위 정보를 유포한 타블로이드지에 소송을 제기했고, 그 출판사를 명예훼손 혐의로 고소했다.

9 ⑨ ┃ 지역사회의 전통과 관습에 대한 변함없는 존중은 여러 세대에 걸쳐 독특한 문화적 정체성을 유지하는 데 도움이 되었다.

10 ⑳ ┃ 보트가 뒤집혀 승객들은 소용돌이 속으로 내던져졌다.

11 ④   **12** ①   **13** ②   **14** ③   **15** ②   **16** ①   **17** ②   **18** ③   **19** ④   **20** ①

[1] Write the meaning of the following words.

☐ inane	☐ stalk
☐ straddle	☐ parlance
☐ deficit	☐ marshal
☐ perpetuate	☐ apostate
☐ unfold	☐ tolerate
☐ euphuism	☐ antidote
☐ refrain	☐ indulgent
☐ callous	☐ jejune
☐ selection	☐ verdict
☐ diminish	☐ garner
☐ malfeasance	☐ commonwealth
☐ separate	☐ perturb
☐ omnipresent	☐ literal
☐ tautology	☐ dehydrate
☐ allocate	☐ precaution
☐ intemperance	☐ vagabond
☐ rotund	☐ blossom
☐ substitute	☐ temporal
☐ wholehearted	☐ abominable
☐ demure	☐ covet
☐ soliloquy	☐ eminent
☐ mingle	☐ labile
☐ heritage	☐ familiarity
☐ flush	☐ bleak
☐ conducive	☐ expel

[2] Select <u>the most</u> appropriate word from the box below. Each word should be used only once.

① apostate	② omnipresent	③ deficit	④ jejune
⑤ perpetuate	⑥ malfeasance	⑦ conducive	⑧ inane
⑨ callous	⑩ allocate	⑪ eminent	⑫ literal
⑬ vagabond	⑭ perturb	⑮ temporal	⑯ garner
⑰ rotund	⑱ intemperance	⑲ marshal	⑳ substitute

1   The judge said he had displayed no empathy and his attitude has been cold and
_____.

2   Rather than giving Clara thoughtful and useful advice, her teacher admonished
her with hollow clichés and _____ platitudes.

3   Since Wikileaks, the term whistleblowing is ubiquitous and has been _____ in
the media.

4   Despite a strong welfare system and an infrastructure _____ to raising children,
Denmark has one of the lowest birth rates in Europe at 1.7 children per family.

5   Iranian media described Mr Rushdie as a(n) _____ — someone who has abandoned
or denied his faith — in their coverage.

6   As predicted, the poet's _____ attempts to illustrate his poetry himself failed
miserably, resulting in amateurish pictures.

7   The eerie silence of the abandoned town was enough to _____ even the most
fearless of explorers.

8   Mr. Nordstrom likes to live in _____ style, traveling all over the world.

9   The private university has produced many _____ scientists including a healthy
crop of Nobel Award winners.

10   The investigation uncovered evidence of _____ within the company, leading to
legal action against several top executives.

[3] Choose the one which is different from the others.

11 ① wholehearted   ② earnest   ③ evasive   ④ sincere

12 ① modest   ② brazen   ③ demure   ④ reserved

13 ① indulgent   ② lenient   ③ tolerant   ④ stringent

14 ① abominable   ② reticent   ③ abhorrent   ④ offensive

15 ① forfeit   ② inheritance   ③ bequest   ④ heritage

16 ① parlance   ② jargon   ③ lingo   ④ hyperbole

17 ① bear   ② tolerate   ③ dodge   ④ endure

18 ① covet   ② spurn   ③ desire   ④ crave

19 ① involuntary   ② labile   ③ unstable   ④ volatile

20 ① expel   ② banish   ③ oust   ④ absorb

✓ Answers

1 ⑨ ㅣ 판사는 그가 아무런 공감도 표현하지 않았고 그의 태도가 차갑고 냉담했다고 말했다.

2 ⑧ ㅣ 클라라(Clara)에게 사려 깊고 쓸모 있는 충고를 하기보다는 그녀의 선생님은 무의미하게 진부한 말과 공허한 상투어로 그녀를 나무랐다.

3 ② ㅣ 위키리크스(Wikileaks) 이후 내부 고발이라는 용어는 어디에나 존재하며 미디어에 편재해있다.

4 ⑦ ㅣ 아이들을 키우는 데 도움이 되는 강력한 복지 제도와 사회기반에도 불구하고, 덴마크는 가족당 자녀 수가 1.7명으로, 유럽에서 출산율이 가장 낮은 나라 중 하나이다.

5 ① ㅣ 이란 언론은 보도에서 러슈디(Rushdie)를 배교자 — 그의 신앙을 포기하거나 부인한 사람 — 로 설명했다.

6 ④ ㅣ 예상했던 대로, 자신의 시에 직접 삽화를 넣으려 했던 그 시인의 미숙한 시도는 형편없는 실패로 끝났으며, 결국 서투른 그림들만 나왔다.

7 ⑭ ㅣ 버려진 마을의 섬뜩한 정적은 가장 겁이 없는 탐험가들조차 불안하게 만들기에 충분했다.

8 ⑬ ㅣ 노드스트롬(Nordstrom) 씨는 방랑 생활을 좋아하며 전 세계를 여행한다.

9 ⑪ ㅣ 그 사립대학교는 수많은 노벨상 수상자를 포함하여 많은 저명한 과학자를 배출했다.

10 ⑥ ㅣ 조사 결과 사내에서 부정행위의 증거가 밝혀졌고 몇몇 최고 경영진을 상대로 법적 조치가 취해졌다.

11 ③   **12** ②   **13** ④   **14** ②   **15** ①   **16** ④   **17** ③   **18** ②   **19** ①   **20** ④

[1] Write the meaning of the following words.

☐ feasible	☐ myriad
☐ portend	☐ pathology
☐ dolt	☐ frown
☐ endorse	☐ auspice
☐ congenital	☐ dismiss
☐ superintend	☐ opaque
☐ infallible	☐ loathe
☐ brand	☐ pathetic
☐ descendant	☐ quantum
☐ Mediterranean	☐ exclude
☐ scintillating	☐ demented
☐ resurrection	☐ audacious
☐ touchy	☐ convalescence
☐ incremental	☐ transcend
☐ attempt	☐ haughty
☐ venal	☐ oblivion
☐ copious	☐ somatic
☐ narcissism	☐ grasp
☐ malleable	☐ enigmatic
☐ uproar	☐ belvedere
☐ rejuvenate	☐ setback
☐ bona fide	☐ appreciate
☐ cram	☐ picayune
☐ stool	☐ supreme
☐ hypochondria	☐ interlude

[2] Select <u>the most</u> appropriate word from the box below. Each word should be used only once.

① congenital	② loathe	③ belvedere	④ malleable
⑤ setback	⑥ feasible	⑦ venal	⑧ myriad
⑨ oblivion	⑩ frown	⑪ branded	⑫ enigmatic
⑬ hypochondria	⑭ somatic	⑮ resurrection	⑯ interlude
⑰ attempted	⑱ pathology	⑲ demented	⑳ transcend

1   The committee members believe that the proposal to redevelop the waterfront area is not _____ due to the extremely high cost.

2   Statistics indicate that children who have _____ myopia are increasingly outnumbered by those who have an acquired form of the disease.

3   Many Muslims have been subjected to prejudice and hostility by being _____ as 'fundamentalists' or 'extremists.'

4   Our dean always seemed to go along with the group and changed his opinion to complement those around him; his _____ nature often irritated his friends.

5   The politician was known for being _____, as his actions often prioritized personal gain over ethical considerations.

6   Prosecutors _____ giving witnesses immunity, particularly in high-profile cases, because it makes it significantly more difficult to prosecute the individual who has received it.

7   If, someday, I am reduced to nothing more than a few words on a page, my body rotted down to dust and my memory faded into _____, I want to at least write some of that story for myself.

8   The _____ existence of extraterrestrial has been one of the deepest mysteries.

9   The breakdown in talks represents a temporary _____ in the peace process.

10   A person with _____ is convinced that her minor symptoms are signs of a more serious illness.

[3] Choose the one which is different from the others.

11 ① portend   ② engulf   ③ augur   ④ foretell

12 ① roundabout   ② faultless   ③ infallible   ④ unerring

13 ① touchy   ② irritable   ③ petulant   ④ cordial

14 ① turmoil   ② commotion   ③ overhaul   ④ uproar

15 ① apocalypse   ② augury   ③ auspice   ④ harbinger

16 ① opaque   ② ambiguous   ③ vague   ④ prominent

17 ① bold   ② daring   ③ audacious   ④ cowardly

18 ① convalescence   ② relapse   ③ recovery   ④ recuperation

19 ① picayune   ② inconsiderable ③ solemn   ④ trivial

20 ① void   ② endorse   ③ approve   ④ ratify

✓**Answers**

1 ⑥ ┃ 위원회의 위원들은 해안지구를 재개발하자는 제안이 비용이 매우 많이 들기 때문에 실행가능성이 없다고 믿는다.

2 ① ┃ 통계에 따르면 선천적인 근시 아동보다 후천적인 근시 아동의 수가 점점 더 많아지고 있다고 한다.

3 ⑪ ┃ 많은 무슬림들은 '근본주의자' 또는 '극단주의자'라는 낙인이 찍혀 편견과 적대감에 시달려왔다.

4 ④ ┃ 우리 학교의 학장은 항상 집단에 동조하는 듯 보였고, 주위 사람들을 보완해주기 위해 자신의 의견을 바꿨다. 그의 유연
        한 성격은 종종 동료들을 화나게 만들었다.

5 ⑦ ┃ 그 정치인은 타산적인 것으로 유명했는데, 그의 행동이 종종 도덕적인 이해보다 개인적인 이익을 우선했기 때문이었다.

6 ② ┃ 검사들은 특히 세간의 주목을 받는 사건에서 증인들에게 면책권을 주는 것을 싫어하는데, 그것은 면책권을 받은 사람을
        기소하는 것을 상당히 어렵게 만들기 때문이다.

7 ⑨ ┃ 만일 어느 날 내가 단지 한 페이지 위에 쓰인 얼마 되지 않은 어휘들이 돼버리고, 나의 몸은 썩어서 먼지가 되고 나의
        기억이 망각 속으로 흐릿해져 간다면, 나는 최소한 나 자신을 위해서 그 이야기의 일부를 쓰고 싶다.

8 ⑫ ┃ 수수께끼 같은 외계인의 존재는 가장 풀리지 않는 미스터리 중 하나이다.

9 ⑤ ┃ 회담 결렬은 평화를 위한 진행 과정에서의 일시적인 차질을 의미한다.

10 ⑬ ┃ 건강염려증이 있는 사람은 자신의 가벼운 증상이 더 심각한 질병의 징후라고 확신한다.

11 ②   12 ①   13 ④   14 ③   15 ①   16 ④   17 ④   18 ②   19 ③   20 ①

[1] Write the meaning of the following words.

☐ alternate	☐ autograph
☐ solidarity	☐ purview
☐ tangible	☐ boast
☐ connoisseur	☐ faction
☐ extensive	☐ questionnaire
☐ relish	☐ enfeeble
☐ bellicose	☐ stable
☐ victim	☐ gallant
☐ measles	☐ device
☐ vary	☐ secrete
☐ maternal	☐ opportunist
☐ strive	☐ consequence
☐ patriarch	☐ temper
☐ hitherto	☐ fluctuate
☐ decent	☐ dint
☐ rosy	☐ intrude
☐ encomium	☐ licentious
☐ savvy	☐ archenemy
☐ appease	☐ tool
☐ laundry	☐ weep
☐ potable	☐ consistent
☐ disperse	☐ meander
☐ intellect	☐ sustainability
☐ unwonted	☐ vocal
☐ comprise	☐ drift

[2] Select <u>the most</u> appropriate word from the box below. Each word should be used only once.

① bellicose	② alternate	③ solidarity	④ secrete
⑤ connoisseur	⑥ strive	⑦ stable	⑧ decent
⑨ appease	⑩ boast	⑪ potable	⑫ enfeebled
⑬ meander	⑭ fluctuate	⑮ temper	⑯ disperse
⑰ drift	⑱ faction	⑲ consistent	⑳ relished

1   The political tension between the two countries has increased since their national leaders exchanged _____ remarks.

2   The student resolved to _____ for excellence in all of her studies so that she could get a high-paying job when she graduates.

3   The water scarcity has driven people out of their homes and into the streets in search of any source, _____ or not.

4   Tear gas was used by the government's military to _____ the protesters.

5   Many species of trees _____ toxic materials into the soil to inhibit the growth of and competition from other plant species.

6   Unlike Niger and two other West African countries run by military juntas, Gabon hasn't been wracked by jihadi violence and has been seen as relatively _____.

7   The supply volume of a product can _____ depending on the market situation.

8   Inconsistent policies are causing affairs of the state to _____ aimlessly.

9   The leader decided to _____ the angry protesters by addressing their concerns and promising to take action.

10   To regain her good will, her husband has pretended to be _____ by a heart attack, but when Maude says she forgives him, he confesses that he's fine.

[3] Choose the one which is different from the others.

11 ① genuine   ② rosy   ③ optimistic   ④ promising

12 ① applause   ② exhortation   ③ encomium   ④ panegyric

13 ① astute   ② shrewd   ③ savvy   ④ guileless

14 ① unbiased   ② unusual   ③ atypical   ④ unwonted

15 ① brave   ② meek   ③ gallant   ④ valiant

16 ① purview   ② extent   ③ range   ④ entity

17 ① trespass   ② encroach   ③ subtract   ④ intrude

18 ① weep   ② praise   ③ sob   ④ lament

19 ① prodigious   ② licentious   ③ promiscuous   ④ wanton

20 ① tangible   ② concrete   ③ substantial   ④ ethereal

✓ Answers

1 ① | 양국 사이의 정치적 긴장은 두 나라의 지도자들이 호전적인 언사를 주고받은 이후 계속 고조되어 왔다.

2 ⑥ | 그 학생은 졸업했을 때 고소득 직장을 얻을 수 있도록 그녀의 모든 학업 분야에서 뛰어나기 위해 노력하기로 결심했다.

3 ⑪ | 물 부족은 사람들을 집 밖으로 내몰아 마실 수 있든 없든 수원을 찾아 거리로 나서게 했다.

4 ⑯ | 정부군은 시위자들을 해산시키기 위해 최루탄을 사용했다.

5 ④ | 많은 종의 나무들은 유독 물질을 토양에 분비해 다른 종의 성장을 억제하고 경쟁을 막는다.

6 ⑦ | 군사 정부에 의해 통치되는 니제르와 다른 두 서아프리카 국가와는 달리, 가봉은 지하드 폭력에 휘말리지 않았으며 상대적으로 안정된 것으로 여겨졌다.

7 ⑭ | 상품의 공급량은 시장의 상황에 따라 변동될 수 있다.

8 ⑰ | 일관성 없는 정책으로 국정이 방향을 잃고 표류하고 있다.

9 ⑨ | 그 지도자는 그들의 우려를 해결하고 조치를 취하겠다고 약속함으로써 분노한 시위자들을 달래기로 했다.

10 ⑫ | 그녀의 호의를 되찾기 위해 그녀의 남편은 심장마비로 쇠약해진 척했지만, 모드(Maude)가 그를 용서한다고 말하자 남편은 괜찮다고 고백한다.

11 ①   **12** ②   **13** ④   **14** ①   **15** ②   **16** ④   **17** ③   **18** ②   **19** ①   **20** ④

ACTUAL TEST

[01-100] Choose the one that is closest in meaning to the underlined part.

01 He has been <u>expelled</u> from the community.
 ① welcomed   ② banished
 ③ afflicted   ④ revenged

02 The uncertainty left everyone confused and <u>testy</u>.
 ① despondent   ② placid
 ③ irritable   ④ perplexed

03 From this data, the brain creates models that simulate <u>tangible</u> objects in the real world.
 ① integral   ② conventional
 ③ expensive   ④ palpable

04 America is the home of the new you, the <u>uncharted</u> land where pilgrims, convicts and Gatsbys set out to remold themselves from scratch.
 ① unknown   ② unconsecrated
 ③ extraordinary   ④ unanimous

05 The water in the jar is <u>potable</u>.
 ① portable   ② transferable
 ③ drinkable   ④ volatile

06 Esperanto is a language that was invented by a man named L. L. Zamenhof in 1887. It is called a <u>constructed</u> language because it didn't develop naturally.

 ① useful   ② substitute
 ③ artificial   ④ surrealistic

07 The <u>unwonted</u> behavior of the animals indicated to the farmer that a storm was approaching.
 ① urgent   ② imperious
 ③ unusual   ④ ancillary

08 The critic's review of the movie seems <u>mawkish</u> and overwrought.
 ① maudlin   ② venial
 ③ parsimonious   ④ torrid

09 The company experienced numerous <u>setbacks</u> before it could finally get the business up and running.
 ① breakthroughs   ② breakaways
 ③ letdowns   ④ turnovers

10 Instead of going forward, he <u>straddled the fence</u> between the life that was familiar and the life he knew deep in his soul he was supposed to lead.
 ① regained his confidence
 ② showed an indecisive attitude
 ③ returned an impartial verdict
 ④ made an arbitrary decision

11 It seems that soliloquy was actively discussed in the late nineteenth and early twentieth century in European psychiatry.
① monologue ② obsession
③ isolation ④ silence

12 Bill's ten previous convictions for larceny made the jury verdict that he is not innocent.
① faith ② theft
③ murder ④ fraud

13 Attitude training is necessary for all who are going to encounter young people as customers.
① attract ② meet
③ guide ④ invite

14 There is little reason to depict the scenes with the salacious, first-person point of views they are treated with, other than to scintillate.
① group with a cause
② help settle differences
③ seize by prior right
④ give off sparks

15 The opera's title reflects a callous worldview that is represented in the music.
① unsympathetic ② tender
③ eerie ④ rapturous

16 While airlines like to cry poor to justify incessant cost-cutting, last year global airlines made profits of $35bn.
① constant ② immediate
③ plausible ④ austere

17 He is not making any attempts to bolster his neighbor's fortitude.
① boost ② impede
③ mitigate ④ extenuate

18 A typical carnivore is an agile runner with sharp teeth and claws, acute hearing and eyesight, and a well-developed sense of smell.
① astute ② nimble
③ arduous ④ nefarious

19 The excitement of starting a new job is always mingled with a certain apprehension.
① mixed ② maxed
③ coaxed ④ coated

20 My timetable for this week is fairly elastic.
① disastrous ② entangled
③ set ④ flexible

21 We would very much deplore it if a popular programme were taken off as a result of political pressure.
① appreciate ② avenge
③ divulge ④ lament

22 During his sojourn in Asia, he learned much about native customs.
① exploration ② brief stay
③ research tour ④ performance

23 Those who had gained rank and power over us during the war were loath to relinquish the prestige they had obtained.
① disliked ② agreed
③ longed ④ bothered

24 After receiving his check, John <u>endorsed</u> it and took it to the bank.

① destroyed ② signed

③ folded   ④ deposited

25 Eberly went into an <u>extemporaneous</u> explanation of his intentions. Speaking off the top of his head, he imparted a rather detailed clarification.

① impromptu ② interesting

③ inadvertent ④ inveterate

26 He was saying no more than the <u>literal</u> truth.

① literary ② coined

③ imaginative ④ unexaggerated

27 While it is <u>feasible</u> to build a balloon and send it up into space, no amateur-made spacecraft has reached the limits of the Earth's atmosphere.

① impractical ② executable

③ inexpensive ④ expensive

28 His reputation as a <u>perspicacious</u> investor has been carefully cultivated over decades.

① greedy ② rewarding

③ discerning ④ courageous

29 The roots of my neighbor's tree began to <u>intrude</u> upon my property.

① preserve ② contain

③ trespass ④ negotiate

30 Some young people consider their nation's traditional values <u>obsolete</u> in this fast-changing age.

① outdated ② absolute

③ meritorious ④ variable

31 So there was this <u>exhilarating</u> sense of mission — of providing the greatness of the Internet through an unheard-of collaboration.

① exciting ② exhaustive

③ gloomy ④ grim

32 Many vegetables are easy to <u>dehydrate</u> and package for future use.

① move ② dry

③ sell   ④ eat

33 The teacher did not <u>tolerate</u> any rude behaviour in his class; as a result all the children behaved very well.

① show   ② encourage

③ put up with ④ recognize

34 Americans have grown accustomed to poor sportsmanship from their sports heroes. On the hard courts, on the clay courts, in the end zones, and on the bases, athletes gloat about their great and minor victories, and they whine when hard luck arrives. To a veteran sports fan, it is a <u>dreary</u> event.

① blithe ② lamentable

③ agreeable ④ gallant

35 First world nations actively, but not necessarily consciously, <u>perpetuate</u> a state of dependency through various policies and initiatives.

① abdicate ② expand

③ maintain ④ terminate

36 Certain amounts can be <u>garnered</u> from the American press, considering its cultural legacy.
① emasculated　② restored
③ hoarded　④ mitigated

37 Summer's heat and humidity shouldn't keep you from exercising — you just need to <u>take precautions</u>.
① avoid going out in the sun
② take measures to avoid possible dangers
③ practice beforehand
④ take every chance

38 <u>A titanic</u> wave battered the small boat and drove it toward the rocks.
① A tremendous　② A stormy
③ A sudden　④ An unexpected

39 The Pentagon's <u>bleak</u> progress report offers good reasons for a speedier withdrawal of American troops from Afghanistan.
① desolate　② bucolic
③ bleary　④ drastic

40 This was <u>an audacious</u> goal, to be sure. Within a few years, it was universally embraced by the First World and many Third World countries as well.
① a special　② a bold
③ a minor　④ an annual

41 In 1833, a small <u>faction</u> agreed to sign a removal agreement: the Treaty of New Echota.
① sect　② insect
③ bisect　④ dissect

42 The European Central Bank promised <u>copious</u> support for 2022, confirming its relaxed view on inflation and indicating that any exit from years of ultra-easy policy will be slow.
① conditional　② abundant
③ imitative　④ frugal

43 The designer has <u>an infallible</u> eye for color.
① a strict　② an effete
③ a hellish　④ an inerrant

44 If the <u>concentration</u> of greenhouse gases in the atmosphere were to increase, then more heat likely would be retained.
① application　② density
③ focus　④ emission

45 The professor's lecture was full of <u>enigmatic</u> references to Greek poetry.
① enlightening　② disturbing
③ entertaining　④ puzzling

46 That is a problem really beyond my <u>grasp</u>.
① comprehension　② imitation
③ concentration　④ imagination

47 Penguins are <u>diminishing</u> in numbers on the Antarctic Continent.
① swelling　② increasing
③ decreasing　④ thriving

48 Foreign policy is about promoting our national interests, a process which is not always <u>compatible</u> with ethical considerations.
① congruous　② ruinous
③ neglectful　④ competitive

49 She walked as demurely as possible, holding the banister with one hand and her gown in the other.
① majestically   ② joyfully
③ modestly   ④ patiently

50 Originally there was enough money to cover all expenses but venal officials took most of it.
① bribable   ② needy
③ violent   ④ greedy

51 Her large weight loss has rejuvenated her.
① slimmed again
② subjugated again
③ made look young again
④ made comfortable again

52 His bellicose personality chafed his colleagues and acquaintances.
① capricious   ② pugnacious
③ conscientious   ④ turbid

53 It was pathetic to watch the cripple struggling to maintain his balance.
① droll   ② pitiable
③ tepid   ④ indiscreet

54 That intelligence tests actually give a measurement of the intelligence of individuals is questioned by some eminent psychologists.
① strong but easily broken
② bold and wicked
③ famous and admired
④ proud and capricious

55 A life of indulgence, a "gay life," as it is falsely called, is a miserable mockery of happiness.
① frugality   ② discipline
③ luxury   ④ complaint

56 This is the author's fourteenth book, and it is clear that his creative power has waned.
① suspended   ② dwindled
③ plunged   ④ kindled

57 Dr. Kim is renowned as a devout person.
① stout   ② resolute
③ frugal   ④ pious

58 Ships passing on the high seas exchange salutes by lowering and raising their flags once.
① information   ② ceremonies
③ greetings   ④ privileges

59 Hiding under furniture while your life is in mortal danger from aerial bombardment is a petrifying experience.
① transcendental   ② exhilarating
③ terrifying   ④ impressionable

60 Whoever did this must have been demented; no sane person would have acted in such a way.
① insane   ② insoluble
③ irrelevant   ④ incessant

61 The archaeologists were baffled by the implications of the find.
① placated   ② elevated
③ puzzled   ④ alleviated

62 It's best not to ask people how their marriage is going if they are touchy about discussing their personal lives.
① sensitive   ② distinctive
③ delighted   ④ sentimental

63 Only a personal apology will appease his rage at having been slighted.
① entrench   ② placate
③ obviate   ④ modify

64 One of the most affecting pieces of film shows soldiers standing around a mass grave.
① interesting   ② loving
③ moving   ④ approving

65 Today there are no drugs which act effectively on the process of the Parkinson's disease, but there are medicines which can palliate the symptoms.
① reiterate   ② exude
③ mitigate   ④ neglect

66 There was something licentious about Laura's smile, and the mothers of teenage boys were concerned when she appeared in Beverley High School.
① promiscuous   ② listless
③ docile   ④ edifying

67 By controlling risk and employing sophisticated software, Stander has emerged from the recession even stronger.
① complex   ② sedentary
③ desultory   ④ timorous

68 What perturbs me is that magazine articles are so much shorter nowadays.
① arouses   ② bothers
③ relieves   ④ liberates

69 I don't relish telling her that her son has been arrested.
① savor   ② inveigh
③ mind   ④ defer

70 Obama's election portends a shift whose magnitude will only be realized as the younger generation comes of age.
① defies   ② belies
③ heralds   ④ implements

71 You are impatient for change now and it is time to act.
① eager   ② tolerant
③ stoic   ④ enduring

72 More and more businesses are beginning to reduce their dependence on oil because it is not a sustainable source of energy.
① suspending   ② reliable
③ alternative   ④ continuous

73 Don't get the idea that the value of music is commensurate with its sensuous appeal or that the loveliest sounding music is made by the greatest composer.
① completed with
② related to
③ applied to
④ proportional to

74 Insisting on a luxury car you cannot afford is fatuous.
① inane　　② avarice
③ pretentious　④ impetuous

75 There is something about the body which leads us to be oblivious of it and pain is the obtrusion of the body into consciousness.
① unaware　② sick
③ familiar　④ conscious

76 The Coriolis force causes all moving projectiles on Earth to be deflected from a straight line.
① reflected　② deviated
③ floated　　④ collided

77 Custody of the child was to alternate between the mother and the father.
① depict　　② prevent
③ interest　④ interchange

78 The old man resumes his career piloting the large passenger planes he had been yearning after.
① simpering　② searching
③ hankering　④ ensuing

79 He said that the development of Israel's giant oil and gas field is dependent on finding a market that is conducive to the cost of its development.
① connected　② proportionate
③ adaptable　④ helpful

80 Today women are well educated, confident and technologically savvy, and they are entering a labor market that still desperately wants them.
① improving　② knowledgeable
③ weak　　　④ pompous

81 John Rolfe, an English settler, became enamored of the Indian Princess Pocahontas and married her.
① surfeited　② transpired
③ captivated　④ envisioned

82 The defendant thought that the jury gave the right verdict.
① decision　② argument
③ testimony　④ volition

83 The new chairman brought about the resurrection of the company by firing a few dozen staffs.
① abandonment　② revival
③ abolishment　④ revolution

84 The currency championed as a source of European solidarity was exposed as an impetus for discord.
① identity　② revenue
③ expertise　④ unification

85 The plaintiff's rule can count as a bona fide authoritative rule because it can completely epistemically guide conduct.
① authentic　② omnipotent
③ immaculate　④ benedictory

86 This challenging experience helped her
    appreciate life more.
    ① undermine   ② value
    ③ regard   ④ overlook

87 After nearly 20 seasons with the Dragons,
    Pete Webster was one of the team's most
    seasoned players, capable of passing on a
    wealth of knowhow to younger members.
    ① sizzling   ② experienced
    ③ tractable   ④ tempered

88 Unfortunately, most of the criminals of these
    abominable crimes are still at large.
    ① miserable   ② minor
    ③ famous   ④ horrible

89 The officer was **gallant** in his behavior toward
    the enemy.
    ① pertinent   ② brave
    ③ obedient   ④ courtly

90 When researchers measured the mosquitos'
    wing lengths, a **substitute** for body size, they
    found the insects grew larger in wet climates.
    ① estimate   ② analogue
    ③ proxy   ④ standard

91 According to a man's experience of life, the
    book will **unfold** new meanings to him.
    ① reveal   ② instruct
    ③ conceal   ④ teach

92 The governor **vigorously** denied any previous
    knowledge of the corruption scandal.
    ① expectedly   ② strongly
    ③ timidly   ④ vaguely

93 According to information from the UNESCO
    Institute for Statistics, while film production
    fluctuates in many nations, only India
    demonstrated a consistent increase in the
    number of films produced from 2005 to
    2011.
    ① lessens   ② dwindles
    ③ varies   ④ increases

94 The money which the legislature appropriated
    for charitable uses has not yet been
    allocated.
    ① allotted   ② recognized
    ③ spent   ④ requested

95 Depression can undermine quality of life and
    contribute to disability, especially in more
    severe or persistent cases. In a given year,
    it's estimated that 1 in 15 adults will
    experience depression or have at least one
    major depressive episode. The mood
    disorder can affect **myriad** aspects of a
    person's life, from one's ability to tackle daily
    activities and work to relationships. Rather
    than involving fleeting sadness, hallmarks
    of the disorder like depressed or low mood
    and loss of interest or pleasure must
    continue for at least two weeks for a
    diagnosis of depression to be made.
    ① countless   ② crucial
    ③ flawless   ④ emotional

96 By the mid 1820s imperial attempts to create a "free market" in labour had an explosive effect on the class relations of a colony dependent on slaves and serfs. New regulations ensured standards of treatment and established equality before the law for "masters" and "servants." Ordinance 50 of 1828, which ensured Khoisan mobility on the labour market, caused an <u>uproar</u>; in 1834 slaves were finally emancipated.

① hubbub   ② humbug

③ hobble   ④ hokum

97 Acquired heart diseases are conditions affecting the heart and its associated blood vessels that develop during a person's lifetime, in contrast to <u>congenital</u> heart diseases, which are present at birth. Acquired heart diseases include coronary artery disease, rheumatic heart disease, diseases of the pulmonary vessels and the aorta, and diseases of the heart valves.

① acute   ② contagious

③ innate   ④ senile

98 In attempting to affirm their whiteness by negating the comparison between themselves and African Americans, southern Jews often <u>capitalized on</u> the fact that their place in southern society was ambiguous, rather than totally marginal.

① dealt with

② drew on

③ took advantage of

④ objected to

99 He that has once done you a kindness will be more ready to do you another, than he whom you yourself have obliged. Human <u>felicity</u> is produced not so much by great pieces of good fortune that seldom happen, as by little advantages that occur every day.

① affliction   ② resolution

③ performance   ④ happiness

100 Sir Arthur Fairbairn was a man great enough to shoulder his responsibilities gracefully, tirelessly, and successfully, leaving behind him some concrete examples of generosity and <u>philanthropy</u> as well as the memory of a genial heart and a simple soul doing good in an aristocratic manner.

① audacity   ② charity

③ publicity   ④ purity

☑ **DAILY CHECKUP**

[1] Write the meaning of the following words.

☐ peripheral	☐ tinge
☐ descend	☐ attribute
☐ vocation	☐ sarcasm
☐ incumbent	☐ decimal
☐ hinder	☐ manipulate
☐ ample	☐ congruent
☐ unseemly	☐ extinguish
☐ commune	☐ supine
☐ immemorial	☐ glossary
☐ enforce	☐ remonstrate
☐ diploma	☐ legacy
☐ nausea	☐ feminine
☐ seclude	☐ belonging
☐ breach	☐ obviate
☐ hymn	☐ certificate
☐ discharge	☐ salvage
☐ straightforward	☐ top-down
☐ paraphernalia	☐ authorize
☐ inept	☐ likeness
☐ jaywalk	☐ mope
☐ vital	☐ renaissance
☐ ensue	☐ contrite
☐ attorney	☐ fertilizer
☐ proffer	☐ preponderant
☐ moving	☐ subside

[2] Select <u>the most</u> appropriate word from the box below. Each word should be used only once.

① incumbent	② moving	③ peripheral	④ glossary
⑤ manipulate	⑥ ensue	⑦ remonstrate	⑧ salvage
⑨ obviate	⑩ seclude	⑪ subside	⑫ contrite
⑬ commune	⑭ immemorial	⑮ straightforward	⑯ enforce
⑰ discharge	⑱ jaywalk	⑲ vital	⑳ decimal

1 Scanners, printers, and speakers are _____ devices for a computer because they aren't central to the working of the computer itself.

2 Battery life is a notoriously misleading statistic, as manufacturers can _____ their in-house tests to produce better numbers.

3 He looked so _____ that she believed he really was sorry about what he had said.

4 A strong U.S. economy usually translates into more votes for the _____ in a presidential election.

5 A Buddhist monk might _____ himself in a remote place to meditate alone for several weeks.

6 The ship was lying in deep water, but we managed to _____ some of its cargo.

7 When you have a favor to ask of a friend, don't beat around the bush — say what you need in a(n) _____ way.

8 New ways to cultivate embryos from mice and stem cells could _____ the need to use real human embryos in some studies.

9 Most respiratory viruses spike in the winter and _____ in the summer, but SARS-CoV-2 has yet to completely fall into the same pattern.

10 The patient eagerly awaited the doctor's approval for _____, hoping to leave the hospital and return to normal daily activities.

[3] Choose the one which is different from the others.

11 ① vocation ② pastime ③ occupation ④ profession

12 ① embrace ② hinder ③ hamper ④ impede

13 ① violation ② infraction ③ breach ④ attachment

14 ① inept ② incompetent ③ dexterous ④ awkward

15 ① stentorian ② negligent ③ indifferent ④ supine

16 ① preponderant ② dominant ③ overriding ④ polemic

17 ① unseemly ② genteel ③ indecent ④ undignified

18 ① proffer ② propose ③ withhold ④ suggest

19 ① divergent ② congruent ③ congruous ④ corresponding

20 ① likeness ② resemblance ③ similarity ④ asymmetry

✓ Answers

1 ③ | 스캐너, 프린터 및 스피커는 컴퓨터 자체가 작동되는 데 있어 중심된 것이 아니기 때문에 컴퓨터의 주변 장치이다.

2 ⑤ | 배터리 수명은 사람들을 호도하는 통계자료로 악명 높은데, 제조업자들이 더 나은 수치를 산출하기 위해 회사 내부의 자체검사를 조작할 수 있기 때문이다.

3 ⑫ | 그가 깊이 뉘우치는 듯이 보여서 그녀는 그가 자신이 한 말에 대해 진심으로 미안해한다고 생각했다.

4 ① | 미국 경제의 호황은 대선에서 보통 현직 대통령에게 더 많은 표가 몰린다는 것을 의미한다.

5 ⑩ | 승려는 혼자 명상하기 위해 몇 주 동안 외딴곳에서 은둔할 수도 있다.

6 ⑧ | 그 배는 바다 밑에 깊이 가라앉아 있었으나 우리는 이럭저럭 일부 화물을 인양해 내었다.

7 ⑮ | 친구에게 부탁할 것이 있다면, 돌려서 말하지 말고 필요한 것을 솔직하게 말하라.

8 ⑨ | 쥐와 줄기세포에서 배아를 배양하는 새로운 방법은 일부 연구에서 실제 인간 배아를 사용할 필요성을 없앨 수 있다.

9 ⑪ | 대부분의 호흡기 바이러스는 겨울에 급증하고 여름에 가라앉지만, SARS-CoV-2(코로나바이러스)는 아직 완전히 같은 패턴에 있지 않다.

10 ⑰ | 그 환자는 병원을 떠나 정상적인 일상 활동으로 복귀하기를 바라며 의사의 퇴원 승인을 간절히 기다렸다.

11 ② **12** ① **13** ④ **14** ③ **15** ① **16** ④ **17** ② **18** ③ **19** ① **20** ④

[1] Write the meaning of the following words.

☐ concise		☐ countervail	
☐ empathy		☐ binge	
☐ betray		☐ conspicuous	
☐ proprietor		☐ off-hand	
☐ sacrifice		☐ ascertain	
☐ incorrigible		☐ gambit	
☐ retreat		☐ depict	
☐ sycophant		☐ veritable	
☐ tart		☐ lapse	
☐ keynote		☐ thermal	
☐ wicked		☐ slant	
☐ disparity		☐ conception	
☐ misty		☐ enrage	
☐ serenity		☐ principal	
☐ abridge		☐ fad	
☐ livery		☐ immerse	
☐ apex		☐ doleful	
☐ reactionary		☐ franchise	
☐ demographic		☐ maggot	
☐ mend		☐ persist	
☐ spooky		☐ auxiliary	
☐ indolence		☐ enroll	
☐ unearth		☐ omnibus	
☐ pedagogy		☐ stir	
☐ temperate		☐ helm	

[2] Select <u>the most</u> appropriate word from the box below. Each word should be used only once.

① concise	② mend	③ doleful	④ sycophant
⑤ auxiliary	⑥ principal	⑦ unearth	⑧ depict
⑨ slant	⑩ abridge	⑪ betray	⑫ retreat
⑬ sacrifice	⑭ disparity	⑮ immerse	⑯ enroll
⑰ conspicuous	⑱ reactionary	⑲ serenity	⑳ omnibus

1   He is a(n) _____ who tries to win favor from the influential politician by flattering her.

2   The 100-word message limit means employees must make emails _____ and to the point, which prevents lengthy communication.

3   Paleontologists started using the method to _____ more bones around the region, including one of the largest dinosaurs in the world.

4   The editor wants to _____ your 1,000-page masterpiece, trimming it down to the more readable essential elements.

5   You've probably heard of "human _____," where a person is killed in a sacred ceremony to please the gods.

6   When they are forced to _____, they just scatter since they have not been instructed how to pull back.

7   The goal of meditation is to reach a state of _____, when your mind is still and perfectly calm.

8   Saudi-Iranian differences run deep along sectarian lines, and it will take more than renewed diplomatic relations to _____ ties.

9   Many streets in San Francisco are so steep that they _____ dramatically upward.

10   Children _____ themselves in a universe out of their parents' reach, a world defined by computer games, TV and movies, where brutality is so common it has become mundane.

[3] Choose the one which is different from the others.

11 ① wicked   ② malevolent   ③ nefarious   ④ obedient

12 ① nadir   ② apex   ③ acme   ④ zenith

13 ① exasperate   ② infuriate   ③ enrage   ④ quell

14 ① acid   ② insipid   ③ tart   ④ sour

15 ① peevish   ② clement   ③ temperate   ④ genial

16 ① gambit   ② artifice   ③ candor   ④ maneuver

17 ① veritable   ② insincere   ③ authentic   ④ factual

18 ① ascertain   ② confirm   ③ verify   ④ refute

19 ① askance   ② off-hand   ③ extempore   ④ impromptu

20 ① countervail   ② offset   ③ countenance   ④ counteract

✓Answers

1 ④ | 그는 그녀에게 아첨하여 그 유력 정치인에게 호감을 얻으려는 아첨꾼이다.

2 ① | 100개의 단어로 메시지에 제한을 둔 것은 직원들이 이메일을 간결하고 명료하게 작성해야 하는 것을 의미하는데, 이것은 장황한 의사소통을 방지한다.

3 ⑦ | 고생물학자들은 그 방법을 사용하여 세계에서 가장 큰 공룡 중 하나를 포함하여 더 많은 뼈를 그 지역 주변에서 발굴하기 시작했다.

4 ⑩ | 편집자는 1,000페이지에 달하는 당신의 걸작을 줄여서 더 읽기 쉬운 필수적 내용이 들어간 글로 다듬기를 원한다.

5 ⑬ | 당신은 신을 달래기 위해 신성한 의식에서 사람을 죽이는 "인간 제물"에 대해 들어본 적이 있을 것이다.

6 ⑫ | 그들은 후퇴하지 않을 수 없을 때, 후퇴하는 법을 지시받지 못했기 때문에 흩어질 뿐이다.

7 ⑲ | 명상의 목표는 마음이 고요하고 완전히 평온한 평정의 상태에 도달하는 것이다.

8 ② | 사우디아라비아와 이란 사이의 이견은 종파적 노선을 따라 깊게 존재하며, 관계를 개선하기 위해서는 외교 관계를 새롭게 하는 것 이상의 것이 필요할 것이다.

9 ⑨ | 샌프란시스코의 많은 거리는 너무 가팔라서 위쪽으로 급격하게 기울어져 있다.

10 ⑮ | 아이들은 부모의 영향이 미치지 않는 세계 즉, 컴퓨터 게임, TV, 영화 등 잔인함이 너무 흔해 일상이 된 세계에 몰입한다.

- -

11 ④   **12** ①   **13** ④   **14** ②   **15** ①   **16** ③   **17** ②   **18** ④   **19** ①   **20** ③

[1] Write the meaning of the following words.

☐ dormant	☐ obstruct
☐ portent	☐ bilingual
☐ grab	☐ terminate
☐ cremation	☐ exiguous
☐ plunge	☐ sordid
☐ sinewy	☐ quarry
☐ indigenous	☐ hardship
☐ merge	☐ effusive
☐ salutary	☐ addict
☐ filthy	☐ vulgar
☐ distribute	☐ dearth
☐ infamous	☐ hitch
☐ strait	☐ tactics
☐ redeem	☐ adjure
☐ vermin	☐ phenomenon
☐ enthrall	☐ berserk
☐ accurate	☐ fathom
☐ malady	☐ pastime
☐ sensuous	☐ tolerant
☐ cramp	☐ confront
☐ surpass	☐ armistice
☐ ulterior	☐ disquiet
☐ negative	☐ mutant
☐ levity	☐ impression
☐ convenient	☐ raven

[2] Select <u>the most</u> appropriate word from the box below. Each word should be used only once.

① sinewy	② plunge	③ dormant	④ distributed
⑤ disquiet	⑥ salutary	⑦ merge	⑧ addict
⑨ sordid	⑩ mutant	⑪ redeem	⑫ surpass
⑬ berserk	⑭ terminated	⑮ strait	⑯ ulterior
⑰ tolerant	⑱ raven	⑲ portent	⑳ sensuous

1   Some researchers urge governments to step up dementia prevention with measures such as public health campaigns that encourage _____ habits.

2   Sherlock Holmes was fed up with the way he had been misrepresented by careless critics, and so he attempted to _____ his reputation by solving his last cold case.

3   In temperate regions, mosquito species are known to go _____ to survive cold winters, which makes sense because insect metabolisms naturally slow when temperatures drop.

4   He claims that his attempts to depose the leader were only for the good of the party, but I suspect he may have some _____ motive.

5   A drunken passenger went _____ on a long haul flight, trying to force open an aircraft door and spitting on passengers.

6   This disastrous summer is yet another _____ of what humanity faces in coming decades if the world does not take dramatic steps to protect ecosystems and curb use of fossil fuels.

7   The French luxury brand _____ its professional relationship with Kanye West because of his antisemitic comments.

8   The actor played a prominent politician who begins a(n) _____ affair with his son's fiancee.

9   He was a drug _____ who had started using drugs at a very young age.

10   If the same medication is used repeatedly, the patient will become _____.

[3] Choose the one which is different from the others.

11	① indigenous	② aboriginal	③ aghast	④ native
12	① notorious	② infamous	③ disreputable	④ militant
13	① meager	② plethora	③ exiguous	④ bare
14	① sincere	② boorish	③ vulgar	④ indecent
15	① deficiency	② scarcity	③ eclectic	④ dearth
16	① armistice	② stalemate	③ cease-fire	④ truce
17	① effusive	② demonstrative	③ gushing	④ apathetic
18	① sterile	② dirty	③ filthy	④ nasty
19	① repel	② enthrall	③ bewitch	④ captivate
20	① adjure	② order	③ shun	④ require

✓Answers

1 ⑥ | 일부 연구자들은 정부가 유익한 습관을 장려하는 공중 보건 캠페인과 같은 조치로 치매 예방을 강화할 것을 촉구한다.

2 ⑪ | 셜록 홈스(Sherlock Holmes)는 부주의한 비평가들이 자신을 잘못 설명해온 것에 넌더리 나서, 그의 마지막 미해결 사건을 해결함으로써 자신의 명성을 되찾으려고 시도했다.

3 ③ | 온대 지방의 모기 종들은 추운 겨울에 살아남기 위해 휴면하는 것으로 알려져 있다. 이것은 온도가 내려갈 때 곤충의 신진대사가 자연스럽게 느려지기 때문에 이치에 맞는다.

4 ⑯ | 그는 자신이 당 대표를 물러나게 하려고 한 것은 오직 당의 이익을 위한 것이었다고 강변하지만, 나는 그에게 숨은 동기가 있을 거라는 의심이 든다.

5 ⑬ | 장거리 여객기에서 술에 취한 승객이 난폭해져서 비행기 문을 열려고 했으며 다른 승객들에게 침을 뱉었다.

6 ⑲ | 피해가 막심한 이번 여름은 생태계를 보호하고 화석 연료의 사용을 억제하기 위해 극단적인 조치를 취하지 않는다면, 인류가 수십 년 안에 직면하게 될 것의 또 다른 전조이다.

7 ⑭ | 그 프랑스 럭셔리 브랜드는 카니예 웨스트(Kanye West)의 반유대주의적 발언으로 인해 그와의 업무 관계를 종료했다.

8 ⑨ | 그 연기자는 아들의 약혼자와 부도덕한 관계를 맺는 저명한 정치가를 연기했다.

9 ⑧ | 그는 아주 어린 나이부터 약물에 손을 댄 약물 중독자였다.

10 ⑰ | 같은 약을 반복해서 사용하면 환자는 내성을 갖게 된다.

- -

11 ③　12 ④　13 ②　14 ①　15 ③　16 ②　17 ④　18 ①　19 ①　20 ③

☑ DAILY CHECKUP

[1] Write the meaning of the following words.

☐ meticulous	☐ fertile
☐ preoccupation	☐ beholden
☐ imprison	☐ pronounce
☐ specter	☐ marble
☐ lengthen	☐ actuate
☐ renowned	☐ trace
☐ paroxysm	☐ cadaverous
☐ segregate	☐ inevitable
☐ genteel	☐ labyrinth
☐ resent	☐ bear
☐ en route	☐ unassuming
☐ statue	☐ fasten
☐ deadly	☐ valor
☐ assault	☐ outward
☐ perfidy	☐ tenor
☐ slang	☐ adorn
☐ communicate	☐ sanctimonious
☐ dose	☐ hiccup
☐ misconstrue	☐ concede
☐ wizened	☐ brawl
☐ jeopardy	☐ entitle
☐ enduring	☐ rapport
☐ occlude	☐ ashamed
☐ donate	☐ infidel
☐ combination	☐ disclaim

[2] Select the most appropriate word from the box below. Each word should be used only once.

① meticulous	② sanctimonious	③ brawl	④ rapport
⑤ infidel	⑥ segregated	⑦ adorn	⑧ wizened
⑨ inevitable	⑩ misconstrue	⑪ fertile	⑫ bear
⑬ assault	⑭ beholden	⑮ ashamed	⑯ resent
⑰ labyrinth	⑱ actuate	⑲ pronounce	⑳ jeopardy

1   The Taliban said women are allowed to study in universities as long as they wear Islamic dress and classrooms are _____ by gender.

2   Rabbits are famously _____ creatures; they can spawn several generations in a matter of months.

3   Some experienced interrogators emphasize the value of establishing _____ with a detainee, and obtaining information on the basis of trust, rather than cruelty.

4   Concert pianists must be _____ because audiences are always listening for wrong notes.

5   I _____ his hypocritical posing as a friend, for I know he is interested only in his own advancement.

6   Some people feel so uncomfortable being _____ to others that they try not to accept assistance from anyone out of worry over what they'd have to do in return.

7   In the late 19th century most scientists believed the brain was composed of a continuous tangle of fibers as serpentine as a(n) _____.

8   An increase in the fiscal deficit is _____ as the country is implementing large-scale stimulus packages to speed up economic recovery.

9   In the Bible, Pharisees were _____ and hypocritical people who made public show of their religious beliefs.

10   A nuclear war between two counties would place the entire planet in _____ by unleashing a climate catastrophe.

[3] Choose the one which is different from the others.

11 ① preoccupation   ② absorption   ③ concentration   ④ nonchalance

12 ① torpid   ② elegant   ③ genteel   ④ refined

13 ① perfidy   ② equity   ③ betrayal   ④ treachery

14 ① famed   ② renowned   ③ trivial   ④ prominent

15 ① lasting   ② ethical   ③ enduring   ④ abiding

16 ① cadaverous   ② wan   ③ pallid   ④ sanguine

17 ① insincere   ② unpretentious   ③ humble   ④ unassuming

18 ① valor   ② fortitude   ③ kinship   ④ gallantry

19 ① acknowledge   ② repudiate   ③ concede   ④ allow

20 ① disclaim   ② deny   ③ refuse   ④ confess

✓ Answers

1 ⑥ | 탈레반은 여성들이 이슬람 복장을 착용하고 교실이 성별로 분리되어 있다면 대학에서 공부할 수 있다고 말했다.

2 ⑪ | 토끼는 번식력이 강한 동물로 유명한데 몇 달 만에 몇 세대의 자손을 낳을 수 있다.

3 ④ | 몇몇 노련한 심문자들은 구류자와 친밀한 관계를 형성하고 무자비함이 아니라 신뢰를 바탕으로 정보를 얻는 것의 가치를 강조한다.

4 ① | 콘서트 피아노 연주가들은 매우 세심한 주의를 기울여야 하는데, 청중은 항상 잘못된 음을 찾아내려고 귀를 기울이기 때문이다.

5 ⑯ | 나는 그가 자신의 출세에만 관심이 있다는 것을 알기 때문에 그가 친구인 척하는 위선적인 모습에 분개한다.

6 ⑭ | 어떤 사람들은 다른 사람들에게 신세를 지는 것에 너무 불편함을 느껴서 그들이 그 대가로 무엇을 해야 할지에 대한 걱정으로 인해 그 누구의 도움도 받지 않으려고 한다.

7 ⑰ | 19세기 후반 대부분의 과학자들은 뇌가 미로처럼 구불구불한 섬유들의 연속적인 엉킴으로 구성되어 있다고 믿었다.

8 ⑨ | 정부가 경제 회복을 가속화하기 위해 대규모의 경기 부양책을 추진함에 따라 재정 적자의 증가가 불가피하다.

9 ② | 성경에서 바리새인들은 자신의 종교적 신념을 공개적으로 드러내는 독실한 척하는 위선적인 사람들이었다.

10 ⑳ | 두 나라 간의 핵전쟁은 기후 재앙을 초래함으로써 전 세계를 위험에 빠뜨릴 것이다.

....

11 ④   **12** ①   **13** ②   **14** ③   **15** ②   **16** ④   **17** ①   **18** ③   **19** ②   **20** ④

[1] Write the meaning of the following words.

☐ genetic	☐ transfer
☐ repercussion	☐ carnivore
☐ secular	☐ emigrate
☐ engross	☐ petty
☐ meritocracy	☐ upshot
☐ project	☐ imitate
☐ dissolute	☐ compulsive
☐ harass	☐ radius
☐ imperceptible	☐ lift
☐ tantrum	☐ fetish
☐ shatter	☐ arrogant
☐ penitent	☐ wager
☐ attain	☐ despair
☐ organism	☐ garment
☐ deem	☐ verify
☐ scathing	☐ hauteur
☐ paradox	☐ disrupt
☐ concomitant	☐ indecision
☐ reliable	☐ fictitious
☐ slumber	☐ bribe
☐ ballyhoo	☐ makeshift
☐ plural	☐ accouter
☐ sag	☐ sketchy
☐ novelty	☐ torpid
☐ apparatus	☐ correspondence

[2] Select the most appropriate word from the box below. Each word should be used only once.

① tantrum	② makeshift	③ dissolute	④ fetish
⑤ verify	⑥ penitent	⑦ meritocracy	⑧ apparatus
⑨ secular	⑩ deem	⑪ imitate	⑫ torpid
⑬ wager	⑭ imperceptible	⑮ compulsive	⑯ emigrate
⑰ bribery	⑱ reliable	⑲ hauteur	⑳ fictitious

1 While a predominately Muslim society, Turkey was founded as a staunchly _____ state that kept most outward signs of religion out of public life.

2 Affected by the capitalist way of living, he committed irregularities and corruption and led a(n) _____ and depraved life.

3 You saw a small child, incapable of expressing the complexities of why she really needed a Barbie doll, erupted into a full-blown _____.

4 The parole board recognized that some crimes are so heinous as to preclude clemency, even when the prisoner is _____ and at death's doorstep.

5 In a(n) _____, individuals are rewarded and promoted based on their skills, abilities, and performance rather than their social connections or background.

6 Rather than showing humility and respect, a despot acted with _____ toward his subjects.

7 The soccer association exonerated their chairman of _____ allegations after he admitted receiving money from Nigeria.

8 Many Haitians have been forced to flee their homes since last year, with some leaving the country and many staying in _____ shelters with deplorable hygiene.

9 The Ramadan fasting season proceeds at a(n) _____ pace beneath the sweltering midsummer sun.

10 Chaucer's peers praised his poetry, which sparked a group of 15th century writers to _____ his writing style.

[3] Choose the one which is different from the others.

11 ① repercussion   ② effect   ③ influence   ④ duplication

12 ① absorb   ② engross   ③ yield   ④ immerse

13 ① acrimonious   ② chivalrous   ③ scathing   ④ vitriolic

14 ① preeminent   ② trivial   ③ petty   ④ insignificant

15 ① indecision   ② perseverance   ③ hesitation   ④ vacillation

16 ① inadequate   ② sketchy   ③ thorough   ④ incomplete

17 ① haughty   ② timid   ③ arrogant   ④ insolent

18 ① originality   ② novelty   ③ uniqueness   ④ likeness

19 ① impetus   ② outcome   ③ upshot   ④ result

20 ① disrupt   ② agitate   ③ tranquilize   ④ disorder

✔ Answers

1 ⑨ ┃ 이슬람교가 주류를 이루고 있는 사회이지만, 터키는 대부분의 외적인 종교적 표지를 공공 생활에서 배제하는 철저한 세속 국가로 설립되었다.

2 ③ ┃ 그는 자본주의적 생활 방식에 영향을 받아 부조리와 부패를 저질렀으며 방탕하고 타락한 삶을 살았다.

3 ① ┃ 당신은 바비 인형이 왜 꼭 필요한지 복잡한 감정을 표현하지 못한 한 아이가 갑자기 짜증을 내는 것을 보았다.

4 ⑥ ┃ 가석방 위원회는 일부 범죄는 수감자가 참회하고 죽음의 문턱에 있을 때조차도 사면을 배제할 정도로 극악하다는 점을 인정했다.

5 ⑦ ┃ 능력주의에서 개인은 사회적 연줄이나 배경보다는 자신의 기량, 능력, 성과에 따라 보상받고 승진한다.

6 ⑲ ┃ 군주는 겸손과 존경심을 표하기보다는 자기 신하들에게 오만하게 행동했다.

7 ⑰ ┃ 축구연맹은 연맹 회장이 나이지리아에서 돈을 받았다고 인정한 뒤에 뇌물혐의를 용서했다.

8 ② ┃ 지난해부터 많은 아이티인들이 고향을 떠나야 했고, 일부는 국외로 떠났고, 다수는 열악한 위생 상태로 임시 보호소에 머물고 있다.

9 ⑫ ┃ 라마단 단식 기간이 무더운 한여름의 태양 아래서 활기 없는 속도로 진행되고 있다.

10 ⑪ ┃ 초서(Chaucer)의 동료들은 그의 시를 높이 평가했으며 이에 따라 15세기 작가들은 그의 문체를 흉내내기 시작했다.

11 ④   **12** ③   **13** ②   **14** ①   **15** ②   **16** ③   **17** ②   **18** ④   **19** ①   **20** ③

ACTUAL TEST

[01-100] Choose the one that is closest in meaning to the underlined part.

01 I <u>conceded</u> that it had failed.
① admitted ② feared
③ announced ④ doubted

02 Tom and Betty were lost in the <u>labyrinth</u> of secret caves.
① maze ② exterior
③ fragrance ④ fluency

03 The project lay <u>dormant</u> for two years until we found a sponsor.
① sedative ② potential
③ confidential ④ sleeping

04 The history of mankind is a history of <u>hardship</u>.
① war ② possession
③ adversity ④ competition

05 The government is prepared for an urban development in the outer <u>peripheral</u> areas of large towns.
① secondary ② marginal
③ superficial ④ insignificant

06 It is not hard to interpret his point in Oedipal terms, as dyadic or imaginary <u>rapport</u> between mother and child is triangulated by the entry of the father upon the scene.
① image ② relation
③ reference ④ memory

07 The punishment had <u>a salutary</u> effect on the boy as he became a model student.
① a useful ② a hygienic
③ a dubious ④ an enforcing

08 There is an economic <u>disparity</u> in our nations.
① inequality ② separation
③ unrest ④ pessimism

09 A compromise agreement reached in the judge's chambers would <u>obviate</u> the need for a long, costly lawsuit.
① repeal ② verify
③ preclude ④ stunt

10 The town is <u>renowned</u> for its clean streets and hospitality.
① famed ② admired
③ envied ④ slighted

11 Stricter anti-pollution laws may <u>cramp</u> economic growth.
① detour ② hinder
③ motivate ④ discord

12 She said nothing about the <u>harassing</u>.
① bullying ② gossiping
③ chatting ④ beating

13 The audience was <u>enthralled</u> by the sheer beauty of the music played by the orchestra.
① shocked   ② stimulated
③ captivated   ④ terrified

14 Just as sports have the ability to make citizens forget about their problems and differences, they can also be used as a tool to <u>manipulate</u> the public or serve political causes.
① relieve   ② handle
③ grasp   ④ tease

15 No one anticipated the unfortunate <u>repercussion</u> of the price freeze.
① strong impact
② symbolic meaning
③ violent protest
④ faint echo

16 We <u>attribute</u> her success to hard work and enthusiasm.
① ascribe   ② contribute
③ insinuate   ④ construe

17 The two businesses have become very powerful since they <u>merged</u> a year ago.
① started   ② changed
③ combined   ④ succeeded

18 In 1861 it seemed <u>inevitable</u> that the Southern states would break away from the Union.
① strange   ② certain
③ inconsistent   ④ proper

19 Being <u>concise</u> is a lot more challenging than being verbose, so this will take effort.
① rational   ② brief
③ coherent   ④ erudite

20 A 'phantom,' in the sense that neurologists use, is a <u>persistent</u> image or memory of part of the body, usually a limb, for months or years after its loss.
① enduring   ② pernicious
③ perplexed   ④ perilous

21 During the Baroque period, European churches were <u>adorned</u> with rich decorative elements, such as twisting columns covered in carvings.
① swaddled   ② dangled
③ embellished   ④ draped

22 She gave a <u>fictitious</u> address on the application.
① forwarding   ② secret
③ private   ④ invented

23 No one had ever <u>unearthed</u> the bones of the dinosaurs lying beneath the soil.
① buried
② discovered
③ paid attention to
④ looked over

24 In frogs and toads, the tongue is fixed to the front of the mouth in order to facilitate <u>projecting</u> it at some distance, greatly aiding in the capture of insects.
① rotating   ② protruding
③ vibrating   ④ contracting

25 Reclaimed rubber is <u>salvaged</u> from worn-out tires, old tubes, and other discarded rubber articles.

① modified   ② recovered

③ dirtied   ④ softened

26 The actor had such an <u>unassuming</u> demeanor that people barely noticed him at events.

① fragile   ② nimble

③ modest   ④ thrifty

27 There is a tendency on the part of the guardians of the elite to be perhaps a little more <u>scathing</u> of someone to whom they haven't given permission to be successful.

① candid   ② ruthless

③ generous   ④ skeptical

28 If I am physically <u>assaulted</u> it will permit me to retaliate with reasonable violence.

① endorsed   ② divulged

③ assailed   ④ curtailed

29 The difference in the greenness of leaves in the morning and in the evening is almost <u>imperceptible</u>.

① naught   ② unnoticeable

③ strange   ④ unattractive

30 People who <u>compulsively</u> seek novelty tend to abuse drugs more than people who are content with old and usual things.

① constantly   ② always

③ irresistibly   ④ invariably

31 Seminal contributions to science are those that change the <u>tenor</u> of the questions asked by succeeding generations.

① result   ② intonation

③ nature   ④ punctuation

32 Wherever we turn up records and artifacts, we usually discover that in every culture, some people were <u>preoccupied</u> with measuring the passage of time.

① absorbed   ② excluded

③ provided   ④ convicted

33 The new coaching staff demanded <u>temperance</u> of the football team during the season.

① humility   ② stigma

③ spontaneity   ④ restraint

34 A high-powered CEO might show <u>hauteur</u> toward the newly hired assistant.

① partiality   ② tenacity

③ arrogance   ④ continence

35 "I will never do it again." she promised <u>contritely</u>.

① smoothly   ② repeatedly

③ repentantly   ④ tiredly

36 The distant rumbling we heard this morning was a <u>portent</u> of the thunderstorm that hit our area this afternoon.

① presage   ② tremor

③ upheaval   ④ plethora

37 Automatons are mechanical objects that become self-operating once they have been underline{actuated}.
① timed   ② constructed
③ cleaned up   ④ set in motion

38 A cut in the budget put 10 percent of the state employees' jobs in jeopardy.
① danger   ② range
③ review   ④ perspective

39 Please understand that we must disclaim all liabilities in this case.
① repudiate   ② arrogate
③ predicate   ④ incriminate

40 More than 50% of all spouses are reported to be victims of infidelity.
① charity   ② torpedo
③ disaster   ④ unfaithfulness

41 There is certainly a chance that we could have as many dying from communicable diseases as from the tsunami.
① adjustable   ② contagious
③ dangerous   ④ incurable

42 The horrid prospect that television opens before us, with nobody speaking and nobody reading, suggests that a bleak and torpid epoch may lie ahead.
① inert   ② dark
③ spectacular   ④ fantastic

43 My uncle has been fired from three jobs for being indolent. He shows up on time, but he does little work and leaves early.
① lazy   ② industrious
③ impudent   ④ vigilant

44 Many homemakers used to save green stamps. Then they would redeem these stamps for all kinds of products.
① revise   ② exchange
③ save   ④ buy

45 A young child will often find it difficult to fully fathom the wisdom of his parents, especially in matters of personal safety.
① trust   ② apply
③ understand   ④ question

46 Too much calcium can hinder a child's growth.
① retard   ② mask
③ reverse   ④ monitor

47 TV has increased the value of reading, since it provides a vulgar alternative.
① holistic   ② substantial
③ remarkable   ④ indecent

48 To some people, art is the depictions of an object — a painting or sculpture of a person, for example. For others, art may be a blank canvas, or a piece of chalk.
① alterations   ② descriptions
③ imitations   ④ symbols

49 These days, Wilma Rudolph is remembered for her inspirational determination to overcome her physical challenges, and for her courage in rising above segregation and racism.
① disturbance   ② restriction
③ interruption   ④ discrimination

50 Choking occurs when the flow of air to the lungs is obstructed.
① restructured   ② debauched
③ vented   ④ blocked

51 It is the duty of the police to protect citizens and enforce the laws.
① overlook   ② carry out
③ give up   ④ alternate

52 Foolishly arrogant as I was, I used to judge the worth of a person by his intellectual power and attainment.
① judicious   ② perceptive
③ imperious   ④ adamant

53 Amid the fog and fury of war, Rivera provided us all with a moment of levity and reason for hope.
① solemnity   ② amusement
③ firmness   ④ gloom

54 Even light physical punishment may provoke resentment and further misbehavior.
① indignation   ② rejection
③ demonstration   ④ impropriety

55 If the leaders of the western countries and those of Russia get berserk, it could bring disaster to the entire world.
① overbearing   ② violent
③ perturbed   ④ stagnant

56 The political incorporation of communities that feel they have a distinct cultural identity provides fertile ground for the emergence of nationalist reaction.
① flamboyant   ② productive
③ imminent   ④ hostile

57 We ought to be modest and remember that life is too short to bore other people with talk of our petty accomplishments.
① insignificant   ② personal
③ stingy   ④ magnificent

58 Colt Telecom Group ended its five month search for a new chief executive by appointing its own chief operating officer, Peter Manning, to the helm.
① committee   ② stock market
③ cabin   ④ controlling position

59 There was no trace of poison in the coffee the chemist analyzed.
① smell   ② indication
③ color   ④ spread

60 The program must be designed to widen the choices available to the market, not to abridge them.
① diversify   ② dictate
③ increase   ④ curtail

61 When treating a patient with a severe injury, doctors may need to <u>occlude</u> a ruptured artery to stop excessive bleeding.

① remove   ② conduct

③ block   ④ transplant

62 Iraq War Veteran Scott Olsen, critically injured at the demonstration, has been on the <u>mend</u> and will return to the protest next week.

① repair   ② change

③ recovery   ④ correction

63 The <u>dearth</u> of rain can create a desert in a few years.

① contamination   ② deficiency

③ equilibrium   ④ abundance

64 Teaism is a cult founded on the adoration of the beautiful among the <u>sordid</u> facts of everyday existence.

① rigorous   ② defiant

③ filthy   ④ impudent

65 Nearly two-thirds of the town's inhabitants are descendants of <u>indigenous</u> civilizations.

① hard-working   ② advanced

③ poor   ④ native

66 China and India, where yearly auto sales of 13.2 million and 12.3 million <u>surpassed</u> the U.S. for the first time during the recession, will continue to be the biggest growth markets as their middle class prospers.

① undermined   ② lost

③ suppressed   ④ excelled

67 Their discussion <u>engrossed</u> his attention.

① attracted   ② suspended

③ bewildered   ④ ignored

68 "No matter what <u>ensues</u>," the heroine said to herself, "I will tell the truth."

① results   ② joins in

③ begins   ④ falls down

69 A groan went through the class when we got the <u>disquieting</u> news that there would be a test later in the week.

① discontented   ② disparate

③ dissembling   ④ uneasy

70 It is <u>incumbent</u> on those holding or seeking high office to be totally accountable to the voters of Illinois.

① irresponsible

② obligatory

③ disadvantageous

④ commandable

71 The most recent violation of the agreement is the apparent extra-judicial detention of five Hong Kong publishers <u>deemed</u> critical of the mainland's leaders.

① prejudiced   ② considered

③ premised   ④ presupposed

72 Korea's economic growth will <u>retreat</u> to 5.7 percent this year from an estimated 9 percent in 2000, following the adverse effects of deteriorating overseas conditions.

① augment   ② recede

③ increase   ④ stagnate

73 Looking into the doleful eyes of the lonely pony, the girl yearned to take him home.
① stressful   ② gleeful
③ wasteful   ④ dirgeful

74 I gave him a difficult problem in algebra and he did it off-hand.
① at all   ② at once
③ by and by   ④ on and off

75 Winston acknowledged that his comments could be construed as racist.
① understood   ② criticized
③ laughed at   ④ reported

76 Even after a century of meticulous investigation, the relation of the solar cycle to terrestrial weather remains enigmatic.
① cursory   ② thorough
③ prolonged   ④ scientific

77 He said that evidently the government had made a plan to seclude us from the young.
① isolate   ② abstain
③ refrain   ④ judge

78 Large groups of carnivores follow more than two million large herbivores during the Great Migrations in Serengeti.
① preys   ② reptiles
③ predators   ④ amphibians

79 The most conspicuous of these industrialized societies that will have to make economic sacrifices are the nations of Eastern Europe.
① modest   ② humble
③ subtle   ④ prominent

80 The preponderance of the 23 million public employees are directly serving the people.
① portent   ② milieu
③ predilection   ④ majority

81 This leaves her ample time to prepare three meals a day.
① rare   ② scanty
③ sufficient   ④ inadequate

82 She thought he was joking but he was deadly serious.
① extremely   ② quietly
③ secretly   ④ mildly

83 We must confront the future of our nation with optimism.
① face   ② avoid
③ evade   ④ conclude

84 The battle was still going on when the armistice was signed.
① arms deal
② military justice
③ military court
④ cease-fire agreement

85 It was a serene summer night as the girl walked by the ocean.
① romantic   ② hot
③ calm   ④ exciting

86 Claiming the murderer did not feel penitent, the victim's family felt his pardon should be denied.
① artificial   ② natural
③ apologetic   ④ generic

87 Marlow refused to abandon their homes before the storm, and his action is regarded as a kind of perfidy.
① betrayal   ② audacity
③ recklessness   ④ agitation

88 The Florentine sculptor had plentiful commissions coming from churches and secular patrons.
① worldly   ② spiritual
③ religious   ④ seductive

89 It is easy to recognize the congruent themes on the two plays.
① incomparable   ② dissimilar
③ indecent   ④ corresponding

90 In many areas of industry, absenteeism and lateness hurt productivity and, since work is specialized, disrupt the regular factory routine.
① prolong   ② tantalize
③ upset   ④ demarcate

91 Some police officers forget to read the Miranda rights to a criminal during an arrest, confuse their undercover identities, and even get fired from their jobs for their inept work.
① clumsy   ② auspicious
③ recluse   ④ merciless

92 This is a makeshift plan until we decided what to do.
① a temporary   ② an urgent
③ an ignoble   ④ an outrageous

93 The police are hoping that the violence will soon subside.
① disapprove   ② diminish
③ subtract   ④ dispel

94 Al Capone was an infamous gangster.
① trivial   ② captivating
③ notorious   ④ terrific

95 She was conditionally discharged after swearing on oath to be of good behaviour.
① humiliated   ② criticized
③ evaluated   ④ released

96 Despite his tantrum, we soon learn that Scrooge's hatred for Christmas is a fabrication.
① apathy   ② mischief
③ brutality   ④ temper

97 In Europe's Romantic Age, men favored the wan, cadaverous look in women. Women sometimes drank vinegar or stayed up all night to look pale and interesting. Fragility was all.
① dangerous   ② charming
③ plump   ④ corpse-like

98 He's an incorrigible liar, but he has great charm.
① a consummate   ② a screwed
③ a rigid   ④ a close

99 When she came home after two days from their dispute over the location of the new house, her husband was on the phone vehemently raising objections to the changed bus route. She pulled out her cellular phone and secretly recorded him as he remonstrated some poor public official. It was so amusing that she posted it in her blog, which eventually resulted in their reconciliation.

① found fault with

② said or pled in protest

③ treated roughly or cruelly

④ kept down or held back

100 The tobacco industry said that while nicotine may be addictive, it is naturally present in vegetables. Jay Leno wondered, "How come you never see people standing outside an office building in the rain eating an eggplant?"

① present in tobacco products

② habit-forming

③ harmful to health

④ remains in our body for a long time

[1] Write the meaning of the following words.

☐ undergo	☐ tremendous
☐ ignominious	☐ district
☐ solemn	☐ astound
☐ manacle	☐ rebate
☐ deride	☐ qualm
☐ spawn	☐ geology
☐ antonym	☐ tackle
☐ confirm	☐ conscience
☐ penurious	☐ advertisement
☐ fabric	☐ endangered
☐ stout	☐ import
☐ electorate	☐ annuity
☐ positive	☐ contend
☐ obedient	☐ variegated
☐ humanity	☐ feud
☐ bestow	☐ slippery
☐ mind-boggling	☐ reimburse
☐ placate	☐ osteoporosis
☐ theory	☐ sedative
☐ languid	☐ abolish
☐ aspect	☐ lousy
☐ enlist	☐ barrier
☐ wobble	☐ patrician
☐ chest	☐ insignificant
☐ reiterate	☐ dismantle

[2] Select <u>the most</u> appropriate word from the box below. Each word should be used only once.

① variegated	② derided	③ obedient	④ dismantle
⑤ placate	⑥ manacle	⑦ languid	⑧ wobble
⑨ sedative	⑩ feud	⑪ qualm	⑫ endangered
⑬ lousy	⑭ slippery	⑮ reiterated	⑯ annuity
⑰ penurious	⑱ enlist	⑲ confirm	⑳ barrier

1 In an effort to _____ the angry customer, the store manager replaced the defective product with a more expensive model at no extra charge.

2 The established axiom is such a manifest, self-evident statement that does not really need to be _____.

3 In William Shakespeare's *Romeo and Juliet*, a long _____ between the Montague and Capulet families disrupts the city of Verona and causes tragic results for Romeo and Juliet.

4 The tent was very complicated to erect but simple enough to _____.

5 The politician _____ the American asylum program, saying migrants fleeing poverty and corruption were a "scam" and a "hoax."

6 He lived a(n)_____ life, eating little, avoiding luxury and dressing in threadbare clothing.

7 His parents wanted him to become a doctor, so the _____ son went to medical school.

8 Most scientists presume that the environment on the sea floor is fairly stable: Temperatures hover near freezing and currents are _____ and steady.

9 The scales of a fish can appear quite _____ from one angle and then strangely uniform from another.

10 If a patient is freaking out about getting an MRI, the doctor might prescribe a(n) _____ to chill him out.

[3] Choose the one which is different from the others.

11　① ignominious　② disgraceful　③ humiliating　④ commendable

12　① corpulent　② stout　③ slight　④ fleshy

13　① frivolous　② serious　③ solemn　④ grave

14　① mind-boggling　② fair to middling　③ astonishing　④ stunning

15　① reimburse　② compensate　③ recoup　④ levy

16　① abrogate　② annul　③ commence　④ abolish

17　① insignificant　② trivial　③ substantial　④ paltry

18　① compete　② surrender　③ contend　④ vie

19　① nominal　② immense　③ enormous　④ tremendous

20　① bestow　② withhold　③ award　④ confer

☑ **DAILY CHECKUP**

[1] Write the meaning of the following words.

☐ absurd	☐ garble
☐ ecstasy	☐ conservative
☐ slander	☐ ward
☐ imposing	☐ urge
☐ offset	☐ arsenal
☐ relentless	☐ dependable
☐ showdown	☐ chart
☐ microscope	☐ plot
☐ headstrong	☐ lateral
☐ affirm	☐ distress
☐ comely	☐ harangue
☐ restore	☐ accomplish
☐ paucity	☐ taxing
☐ exempt	☐ maneuver
☐ incur	☐ cannibalism
☐ solitary	☐ vicious
☐ trafficking	☐ spell
☐ informal	☐ bedizen
☐ visage	☐ landscape
☐ pith	☐ amerce
☐ stammer	☐ cluster
☐ neutral	☐ flip-flop
☐ entrench	☐ peremptory
☐ bucolic	☐ track
☐ deliberate	☐ remorse

[2] Select <u>the most</u> appropriate word from the box below. Each word should be used only once.

① absurd	② visage	③ lateral	④ solitary
⑤ garble	⑥ deliberate	⑦ headstrong	⑧ exempt
⑨ accomplish	⑩ paucity	⑪ imposing	⑫ distress
⑬ neutral	⑭ restore	⑮ amerce	⑯ taxing
⑰ offset	⑱ remorse	⑲ bedizen	⑳ spell

1 Quantum theory was initially regarded as _____ and incompatible with common sense.

2 Being a(n) _____ person, he insisted at the conference that when he spoke he was not to be interrupted.

3 The extreme _____ of allusions to umbrellas throughout the Middle Ages shows that they were not in common use.

4 Inmates on Alcatraz who were deemed too dangerous to mingle with their fellows were put in _____ confinement cells.

5 Myron was able to remain completely _____; he never took sides in any of the disagreements around the house.

6 The British tourist who went viral for etching his name into the side of Rome's historic Colosseum is expressing "sincere _____" for his potentially criminal actions.

7 Today when courts _____ someone, it legally orders them to pay a fine after finding them guilty of wrongdoing.

8 Being exposed to an industrial disaster is anxiety-inducing, and yet this _____ routine is sadly becoming more quotidian.

9 Winning a medal in the Olympic Games is one of the highest achievements an athlete can _____.

10 Children suffer emotional _____ when their parents get divorced.

[3] Choose the one which is different from the others.

11 ① besmirch   ② slander   ③ libel   ④ extol

12 ① relentless   ② intermittent   ③ sustained   ④ constant

13 ① puerile   ② attractive   ③ comely   ④ winsome

14 ① falter   ② stutter   ③ stammer   ④ enunciate

15 ① idyllic   ② bucolic   ③ classy   ④ rustic

16 ① faithful   ② credulous   ③ reliable   ④ dependable

17 ① virtuous   ② vicious   ③ malicious   ④ wicked

18 ① peremptory   ② overbearing   ③ indulgent   ④ authoritative

19 ① succumb   ② maneuver   ③ exploit   ④ manipulate

20 ① harangue   ② omission   ③ screed   ④ tirade

✔ Answers

1 ① | 양자론은 처음에는 불합리하고 상식에 부합하지 않는 것으로 여겨졌다.

2 ⑦ | 그는 고집이 센 사람이었기 때문에, 회의에서 자신이 발언할 때 방해받아서는 안 된다고 주장했다.

3 ⑩ | 중세 시대 동안 우산에 대한 언급이 극도로 적은 것은 우산이 일상적으로 사용되지 않았다는 것을 보여준다.

4 ④ | 동료 수감자들과 섞이기에는 너무 위험하다고 여겨진 앨커트래즈의 수감자들은 독방에 수감되었다.

5 ⑬ | 마이론(Myron)은 언제나 완전히 중립적인 태도를 유지할 수 있었다. 그는 집안의 그 어떤 논쟁에서도 누구의 편도 들지 않았다.

6 ⑱ | 로마의 역사적인 콜로세움 측면에 자신의 이름을 새긴 것으로 소문이 난 영국인 관광객은 자신의 범죄일 수 있는 행위에 대해 "진심어린 후회"를 표명했다.

7 ⑮ | 오늘날 법원이 누군가에게 벌금을 과한다면, 불법 행위에 대해 유죄임을 확인한 후 그들에게 벌금을 내도록 법적으로 명한다.

8 ⑯ | 산업 재해에 노출되는 것은 불안을 야기하지만, 이러한 부담스러운 일상은 유감스럽게도 점점 일상화되고 있다.

9 ⑨ | 올림픽에서 금메달을 따는 것은 운동선수가 성취할 수 있는 가장 높은 업적 중 하나이다.

10 ⑫ | 부모가 이혼하면 아이들은 정신적 고통을 겪는다.

11 ④   **12** ②   **13** ①   **14** ④   **15** ③   **16** ②   **17** ①   **18** ③   **19** ①   **20** ②

☑ DAILY CHECKUP

[1] Write the meaning of the following words.

☐ bewilder		☐ preach	
☐ inclement		☐ tawdry	
☐ martyr		☐ outrun	
☐ earthly		☐ exception	
☐ shimmer		☐ castigate	
☐ petition		☐ hypocrisy	
☐ remiss		☐ condign	
☐ finagle		☐ lavish	
☐ sue		☐ dimension	
☐ accessory		☐ fair	
☐ jest		☐ controversy	
☐ sought-after		☐ vainglorious	
☐ tease		☐ identify	
☐ phony		☐ compartment	
☐ relate		☐ address	
☐ snug		☐ indelible	
☐ autism		☐ bishop	
☐ crude		☐ meager	
☐ newfangled		☐ panegyric	
☐ emblazon		☐ degrade	
☐ decree		☐ longevity	
☐ slovenly		☐ raze	
☐ gizmo		☐ omnipotent	
☐ unintended		☐ avert	
☐ angst		☐ torso	

[2] Select <u>the most</u> appropriate word from the box below. Each word should be used only once.

① martyr	② avert	③ hypocrisy	④ bewilder
⑤ longevity	⑥ petition	⑦ remiss	⑧ lavish
⑨ teasing	⑩ inclement	⑪ shimmer	⑫ angst
⑬ sued	⑭ decree	⑮ preach	⑯ indelible
⑰ meager	⑱ emblazoned	⑲ tawdry	⑳ condign

1   If someone you know died in a freak accident, that would _____ you in a very sad way.

2   Children and adolescents with obesity often experience _____ and bullying, which contribute to "binge eating and decreased physical activity."

3   Due to _____ weather conditions as a result of hurricane, most flights into and out of John F. Kennedy International Airport may be delayed or cancelled.

4   Colleges and universities frequently sell sweatshirts and hats _____ with their logos.

5   He condemned the _____ of those politicians who do one thing and say another.

6   Living memories of the annihilating Great Depression grow faint, but the recorded histories are _____.

7   Well-informed and adequately prepared employees are more likely to _____ accidents and respond efficiently during emergencies.

8   The diet of developing nations has changed greatly since World War II, having a tremendous effect on the health and _____ of their populations.

9   In spite of the importance of research on universal vaccines and the variety of approaches, there is surprisingly _____ federal research funding in this area.

10   Luxury retailers are rushing to open new and increasingly _____ stores in suburbs and the vacation hot spots.

[3] Choose the one which is different from the others.

11 ① earthly   ② secular   ③ heavenly   ④ worldly

12 ① bogus   ② sincere   ③ phony   ④ counterfeit

13 ① outmoded   ② in vogue   ③ fashionable   ④ newfangled

14 ① all-powerful   ② omnipotent   ③ almighty   ④ impotent

15 ① panegyric   ② opprobrium   ③ praise   ④ encomium

16 ① hubristic   ② conceited   ③ furtive   ④ vainglorious

17 ① castigate   ② rebuke   ③ reprimand   ④ extol

18 ① raw   ② uncommon   ③ crude   ④ unrefined

19 ① unctuous   ② slovenly   ③ unkempt   ④ untidy

20 ① gizmo   ② gadget   ③ gimmick   ④ ramification

✓ Answers

1 ④ | 만약 당신의 지인이 기이한 사고로 죽었다면, 그것으로 당신은 매우 슬프게 당황해질 것이다.

2 ⑨ | 비만이 있는 어린이와 청소년은 종종 놀림과 따돌림을 겪는데, 이는 "폭식과 신체 활동 감소"의 원인이 된다.

3 ⑩ | 허리케인으로 인한 험악한 날씨 여건 때문에 JFK국제공항에 이착륙하는 대부분의 비행편이 지연되거나 취소될지도 모른다.

4 ⑱ | 대학들은 종종 학교의 로고가 새겨진 스웨트셔츠와 모자를 판매한다.

5 ③ | 그는 말과 행동이 다른 정치인들의 위선을 비난했다.

6 ⑯ | 전멸적인 대공황의 생생한 기억이 점점 희미해지고 있지만, 기록된 역사는 지워지지 않는다.

7 ② | 정보를 잘 알고 있고 준비가 충분히 되어 있는 직원은 비상시에 사고를 막고 효율적으로 대응할 가능성이 높다.

8 ⑤ | 제2차 세계대전 후 개발도상국의 식생활은 크게 바뀌어서 국민들의 건강과 수명에 막대한 영향을 끼쳤다.

9 ⑰ | 범용 백신에 관한 연구의 중요성과 다양한 접근법에도 불구하고, 이 분야에는 놀랍게도 연방 연구 자금이 부족하다.

10 ⑧ | 명품 업체들은 교외와 휴가 명소에 점점 더 호화로운 신규 매장을 열기 위해 서두르고 있다.

- -

11 ③   **12** ②   **13** ①   **14** ④   **15** ②   **16** ③   **17** ④   **18** ②   **19** ①   **20** ④

MVP **34** ☑ **DAILY CHECKUP**

[1] Write the meaning of the following words.

☐ well-to-do

☐ correspond

☐ perverse

☐ magnate

☐ spacious

☐ alien

☐ deduce

☐ pier

☐ impecunious

☐ vogue

☐ bespeak

☐ sortition

☐ cognizant

☐ hegemony

☐ distinguished

☐ rancor

☐ ooze

☐ infectious

☐ filial

☐ bias

☐ germinate

☐ advisable

☐ retard

☐ kickback

☐ teem

☐ canine

☐ leftover

☐ acclimate

☐ repellent

☐ dictator

☐ shiver

☐ outright

☐ crisscross

☐ anarchy

☐ extend

☐ sanguinary

☐ underlie

☐ function

☐ penitentiary

☐ elated

☐ impulse

☐ throb

☐ starry-eyed

☐ colony

☐ hardwired

☐ appropriate

☐ tenure

☐ paramount

☐ meet

☐ ensconce

[2] Select <u>the most</u> appropriate word from the box below. Each word should be used only once.

① alien	② rancorous	③ sortition	④ infectious
⑤ hegemony	⑥ retard	⑦ sanguinary	⑧ penitentiary
⑨ spacious	⑩ underlie	⑪ ensconced	⑫ kickback
⑬ tenure	⑭ anarchy	⑮ function	⑯ hardwired
⑰ heartthrob	⑱ acclimate	⑲ elated	⑳ filial

1 The society's members were so divided on the subject and the debate was so _____ that they finally gave up on trying to reach a consensus.

2 In the 1860s, author Leo Tolstoy was _____ with his family in the Tula region of Russia; while comfortably established there, he wrote *War and Peace*.

3 They have more _____ accommodation here than they had in Tokyo where their flat was very small.

4 In the early part of the 1800s, the thought of women having the right to vote in the United Kingdom was completely _____ to many. In 1831, only a tiny part of British society could take part in parliamentary elections.

5 Wealthy lender nations hoping to determine political outcomes and trade decisions have established _____ over the debtor nations they lend to.

6 Those suffering from _____ diseases were separated from the other patients.

7 Those organisms who were not able to _____ themselves to their new surroundings quickly died out and became extinct.

8 Jazz is all about rule-breaking, tossing out the conventional structure of music and replacing it with something closer to improvisational _____.

9 Robert Pattinson immediately became an international star and _____ who has fans of all ages after his movie became a hit.

10 Amgen is accused of offering a(n) _____ to doctors and clinics to induce them to use its drugs.

[3] Choose the one which is different from the others.

11 ① impecunious ② gullible ③ penniless ④ penurious

12 ① eminent ② distinguished ③ notable ④ coarse

13 ① preconception ② prerogative ③ bias ④ prejudice

14 ① loathsome ② repellent ③ punctual ④ unpleasant

15 ① tranquilize ② quiver ③ shudder ④ shiver

16 ① prime ② principal ③ paramount ④ trivial

17 ① starry-eyed ② quixotic ③ utilitarian ④ impractical

18 ① conserve ② germinate ③ bud ④ sprout

19 ① advisable ② desirable ③ prudent ④ extravagant

20 ① vogue ② hype ③ popularity ④ trend

[1] Write the meaning of the following words.

☐ fascinate	☐ utterly
☐ disgust	☐ victual
☐ indispensable	☐ pernicious
☐ pathos	☐ administer
☐ compute	☐ laissez-faire
☐ watchword	☐ evolution
☐ sheer	☐ saturate
☐ elapse	☐ metastasis
☐ pirate	☐ depreciate
☐ nonpareil	☐ rash
☐ summary	☐ credo
☐ maritime	☐ obscure
☐ impair	☐ gale
☐ amiable	☐ bankruptcy
☐ sharpen	☐ hermetic
☐ remuneration	☐ dodge
☐ deliver	☐ calumniate
☐ audible	☐ thick
☐ recede	☐ fowl
☐ somnolent	☐ lessen
☐ bemoan	☐ pageant
☐ pending	☐ common
☐ swift	☐ topography
☐ thrall	☐ embroil
☐ altitude	☐ inexhaustible

[2] Select the most appropriate word from the box below. Each word should be used only once.

① amiable	② swift	③ pirate	④ sharpening
⑤ indispensable	⑥ hermetic	⑦ victual	⑧ dodge
⑨ saturate	⑩ laissez-faire	⑪ remunerative	⑫ pageant
⑬ obscure	⑭ gale	⑮ recede	⑯ elapse
⑰ thrall	⑱ impair	⑲ bankruptcy	⑳ pending

1 An insulin pill to replace needles has proved difficult for researchers, as insulin is destroyed in the stomach. For now, insulin injections seem _____ for the health of diabetics across the world.

2 Her _____ personality was a welcome addition to the gloomy atmosphere at the annual meeting.

3 As the pandemic continues to _____, more and more employers are bringing their employees back to the office.

4 A king cobra moves very fast, but the mongoose has quicker reflexes and can _____ the cobra's attack.

5 His style is frequently concise but ambiguous, which makes it somewhat _____.

6 Though many consumers still _____ the music, a portion of music consumers are willing to pay a positive amount to download music legally.

7 Many experts are concerned that coffee can _____ the body's absorption of calcium and thus become a significant risk factor for osteoporosis.

8 The U.S. and South Korea held a simulation in Washington aimed at _____ their response to North Korean nuclear threats.

9 Women in less _____ occupations are often forced to choose between making do with long hours or finding part-time jobs that pay even more poorly.

10 Although results from clinical trials are still _____, Ghana has become the first country to approve a new malaria vaccine.

[3] Choose the one which is different from the others.

11 ① charm ② fascinate ③ irritate ④ captivate

12 ① infinite ② groundless ③ inexhaustible ④ limitless

13 ① exclude ② involve ③ entangle ④ embroil

14 ① libel ② slander ③ calumniate ④ crawl

15 ① belief ② creed ③ quandary ④ credo

16 ① hatred ② relish ③ disgust ④ loathing

17 ① nonpareil ② unparalleled ③ inexperienced ④ incomparable

18 ① vigilant ② somnolent ③ sleepy ④ soporific

19 ① deplore ② rejoice ③ bemoan ④ lament

20 ① pernicious ② baneful ③ preposterous ④ harmful

✔ Answers

1 ⑤ | 인슐린은 위에서 파괴되므로 주사를 대신할 인슐린 정제는 연구자들이 인정하기 어려운 것으로 판명되었다. 지금으로서는, 인슐린 주사가 전 세계 당뇨병 환자들의 건강을 위해 필수불가결한 것 같다.

2 ① | 그녀의 쾌활한 성격은 연례회의장의 우울한 분위기에 더해지기에 환영할만한 것이었다.

3 ⑮ | 팬데믹이 계속해서 약해짐에 따라, 점점 더 많은 고용주들이 그들의 직원들을 사무실로 복귀시키고 있다.

4 ⑧ | 킹코브라는 움직임이 매우 빠르지만, 몽구스는 더 빠른 반사 신경을 가지고 있어 코브라의 공격을 피할 수 있다.

5 ⑬ | 그의 문체는 아주 짧고 모호해서 약간 불분명한 느낌을 준다.

6 ③ | 많은 소비자가 여전히 음악을 불법 복제하지만 일부 음악 소비자는 음악을 합법적으로 다운로드하기 위해 기꺼이 상당한 금액을 지불한다.

7 ⑱ | 많은 전문가들은 커피가 신체의 칼슘 흡수를 방해하여 골다공증에 걸릴 확률을 현저하게 높일 수 있는 점을 우려하고 있다.

8 ④ | 미국과 한국은 북한의 핵 위협에 대한 대응을 강화하기 위한 모의 훈련을 워싱턴에서 열었다.

9 ⑪ | 보수가 낮은 직업에 종사하는 여성들은 종종 장시간의 근무와 급여가 낮은 시간제 근무 사이에서 선택을 강요당한다.

10 ⑳ | 아직 임상시험 결과가 미결정 상태이지만, 가나는 새로운 말라리아 백신을 승인한 첫 번째 국가가 되었다.

11 ③ **12** ② **13** ① **14** ④ **15** ③ **16** ② **17** ③ **18** ① **19** ② **20** ③

ACTUAL TEST

문항수 / 시간 100문항 ⏱60분

▶▶▶ ANSWERS P.364

[01-100] Choose the one that is closest in meaning to the underlined part.

01 Her <u>visage</u> was one of a self-fulfilled woman.
① look ② apparel
③ conduct ④ knack

02 Physics does not lend itself to <u>pithy</u> introductions.
① laconic ② jejune
③ erratic ④ opulent

03 She <u>underwent</u> a thorough examination at the hospital.
① confided ② exasperated
③ unearthed ④ experienced

04 Different kinds of beads are used to <u>ward off</u> evil.
① avert ② conduce
③ anticipate ④ resume

05 Early log cabins were <u>crude</u> if sturdy structures.
① painted ② resilient
③ unseasoned ④ rough

06 She was a <u>vainglorious</u> person.
① an invalid
② a polished
③ an outrageous
④ a haughty

07 The family's <u>penurious</u> nature made it difficult for them to enjoy the simple pleasures in life.
① stingy ② shrewd
③ flippant ④ truculent

08 An attempt to harmonize the imbalances in my character by means of harsh discipline nearly led me to the same <u>ignominious</u> end.
① disgraceful ② pitiless
③ honorable ④ dangerous

09 Many doctors and nurses were <u>utterly</u> convinced of the medicine's effect.
① hardly ② finally
③ rapidly ④ completely

10 Political boundaries can act as barriers to the spread of ideas or knowledge, thereby <u>retarding</u> cultural diffusion.
① deferring ② replenishing
③ facilitating ④ blurring

11 To understand this <u>mind-boggling</u> idea, consider a black hole floating in space.
① spontaneous ② sophisticated
③ incredible ④ poignant

12 The government has declared <u>solemn</u> pledge to root out corruption among public officials.
① serious ② suitable
③ fitful ④ ruthless

13 Because he had so many problems on his mind, he was remiss in performing his duties.
① negligent   ② scrupulous
③ attentive   ④ careful

14 It is very dangerous idea that science has become omnipotent.
① means of life   ② aggrandizement
③ almighty   ④ ultimate target

15 A day after the April check got cashed, we got a notice stating we had to move; they were going to raze the house.
① demolish   ② rent
③ purchase   ④ enlarge

16 California real estate is among the most expensive in the world. The state's millions of residents have decided that the pleasures of West Coast life offset the danger of living along a fault line.
① overweigh   ② outlive
③ hazard   ④ underscore

17 The spore of the blight fungus is water-borne; when it moves it swims, therefore, to germinate effectively it needs a drop of moisture.
① grow   ② decay
③ infect   ④ recover

18 Most often, managers bullied subordinates for the sheer pleasure of exercising power.
① pure   ② decent
③ scanty   ④ transparent

19 They were amazed by the breathtaking landscape.
① venue   ② geography
③ scenery   ④ vignette

20 There were always esoteric movies that pleased critics but left the public bewildered.
① terrified   ② puzzled
③ fascinated   ④ bruised

21 Arthur's impulse to board the train while in motion almost cost him his life.
① trickery   ② soot
③ allowance   ④ desire

22 The judge said he was not cognizant of the case.
① legally responsible
② very careful
③ aware of
④ careless about

23 When he was an executive of the company, his first accomplishment was to bring about better working conditions.
① duty   ② achievement
③ accumulation   ④ imposition

24 People who spend more than they earn are said to be undependable about money.
① grave   ② crumpled
③ irresponsible   ④ shambled

25 It was difficult to maneuver the car in such a small space.
① manipulate   ② fare
③ shake   ④ chop

26 Although old threats have disappeared or receded, new ones have arisen.
① renovated　② rearranged
③ withdrawn　④ withstood

27 An authoritarian style appears to be more effective in emergency situations, a democratic style works best for most situations, and a laissez-faire style is usually ineffective.
① interventional　② permissive
③ disrupted　④ anarchic

28 He discovered that bad investments had made him impecunious overnight.
① transitory　② penniless
③ imminent　④ affluent

29 During the five-day meeting of the International Whaling Commission, Japan derided the delegates of anti-whaling nations as "mimics for Greenpeace."
① ridiculed　② designated
③ named　④ degenerated

30 Historical records reveal that Jefferson reiterated his ideas about a meritocracy.
① withdrew　② repeated
③ emphasized　④ published

31 Scientists will have all the time they need to tease out richer science from the data that Huygens left them.
① validate　② uncover
③ manipulate　④ distort

32 Many scientists talk with relish about how insignificant we humans are when placed against the time — scale of geology and the cosmos.
① trivial　② uncivilized
③ unfathomable　④ short-sighted

33 It is not widely known that flu medication impairs the ability to operate machinery including motor vehicles.
① undermines　② enhances
③ influences　④ restores

34 He attempted suicide after being relentlessly bullied at school.
① incessantly　② accurately
③ moderately　④ whimsically

35 Many people are still fascinated by the Internet because it has been particularly important in shaping the new millenium global values.
① attracted　③ informed
③ improved　④ fashioned

36 The C.E.O. accused of plagiarism rejected outright the slanderous accusations.
① infelicitous　② parsimonious
③ defamatory　④ untrustworthy

37 Antioxidants such as vitamins A, C, and E are indispensable in countering the potential harm of chemicals known as free radicals.
① vital　② indigenous
③ unperturbed　④ superfluous

38 The company temporarily <u>averted</u> disaster by stealing several ten dollars from the employees' pension fund.
① diverted   ② induced
③ avoided   ④ caused

39 In appearance she was <u>imposing</u> rather than attractive.
① trifling   ② massive
③ bewildering   ④ notorious

40 The movie's Christ Kyle has no <u>qualms</u> about killing her in his rifle sight.
① aplomb   ② indulgence
③ compunction   ④ equilibrium

41 Marvel changed the ethnicity of a character from Tibetan to Celtic to <u>placate</u> Chinese censors and audiences.
① pacify   ② specify
③ duplicate   ④ implicate

42 A bursary is <u>bestowed</u> annually on the student gaining the highest marks in the entrance examination.
① conferred   ② scheduled
③ palliated   ④ repudiated

43 Scientists were able to <u>identify</u> the chemicals that give fetal cells their regenerative powers.
① recognize   ② intensify
③ standardize   ④ exemplify

44 He has an <u>infectious</u> laugh; when he starts laughing, everyone starts laughing.
① thundering   ② mischievous
③ hearty   ④ contagious

45 She has been the victim of a series of completely unjustified <u>calumnies</u>.
① phrases   ② credos
③ vestiges   ④ slanders

46 If your husband won't leave, then you go. You are now an <u>accessory</u> after the fact. You are answerable. You, your children, could lose everything you own.
① misogynist   ② misanthrope
③ humanitarian ④ accomplice

47 If Space X is able to <u>restore</u> and reuse its first stages routinely, it could greatly reduce the cost of launching things into space.
① refurbish   ② replace
③ allocate   ④ reciprocate

48 Starting from this year, students from low-income families will be <u>exempt</u> from paying interest on their student loans while they are serving in the military, the Ministry of National Defense said yesterday.
① depressed   ② excluded
③ isolated   ④ agonized

49 Officials say the cause of his death is unknown, and results of an autopsy are <u>pending</u>.
① released   ② determined
③ anticipated   ④ undecided

50 I could submit and live the life of an amiable slave, but that was impossible.

① servile   ② agreeable

③ shrewd   ④ wretched

51 It is not right to contend that children are good rote learners, that they make good use of meaningless repetition and mimicking.

① report   ② claim

③ conform   ④ counter

52 A couple of giraffes languidly picking at some leaves and a glimpse of a few more impalas represented our last look at game.

① incessantly   ② hilariously

③ aggressively   ④ feebly

53 Even reasonable men sometimes do absurd thing.

① serious   ② foolish

③ strange   ④ pleasant

54 The unknown about what society will be like after the coronavirus pandemic ends is taxing.

① burdensome   ② terrifying

③ soluble   ④ stagnant

55 One of the responsibilities of the Coast Guard is to make sure that all ships obediently follow traffic rules in busy harbors.

① skillfully   ② safely

③ dutifully   ④ currently

56 Drought and soil erosion spawned dust storms across the Great Plains in the 1930s.

① followed   ② generated

③ indicated   ④ intensified

57 Even when a willing storyteller was available, an hour or so a day was more time than most children spent ensconced in the imagination of others.

① enforced   ② dazzled

③ settled   ④ eclipsed

58 The meager nature of his salary did not negatively affect his generosity.

① good   ② mediocre

③ sympathetic   ④ scanty

59 Three months have elapsed since she went away.

① gone by   ② been wasted

③ been saved   ④ been lonesome

60 Researchers found that Zika virus can affect embryonic cells that help form the brain and kill some of them outright.

① utterly   ② harshly

③ zealously   ④ dejectedly

61 The water table has a level called the zone of saturation.

① freezing   ② humidity

③ soaking   ④ dryness

62 His novel is weirdly <u>somnolent</u> given how portentously it primes us for danger, for the burning of mosques and blood in the streets.
① languid
② elliptical
③ ecstatic
④ shifty

63 By focusing on imaginary dangers managed in a comical and <u>peremptory</u> way, he discredited the cause of the Republican Party.
① dictatorial
② capricious
③ indecisive
④ eccentric

64 It may be easier to <u>track</u> an animal after rain because paw prints will show up in wet ground.
① follow
② classify
③ catch
④ train

65 The odds of home assistants accidentally recording conversations are low, and the devices should ask for <u>confirmation</u> before sending information to a third party.
① authorization
② advice
③ connection
④ privacy

66 Joyce has attempted in *Ulysses* to render as <u>exhaustively</u>, as precisely and as directly as it is possible in words to do, what our participation in life is like — or rather, what it seems to us like as from moment to moment we live.
① tiredly
② enthusiastically
③ descriptively
④ thoroughly

67 In his definition of phenomenology, Merleau-Ponty asserts "the body is not negligible, but <u>paramount</u>."
① preponderant
② mephitic
③ craven
④ arcuated

68 Previous economic crises in the U.S. have put men out of work, and we have <u>bemoaned</u> the hit to masculinity.
① resisted
② venerated
③ bewildered
④ bewailed

69 The minister was found to have <u>appropriated</u> a great deal of government money.
① donated
② saved
③ stolen
④ borrowed

70 The members of Mary Wilcher's family were notorious for their <u>headstrong</u> temperaments.
① stubborn
② rash
③ snobbish
④ intellectual

71 The present five-year-single-term presidential <u>tenure</u> was set to block dictatorship.
① approval
② statement
③ term
④ legacy

72 It is time to <u>abolish</u> our conception of what it means to be a mother in America and rebuild it on a policy level.
① abrogate
② surrogate
③ subjugate
④ congregate

73 Unlike the unequivocal accounts provided by eyewitnesses, the evidence provided by the flight recorder was more controvertible, leading to the development of several different theories to explain the crash.

① lucid   ② ambiguous

③ infallible   ④ theoretical

74 They give you the chance to learn new skills in a friendly and informal, yet professional atmosphere.

① casual   ② conventional

③ official   ④ illegal

75 The changing of the autumn leaves, old stone walls, distant views, and horses grazing in green meadows are examples of bucolic splendor.

① craven   ② rustic

③ servile   ④ querulous

76 The private Paley was aloof with employees, cold to his children and lavish in his personal lifestyle.

① frugal   ② prodigal

③ hygienic   ④ abstinent

77 As the kidnapper's actions were so repellent, it was hard to have any sympathy for her.

① reserved   ② insincere

③ aggressive   ④ unpleasant

78 The dean's spacious new office overlooked the campus.

① comfortable   ② luxurious

③ roomy   ④ quiet

79 By now he had exhausted his funds to the degree that he could not even pay his own mother the current installment of her annuity.

① debt   ② pension

③ lease   ④ investment

80 As soon as you drive it off the lot, your new car has already depreciated by several thousand dollars.

① devalued   ② denoted

③ assessed   ④ exalted

81 It is perverse of Tim to insist on having the window seat, since looking down from great heights makes him airsick.

① kind   ② generous

③ contrary   ④ interesting

82 Cocaine addicts and sticky-fingered finaglers are harmful to the best interests of the community.

① peddlers   ② swindlers

③ wanderers   ④ gamblers

83 Mary Tyler Moore is most remembered for two indelible sitcom roles: Laura Petrie on "The Dick Van Dyke Show" and Mary Richards on "The Mary Tyler Moore Show."

① incomparable   ② unforgettable

③ impressionable ④ indistinguishable

84 Tom Johnson was distinguished both as a critic and as a writer.

① eminent   ② inventive

③ dynamic   ④ enthusiastic

85 In A. D. 394, Emperor Theodosius I of Rome decreed that the Olympic Games should cease to take place.
① predicted   ② ordered
③ decided   ④ resolved

86 The current vogue of country music originated primarily in Tennessee.
① voice   ② popularity
③ sound   ④ tempo

87 Archaeologists study the material remains of past human life and materials to deduce how prehistoric people lived.
① reduce   ② infer
③ produce   ④ report

88 He seems to castigate tolerance as the "intellectual charity" of the powerful.
① aspirate   ② rebuke
③ culminate   ④ alleviate

89 Expense reports would show that the man who bought the drinks was reimbursed by the company for those purchases.
① withhold   ② reduced
③ waned   ④ refunded

90 The idea has been fascinating astronomers since the late 18th century, suggesting images of unimaginably strong cosmic whirlpools sucking up space matter and consigning it to oblivion.
① comparing   ② committing
③ compiling   ④ conserving

91 Such pernicious behavior got him sent to prison.
① costly   ② disgusting
③ harmful   ④ healthful

92 The extreme seriousness of desertification results from the vast areas of land and the tremendous numbers of people affected, as well as from the great difficulty of reversing or even slowing the process.
① augmented   ② unacceptable
③ inadequate   ④ enormous

93 The red juice oozed through the cloth and made a big round stain.
① absolved   ② exuded
③ absorbed   ④ consumed

94 While the surface of Antarctica is inhospitable to most living things, the water surrounding the continent is teeming with living creatures.
① crowded   ② magnificent
③ enormous   ④ colossal

95 Laser applications have increased swiftly in such areas as surgery, welding and metal cutting, and sound and video recording.
① universally   ② sweetly
③ quickly   ④ usefully

96 Do I exist? Am I real? Is what I see and touch real? Human beings are different from animals in that they raise questions about the meaning of life. People always come across new problems. Whether they are light or serious, the understanding of the relationship between self and the world is the base for one to tackle problems.
① complicate   ② correct
③ analyze   ④ undertake

97 AIDS, especially in the early years, primarily affected three groups: gay men, Haitians and intravenous drug users. As such, it served to inflame existing stigma, amplifying already entrenched homophobia, racism and contempt for addicts.
① eschewed   ② established
③ encroached   ④ endangered

98 Before the famous Egyptian feminist Hoda Shaarawi deliberately removed her veil in 1922, it was worn in public by all respectable middle class and upper class women. By 1935, however, veils were optional in Egypt. On the other hand, they have remained obligatory in the Arabian Peninsula to this day.
① seriously   ② carefully
③ intentionally ④ reluctantly

99 The global nature of climate change arises from the fact that irrespective of where on earth greenhouse gases are emitted they are rapidly absorbed into the atmosphere and spread around the earth. The consequences of the resulting global climate change, however, are projected to be far from uniform, with some countries expected to suffer far greater adverse impacts than others. In addition, unilateral action by any one country cannot alter this situation significantly. It therefore requires concerted remedial cooperative action at the international level to address the problem.
① unauthorized ② zero-sum
③ conventional ④ one-sided

100 Enthusiasm, appreciation and participation were the watchwords at the festival.
① words that sum up their attitude to a particular subject
② statements or principles that are generally accepted to be true
③ units of language that can be represented in writing or speech
④ words that you must know in order to be allowed to enter a place

[1] Write the meaning of the following words.

☐ circulate	☐ opposite
☐ unflagging	☐ versatile
☐ denotation	☐ caliber
☐ navigate	☐ employ
☐ acoustic	☐ shortsighted
☐ skip	☐ procession
☐ longitude	☐ mediocre
☐ corrupt	☐ hazy
☐ waterproof	☐ trance
☐ skittish	☐ liberate
☐ implement	☐ apostle
☐ errand	☐ recumbent
☐ dread	☐ sentiment
☐ sartorial	☐ peel
☐ flaw	☐ majority
☐ bent	☐ ferocious
☐ antipathy	☐ abuse
☐ durable	☐ centennial
☐ infinite	☐ obstetrician
☐ hurl	☐ replace
☐ collapse	☐ blithe
☐ geography	☐ red tape
☐ advocate	☐ palatial
☐ inverse	☐ screen
☐ perplex	☐ toll

[2] Select <u>the most</u> appropriate word from the box below. Each word should be used only once.

① liberate	② sartorial	③ screened	④ circulate
⑤ mediocre	⑥ denotation	⑦ errand	⑧ perplexed
⑨ dread	⑩ red tape	⑪ bent	⑫ navigate
⑬ versatile	⑭ skip	⑮ shortsighted	⑯ employ
⑰ centennial	⑱ palatial	⑲ durable	⑳ recumbent

1 The film was not very impressive; its plot was predictable and the acting was
_____.

2 All employees may be _____ for drugs and alcohol as well as a personality test,
which can be used to determine the applicant's integrity or emotional intelligence.

3 The _____ involved in conducting business here is unacceptably burdensome and
is becoming worse.

4 There are rebel groups in foreign countries striving to _____ their people who
are denied freedom by their governments.

5 His _____ attitude prevented him from recognizing the potential benefits of a
long-term investment.

6 Embryonic stem cells have the benefit of being highly _____ because scientists
can program them to become many different types of cells, including nerve or
heart cells.

7 When the U.S. government released a much-anticipated report on UFOs a year
ago, many were _____ that it couldn't explain 143 of the 144 sightings it examined.

8 The parts of the machine which experience a lot of friction have to be made from
_____ materials.

9 I'm a chemist that is in the prime of his career and I am _____ on achieving
my goals.

10 The enemies the companies _____ are potential internal informers.

[3] Choose the one which is different from the others.

11 ① blithe   ② jaunty   ③ jovial   ④ lethargic

12 ① extinct   ② ferocious   ③ savage   ④ fierce

13 ① competence   ② coalition   ③ caliber   ④ capacity

14 ① advocate   ② defender   ③ assailant   ④ proponent

15 ① antipathy   ② abhorrence   ③ hatred   ④ rapport

16 ① erratic   ② indefatigable   ③ unflagging   ④ tireless

17 ① skittish   ② nervous   ③ spooky   ④ impertinent

18 ① implement   ② execute   ③ halt   ④ fulfil

19 ① corrupt   ② chaste   ③ fraudulent   ④ venal

20 ① penetrate   ② collapse   ③ crumple   ④ disintegrate

✓ Answers

1 ⑤ | 그 영화는 그다지 인상적이지 않았다. 줄거리는 예상할 수 있었고 연기도 평범했다.

2 ③ | 모든 직원은 인성 검사뿐만 아니라 약물 및 알코올에 대한 검사를 받을 수도 있는데, 이는 지원자의 성실성이나 정서 지능을 판단하는 데 사용될 수 있다.

3 ⑩ | 이곳에서 업무를 수행하는 데 수반되는 불필요한 요식이 받아들일 수 없을 만큼 부담스러우며 날로 악화되고 있다.

4 ① | 외국에는 정부에 의해 자유를 거부당한 국민들을 해방시키려고 애쓰는 반군들이 있다.

5 ⑮ | 그의 근시안적인 태도로 인해 그는 장기 투자의 잠재적인 이점을 인식하지 못했다.

6 ⑬ | 배아 줄기세포는 과학자들이 신경 세포나 심장 세포를 포함하여 다양한 유형의 세포가 되도록 배아 줄기세포를 프로그램할 수 있기 때문에 매우 용도가 많다는 이점이 있다.

7 ⑧ | 1년 전 미국 정부가 많은 기대를 모았던 UFO(미확인 비행 물체)에 대한 보고서를 발표했을 때, 많은 사람들은 정부가 조사한 144건의 목격 사례 중 143건을 설명할 수 없다는 사실에 당황했다.

8 ⑲ | 많은 마찰을 겪는 기계 부품은 내구성 있는 소재로 만들어야 한다.

9 ⑪ | 나는 내 경력의 전성기에 있는 화학자이며 목표 달성을 위해 전념하고 있다.

10 ⑨ | 기업이 두려워하는 적은 잠재적인 내부 고발자이다.

- -

11 ④   **12** ①   **13** ②   **14** ③   **15** ④   **16** ①   **17** ④   **18** ③   **19** ②   **20** ①

☑ **DAILY CHECKUP**

[1] Write the meaning of the following words.

☐ valid	☐ fancy
☐ amass	☐ actually
☐ emblem	☐ clamor
☐ coin	☐ indifferent
☐ sentinel	☐ pertain
☐ impervious	☐ sticky
☐ timber	☐ jockey
☐ relieve	☐ vengeance
☐ eponymous	☐ applicable
☐ superb	☐ downfall
☐ woo	☐ spangle
☐ pessimistic	☐ moody
☐ encapsulate	☐ garland
☐ refrigerate	☐ confident
☐ caprice	☐ obtuse
☐ halcyon	☐ stretch
☐ blackmail	☐ malingerer
☐ premier	☐ inborn
☐ atheist	☐ paranoia
☐ derive	☐ cosset
☐ ramification	☐ forefather
☐ undue	☐ tailor-made
☐ bombshell	☐ agenda
☐ disconsolate	☐ lame
☐ legible	☐ draft

[2] Select <u>the most</u> appropriate word from the box below. Each word should be used only once.

① impervious	② eponymous	③ relieve	④ ramification
⑤ vengeance	⑥ blackmailing	⑦ superb	⑧ atheist
⑨ caprice	⑩ woo	⑪ halcyon	⑫ derive
⑬ applicable	⑭ legible	⑮ sticky	⑯ moody
⑰ obtuse	⑱ downfall	⑲ draft	⑳ stretch

1   Clay is paradoxical: it can hold a lot of water when loose, but when it is compacted it becomes almost _____.

2   The nurses massaged her lower back to try to _____ her back labor.

3   You need a system that protects the majority from the whim and _____ of the minority.

4   The _____ period of peace and prosperity was a welcome contrast to the turbulent years that had come before.

5   The next day he was arraigned but denied bail because he was suspected of _____ the actor and actresses.

6   A monotheist is someone who believes in a single god, a polytheist is someone who believes in many gods, and a(n) _____ is someone who believes there is no god at all.

7   The poster was written in letters big enough to be _____ across the room.

8   He was so _____ that he couldn't follow his teacher, so he asked some stupid questions.

9   The monotonous routine of hospital life induced a feeling of ennui which made him _____ and irritable.

10   The president of the company takes _____ on staffs who divulge his management problems.

[3] Choose the one which is different from the others.

11 ① dissipate   ② accumulate   ③ amass   ④ garner

12 ① undue   ② temperate   ③ excessive   ④ immoderate

13 ① desolate   ② disconsolate   ③ cowardly   ④ forlorn

14 ① uproar   ② outcry   ③ clamor   ④ serenity

15 ① inborn   ② congenital   ③ acquired   ④ innate

16 ① coddle   ② mimic   ③ cosset   ④ pamper

17 ① amplify   ② epitomize   ③ encapsulate   ④ condense

18 ① indifferent   ② apathetic   ③ nonchalant   ④ unyielding

19 ① lame   ② flimsy   ③ sturdy   ④ inadequate

20 ① pessimistic   ② fearless   ③ bleak   ④ gloomy

✓Answers

1 ① ┃ 점토는 역설적이다. 점토가 푸석푸석하면 많은 물을 머금을 수 있지만, 속이 꽉 차면 거의 물을 통과시키지 않는다.

2 ③ ┃ 간호사들은 그녀의 (출산 중의) 허리 진통을 완화하기 위해 그녀의 허리를 마사지했다.

3 ⑨ ┃ 소수의 일시적인 기분과 변덕으로부터 다수를 보호하는 시스템이 필요하다.

4 ⑪ ┃ 평화와 번영의 평온한 시기는 이전에 있었던 격동의 시기와 반가운 대조를 이루었다.

5 ⑥ ┃ 그는 그 배우와 여배우들을 갈취한 혐의를 받았기 때문에 다음날 법원에 소환되어 심문받았지만 보석이 거부되었다.

6 ⑧ ┃ 일신론자는 유일신을 믿는 사람이고, 다신론자는 여러 신을 믿는 사람이고, 무신론자는 신이 전혀 없다고 믿는 사람이다.

7 ⑭ ┃ 그 포스터는 그 방 어디서나 읽을 수 있을 정도로 충분히 큰 글씨로 쓰여 있었다.

8 ⑰ ┃ 그는 너무 우둔해서 선생님 말씀을 이해하지 못하고 바보 같은 질문들을 했다.

9 ⑯ ┃ 병원 생활의 단조로운 일상은 권태감을 유발해 그를 우울하고 신경질적으로 만들었다.

10 ⑤ ┃ 그 회사의 사장은 자신의 경영 문제를 폭로한 직원들에게 복수를 했다.

- -

11 ①   **12** ②   **13** ③   **14** ④   **15** ③   **16** ②   **17** ①   **18** ④   **19** ③   **20** ②

[1] Write the meaning of the following words.

☐ ambiguous	☐ remain
☐ embed	☐ sciolism
☐ regal	☐ quash
☐ impersonation	☐ vile
☐ spark	☐ enslave
☐ parsimonious	☐ discerning
☐ heredity	☐ savor
☐ becoming	☐ deter
☐ claim	☐ workout
☐ uneven	☐ extent
☐ delude	☐ concur
☐ perseverance	☐ comprehend
☐ singular	☐ tenet
☐ autobiography	☐ gauche
☐ veteran	☐ shaggy
☐ hamper	☐ discord
☐ tame	☐ ache
☐ pompous	☐ leak
☐ oligarchy	☐ manifold
☐ rational	☐ chamber
☐ bombard	☐ induce
☐ candidate	☐ parole
☐ fiscal	☐ feline
☐ mutter	☐ captive
☐ alchemy	☐ semantic

[2] Select <u>the most</u> appropriate word from the box below. Each word should be used only once.

① deluded	② ambiguous	③ parole	④ discerning
⑤ chamber	⑥ leaked	⑦ parsimonious	⑧ sciolism
⑨ rational	⑩ discord	⑪ bombard	⑫ hamper
⑬ tame	⑭ quash	⑮ candidate	⑯ becoming
⑰ fiscal	⑱ manifold	⑲ muttered	⑳ comprehend

1 Germany's neighbours in the European Union have long wished that its _____ citizens would save less and spend more, to boost the economy of the whole region.

2 The author purposely left the ending of his novel _____ so readers would have to decide for themselves what happened.

3 The cult leader _____ his followers into thinking that he possessed supernatural powers, leading them to blindly follow his every command.

4 Federal efforts to help develop next-generation vaccines are running into bureaucratic hurdles that may _____ efforts to fight future pandemics.

5 Given that the reality is that we're judged on our appearance all the time, it's perfectly _____ to want to look good.

6 Misinformation has been widely shared, despite attempts by authorities to _____ it by restricting internet access.

7 Mrs. Amherst was such a sensitive and _____ librarian that she had the ability to know exactly which book would suit each one of the students.

8 Marital _____ is the term used in society to describe these disagreements between husband and wife.

9 Samsung stopped its workers' use of generative AI tools this year after discovering its employees inadvertently _____ sensitive data to ChatGPT.

10 An irritable teenager _____ when her parents made her get off the couch and mow the lawn.

[3] Choose the one which is different from the others.

11 ① uneven   ② reciprocal   ③ bumpy   ④ rough

12 ① reluctance   ② perseverance   ③ endurance   ④ tenacity

13 ① pompous   ② arrogant   ③ pretentious   ④ humble

14 ① obsolescent   ② gauche   ③ awkward   ④ clumsy

15 ① tenet   ② creed   ③ conundrum   ④ dogma

16 ① contemptible   ② virtuous   ③ vile   ④ despicable

17 ① trigger   ② provoke   ③ spark   ④ culminate

18 ① singular   ② aberrant   ③ extraordinary ④ remarkable

19 ① savor   ② flavor   ③ connoisseur   ④ relish

20 ① insult   ② deter   ③ discourage   ④ dissuade

✔ **Answers**

1 ⑦ | 유럽연합에 있는 독일의 이웃 국가들은 전체 지역의 경제를 활성화하기 위해 인색한 독일 시민들이 덜 저축하고 더 많이 지출하기를 오랫동안 바랐다.

2 ② | 그 저자는 그의 소설의 결말을 의도적으로 애매모호한 상태로 두어서 독자들이 어떤 일이 일어났는지 스스로 판단해야 했다.

3 ① | 그 사이비 교주는 신도들을 속여 자신이 초능력을 가지고 있다고 생각하게 하여 맹목적으로 그의 모든 명령을 따르도록 했다.

4 ⑫ | 차세대 백신 개발을 돕기 위한 연방 정부의 노력은 미래의 전염병에 맞서 싸우려는 노력을 방해할 수도 있는 관료적 장애물에 부딪히고 있다.

5 ⑨ | 우리가 늘 외모로 평가받는 현실을 생각하면, 멋져 보이기를 원하는 것은 지극히 합리적인 것이다.

6 ⑭ | 인터넷 접속을 제한함으로써 잘못된 정보를 잠재우려는 당국의 노력에도 불구하고 잘못된 정보는 널리 공유되었다.

7 ④ | 애머스트(Amherst) 여사는 매우 세심하고 안목 있는 사서였기 때문에 학생들 각자에게 어떤 책이 맞는지를 정확히 알 수 있는 능력이 있었다.

8 ⑩ | 부부 사이 불화는 남편과 아내 사이의 다툼을 설명하기 위해 사회에서 사용되는 용어이다.

9 ⑥ | 삼성은 직원들이 ChatGPT에 민감한 데이터를 무심코 유출한 사실을 발견한 후 올해 직원들의 생성형 인공지능의 사용을 막았다.

10 ⑲ | 부모님이 소파에서 일어나 잔디를 깎으라고 하자 짜증이 난 십 대 소녀가 투덜거렸다.

- -

11 ②   **12** ①   **13** ④   **14** ①   **15** ③   **16** ②   **17** ④   **18** ②   **19** ③   **20** ①

☑ DAILY CHECKUP

[1] Write the meaning of the following words.

☐ encompass	☐ bachelor
☐ unique	☐ high-profile
☐ philistine	☐ vagary
☐ season	☐ obtrusive
☐ dubious	☐ parade
☐ reorganize	☐ arbiter
☐ significance	☐ thwart
☐ populous	☐ faucet
☐ avoidance	☐ comply
☐ reckless	☐ loom
☐ coexist	☐ saturnine
☐ neurosis	☐ eruption
☐ behold	☐ inalienable
☐ accustomed	☐ merchandise
☐ wanton	☐ fitful
☐ intimate	☐ delete
☐ effervescent	☐ stock
☐ budget	☐ imponderable
☐ glib	☐ prestige
☐ desert	☐ rehabilitate
☐ chisel	☐ traitor
☐ layoff	☐ adopt
☐ obfuscate	☐ matrimonial
☐ conceit	☐ slump
☐ averse	☐ canard

[2] Select <u>the most</u> appropriate word from the box below. Each word should be used only once.

① reckless	② canard	③ vagary	④ philistines
⑤ slump	⑥ obfuscated	⑦ matrimonial	⑧ stock
⑨ inalienable	⑩ faucet	⑪ layoff	⑫ loom
⑬ accustomed	⑭ rehabilitate	⑮ chisel	⑯ conceited
⑰ thwarts	⑱ populous	⑲ reorganize	⑳ averse

1   We need more men and women of culture and enlightenment in our society; we have too many _____ among us.

2   _____ destruction of nature by human beings has brought ecological catastrophe.

3   The author's use of complex metaphors and cryptic symbols often _____ the true meaning of his work, leaving readers perplexed.

4   The decreased export of electronic goods resulted in the _____ of numerous employees.

5   He had always had a good opinion of himself, but after the publication of his best selling novel he became unbearably _____.

6   The weather pattern has shifted that there is the _____ about today being very cold and tomorrow being very hot.

7   Harvard, committed only to avoiding bad publicity, _____ a police investigation, protects the suspected professor and silences the press.

8   In the Declaration of Independence, Thomas Jefferson wrote that all men are "endowed by their Creator with certain _____ rights" including "life, liberty and the pursuit of happiness."

9   Those who committed crimes against the public have to be ostracized from society for a certain amount of time until they _____.

10   During a political campaign, you will often hear on TV commercials some _____ about the opponent. This is a false statement designed to confuse the voters.

[3] Choose the one which is different from the others.

11 ① wanton   ② thrifty   ③ lewd   ④ profligate

12 ① dismal   ② saturnine   ③ reluctant   ④ gloomy

13 ① traitor   ② renegade   ③ betrayer   ④ fugitive

14 ① indulgence   ② reputation   ③ prestige   ④ standing

15 ① intermittent   ② consecutive   ③ sporadic   ④ fitful

16 ① prudent   ② intrusive   ③ obtrusive   ④ officious

17 ① eloquent   ② glib   ③ stuttering   ④ fluent

18 ① effervescent   ② ascetic   ③ buoyant   ④ ebullient

19 ① doubtful   ② skeptical   ③ dubious   ④ imperious

20 ① definite   ② intimate   ③ close   ④ familiar

✓Answers

1 ④ ｜ 우리 사회에는 교양 있고 개화된 사람들이 더 필요하다. 왜냐하면 우리들 사이에는 속물들이 너무 많기 때문이다.

2 ① ｜ 인간에 의한 무분별한 자연 파괴는 생태계의 재앙을 가져왔다.

3 ⑥ ｜ 작가의 복잡한 은유와 수수께끼 같은 상징의 사용은 종종 그의 작품의 진정한 의미를 혼란스럽게 만들어 독자들을 당황하게 했다.

4 ⑪ ｜ 전자 제품의 수출 감소로 수많은 직원이 정리 해고되었다.

5 ⑯ ｜ 그가 항상 자신을 좋게 평가해왔지만, 그의 베스트셀러 소설이 출판된 후에는 참을 수 없을 만큼 우쭐해졌다.

6 ③ ｜ 날씨 패턴이 바뀌어서 오늘은 매우 춥다가 내일은 매우 더운 변덕스러운 현상이 일어나고 있다.

7 ⑰ ｜ 나쁜 평판을 피하는 일에만 몰두한 하버드대학교는 경찰 조사를 방해하고 혐의를 받고 있는 그 교수를 보호하고 있으며 언론을 침묵시키고 있다.

8 ⑨ ｜ 토머스 제퍼슨(Thomas Jefferson)은 독립선언문에서 모든 사람은 "생명, 자유, 행복 추구"를 포함하여 "양도할 수 없는 특정한 권리를 창조주에 의해 부여받았다"라고 썼다.

9 ⑭ ｜ 국민을 상대로 범죄를 저지른 사람은 사회에 복귀할 때까지 일정 기간 동안 사회에서 격리되어야 한다.

10 ② ｜ 선거 운동 기간에, 당신은 TV 광고에서 종종 상대편에 대한 유언비어를 들을 것이다. 이것은 유권자들을 혼란스럽게 하도록 의도된 거짓 진술이다.

11 ②   **12** ③   **13** ④   **14** ①   **15** ②   **16** ①   **17** ③   **18** ②   **19** ④   **20** ①

☑ DAILY CHECKUP

[1] Write the meaning of the following words.

☐ uncouth	☐ ductile
☐ define	☐ enhance
☐ pedestal	☐ genesis
☐ salacious	☐ sentence
☐ restrain	☐ pandemic
☐ ingrained	☐ comb
☐ critical	☐ barbarian
☐ reparation	☐ expiate
☐ postpone	☐ antipodes
☐ maxim	☐ weave
☐ ajar	☐ sour
☐ element	☐ zephyr
☐ launch	☐ harbor
☐ obituary	☐ absolute
☐ afford	☐ stride
☐ fickle	☐ vest
☐ vibrate	☐ faint
☐ bigamy	☐ choir
☐ dated	☐ discriminate
☐ ascribe	☐ intermediate
☐ literate	☐ proportion
☐ calligraphy	☐ minuscule
☐ theatrical	☐ ratify
☐ hit-or-miss	☐ threshold
☐ counterpart	☐ scream

[2] Select <u>the most</u> appropriate word from the box below. Each word should be used only once.

① pedestal	② threshold	③ reparation	④ minuscule
⑤ ductile	⑥ fickle	⑦ discriminate	⑧ vest
⑨ ratified	⑩ postponed	⑪ intermediate	⑫ obituary
⑬ stride	⑭ literate	⑮ expiate	⑯ maxim
⑰ uncouth	⑱ ingrained	⑲ launch	⑳ dated

1   Across hygiene-conscious Eastern Europe, many people consider it _____ and unsanitary to eat a burger with their bare hands.

2   After the accident we sought _____ in court, but our lawyer was not competent and we didn't win a cent.

3   Due to the worsening weather conditions, all flights from the snow-bound airport have been _____ until further notice.

4   People who are _____ change their minds so much you can't rely on them.

5   The usual details of a(n) _____ — the date, location and cause of death — were missing.

6   The 3D printed stainless steels were up to three times stronger than steels made by conventional techniques and yet still _____.

7   The oracle at Delphi assigned Hercules a series of labors to _____ the sin of murdering his family.

8   Some people take it too far and _____ against other people, treating them differently based on their physical characteristics or abilities.

9   A high pain _____ means we are not experiencing pain, despite pain signals being activated.

10   An amendment to the U.S. Constitution must be _____ by three-fourths of the states, either passed by the state legislatures or by state conventions.

[3] Choose the one which is different from the others.

11 ① salacious ② lecherous ③ libertine ④ unfledged

12 ① accentuate ② vibrate ③ shake ④ quiver

13 ① hit-or-miss ② even-handed ③ careless ④ desultory

14 ① improve ② heighten ③ subtract ④ enhance

15 ① harbor ② validate ③ conceal ④ hide

16 ① faint ② feeble ③ resolute ④ weak

17 ① bland ② sour ③ acid ④ tart

18 ① sentence ② exonerate ③ condemn ④ convict

19 ① attribute ② ascribe ③ proscribe ④ impute

20 ① forsake ② restrain ③ inhibit ④ repress

✓ Answers

1 ⑰ | 위생에 민감한 동유럽 전역에서, 많은 사람들은 맨손으로 햄버거를 먹는 것이 무례하고 비위생적이라고 생각한다.

2 ③ | 사고 후에 법정에서 배상을 받으려 했지만, 우리 변호사가 유능하지 않아서 우리는 단 한 푼도 받지 못했다.

3 ⑩ | 악화되고 있는 기상 상태 때문에, 눈에 갇힌 공항의 모든 비행편이 추후 통지가 있을 때까지 연기되었다.

4 ⑥ | 변덕스러운 사람들은 마음을 너무 바꾸어서 의지할 수 없다.

5 ⑫ | 사망 날짜, 장소, 원인 등 사망 기사의 일반적인 세부 정보가 누락되었다.

6 ⑤ | 3D 프린팅된 스테인리스강은 기존 기술로 만든 강철보다 최대 3배 강하면서도 여전히 연성이 있다(유연하다).

7 ⑮ | 델포이의 신탁은 헤라클레스에게 가족을 살해한 죗값을 치르는 일련의 고된 노동을 부과했다.

8 ⑦ | 어떤 사람들은 도가 지나쳐 다른 사람을 차별하여 신체적 특성이나 능력에 따라 사람들을 다르게 대우한다.

9 ② | 고통을 느끼는 한계점이 높다는 것은 통증 신호가 활성화되었음에도 우리가 통증을 겪고 있지 않다는 것을 의미한다.

10 ⑨ | 미국 헌법 수정안은 주 의회나 주 협약에 의해 통과된 주의 4분의 3의 비준을 받아야 한다.

- -

11 ④ **12** ① **13** ② **14** ③ **15** ② **16** ③ **17** ① **18** ② **19** ③ **20** ①

ACTUAL TEST

[01-100] Choose the one that is closest in meaning to the underlined part.

01 She left the door ajar so as to let the cat go in.
① slightly open ② widely open
③ unlocked ④ unfixed

02 Fine bone china is eminently practical, because it is strong and durable.
① sturdy ② impeccable
③ elastic ④ brittle

03 Cobalt in infinitesimal amounts is one of the metals essential to life.
① minute ② prescribed
③ limited ④ restricted

04 The middle class has taken the brunt of the currency and stock market collapse.
① construction ② intrusion
③ breakdown ④ change

05 He made some blithe remarks about the coming hurricane.
① careless ② defensive
③ discreet ④ ungrounded

06 Tom says that this place is the palatial home of celebrities.
① attractive ② comfortable
③ friendly ④ grand

07 The film's plot is predictable and the acting is mediocre.
① potent ② peculiar
③ impressive ④ undistinguished

08 Real or imagined, Nessie has long been a Scottish emblem.
① symbol ② falsehood
③ disgrace ④ boast

09 In defence industries, sudden layoffs are common.
① bankruptcies ② redundancies
③ innovations ④ advances

10 Do not obfuscate the issues by dragging in irrelevant argument.
① detonate ② illumine
③ elucidate ④ obscure

11 The latest revelation certainly won't enhance her image.
① increase ② influence
③ develop ④ improve

12 Rain forced a postponement of the match.
① delay ② rain check
③ cancellation ④ vengeance

13 Due to the <u>unflagging</u> efforts of the rescue team, the children were found after a few hours.

① brave   ② unified

③ hurried   ④ indefatigable

14 The small gold emblem on the bottom of the tableware <u>denotes</u> quality and excellence.

① surfaces   ② treasures

③ indicates   ④ retails

15 We plan to <u>implement</u> a policy allowing students to choose a humane alternative.

① make up

② stand for

③ put into action

④ ask for

16 Maslow's attitude is partly due to the <u>dread</u> of further contention between his friends and his sisters.

① boredom   ② admiration

③ fear   ④ native

17 Certain <u>acoustic</u> problems often result from improper design or from construction limitations. If large echoes are to be avoided, focusing of the sound wave must be avoided.

① sensory   ② tactile

③ visible   ④ auditory

18 We all come into this life with a natural <u>bent</u> toward credulity, toward believing what others tell us.

① disposition   ② abhorrence

③ undeviating   ④ curiosity

19 We were amazed at the seemingly <u>infinite</u> assortment of fruits and vegetables in so small a market.

① erudite   ② numerous

③ exclusive   ④ adroit

20 Unique to its era, the fate of the dinosaurs has <u>perplexed</u> scientists for more than a century.

① discovered   ② called

③ puzzled   ④ dubbed

21 The author's analysis and the scientific evidence <u>validate</u> the position that individuals do not need the same amount of leisure time to be satisfied.

① refute   ② challenge

③ justify   ④ neutralize

22 He may not be much of an artist, but he is an exceptionally <u>versatile</u> man.

① creative   ② energetic

③ many-sided   ④ long-lasting

23 Barracudas are <u>ferocious</u> predators, sometimes called the tigers of tropical waters.

① savage   ② indistinct

③ flagrant   ④ lavish

24 Large corporations cannot interview all the people who wish to work for them, so they <u>screen</u> the resumé first, often by computer, to choose the best applicants.

① filter   ② block

③ investigate   ④ show

25 Tom encapsulated a 500-page report into an accessible 25-page summary.
① condensed ② featured
③ reduced ④ located

26 In democratic countries any efforts to restrict the freedom of the press are rightly condemned. However, this freedom can easily be abused.
① preserved ② demystified
③ misused ④ denounced

27 Karen's aptitude for business enabled her to amass a small fortune before she was thirty.
① accumulate ② deplete
③ bequeath ④ donate

28 Being impervious to rain, the tent made a fine shelter during the storm.
① antagonistic ② precarious
③ peripatetic ④ resistant

29 Two new elementary schools will relieve crowding in Palm Beach County, Florida.
① induce ② reinforce
③ allay ④ intensify

30 It is more preferable to be poor, but the master of one's destiny, than to be wealthy, but living at the caprice of such an unpredictable king.
① whim ② prestige
③ blessing ④ introspection

31 The immigration debate is heating up on both sides of the Atlantic, pitting advocates for legalizing illegal immigrants against those who support stronger anti-immigration measures.
① adversaries ② rebels
③ proponents ④ priests

32 The robbers have been involved in wanton beating of innocent people and deliberate destruction of bank building.
① illegal ② unruly
③ intentional ④ stubborn

33 I'm sorry but those items are temporarily out of stock.
① unavailable ② overpriced
③ not for sale ④ the wrong size

34 The men and boys of West Africa have to leave home because the rains have become so fickle, the days measurably hotter, the droughts more frequent, making it impossible to grow enough food on their land.
① scanty ② perpetual
③ voracious ④ capricious

35 Alienated and unsettled by Tokyo's clamorous high-rise strangeness, Charlotte experiences a flash of panic about her own life.
① noisy ② glamourous
③ cumbersome ④ skeletal

36 The industry <u>encompasses</u> the design, manufacturing, distribution, marketing, retailing, advertising, and promotion of all types of apparel.
① covers   ② encounters
③ compares   ④ spurs

37 He's always <u>moody</u> because things aren't working out at home.
① romantic   ② depressed
③ foolish   ④ numb

38 The artist's fanciful dreams led to <u>delude</u> himself and his family.
① vindicate   ② acquit
③ fool   ④ execute

39 His business is still a far cry from returning to the <u>halcyon</u> days of the early 1990s.
① prosperous   ② turbulent
③ impoverished   ④ embryonic

40 WHO has <u>launched</u> a new initiative to tackle the growing problem of counterfeit and substandard drugs.
① modified   ② announced
③ commenced   ④ examined

41 This is the third time today my dad has given us an <u>ambiguous</u> reply.
① angry   ② uncertain
③ clear   ④ humorous

42 His discussion of white hiphop consumers makes the point that to an unprecedented <u>extent</u> white youth are listening to an explicit critique of "white" society.
① quality   ② extant
③ extra   ④ degree

43 Nobody in that company seemed to <u>concur with</u> Johnson.
① occur to   ② dispute with
③ agree with   ④ recur to

44 Convicted thieves and counterfeiters often received the death penalty, which was thought to be a <u>deterrent</u> to other criminals.
① beacon   ② amphibian
③ eminence   ④ hindrance

45 When the time came for him to be <u>sentenced</u>, his father pleaded for leniency.
① nominated   ② investigated
③ arrested   ④ condemned

46 "Enough with the <u>obituary</u> ideas!" she said.
① outlandish   ② difficult
③ cheap   ④ dead

47 In the novel *Silent Spring*, Rachel Carson forcefully decried the <u>indiscriminate</u> use of pesticides.
① haphazard   ② innovative
③ unpleasant   ④ indispensable

48 The committee members have not decided which of the two strategies they should <u>adopt</u> to successfully complete the task.
① expedite ② employ
③ manipulate ④ abandon

49 A customer who bought a book from me through Amazon.com left a poor rating, along with a complaint about the book being "too <u>dated</u>".
① damaged ② monotonous
③ old-fashioned ④ poorly designed

50 She found it difficult to talk about her achievements without sounding <u>pompous</u>.
① tolerant ② variant
③ compliant ④ arrogant

51 There must be indeed morality; but it must be <u>tailor-made</u> for one's inimitable personality, not off-the-peg.
① off-the-rack ② custom-built
③ ready-made ④ incomparable

52 It is a theme which commonly gets <u>salacious</u> treatment in the mass media.
① obscene ② incorrigible
③ scathing ④ malicious

53 The administration could <u>rehabilitate</u> its image by taking bold action to remove the tariff.
① concoct ② restore
③ compensate ④ imagine

54 Anxiety arises in response to inner stimuli which <u>obtrude</u> from the unconscious levels of the mind.
① vanish ② relinquish
③ suffer ④ emerge

55 John's composition was poorly organized but at least it was <u>legible</u>.
① conclusive ② comprehensible
③ audible ④ valiant

56 Although a Canadian nation had been formed by the end of the 19th century, separate political, economic, and geographic influences continued through the 20th century to <u>restrain</u> unified educational development.
① release ② curb
③ distract ④ promote

57 The public was so <u>indifferent</u> to the outcome of the baseball match that few even bothered to read about it in the news the next day.
① amenable ② apathetic
③ congenial ④ cogent

58 It is the very pursuit of happiness that <u>thwarts</u> happiness.
① compels ② impedes
③ spawns ④ augments

59 Not surprisingly, those who are <u>averse</u> to surrendering their sovereignty have become increasingly restive of late.
① determined ② obedient
③ hostile ④ agreeable

60 All men are endowed with inalienable rights to the pursuit of happiness.
① irreverent ② discriminatory
③ nontransferable ④ statutory

61 In certain types of poisoning, immediately give large quantities of soapy or salty water in order to induce vomiting.
① control ② lessen
③ stop ④ cause

62 The eye-witness account was somewhat hazy, as he struggled to recall specific details due to the passage of time.
① scanty ② impetuous
③ nebulous ④ surreal

63 It's one of the most prestigious schools in the country.
① repugnant ② reputable
③ susceptive ④ presumptuous

64 They may not be unduly apprehensive about climate change, but they know about the greenhouse effect and how the state of the world and their own localities impinges on their lives.
① excessively ② tellingly
③ flagrantly ④ forthrightly

65 We hope that the republics will ratify the treaty.
① deny ② purge
③ approve ④ elucidate

66 Pure silver is nearly white, lustrous, soft, and very ductile.
① versatile ② pliable
③ serviceable ④ shiny

67 Dr. Haycock prescribed a mixture of ammonium chloride and sugar which was the stock remedy for malingerers in the army.
① placebos ② troopers
③ mercenaries ④ shirkers

68 The professor criticized the hit-or-miss quality of our research.
① lucrative ② attentive
③ targeted ④ careless

69 The climbers were astonished to see the peak of the mountain loom before them.
① shake ② collapse
③ explode ④ emerge

70 Reckless distribution of complicated derivative products throughout the global market, detached from the real economy, put the global financial market into crisis.
① unoriginal ② disingenuous
③ foreign ④ speculative

71 Perhaps the most high-profile supporter of creatine supplements is professional baseball player Mark McGuire.
① ardent ② renowned
③ stern ④ sophisticated

72 Mandy's performance on the math test was <u>hampered</u> because her attention was focused on the party she was attending on that weekend.
① intensified   ② endowed
③ obstructed   ④ occupied

73 He made <u>a critical</u> mistake and failed the exam.
① an ambiguous   ② a surprising
③ a conditional   ④ a crucial

74 It was inevitable that the pent-up emotion would <u>erupt</u> into violence.
① go off   ② come off
③ bring into   ④ come about

75 The public is very <u>dubious</u> about the governor's plans for a tax cut.
① delightful   ② creditable
③ doubtful   ④ trustful

76 It proved how much harm was done by the uncontrolled, <u>reckless</u> use of insecticides.
① unnecessary   ② limited
③ irresponsible   ④ continuous

77 The history of the exploration of Antarctica recounts many tales of <u>perseverance</u> and suffering.
① endurance   ② skill
③ generosity   ④ disturbance

78 Tom's smart cousin had been a perpetual obstacle in the path of his <u>uncouth</u> ambitions.
① crude   ② noble
③ undaunted   ④ laudable

79 You <u>fancy</u> me mad. Mad men know nothing. But I know everything from A to Z.
① like   ② imagine
③ trust   ④ declare

80 There is a military <u>maxim</u> that a commander is responsible for everything his or her subordinates do, or fail to do.
① police   ② principle
③ tradition   ④ service

81 In his novels, Upton Beall Sinclair showed his <u>unique</u> genius for recreating social history.
① proven   ② peerless
③ understated   ④ understandable

82 It is considered almost <u>gauche</u> to wave the flag of general suffering in other people's faces.
① awkward   ② sophisticated
③ brave   ④ painful

83 In the play, Huston's <u>saturnine</u> patrician and Jacob's plaintive everyman never faltered.
① sullen   ② dissident
③ sinistral   ④ foolhardy

84 Her decision to wear only red dress was pure <u>vagary</u>.
① good manners
② caprice
③ up to date fashion
④ attitude

85 Much of this <u>obtuseness</u> sprang from the fanatical faith of mid-nineteenth century British politicians in the economic doctrine of *laissez-faire,* no interference by government.
① acuity ② enmity
③ enthusiasm ④ callousness

86 I find the content and approach of his story <u>unsavory</u>.
① confusing ② diverse
③ unpleasant ④ predictable

87 This novel is too difficult for <u>intermediate</u> students of English.
① meridian ② average
③ advanced ④ introductory

88 Preserving wilderness has for decades been a fundamental <u>tenet</u> of the environmental movement in the US.
① principle ② benefit
③ privilege ④ strength

89 <u>Intimacy</u> is valuable currency when an artist's identity and image hinge on hired-gun hitmakers and airbrushed photo shoots and social-media posts.
① friendliness ② popularity
③ resemblance ④ similarity

90 It is now evident that neither <u>heredity</u> alone nor experience alone can account for individual differences.
① archetype ② genetics
③ milieu ④ constitution

91 It came as a joyous daybreak to end the long night of their <u>captivity</u>.
① imprisonment ② captivation
③ capturing ④ capacity

92 The worst flu <u>pandemic</u> on record was that caused by the infamous Spanish flu which killed many people.
① widespread
② locally spread
③ quickly spread
④ aerially spread

93 The idea that today's failing funds are proverbial canaries in the coal mine looks more like a(n) <u>false report</u>.
① canard ② ascription
③ recapitulation ④ dispatch

94 The defeated country demanded <u>reparations</u> for the destruction it had suffered at the hands of the victorious army.
① restraints ② extortions
③ quittances ④ disadvantages

95 Israel's security cabinet decided yesterday on a number of measures to <u>deter</u> new Palestinian attacks.
① repay ② criticize
③ anticipate ④ prevent

96 Despite my close familiarity with the wolf family, this was the kind of situation where irrational but deeply <u>ingrained</u> prejudices completely overmaster reason and experience.
① infringed ② embedded
③ intimidated ④ encountered

97 When the historian <u>ascribed</u> the brick to the historic structure, Hadrian's Wall, none of his colleagues believed him.

① prescribed   ② attributed

③ conscripted   ④ contributed

98 If you want to run a kindergarten, you must <u>comply with</u> the conditions laid down by the authorities.

① obey   ② presume

③ improve with   ④ agree with

99 Our ranking is a strong indication of the <u>caliber</u> of our student body, the dedication of our faculty, and the strength of our academic programs and reflects our continuing commitment to provide our students with a superior education.

① quantity   ② quality

③ motivation   ④ background

100 The earliest quilts were fashioned with relatively simple designs and were made to be primarily functional rather than to serve as a means of elaborate artistic expression. <u>Parsimonious</u> women recycled highly valued scraps of materials to make and repair the quilts.

① Frugal   ② Notorious

③ Capricious   ④ Rancorous

☑ DAILY CHECKUP

[1] Write the meaning of the following words.

☐ kidnap	☐ terror
☐ defiant	☐ cement
☐ menial	☐ despise
☐ subscribe	☐ lanky
☐ acumen	☐ impact
☐ endeavor	☐ beckon
☐ somnambulism	☐ foundation
☐ official	☐ pertinent
☐ impound	☐ arrant
☐ character	☐ omit
☐ workaday	☐ tardy
☐ luggage	☐ entomology
☐ ply	☐ recant
☐ incisive	☐ pertinacious
☐ microbe	☐ compose
☐ bravery	☐ serendipity
☐ cynical	☐ rag
☐ playwright	☐ martial
☐ abreast	☐ garret
☐ calling	☐ vouch
☐ refined	☐ patrimony
☐ sabotage	☐ amazing
☐ fawning	☐ scrub
☐ disqualify	☐ homicide
☐ umbrage	☐ excuse

[2] Select <u>the most</u> appropriate word from the box below. Each word should be used only once.

① acumen	② tardy	③ amazing	④ umbrage
⑤ beckon	⑥ menial	⑦ patrimony	⑧ cement
⑨ recant	⑩ impound	⑪ refined	⑫ disqualify
⑬ endeavor	⑭ omit	⑮ cynical	⑯ garret
⑰ vouch	⑱ serendipity	⑲ subscribe	⑳ pertinent

1 Jack's business _____ became apparent when he rescued his company by finding an appropriate partner for a merger.

2 Instead of being assigned important jobs by their bosses, they were often given _____ tasks such as getting coffee and doing photocopying.

3 When a driver repeatedly ignores parking regulations and accumulates multiple fines, the city authorities may _____ a driver's car.

4 The political corruption scandal left many Americans with a strong distrust of the U.S. government and a(n) _____ view of politicians and lawyers.

5 Protesters took particular _____ at an incident in which officers detained an innocent black man and patted him down.

6 The scope of the journal is quite restricted; they publish only articles _____ to education policies.

7 Indian criminal justice is known for being _____ and many citizens say they resent the fact that court cases often go on for years, even decades.

8 Mr. Protasevich later renounced his political activism and was released from jail into house arrest, although many believe he was coerced to _____.

9 Many scientific discoveries are a matter of _____: Newton was not sitting on the ground thinking about gravity when the apple dropped on his head.

10 In Argentina, national oil company is generally viewed as a national _____ and off-limits to outsiders.

[3] Choose the one which is different from the others.

11 ① indulgent   ② defiant   ③ disobedient   ④ inflexible

12 ① bravery   ② fury   ③ courage   ④ valor

13 ① profession   ② calling   ③ pastime   ④ vocation

14 ① despise   ② disdain   ③ scorn   ④ cherish

15 ① lean   ② squat   ③ lanky   ④ gaunt

16 ① arrant   ② flagrant   ③ dissimilar   ④ notorious

17 ① excuse   ② pardon   ③ forgive   ④ accuse

18 ① venturesome   ② pertinacious   ③ stubborn   ④ persistent

19 ① incisive   ② superficial   ③ acute   ④ trenchant

20 ① fawning   ② flattering   ③ pugnacious   ④ obsequious

✓ Answers

1 ① │ 잭(Jack)이 가진 사업상의 날카로운 통찰력은 그가 회사 합병의 적절한 파트너를 찾아 그의 회사를 구했을 때 명백해졌다.

2 ⑥ │ 그들은 상사에게 중요한 일을 배정받는 대신 커피를 타거나 복사를 하는 등의 사소한 일들을 받는 경우가 종종 있었다.

3 ⑩ │ 운전자가 반복적으로 주차 규정을 무시하고 많은 벌금이 쌓이면 시 당국은 운전자의 차량을 압수할 수도 있다.

4 ⑮ │ 정치 부패 스캔들은 많은 미국인에게 미국 정부에 대한 강한 불신을 남겼고, 정치인과 법률가들에 대해 냉소적 시각을 갖도록 만들었다.

5 ④ │ 시위자들은 경찰이 한 무고한 흑인 남성을 구금해서 몸을 수색했던 사건에 특히 분노했다.

6 ⑳ │ 그 저널의 범위는 꽤 제한적인데, 그들은 교육정책과 관계있는 기사만 게재한다.

7 ② │ 인도의 형사 사법제도는 더딘 것으로 알려져 있으며 많은 시민들은 법원 소송이 종종 수년, 심지어 수십 년 동안 지속되는 경우가 많다는 사실에 분개하고 있다고 말한다.

8 ⑨ │ 프로타세비치(Protasevich)는 이후 정치적 행동주의를 포기하고 감옥에서 가택연금 상태로 풀려났지만, 많은 사람들은 그가 발언을 철회하도록 강요받았다고 믿고 있다.

9 ⑱ │ 많은 과학적인 발견들은 뜻밖의 발견의 문제다. 뉴턴(Newton)이 중력에 대해 생각하면서 땅바닥에 앉아 있는 바로 그때 사과가 머리에 떨어진 것은 아니었다.

10 ⑦ │ 아르헨티나에서 국영 석유회사는 국가적인 유산으로 외국인들이 넘볼 수 없는 것으로 일반적으로 여겨진다.

- - - - - - - - - -

11 ①   **12** ②   **13** ③   **14** ④   **15** ②   **16** ③   **17** ④   **18** ①   **19** ②   **20** ③

☑ **DAILY CHECKUP**

[1] Write the meaning of the following words.

☐ compensate	☐ passion
☐ sanity	☐ exorcise
☐ impenetrable	☐ tolerance
☐ eugenics	☐ dexterous
☐ pivotal	☐ endow
☐ ancestor	☐ belabor
☐ detract	☐ hypothesis
☐ raw	☐ viper
☐ jocose	☐ campaign
☐ penance	☐ allegedly
☐ retire	☐ shutdown
☐ meek	☐ fierce
☐ occupation	☐ gentry
☐ interject	☐ bold
☐ mainstream	☐ lade
☐ pine	☐ decade
☐ solitude	☐ coarse
☐ narcotic	☐ application
☐ acquire	☐ militant
☐ condolence	☐ recrimination
☐ perceive	☐ valedictory
☐ feckless	☐ conserve
☐ spire	☐ seminal
☐ undermine	☐ inroad
☐ hapless	☐ taut

[2] Select <u>the most</u> appropriate word from the box below. Each word should be used only once.

① impenetrable	② penance	③ sanity	④ fierce
⑤ detract	⑥ mainstream	⑦ eugenics	⑧ narcotic
⑨ compensate	⑩ spire	⑪ tolerance	⑫ retire
⑬ hypothesis	⑭ undermine	⑮ valedictory	⑯ inroad
⑰ recrimination	⑱ conserve	⑲ campaign	⑳ solitude

1 Most travel insurance companies and airlines will not _____ for situations beyond their control.

2 Banks maintain that they have built _____ walls in their organizations to prevent seepage of material information.

3 During the end of the late 19th century, Japanese scholars began to think about _____, or the breeding of human beings through controlled marriages.

4 Many Filipinos perform religious _____ in the week leading to Easter in the hope they will be cleansed of sins and their wishes might be granted.

5 We live exclusively in relation to others, and what disappears from our lives is _____. Technology is taking away our privacy and our concentration, but it is also taking away our ability to be alone.

6 The availability of fake IDs on the Internet could _____ the efforts to stop underage drinking.

7 Sometimes patients will find that one medicine works well for a few years and then their body seems to build up a(n) _____ and that medicine no longer controls symptoms.

8 The UK Dangerous Dogs Act prohibits breeding certain _____ dogs such as Pit Bull Terriers.

9 The nationalists are very keen to _____ their customs and language.

10 His sudden decision to _____ brought down the curtain on a distinguished career.

[3] Choose the one which is different from the others.

11 ① pivotal ② ulterior ③ crucial ④ important

12 ① vehement ② meek ③ docile ④ gentle

13 ① unfortunate ② unlucky ③ hapless ④ impeccable

14 ① bellicose ② aggressive ③ submissive ④ militant

15 ① feckless ② inept ③ incompetent ④ palliative

16 ① adroit ② cumbersome ③ dexterous ④ deft

17 ① bold ② audacious ③ cowardly ④ daring

18 ① refined ② coarse ③ rude ④ vulgar

19 ① jocose ② solemn ③ facetious ④ jocular

20 ① solace ② compassion ③ condolence ④ conceit

✔ Answers

1 ⑨ | 대부분의 여행 보험 회사와 항공사는 그들이 통제할 수 없는 상황에 대해 보상하지 않을 것이다.

2 ① | 은행은 중요한 정보가 유출되는 것을 방지하기 위해 사내에 뚫을 수 없는 벽을 구축했다고 주장한다.

3 ⑦ | 19세기 말, 일본의 학자들은 우생학, 즉 통제된 혼인을 통한 인간의 형질 개량에 대해 생각하기 시작했다.

4 ② | 많은 필리핀 사람들은 부활절로 이어지는 한 주 동안 그들이 지은 죄가 깨끗이 씻겨지고 그들의 소원이 이루어지길
바라는 마음에서 종교적인 참회를 한다.

5 ⑳ | 우리는 오로지 타인과 관계를 맺으며 살아간다. 그리고 우리의 삶에서 사라지는 것은 고독이다. 기술은 우리의 사생활과
집중력을 앗아가고 있지만 혼자 있을 수 있는 능력마저도 앗아가고 있다.

6 ⑭ | 인터넷상에서 가짜 신분증을 구할 수 있다는 것은 미성년자의 음주를 막으려는 노력을 저해할 수 있을 것이다.

7 ⑪ | 때때로 환자들은 한 약물이 몇 년 동안은 잘 듣지만 그 이후에는 환자의 체내에 내성이 쌓이는 것 같아서 그 약물이 더
이상 증상을 억제하지 못한다는 것을 알게 될 것이다.

8 ④ | 영국 맹견 법은 핏불테리어와 같은 특정 맹견의 사육을 금한다.

9 ⑱ | 민족주의자들은 자신들의 관습과 언어를 보존하는 데 매우 열심이다.

10 ⑫ | 그의 갑작스러운 은퇴 결심으로 훌륭한 경력이 막을 내렸다.

- -

11 ② **12** ① **13** ④ **14** ③ **15** ④ **16** ② **17** ③ **18** ① **19** ② **20** ④

[1] Write the meaning of the following words.

☐ lethal	☐ convert
☐ safeguard	☐ quay
☐ enlighten	☐ unite
☐ parturition	☐ incognito
☐ urban	☐ recession
☐ ballot	☐ malign
☐ absorb	☐ shore
☐ closet	☐ vista
☐ perpetual	☐ objective
☐ top-notch	☐ accord
☐ interpret	☐ constable
☐ enmity	☐ exchange
☐ disband	☐ onset
☐ conscious	☐ rake
☐ naturalize	☐ homogeneous
☐ desperate	☐ pinnacle
☐ garnish	☐ feign
☐ stand	☐ impregnable
☐ muddy	☐ medium
☐ cast	☐ servile
☐ adamant	☐ loophole
☐ glee	☐ bland
☐ process	☐ tyro
☐ sleek	☐ penny-pinching
☐ dyslexia	☐ assemble

[2] Select <u>the most</u> appropriate word from the box below. Each word should be used only once.

① enmity	② convert	③ loophole	④ incognito
⑤ servile	⑥ pinnacle	⑦ lethal	⑧ recession
⑨ enlightened	⑩ adamant	⑪ exchange	⑫ garnish
⑬ homogeneous	⑭ disband	⑮ stand	⑯ impregnable
⑰ unite	⑱ naturalize	⑲ interpret	⑳ safeguard

1 Celebrities often try to go out or travel _____ so that they may have some privacy.

2 Although they might bring on an adrenaline rush of a lifetime, extreme sports are highly risky and can even be _____.

3 The Renaissance was a period of great intellectual and artistic growth, often characterized as a(n) _____ era that celebrated human achievement and knowledge.

4 Sometimes police officers or government officials _____ groups they believe are a nuisance or a threat.

5 Building a fence to stop illegal crossings has drawn praise from some of communities adjoining the border, but it is viewed with _____ by many Mexicans.

6 Her behavior at work, marked by an excessive desire to please her superiors, was often described as highly _____.

7 Critics argue that missionaries are being disrespectful of other cultures when trying to _____ Muslims to Christianity.

8 The _____ knocked on the head any idea of expanding the business.

9 The medieval fortress was so strong that it remained _____ to the enemy troops, no matter what tactics or weapons they used.

10 A(n) _____ in the International Whaling Commission's moratorium on commercial whaling allows Japan to hunt whales for scientific purposes, although many view the country's whale study as a poorly disguised excuse to hunt the protected animals for their meat.

[3] Choose the one which is different from the others.

11 ① tyro   ② novice   ③ foreman   ④ neophyte

12 ① profligate   ② stingy   ③ parsimonious   ④ penny-pinching

13 ① accord   ② withhold   ③ bestow   ④ confer

14 ① impartial   ② unbiased   ③ objective   ④ prejudiced

15 ① malign   ② slander   ③ traduce   ④ commend

16 ① delight   ② gloom   ③ glee   ④ mirth

17 ① lackluster   ② lustrous   ③ glossy   ④ sleek

18 ① constant   ② transitory   ③ perpetual   ④ endless

19 ① assemble   ② congregate   ③ disperse   ④ convene

20 ① feign   ② pretend   ③ assume   ④ abdicate

✓ Answers

1 ④ ∣ 유명인사들은 종종 자신들의 프라이버시를 위해 신분을 숨기고 밖에 나가거나 여행을 한다.

2 ⑦ ∣ 비록 이것들이 일생 최대의 아드레날린을 솟구치게 하지만, 익스트림 스포츠들은 굉장히 위험하고 심지어 치명적일 수 있다.

3 ⑨ ∣ 르네상스는 지적, 예술적으로 크게 성장한 시기로, 종종 인간의 성취와 지식을 찬양한 계몽된 시대로 간주된다.

4 ⑭ ∣ 때때로 경찰관이나 공무원들은 방해가 되거나 위협이 된다고 생각하는 단체들을 해산한다.

5 ① ∣ 불법 월경을 막기 위해 방벽을 세우는 것은 국경에 인접한 일부 지역에서 칭찬받았지만, 많은 멕시코인들은 이를 적대적인 시각으로 바라보고 있다.

6 ⑤ ∣ 직장에서 상사의 기분을 맞추려는 지나친 욕구로 특징지어지는 그녀의 행동은 종종 매우 비굴한 것으로 평해진다.

7 ② ∣ 비판자들은 선교사들이 회교도들을 기독교인으로 개종시키려고 할 때 다른 문화를 존중하지 않는다고 주장한다.

8 ⑧ ∣ 경기 침체로 사업을 확장하려던 모든 생각이 좌절되었다.

9 ⑯ ∣ 그 중세의 요새는 너무도 튼튼해서 적군이 그 어떤 전술이나 무기를 사용하더라도 적군에게는 난공불락의 상태로 남아있었다.

10 ③ ∣ 국제포경위원회(International Whaling Commission)의 상업적 포경 중단 조치의 허점으로 인해 일본은 과학적 목적으로 고래를 사냥할 수 있다. 그러나 많은 사람들은 일본의 고래 연구를 고기를 얻기 위해 보호받는 동물을 사냥하기 위한 허술한 변명으로 보고 있다.

- -

11 ③   **12** ①   **13** ②   **14** ④   **15** ④   **16** ②   **17** ①   **18** ②   **19** ③   **20** ④

[1] Write the meaning of the following words.

☐ wary	☐ harbinger
☐ impeach	☐ mar
☐ recluse	☐ debate
☐ sever	☐ incursion
☐ privy	☐ gratitude
☐ chagrin	☐ vaunt
☐ aggrieve	☐ merit
☐ parley	☐ dense
☐ morose	☐ autodidact
☐ establish	☐ lenient
☐ beneficiary	☐ uterus
☐ complaisant	☐ elusive
☐ semester	☐ quibble
☐ nettle	☐ facility
☐ alternative	☐ desist
☐ optimal	☐ conglomeration
☐ amusement	☐ retrench
☐ sieve	☐ initial
☐ petulant	☐ harry
☐ bend	☐ civilian
☐ egoism	☐ breeze
☐ tiresome	☐ placid
☐ forswear	☐ transport
☐ spectacular	☐ sallow
☐ conceive	☐ reconnaissance

[2] Select <u>the most</u> appropriate word from the box below. Each word should be used only once.

① lenient	② wary	③ recluse	④ sallow
⑤ chagrin	⑥ impeached	⑦ parley	⑧ tiresome
⑨ beneficiary	⑩ alternative	⑪ optimal	⑫ elusive
⑬ spectacular	⑭ dense	⑮ retrenching	⑯ placid
⑰ harbinger	⑱ facility	⑲ harry	⑳ nettle

1 Most of those polled stated that they would vote to reelect their legislator; this response showed the public was _____ of a change in leadership.

2 Trump became the third U.S. president to be _____, but the Republican-controlled Senate is widely expected not to convict him.

3 Emily Dickinson did not belong to any literary movement or school; she lived as a(n) _____ and wrote highly individual and idiosyncratic poetry.

4 After an adolescence immersed in his father's creed of utilitarianism, Mill realized, to his father's great _____, that its promise of happiness was chimerical.

5 The early signs of economic decline, such as rising unemployment rates and falling stock prices, are often considered _____ of an impending recession.

6 The justice system is too _____ toward criminals in the country. Many judges let a lot of criminals go with a slap on the wrist.

7 Autopsies are often done when the cause of death is _____ and for COVID-related deaths — the third most common cause of death in 2020 — an autopsy would not necessarily have provided any new information.

8 Companies in the process of _____ are usually laying off staff or cutting back on employee benefits.

9 His smile was as engaging as ever, but from his _____ complexion, I knew he was sick.

10 Pasta straws are suggested as a novel _____ to plastic straws.

[3] Choose the one which is different from the others.

11 ① blithe   ② morose   ③ moody   ④ sullen
12 ① complaisant   ② specious   ③ compliant   ④ obedient
13 ① irritable   ② peevish   ③ amiable   ④ petulant
14 ① forswear   ② abandon   ③ renounce   ④ revert
15 ① incursion   ② retreat   ③ foray   ④ raid
16 ① precipitate   ② desist   ③ abstain   ④ refrain
17 ① brag   ② boast   ③ deprecate   ④ vaunt
18 ① mar   ② mend   ③ blight   ④ ruin
19 ① console   ② aggrieve   ③ afflict   ④ distress
20 ① privy   ② covert   ③ secret   ④ compatible

✓ Answers

1 ② | 여론조사에 참여한 사람들 대부분은 현역 의원을 재선출할 거라 말했는데, 이런 반응은 대중들이 지도자가 바뀌는 것을 경계하고 있다는 것을 보여주었다.

2 ⑥ | 트럼프(Trump)는 탄핵당한 세 번째 미국 대통령이 되었지만, 공화당이 장악한 상원은 그에게 유죄를 선고하지는 않을 것으로 널리 예상된다.

3 ③ | 에밀리 디킨슨(Emily Dickinson)은 그 어떤 문학 운동(사조)이나 유파에도 속하지 않았다. 그녀는 은둔자로 살았고 매우 개인적이고 특이한 시를 썼다.

4 ⑤ | 그의 아버지의 공리주의 신조에 깊이 빠져있던 청소년기를 지난 뒤, 밀(Mill)은 그의 아버지에게는 매우 유감스럽게도 불구하고 공리주의가 약속하는 행복이 허무맹랑하다는 것을 깨달았다.

5 ⑰ | 실업률 상승과 주가 하락과 같은 경기 하락의 초기 신호는 종종 임박한 경기 침체의 전조로 간주된다.

6 ① | 이 나라의 사법제도는 범인들에 대해 너무 관대하다. 많은 판사들이 수많은 범인들에게 가벼운 처벌을 내리고 있다.

7 ⑫ | 부검은 사망 원인이 알기 어려울 때 시행되는 경우가 많으며, 2020년 세 번째로 가장 흔한 사망 원인인 코로나바이러스 관련 사망의 경우에는 부검이 반드시 새로운 정보를 제공하지는 않았을 것이다.

8 ⑮ | 비용을 줄이는 상황에 있는 기업들은 대개 직원을 해고하거나 직원 혜택을 삭감하고 있다.

9 ④ | 그의 미소는 여느 때와 마찬가지로 매력적이었지만, 그의 창백한 안색으로 보아 그가 아프다는 것을 알았다.

10 ⑩ | 파스타 면으로 만든 (친환경) 빨대는 플라스틱 빨대의 새로운 대안으로 제시된다.

11 ① **12** ② **13** ③ **14** ④ **15** ② **16** ① **17** ③ **18** ② **19** ① **20** ④

[1] Write the meaning of the following words.

☐ grateful	☐ innocuous
☐ rage	☐ transform
☐ neglect	☐ auction
☐ soggy	☐ fissure
☐ pariah	☐ breakthrough
☐ even-handed	☐ perpetrate
☐ torrent	☐ opus
☐ access	☐ haunt
☐ confine	☐ indomitable
☐ lush	☐ maim
☐ elicit	☐ larva
☐ warden	☐ derail
☐ slash	☐ premeditated
☐ uncanny	☐ ruin
☐ impute	☐ misogamy
☐ din	☐ pamper
☐ mock	☐ fit
☐ superlative	☐ asteroid
☐ expensive	☐ sanction
☐ tint	☐ practicable
☐ adverse	☐ berate
☐ gestation	☐ restless
☐ visible	☐ compassion
☐ dwindle	☐ sepulchral
☐ coroner	☐ ensure

[2] Select the most appropriate word from the box below. Each word should be used only once.

① elicited	② sepulchral	③ adverse	④ rage
⑤ berated	⑥ compassion	⑦ perpetrated	⑧ fissure
⑨ pariah	⑩ innocuous	⑪ premeditated	⑫ impute
⑬ lush	⑭ superlative	⑮ neglect	⑯ warden
⑰ pamper	⑱ gestation	⑲ tint	⑳ derailed

1 Some frustrated drivers let their emotions boil over into road _____ when another car cuts them off.

2 The invasion prompted the United States and European countries to tighten sanctions on Russia, effectively turning it into a(n) _____ state.

3 Congressional plans to tax the endowments of wealthy private universities have _____ outrage from them.

4 Scientists _____ dental decay to high consumption of sugar, cautioning the public that children are not the only offenders.

5 Excessive fluctuation in exchange rates would certainly have _____ effects on exports.

6 Some predators masquerade as common objects in their surroundings to appear _____ to unsuspecting prey.

7 Honor killing is _____ by people who claim to be upholding the so-called honor of a family or community.

8 Some people love to _____ their pets, cooking them special food and buying them expensive collars and toys.

9 The carefully planned itinerary for the trip was unexpectedly _____ due to bad weather conditions.

10 The senior North Korean military official _____ the combined U.S.-South Korean military exercises, which Pyongyang has long described as invasion rehearsals.

[3] Choose the one which is different from the others.

11 ① grateful   ② thankful   ③ appreciative   ④ deliberate

12 ① hortatory   ② even-handed   ③ fair   ④ impartial

13 ① extraordinary   ② incontrovertible   ③ supernatural   ④ uncanny

14 ① indomitable   ② impregnable   ③ impermissible   ④ invincible

15 ① restless   ② laid-back   ③ restive   ④ fidgety

16 ① practicable   ② feasible   ③ possible   ④ malleable

17 ① advance   ② accolade   ③ breakthrough   ④ leap

18 ① sterile   ② soggy   ③ drenched   ④ soaked

19 ① mock   ② deride   ③ insult   ④ exalt

20 ① noise   ② din   ③ serenity   ④ racket

✓ Answers

1 ④ ┃ 일부 불만감을 느끼는 운전자들은 다른 차가 그들을 가로막으면 그들의 감정을 도로에서 분노로 표출한다.

2 ⑨ ┃ 이 침공으로 인해 미국과 유럽 국가들은 러시아에 대한 제재를 강화했고, 러시아를 사실상 따돌림받는 국가로 만들었다.

3 ① ┃ 부유한 사립대학들의 기부금에 세금을 부과하려는 의회의 계획은 그 대학들로부터 분노를 불러일으켰다.

4 ⑫ ┃ 과학자들은 어린이들만이 잘못을 저지르는 게 아니라고 대중들에게 경고하면서 충치를 설탕을 많이 소비한 탓으로 돌린다.

5 ③ ┃ 환율의 지나친 변동은 분명히 수출에 부정적인 영향을 끼칠 것이다.

6 ⑩ ┃ 일부 포식자는 의심하지 않는 먹이에 무해한 것처럼 보이기 위해 주변에 있는 흔한 물체로 위장한다.

7 ⑦ ┃ 명예 살인은 소위 가족이나 지역사회의 명예를 지킨다고 주장하는 사람들에 의해 자행된다.

8 ⑰ ┃ 어떤 사람들은 애완동물에게 특별한 음식을 요리해주고, 값비싼 목걸이와 장난감을 사주면서, 그들에게 좋은 것을 다 해주기를 좋아한다.

9 ⑳ ┃ 신중하게 계획된 여행 일정이 악천후로 인해 예기치 않게 틀어지게 되었다.

10 ⑤ ┃ 북한군 고위 관계자는 한미연합훈련을 비난했는데, 북한은 이 훈련을 오랫동안 침략 예행연습이라고 말해왔다.

- -

11 ④   **12** ①   **13** ②   **14** ③   **15** ②   **16** ④   **17** ②   **18** ①   **19** ④   **20** ③

ACTUAL TEST

[01-100] Choose the one that is closest in meaning to the underlined part.

01 She <u>despised</u> him just because he was poor.
① put up
② looked down upon
③ kept off
④ got out of

02 The man quickly squandered his <u>patrimony</u>.
① savings   ② plethora
③ dividends   ④ inheritance

03 The salesman was <u>a jocose</u> person.
① a venomous   ② a facetious
③ an intuitive ④ a sober

04 The company has just <u>acquired</u> a further 5% of the shares.
① inquired   ② obtained
③ sold   ④ given up

05 He agreed to the plan <u>of his own accord</u>.
① enthusiastically
② unwillingly
③ unhesitatingly
④ voluntarily

06 He would rather hear applause for his accomplishments than have you <u>fawning</u> all over him and catering to his needs.
① denouncing   ② flattering
③ considering ④ summoning

07 She recruited teachers who would <u>forswear</u> corporal punishment and encourage creativity rather than rote learning.
① abandon   ② reform
③ inflict   ④ endure

08 Do you actually believe you'll win praise for being so <u>negligent</u>?
① unpleasant   ② ambitious
③ careful   ④ forgetful

09 She was quiet for a long time, then <u>interjected</u> a few remarks at the end of the meeting.
① interpolated ② interrupted
③ interpreted ④ interested

10 The function of ears in hearing is to <u>convert</u> the sound waves to nerve impulses.
① transmit   ② represent
③ change   ④ manufacture

11 Striving for maximum profit can also <u>derail</u> sustainable development.
① alleviate   ② rationalize
③ evaluate   ④ thwart

12 Millions of singles yearning for escape zones for <u>solitude</u> are straining Europe's city housing markets.
① amity   ② isolation
③ indolence   ④ vanity

13 Some contemporary theories of criticism assert that the only reliable reading of a text is misreading, that the only existence of a text is given by the chain of responses it <u>elicits</u>.

① bans   ② counters

③ draws   ④ grills

14 We climbed to our peanut gallery seats just as Miss Rodeo America, a <u>lanky</u> brunette swaddled in a lavender pantsuit, gloves, and a cowboy hat, loped across the arena.

① plump   ② beautiful

③ dainty   ④ lean

15 You'll have to hurry up to <u>compensate for</u> the time you lost.

① make the best of

② make up for

③ make it up with

④ be punished for

16 She tried her best, but she knew that her efforts to <u>feign</u> cheerfulness weren't convincing.

① pretend   ② boost

③ dodge   ④ surrender

17 He believes his country's nuclear arsenal will <u>shore up</u> his regime in the face of growing discontent among the impoverished public.

① undermine   ② buttress

③ maneuver   ④ publicize

18 The bad boys <u>mocked</u> the blind woman when they passed by her.

① mobbed   ② ridiculed

③ struck   ④ helped

19 Learning by rote is understandably reckoned to be a <u>tiresome</u> thing, however necessary it might occasionally be.

① annoying   ② clumsy

④ trivial   ③ plausible

20 Because the city is slow in <u>processing</u> applications, many of the elderly do not get housing benefits.

① trying   ② providing

③ working on   ④ raising

21 The thieves were trying to <u>perpetrate</u> a robbery in the office building.

① stop   ② view

③ commit   ④ interfere with

22 Columbia, <u>established</u> in New York, is one of the oldest colleges in America, along with Harvard established in 1636.

① authorized   ② founded

③ constructed   ④ understood

23 Education has been widely recognised as a tool to <u>enlighten</u> the ignorant.

① despise   ② simulate

③ surpass   ④ instruct

24 The court has ordered him to <u>desist</u> from bothering his neighbor.

① cease   ② inflate

③ standardize   ④ express

25 Among all societies legal marriage is usually accomplished by some kind of ceremony that expresses group sanction of the union.
① opinion   ② coercion
③ approval   ④ insistence

26 We should not impute false motives to those who are kind.
① notify   ② proclaim
③ ascertain   ④ ascribe

27 S. Freud's psychoanalysis starts on the hypothesis that the origins of paranoia of adults may be found in the experiences of oppression of the unconscious in their childhood.
① hyperbole   ② argument
③ assumption   ④ confluence

28 She had no sooner quitted the room than Mrs. Drukker leaned over the table and said to Markham in a sepulchral whisper.
① husky   ② fierce
③ inaudible   ④ dismal

29 With just five seconds remaining, the basketball star snatched the ball and defiantly threw it into the basket.
① boldly   ② daintily
③ hastily   ④ precisely

30 An important aspect of direct carving is the artist's commitment to presenting the nature of the medium, working to reveal its appealing aesthetic and textural qualities.
① component   ② aspect
③ subject   ④ material

31 The densely populated area is hard to live in.
① sloppily   ② sparsely
③ improperly   ④ heavily

32 The social worker's incisive observations clearly identified the girl's problem.
① sharp   ② derelict
③ empirical   ④ incessant

33 The jury awarded ten million dollars to the aggrieved former employees of the company.
① laid-off   ② retired
③ mourned   ④ mistreated

34 About 60 percent of participants were prepared to deliver what they thought was a potentially lethal shock to the hapless victim.
① unlucky   ② patient
③ weak   ④ apparent

35 John Adams sought to sever his personal ties with the British King.
① improve   ② proclaim
③ dissolve   ④ embellish

36 Most of America's mission-critical work calls for leadership and character more than political acumen.
① eminence   ② ethics
③ activity   ④ insight

37 Doctors believe they've made a breakthrough in the treatment of breast cancer using drugs instead of surgery.
① panacea ② device
③ sample ④ advance

38 He was very adamant about the way I looked, the way I should look.
① flexible ② indecisive
③ pessimistic ④ unyielding

39 Flatboats transport cars on the Great Lakes between the United States and Canada.
① load ② ferry
③ pursue ④ inspect

40 She found dayworkers' laughter and noisy games coarse and rather vulgar.
① unimportant ② unrealistic
③ uncouth ④ unguarded

41 Charles nettled the president with sarcastic comments.
① vexed ② endued
③ palpated ④ ascertained

42 Efforts to prevent small companies being abused by large customers are being undermined by a lack of resources and the indifference of the officials.
① damaged ② backed
③ rewarded ④ delayed

43 I hadn't paid any of the parking fines in the past year and now, the authorities want to impound my car.

① confine ② reproach
③ confiscate ④ lubricate

44 The article reports that the Dalai Lama stressed compassion in dealing with other human begins while speaking on Ethics and Business at the Indian Institute of Management-Ahmedabad (IIM-A) on January 18, 2008.
① condolence ② sympathy
③ composure ④ digression

45 There was nothing remarkable about the man save his blazing red head, and the expression of extreme chagrin and discontent upon his features.
① embarrassment ② pride
③ satisfaction ④ distraction

46 Many urban blacks still live in depressingly poor conditions.
① lacking self-confidence
② in the lowest position
③ of a town or city
④ ready to quarrel or attack

47 The lover of democracy has an enmity to totalitarianism.
① repugnance ② empathy
③ sympathy ④ antipodes

48 While studying the history of the world's 200 countries, he tried to find countries that had never experienced an incursion by Britain.
① an assistance ② an assault
③ a withdrawal ④ a reconstruction

49 The pertinent question is not how to do things right but how to find the right things to do.
① obliging   ② apt
③ veracious   ④ illusory

50 After a rape accusation against the two athletes was recanted, questions arise on the news media's reporting of the case.
① criticized   ② reinforced
③ repeated   ④ withdrawn

51 Because the speaker belabored every point of his speech, the exhausted audience lost interest in everything he had to say.
① elaborated   ② summarized
③ put off   ④ refrained

52 Rumors abroad say that the leader may declare presidential rule and disband the Congress.
① dissolve   ② banter
③ inspect   ④ convene

53 Ironically, professional scientists berated the early evolutionists such as Lamarck and Chambers for overindulgence in the imagination.
① advocated   ② adored
③ charmed   ④ chided

54 The cars ahead were not visible, being hidden by thick clouds that descended on the road.
① discernible   ② coincident
③ grotesque   ④ gallant

55 Few people know the cultural and ethnic terrain of the cafeteria as well as John Watson, a dean of boys, who presides over the din of lunchtime.
① place   ② noise
③ rule   ④ start

56 He is a writer who has an uncanny power to see through the psychic domain of man.
① a beautiful
② an intelligent
③ an extraordinary
④ a natural

57 The most disturbing picture of presidential drinking is provided by Richard Nixon, a man prone to morose self-pity.
① egoistic   ② solitary
③ dour   ④ impulsive

58 The knight obeyed the king's orders in a complaisant manner.
① sluggish   ② submissive
③ belligerent   ④ truthful

59 Meanness and generosity, prudence and boldness, courage and timidity, weakness and strength; men show all these at the card table according to their natures.
① admiration   ② audacity
③ seclusion   ④ cleanness

60 The President's visit was intended to cement the alliance between the two countries.
① delegate   ② consolidate
③ scrutinize   ④ renounce

61 A small group of the soldiers reconnoitered the territory before the attack.
① retained   ② subsided
③ scouted   ④ allocated

62 As the world becomes increasingly homogenized and ancient cultures disappear, some people strive to keep alive a knowledge of their past.
① artificial   ② new-fashioned
③ identical   ④ mechanical

63 His remarks totally shake mutual trust, the most pivotal element in the alliance.
① crucial   ② elementary
③ perspicuous   ④ vulnerable

64 Even though the ambassador's comments were mostly innocuous, they caused a diplomatic dispute between the two countries.
① vague   ② gracious
③ harmless   ④ incompetent

65 In times of war, we must take precautions against acts of sabotage as well as of direct violence.
① subversion   ② heinousness
③ subterfuge   ④ infiltration

66 California's drought is a harbinger of things to come around the world, wherever population and industries are growing.
① mishap   ② hoax
③ precursor   ④ repercussion

67 He could not say no to the request because he is a meek person.
① a humble   ② an aggressive
③ an endearing ④ a patient

68 A reclusive author could be pallid from spending too much time indoors.
① anonymous   ② hermitic
③ ardent   ④ pretentious

69 There are three types of scorpions found in Australia, and the most deadly one is the most elusive.
① tremendous   ② tricky
③ insignificant ④ scarce

70 He showed his gratitude for receiving such excellent care in the hospital by making a large donation.
① asset   ② contribution
③ scarcity   ④ appreciation

71 A lover who is tender and affectionate and then petulant and judgmental arouses love and devotion and also frustration and anger.
① decided   ② steadfast
③ peevish   ④ predictable

72 He exheredated his daughter with rage when she married the man.
① qualification ② fury
③ eternity   ④ impulse

73 Again and again, the army unsuccessfully attacked the fortress, only to conclude that it was impregnable.
① unconquerable ② implicit
③ fragile ④ phenomenal

74 American jazz is a conglomeration of sounds borrowed from such varied sources as American and African folk music, European classical music, and Christian gospel songs.
① organization ② symmetry
③ combination ④ illustration

75 Servile people tend to cheapen themselves by bowing to authority to make a living.
① preposterous ② fawning
③ prodigal ④ reticent

76 The smooth surface of the placid lake mirrored the surrounding mountains.
① perturbed ② tranquil
③ frozen ④ clean

77 One might have expected Egyptians to be especially wary of military intervention.
① cautious of
② familiar with
③ insensitive to
④ displeased with

78 They were fought back and retreated, but managed to complete their objective.
① mission ② invasion
③ conquest ④ conflict

79 Scientific knowledge may help a person to restore health but it may also be used to maim men.
① kill ② disable
③ cure ④ disrupt

80 This leaves his speeches open to all sorts of malign interpretation.
① evil ② benign
③ flattering ④ exaggerate

81 The sudden onset of Web culture is really a dramatic turn in the timeless question of what it means to be a human being.
① beginning ② decline
③ transformation ④ expansion

82 Children become spoiled if the parents pamper them too much.
① discipline ② overlook
③ coddle ④ scold

83 His opponents tried to ruin the candidate's reputation by spreading rumors about his past.
① induce ② transact
③ transcribe ④ vilify

84 His decisiveness and even-handed approach have earned him far more devotees than detractors.
① ambidextrous ② participatory
③ pretentious ④ impartial

85 The flight was delayed because of adverse weather.
① authentic　　② unfavorable
③ averse　　　④ apparent

86 The White Sox, cruising through a vacuum left by a surprisingly flat Yankee campaign and pursued by a fierce but ultimately feckless Cleveland Indians team, are closing in on the pennant.
① operant　　　② dexterous
③ ineffective　　④ inexpensive

87 The military-backed government that replaced Mohamed Morsi launched a lethal crackdown on his Islamist supporters and other political opponents.
① irritable　　② legal
③ lawful　　　④ deadly

88 He was somewhat sallow, with very high forehead and small deep-set eyes.
① bereft　　　　② indiscreet
③ unassuming　④ pasty

89 My leg kept bouncing as I felt restless waiting for my turn in the interview room.
① slackened　② languid
③ uneasy　　　④ exuberant

90 Many immigrants, when they first arrived in the United States, were forced to engage in menial jobs.
① significant　② lowly
③ rough　　　④ remedial

91 Without perpetual temptation no human spirit can ever be tempered and fortified.
① continual　② practical
③ credible　　④ ingenuous

92 The students are going to study how insects perceive the world.
① affect　　　② betray
③ grumble　　④ understand

93 The window had been left open during the storm, and the papers on my desk were a soggy mess.
① impetuous　② soaked
③ desiccated　④ limpid

94 Many people thought that the punishment of the rude student was too lenient.
① generous　② ridiculous
③ harsh　　　④ unexpectant

95 Their facilities to connect the unconnected enables geniuses to see thing others miss.
① ability　　② convenience
③ imagination　④ ease

96 The magician was so dexterous that we could not follow him as he performed his tricks.
① sluggish　② nimble
③ wary　　　④ inept

97 The graduate committee must be in full accord in their approval of a dissertation.
① indecisive　② shrewd
③ vulnerable　④ unanimous

98 His intention is very far from being <u>confined</u> to provide only for the children of professed beggars.

① expanded   ② entitled

③ inclined   ④ restricted

99 Mary Travers was known for being charismatic, <u>indomitable</u>, and beautiful because she inspired people to confront racial segregation, to halt an immoral war in Vietnam, and to right much of the historical inequity between men and women.

① ingenuous   ② invidious

③ invincible   ④ ingenious

100 *Blacks want to be treated like men*: a perfectly straightforward statement, containing only seven words. People who have mastered Kant, Hegel, Shakespeare, Marx, Freud, and the Bible find this statement utterly <u>impenetrable</u>. The idea seems to threaten profound, barely conscious assumptions.

① debonair   ② irksome

③ congenital   ④ incomprehensible

[1] Write the meaning of the following words.

☐ universal	☐ pestilence
☐ solace	☐ adhere
☐ entourage	☐ gridlock
☐ incredible	☐ vast
☐ magnet	☐ monologue
☐ deceive	☐ empower
☐ bully	☐ chorus
☐ posterity	☐ astray
☐ dismay	☐ exaggerate
☐ collateral	☐ hectic
☐ ration	☐ obsession
☐ incantation	☐ platonic
☐ attract	☐ defeat
☐ recidivism	☐ minute
☐ paltry	☐ shift
☐ quandary	☐ leverage
☐ contain	☐ recusant
☐ osseous	☐ swamp
☐ hatred	☐ frequent
☐ invoke	☐ scourge
☐ leech	☐ alms
☐ delicate	☐ perish
☐ bovine	☐ toxic
☐ temptation	☐ conduct
☐ negligent	☐ spill

[2] Select <u>the most</u> appropriate word from the box below. Each word should be used only once.

① recidivism	② deceived	③ scourge	④ hectic
⑤ gridlock	⑥ entourage	⑦ bullied	⑧ dismay
⑨ collateral	⑩ osseous	⑪ bovine	⑫ delicate
⑬ adhere	⑭ paltry	⑮ recusant	⑯ leverage
⑰ empowered	⑱ obsession	⑲ ration	⑳ universal

1   Ms. Holmes intentionally _____ investors and commercial partners by forging financial reports.

2   He is now _____ at school and called "chicken" by the other children.

3   Iran often orders athletes who go abroad to compete in international competitions to leave _____ to guarantee they will come back.

4   With risk-free savings offering _____ returns, investors flocked to these higher-risk alternatives.

5   Jail has a criminogenic effect because of loss of contact, loss of jobs, loss of housing — all these things that actually creates _____ down the road.

6   Because a baby's skin is so _____, it can be easily damaged by the sun.

7   While federal agencies have filed antitrust lawsuits against tech companies, congressional efforts to pass new laws that would bolster anti-competition standards have languished amid political _____.

8   Between the 16th and 18th centuries, anyone who broke church rules by refusing to attend services would be labeled a(n) _____ by the Church of England.

9   Cutting the city's transportation budget will do nothing but _____ people without cars.

10   In the 1960s, when women felt like second-class citizens, the women's movement _____ them to stand up and demand their equal rights.

[3] Choose the one which is different from the others.

11 ① widespread   ② incredible   ③ enormous   ④ tremendous

12 ① solace   ② malice   ③ comfort   ④ consolation

13 ① descendant   ② offspring   ③ posterity   ④ predecessor

14 ① quandary   ② dilemma   ③ boon   ④ impasse

15 ① rancor   ② munificence   ③ hatred   ④ contempt

16 ① allurement   ② temptation   ③ enticement   ④ superstition

17 ① diligent   ② negligent   ③ careless   ④ remiss

18 ① exaggerate   ② abridge   ③ magnify   ④ overstate

19 ① spill   ② divulge   ③ secrete   ④ disclose

20 ① noxious   ② virulent   ③ toxic   ④ wholesome

✓ Answers

1 ② | 홈즈(Holmes) 씨는 재무보고서를 위조하여 투자자와 거래처를 의도적으로 속였다.

2 ⑦ | 그는 현재 학교에서 괴롭힘을 당하고 있으며 다른 아이들로부터 "겁쟁이"라고 불린다.

3 ⑨ | 이란은 종종 국제 대회에 출전하기 위해 외국에 나가는 선수들에게 그들이 돌아올 것을 확실히 하기 위해 담보를 맡기라고 명한다.

4 ⑭ | 안전한 저축이 보잘것없는 수익을 제공하자 투자자들은 이러한 고위험 대안 투자로 몰려들었다.

5 ① | 감옥에 들어갔다 나오면 연락이 두절되고, 일자리를 잃고 집이 없어지기 때문에 감옥은 범죄를 야기하는 효과가 있다. 이러한 모든 요인은 실제로 향후 재범의 가능성을 높인다.

6 ⑫ | 아기의 피부는 너무 연약해서 햇볕에 쉽게 손상된다.

7 ⑤ | 연방정부 기관들이 기술회사들을 상대로 반독점 소송을 제기했지만, 반경쟁 기준을 강화하는 새로운 법을 통과시키려는 의회의 노력은 정치적 교착상태 속에서 지지부진해졌다.

8 ⑮ | 16세기와 18세기 사이에, 예배에 참석하는 것을 거부함으로써 교회 규칙을 어긴 사람은 영국 교회에 의해 국교를 거부한 사람으로 분류되었다.

9 ③ | 도시의 교통 예산 삭감은 자동차가 없는 사람들을 괴롭힐 뿐이다.

10 ⑰ | 여성들이 이등 시민처럼 느껴지던 1960년대에, 여성운동은 이들이 일어나 동등한 권리를 요구할 수 있게 해주었다.

11 ①   12 ②   13 ④   14 ③   15 ②   16 ④   17 ①   18 ②   19 ③   20 ④

[1] Write the meaning of the following words.

☐ manifest	☐ enthusiasm
☐ seal	☐ mimic
☐ chaos	☐ genus
☐ edit	☐ abort
☐ platitude	☐ tone
☐ jocund	☐ verbose
☐ smack	☐ solicit
☐ influence	☐ vis-à-vis
☐ paranoid	☐ frustration
☐ board	☐ levy
☐ scoundrel	☐ organ
☐ excommunication	☐ falter
☐ imperial	☐ antagonist
☐ penetrate	☐ horrendous
☐ integral	☐ portal
☐ diagnosis	☐ embroider
☐ wraith	☐ contrast
☐ underscore	☐ peevish
☐ laureate	☐ bicker
☐ awkward	☐ incident
☐ diameter	☐ aviation
☐ produce	☐ considerable
☐ recondite	☐ molecule
☐ decomposition	☐ rotate
☐ caress	☐ tarry

[2] Select <u>the most</u> appropriate word from the box below. Each word should be used only once.

① solicit	② chaos	③ edit	④ bicker
⑤ penetrate	⑥ levy	⑦ recondite	⑧ mimic
⑨ awkward	⑩ laureate	⑪ verbose	⑫ frustration
⑬ seal	⑭ peevish	⑮ rotate	⑯ wraith
⑰ jocund	⑱ underscore	⑲ decomposition	⑳ caress

1 Confucius believed that people needed to stop all the fighting and that people needed a ruler who could replace _____ with order.

2 During a job interview, applicants want to _____ any experience that relates to the job they are applying for.

3 He found himself in the _____ position of appearing to support a point of view which he abhorred.

4 As a non-mathematician, he appreciates the difficulty of explaining a(n) _____ mathematical problem to a general audience.

5 A(n) _____ book report goes on and on and is packed with long, complicated words that aren't at all necessary.

6 It is illegal for public officials to _____ gifts or money in exchange for favors.

7 The government has announced a series of tax-raising measures, including an increase in corporation tax from 19% to 25%, and the _____ on profits made by energy companies.

8 Despite their best efforts to appease the demanding customer, the client remained persistently _____ during the entire negotiation.

9 The team members often struggled to collaborate effectively and would frequently _____ during meetings.

10 After receiving the unexpected promotion at work, Sarah's face lit up with a(n) _____ expression.

[3] Choose the one which is different from the others.

11 ① coinage ② banality ③ cliché ④ platitude

12 ① scoundrel ② pathfinder ③ rogue ④ villain

13 ① delirium ② ardor ③ enthusiasm ④ fervor

14 ① awful ② appalling ③ felicitous ④ horrendous

15 ① tarry ② dawdle ③ loiter ④ precipitate

16 ① manifest ② apparent ③ evident ④ ambiguous

17 ① essential ② integral ③ fractional ④ indispensable

18 ① abort ② abduct ③ halt ④ interrupt

19 ① ally ② antagonist ③ foe ④ enemy

20 ① excommunication ② dismissal ③ retention ④ expulsion

✔ Answers

1 ② ┃ 공자는 사람들이 싸움을 멈추어야 하고 혼란을 질서로 대체할 수 있는 지도자가 사람들에게 필요하다고 생각했다.

2 ⑱ ┃ 취업면접 시 지원자는 지원하는 직무와 관련된 모든 경험을 강조하고 싶어 한다.

3 ⑨ ┃ 그는 자신이 아주 싫어하던 견해를 지지하는 것처럼 보이는 난처한 입장에 처해 있다는 것을 알았다.

4 ⑦ ┃ 수학자가 아닌 그는 일반 청중에게 난해한 수학적 문제를 설명하는 것의 어려움을 알고 있다.

5 ⑪ ┃ 장황한 독후감은 그칠 줄 모르고 이어지고 전혀 필요 없는 길고 복잡한 단어들로 가득 차 있다.

6 ① ┃ 공무원들이 청탁을 들어주는 대가로 선물이나 돈을 요구하는 것은 불법이다.

7 ⑥ ┃ 정부는 법인세를 19%에서 25%로 인상하고, 에너지 기업이 벌어들이는 이익에 대한 과세하는 등 일련의 증세 방안을 발표했다.

8 ⑭ ┃ 까다로운 고객을 달래기 위한 최선의 노력에도 불구하고 고객은 협상 내내 계속해서 역정을 냈다.

9 ④ ┃ 팀원들은 효과적으로 협업하는 데 어려움을 겪는 경우가 많았고 회의 중에 말다툼을 벌이는 일도 잦았다.

10 ⑰ ┃ 직장에서 예기치 않게 승진한 사라(Sarah)의 얼굴은 즐거운 표정으로 환해졌다.

- -

11 ① **12** ② **13** ① **14** ③ **15** ④ **16** ④ **17** ③ **18** ② **19** ① **20** ③

[1] Write the meaning of the following words.

☐ obstinate	☐ asylum
☐ celebrity	☐ retail
☐ defuse	☐ point-blank
☐ misery	☐ stature
☐ rant	☐ halt
☐ perspicuous	☐ complication
☐ extinct	☐ supposedly
☐ tramp	☐ fallow
☐ devaluation	☐ recess
☐ bane	☐ proctor
☐ acclaim	☐ intensive
☐ hamlet	☐ obsolescence
☐ constant	☐ understate
☐ wrap	☐ reign
☐ impediment	☐ gratuity
☐ version	☐ plain
☐ patent	☐ inexplicable
☐ align	☐ masquerade
☐ craftsman	☐ reluctant
☐ lewd	☐ physiology
☐ disturb	☐ senile
☐ bid	☐ furor
☐ sneer	☐ entail
☐ kinetic	☐ towering
☐ complement	☐ arsenic

[2] Select <u>the most</u> appropriate word from the box below. Each word should be used only once.

① defuse	② entail	③ gratuity	④ perspicuous
⑤ complement	⑥ impediment	⑦ recess	⑧ tramp
⑨ misery	⑩ point-blank	⑪ disturb	⑫ rant
⑬ fallow	⑭ kinetic	⑮ obsolescence	⑯ reluctant
⑰ complication	⑱ extinction	⑲ understate	⑳ senile

1 In the tense negotiation, it was essential for the skilled mediator to find a way to calmly and diplomatically _____ the escalating conflict.

2 In order to ensure that her presentation was easily understandable to the diverse audience, she worked hard to make her slides and explanations as _____ as possible.

3 The country's chronic debt problems have been a(n) _____ to development.

4 Some say GM food can violate the rule of nature and _____ our ecosystem.

5 Rather than planting crops every year, farmers leave their fields _____ occasionally so that the soil can regain nutrients.

6 As oil companies face a mounting pile of climate-related lawsuits, some young lawyers may be _____ to defend them.

7 In the United States, waiters and waitresses typically expect a(n) _____ of between 18 and 20 percent of the total cost of a meal.

8 According to the Foundation for Endangered Languages, the majority of languages are vulnerable not just to decline but to _____.

9 In the culinary arts, selecting the right wine to _____ the flavors of a dish is considered an art form by many sommeliers.

10 Business owners might _____ their financial problems when they're applying for a bank loan.

[3] Choose the one which is different from the others.

11 ① obstinate   ② stubborn   ③ ductile   ④ determined

12 ① bane   ② calamity   ③ exorbitance   ④ curse

13 ① lewd   ② lascivious   ③ promiscuous   ④ salubrious

14 ① vitiate   ② acclaim   ③ applaud   ④ compliment

15 ① sneer   ② blandish   ③ deride   ④ scoff

16 ① eminence   ② stature   ③ milieu   ④ prominence

17 ① replicate   ② masquerade   ③ dissemble   ④ disguise

18 ① furor   ② craze   ③ tranquility   ④ enthusiasm

19 ① unaccountable   ② enigmatic   ③ inexplicable   ④ fathomable

20 ① halt   ② commence   ③ cease   ④ pause

✔ Answers

1 ① | 긴장감이 감도는 협상에서, 노련한 중재자는 고조되는 갈등을 차분하고 외교적으로 완화할 수 있는 방법을 찾는 것이 필수적이었다.

2 ④ | 다양한 청중들이 그녀의 발표를 쉽게 이해할 수 있도록 그녀는 슬라이드와 설명을 최대한 명료하게 만들기 위해 열심히 노력했다.

3 ⑥ | 그 나라의 만성적인 부채 문제가 발전의 걸림돌이 되어왔다.

4 ⑪ | 어떤 사람들은 유전자 변형 식품이 자연의 법칙에 위배되며 우리의 생태계를 혼란시킨다고 말한다.

5 ⑬ | 농부들은 매년 농작물을 심기보다 때때로 그들의 농지를 놀림으로써 땅은 다시 영양분을 되찾을 수 있다.

6 ⑯ | 석유회사들이 증가하는 기후 관련 소송에 직면하면서, 일부 젊은 변호사들은 그 회사들을 변호하는 것을 꺼릴 수도 있다.

7 ③ | 미국에서 웨이터와 웨이트리스들은 일반적으로 총 식사비용의 18%에서 20%의 팁을 기대한다.

8 ⑱ | 멸종위기언어재단(FEL)에 따르면, 대다수의 언어가 언어의 쇠퇴뿐 아니라, 언어의 소멸에도 취약하다고 한다.

9 ⑤ | 요리에서 요리 음식의 풍미를 보완하는 올바른 와인을 선택하는 것은 많은 소믈리에게 예술 형태로 간주된다.

10 ⑲ | 사업주들은 은행 대출을 신청할 때 그들의 재정적인 문제를 줄여서 말할지도 모른다.

11 ③   **12** ③   **13** ④   **14** ①   **15** ②   **16** ③   **17** ①   **18** ③   **19** ④   **20** ②

[1] Write the meaning of the following words.

☐ sedentary	☐ confederation
☐ congregate	☐ entice
☐ meteorology	☐ gem
☐ reflect	☐ landmark
☐ illegitimate	☐ renounce
☐ dilute	☐ pack
☐ unflinching	☐ malevolent
☐ eternity	☐ puzzling
☐ succor	☐ rack
☐ corrosive	☐ fetus
☐ vanish	☐ blend
☐ pejorative	☐ intercourse
☐ sneak	☐ demolish
☐ ontology	☐ oblique
☐ reputation	☐ deception
☐ eject	☐ leaven
☐ neighborhood	☐ rookie
☐ truculent	☐ appoint
☐ companion	☐ toil
☐ blush	☐ fake
☐ available	☐ incarcerate
☐ polymath	☐ basin
☐ stagnation	☐ politic
☐ queasy	☐ section
☐ hatch	☐ clash

[2] Select <u>the most</u> appropriate word from the box below. Each word should be used only once.

① truculent	② leaven	③ sedentary	④ sneak
⑤ hatch	⑥ diluted	⑦ deception	⑧ entice
⑨ pejorative	⑩ incarcerated	⑪ demolish	⑫ stagnation
⑬ puzzling	⑭ rack	⑮ renounce	⑯ blushed
⑰ illegitimate	⑱ vanish	⑲ reflected	⑳ appoint

1 Norwegian children now spend more time indoors in _____ activities, such as watching television or DVDs and playing computer games, than they do outdoors.

2 Japan said discharging the nuclear wastewater into the ocean would be carefully managed and the water would be further _____ by seawater before being released.

3 Some critics argue that labeling certain cultural practices as 'primitive' is a(n) _____ way to assess their value and significance.

4 In the face of adversity, some individuals adopt a(n) _____ attitude, displaying aggression and hostility as their primary response.

5 A prince who's tired of the royal life could _____ his title and become a commoner.

6 He was arrested and _____, but his direct participation in the uprising was never proven.

7 The marketing team worked tirelessly to craft an advertising campaign that would _____ potential customers.

8 The intricate pattern of symbols on the ancient artifact proved to be utterly _____, leaving archaeologists and historians perplexed about its meaning.

9 If climate change continues, sea levels will keep rising, eventually causing some cities and nations to _____.

10 The old building was scheduled for renovation, but due to its deteriorating condition, they decided to _____ it instead.

[3] Choose the one which is different from the others.

11	① congregate	② assemble	③ migrate	④ gather
12	① unflinching	② abstruse	③ adamant	④ resolute
13	① vicious	② malicious	③ malevolent	④ evasive
14	① distraction	② toil	③ exertion	④ effort
15	① oblique	② impeccable	③ indirect	④ roundabout
16	① politic	② sensible	③ wise	④ indecisive
17	① succor	② aid	③ indulgence	④ assistance
18	① fake	② bogus	③ ingenuous	④ spurious
19	① abstinence	② eternity	③ aeon	④ perpetuity
20	① eject	② embrace	③ expel	④ oust

✓ **Answers**

1 ③ | 노르웨이 어린이들은 이제 야외활동을 하는 것보다 TV나 DVD를 보거나 컴퓨터 게임을 하는 것과 같이 앉아서 하는 실내 활동에 더 많은 시간을 보낸다.

2 ⑥ | 일본은 핵 폐수를 바다로 방류하는 것이 신중하게 관리될 것이며, 방류되기 전에 물은 바닷물로 더 희석될 것이라고 말했다.

3 ⑨ | 일부 비평가들은 특정 문화적 관행을 '원시적'이라고 분류하는 것이 그 관행의 가치와 중요성을 평가하는 경멸적인 방법이라고 주장한다.

4 ① | 역경에 직면했을 때, 어떤 사람들은 공격성과 적대감을 우선적인 반응으로 보여주며 공격적인 태도를 취한다.

5 ⑮ | 왕실 생활에 싫증이 났던 한 왕자는 작위를 포기해서 평민이 될 수 있었다.

6 ⑩ | 그는 체포되어 투옥되었지만, 그가 직접 봉기에 참여했다는 사실은 입증되지 않았다.

7 ⑧ | 마케팅팀은 잠재 고객을 유인할 수 있는 광고캠페인을 만들기 위해 부단히 노력했다.

8 ⑬ | 고대 유물에 새겨진 복잡한 상징 패턴은 완전히 수수께끼 같은 것으로 판명되었고 고고학자와 역사가들은 그 의미에 대해 어찌할 바를 몰랐다.

9 ⑱ | 기후변화가 계속되면 해수면은 계속 상승할 것이고 결국 일부 도시와 국가는 사라질 것이다.

10 ⑪ | 그 오래된 건물은 리모델링 예정이었으나 노후화로 인해 그 대신 철거하기로 했다.

11 ③ 12 ② 13 ④ 14 ① 15 ② 16 ④ 17 ③ 18 ③ 19 ① 20 ②

[1] Write the meaning of the following words.

☐ immune	☐ enervate
☐ sparse	☐ masterpiece
☐ waive	☐ vent
☐ distraction	☐ optional
☐ peripatetic	☐ filter
☐ reckon	☐ concord
☐ mean	☐ incubate
☐ perforate	☐ hieroglyph
☐ redundant	☐ prop
☐ chatterbox	☐ trail
☐ ponder	☐ commend
☐ uniform	☐ innumerable
☐ eclogue	☐ relax
☐ rotten	☐ libel
☐ appall	☐ shambles
☐ scar	☐ faculty
☐ naught	☐ air
☐ haggle	☐ paragon
☐ agony	☐ due
☐ booty	☐ temerity
☐ discard	☐ current
☐ graphic	☐ rapscallion
☐ convince	☐ befit
☐ optician	☐ stubby
☐ ardent	☐ planet

[2] Select <u>the most</u> appropriate word from the box below. Each word should be used only once.

① immune	② stubby	③ ardent	④ redundant
⑤ commend	⑥ libel	⑦ appalled	⑧ befit
⑨ distraction	⑩ waive	⑪ optional	⑫ rotten
⑬ haggle	⑭ vented	⑮ perforate	⑯ reckon
⑰ booty	⑱ sparse	⑲ enervate	⑳ filter

1   Being a diplomat makes people _____ to certain laws of a foreign jurisdiction.

2   To help students facing financial hardship, the university decided to _____ the tuition fees for the upcoming semester.

3   The company tried to eliminate _____ jobs such as two marketing teams that handle the same event.

4   While it is true that some Romans enjoyed combat sports, many were so _____ by the violence that they refused to attend these events.

5   You can _____ at a flea market or anywhere where the price of items is flexible.

6   The fans of the sports team were known for their _____ support, never missing a game and always cheering passionately for their favorite players.

7   The long and exhausting journey through the desert began to _____ the group, sapping their energy and motivation.

8   The newspaper faced legal action for publishing a damaging article that was considered _____ by the public figure mentioned in the story.

9   In the arid desert, vegetation is typically _____ due to the limited availability of water.

10   Our politicians become so _____ that brazen acts of corruption and venality hardly elicit public outrage anymore.

[3] Choose the one which is different from the others.

11 ① peripatetic ② itinerant ③ roving ④ indigenous

12 ① nervous ② mean ③ hostile ④ rude

13 ① agony ② propensity ③ anguish ④ distress

14 ① discard ② dispose of ③ hoard ④ jettison

15 ① harmony ② agreement ③ cacophony ④ concord

16 ① vituperation ② paragon ③ epitome ④ exemplar

17 ① temerity ② felicity ③ audacity ④ boldness

18 ① rogue ② knave ③ rapscallion ④ pilgrim

19 ① myriad ② innumerable ③ measurable ④ numerous

20 ① incubate ② brood ③ hatch ④ conceive

✓ Answers

1 ① ┃ 외교관이 되면 사람들은 외국 사법권의 특정한 법률로부터 면제된다.

2 ⑩ ┃ 경제적 어려움을 겪고 있는 학생들을 돕기 위해 그 대학은 다음 학기 등록금을 생략하기로 결정했다.

3 ④ ┃ 그 회사는 같은 행사를 처리하는 두 개의 마케팅팀과 같은 중복되는 일자리를 없애기 위해 노력했다.

4 ⑦ ┃ 일부 로마인들이 전투 스포츠를 즐겼다는 것이 사실이지만, 많은 로마인들은 그 폭력에 너무나 경악해서 이런 시합에 참여하는 것을 거부했다.

5 ⑬ ┃ 벼룩시장이나 물건 가격이 정해진 곳이 아니면 어디든 흥정할 수 있다.

6 ③ ┃ 그 스포츠팀의 팬들은 열렬한 응원으로 유명했으며 경기를 한 번도 놓치지 않고 자신이 좋아하는 선수들을 항상 열렬히 응원했다.

7 ⑲ ┃ 사막을 가로지르는 길고 고단한 여행은 그 무리의 기력을 떨어뜨리고 에너지와 동기를 약화시키기 시작했다.

8 ⑥ ┃ 그 신문은 이 기사에 언급된 공인이 명예훼손으로 간주한 피해를 주는 기사를 게재한 것에 대해 법적 소송에 직면했다.

9 ⑱ ┃ 건조한 사막에서는 물의 가용성이 제한되어 있기 때문에 일반적으로 초목이 드물다.

10 ⑫ ┃ 우리 정치인들은 너무나 부패해서 부패와 금품수수와 같은 뻔뻔스러운 행동은 더 이상 대중의 분노를 이끌어내기 힘들다.

11 ④ 12 ① 13 ② 14 ③ 15 ③ 16 ① 17 ② 18 ④ 19 ③ 20 ④

ACTUAL TEST

[01-100] Choose the one that is closest in meaning to the underlined part.

01 The film was considered <u>lewd</u> by some people.
① prim   ② decent
③ obscene   ④ vigorous

02 He looked at me with intense <u>hatred</u>.
① eagerness   ② obsession
③ charm   ④ contempt

03 The state government <u>empowered</u> him to negotiate the contract.
① authorized   ② ordered
③ motivated   ④ forbade

04 The king <u>manifested</u> his pleasure with a hearty laugh.
① denied   ② hid
③ showed   ④ emphasized

05 She <u>smacked</u> her books down on the table.
① tore   ② slanted
③ bashed   ④ slashed

06 During the recent petroleum embargo, motor fuels had to be <u>rationed</u>.
① located   ② allotted
③ doled   ④ confiscated

07 The antics of the monkey seemed to <u>attract</u> a large crowd.
① engross   ② bore
③ turn off   ④ turn up

08 Religion has arisen from people's need to <u>ponder</u> their origins.
① deny   ② justify
③ think about   ④ cherish

09 Caudate amphibians such as newts mostly have long tails and <u>stubby</u> legs.
① long and thin
② undeveloped
③ thick and short
④ powerful

10 At one time a composer of abstract music, Aaron Copland later <u>shifted to</u> a style that more people could understand.
① exaggerated
② converted to
③ imitated
④ refused to work with

11 Not wanting to face the dire consequences of her actions, Jane <u>tarried</u> as long as she could before she appeared in front of the committee.
① officiated   ② waned
③ skittered   ④ delayed

12 Plays that <u>entail</u> direct interaction between actor and audience present no unusual difficulties for actors.
① advocate   ② involve
③ exaggerate   ④ announce

13 The scholarly journal was so recondite as to be utterly incomprehensible.
① contradictory ② obscure
③ abstruse ④ provocative

14 A kinetic learner learns chiefly by doing; this individual prefers to perform a task individually without directions or instructions.
① active ② introspective
③ auditory ④ visual

15 The author's new book was acclaimed by all the important reviewers.
① applauded ② understood
③ reflected ④ criticized

16 She was graceful and never moved awkwardly.
① joyfully ② clumsily
③ smoothly ④ tactfully

17 These chemicals have been found to be toxic to human life.
① textual ② poisonous
③ useful ④ harmless

18 I always thought his line about watching his mother haggle with the healthcare companies while she was dying of cancer was one of the more genuinely moving sections of his speech.
① suffer from ② support
③ argue with ④ get the help from

19 The attempt proved completely abortive.
① immature ② imperfect
③ unsuccessful ④ experimental

20 It's incredible how much Tom has been changed since he met Sally.
① incredulous ② unbelievable
③ uncertain ④ undoubtful

21 The politician is unflinching in standing up for social-value issues as a political as well as moral imperative.
① pompous ② resolute
③ formidable ④ incessant

22 We only fulfill our nature when we exercise our faculty of language, which requires in turn that we deliberate with others about right and wrong, good and evil, justice and injustice.
① aptitude ② capacity
③ intelligence ④ professor

23 In the novel, the protagonist is depicted as a paragon of purity and perfection.
① creator ② paradox
③ exemplar ④ advocate

24 Experiments are often conducted in a laboratory under controlled conditions.
① discussed ② performed
③ debated ④ started

25 The human cost of this scourge becomes apparent to any visitor to Cambodia — the pockmarked nation has an estimated 40,000 amputees.
① chastisement ② vicissitude
③ upheaval ④ turmoil

26 Foyot's is a restaurant at which the French senators eat and it was so far beyond my <u>means</u> that I had never even thought of going there.

① intention   ② device

③ lowliness   ④ affordability

27 The art gallery was <u>frequented</u> by some of the most influential artists of the time.

① founded   ② favored

③ supported   ④ visited

28 Experiments are also under way to allow private farmers to use <u>fallow</u> government land and keep the profits.

① unexploited   ② productive

③ multifarious   ④ unvaried

29 No matter how extensive their efforts, the blame and responsibility will be <u>levied</u> on those who fail.

① predicted   ② imposed

③ repulsed   ④ supplicated

30 He is an obstinate <u>recusant</u> and will by no means take the oath.

① bandit   ② dissident

③ vagabond   ④ sophist

31 The laborer received a <u>paltry</u> wage for a week's work, barely enough to feed his family.

① solvent   ② significant

③ meager   ④ replete

32 The mayor was thoroughly <u>dismayed</u> by the lack of public support for his new project.

① disrupted   ② disavowed

③ disappointed   ④ disabled

33 But somehow I had never quite sensed its <u>appalling</u> desolation.

① accepting   ② asymmetric

③ dreadful   ④ crazy

34 Doctors report that weight-loss claims by the diet's promoters are greatly <u>exaggerated</u>.

① abridged   ② inconstant

③ unreliable   ④ overestimated

35 Theresa would often <u>give vent to</u> her annoyance even in public places. She needs to learn to control her temper.

① masquerade   ② extinguish

③ suppress   ④ express

36 She had <u>an obsession</u> to read the obituary section every day.

① a sequence

② a promulgation

③ an interpellation

④ a fixation

37 "Why does the apple fall down rather than go up?" Many children find this question <u>puzzling</u>.

① penetrating   ② perplexing

③ strange   ④ attractive

38 The restaurant's serving staff has become redundant with the introduction of the new serving robots.

① superfluous   ② plausible

③ sarcastic   ④ liable

39 It is easy for the sophisticated marketer or businessman today to sneer at the primitiveness of the production-led approach.

① to pay no attention to

② to show contempt by means of a derisive smile

③ to decide that something is not worth considering

④ to think something is more important than it really is

40 Incidentally, some Native Americans are still members of separate and distinct Indian nations, each with its own language, culture, traditions, and even government.

① Additionally   ② Consequently

③ Likewise   ④ On the contrary

41 In the face of a howling mob he refused to renounce either his religion or his office.

① abjure   ② blanch

③ prognosticate   ④ decussate

42 When her grandmother passed away after a long fight with a cancer, Jennifer found solace in her memories of their time together.

① wealth   ② esteem

③ consolation   ④ solitude

43 It is hard to understand how any educated person of the present age could have the temerity to declare that members of one ethnic group are invariably more intelligent than those of another.

① ignorance   ② distress

③ audacity   ④ affectivity

44 Because of the medication's corrosive nature, people who take the drug must take steps to prevent the throat from becoming inflamed.

① provocative   ② psychoactive

③ caustic   ④ lethal

45 Within the next twenty or thirty years, most glaciers in Africa and South America will vanish completely.

① freeze   ② activate

③ disappear   ④ impact

46 The bouncer arrived in time to eject the men who were getting ready for a fistfight.

① modify   ② criticize

③ beat   ④ banish

47 They preserved a large number of rare books for posterity.

① descendants   ② neighbors

③ fortune   ④ youth

48 She is rather antagonistic to the church members.

① opposed   ② ignorant

③ charitable   ④ curious

49 A spirit of unruliness diffused itself among us and, under its influence, differences of culture and constitution were <u>waived</u>.

① pursued   ② put aside

③ fluctuated   ④ spread

50 If a fisherman sitting on the dock tells you about the 38 inch striped bass he almost caught this morning, he may have found a way to <u>embroider</u> the truth.

① disclose   ② embellish

③ reiterate   ④ clarify

51 This writing is <u>verbose</u>; we need to edit it.

① obtuse   ② nefarious

③ intractable   ④ wordy

52 His stare was <u>malevolent</u>, his mouth a thin line, but his eyes bright and glittering.

① violent   ② friendly

③ scary   ④ wicked

53 Her <u>perspicuous</u> comments eliminated all possibility of misinterpretation.

① muddied   ② twisted

③ clear   ④ confusing

54 In the Chinese tradition, humidity and <u>stagnant</u> water are considered as the source of endemic and epidemic illness.

① mobile   ② warm

③ static   ④ tepid

55 We are planning a surprise party for Jane. Don't <u>spill the beans</u>.

① let the cat out of the bag

② make a big deal

③ do in her shoes

④ observe the secret

56 Soak this sponge in hot water another ten to twenty minutes, then you need to <u>discard</u> the water.

① dispose of   ② disregard

③ disseminate   ④ dissolve

57 The overall population is becoming overweight, due to poor eating habits, lack of exercise, and a <u>sedentary</u> lifestyle.

① immobile   ② quiet

③ serene   ④ surreptitious

58 A laser beam is used to <u>penetrate</u> even the hardest substances.

① light up   ② identify

③ repair   ④ pass through

59 Given the existence of so many factions in the field, it was unrealistic of Anna Freud to expect any <u>uniformity</u> of opinion.

① consensus   ② shortage

③ constancy   ④ diversity

60 The students were <u>reluctant</u> at first to listen to the young teacher.

① indifferent   ② interested

③ impatient   ④ hesitant

61 Magnesium has <u>innumerable</u> uses in many countries where a light weight metal is desired.
① too many to be counted
② less valuable
③ uproarious
④ trustworthy

62 It's a rare thing to witness the <u>extinction</u> of an entire class of animal.
① subsidence   ② augmentation
③ extermination   ④ propagation

63 We are left with <u>platitudes</u> about being empirical, nuanced, and avoiding dogmatism, without a serious discussion of the important questions that are so carelessly glossed over.
① plethora   ② glitches
③ banalities   ④ trappings

64 Sincere apologies signal government commitment to redress economic conditions and may <u>entice</u> production investment.
① lure   ② appease
③ defile   ④ undermine

65 Many people think that Jackson is the most <u>considerate</u> one of them all.
① considerable   ② thoughtful
③ peevish   ④ dominant

66 They are among the 9,500 volunteers who have signed up to <u>solicit</u> their friends and families by hosting individual fund-raising Web pages for Obama.
① offer   ② accuse
③ entreat   ④ inquire

67 Forests are <u>delicate</u> systems that, if disturbed, can be permanently destroyed.
① fragile   ② expansive
③ complex   ④ unusual

68 India has long resisted environmental restrictions as <u>impediments</u> to economic growth.
① priorities   ② measures
③ stimulants   ④ hindrances

69 The word of an English gentleman was as good as a bond <u>sealed</u> in blood.
① attached   ② written
③ endorsed   ④ issued

70 The government appears to be in a <u>quandary</u> about what to do with so many people.
① insolvency   ② delusion
③ collocation   ④ plight

71 Angry at what the newspaper had printed, she sued for <u>libel</u>.
① ferocity   ② slander
③ propensity   ④ arson

72 It is certain that his theoretical caprices had a <u>baneful</u> influence on Byron's Italian dramas.
① baleful   ② lachrymose
③ rattling   ④ redoubtable

73 Choppy sea <u>brings halt to</u> oil skimming efforts around Mississippi coasts.
① discontinues   ② reinforces
③ consolidates   ④ fatigues

74 Coca-Cola has for years attempted to <u>deceive</u> the public on the links between sugary sodas and conditions like obesity, diabetes and heart disease.

① put off   ② take in

③ back up   ④ turn down

75 Yet the continent is far from <u>immune</u> to the forces of extremism.

① insidious   ② immanent

③ endangered   ④ unsusceptible

76 The Senate approved the bill to <u>incarcerate</u> those who committed small crimes like pilfering and misdemeanor.

① exonerate   ② put on probation

③ fine   ④ put in prison

77 The low price is <u>deceptive</u>. Many fees are added to it before the purchase is complete.

① misleading   ② conducive

③ reasonable   ④ lucrative

78 Some wonder if the Internet has made it more difficult to concentrate on one task without getting <u>distracted</u> by other things.

① daunted   ② diverted

③ disclosed   ④ devoured

79 Today's fatal shooting <u>underscores</u> the need for stricter gun control legislation.

① emphasizes   ② eliminates

③ ignores   ④ undermines

80 Local police are trying to <u>defuse</u> racial tensions in the community.

① calm   ② ignite

③ aggravate   ④ disconnect

81 The <u>pejorative</u> sense of the invention of tradition implies manipulation and mystification and should not be taken as characteristic of traditions in general.

① critical   ② permeable

③ lucid   ④ ludicrous

82 Part of the reason for this greater participation of women is that technological advances replaced purely physical strength in many military operations, allowing women to fill new roles in jobs where their participation had been very <u>sparse</u>.

① affluent   ② effeminate

③ scanty   ④ loathsome

83 Her orange juice was too sweet, so Ellen <u>diluted</u> it with water.

① deleted   ② soaked

③ weakened   ④ fortified

84 When Hollywood got on the patriotic bandwagon and produced *Why We Fight for*, a documentary film about the armed forces of the Second World War, it found that the <u>graphic</u> depiction of enemy atrocities actually drove enrollments down.

① vivid   ② deprecated

③ drawn   ④ speechless

85 The President has the power to <u>appoint</u> ambassadors.
   ① acquit   ② promote
   ③ condemn   ④ designate

86 "What's the matter with you?" he <u>faltered</u>.
   ① exclaimed   ② stammered
   ③ screamed   ④ yelled

87 The major themes in Robert Hayden's poetry are <u>obliquely</u> stated.
   ① powerfully   ② elaborately
   ③ indirectly   ④ uncompromisingly

88 He couldn't <u>convince</u> us to abandon our hopes of finding our missing child.
   ① dominate   ② nibble
   ③ ridicule   ④ induce

89 Workaholics usually prefer not to quit. They are still <u>ardent</u> about work even in their eighties and nineties.
   ① apathetic   ② flabby
   ③ diligent   ④ enthusiastic

90 By beginning of last year, part of the school had to be <u>demolished</u> as its foundation had become too unstable.
   ① rebuilt   ② moved
   ③ destroyed   ④ remodeled

91 The scientists are busy finding out some evidence to <u>prop up</u> the hypothesis.
   ① realize   ② support
   ③ repudiate   ④ cultivate

92 A marathon is about enduring <u>agony</u> and somehow finding the strength to keep putting one foot in front of the other.
   ① boredom   ② suffering
   ③ drawback   ④ spirit

93 Bacteria are an <u>integral</u> part of a healthy life. Most of the bacteria help with digestion, making vitamins, shaping the immune system, and keeping us healthy.
   ① trivial   ② furtive
   ③ virulent   ④ essential

94 A <u>collateral</u> aim of the government's industrial strategy is to increase employment.
   ① additional   ② complimentary
   ③ major   ④ reciprocal

95 Brown and his wife are always <u>bickering</u>.
   ① hugging   ② joking
   ③ referring   ④ arguing

96 She couldn't stand the thought of being without the telephone and her car, which she had only just learned to drive, so she refused <u>point-blank</u> to join in.
   ① angrily   ② indifferently
   ③ directly   ④ politely

97 Warm winds make many people feel <u>enervated</u> and depressed; that is why the folks here are lethargic during this period.
   ① energized   ② refreshed
   ③ unsatisfied   ④ tired

98 Jerry Wyckoff, a family psychologist, said the hectic pace of life keeps spanking alive. "We've sort of lost touch with strategies," he said. "People are frustrated, they don't have a lot of time, and they want results now."

① hasty   ② burning

③ terrific   ④ formidable

99 With computers being used to design computers, the pace of change became so fast that hardware and software suffered obsolescence every five years or less. No other technology has ever increased the productivity of mankind more or faster.

① onset   ② grind

③ lull   ④ wane

100 Despite the violence around the black hole, the galactic core is a fertile place. Stars congregate at the galaxy's center, so the life-giving heavy elements they create are most plentiful there. Even the newborn stars near our sun — halfway between the black hole and the edge of the galaxy — possess orbiting disks of gas and dust that survive long enough to give birth to planets.

① disperse   ② expand

③ gather   ④ revolve

[1] Write the meaning of the following words.

☐ queer		☐ craft	
☐ extirpate		☐ accommodation	
☐ rustic		☐ genial	
☐ soothe		☐ fare	
☐ palaver		☐ pointed	
☐ mute		☐ reptile	
☐ spout		☐ banner	
☐ circumference		☐ anonymous	
☐ devote		☐ regenerate	
☐ understudy		☐ leprosy	
☐ allot		☐ prosecute	
☐ topsy-turvy		☐ censor	
☐ disdain		☐ mature	
☐ latent		☐ indefatigable	
☐ compromise		☐ swing	
☐ intelligence		☐ vice	
☐ wiseacre		☐ obverse	
☐ embody		☐ resist	
☐ attachment		☐ polygraph	
☐ install		☐ humid	
☐ territory		☐ funeral	
☐ contrary		☐ permissive	
☐ brew		☐ stuff	
☐ plight		☐ rampart	
☐ onerous		☐ dwell	

[2] Select <u>the most</u> appropriate word from the box below. Each word should be used only once.

① palaver	② topsy-turvy	③ genial	④ wiseacre
⑤ craft	⑥ extirpated	⑦ rampart	⑧ censor
⑨ latent	⑩ regenerate	⑪ muted	⑫ pointed
⑬ embody	⑭ onerous	⑮ spout	⑯ mature
⑰ leprosy	⑱ devote	⑲ vice	⑳ anonymous

1 The dodo bird was _____ due to hunting and the introduction of predators in their habitat.

2 In diplomatic negotiations, it's not uncommon for parties to engage in lengthy _____ before reaching an agreement.

3 Some people in abusive situations have secret cellphones — usually with notifications _____ — hidden from their abuser that allow them to keep contact with the outside world.

4 After the hurricane passed through, the neighborhood was left in a(n) _____ state, with houses and trees strewn about in all directions.

5 Antiviral drugs prevent HIV from replicating, but the virus can hide in the cells of infected individuals in a non-replicating, _____ form.

6 The complex legal paperwork and numerous regulations made starting a new business in that country a(n) _____ undertaking.

7 During certain stages of hibernation, some animals have the astonishing capability to enter a state where their cells can pause, repair, and _____.

8 Most former employees who spoke with The New York Times asked to remain _____ because they feared retaliation.

9 In some countries, the government has the authority to _____ certain content in the media, controlling what information is accessible to the public.

10 The film ended most satisfactorily: _____ punished and virtue rewarded.

[3] Choose the one which is different from the others.

11 ① queer ② eccentric ③ odd ④ conventional

12 ① exquisite ② rustic ③ bucolic ④ rural

13 ① calm ② provoke ③ soothe ④ appease

14 ① disdain ② contempt ③ concern ④ scorn

15 ① quandary ② largess ③ plight ④ predicament

16 ① indefatigable ② tireless ③ unflagging ④ weary

17 ① damp ② humid ③ sultry ④ dank

18 ① arraign ② litigate ③ prosecute ④ exonerate

19 ① aversion ② attachment ③ affection ④ affinity

20 ① allot ② ascribe ③ allocate ④ apportion

✓Answers

1 ⑥ | 도도새는 사냥과 포식자의 서식지 유입으로 인해 멸종되었다.

2 ① | 외교 협상에서 당사자들이 합의에 이르기 전에 긴 시간 동안 교섭을 하는 것은 드문 일이 아니다.

3 ⑪ | 학대받는 상황에 처한 일부 사람들은 외부 세계와 계속 연락할 수 있도록 학대하는 사람에게 숨긴 비밀 휴대폰 — 보통 알림이 음소거됨 — 을 가지고 있다.

4 ② | 허리케인이 지나간 후, 그 동네는 사방에 흩어져 있는 집과 나무로 엉망진창인 상태가 되었다.

5 ⑨ | 항바이러스제는 HIV 바이러스의 복제를 막지만, 그 바이러스는 감염된 사람의 세포 속에 복제되지 않는 잠재된 형태로 숨어있을 수 있다.

6 ⑭ | 복잡한 법적 서류와 수많은 규정은 그 국가에서 새로운 사업을 시작하는 것을 어려운 일로 만들었다.

7 ⑩ | 동면의 특정 단계에서 일부 동물은 세포가 일시 멈추고, 복구 및 재생할 수 있는 상태로 들어가는 놀라운 능력을 지니고 있다.

8 ⑳ | 뉴욕타임스와 인터뷰한 대부분의 전(前) 직원들은 보복이 두려워 익명을 요구했다.

9 ⑧ | 일부 국가에서는 정부가 대중이 접근할 수 있는 정보를 통제하면서 미디어의 특정 콘텐츠를 검열할 수 있는 권한을 가지고 있다.

10 ⑲ | 그 영화는 아주 만족스럽게 끝을 맺었는데 악은 처벌받고 선은 보상을 받았다.

- -

11 ④ **12** ① **13** ② **14** ③ **15** ② **16** ④ **17** ③ **18** ④ **19** ① **20** ②

☑ **DAILY CHECKUP**

[1] Write the meaning of the following words.

☐ thrive	☐ venomous
☐ bitter	☐ loyalty
☐ sear	☐ framework
☐ perk	☐ advent
☐ sole	☐ pliable
☐ rebut	☐ represent
☐ profession	☐ yeast
☐ entrenched	☐ facile
☐ incentive	☐ vortex
☐ meddle	☐ consent
☐ surge	☐ osmosis
☐ rendezvous	☐ ultimate
☐ winsome	☐ cough
☐ discern	☐ dilemma
☐ conifer	☐ aloft
☐ bloom	☐ emancipate
☐ peasant	☐ beacon
☐ regress	☐ independent
☐ polarize	☐ marrow
☐ harrowing	☐ pardon
☐ intoxicate	☐ transfigure
☐ glue	☐ compulsory
☐ coax	☐ retention
☐ hallmark	☐ scanty
☐ award	☐ dent

[2] Select <u>the most</u> appropriate word from the box below. Each word should be used only once.

① entrenched	② meddlesome	③ emancipated	④ coax
⑤ beacon	⑥ dilemma	⑦ dent	⑧ retention
⑨ regressive	⑩ vortex	⑪ rebut	⑫ thrive
⑬ pliable	⑭ intoxicate	⑮ represent	⑯ polarized
⑰ compulsory	⑱ sole	⑲ surge	⑳ discern

1 During the debate, the opposition will have the chance to _____ the arguments put forth by the proponents of the new policy.

2 Having turkey on Thanksgiving is a tradition that's _____ in American culture — it's long been established and isn't going anywhere.

3 Pope Francis — the most overtly partisan and politically _____ pontiff in recent history — tried to pretend he was not really interested in playing politics.

4 Women are vastly underrepresented in positions of power in Japan, which is the world's third-largest economy but consistently ranks as the most _____ developed nation on gender equality.

5 Before the Civil War, the issue of slavery _____ Americans into two groups: those who defended the South's peculiar institution and those who demanded that slavery be abolished.

6 Alcohol's effect on most people, especially when they drink too much of it, is to _____ them.

7 Using a soft tone, he tried to _____ a scared puppy out of its hiding spot.

8 Mary found herself on the horns of a(n) _____. She didn't know which to choose.

9 At the end of the Civil War, slaves were _____ and became free men and women.

10 In many places, wearing a seatbelt while driving is _____ by law to enhance road safety.

[3] Choose the one which is different from the others.

11 ① winsome ② attractive ③ charming ④ infatuated

12 ① harrowing ② fledgling ③ distressing ④ disturbing

13 ① insidious ② noxious ③ venomous ④ poisonous

14 ① advent ② affront ③ appearance ④ emergence

15 ① facile ② easy ③ arduous ④ effortless

16 ① scanty ② meager ③ insufficient ④ commodious

17 ① condone ② condemn ③ pardon ④ forgive

18 ① consent ② assent ③ repudiate ④ concur

19 ① fringe ② perk ③ benefit ④ perquisite

20 ① bitter ② cynical ③ sarcastic ④ abstruse

✓ Answers

1 ⑪ ┃ 토론이 진행되는 동안, 반대측은 새로운 정책의 지지자들이 제시한 주장을 반박할 기회를 갖게 될 것이다.

2 ① ┃ 추수감사절에 칠면조를 먹는 것은 미국 문화에 자리잡은 전통이다. 이것은 오랫동안 확립되어 없어지지 않을 것이다.

3 ② ┃ 근래 역사상 가장 공공연하게 당파적이고 정치적으로 간섭하기를 좋아하는 교황인 프란치스코(Francis) 교황은 정치에는 실제로 관심이 없는 듯이 보이려고 애썼다.

4 ⑨ ┃ 세계 3위의 경제 대국이지만 성평등 측면에서 가장 퇴보한 선진국으로 꾸준히 평가되는 일본에서는 여성이 권력 있는 직위에 오르는 예가 매우 드물다.

5 ⑯ ┃ 남북전쟁 이전에 노예 제도 문제는 미국인들을 두 개의 집단으로 분열시켰는데, 남부의 흑인 노예 제도를 옹호하는 사람들과 노예 제도를 철폐해야 한다고 요구하는 사람들로 나뉘어졌다.

6 ⑭ ┃ 알코올이 대부분의 사람들에게 미치는 영향은, 특히 그들이 술을 너무 많이 마실 때, 그들을 취하게 하는 것이다.

7 ④ ┃ 그는 부드러운 어조로 겁에 질린 강아지를 달래어 숨어있던 곳에서 끌어내려고 애썼다.

8 ⑥ ┃ 메리(Mary)는 딜레마에 빠져 있었다. 그녀는 어느 쪽을 골라야 하는지 몰랐다.

9 ③ ┃ 남북전쟁이 끝나자 노예들은 해방되어 자유인이 되었다.

10 ⑰ ┃ 많은 곳에서 도로 안전을 강화하기 위해 운전 중 안전벨트 착용이 법으로 의무화되어 있다.

11 ④ **12** ② **13** ① **14** ② **15** ③ **16** ④ **17** ② **18** ③ **19** ① **20** ④

☑ **DAILY CHECKUP**

[1] Write the meaning of the following words.

☐ fatal	☐ domineer
☐ enclose	☐ convolution
☐ speck	☐ resolve
☐ pang	☐ jovial
☐ inferior	☐ contact
☐ rectify	☐ largess
☐ slight	☐ preen
☐ bargain	☐ treat
☐ allure	☐ aura
☐ crevice	☐ invaluable
☐ pervade	☐ furnace
☐ malfunction	☐ philately
☐ strict	☐ opulent
☐ hidebound	☐ vicinity
☐ gravity	☐ sap
☐ mercantile	☐ repertoire
☐ potent	☐ loan
☐ regime	☐ err
☐ dally	☐ throng
☐ arable	☐ confound
☐ cohesion	☐ incubus
☐ usher	☐ brand-new
☐ dispute	☐ recoup
☐ olfactory	☐ sore
☐ narrative	☐ plagiarism

[2] Select the most appropriate word from the box below. Each word should be used only once.

① fatal	② err	③ plagiarism	④ hidebound
⑤ convolution	⑥ rectify	⑦ arable	⑧ enclose
⑨ preen	⑩ opulent	⑪ allure	⑫ gravity
⑬ confounding	⑭ usher	⑮ incubus	⑯ malfunction
⑰ dispute	⑱ recoup	⑲ dally	⑳ inferior

1 A(n) _____ defect in the construction design caused the building to collapse.

2 After the construction error was discovered, the construction team had to work overtime to _____ the structural problem in the building.

3 The mysterious aura and captivating beauty of the ancient castle held a strong _____ for those interested in history and folklore.

4 A passenger aircraft Boeing 777 made an emergency landing at the Narita Airport due to a(n) _____ in the plane's left engine.

5 The company's _____ approach to innovation hindered its ability to adapt to changing market trends.

6 When there is a world shortage of food, taking good _____ land out of use is a sin.

7 He has been called the world's poorest President for his modest lifestyle. He doesn't ride around in limousines, nor does he live in a(n) _____ official residence.

8 All study participants were white Caucasian to attain a homogeneous sample and avoid _____ by ethnicity.

9 Businesses that lose huge amounts of money try to _____ it by throwing a sale or cutting their budget.

10 Cutting-edge AI programs mask _____ through liberal use of a thesaurus; replace enough words with synonyms and hopefully nobody will ever find the original source.

[3] Choose the one which is different from the others.

11 ① cavity   ② speck   ③ blot   ④ stain

12 ① ache   ② scab   ③ pain   ④ pang

13 ① strict   ② austere   ③ lenient   ④ stern

14 ① resolve   ② decide   ③ determine   ④ embroil

15 ① pensive   ② jovial   ③ cheerful   ④ merry

16 ① sap   ② invigorate   ③ drain   ④ undermine

17 ① slight   ② trivial   ③ negligible   ④ tangible

18 ① haggle   ② dicker   ③ designate   ④ bargain

19 ① frugality   ② largess   ③ generosity   ④ munificence

20 ① invaluable   ② modest   ③ precious   ④ priceless

✓Answers

1 ① | 건축 설계상의 치명적인 결함이 건물 붕괴의 원인이 되었다.

2 ⑥ | 시공 오류가 발견된 후, 건설팀은 건물의 구조적인 문제를 해결하기 위해 초과 근무를 해야 했다.

3 ⑪ | 고성의 신비로운 분위기와 매혹적인 아름다움은 역사와 민속에 관심이 있는 사람들에게 강한 매력을 가지고 있다.

4 ⑯ | 보잉 777 여객기가 왼쪽 엔진 기능장애로 나리타 공항에 비상착륙했다.

5 ④ | 혁신에 대한 그 회사의 고루한 접근 방식은 변화하는 시장 동향에 적응하는 능력을 방해했다.

6 ⑦ | 식량이 세계적으로 부족할 때, 좋은 경작지를 사용하지 않는 것은 잘못된 것이다.

7 ⑩ | 그는 수수한 생활방식 때문에 세계에서 가장 가난한 대통령으로 불려 왔다. 그는 리무진을 타고 다니지도 않고, 호화로운 대통령 관저에 살지도 않는다.

8 ⑬ | 모든 연구 참가자는 동일한 표본을 얻고 인종이 뒤섞이는 것을 피하기 위해 백인이었다.

9 ⑱ | 막대한 자금을 잃은 기업들은 매각을 하거나 예산을 삭감함으로써 이를 벌충하려고 한다.

10 ③ | 최첨단 AI 프로그램은 동의어 사전을 자유롭게 사용하여 표절을 숨기는데, 충분한 단어를 동의어로 대체하며 잘되면 아마도 아무도 원전을 찾지 않을 것이다.

....

11 ①   **12** ②   **13** ③   **14** ④   **15** ①   **16** ②   **17** ④   **18** ③   **19** ①   **20** ②

☑ DAILY CHECKUP

[1] Write the meaning of the following words.

☐ valiant	☐ persecute
☐ pile	☐ hindsight
☐ refute	☐ trap
☐ podium	☐ augur
☐ syllabus	☐ crop
☐ dismal	☐ incriminate
☐ parable	☐ refuge
☐ cloy	☐ sinister
☐ substance	☐ geometry
☐ mandate	☐ heedless
☐ anemia	☐ emit
☐ contaminate	☐ breakdown
☐ proselyte	☐ delegate
☐ recall	☐ limb
☐ irreparable	☐ melt
☐ smear	☐ fervent
☐ obstacle	☐ liability
☐ kidney	☐ betoken
☐ entangle	☐ component
☐ remnant	☐ stutter
☐ nibble	☐ pawn
☐ contract	☐ appreciably
☐ obeisance	☐ roost
☐ undertake	☐ dysfunction
☐ autonomy	☐ instruct

[2] Select the most appropriate word from the box below. Each word should be used only once.

① contaminating	② valiant	③ instruct	④ incriminate
⑤ cloy	⑥ delegate	⑦ irreparable	⑧ liability
⑨ parable	⑩ stutter	⑪ substance	⑫ recall
⑬ autonomy	⑭ mandate	⑮ augur	⑯ remnant
⑰ obeisance	⑱ dismal	⑲ trap	⑳ entangle

1 The team's performance was utterly _____ as they failed to secure a single victory throughout the entire season.

2 The soldier's _____ sacrifice on the battlefield was honored with a medal for bravery.

3 The massive earthquake and tsunami on March 11, 2011, destroyed the Fukushima Daiichi plant's cooling systems, causing three reactors to melt and _____ their cooling water.

4 The elderly woman's memory was starting to fade, making it difficult for her to _____ past events with clarity.

5 When the heart stops and blood stops circulating, the brain quickly becomes starved of oxygen, suffering _____ damage within about five minutes.

6 Notice how politicians usually reflect dominant belief systems and reigning ideologies within the culture. That is, note how they lack intellectual _____.

7 The dark clouds and thunder in the distance seemed to _____ an approaching storm.

8 In the American judicial system, defendants have the right not to _____ themselves, and so may refuse to answer compromising questions.

9 The nervous public speaker struggled to maintain composure and avoid _____ while delivering the important presentation.

10 The president can _____ authority to the vice president in emergency.

[3] Choose the one which is different from the others.

11	① smear	② besiege	③ slander	④ vilify
12	① plethora	② obstacle	③ hindrance	④ impediment
13	① abuse	② maltreat	③ relinquish	④ persecute
14	① sinister	② malignant	③ diabolic	④ frenetic
15	① heedless	② ceaseless	③ careless	④ reckless
16	① take in	② emit	③ give off	④ discharge
17	① ardent	② fervent	③ fervid	④ pompous
18	① proselyte	② convert	③ orthodox	④ neophyte
19	① coagulate	② melt	③ dissolve	④ thaw
20	① contradict	② speculate	③ refute	④ disprove

✔Answers

1 ⑱ │ 그 팀의 성적은 완전히 비참했는데, 시즌 내내 단 한 번의 승리도 거두지 못했다.

2 ② │ 그 병사는 전장에서 용감하게 희생한 공로로 무공 훈장을 받았다.

3 ① │ 2011년 3월 11일 발생한 대규모 지진과 쓰나미로 인해 후쿠시마 다이이치 원전의 냉각 시스템이 파괴되어 원자로 3기가 녹아 냉각수가 오염되었다.

4 ⑫ │ 나이든 여성의 기억력이 희미해지기 시작하면서 과거의 일을 분명히 기억하는 것이 어려워졌다.

5 ⑦ │ 심장이 정지하고 혈액순환이 멈추면 뇌는 빠르게 산소가 부족해지며 약 5분 이내에 회복할 수 없는 손상을 입는다.

6 ⑬ │ 대개 정치인들이 어떻게 그 문화 내의 지배적인 신념 체계와 군림하는 이데올로기를 반영하는지를 주목하라. 다시 말해, 정치인들이 얼마나 지적 자율성이 부족한지를 주목하라.

7 ⑮ │ 멀리서 보이는 검은 구름과 천둥소리는 다가오는 폭풍을 예고하는 것처럼 보였다.

8 ④ │ 미국 사법 제도에서는 피고들이 자신들에게 불리한 진술을 하지 않을 권리가 있기 때문에, 자신이 의심받을 수 있는 질문에 답하는 것을 거부할 수 있다.

9 ⑩ │ 긴장한 연설자는 중요한 프레젠테이션을 하면서 침착함을 유지하고 말을 더듬지 않으려고 애썼다.

10 ⑥ │ 대통령은 비상시 부통령에게 권한을 위임할 수 있다.

11 ② 　 12 ① 　 13 ③ 　 14 ④ 　 15 ② 　 16 ① 　 17 ④ 　 18 ③ 　 19 ① 　 20 ②

[1] Write the meaning of the following words.

☐ partial	☐ bowdlerize
☐ reinstate	☐ fiasco
☐ derogatory	☐ transmit
☐ stink	☐ ruffian
☐ akin	☐ synchronize
☐ commencement	☐ cradle
☐ wax	☐ nonage
☐ ingenious	☐ quench
☐ soak	☐ layman
☐ habiliment	☐ intent
☐ repent	☐ enrapture
☐ premonition	☐ obscene
☐ deposit	☐ barricade
☐ issue	☐ locate
☐ affiliate	☐ continent
☐ vulnerable	☐ realm
☐ credence	☐ grime
☐ disclose	☐ prologue
☐ argot	☐ condition
☐ steep	☐ alias
☐ embezzle	☐ demerit
☐ proposition	☐ vault
☐ redress	☐ mob
☐ tip	☐ plume
☐ seduce	☐ fatigue

[2] Select the most appropriate word from the box below. Each word should be used only once.

① vulnerable	② bowdlerize	③ embezzle	④ ingenious
⑤ deposit	⑥ derogatory	⑦ credence	⑧ repent
⑨ redress	⑩ affiliate	⑪ obscene	⑫ seduce
⑬ synchronize	⑭ disclose	⑮ grime	⑯ vault
⑰ quench	⑱ plume	⑲ reinstate	⑳ habiliment

1   Her _____ idea for a sustainable energy source could revolutionize the way we power our homes and cities.

2   In many religious traditions, individuals are encouraged to _____ for their sins and seek forgiveness as a path to redemption.

3   He is not technically crazy, but he is so highly neurotic and unstable a personality as to be quite _____ to certain kinds of psychological pressure.

4   Most employment agreements contain some form of a confidentiality clause that obliges employees not to _____ company information.

5   The accountant was caught attempting to _____ company funds for personal gain.

6   The company offered her a large sum of money to _____ the harm that their hair care product had done to her.

7   Publishers may choose to _____ controversial content from a book in order to make it more suitable for a younger audience.

8   Coffee and alcohol should be avoided because they will actually cause dehydration rather than _____ thirst.

9   The explicit content in the film caused it to receive a(n) _____ rating, restricting its audience to adults.

10   After a thorough investigation, the company decided to _____ the employee who had been wrongfully terminated.

[3] Choose the one which is different from the others.

11 ① partial   ② reciprocal   ③ biased   ④ prejudiced

12 ① agony   ② premonition   ③ foreboding   ④ portent

13 ① washout   ② debacle   ③ fiasco   ④ boon

14 ① continent   ② impure   ③ ascetic   ④ abstemious

15 ① fault   ② demerit   ③ indulgence   ④ defect

16 ① pedant   ② ruffian   ③ scoundrel   ④ hoodlum

17 ① steep   ② perpendicular   ③ vibrant   ④ precipitous

18 ① enrapture   ② captivate   ③ enchant   ④ imbue

19 ① argot   ② canard   ③ jargon   ④ slang

20 ① eminence   ② nonage   ③ immaturity   ④ inexperience

✓ Answers

1 ④ │ 지속 가능한 에너지원에 대한 그녀의 기발한 생각은 우리가 가정과 도시에 전력을 공급하는 방식에 대변혁을 일으킬 수 있을 것이다.

2 ⑧ │ 많은 종교 전통에서 사람들은 구원의 길로서 그들의 죄를 회개하고 용서를 빌도록 격려된다.

3 ① │ 그는 전문 용어로 말해 미친 것은 아니지만, 너무나 신경과민하고 불안정한 인물이어서 특정한 종류의 심리적 압박에 아주 취약하다.

4 ⑭ │ 대부분의 고용 계약서에는 직원들이 회사 정보를 공개하지 않도록 의무화하는 일종의 비밀 유지 조항이 포함되어 있다.

5 ③ │ 그 회계사는 사적인 이익을 위해 회사 자금을 횡령하려다가 적발됐다.

6 ⑨ │ 그 회사는 자사의 모발 보호제가 그녀에게 끼친 손해를 배상하고자 그녀에게 거액의 돈을 지불했다.

7 ② │ 출판사들은 어린 독자들에게 읽기에 적합하도록 책에서 논란이 되고 있는 내용을 삭제하는 선택을 할 수도 있다.

8 ⑰ │ 커피와 알코올은 실제로 갈증을 해소하기보다는 탈수를 유발하므로 피해야 한다.

9 ⑪ │ 그 영화의 노골적인 내용으로 인해 음란 등급을 받아 관객이 성인으로 제한되었다.

10 ⑲ │ 회사 측은 철저한 조사 끝에 부당 해고된 그 직원을 복직시키기로 결정했다.

11 ②   12 ①   13 ④   14 ②   15 ③   16 ①   17 ③   18 ④   19 ②   20 ①

ACTUAL TEST

▶ ▶ ▶ ANSWERS P.404

[01-100] Choose the one that is closest in meaning to the underlined part.

01 We are driven by underlined{incentives}.
① requests   ② instincts
③ desires   ④ motives

02 The professor received an anonymous letter.
① a friendly   ② an unsigned
③ a hostile   ④ a congratulatory

03 Metals rust most rapidly in humid regions.
① damp   ② hot
③ cold   ④ warm

04 We will not dwell on the unpleasant subject.
① contemplate   ② reside
③ speak   ④ enter

05 Species evolve and the ones best adapted to their environment thrive and leave more offspring.
① surpass   ② survive
③ develop   ④ flourish

06 What he did was contrary to what he said.
① pertinent   ② similar
③ opposite   ④ relevant

07 He resolved to act at once.
① hesitated   ② offered
③ refused   ④ determined

08 Your anxiety is sure to melt away once you consult your doctor.
① solve   ② disappear
③ increase   ④ incite

09 The perk of being a student is an inexpensive flight fee.
① perquisite   ② blunder
③ prevision   ④ amercement

10 The young hiker, heedless of the trail warnings, ventured deeper into the forest.
① wary   ② meticulous
③ inattentive   ④ dauntless

11 Businesses will frequently seek to capitalize on the rebellious allure of subcultures.
① faction   ② exclusivity
③ charm   ④ vivacity

12 Japan is a society whose culture is steeped in the traditions and symbols of the past.
① inclined to
② permeated with
③ obsessed with
④ indebted to

13 Her voice was intoxicating, though I'd heard the tale several times before.
① drunken   ② captivating
③ intimidating   ④ poisonous

14 *Car Buyer's Guide* includes everything you need to know about car shopping, including <u>invaluable tips</u> on haggling for the best possible price.
① important hints
② unworthy helps
③ unnecessary contents
④ profitable bargains

15 The scientist is as <u>impartial</u> as Nature in Turgenev's poem.
① indifferent   ② useless
③ skillful   ④ ideal

16 The surgeon tried to describe the procedure in terms of a <u>layman</u>, but he used so much medical jargon that I had no idea what he was talking about.
① expert   ② mentor
③ non-specialist   ④ misanthrope

17 In every culture it seems that one or two animals are considered <u>crafty</u> while others are looked upon as lacking in intelligence.
① artistic   ② humanistic
③ capable   ④ cunning

18 He attacks the newspapers for their uncritical <u>obeisance</u> to the rich and the powerful.
① interpretation   ② reverence
③ rapture   ④ deviance

19 Of course, many people would not want this job — its <u>searing</u> solitude, the haranguing drills of a sole sentence's fate, and the inescapability of relentless autocritique.
① sealing   ② parching
③ sorrowful   ④ frigid

20 Hitler wanted to <u>extirpate</u> the Catholic Church because he thought that Catholics and Jews were the source of every evil.
① subsidize   ② deprecate
③ ameliorate   ④ uproot

21 He spent most of his speech <u>rebutting</u> criticisms of his foreign policy.
① spurring   ② vacating
③ grieving   ④ disproving

22 A Rube Goldberg device performs a very simple task in a very indirect and <u>convoluted</u> way.
① circuitous   ② subtle
③ crafty   ④ intricate

23 He was surprised by the <u>venomous</u> tone of the anonymous calls.
① affectionate   ② complementary
③ flattering   ④ spiteful

24 European leaders are attempting to distance themselves from the Afghanistan <u>fiasco</u> despite generally supporting the decision to leave.
① alliance   ② debacle
③ withdrawal   ④ liberation

25 His latest film is about the experience of being <u>persecuted</u> for being gay.
① pampered   ② accommodated
③ wronged   ④ indulged

26 The investor recouped her previous losses by making several well-timed investments later.
① got back   ② explained away
③ paid off   ④ looked into

27 Nearly 9 in 10 dark-money spots are negative, and an analysis by the Annenberg Public Policy Center found that 26% of the ads are deceptive, a slightly higher rate than that for ads by groups that disclose their donor's identities.
① reveal   ② discover
③ disqualify   ④ repudiate

28 She had a premonition that her cat would somehow get hurt that day.
① hindsight   ② sign
③ foreboding   ④ peroration

29 People forget their childhood, no doubt, and it is a loss which, no matter how lightly they take it, is irreparable.
① irreproachable   ② irrecognizable
③ irresistible   ④ irretrievable

30 The explorer stopped to quench her thirst at the stream but was scared away by an enraged bear.
① satiate   ② absorb
③ savor   ④ curb

31 He coaxed his friend into buying his company's products.
① haggled   ② directed
③ blandished   ④ rendered

32 In the minds of many Americans, this ethno-racial transition betokens political, cultural, and social upheaval.
① declares   ② signifies
③ ascribes   ④ aggrandizes

33 *The Herald* had been prosecuted for printing obscene and indecent advertising.
① chaste   ② salacious
③ arrogant   ④ despicable

34 He was an indefatigable worker, a rousing public speaker, and a decisive administrator.
① sociable   ② tireless
③ persuasive   ④ reasonable

35 The tip of each device is made with soft pliable materials in a universal size.
① movable   ② plastic
③ unadaptable   ④ inflexible

36 Analysts say the recession in Japan has sapped investor confidence.
① jeopardized
② enviously challenged
③ stirred up
④ gradually weakened

37 If white people in political leadership are truly repentant, they will listen to black and other marginalized people in our society.
① elusive   ② penitent
③ sagacious   ④ adamant

38 The stories are harrowing, often producing tears among the participants themselves and from the invited audiences.
① frustrating ② irritating
③ distressing ④ aggravating

39 An newspaper article has caused fears that heating plastics in the microwave can contaminate food with dioxins, a group of carcinogens.
① preserve ② spoil
③ reheat ④ keep

40 Although he lacked formal education, he had an amazingly retentive memory and a passion for learning.
① absurd ② recollective
③ distinct ④ infinite

41 The novelist is here expressing the doctrine of industriousness — a pervasive notion that inspired his contemporaries.
① petrifying ② pejorative
③ pernicious ④ permeating

42 The scene appeared calm and jovial, and police stationed nearby said the visitors were largely behaving themselves.
① serene ② cheerful
③ deliberate ④ monotonous

43 The service of the restaurant was courteous but not cloying.
① nugatory ② phlegmatic
③ mawkish ④ obstreperous

44 A throng of bearded men in sad-colored garments and gray, steeple-crowned hats was assembled in front of a wooden edifice.
① crowd ② member
③ number ④ row

45 Ushered into a waiting car, he was driven for two hours into the Bavarian countryside.
① Announced ② Pushed
③ Guided ④ Forced

46 A grocery store is in the vicinity of your home.
① distance ② end
③ rear ④ proximity

47 This textbook encloses the information you will have to master to get good grades in the final exam.
① empowers ② encompasses
③ encumbers ④ obligates

48 Hotels and restaurants are acutely vulnerable to recession.
① weak ② strong
③ resistive ④ formidable

49 The new housekeeper proved to be a fine cook into the bargain.
① at a discount ② as well
③ in business ④ for a nominal wage

50 America's vaunted emancipation in the workplace is well known to the world.
① liberation ② enthusiasm
③ infringement ④ mantra

51 The soldier was treated with disdain by his comrades because he fled the battle after the first shot was fired.
① respect
② scorn
③ ambivalence
④ authority

52 There was a rather sinister figure walking behind the bushes.
① indigenous
② suspicious
③ conspicuous
④ unknown

53 Fifty years later he knew, and they knew as well, that there was no way to rectify his betrayal.
① correct
② qualify
③ integrate
④ disdain

54 While it is sadly too late for John, there is hope beyond these dismal facts.
① depressing
② attested
③ undeniable
④ complicated

55 For boys, impulsivity in the early years may augur a heightened risk of delinquency or violence.
① augment
② formulate
③ herald
④ mask

56 For children, playing is an automatic and integral component of growing up.
① reminder
② decision
③ result
④ part

57 After 1850, various states in the United States began to pass compulsory school attendance laws.
① harsh
② diversified
③ mandatory
④ complicated

58 Native American nations are regarded as autonomous in many respects and thus not subject to a number of state laws.
① supportive
② independent
③ resistant
④ interfering

59 Australia's current drought is not yet the longest, but it is the hottest — and it has devastated cattle and ranches, sheep farms and swaths of arable land across the nation.
① abominable
② barren
③ sterile
④ tillable

60 In the past century, homosexuality was often regarded as a serious form of deviance and in some cases prosecuted and punished by law.
① restrained
② offended
③ indicted
④ affronted

61 The innocent man refuted the accusation.
① extenuated
② fought
③ disproved
④ avoided

62 The number of vehicles on the road is dramatically increasing in many countries, and the roads often haven't kept pace with this sudden surge in drivers.
① menacing behavior
② sharp growth
③ mysterious decrease
④ urge to race

63 In the past few years, there have been appreciably lower temperatures during the winter months than are usual in this part of the region.

① abundantly   ② immeasurably
③ unendingly   ④ noticeably

64 The sudden fall in share prices has confounded economists.

① disseminated   ② deduced
③ baffled   ④ demeaned

65 The current leadership tried to redress the dire economic condition by revaluing the currency, but that only made the situation worse.

① correct   ② defy
③ assess   ④ justify

66 Congressman Hamilton was spared the liability of signing the surrender document, as he relegated this assignment to his political advisors.

① recrudescence   ② palimpsest
③ burden   ④ impunity

67 For example, one typically assumes that the line connecting two data points is continuous with earlier segments of the line, but that is an assumption, not a hidebound reality.

① innocuous   ② indolent
③ intolerant   ④ indifferent

68 Smallpox remained a dreaded, often fatal illness until very recently.

① anxious   ② mortal
③ acute   ④ sharp

69 The stern parent had reason not to consent to his daughter's marriage.

① agree   ② assemble
③ convene   ④ refrain

70 In the past, new immigrants were often able to obtain jobs easily. Now the advent of new technologies requires the newcomers to obtain more education to be recruited.

① outdating   ② appearance
③ retrogression   ④ retardation

71 He plumes himself on his quick promotion in his firm.

① feels lucky
② prides himself on
③ doubts himself
④ hardly believes

72 A good statesman, like any other sensible human being, always learns more from his opponents than from his fervent supporters.

① voracious   ② acute
③ ferocious   ④ passionate

73 Once the hope for democracy in the tiny island nation, Aristide has recently come to be seen as the cause of the people's plight rather than their salvation.

① hardship   ② whim
③ anger   ④ curse

74 It is necessary to distinguish between the manifest dream and the latent dream.

① dormant   ② exposed
③ imposed   ④ fake

75 The poet transforms a <u>genial</u> social performance into a passionate lyric utterance.
① delicate   ② friendly
③ religious   ④ insistent

76 World leaders suddenly seem more concerned with the irrational excitement of tomorrow than the <u>anemic</u> economy of today.
① abnormal   ② pathological
③ feeble   ④ irregular

77 She devised an <u>ingenious</u> solution to the problem.
① genuine   ② influential
③ original   ④ indifferent

78 Many families could take advantage of previously unavailable fruits, vegetables, and dairy products to achieve more varied <u>fare</u>.
① fee   ② rate
③ charge   ④ diet

79 Astronomers have difficulty detecting black holes since they <u>emit</u> no electronic radiation. Therefore, their presence is inferred by the absence of such radiation or by the drawing of material from a nearby cloud of interstellar matter toward the black hole.
① expand   ② condense
③ release   ④ exhaust

80 Mrs. Smith is <u>meddlesome</u> in the affairs of her cousin, but loves her dearly.
① assiduous   ② instructive
③ officious   ④ official

81 His extreme antipathy to <u>dispute</u> caused him to avoid argumentative discussions with his friends.
① assent   ② discourse
③ altercate   ④ repute

82 The story was an attempt to <u>smear</u> the leader of the opposition.
① slander   ② squash
③ elevate   ④ muzzle

83 As chairman, you will have to <u>delegate</u> responsibility to each of the committee members.
① demand   ② align
③ share   ④ assign

84 From 1775 to 1776 the Americans <u>undertook</u> an unsuccessful campaign against the British in Canada.
① waged   ② headed
③ computed   ④ haunted

85 Fifty-nine years after Congress outlawed child labor in its most <u>onerous</u> forms, underage workers still toil in fields and factories scattered throughout America.
① liberal   ② demanding
③ profuse   ④ extravagant

86 The company's latest big push is to address body shaming by imposing a ban on "unsolicited and <u>derogatory</u> comments made about someone's appearance, body shape, size or health."
① arrogant   ② provocative
③ disparaging   ④ conclusive

87 The tendency of the human body to reject foreign matter is the main obstacle to successful tissue transportation.
① factor in
② impediment to
③ occurrence in
④ phenomenon of

88 Our knowledge of at least two-thirds of the world's languages remains scanty.
① theoretical
② meager
③ indeterminate
④ implicit

89 The muffler on a car conducts exhaust gases around a series of obstacles called baffles, soaking up the noise.
① absorbing
② echoing
③ deflecting
④ releasing

90 The politician seemed so sincere that one couldn't help but give credence to his statements.
① invocation
② nonchalance
③ confidence
④ misgiving

91 The chairman of SK Group will be summoned for interrogation over allegations that he embezzled a massive amount of company funds.
① inadvertently invested
② took as a bribe
③ illegally confiscated
④ diverted fraudulently

92 At those times, there were impotent aristocrats talking regularly about the code of chivalry but unable to bring it to life.
① powerless
② dictatorial
③ impartial
④ tainted

93 The hallmark of Jefferson's life was self-confidence.
① reason for success
② guiding light
③ distinguishing characteristic
④ mark of excellence

94 In the past, religions were very important to disentangle the complicated problems faced by society.
① unravel
② coordinate
③ abolish
④ underrate

95 Hans Makart exploited the potential of theatrical spectacle and swept his audiences into opulent fantasy worlds.
① excessive
② rich
③ unfamiliar
④ mysterious

96 After the election the government commenced to develop the new highway.
① agreed
② planned
③ decided
④ started

97 The audience was enraptured by the young soloist's performance.
① resuscitated
② mollified
③ enchanted
④ convinced

98 Repairs began immediately on the dam, whose structural integrity had been <u>compromised</u> by the earthquake.
① measured   ② shattered
③ harassed   ④ impaired

99 Many royalist men who escaped to the continent left behind wives and families who struggled <u>valiantly</u>.
① dauntlessly   ② ceaselessly
③ languidly   ④ surreptitiously

100 As in the "superpredator" era, some politicians are leaping to <u>facile</u> conclusions and taking it out on an easy target — young people of color.
① virile   ② effortless
③ convincing   ④ vote-catching

[1] Write the meaning of the following words.

☐ incorporate	☐ trait
☐ felony	☐ obnoxious
☐ rebuff	☐ fabrication
☐ sloth	☐ negate
☐ preternatural	☐ animosity
☐ estimate	☐ vertebrate
☐ misgiving	☐ congestion
☐ suit	☐ gratis
☐ assassinate	☐ restrict
☐ elf	☐ priest
☐ random	☐ detain
☐ skyrocket	☐ temperament
☐ peer	☐ insight
☐ dip	☐ conjure
☐ coverage	☐ rend
☐ bumble	☐ obvious
☐ spread	☐ mantle
☐ providence	☐ inspire
☐ upbeat	☐ havoc
☐ crave	☐ audit
☐ lexicon	☐ prostitute
☐ hallow	☐ capsize
☐ brink	☐ endemic
☐ pillory	☐ remit
☐ wardrobe	☐ diversity

[2] Select <u>the most</u> appropriate word from the box below. Each word should be used only once.

① preternatural	② incorporate	③ pillory	④ inspire
⑤ negated	⑥ random	⑦ havoc	⑧ felony
⑨ sloth	⑩ crave	⑪ congestion	⑫ rend
⑬ capsize	⑭ diversity	⑮ fabrication	⑯ animosity
⑰ detaining	⑱ remit	⑲ mantle	⑳ conjure

1 Because of its strength, adhesiveness, and invaluable qualities as a nest building material, many species of birds _____ silk into their nests.

2 Unlike a misdemeanor, a(n) _____ is a serious crime that may result in a long prison sentence if convicted.

3 He always procrastinates; his _____ only augments the problem of the impending deadline.

4 The computer algorithm generates _____ numbers, making it impossible to predict the next outcome in the sequence.

5 The detective suspected that the suspect's alibi was a(n) _____ and set out to uncover the truth.

6 The discovery of one dinosaur jaw _____ the conventional wisdom that all dinosaurs were vegetarians, since the tooth structure proved that guy definitely ate meat.

7 Having experienced Japanese colonial rule, many Koreans still harbor _____ toward Japan.

8 Amnesty International has accused the police of beating protesters as well as unlawfully arresting and _____ them.

9 For many British people the ideal place to live is a village set in attractive countryside. To those living in towns, villages _____ up images of peace, a slow pace of life and pretty cottages.

10 Continuing strikes are beginning to play _____ with the national economy.

[3] Choose the one which is different from the others.

11 ① rebuff   ② refuse   ③ snub   ④ spur

12 ① sordid   ② upbeat   ③ optimistic   ④ sanguine

13 ① offensive   ② loathsome   ③ obnoxious   ④ precipitous

14 ① insight   ② candor   ③ acumen   ④ intuition

15 ① circumscribe   ② restrict   ③ distract   ④ curb

16 ① impure   ② apparent   ③ obvious   ④ evident

17 ① estimate   ② swindle   ③ assess   ④ guess

18 ① hallow   ② consecrate   ③ harangue   ④ sanctify

19 ① gratis   ② complimentary   ③ for nothing   ④ customary

20 ① trait   ② competence   ③ characteristic   ④ feature

✓Answers

1 ② ㅣ 내구력, 접착력, 그리고 둥지를 짓는 재료로서의 중요한 특성 때문에, 많은 종류의 새들이 비단을 둥지에 섞어 넣는다.

2 ⑧ ㅣ 경범죄와 달리, 중죄는 유죄 판결을 받게 되면 장기 징역형에 처할 수 있는 중대한 범죄이다.

3 ⑨ ㅣ 그는 항상 꾸물거린다. 그의 게으름은 마감 시간이 임박한 문제를 증가시킬 뿐이었다.

4 ⑥ ㅣ 컴퓨터 알고리즘은 난수(亂數)를 생성하므로 순서상 다음 결과(수)를 예측하는 것이 불가능하다.

5 ⑮ ㅣ 형사는 용의자의 알리바이가 조작된 것이라고 의심하고 진실을 밝히기 위해 나섰다.

6 ⑤ ㅣ 한 공룡턱의 발견은 모든 공룡이 채식주의를 했다는 통념을 부정하는 것이었는데, 치아 구조를 통해 공룡이 확실히 고기를 먹었다는 것이 입증되었기 때문이다.

7 ⑯ ㅣ 일본의 식민 지배를 겪은 많은 한국인들은 여전히 일본에 대한 적개심을 품고 있다.

8 ⑰ ㅣ 국제앰네스티는 경찰이 시위자들을 구타하고 불법적으로 체포하고 구금했다고 비난했다.

9 ⑳ ㅣ 많은 영국인들에게, 살기에 이상적인 곳은 매력적인 시골에 자리 잡고 있는 마을이다. 도시에 살고 있는 사람들에게, 마을은 평화, 느릿느릿한 생활 속도, 예쁜 오두막집의 이미지를 떠올리게 한다.

10 ⑦ ㅣ 계속되는 파업이 국가 경제를 혼란에 빠뜨리기 시작하고 있다.

11 ④   **12** ①   **13** ④   **14** ②   **15** ③   **16** ①   **17** ②   **18** ③   **19** ④   **20** ②

[1] Write the meaning of the following words.

☐ hesitate	☐ strain
☐ circumspect	☐ budge
☐ reservoir	☐ remedy
☐ designate	☐ apparel
☐ pusillanimous	☐ threadbare
☐ spearhead	☐ portray
☐ marked	☐ corridor
☐ dermatologist	☐ oblige
☐ erase	☐ luminary
☐ attrition	☐ concern
☐ suppurate	☐ hull
☐ listless	☐ assign
☐ patron	☐ unbridled
☐ inject	☐ straitjacket
☐ motto	☐ transition
☐ wreath	☐ ferret
☐ annul	☐ eloquence
☐ conclusion	☐ relegate
☐ enmesh	☐ gourmand
☐ judicial	☐ count
☐ drip	☐ fable
☐ moderate	☐ privatize
☐ veneer	☐ rupture
☐ inherent	☐ blast
☐ profile	☐ snoop

[2] Select the most appropriate word from the box below. Each word should be used only once.

① suppurate	② ferret	③ wreath	④ relegate
⑤ privatize	⑥ spearhead	⑦ rupture	⑧ veneer
⑨ reservoir	⑩ judicial	⑪ annul	⑫ moderate
⑬ assign	⑭ listless	⑮ remedy	⑯ count
⑰ circumspect	⑱ snoop	⑲ luminary	⑳ unbridled

1   In a world where information travels quickly, it's important to be _____ about sharing personal details online to protect your privacy.

2   The scorching heat and lack of activity made everyone feel _____ on the lazy summer afternoon.

3   New government officials often want to _____ laws and policies of the previous post-holder, effectively reversing their work.

4   Despite her polite _____, it was clear to those who knew her well that her outward pretense concealed a more complex personality.

5   In his youth, he was known for his _____ enthusiasm and boundless energy, which often led to daring adventures.

6   The government has to walk the fine line of ensuring the rights of the defectors and at the same time doing its best to _____ out potential spies among them.

7   If we _____ these experienced people to positions of unimportance because of their political persuasions, we shall lose the services of valuably trained personnel.

8   The proposal to _____ the state-owned healthcare system has sparked a heated debate on the role of government in providing medical services.

9   The escalating tension between the two nations could lead to a diplomatic _____ if not resolved soon.

10   During periods of drought, the levels in the _____ may decrease significantly, impacting the region's water supply.

[3] Choose the one which is different from the others.

11 ① expedite ② hesitate ③ waver ④ falter

12 ① pusillanimous ② craven ③ timid ④ discreet

13 ① embroil ② enmesh ③ enforce ④ entangle

14 ① assign ② appoint ③ designate ④ nudge

15 ① expunge ② extricate ③ delete ④ erase

16 ① patron ② benefactor ③ comrade ④ sponsor

17 ① overt ② threadbare ③ banal ④ hackneyed

18 ① eloquence ② fluency ③ contempt ④ oratory

19 ① detonation ② furnace ③ explosion ④ blast

20 ① tranquility ② strain ③ burden ④ pressure

[1] Write the meaning of the following words.

☐ relevant	☐ flamboyant
☐ domesticate	☐ rein
☐ convent	☐ gazette
☐ stumble	☐ contest
☐ menace	☐ book
☐ supervene	☐ proper
☐ perdition	☐ torpedo
☐ intrigue	☐ officious
☐ degenerate	☐ apartheid
☐ survey	☐ eclipse
☐ querulous	☐ vantage
☐ pitch	☐ putrefy
☐ coup	☐ descent
☐ arbitrate	☐ expand
☐ habitat	☐ bumptious
☐ veer	☐ interrogate
☐ nerve	☐ relinquish
☐ traduce	☐ context
☐ untold	☐ attest
☐ stoop	☐ litigation
☐ pledge	☐ redound
☐ azure	☐ mint
☐ loot	☐ enfetter
☐ cognomen	☐ repetitive
☐ submit	☐ feast

[2] Select <u>the most</u> appropriate word from the box below. Each word should be used only once.

① gazette	② feast	③ stumble	④ pitch
⑤ coup	⑥ azure	⑦ submit	⑧ traduce
⑨ officious	⑩ arbitrate	⑪ pledge	⑫ loot
⑬ flamboyant	⑭ torpedo	⑮ interrogate	⑯ redound
⑰ context	⑱ domesticate	⑲ putrefy	⑳ relinquish

1 When the parties could not reach a consensus, a labor specialist was asked to _____ in the dispute between workers and management.

2 The tabloid newspaper attempted to _____ the reputation of the celebrity with false and damaging stories.

3 The artist's _____ paintings, filled with vibrant colors and bold strokes, captured the attention of art enthusiasts worldwide.

4 The manager's _____ behavior, constantly micromanaging the team's tasks, created tension and frustration among the employees.

5 After apprehending the prime suspect, the detective prepared to _____ him in order to unravel the details of the crime.

6 The company's decision to _____ its hold on the struggling division was seen as a strategic move to focus on more profitable ventures.

7 To celebrate their anniversary, the couple decided to prepare a lavish and extravagant _____ for their friends and family.

8 The process of selective breeding over generations helped humans _____ wild animals into more docile and suitable companions.

9 The pirates sailed away with their _____ after raiding the coastal village.

10 The stagnant water in the pond began to _____, creating an unpleasant environment for nearby wildlife.

[3] Choose the one which is different from the others.

11 ① gasp ② menace ③ intimidation ④ threat

12 ① relevant ② germane ③ pertinent ④ incessant

13 ① machination ② intrigue ③ contrition ④ conspiracy

14 ① bumptious ② derisive ③ arrogant ④ haughty

15 ① tawdry ② querulous ③ complaining ④ irritable

16 ① untold ② immense ③ numerable ④ incalculable

17 ① ensue ② follow ③ supervene ④ precede

18 ① attest ② glimpse ③ confirm ④ verify

19 ① revolve ② veer ③ shift ④ swerve

20 ① constrain ② shackle ③ dissipate ④ enfetter

✔ Answers

1 ⑩ | 당사자들이 합의에 이르지 못하자, 노동 전문가에게 근로자들과 경영진 사이의 분쟁을 중재하도록 요청했다.

2 ⑧ | 그 타블로이드 신문은 사실이 아닌 피해를 주는 이야기로 그 유명인의 명성을 비방하려고 시도했다.

3 ⑬ | 강렬한 색과 대담한 화법으로 가득한 그 화가의 화려한 그림은 전 세계 미술 애호가들의 관심을 사로잡았다.

4 ⑨ | 팀의 업무를 끊임없이 세세한 점까지 관리하는 관리자의 참견하기 좋아하는 행동은 직원들 사이에 긴장과 좌절감을 불러일으켰다.

5 ⑮ | 형사는 유력 용의자를 체포한 후 범행의 경위를 밝히기 위해 그를 심문할 준비를 했다.

6 ⑳ | 어려움을 겪고 있는 사업부에 대한 소유권 보유를 포기하기로 한 회사의 결정은 수익성이 더 높은 신규 개발 사업에 집중하기 위한 전략적 움직임으로 간주되었다.

7 ② | 기념일을 축하하기 위해 그 부부는 친구와 가족을 위해 풍성하고 호화로운 잔치를 준비하기로 결정했다.

8 ⑱ | 여러 세대에 걸쳐 선발 육종을 하는 과정은 인간이 야생 동물을 더 유순하고 적합한 반려동물로 길들이는 데 도움이 되었다.

9 ⑫ | 해적들은 해안 마을을 습격한 후 약탈품을 가지고 달아났다.

10 ⑲ | 연못에 고인 물이 썩기 시작하여 인근 야생동물에게 불쾌한 환경이 조성됐다.

- -

11 ① **12** ④ **13** ③ **14** ② **15** ① **16** ③ **17** ④ **18** ② **19** ① **20** ③

☑ **DAILY CHECKUP**

[1] Write the meaning of the following words.

☐ shun	☐ ambush
☐ anthropoid	☐ bullion
☐ expose	☐ credit
☐ nefarious	☐ occupy
☐ disgrace	☐ congress
☐ response	☐ swap
☐ plaster	☐ layout
☐ render	☐ gravid
☐ myth	☐ verisimilitude
☐ civil	☐ pursue
☐ engender	☐ farce
☐ indigence	☐ expedite
☐ mutual	☐ bridle
☐ suffice	☐ deracinate
☐ aeon	☐ herd
☐ disillusion	☐ revel
☐ plump	☐ console
☐ stroll	☐ regurgitate
☐ odds	☐ procedure
☐ trounce	☐ limpid
☐ bud	☐ assert
☐ jettison	☐ squeamish
☐ flair	☐ testimony
☐ customize	☐ redolent
☐ upright	☐ incline

[2] Select <u>the most</u> appropriate word from the box below. Each word should be used only once.

① limpid	② squeamish	③ render	④ ambushed
⑤ pursue	⑥ indigence	⑦ plump	⑧ engender
⑨ myth	⑩ customize	⑪ upright	⑫ nefarious
⑬ jettison	⑭ verisimilitude	⑮ credit	⑯ layout
⑰ herd	⑱ regurgitated	⑲ revel	⑳ expedite

1   News reporters investigate corrupt politicians in order to uncover their _____ activities.

2   The charity organization's mission is to provide support and resources to families facing financial hardship and _____.

3   If an aircraft is heavily loaded with fuel, it will need to lose weight in order to land safely. It's rare, because of fuel costs, but pilots may _____ fuel to lighten their load.

4   As they ventured deeper into the forest, they were suddenly _____ by a group of bandits hiding among the trees.

5   The author's use of vivid descriptions and realistic dialogue added to the novel's sense of _____.

6   Despite facing obstacles, he was determined to _____ his dream of becoming a professional musician.

7   The _____ waters of the mountain lake were so transparent that you could see the fish swimming beneath the surface.

8   Some people feel _____ at the sight of blood, while others can handle medical procedures without any discomfort.

9   Despite the _____ that alligators are dangerous to humans, they generally avoid human contact and rarely pose a threat.

10   He was praised for his _____ character, always doing what he believed was right.

[3] Choose the one which is different from the others.

11 ① avoid   ② shun   ③ dodge   ④ confront

12 ① epoch   ② aeon   ③ eternity   ④ perpetuity

13 ① ominous   ② foreboding   ③ imperative   ④ gravid

14 ① deracinate   ② delineate   ③ eradicate   ④ uproot

15 ① swap   ② deviate   ③ barter   ④ exchange

16 ① detached   ② mutual   ③ bilateral   ④ reciprocal

17 ① odds   ② probability   ③ likelihood   ④ resemblance

18 ① talent   ② flair   ③ instinct   ④ gift

19 ① soothe   ② denote   ③ comfort   ④ console

20 ① tactile   ② redolent   ③ fragrant   ④ scented

✓ Answers

1 ⑫ ▎뉴스 기자들은 부패한 정치인들의 사악한 범죄 행위를 밝혀내기 그들을 조사한다.

2 ⑥ ▎그 자선 단체의 임무는 경제적 어려움과 빈곤에 처한 가족들에게 지원과 재원을 제공하는 것이다.

3 ⑬ ▎항공기에 연료가 많이 실리면, 안전하게 착륙하기 위해 무게를 줄일 필요가 있을 것이다. 연료 비용 때문에 이런 일은 드물지만, 조종사는 항공기의 무게를 가볍게 하기 위해 연료를 버릴지도 모른다.

4 ④ ▎그들이 숲속으로 더 깊이 들어가자 갑자기 나무 사이에 숨어있던 한 무리의 도적 떼의 습격을 받았다.

5 ⑭ ▎작가의 생생한 묘사와 사실적인 대화의 사용은 소설의 사실감을 더했다.

6 ⑤ ▎여러 어려움에 직면해서도 그는 전문 음악가가 되겠다는 꿈을 추구하기로 결심했다.

7 ① ▎산속 호수의 맑은 물은 너무 투명해서 수면 밑에 있는 물고기가 헤엄치는 모습을 볼 수 있다.

8 ② ▎어떤 사람들은 피를 보는 것에 대해 메스꺼움을 느끼지만, 다른 사람들은 아무런 불편함 없이 시술을 할 수 있다.

9 ⑨ ▎악어가 인간에게 위험하다는 근거없는 믿음에도 불구하고 일반적으로 악어는 인간과의 접촉을 피하고 위협을 가하는 경우가 거의 없다.

10 ⑪ ▎그는 항상 옳다고 믿은 일을 행하는 곧은 성품으로 칭찬받았다.

11 ④   **12** ①   **13** ③   **14** ②   **15** ②   **16** ①   **17** ④   **18** ③   **19** ②   **20** ①

[1] Write the meaning of the following words.

☐ tenacious	☐ venue
☐ envelop	☐ polish
☐ siege	☐ gaudy
☐ assess	☐ retort
☐ portable	☐ asset
☐ recital	☐ pore
☐ startle	☐ indisputable
☐ morsel	☐ crucify
☐ annex	☐ loaf
☐ contagion	☐ brunt
☐ spiritual	☐ grant
☐ maul	☐ finesse
☐ uneasy	☐ conquer
☐ eliminate	☐ poach
☐ spice	☐ onus
☐ inaugurate	☐ authenticate
☐ hermit	☐ precinct
☐ reserve	☐ forerunner
☐ decisive	☐ repeal
☐ nicety	☐ buoy
☐ digress	☐ dissimulate
☐ anachronism	☐ surname
☐ waver	☐ corporation
☐ terrestrial	☐ encumber
☐ convict	☐ logrolling

[2] Select <u>the most</u> appropriate word from the box below. Each word should be used only once.

① logrolling	② encumber	③ annex	④ buoyed
⑤ digress	⑥ terrestrial	⑦ eliminate	⑧ polish
⑨ brunt	⑩ reserve	⑪ authenticate	⑫ convict
⑬ repealed	⑭ decisive	⑮ retorted	⑯ grant
⑰ hermit	⑱ portable	⑲ siege	⑳ poach

1   The complex legal procedures often _____ small business owners, preventing them from focusing on their core operations.

2   The isolated outpost was under _____ by hostile forces, and the soldiers inside were running low on supplies.

3   In order to improve efficiency, the company implemented a new system to _____ unnecessary bottlenecks in the production process.

4   A life of solitude isn't for everyone, but a(n) _____ chooses it for any number of reasons.

5   The problem is that most people are _____ in their false religion, stubborn against the truth and unwilling to admit that they're wrong.

6   When asked about the controversial decision, she _____ with a sharp and impassioned response, defending her stance.

7   The problem was that the meeting was running late and there was no time to let you _____. I had to pull you back to the main topic.

8   In the United States the tax on distilled spirits was _____ in 1817, but was reimposed at the outbreak of the Civil War in 1861.

9   In his heartfelt apology, he expressed his regret and remorse without _____, leaving no doubt about the sincerity of his words.

10   _____ by the positive feedback from the audience, the young musician gained the confidence to pursue a career in music.

[3] Choose the one which is different from the others.

11 ① onus   ② burden   ③ root   ④ weight

12 ① obstinate   ② tenacious   ③ stubborn   ④ versatile

13 ① familiarize   ② startle   ③ astonish   ④ surprise

14 ① waver   ② elicit   ③ dither   ④ falter

15 ① tidy   ② gaudy   ③ garish   ④ showy

16 ① crucify   ② excruciate   ③ abduct   ④ torment

17 ① skill   ② acumen   ③ finesse   ④ hyperbole

18 ① dissimulate   ② deprecate   ③ dissemble   ④ conceal

19 ① nicety   ② nuance   ③ subtlety   ④ proxy

20 ① unwitting   ② indisputable   ③ incontrovertible   ④ unquestionable

✓ Answers

1 ② ┃ 복잡한 법적 절차는 소규모 사업주들을 종종 방해하여 그들이 핵심 사업에 집중하지 못하게 한다.

2 ⑲ ┃ 고립된 전초기지는 적군에 의해 포위되었고, 내부의 병사들은 보급품이 부족해졌다.

3 ⑦ ┃ 효율성을 높이기 위해 그 회사는 생산 과정에서 불필요한 병목 현상을 없애기 위해 새로운 시스템을 실행했다.

4 ⑰ ┃ 고독한 삶은 모든 사람을 위한 것은 아니지만, 은둔자는 여러 가지 이유로 고독한 삶을 선택한다.

5 ⑭ ┃ 문제는 대부분의 사람들이 자신들의 사이비 종교에 대해 확고한 태도를 취하고 있으며 진실에 대해 완고하게 굴며 그들이 잘못됐다는 것을 인정하고 싶어 하지 않는다는 데 있다.

6 ⑮ ┃ 논란의 여지가 있는 결정을 질문받자 그녀는 날카롭고 열정적인 반응으로 반박하며 자신의 입장을 변호했다.

7 ⑤ ┃ 문제는 회의가 늦어지고 있어서 당신이 본제를 벗어나 다른 말을 하게 할 시간이 없었다. 나는 당신을 다시 본 주제로 끌어들여야 했다.

8 ⑬ ┃ 미국에서는 1817년에 증류주에 대한 세금이 폐지되었으나 1861년에 남북전쟁이 발발하면서 다시 부과되었다.

9 ⑩ ┃ 그는 진심 어린 사과문에서 후회와 반성의 뜻을 솔직히 표현하며 자신의 말의 진정성에 의심의 여지를 남기지 않았다.

10 ④ ┃ 관객의 긍정적인 피드백에 힘입어 젊은 음악가는 음악 분야에서 경력을 쌓을 자신감을 얻었다.

....

11 ③   **12** ④   **13** ①   **14** ②   **15** ①   **16** ③   **17** ④   **18** ②   **19** ④   **20** ①

▶▶▶ ANSWERS P.414

[01-100] Choose the one that is closest in meaning to the underlined part.

01 Shooting stars are <u>unsuitably</u> named as they are not stars at all.
① illogically
② unrealistically
③ indiscreetly
④ inappropriately

02 He asked a lot of questions <u>at random</u>.
① on purpose
② painstakingly
③ aimlessly
④ to the point

03 My brother became more <u>temperamental</u> after he got a better job.
① understanding
② emotional
③ confident
④ hardworking

04 The hurricane caused great <u>havoc</u> on the island.
① winds
② treatment
③ destruction
④ immersion

05 John said he was <u>obliged</u> to his neighbors for all their help.
① polite
② opposed
③ accepted
④ thankful

06 She has <u>relinquished</u> all hope of going to Europe this year.
① abandoned
② regretted
③ secured
④ pursued

07 The young man's ability was <u>attested</u> by his rapid promotion.
① confirmed
② impeached
③ protruded
④ stipulated

08 At all stages, investors will conduct credit analysis to <u>assess</u> a company's ability to repay its debt.
① facilitate
② contract
③ appraise
④ deteriorate

09 The <u>undomesticated</u> cat would not allow us to pet it.
① fatuous
② feral
③ prodigal
④ preposterous

10 The coach of a team or a leader of any organization should always be <u>moderate</u> in showing enthusiasm.
① skillful
② honest
③ passionate
④ reasonable

11 The children had been dragged to so many museums that by the time they reached the dinosaur exhibit, their response was disappointingly <u>listless</u>.
① neurotic
② pointless
③ unconcerned
④ repulsive

12 At the party, Mr. Whitaker drank whisky rather than beer, so his friends <u>designated</u> his driver for the trip home.
① appointed   ② discharged
③ deluded   ④ collected

13 Sympathy often <u>engenders</u> love.
① begets   ② beguiles
③ embroiders   ④ enlightens

14 The nature hike featured several <u>endemic</u> plants, which the guide was eager to point out.
① indigenous   ② tropical
③ significant   ④ giant

15 There is something <u>flamboyant</u> about these boots that does not suit the average Englishwoman.
① somber   ② subdued
③ showy   ④ petulant

16 She tried to <u>console</u> the people who were letting out the frantic cries but, after a while, everything fell silent.
① seduce   ② persuade
③ repress   ④ soothe

17 If the politicians make that response to these advances, everything will <u>redound</u> to their credit.
① contribute   ② overflow
③ subtract   ④ deprive

18 Juana fails to regain the affections of her <u>bumptious</u> lover Don Gil who abandons her in pursuit of a more affluent Dona Ines.
① indecisive   ② cunning
③ arrogant   ④ brutal

19 Classic operas concern themselves not with the <u>verisimilitude</u> of human emotions but with spectacle, intrigue and fate.
① abyss   ② similarity
③ authenticity   ④ vicissitude

20 Tom spent the whole day <u>polishing</u> the statue because of the misguided direction from his boss.
① offering   ② burnishing
③ capturing   ④ picturing

21 His <u>upbeat</u> attitude and preeminent work habits have been an inspiration to all of us.
① belligerent   ② laid-back
③ optimistic   ④ obsequious

22 That, of course, wasn't as clever an ending as the writer cooked up for his onstage alter ego, and he stands by the <u>assertion</u> that most of his online dating experience was awful.
① claim   ② excuse
③ suspicion   ④ brag

23 I knew that she was <u>bridled</u> by the news of my staying.
① relieved   ② surprised
③ offended   ④ saddened

24 The author wrote in a <u>limpid</u> style.
① lofty
② literary
③ lucid
④ lukewarm

25 Congress plans to <u>incorporate</u> several new provisions into the revenue bill.
① degenerate
② puncture
③ flirt
④ integrate

26 Allowing students to simply <u>regurgitate</u> the facts and figures that they find on websites like Wikipedia only dulls their critical thinking.
① repeat
② manipulate
③ distort
④ obliterate

27 A new study shows that robots are more persuasive when they're presented as a <u>peer</u>, as opposed to an authority figure.
① collage
② conductor
③ college
④ colleague

28 Many of San Francisco's <u>gaudy</u> 19th century Victorian houses were lost in the 1906 earthquake.
① showy
② enormous
③ antiquated
④ simple

29 Those who work side by side with their Russian counterparts say that strong relationships and <u>mutual</u> respect have resulted from the many years of collaboration.
① burdensome
② reciprocal
③ dithery
④ generous

30 Suspicious of too powerful a President, Americans nonetheless are <u>uneasy</u> when a President does not act decisively.
① adamant
② indifferent
③ united
④ anxious

31 The extremist organization has <u>shunned</u> conventional politics.
① thrived on
② lacked
③ demanded
④ avoided

32 The notion that income is a remedy for <u>indigence</u> has a certain forthright appeal.
① hardship
② poverty
③ industry
④ anguish

33 The Western Baseball League was a 19th-century <u>forerunner</u> of the modern major leagues.
① player
② dictator
③ transformer
④ ancestor

34 Throughout history, women have been <u>traduced</u> and silenced. Now, it's our time to tell our own stories in our own words.
① titillated
② quelled
③ maligned
④ embraced

35 For years, against all odds, women <u>tenaciously</u> fought for the right to vote.
① doggedly
② indefinitely
③ perfunctorily
④ waveringly

36 It's a <u>startling</u> statistic: the fastest-growing segment of the world population is the very old.

① emerging   ② surprising

③ pessimistic   ④ shining

37 Perhaps some will say that animals have some <u>inherent</u> value, only less than we have.

① inborn   ② superficial

③ inhuman   ④ intelligent

38 Some of technology's negative aspects are extremely hard to <u>remedy</u>.

① understand   ② identify

③ utilize   ④ correct

39 The new contract will <u>annul</u> the previous agreement between the two companies.

① support   ② avert

③ abominate   ④ nullify

40 If he'd grown up as a half-black child in South Korea, he likely would have been <u>relegated</u> to a second-class existence.

① besieged   ② terrified

③ integrated   ④ demoted

41 It was about ten years ago that Tony Adams first detected Kevin Keegan's <u>unbridled</u> passion for football.

① crafty   ② involuntary

③ unrestrained   ④ lucrative

42 Researchers <u>eliminated</u> those who reported during the interview that they never yelled at home.

① recognized   ② studied

③ experimented   ④ excluded

43 We can do far more than we think to improve our <u>odds</u> of preventing the most horrendous of catastrophes.

① endeavor   ② likelihood

③ provocation   ④ apathy

44 Young Indian girls are raised by parents who teach them not to <u>retort</u> no matter how humiliated you feel.

① ignore   ② respond

③ denounce   ④ forget

45 Last year, we would have been overjoyed to have the economic <u>buoyancy</u> we are seeing now.

① resilience   ② breach

③ potential   ④ depression

46 They had selected Harold as their director last season and he had <u>ferreted out</u> some scripts that he thought the members might like to perform.

① chimed in   ② written up

③ referred to   ④ searched for

47 Some historians argue that the British Commonwealth is a marvelous <u>testimony</u> to how injustice and oppression can be transformed into co-operation and harmony.

① exam   ② accusation

③ phenomenon   ④ proof

48 The jury will undoubtedly <u>convict</u> the culprit of grand larceny.

① condemn   ② extend

③ scorch   ④ supplant

49 Mexico seems to have failed to take quick and <u>decisive</u> action in detecting the flu epidemic and preventing its spread.

① nimble   ② unilateral

③ vigilant   ④ resolute

50 During a ten-year period, Napoleon <u>conquered</u> most of the Baltic States and Spain.

① vanquished   ② forfeited

③ transcended   ④ refuted

51 Winston Churchill is best known as a wartime leader, a clear-eyed historian and <u>an eloquent</u> orator.

① a calm   ② a fluent

③ a rational   ④ a candid

52 Since coming to a head in 2004, the high fructose corn syrup crisis and its role in the emergent obesity epidemic has faced <u>unwavering</u> denial from the food industry.

① fluctuating   ② partial

③ steadfast   ④ unprecedented

53 The fame of the film *Forrest Gump* easily <u>eclipsed</u> that of the novel on which it was based.

① exposed   ② hampered

③ mustered   ④ surpassed

54 We must prevent one person from <u>mauling</u> another.

① beating   ② cuddling

③ throwing   ④ trapping

55 A person of <u>diverse</u> interests can talk on many subjects.

① common   ② stubborn

③ different   ④ concentrated

56 The country has publicly <u>negated</u> paying any ransom money to kidnappers to secure the release of its citizens.

① validated   ② repudiated

③ accredited   ④ acquainted

57 The authors were never <u>encumbered</u> by the weight of what they did before.

① hampered   ② pampered

③ contemplated   ④ modified

58 As a work of art contains its verification in itself, <u>strained</u> concepts do not withstand the test of being turned into images.

① direct   ② not familiar

③ opposite   ④ not natural

59 The judge clearly said that the dispute should be <u>arbitrated</u>, and we should comply with that.

① determined   ② engaged

③ avoided   ④ mediated

60 Disagreement over the impending treaty caused a <u>rupture</u> in the relations of the two nations.

① fan   ② lore

③ crack   ④ crank

61 Didn't his colleagues insist his recent experiment was a <u>fabrication</u>?

① invention   ② mystery

③ failure   ④ sensation

62 You have to remember the biggest <u>asset</u> you have is your credibility.

① exhibition   ② property

③ attribute   ④ obligation

63 The cause of radical, violent anti-Westernism — the one ideological <u>trait</u> that is shared by them all — would be dealt a severe blow.

① trade   ② hostility

③ tendency   ④ sycophant

64 If the board could look past her <u>obvious</u> flaws as a candidate, they would see she has tremendous potential in the role.

① manifest   ② resplendent

③ critical   ④ composite

65 Native Americans refer to Americans of Indian <u>descent</u>.

① character   ② temperament

③ alliance   ④ lineage

66 In many problem situations, it is tempting to <u>jump to a conclusion</u> in order to quickly build a solution.

① reconsider a conclusion

② draw a rash conclusion

③ change a previous conclusion

④ fail to reach a conclusion

67 The helicopter offers a viable alternative to the often <u>congested</u> surface transportation.

① subsonic   ② meddling

③ free   ④ jammed

68 Despite any <u>nefarious</u> behavior, real or perceived, my decision to quit was actually far less sophisticated.

① stolid   ② iniquitous

③ boorish   ④ churlish

69 Opponents of nuclear energy have deep <u>misgivings</u> about its safety.

① distrust   ② mischief

③ misconception   ④ disenchantment

70 He has been charged with aggravated assault according to <u>judicial</u> sources.

① fractional   ② official

③ legal   ④ exact

71 We <u>pledge</u> our best offers to help them for whatever period is required.

① make a solemn promise of

② make a serious request for

③ recommend in a good will

④ provide a suitable solution for

72 In two-party systems, like the United States and Britain, the right is in power, but only by jettisoning the values that used to define it.
① defending   ② revising
③ discarding   ④ asserting

73 Israeli and Palestinian negotiators working with American mediators pored over every dot and comma in their drafts, delaying again an elusive agreement on Hebron.
① changed
② overlooked
③ recapitulated
④ gave close attention to

74 They would gladly purchase the emperor's protection by the sacrifice of an obnoxious fugitive.
① a lustrous   ② an anomalous
③ a disagreeable ④ a hypocritical

75 The mayor's refusal to meet with the grief-stricken family was the ultimate pusillanimous act.
① cowardly   ② treacherous
③ political   ④ immoral

76 The dealer advertised the small television set as being portable.
① movable   ② relievable
③ vivid   ④ elastic

77 We should repeal the law that gives social media sites immunity for anything their users post.
① abolish   ② enact
③ revise   ④ oppose

78 Danny's father hit the ceiling when he was informed that his son had been detained by the police for disorderly conduct.
① charged   ② murdered
③ imprisoned   ④ tormented

79 The violinist gave a creditable rendition of the concerto.
① a nonsensical   ② a laudable
③ a calamitous   ④ an inadvertent

80 His grief, which has abated for a short while, returns and rends his heart with greater force.
① fills   ② tears
③ packs   ④ reminds

81 The querulous voices of the students, who believed that their quizzes had been graded too harshly, could be heard all the way at the other end of the school building.
① sanguine   ② avaricious
③ whining   ④ servile

82 Sometimes, while living in a foreign country, one craves a special dish from home.
① eats   ② desires
③ prepares   ④ looks for

83 Citizens of India have to apply for tourist visas but this visa is issued gratis.
① in confidence   ② at random
③ for free   ④ for credit

84 The winters in Scotland are longer and darker, so hard, warm liquor provides light and respite, no matter how <u>transitory</u>.

① transcendental   ② deceptive

③ fleeting   ④ translucent

85 With so many of the world's economies in tatters, the combined might of China and India could <u>spearhead</u> global growth in the coming decades.

① endanger   ② lead

③ slow down   ④ speed up

86 We were worried that he might get hurt in training or <u>ambushed</u> by the terrorists on his journey to and back from the camp.

① hidden from sight

② spied on from afar

③ attacked by surprise

④ shadowed on sight

87 By 1929, two years after the start of the "talkies," motion picture theaters in the United States were attracting 100 million <u>patrons</u> every week.

① owners   ② actors

③ customers   ④ critics

88 To <u>expedite</u> the immigration check, please have your arrival card filled out before you approach the window.

① certify   ② prompt

③ hasten   ④ impose

89 Critics say the law is too easy to bypass because it places the <u>onus</u> on offenders to report changes in their circumstances.

① favor   ② menace

③ liability   ④ nuisance

90 I dreamt of becoming a librarian. <u>Sloth</u> and an ill-restrained fondness for travel decided otherwise.

① Indolence   ② Illness

③ Inhibition   ④ Industry

91 More than 3,000 years ago, ancient people <u>stumbled upon</u> the fact that some molds could cure disease.

① were aware of

② were intrigued by

③ learned by experimentation

④ discovered by accident

92 His strong dark eyebrows give his face an oddly <u>menacing</u> look.

① sturdy   ② gloomy

③ friendly   ④ threatening

93 U.S. military forces are getting more deeply <u>enmeshed</u> in Columbia's bloody civil war.

① encroached   ② entangled

③ embittered   ④ enlightened

94 His reasoning proved <u>needlessly repetitive</u> in its harking on the same idea.

① pathological   ② adnominal

③ dolose   ④ tautological

95 An economic model's power stems from the elimination of <u>irrelevant</u> details, which allows the economist to focus on the essential features of the economic reality he or she is attempting to understand.

① complex   ② confusing

③ specific   ④ trivial

96 The president was <u>circumspect</u> in choosing his advisors, as he knew that he would have to rely heavily on their counsel.

① cautious   ② devious

③ genuine   ④ industrious

97 The mystics have speculated about the possible existence of other worlds for a long time. They have been <u>intrigued</u> by the possibility that these unexplored, nether worlds may even be tantalizingly close, yet just beyond our physical grasp and eluding our senses.

① beleaguered   ② fascinated

③ dumbfounded   ④ nonplussed

98 The many thousands of Egyptians queueing patiently outside balloting stations for the elections that began on Nov. 28, 2011 knew they were making history: for the first time in living memory, they were being asked to vote without already knowing the outcome — a happy contrast with the electoral <u>farces</u> staged by the regime of ousted President Hosni Mubarak.

① reform   ② coup

③ process   ④ comedy

99 I felt offended when some stranger tried to be <u>officious</u> by asking private questions while waiting for the bank service. She kept offering unwanted advice about my career, and even tried to advise me about my marriage, telling me about dos and don'ts.

① judicious   ② convivial

③ courteous   ④ meddlesome

100 Columbia University, which faces a $50 million deficit, will probably <u>follow suit</u>, although the heads of 26 arts-and-sciences departments have threatened to quit if the cutbacks are too harsh.

① argue against other suggestions

② do the same as another has done

③ not have the right qualities

④ carry out legal actions

MVP

Vol.1 워크북

ACTUAL TEST
정답

MVP 01-05 ACTUAL TEST

01 ①	02 ②	03 ①	04 ①	05 ①	06 ①	07 ①	08 ①	09 ①	10 ②
11 ④	12 ③	13 ③	14 ③	15 ③	16 ④	17 ②	18 ②	19 ①	20 ①
21 ②	22 ②	23 ①	24 ①	25 ④	26 ①	27 ②	28 ②	29 ②	30 ②
31 ①	32 ④	33 ②	34 ①	35 ②	36 ①	37 ①	38 ②	39 ④	40 ④
41 ②	42 ①	43 ③	44 ③	45 ③	46 ①	47 ④	48 ③	49 ③	50 ③
51 ②	52 ①	53 ②	54 ①	55 ①	56 ④	57 ④	58 ②	59 ②	60 ①
61 ②	62 ④	63 ③	64 ④	65 ②	66 ①	67 ②	68 ①	69 ②	70 ①
71 ①	72 ③	73 ①	74 ①	75 ②	76 ②	77 ④	78 ④	79 ④	80 ②
81 ②	82 ④	83 ④	84 ④	85 ①	86 ②	87 ④	88 ②	89 ②	90 ③
91 ①	92 ④	93 ②	94 ④	95 ③	96 ④	97 ②	98 ②	99 ③	100 ①

01 ①

☐ fastidious a. 까다로운, 꼼꼼한(=meticulous) ☐ perfect a. 완벽한, 결점이 없는 ☐ tenacious a. 고집이 센, 완강한 ☐ fractious a. 성[짜증]을 잘 내는, 괴팍한

그는 창작할 때 느리고 꼼꼼했고, 그래서 그의 시는 과도할 정도의 마무리 과정을 겪었다.

02 ②

☐ cogent a. 설득력 있는(=convincing); 적절한 ☐ full of meaning 의미심장한 ☐ illustrate v. 설명하다 ☐ concise a. 간결한, 간명한 ☐ confounding a. 어리둥절하게 만드는 ☐ controversial a. 논쟁의, 논란이 많은

그 어떤 단 하나의 문장도, 아무리 그것이 설득력 있고 의미심장할지라도, 크고 중심이 되는 진실의 한 가지 측면을 설명하는 것 이상을 해낼 수는 없다.

03 ①

☐ cache v. (은닉처에) 저장하다, 숨기다(=hide) ☐ wax-moth n. 벌집나방 ☐ larva n. 애벌레, 유충(pl. larvae) ☐ taste v. 맛보다, 시식하다; 경험하다 ☐ take v. 쥐다; 획득하다 ☐ choose v. 선택하다, 고르다

그 연구에서, 그 새들은 두 종류의 먹이를 숨길 수 있었는데, 그것은 땅콩과 벌집나방 애벌레로, 그 새들이 매우 좋아하는 것들이었다.

04 ①

☐ efface v. 지우다, 삭제하다(=erase) ☐ convulse v. 진동시키다; 대소동을 일으키다 ☐ edify v. 교화하다, 계발하다 ☐ elude v. 교묘히 피하다, 벗어나다

기억을 지우는 데는 오랜 시간이 걸린다.

05 ①

☐ quote v. 인용하다, (남의 말을 그대로) 전달하다 ☐ sagacious a. 총명한, 현명한; 영리한(=wise) ☐ timid a. 겁 많은, 두려워하는, 소심한 ☐ attractive a. 사람의 마음을 끄는; 매력적인 ☐ flamboyant a. 현란한, 화려한; (색이) 혼란한

토머스(Thomas) 씨는 그 위원회에서 가장 영리한 위원으로 인용되었다.

06 ①

☐ poignant a. 통렬한, 날카로운(=sharp) ☐ racialize v. 인종화하다, 인종적 특징을 부여하다 ☐ matrix n. 매트릭스, (발생, 성장의) 모체 ☐ preposterous a. 불합리한, 비상식적인, 터무니없는 ☐ significant a. 중대한, 중요한 ☐ blended a. 혼합된

이런 선택은 특히 통렬한데, 그 영화가 매트릭스 세계와 현실 세계에 인종적 특징을 부여하기 때문이다.

07 ①

☐ discernible a. 분간할 수 있는, 인식할 수 있는; 분명한(=obvious) ☐ diagnostic a. 진단상의, 증상을 나타내는; 특징적인 ☐ careful a. 조심성 있는, 주의 깊은, 신중한 ☐ competent a. 적임의, 유능한; 적당한, 충분한

이 직원은 현재 컴퓨터 업무를 하는 데 있어서 두드러진 기술을 갖고 있지 못하지만, 우리는 그녀를 빨리 가르칠 수 있을 것이다.

08 ①

☐ damp a. 축축한, 습기찬(=dank) ☐ hot a. 뜨거운, 더운; 열렬한
☐ cold a. 추운, 찬; 냉정한 ☐ warm a. 따뜻한; 열렬한

그 성냥은 눅눅해서 그가 그것들로 불을 켤 수가 없었다.

09 ①

☐ consecutive a. 연속적인, 계속되는; 시종일관(=straight) ☐ leap
v. 뛰어오르다, 도약하다 ☐ preceding a. 앞선, 선행하는; 바로 앞의
☐ descending a. 내려가는, 강하하는

업무 경력을 쌓는 것에 대한 대학 신입생들의 관심이 4년 연속 계속해서
하락했다.

10 ②

☐ sediment n. 침전물, 앙금, 퇴적물(=deposition) ☐ ensilage n. (생
목초 따위의) 신선 보존법; (신선하게 저장된) 목초 ☐ embayment n.
만(灣) ☐ dolmen n. 고인돌

1830년 이후로, 그 강 속의 부유 퇴적물이 계속해서 늘어났다.

11 ④

☐ backbite v. 뒤에서 험담하다, 중상하다(=defame) ☐ reign v. 군림하
다, 지배하다 ☐ writhe v. 몸부림치다 ☐ dissemble v. (진짜 감정·의도
를) 숨기다, 가식적으로 꾸미다

사람들은 때때로 다른 사람들에 대해 불친절한 말을 하며 험담하는 경향
이 있다.

12 ③

☐ agitate v. 선동하다, 교란하다, 동요시키다(=disturb) ☐ irritate v.
초조하게 하다, 안달하게 하다 ☐ scare v. 위협하다, 깜짝 놀라게 하다
☐ confuse v. 혼동하다, 당황하게 하다

할머니가 돌아가시면 칼(Carl)과 마틴(Martin)이 재산을 상속받을 것이
다. 이 생각은 그녀를 심란하게 한다.

13 ③

☐ spontaneously ad. 자발적으로, 자연스럽게(=without being forced)
☐ excluding prep. ~을 제외하고 ☐ exceptional a. 예외적인 ☐
with great pleasure 대단히 기쁘게 ☐ with much difficulty 간신히,
겨우 ☐ at an unbelievable speed 믿을 수 없는 속도로

예외적인 상황을 제외하면, 어릴 적에 아이들은 자연적으로 언어를 습
득한다.

14 ③

☐ genial a. 상냥한 ☐ perennial a. (아주 오랫동안) 지속되는(=lasting)
☐ contestant n. (대회 등의) 참가자 ☐ industrious a. 부지런한
☐ willing a. 기꺼이 하는 ☐ indulgent a. 멋대로 하게 하는

항상 상냥했고 공정했지만, 그는 학생들이 자기를 좋아하게 만들려고
시도하지 않았다. 그는 마치 인기 경연대회의 지속적인 참가자이기라도
한 것처럼 행동하지는 않았다.

15 ③

☐ kidnapping n. 유괴, 납치 ☐ malefactor n. 죄인, 범인, 악인
(=culprit) ☐ insurgent n. 폭도, 반란자 ☐ dilettante n. 아마추어
애호가 ☐ agitator n. 선동자, (정치) 운동자

유괴 사건을 수사하고 있던 경찰은 범인의 신원을 확인하지 못했다.

16 ④

☐ imperative n. 명령; 필요(성), 의무, 책무(=demand) ☐ purpose
n. 목적, 의지, 용도, 요점 ☐ impact n. 충돌; 충격; 영향(력) ☐
comment n. 논평, 주석, 설명

유색 인종과 여성에 관해 글을 쓴 작가들은, 자신들과 또 자신들처럼 역
사 속에서 침묵을 지켜왔던 다른 사람들을 대변해달라는 요구에 점차
더 응하게 되었다.

17 ②

☐ acerbic a. (성질, 표현 등이) 가혹한, 신랄한(=pungent) ☐ submit
v. 제출하다 ☐ previous a. 앞의, 이전의; 사전의 ☐ slovenly a. 단정치
못한 ☐ verbose a. 장황한 ☐ irrelevant a. 무관한, 상관없는

신문이 그의 편지를 싣지 않았는데, 편지 내용이 너무 신랄하기 때문이
거나 지난번 편지가 실린 후 너무 일찍 또 제출되었기 때문이다.

18 ②

☐ solidify v. 공고히 하다, 강화하다(=strengthen) ☐ dissolve v. 녹이
다, 용해하다; 해산하다 ☐ embrace v. 받아들이다, 수용하다 ☐
paralyze v. 마비시키다; 무력하게 하다

치누아 아체베(Chinua Achebe)는 나이지리아의 수많은 문제들이 여
전히 해결되지 않은 상태로 남아있다는 이유로 나이지리아 정부의 국가
훈장을 두 번이나 거부했다. 이는 원칙을 궁극적으로 고수하는 사람이
라는 그의 평판을 오히려 더 확고하게 해주었다.

19 ①

☐ negotiator n. 교섭자, 협상자 ☐ mediate v. 조정하다, 중재하다, 화해시키다(=interpose) ☐ intercept v. 도중에서 잡다, 빼앗다, 가로채다 ☐ immediate a. 즉석[즉시]의; 당면한 ☐ impose v. 지우다, 부과하다; 강요[강제]하다

양쪽의 중재를 위해 협상자들을 불러들였다.

20 ①

☐ elaborate v. 상세히 설명하다, 부연하다(=explain) ☐ give up 단념하다, 체념하다; 항복하다 ☐ sue v. 고소하다, 소송을 제기하다 ☐ criticize v. 비평하다; 비난하다

모하마디 애쉬티아니(Mohammadi Ashtiani)는 취재기자들에게 (독일 주간지) 빌트 암 존탁(Bild am Sonntag) 기자들이 자신을 '당황하게 했었다'라고 말했지만 상세히 설명하기를 거절했다.

21 ②

☐ plebeian a. 평민의, 서민의(=common) ☐ patrician a. 귀족의, 귀족적인 ☐ lugubrious a. 침울한, 가련한, 애처로운 ☐ cordial a. 화기애애한, 다정한

그의 연설은 서민의 정신과 감정을 겨냥한 것이었다.

22 ②

☐ emaciated a. 수척한, 야윈(=lean) ☐ corpulent a. 뚱뚱한, 살찐, 비만한 ☐ lucrative a. 유리한, 수지맞는, 돈이 벌리는 ☐ charming a. 매력적인, 아름다운

대중문화에서, 야윈 패션모델들은 여성의 아름다움에 대한 기준으로 간주된다.

23 ①

☐ knack n. 숙련된 기교, 솜씨; 요령 ☐ legerdemain n. 재주; 속임수(=trickery) ☐ trend n. 경향, 동향, 추세 ☐ glibness n. 말을 잘함, 입심이 좋음; 경박함 ☐ logic n. 논리, 논법

논쟁에 어떤 요령이나 속임수가 있다.

24 ①

☐ chlorofluorocarbon n. 염화불화탄소 화합물, 프레온 가스(Freon gas) ☐ imminent a. 금방이라도 닥칠 듯한, 임박한(=impending) ☐ feel compelled to ~를 꼭 해야 한다, ~하지 않으면 안 된다고 생각하다 ☐ distant a. 거리가 먼, 동떨어진 ☐ delayed a. 지연된 ☐ avoidable a. 피할 수 있는

그 발견은 프레온 가스 생산을 중단시키기 위한 강력한 정치적 조치가 임박했음을 암시했는데, 다행스럽게도 화학업계는 더 이상 그러한 조치에 반대해야 한다고 생각하지 않았다.

25 ④

☐ semblance n. 외형, 외관, 겉모습(=appearance) ☐ serenity n. 평온, 차분 ☐ take hold 뿌리내리다, 자리 잡다 ☐ enmity n. 증오, 원한 ☐ assembly n. 집회; 의회 ☐ ensemble n. 합창[합주]; 합창단

우리의 인생이 평온한 모습이어야 한다는 생각이 자리를 잡아가는 것 같다.

26 ①

☐ exceed v. 넘다, 초과하다(=be more than) ☐ be less than ~보다 적다, ~보다 덜하다 ☐ equal v. ~와 같다, 필적하다, 못지않다 ☐ approach v. 가까이 가다, 접근하다

2000년까지 저 수치는 15억을 넘을 것 같다.

27 ②

☐ ensure v. 반드시 ~하게 하다, 보장[보증]하다 ☐ perspective n. 관점, 견지, 시각(=overview) ☐ conviction n. 신념, 확신; 유죄 판결 ☐ interpretation n. 해석, 이해, 설명 ☐ appreciation n. (올바른) 평가, 판단; 진가의 인정; 감상

훈련은 한 개인이 자기 주변에서 일어나는 일들에 대해 올바른 관점을 가질 수 있게 해주는 비결이다.

28 ②

☐ PAS 파스(결핵의 특효약, para-aminosalicylic acid) ☐ spiritual a. 정신의; 영적인 ☐ intuition n. 직관(력); 직관적 통찰(=hunch) ☐ falsification n. 위조, 변조 ☐ reason n. 이유, 동기 ☐ calculation n. 계산; 추정

PAS의 발견에 대한 그의 이야기는 체계적인 추론보다 과학적인 직관에 기초한 영적인 비전에 더 가깝게 읽혀진다.

29 ②

☐ definite a. 한정된, 확정된, 일정한; 명확한(=obvious) ☐ careful a. 조심성 있는, 주의 깊은 ☐ minor a. 작은, 적은 편의; 중요치 않은 ☐ vague a. 막연한, 모호한, 애매한

그녀의 얼굴 표정은 뭔가가 잘못되었음을 분명히 드러냈다.

30 ②

□ deadlock n. 막힘, 막다른 골목; 교착 상태(=standstill) □ majority n. 대부분, 대다수, 과반수 □ turning point n. 전환점; 전환기; 위기, 고비 □ upgrade n. 오르막; 증가, 향상, 상승

국회로부터의 소식은 일종의 정치적 교착상태의 신호일 것이다.

31 ①

□ publicly ad. 공공연하게, 공개적으로 □ denounce v. 비난하다; 고발하다(=condemn) □ celebrate v. 축하하다, 기리다 □ depict v. 그리다, 묘사하다 □ acknowledge v. 인정하다, 승인하다 □ humiliate v. 굴욕감을 느끼게 하다, 창피를 주다

대통령은 미중앙정보부(CIA) 국장의 불법 행동을 공식적으로는 비난했지만 사적으로는 칭찬했다.

32 ④

□ plummet v. 떨어지다; 폭락[급락]하다(=decline) □ establish v. 설립하다, 수립하다 □ resume v. 재개하다, 다시 시작하다 □ grow v. 커지다, 자라다, 증가하다

그의 주변의 경기는 곤두박질쳤지만, 그 회사의 사업은 호황을 누리고 있었다.

33 ②

□ penchant n. 경향; 기호(=definite liking) □ tidbit n. 맛있는 가벼운 음식, (맛있는 것의) 한 입 □ leap v. 뛰어오르다 □ windowsill n. 창턱, 창 아래틀 □ discipline n. 훈련; 학문 □ lack of appreciation 감사의 결여 □ abhorrence n. 혐오, 증오

분명히 그 고양이는 햇살이 비치는 창과 참치 음식을 좋아한다. 그 고양이는 생선 냄새를 맡으면 언제나 부엌 창턱에서 뛰어내려 자기 음식으로 뛰어간다.

34 ①

□ ambivalence n. 반대 감정의 공존, 애증, 양면가치(=indecision) □ atrophy n. 위축(증); 쇠약 □ apathy n. 무관심, 냉담 □ cynicism n. 냉소, 비꼼

작가들은 종종 반대나 동의를 표현하는 것에 대해서 만큼이나 양쪽 모두를(양쪽 사이에서 주저함을) 표현하는 것에 대해서도 많이 우려한다.

35 ②

□ languish v. 쇠약해지다, 시들다(=decline) □ filthy a. 불결한, 더러운; 부정한 □ abuse n. 남용, 오용, 학대 □ brutality n. 잔인, 무자비;

야만적 행위 □ flourish v. 번영하다, 번성하다 □ ameliorate v. 좋아지다, 고쳐지다 □ degrade v. 지위가 떨어지다, 타락하다

경찰의 학대와 만행을 겪으며 그들은 더러운 교도소 안에서 쇠약해졌다.

36 ①

□ ingenuous a. 솔직담백한; 순진한(=guileless) □ intrepid a. 대담한, 용기 있는 □ unscientific a. 비과학적인; 과학적 지식이 없는 □ fanciful a. 공상에 잠기는; 변덕스러운

당신이 그와 같은 어리석은 이야기를 믿으려면 아주 순진해야 할 것이다.

37 ①

□ veganism n. 채식주의 □ virtuous a. 도덕적인, 고결한 □ vanity n. 자만심, 허영심(=conceit) □ undeniable a. 부인[부정]할 수 없는 □ obesity n. 비만 □ impulse n. 충동 □ circumstance n. 상황, 환경

사람들은 도덕적인 이유들로 엄격한 채식주의를 하지만, 허영심 또한 부인할 수 없는 역할을 한다.

38 ②

□ whimsical a. 변덕스러운; 엉뚱한 □ zeal n. 열중, 열의, 열심; 열정(=passion) □ rehabilitate v. 명예[평판]를 회복시키다 □ direction n. 지도; 감독; 방향 □ requirement n. 요구, 필요; 필요조건, 자격 □ tendency n. 경향, 풍조

역사가 안내자라면, 오바마(Obama)가 최고사령관으로서 더 나쁘게 지낼수록, 전직 최고사령관으로서는 더 잘 빛날 것이다. "엉뚱하게 들리겠지만, 사실입니다"라고 역사가 리처드 노튼 스미스(Richard Norton Smith)는 말한다. 좋지 않게 끝을 맺는 행정부는 유산을 원래대로 회복시키려는 동등한 크기의 정반대의 열정을 만들어낸다고 스미스는 말하고 있다.

39 ④

□ impose v. 지우다, 부과하다; 강요하다(=force) □ lift v. 들어올리다, 추켜올리다; 향상시키다 □ imply v. 함축하다, 암시하다; 의미하다 □ change v. 바꾸다, 변경하다, 고치다

너의 요구를 우리에게 떠맡기지 마라.

40 ④

☐ generate v. 일으키다, 초래하다(=bring about) ☐ improvement n. 개선, 진보, 향상 ☐ carry on ~을 계속하다 ☐ count on ~을 믿다, 의지하다 ☐ come across 마주치다; 우연히 발견하다

효과적인 분석과 공인받은 기술이 큰 발전을 가져올 수 있다.

41 ②

☐ gadget n. 간단한 장치; 도구, 부속품(=gizmo) ☐ bits of 하찮은, 조그마한 ☐ wizardry n. 마법, 마술; 뛰어난 묘기; 하이테크 제품 ☐ chew up 소비하다, 먹어치우다 ☐ molder v. 썩다, 타락하다; 하는 일 없이 때를 보내다 ☐ scythe v. ~을 큰 낫으로 베다 ☐ commodity n. 일용품, 필수품, 물자 ☐ technique n. (전문) 기술; 기법 ☐ ganoid n. <어류> 경린어(硬鱗魚)

그러한 모든 시간 절약 장치에 관해, 많은 사람들은 자신들이 교통체증에 갇혀 하는 일 없이 시간을 보내고 있든, 자동 음성 메시지 시스템을 탐색하고 있든, 혹은 이메일을 삭제하고 있든, 이들 작은 첨단제품이 너무 많은 시간을 소비하게 만든다고 불평한다.

42 ①

☐ embody v. 구체화하다, 구체적으로 나타내다 ☐ flagrant a. 명백한; 악명 높은, 이름난(=blatant) ☐ hypocrisy n. 위선; 위선적 행위 ☐ contradictory a. 모순된, 양립하지 않는 ☐ flaming a. 불타는, 과장된, 현란한 ☐ unethical a. 비윤리적인, 도리에 어긋나는

병이 낫기를 애쓰는 내가 담배를 피우고 있으니 이게 뭐하는 짓이지? 이런 행위는 명백한 위선이야!

43 ③

☐ pecuniary a. 금전상의, 재정상의(=monetary); 벌금형의 ☐ strict a. 엄격한; 꼼꼼한 ☐ civil a. 시민의, 문명의, 민정의 ☐ discretionary a. 임의의, 자유재량의

형법에서 벌금형이란 법원의 결정에 따라 범죄자에게 부과되는 금전상의 형벌이다.

44 ③

☐ miscellaneous a. 여러 가지 종류의, 이것저것 잡다한(=diverse) ☐ rare a. 드문, 진기한 ☐ sound a. 건전한, 정상적인 ☐ interesting a. 흥미 있는, 재미있는

22개 언어로 된 다양한 수준의 시청각 학습강좌와 몇몇 언어로 된 문학 자료, 역사학 자료, 정치학 자료, 문화 자료를 포함한 많은 양의 다양한 기록물 소장품을 잘 갖춘 CD 도서관이 있다.

45 ③

☐ tamper v. 간섭하다; (서류 등을) 함부로 변경하다(=interfere) ☐ solemnly ad. 장엄하게; 진지하게 ☐ deliberation n. 심의 ☐ amend v. 개정하다; 고치다 ☐ upgrade v. 개선하다, 품질을 높이다 ☐ imply v. 넌지시 나타내다, 암시하다 ☐ guarantee v. 보장하다, 약속하다

그들은 이 중요한 문서가 가볍게 변경되지 말고, 진지하게 적절한 공지와 심의를 거쳐 조심스럽게 수정되는 것을 원할지도 모른다.

46 ①

☐ subsystem n. 하부조직, 하부시스템 ☐ nascent a. 발생하려고 하는, 초기의(=dawning) ☐ have ~ in common 공통으로[공동으로] 갖고 있다 ☐ confidential a. 은밀한, 기밀의 ☐ expensive a. 값비싼; 사치스러운 ☐ dangerous a. 위험한, 위태로운

이들 하위 시스템 각각에는 두 가지 신생 기술이 공통적으로 들어 있다.

47 ④

☐ acceptable a. 받아들일 수 있는; 허용[용인]되는 ☐ abbreviate v. 단축하다(=shorten), 생략하다 ☐ omit v. 빠뜨리다, 생략하다 ☐ explain v. 설명하다 ☐ forge v. 꾸며내다, 날조하다

공식적인 글에서 단어를 축약해서 쓰는 것은 거의 용인되지 않는다.

48 ③

☐ have a way of ~ing ~하는 습관을 갖고 있다 ☐ ceaseless a. 끊임없는, 부단한(=continuous) ☐ nervous tension 신경의 긴장 ☐ serious a. 진지한, 심각한 ☐ anxious a. 걱정스러운, 불안한 ☐ emotional a. 감정적인, 정서의

로렌(Lauren)은 고개를 들고 두리번거리는 습관이 있었는데 이것은 조심성을 암시하기보다는 일종의 끊임없는 신경의 긴장을 암시하는 행동이었다.

49 ③

☐ wayward a. 제멋대로인; 변덕스러운(=erratic) ☐ discursive a. 두서없는, 산만한 ☐ inquisitive a. 탐구심이 많은 ☐ prosaic a. 평범한; 세속적인

그의 변덕스러운 행동은 사람들이 그를 판단할 때 종종 혼란스럽게 만든다.

50 ③

□ elect v. (투표 따위로) 선거하다, 선임하다 □ hold ~ accountable for … …의 책임을 ~에게 지우다 □ accountable a. (행위 등에 대해) 책임이 있는(=responsible) □ corruption n. 타락; 부패(행위) □ predictable a. 예언[예상]할 수 있는 □ appropriate a. 적합한, 적절한 □ grateful a. 감사하고 있는, 고마워하는

우리가 선출된 대표들에게 그들의 행동에 대한 책임을 지우지 않는다면, 정치권의 부패는 계속될 것이다.

51 ②

□ tactile a. 촉각의, 만질 수 있는(=touchable) □ statue n. 상(像), 조각상 □ twirl v. 빙빙 돌리다 □ sensible a. 분별 있는 □ flexible a. 구부리기 쉬운; 유연성이 있는 □ valuable a. 귀중한; 값비싼

그 아동 미술관은 기어오를 수 있는 조각상과 빙글빙글 돌릴 수 있는 모빌 같이 만질 수 있는 예술품으로 가득 차 있었다.

52 ①

□ hideous a. 무서운, 두려운; 끔찍스러운, 무시무시한(=dreadful) □ howl v. (개, 이리가) 울다, 울부짖다 □ lodge n. 오두막, 산장

오두막집 문가에서 울부짖는 늑대 소리에 그날 밤은 끔찍했다.

53 ②

□ amenable a. 순종하는, 따르는(=agreeable) □ visible a. 눈에 보이는; 명백한 □ feasible a. 실행할 수 있는; 그럴듯한 □ audible a. 들리는, 청취할 수 있는

인도에서 갤럽 조사에 따르면, 인도인들은 중국과의 관계 개선에 적대적이기보다 호의적으로 받아들이고 있으며, 중국의 영향력 증대가 인도에 이익이 된다는 것을 보여준다.

54 ①

□ unanimous a. 만장일치의, 이의 없는 □ hail v. 환호하며 맞이하다; 축하하다(=applaud) □ libertarian n. 자유론자(시민의 자유를 옹호하는 자) □ forestall v. 미연에 방지하다, 기선을 제압하다 □ repulse v. 논박하다; 거절하다 □ overturn v. 뒤집어엎다, 전복시키다

그 만장일치의 판결은 언론의 자유를 쟁취하기 위한 투쟁에 있어 주목할 만한 순간으로 시민권 옹호자들에게 환영받았다.

55 ①

□ timidity n. 겁 많음; 소심, 수줍음(=fearfulness) □ try somebody/something out ~을 (~에게) 테스트해[시험적으로 사용해] 보다 □

□ reverence n. 숭상, 존경; 경의, 경외 □ inclination n. 경향, 기질, 성향 □ impulse n. 추진(력); 자극; 충동; 욕구

그 수줍은 아이의 타고난 겁이 많은 성격은 그녀가 그 팀에 들어가기 위한 적격 시험을 보는 것을 두려워하게 만들었다.

56 ④

□ delegate n. 대표자, 대리(인) □ hammer out ~에 대해 타결을 보다 □ shrewd a. 빈틈없는, 기민한, 약삭빠른, 영리한(=clever) □ practical a. 실제의; 실용적인; 실질적인 □ unfair a. 공정치 못한; 부정한, 부정직한 □ important a. 중요한, 의미 있는; 유력한

대표자들은 고생하며 생각한 끝에 합의에 도달했지만 사실은 약삭빠른 타협이었다.

57 ④

□ aggravate v. 악화시키다(=worsen) □ impede v. 지연시키다, 방해하다 □ prevent v. 막다, 방지하다 □ destroy v. 파괴하다, 말살하다

야당은 그 새로운 조치가 이미 불안정한 상태에 있는 국내 노동 시장을 악화시키고 노동자들의 생계를 위협할 것이라고 주장한다.

58 ③

□ calamity n. 재난, 불행(=mishap) □ acuity n. 명민함, (사고·시각·청각의) 예리함 □ discernment n. 식별, 인식; 통찰력 □ prospect n. 가망, 예상

한 평론가는 그녀의 비할 데 없는 불행에 대해 다음과 같이 적었다. "당신은 이 인간 파멸의 소재(이야기)를 잊기 힘들 것입니다."

59 ②

□ tenet n. 주의(主義); 교의(敎義)(=doctrine) □ traitor n. 배반자, 반역자 □ figure n. 숫자; 형태, 형상 □ core n. 핵심, 중심

우리가 가진 전략의 주된 신조는 각종 보안책임을 이라크 군에 넘기는 것이다.

60 ①

□ adversary n. 적, 반대자; 상대편(=enemy) □ speaker n. 말하는 사람, 연설자 □ partner n. 동료, 협력자 □ observer n. 관찰자; 관측자

베트남 전쟁과 워터게이트 사건 이후로 저널리스트들은 정부의 적이 되었다.

61 ②

☐ traditional a. 전통적인 ☐ reluctance n. 마지못해 함, (하기)싫음 ☐ turn away 외면하다, 쫓아버리다 ☐ thrifty a. 검소한, 절약하는 (=frugal) ☐ prospective a. 가망이 있는; 장래의 ☐ scrupulous a. 세심한, 꼼꼼한 ☐ demanding a. 너무 많은 요구를 하는

그 회사가 전통적으로 판촉 상품을 제공하는 것을 주저하는 것은 검소한 소비자들을 외면하는 것이었다.

62 ④

☐ macabre a. 섬뜩한, 으스스한(=grisly) ☐ stodgy a. 소화가 잘 안 되는; 지루한 ☐ paranormal a. 과학으로는 설명할 수 없는 ☐ riveting a. 황홀케 하는, 매혹적인

그 화가의 그림들은 종종 무시무시하고 불안한 이미지를 특징으로 하는 섬뜩한 분위기의 장면들을 묘사했다.

63 ③

☐ the following year 이듬해, 그 다음해 ☐ elevate v. (들어) 올리다; 승진[승격]시키다 ☐ cause n. 사회적 이상, 대의명분 ☐ respite n. 일시적 중단[휴지]; 연기; (사형의) 집행유예(=reprieve) ☐ respect n. 존경, 존중 ☐ recognition n. 인식, 인정 ☐ rejection n. 거절, 거부

이듬해 그가 받은 노벨 평화상은 그의 대의명분을 세계에 드높였지만, 그것이 그에게 중국 정부의 형 집행유예를 가져다주지는 못했다.

64 ④

☐ celebrity n. 연예인 ☐ gossip n. (나쁜 의미로) 남에 대한 소문, 험담 ☐ mendacious a. 거짓의, 허위인(=deceitful) ☐ propaganda n. 선전 ☐ provocative a. 도발적인, 자극적인 ☐ reasonable a. 합리적인, 분별 있는 ☐ aggressive a. 공격적인, 호전적인

인터넷 뉴스는 사실이라기보다는 연예인들에 대한 무의미한 가십과 거짓된 정치선전으로 넘쳐나고 있다.

65 ②

☐ lackadaisical a. 부주의한, 게으른, 나태한, 기력이 없는(=languid) ☐ tranquil a. 고요한, 평범한 ☐ vigilant a. 바짝 경계하는, 조금도 방심하지 않는 ☐ attentive a. 주의[귀]를 기울이는; 배려하는

경기 후 감독은 선수들의 정신이 나태한 모습을 질책했다.

66 ①

☐ polemic n. 논쟁, 반론(=contention) ☐ chatter n. 수다, 지껄임 ☐ scrutiny n. 정밀 조사, 철저한 검토 ☐ escapade n. 무모한 장난

그 주제는 우리가 논쟁을 벌이기에는 너무 중대한 것이다.

67 ②

☐ pretext n. 구실, 핑계 ☐ smugly ad. 잘난 체하며 ☐ scoff at 비웃다, 조소하다(=sneer at) ☐ contemplate v. 고려하다, 심사숙고하다 ☐ notice v. 주목하다, 관심을 기울이다 ☐ denounce v. 맹렬히 비난하다

적어도 일부 사람들에게 브렉시트(Brexit)는 현재 다수가 그것에 찬성했던 지역들의 운명에 대해 그저 뒤로 물러서서 잘난 체하며 비웃을 수 있는 구실이다.

68 ①

☐ negotiate v. 교섭하다, 협상하다(=discuss) ☐ nibble v. 조금씩 물어뜯다, 갉아먹다; 서서히 잠식하다 ☐ inform v. 알리다, 통지하다; 정보를 제공하다 ☐ agree v. 동의하다, 찬성하다

우리는 마을까지 요금이 적게 드는 가격으로 갈 수 있도록 택시 기사와 흥정하기로 했다.

69 ②

☐ ponderous a. 대단히 무거운; 답답한, 지루한(=dull) ☐ intricate a. 뒤얽힌, 얽히고설킨; 착잡한 ☐ meticulous a. 지나치게 세심한, 매우 신중한; 소심한 ☐ critical a. 비평의, 평론의; 비판적인

학자로서 그녀는 영국의 도덕과 풍습에 관한 장황한 논문을 많이 썼지만, 그녀는 가벼운 추리소설을 쓰는 베스트셀러 소설가로 부(富)를 축적했다.

70 ①

☐ salubrious a. (기후, 토지 따위가) 건강에 좋은, 살기 좋은(=pleasant) ☐ frigid a. 추운, 극한의; 냉담한 ☐ variable a. 변하기 쉬운, 변덕스러운; 변화무쌍한 ☐ inhospitable a. 대접이 나쁜, 불친절한; 비바람을 피할 데가 없는, 황량한

그 지역은 겨울에 특히 쾌적했다.

71 ①

☐ receiving line (리셉션 따위에서의) 손님을 영접하는 주최자들의 늘어선 열(列) ☐ trite a. 흔해 빠진, 진부한, 케케묵은(=hackneyed) ☐ exhausted a. 소모된; 고갈된; 기운이 빠진 ☐ vacant a. 공허한, 비어 있는 ☐ tepid a. 미지근한; 열의 없는

하객들이 늘어선 줄이 끝나갈 무렵엔, 신랑과 신부의 감사 인사가 진부하고 지친 듯이 들렸다.

72 ③

☐ abhor v. 몹시 싫어하다, 혐오하다(=hate) ☐ physical appearance 신체적 외모 ☐ prefer v. 더 좋아하다, 선호하다 ☐ reconcile v. 화해시키다, 조화시키다 ☐ imagine v. 상상하다, 가정하다

대부분의 여권주의자들은 여성이 신체 외모로 판단된다는 생각을 혐오한다.

73 ①

☐ boorish a. 투박한, 교양 없는(=unrefined) ☐ retentive a. 기억력이 좋은 ☐ susceptible a. 민감한, 예민한 ☐ unilateral a. 일방적인, 단독의

정찬에서 그가 보인 교양 없는 행동은 그가 그러한 자리에 올바른 예의가 부족하다는 것을 분명히 보여줬다.

74 ①

☐ formulate v. 공식화하다 ☐ in earnest 진지하게, 진심으로 (=seriously); 본격적으로 ☐ originally ad. 원래; 최초에; 최초부터 ☐ theoretically ad. 이론상으로 ☐ primarily ad. 첫째로, 우선; 본래

미국 여성들에 의한 선거권 요구는 세네카 폭포 회의(Seneca Falls Convention)에서 최초로 진지하게 공식화되었다.

75 ③

☐ scold v. 야단치다, 꾸짖다(=chide) ☐ shout out 큰소리로 말하다 ☐ corrugate v. 물결 모양으로 주름 잡다, 주름지게 하다 ☐ consort v. 조화하다; 교제하다 ☐ cinch v. ~을 허리에 단단히 매다; ~을 확실히 하다

교사들은 특히 수학과 과학 수업시간에 큰소리로 답하는 여학생들을 꾸짖는 경향이 있었다.

76 ②

☐ secede from ~에서 정식으로 탈퇴하다(=withdraw from) ☐ benefit from ~으로부터 이익을 얻다 ☐ terminate v. 끝나다, 종결하다 ☐ discriminate against 차별대우를 하다

미국 남부 여러 주(州)는 1860년에 미합중국 연방으로부터 탈퇴했다.

77 ④

☐ camouflage v. 위장하다; 눈가림하다(=conceal) ☐ captivate v. 현혹시키다, 매혹하다, 마음을 사로잡다 ☐ care for ~을 돌보다; 좋아하다, 바라다 ☐ confident a. 확신하는; 자신 있는, 자신만만한

뱀의 나머지 부분은 마른 잎으로 잘 위장되기 때문에, 개구리나 도마뱀이 뱀 꼬리에 관심을 집중하고 그 꼬리를 먹을 수 있는 어떤 것으로 오인할 때 뱀의 먹이가 된다.

78 ④

☐ simultaneously ad. 동시에, 일제히(=concurrently) ☐ respectively ad. 각각, 제각기 ☐ in turn 차례로 ☐ immediately ad. 곧, 즉각

두 어린이가 선생님의 질문에 동시에 대답했다.

79 ④

☐ civilization n. 문명 ☐ affair n. 일, 사건, 행사 ☐ illustrate v. 설명하다, 예증하다 ☐ aspiration n. 포부, 대망, 열망(=desire) ☐ suspicion n. 혐의, 용의, 의심 ☐ inspiration n. 영감; 고취, 고무, 격려 ☐ articulation n. 또렷한 발음; 명확한 표현

새로운 문명은 항상 만들어지고 있다. 오늘날 우리가 향유하고 있는 상황은 더 나은 문명을 위한 각 세대의 열망에 어떤 일이 일어나는지를 설명해준다.

80 ②

☐ tacit a. 암묵적인, 무언의(=implied) ☐ expressed a. 표현된 ☐ outspoken a. 거침없이 말하는 ☐ unanimous a. 만장일치의

그들이 겪었던 대단히 충격적인 경험을 언급하지 말자는 암묵적인 합의가 생존자들 사이에 있었다.

81 ②

☐ facilitate v. 가능하게[용이하게] 하다(=make easy) ☐ optimum a. 가장 알맞은, 최적의 ☐ fabrication n. 제작, 구성 ☐ autonomous driving 자율 주행 ☐ go along with 찬성하다, 동조하다 ☐ put into action 행동에 옮기다 ☐ put in jeopardy 위험에 빠뜨리다

그 결과는 안전한 자율 주행을 위해 요구되는 감지 장치의 최적 설계와 제작을 용이하게 할지도 모른다.

82 ④

☐ facade n. 표면, 외관, 겉보기(=appearance) ☐ calmness n. 평온, 침착 ☐ dimension n. 차원; 크기, 부피 ☐ beauty n. 아름다움, 미(美)

외면과 내적 갈등 사이의 긴장은 문학과 심리학의 중심 주제이다.

83 ④

□ corpulent a. 뚱뚱한, 비만한(=obese) □ susceptible a. 여지가 있는; 민감한; 감염되기 쉬운 □ heart disease 심장병 □ hazardous a. 모험적인, 위험한, 운에 맡기는 □ misguided a. 잘못 지도된, 잘못 안 □ boring a. 지루한, 따분한

살찐 사람은 대개 심장병에 더 걸리기 쉽다.

84 ④

□ envision v. 마음속에 그리다[상상하다] □ dodge v. 기피[회피]하다 □ pitfall n. 함정, 곤란(=peril) □ query n. 문의, 의문 □ qualm n. 불안, 염려 □ restraint n. 규제, 통제

성공은 때때로 먼 꿈처럼 보일 수 있지만, 그는 모든 어려움을 피하는 자신을 상상한다.

85 ①

□ accuse v. 고발[기소, 비난]하다, 혐의를 제기하다 □ vulnerability n. 약점이 있음, 취약성 □ illicit a. 불법의, 부정한(=illegal) □ imminent a. 절박한, 급박한 □ irresponsible a. 책임이 없는; 무책임한 □ immediate a. 즉각적인; 당면한, 목전의

화웨이(Huawei)는 소프트웨어와 하드웨어에 비밀스러운 취약점인 '백도어(뒷문)'를 남겨두어 개인 정보에의 불법적인 접근을 허용했다는 비난을 오랫동안 받아왔다.

86 ②

□ treaty n. 협정, 조약 □ adjacent a. 부근의, 인접한(=neighboring) □ demilitarize v. 비무장화하다 □ border n. 경계, 국경 □ warring a. 서로 싸우는; 적대하는 □ affiliated a. 관련 있는; 가맹[가입]한; 제휴[합병]한 □ protracted a. (예상·평상시보다) 오래 끈[오래 계속된]

평화조약에 서명한 후, 두 인접 국가들은 그들이 공유하고 있는 국경을 비무장지대로 만들었다.

87 ④

□ hermit n. 수행자; 은자 □ abandon v. 그만두다, 포기하다(=give up) □ earthly a. 세속적인, 속세의 □ postpone v. 연기하다 □ curse v. 저주하다 □ anticipate v. 예상하다

영적인 자유를 얻기 위하여 그 은자는 세속적 쾌락을 포기한다.

88 ②

□ sacred a. 신성한; 존중받는(=treated with great reverence) □ based on moral obligation 도덕적 의무에 근거를 둔 □ very distinguished 아주 두드러진, 현저한 □ introspect v. 자기 반성하다

고대 그리스인들에게 신성한 곳이라 여겨졌던 델로스 섬은 큰 노예시장이 되었다.

89 ②

□ illuminate v. 조명하다; (문제 따위를) 설명[해명]하다(=elucidate) □ exclude v. 제외하다, 배제하다 □ disguise v. 변장하다, 가장하다 □ obfuscate v. (마음·머리를) 어둡게 하다

그 토론의 세부사항들은 전 세계 국가들이 에너지 조합에서 석탄을 제거할 때 직면하게 될 주된 장애들을 설명한다.

90 ③

□ sanitary a. 위생의, 보건상의; 위생적인(=hygienic) □ quiet a. 조용한, 고요한 □ bright a. 빛나는; 맑은 □ reasonable a. 분별 있는

나는 광주의 작고 그다지 위생적이지 않은 한 카페에 앉아 있었다.

91 ①

□ chew v. (음식을) 씹다(=masticate) □ swallow v. 삼키다; 곧이곧대로 믿다 □ abacinate v. (처벌이나 고문으로) 눈이 멀게하다 □ fornicate v. 간통하다, 간음하다 □ impennate a. (새가) 날 수 없는

좋은 부모라면 모두가 자녀들이 음식을 삼키기 전에 잘 씹도록 가르쳐야 한다.

92 ④

□ extent n. 정도; 범위, 한도 □ capacity n. 수용력 □ negotiate v. 협상하다, 교섭하다 □ bilateral a. 쌍방의, 쌍무적인; 양쪽의(=mutual) □ active a. 활동적인; 적극적인 □ multilateral a. 다자간의 □ concentrated a. 집중적인, 결연한

수용양의 한도는 상호간의 협정을 통해 결정될 예정이었다.

93 ②

□ face to face 마주 대하여; ~에 직면하여; ~와 충돌하여 □ obdurate a. 고집 센, 완강한(=unyielding) □ sacrifice v. 희생시키다; 단념하다 □ innocent n. 결백한 사람; 순결한 사람 □ odious a. 혐오스러운, 끔찍한; 불쾌한 □ obsequious a. 아첨하는; 비굴한 □ insidious a. 음흉한, 방심할 수 없는 □ uncanny a. 이상한, 묘한

우리는 그의 끔찍한 목표를 실현시키기 위해서 군인과 무고한 사람들 모두의 목숨을 희생시킬 준비가 되어있음을 스스로 입증한 완강한 적과 다시 한번 마주하고 있다.

94   ④

☐ plausible a. 그럴듯한, 타당한, 진실 같은(=reasonable) ☐ urgent a. 긴급한, 절박한 ☐ modest a. 겸손한, 신중한 ☐ impolite a. 버릇없는, 무례한

차가 고장이 나서, 그는 늦은 이유에 관한 그럴듯한 변명거리가 있다.

95   ③

☐ damn v. 비난하다, 혹평하다 ☐ indolence n. 나태, 게으름 ☐ mourn v. 슬퍼하다; 죽음을 애통해 하다, 애도하다(=lament) ☐ express v. 표현하다, 표명하다; 나타내다 ☐ accept v. 받아들이다, 수락하다; 인정하다 ☐ glorify v. 찬미하다, 찬양하다

그는 그의 국민의 칭찬받을 점을 예찬하고, 그들의 나태를 비난하고, 그들의 슬픔을 애도한다.

96   ④

☐ acclaimed a. 호평을 받은 ☐ artless a. 꾸밈없는 ☐ style n. 문체 ☐ recuperate v. 회복하다, 재기하다(=recover) ☐ recurring a. 반복되는 ☐ motif n. 모티프, 주제 ☐ revere v. 존경하다, 숭배하다 ☐ revolve v. 회전하다, 선회하다 ☐ retract v. 취소하다, 철회하다

간결하고 꾸밈없는 문체로 널리 호평을 받은 헤밍웨이(Hemingway)의 소설들에서, 자연은 인간이 만사를 회복할 수 있는 곳이라는 생각이 (그의 소설들에서) 반복되는 주제이다.

97   ②

☐ barge v. 억지로 들어가다, 끼어들다(in, into) ☐ belie v. 거짓[잘못] 전하다; ~의 그릇됨을 드러내다; ~와 모순되다(=contradict) ☐ degrade v. ~의 품위[평판]를 떨어뜨리다 ☐ manifest v. 명백히 하다, 분명히 나타내다 ☐ presage v. 전조가 되다; 예언하다

백설공주가 일곱 난쟁이의 집에 초대 없이 들어가기로 한 결정은 그녀의 부드러운 성품과 모순되었다.

98   ②

☐ impassive a. 무표정한, 아무런 감정이 없는(=reserved) ☐ undemonstrative a. 감정(등)을 나타내지 않는, 내색하지 않는 ☐ stoical a. 자제[극기(克己)]심이 강한; 냉철한 ☐ disruptive a. 분열시키는, 파괴적인 ☐ ruthless a. 무자비한, 잔인한 ☐ belligerent a. 호전적인, 싸우기 좋아하는

미국 인디언들은 감정이 없고, 내색하지 않고, 자제심이 강한 사람들로 간주되어왔다.

99   ③

☐ earmark v. (가축에) 귀표를 하다; (자금 따위를) 책정하다, 배당하다(=allocate) ☐ embark v. 승선하다; 착수하다; 투자하다 ☐ pinpoint v. 정확히 나타내다, 겨누다 ☐ replace v. 대체하다; 제자리에 다시 놓다

극장 옆에 있는 쓰레기 매립지가 사무실 개발 부지로 할당되었다.

100   ①

☐ universally ad. 일반적으로, 누구에게서나; 널리 ☐ recognizable a. 쉽게 알 수 있는, 인식[인지] 가능한 ☐ ominous a. 불길한, 나쁜 징조의(=threatening) ☐ overtone n. (사상, 언어 등의) 부대적 의미, 함축, 뉘앙스 ☐ enhancing a. 향상시키는 ☐ restraining a. 제한하는 ☐ disturbing a. 불안하게 하는, 충격적인

20세기 동안 일반적으로 알아볼 수 있게 된 집단들은 많지 않았는데, 그렇게 된 집단들은 종종 마피아와 같은 그런 불길한(위험스러운) 의미를 갖고 있었다.

01 ②	02 ①	03 ①	04 ④	05 ③	06 ③	07 ①	08 ④	09 ①	10 ③
11 ②	12 ④	13 ①	14 ①	15 ③	16 ③	17 ④	18 ②	19 ②	20 ①
21 ①	22 ④	23 ③	24 ①	25 ④	26 ①	27 ③	28 ②	29 ③	30 ④
31 ①	32 ③	33 ③	34 ④	35 ①	36 ③	37 ①	38 ②	39 ③	40 ④
41 ③	42 ②	43 ①	44 ④	45 ④	46 ③	47 ①	48 ④	49 ④	50 ③
51 ④	52 ②	53 ①	54 ④	55 ③	56 ④	57 ④	58 ①	59 ②	60 ③
61 ①	62 ④	63 ④	64 ④	65 ①	66 ①	67 ①	68 ①	69 ①	70 ①
71 ④	72 ①	73 ①	74 ④	75 ②	76 ②	77 ②	78 ④	79 ④	80 ①
81 ④	82 ④	83 ④	84 ②	85 ①	86 ①	87 ③	88 ①	89 ④	90 ②
91 ②	92 ④	93 ④	94 ③	95 ③	96 ④	97 ④	98 ④	99 ④	100 ③

01
②

☐ linger v. 남다, 계속되다(=remain) ☐ strike v. 치다, 두드리다 ☐ hide v. 숨기다, 감추다 ☐ fade v. 바래다, 희미해지다

너무나 많은 시간이 흘렀고, 처음으로 한 일이 너무나 많았다. 그러나 내 마음에 여전히 남아있는 질문이 있다. 만약 내가 그녀를 데려갔더라면 그가 나를 더 사랑할 것인지 나는 궁금할 것이다. 우리의 유대가 더 단단해질까?

02
①

☐ rulebook n. 규정집, 세부이행지침 ☐ palatable a. 입맛에 맞는; 마음에 드는(=acceptable) ☐ ratify v. 비준하다 ☐ sustainable a. 지속 가능한 ☐ recoverable a. 회복할 수 있는 ☐ irrevocable a. 돌이킬 수 없는

제24차 유엔기후변화협약 당사국총회(COP24)에서는 파리협정을 비준한 183개 국가 모두의 입맛에 맞는 세부이행지침에 국가 간 합의가 있어야 한다.

03
①

☐ mitigate v. 누그러뜨리다, 완화시키다(=alleviate) ☐ clarify v. 분명히 하다; 정화하다 ☐ impose v. 부과하다; 강요하다 ☐ discuss v. 논의하다, 토의하다

이것들은 만일 적절하게 완화되어야 한다면, 이해되어야 한다.

04
④

☐ specious a. 외양만 좋은, 그럴듯한(=misleading) ☐ professional a. 직업의, 직업상의, 전문직의 ☐ diverse a. 다양한, 여러 방면의 ☐

aggressive a. 공격적인; 적극적인

우리는 그러한 허울만 좋은 주장에 대해 논의할 시간이 없다.

05
③

☐ motley a. 잡다한(=variegated) ☐ flock v. 떼 지어 몰려들다 ☐ bloated a. 거만한 ☐ minuscule a. 작은 ☐ destitute a. 가난한

그들은 그의 주위에 몰려들어 그가 유럽의 철학을 만들도록 도운 잡다한 무리의 젊은이들이었다.

06
③

☐ insecurity n. 불안정; 불안(감) ☐ breakdown n. 파손, 붕괴 ☐ rampant a. 사나운; 자유분방한; 만연한(=prevalent) ☐ gossip v. 잡담하다; 험담을 퍼뜨리다 ☐ obstinate a. 완고한; (병이) 난치의 ☐ troublesome a. 성가신, 귀찮은

사무직 노동자들 사이에서는 불안감, 걱정, 신경쇠약이 널리 퍼져있다.

07
①

☐ champion v. ~을 위해 싸우다; 옹호하다(=patronize) ☐ ratify v. 비준하다, 재가하다 ☐ take office 취임하다 ☐ repeal v. 무효로 하다, 폐지[폐기, 철회]하다 ☐ monopolize v. 독점하다, 전유하다 ☐ defeat v. ~을 패배시키다, 무찌르다

취임 이래로, 그 주지사는 평등권 개정안 비준 운동을 지지해왔다.

08 ④

☐ impeccable a. 나무랄 데[결점] 없는; 완벽한(=excellent) ☐ naive a. 순진한; 고지식한 ☐ horrible a. 무서운, 끔찍한; 몹시 불쾌한 ☐ peculiar a. 독특한; 고유의, 독자적인

그녀는 옷에 대해 완벽한 안목이 있었다.

09 ①

☐ sanctuary n. (동물) 보호구역; 피난처(=shelter); 신성한 곳 ☐ inhabitant n. 주민, 거주자; 서식동물 ☐ wasteland n. 황무지, 불모지 ☐ institution n. 제도, 협회, 기관

세계에서 가장 큰 야생동물보호구역 중 하나는 치앙마이 근처에 있다.

10 ③

☐ colloquial a. 구어(口語)의, 일상 회화의 ☐ blurred a. 희미한, 흐릿한(=indistinct) ☐ exaggerated a. 과장된; 비대한 ☐ reversed a. 거꾸로 한, 뒤집은; 취소된 ☐ unintentional a. 고의가 아닌, 무심코 한

오늘날의 저작물에서 문학적 표현과 구어체 표현 사이의 구별은 종종 분명치 않다.

11 ②

☐ transfer v. 옮기다; 변환하다; 이체하다 ☐ eligible a. 적격의, 적임의; 바람직한, 적합한(=entitled) ☐ fortune n. 행운; 재산 ☐ responsible a. 책임이 있는; 신뢰할 수 있는 ☐ guilty a. 죄를 범한, 유죄의 ☐ sufficient a. 충분한

만일 당신이 그들에게 그 돈을 당신의 은행 계좌로 이체하도록 허용한다면, 당신은 10%의 이윤을 받을 자격이 될 것입니다.

12 ④

☐ furious a. 성난, 격노한; 맹렬한, 격렬한(=angry) ☐ drowsy a. 졸리는, 활기 없는; 완만한 ☐ sympathetic a. 동정심 있는, 동정적인 ☐ surprised a. 놀란; 놀라움을 나타내는

내가 또 학교에서 퇴학당했다고 말씀드렸을 때 아버지께서는 매우 화를 내셨다.

13 ①

☐ ebullient a. 끓어 넘치는; 원기 왕성한, 열광적인(=exuberant) ☐ repress v. 억누르다, 저지하다 ☐ gay a. 명랑한, 즐거운 ☐ quixotic a. 돈키호테식의; 비실제적인 ☐ placid a. 평온한, 조용한, 침착한; 매우 만족한 ☐ incandescent a. 백열의; 눈부신, 빛나는; 열렬한

그녀의 생기 넘치는 성격은 억제될 수가 없었다. 그녀는 항상 웃음을 짓고 즐거워했다.

14 ①

☐ crackdown n. 엄중 단속, 강력 탄압 ☐ topple v. 비틀거리다, 무너지다; 전복시키다(=overturn) ☐ defile v. 더럽히다; (신성을) 모독하다 ☐ slander v. 중상하다, 비방하다 ☐ vilify v. 비방하다, 중상하다, 헐뜯다, 욕하다

중국의 전 지도자 덩샤오핑(Deng Xiaoping)은 시위 참가자들이 공산당을 전복시킬 수 있다는 두려움 때문에 1989년 천안문 광장 사태를 폭력으로 진압하라고 명령했다.

15 ③

☐ feature v. 특별히 포함하다, 특징으로 삼다(=highlight) ☐ create v. 창조하다, 창작하다 ☐ liquidate v. 청산[정리]하다 ☐ distribute v. 분배하다

2009년 미국의 한 장난감 회사가 중국 대도시의 주요 쇼핑 거리에 거대한 상점을 열었고, 그 상점은 이 회사의 유명한 인형을 특징적인 인기물로 삼았다.

16 ③

☐ austerity n. 검소, 내핍, 긴축(=abstention) ☐ ingenuity n. 기발한 재주, 재간, 독창성 ☐ convention n. 협정; 풍습, 관례 ☐ tenacity n. 고집, 끈기

대체로, 일본이 친환경 자동차 기술에서 앞서 나가고 있는 것은 일본의 오랜 내핍(절제) 생활의 산물이다.

17 ④

☐ merciless a. 무자비한, 잔인한(=pitiless) ☐ compassionate a. 인정 많은, 동정심 있는 ☐ lenient a. 너그러운, 인자한 ☐ relenting a. (화, 흥분 등이) 가라앉는; 약해지는

그 낯선 사람들은 결국 잔인한 살인자들로 밝혀졌다.

18 ②

☐ haggard a. 야윈, 수척한, 초췌한(=gaunt) ☐ bold a. 대담한, 담력이 있는 ☐ vigorous a. 원기 왕성한, 강력한 ☐ daring a. 대담한, 용감한

자신을 쳐다보는 화난 얼굴들을 힐끗 봤을 때 그는 창백하고 약간 수척했다.

19 ②

☐ phenomenal a. 놀라운, 굉장한, 거대한(=great); 현상의 ☐ secular a. 현세의, 세속의 ☐ superficial a. 표면(상)의; 피상적인 ☐ terrible a. 무서운

나는 그가 단연 뛰어난 재능을 가진 피아니스트라고 생각한다.

20 ①

☐ promptly ad. 신속히; 즉석에서(=quickly) ☐ patriotically ad. 애국적으로 , 애국심이 강하게 ☐ unanimously ad. 만장일치로; 전원 합의로 ☐ ideally ad. 관념적으로; 전형적으로; 이상적으로 ☐ definitely ad. 한정적으로; 명확히, 확실히

두 번째 조치는 의회에 의해 신속하고 애국적 차원에서 통과된 법률이었다.

21 ①

☐ tarnish v. 흐리게 하다; 녹슬게 하다; 변색시키다; ~의 가치를 저하시키다(=blemish) ☐ enhance v. 향상하다, 높이다, 늘리다 ☐ question v. 질문하다, 묻다; 심문하다 ☐ shatter v. 부서지다, 산산조각이 나다

블레어(Blair)의 신뢰도가 손상된다면, 유럽 전역에서의 그의 영향력도 감소될 것이다.

22 ④

☐ cozy a. 기분 좋은, 편안한, 아늑한(=comfortable) ☐ light a. 밝은; 옅은; 가벼운 ☐ roomy a. 널찍한, 여유가 있는 ☐ cluttered a. 어수선한, 혼란한

어떤 색깔은 방의 장식과 합해지면 아늑한 분위기를 만들어낼 수 있다.

23 ③

☐ Popsicle n. (가는 막대기에 얼린) 아이스캔디 ☐ ambience n. 환경; 분위기(=atmosphere) ☐ delight v. 매우 기쁘게 하다 ☐ oblivion n. 망각, 잊혀짐 ☐ extravaganza n. 화려한 쇼; 광상곡 ☐ audacity n. 대담함; 무모함

플레밍(Flemmings) 부부는 비닐로 된 비치볼과 아이스캔디 스틱으로 집을 꾸며서 어린 자녀가 즐거워할 만한 친근한 분위기를 만들었다.

24 ①

☐ comprehend v. 이해하다, 파악하다; 포함하다 ☐ appellation n. 명칭, 호칭(=label) ☐ view n. 시야; 견해, 의견 ☐ apparatus n. 장치, 기구 ☐ condition n. 조건; 상태

언어는 다수의 유사한 것들을 동일한 명칭 하에 포함할 때야 비로소 본연의 역할을 하고 있는 것이다.

25 ④

☐ post v. (정보를) 게시하다 ☐ ample a. 많은 ☐ contemplate v. 눈여겨보다, 주의 깊게 관찰하다 ☐ track down ~을 찾아내다, 추적하다 ☐ recalcitrant a. 저항하는; 다루기 어려운(=stubborn) ☐ contrite a. 죄를 뉘우치는, 회한에 찬 ☐ frantic a. 제정신이 아닌, 극도로 흥분한 ☐ grateful a. 감사하고 있는, 고마워하는

학생들이 페이스북 페이지에 많은 연락정보를 남겨서, 나는 내가 맡은 반에서 다루기 힘든 지도받는 학생들과 잦은 결석자들을 찾아내는 것과 같은 페이스북 페이지의 다른 용도들을 생각해보게 된다.

26 ①

☐ edible a. 먹을 수 있는, 식용에 알맞은(=eatable) ☐ ripen a. (과일, 곡물) 익은, 숙성된 ☐ delicious a. 맛있는, 맛 좋은; 향기로운 ☐ blazing a. 타오르는, 타는 듯한; 빛나는

먹을 수 있는 것처럼 보일지라도 절대로 야생 버섯을 먹지 마라. 야생 버섯에는 독이 있을 수 있다.

27 ③

☐ sequester v. 격리시키다(=confine) ☐ facilitate v. 용이하게 하다 ☐ evict v. 쫓아내다, 퇴거시키다 ☐ vest v. (권리를) 주다, 부여하다; 의복을 입히다

그 알코올 중독 가수의 관리팀은 그를 재활원에 격리시키는 한편 대중들에게는 그가 신곡 제작에 바쁘다고 이야기했다.

28 ②

☐ excoriate v. (피부가) 벗겨지게 하다; 심하게 비난하다(=denounce) ☐ compliment v. ~에게 찬사를 말하다, 칭찬하다 ☐ accommodate v. 수용하다, 편의를 도모하다 ☐ ratify v. 비준하다, 재가하다

편집장에게 온 그 3쪽 분량의 편지는 그 소문의 출처를 확인도 하지 않고 활자화한 데 대해 그 간행물을 강도 높게 비난했다.

29 ③

☐ dweller n. 거주자, 주민 ☐ vacant a. 빈, 사는 사람이 없는(=empty) ☐ lot n. 토지, 지구; 땅 ☐ small a. 작은, 소형의 ☐ shady a. 그늘이 많은, 응달진 ☐ costly a. 값비싼, 비용이 많이 드는

많은 시민들이 공터를 북적거리는 유원지로 바꾸고 있다.

30
④

☐ ascetic a. 고행의; 금욕적인(=puritanical) ☐ Hell's angel 폭주족
☐ prurient a. 외설적인, 호색의 ☐ preposterous a. 말도 안 되는,
터무니없는 ☐ profligate a. 낭비하는

몰리(Molly)는 자신이 엄격한 생활을 한다고 생각되지 않기를 너무나
바라서 오토바이 폭주족 회원에게 자신도 라스베이거스에서 그들과 함
께 주말을 보내고 싶다고 말했다.

31
②

☐ galvanize v. 갑자기 활기를 띠게 하다, 자극하다(=energize) ☐
relegate v. 격하하다, 좌천시키다 ☐ emancipate v. 해방시키다, 석방
하다 ☐ sanction v. 재가하다; 제재를 가하다

수십 년 동안 민권 단체들의 진전은 고통스러울 정도로 느렸다. 마틴 루
터 킹(Martin Luther King Jr.) 박사의 언행으로 인해 민권 운동은 재개
되고 활기를 띠게 되었다.

32
③

☐ pensive a. 생각에 잠긴, 수심에 잠긴(=thoughtful) ☐ cheerful a.
기분 좋은, 마음을 밝게 하는 ☐ depressed a. 내리눌린; 우울한, 풀이
죽은 ☐ fresh a. 새로운, 갓 만들어진; 신선한

달리(Dali)의 그림들은 사색적인 느낌을 일으킨다.

33
②

☐ neologism n. 신조어, 새로운 표현(=coinage) ☐ simile n. 직유
☐ epigram n. 경구, 금언 ☐ shibboleth n. 진부한[구식의] 문구

'강남스타일'이란 표현은 서울의 강남 지역과 관련된 라이프 스타일을
일컫는 한국어의 신조어이다.

34
④

☐ pronouncement n. 선언, 발표 ☐ scrutinize v. (면밀하게) 검토하
다(=examine) ☐ ascertain v. (조사 등으로) 확인하다, 규명하다 ☐
methodology n. 방법론 ☐ utilize v. 이용하다, 활용하다 ☐ select
v. 선택하다, 고르다 ☐ systemize v. 체계화하다, 조직화하다

교육 공학에 관한 모든 발표는 기계, 소프트웨어, 방법론 등, 프로세스의
어떤 부분이 관련돼 있는지를 확인하기 위해 매우 신중하게 검토되어야
한다.

35
①

☐ subdue v. 정복하다, 진압하다 ☐ acme n. 절정, 극점, 극치, 전성기
(=culmination) ☐ subjugation n. 정복, 예속 ☐ qualification n.

자격 부여, 자격 증명; 적성, 능력 ☐ protestation n. 항의, 이의(의
제기), 불복

손자(Sun Tzu)는 2,000여 년 전에 "모든 전쟁은 속임수이며, 싸우지
않고 적을 제압하는 것이 전술의 극치다."라고 전사들에게 말했다.

36
③

☐ dune n. 모래 언덕 ☐ obviously ad. 명백하게 ☐ factitious a.
인위적인, 인공적인(=artificial) ☐ dig v. (땅 따위를) 파다; (구멍·무덤을)
파다 ☐ bury v. 묻다; (흙 따위를) 덮다; 매장하다 ☐ clean a. 깨끗한,
깔끔한 ☐ truthful a. 정직한; 진실한 ☐ attractive a. 사람의 마음을
끄는, 매력적인

사막의 모래 언덕들 중 몇몇은 분명히 인공적인 것들이다. 그래서 만약
내가 매장된 보물을 찾아 땅을 파게 된다면, 나는 거기서부터 시작할 것
이다.

37
①

☐ entail v. 수반하다; 부과하다 ☐ expenditure n. 경비, 지출, 소비
(=expense) ☐ expertise n. 전문적 기술 ☐ rationale n. 이론적 해설
[근거, 설명] ☐ exposure n. 노출, 드러남, 쬠

그 프로젝트는 많은 에너지 소비를 필요로 했다.

38
②

☐ contradiction n. 모순 ☐ radical a. 근본적인(=fundamental) ☐
resolve v. 풀다, 해결하다 ☐ practical a. 실제적인, 실용적인 ☐
conventional a. 관례적인 ☐ occasional a. 가끔의

모든 혁명은 첨예한 계급 모순의 표현임과 동시에 그 모순을 해결하려는
근본적인 시도이다.

39
③

☐ adjourn v. (재판·회의 등을) 중단하다, 휴정[휴회]하다(=suspend)
☐ submerge v. 물속에 잠기다, 침몰하다 ☐ hasten v. 서두르다; 서둘
러 하다 ☐ renovate v. 수선하다, 수리하다

법정은 천장에서 빗물이 떨어지기 시작하자 휴회할 수밖에 없었다.

40
④

☐ panacea n. 만병통치약; 모든 문제의 해결책(=solution) ☐
challenge n. 도전, 과제, 난제 ☐ implementation n. 이행, 실행; 완성
☐ mechanism n. 기계 장치[기구], 방법

공정무역이 분명히 만병통치약은 아니지만, 국제 교역의 규제와 통합을
촉진할 수는 있다.

41
③

☐ **bizarre** a. 기이한, 특이한, 별난(=crazy) ☐ **cruel** a. 잔혹한, 무정한; 비참한 ☐ **suspicious** a. 의심스러운, 수상쩍은; 의심 많은 ☐ **asserted** a. (확증 없이) 주장된, 단언된

그들의 기이한 태도는 결국 예상치 못한 반응을 불러일으켰다.

42
②

☐ **commodity** n. 상품, 일용품, 물품(=goods) ☐ **foundry** n. 주조; 주조 공장 ☐ **subsidy** n. 보조금, 장려금; 기부금 ☐ **embargo** n. 금수 조치, 통상 금지령

노동력은 다른 일용품처럼 사고 팔린다.

43
①

☐ **speak out** 공개적으로 말하다[밝히다] ☐ **embellish** v. 장식하다, 꾸미다(=decorate) ☐ **credential** n. 신임장; 자격, 적격; 자격 증명서 ☐ **cook up** 날조하다, 조작하다 ☐ **destroy** v. 파괴하다, 말살하다 ☐ **compile** v. 편집하다, 수집하다 ☐ **install** v. 설치하다, 장치하다

그는 관리들이 통계 자료를 조작하는 방법으로 그들의 이력을 보기 좋게 꾸미는 것에 반대의 뜻을 공개적으로 밝혀왔다.

44
④

☐ **celebrity** n. 유명인, 명사 ☐ **donor** n. 기부자, 기증자 ☐ **pique** v. (흥미, 호기심 따위를) 불러일으키다(=incite) ☐ **tailor** v. (특정한 목적, 사람 등에) 맞추다 ☐ **fudge** v. 날조하다 ☐ **smother** v. 감추다, 은폐하다; ~을 숨막히게 하다

유명한 연사들의 강연을 위해 비용을 지불하는 대학들은 그들이 기부자들에게 깊은 인상을 줄 수 있고 입학하길 희망하는 학생들의 관심을 불러일으킬 수 있다고 말한다.

45
④

☐ **illustrious** a. 뛰어난, 저명한; (행위 등이) 빛나는(=remarkable) ☐ **insignificant** a. 하찮은, 사소한, 무가치한 ☐ **nasty** a. 더러운, 불쾌한 ☐ **notorious** a. 악명 높은; 소문난, 유명한

1998년 월드컵 우승자인 34세의 미드필더는 빛나는 선수 생활의 마지막 경기를 하고 있었다.

46
③

☐ **dilettante** n. 문학·예술의 애호가; 아마추어 평론가(=tyro) ☐ **zealot** n. 열중하는 사람; 열광자 ☐ **altruist** n. 이타주의자 ☐ **renegade** n. 변절자, 탈당자; 배교자

사람들은 윈스턴 처칠(Winston Churchill)이 자신의 그림을 가볍게 여길 것이라고 생각했지만, 아마추어 예술가가 아니었던 처칠은 자신의 예술적인 노력을 실제로 매우 진지하게 생각했다.

47
①

☐ **sweeping** a. 일소하는; 포괄적인(=overall) ☐ **regional** a. 지방의; 지역적인 ☐ **smooth** a. 매끈한, 매끄러운; 잔잔한 ☐ **impressive** a. 인상적인; 감동적인

아마도 어떤 주제에 관한 전통적인 사고방식에 대해 과학이 지금보다 더 총체적인 변화를 요구한 적은 없었을 것이고, 또한 이보다 더 중요한 주제는 없었을 것이다.

48
④

☐ **adept** a. 숙달한, 정통한(=skillful) ☐ **immature** a. 미숙한, 미완성의 ☐ **impatient** a. 참을성 없는, 성급한 ☐ **earnest** a. 진지한, 열심인 ☐ **sincere** a. 성실한, 참된

그들은 원하는 것을 얻는 많은 기술들에 있어 그들 스스로 능숙함을 보여주었다.

49
④

☐ **fury** n. (병, 날씨, 전쟁 따위의) 격심함, 맹렬함 ☐ **blizzard** n. 강한 눈보라 ☐ **abate** v. 약해지다, 누그러지다(=lessen) ☐ **adjourn** v. 중단하다, 휴정하다 ☐ **assent** v. 동의하다, 찬성하다 ☐ **loiter** v. 빈둥거리다; 배회하다

몇 번이고 그는 사나운 눈보라가 약해지기를 소망했다.

50
③

☐ **rancid** a. 고약한 냄새가 나는, 불쾌한, (맛이) 고약한(=spoiled) ☐ **discolored** a. 변색된, 퇴색한 ☐ **fresh** a. 새로운; 신선한 ☐ **organic** a. 유기체의; 유기적인

케이크를 구울 때 사용했던 버터가 상했음이 분명하다.

51
④

☐ **taciturn** a. 과묵한, 말없는(=reserved) ☐ **disconcerted** a. 당황한, 당혹한 ☐ **undaunted** a. 불굴의, 기가 꺾이지 않는 ☐ **astounded** a. 몹시 놀란, 큰 충격을 받은

그 여자가 자유롭게 이야기하는 것을 즐긴 반면, 그녀의 남편은 듣는 것을 선호하는 과묵한 남자였다.

52 ②

□ drawback n. 약점, 결점; 고장(=disadvantage) □ feature n. 얼굴의 생김새, 용모; 특징, 특색 □ version n. 번역; 번역문서; 각색 □ withdrawal n. 움츠림; 물러남, 철수, 퇴학

어떤 부기 시스템이나 단점은 있다.

53 ①

□ solecism n. 실수, 결례(=gaffe) □ harangue n. 장황한 이야기, 장광설 □ disdain n. 경멸, 모멸; 오만 □ stalemate n. 교착 상태, 곤경

전 세계에서 수십억 명의 시선이 그를 주시하고 있던 화요일 밤에 그는 취임 파티석상에서 무례한 실수를 반복했다.

54 ④

□ ransack v. 샅샅이 뒤지다; 빼앗다, 약탈하다(=rob) □ abandon v. 버리다, 유기하다; 그만두다, 단념하다 □ repair v. 수선하다, 수리하다; 회복하다 □ paint v. 페인트칠하다; 그리다

사무실은 약탈당했고, 회사 차들은 도둑맞았고, 통신장비들은 파괴되었다.

55 ③

□ ban n. 금지(령)(=restriction) □ behind the wheel (자동차의) 핸들을 잡고; 운전하여 □ be on the rise 증가하고 있다 □ offer n. 제의, 제안 □ permit n. 허가; 허가증 □ institution n. 기관; 제도

운전 중에 휴대 전화를 이용하여 문자 메시지를 주고받는 것을 막기 위한 여러 주법(州法)의 금지규정과 전국적인 캠페인에도 불구하고, 운전 중에 문자메시지를 주고받는 사람들의 수가 실제로 증가하고 있다는 것을 새로운 연구는 보여준다.

56 ④

□ generous a. 관대한, 아량 있는(=capacious) □ endless a. 끝없는, 무한한 □ cadaverous a. 시체 같은; 창백한; 수척한 □ careless a. 부주의한, 경솔한 □ captive a. 포로의; 사로잡힌, 매혹된

그녀는 모든 분야의 끝없는 지식과 생각들을 수용할 수 있는 포용력 있는 마음을 가지고 있다.

57 ④

□ abruptly ad. 갑자기, 뜻밖에(=unexpectedly) □ sadly ad. 슬프게, 애처롭게 □ shortly ad. 곧, 얼마 안 있어; 간단히 □ gradually ad. 차차, 점차로

그녀의 다음 발언으로 대화가 갑자기 중단됐다.

58 ①

□ debacle n. (정부 등의) 붕괴; (시장의) 폭락(=disruption) □ lie with ~의 의무[책임]이다 □ call on (연설 등을) ~에게 청하다; 요구하다 □ on behalf of ~을 대신[대표]하여 □ opulence n. 풍부; 부유 □ lowness n. 낮음; 미천 □ squalidness n. 더러움, 불결함

그 보고서는 실패의 주된 책임이 정부에 있다고 밝혔으며, 현 장관에게 정부를 대신하여 책임질 것을 요구했다.

59 ②

□ confidential a. 기밀의, 내밀한(=undisclosed) □ submit v. 복종시키다; 제출하다 □ vociferous a. 큰 소리로 외치는, 소란한, 시끄러운 □ reproachful a. 나무라는, 비난하는 □ agitative a. 선동적인

아주 민감한 종류의 기밀 보고서가 위원회에 제출되었다.

60 ③

□ lure v. 유혹하다, 꾀어내다; 불러내다(=entice) □ refer v. 보내다, 조회하다; 위탁[부탁]하다, 맡기다 □ employ v. 쓰다, 고용하다; 소비하다 □ transform v. 변형시키다, 바꾸다

좀 더 배려심 있는 사람들을 현장으로 끌어들이기 위해, 학부는 비과학 전공자들뿐만 아니라 나이 든 학생들도 찾고 있다.

61 ③

□ monotonous a. 단조로운; 지루한 □ torpor n. 무기력(=lethargy) □ pabulum n. 음식물; 마음의 양식 □ disorder n. 무질서; 장애 □ acuity n. 명민한, 예리함

길고 단조로운 일과를 마치고 나면 사람들은 정신적으로 무기력한 상태에 빠지게 된다.

62 ④

□ exert v. (권력·영향력을) 가하다[행사하다] □ cajole v. 부추기다, 꼬드기다, 회유하다(=coax) □ summit n. 정상; 정상회담 □ agenda n. 안건, 의제 □ yank v. 해임하다; 체포하다 □ dodge v. (몸을) 재빨리[휙] 움직이다; 회피하다 □ tout v. 졸라대다; 극구 칭찬[선전]하다

대통령은 정상회담에 참석한 다른 지도자들을 회유하여 자신의 의제를 지지하도록 영향력을 행사했다.

63　　　④

☐ flee v. 달아나다, 도망하다　☐ detailed a. 상세한　☐ account n. 설명, (자세한) 이야기　☐ ordeal n. 호된 시련(=trial)　☐ lynching n. 린치, 폭력적인 사적 제재　☐ slur n. 중상, 비방　☐ experience n. 경험; 경력　☐ challenge n. 도전　☐ action n. 활동

분노한 트럼프 지지자들의 살해 위협으로 인해 조지아(Georgia)주의 선거 감독관 루비 프리먼(Ruby Freeman)은 자신이 20년 동안 살던 집을 떠나야 했다. 이 여성은 자신이 겪은 시련에 대해 처음으로 자세히 설명하면서, 린치를 가하겠다는 위협, 인종차별적인 비방, 그리고 낯선 사람들이 프리먼과 그녀의 어머니의 집을 찾아와서 불안에 떨게 한 것에 대해 로이터 통신에 이야기했다.

64　　　④

☐ absorb v. 흡수하다　☐ scatter v. 흩뿌리다, 흩어버리다　☐ harmful a. 해로운(=pernicious)　☐ radiation n. 방사; 복사선　☐ perpetual a. 영속하는　☐ addictive a. 습관성의, 중독성의　☐ benevolent a. 자비로운

대기는 또한 태양이나 우주로부터 오는 해로운 복사에너지를 흡수하고 발산함으로써 우리를 보호한다.

65　　　①

☐ haphazard a. 우연한; 되는 대로의, 무계획의(=random)　☐ neat a. 정돈된; 깔끔한, 단정한　☐ ordered a. 정돈된, 질서가 잡힌　☐ scattered a. 뿔뿔이 흩어진, 산재해 있는; 산발적인

책들이 아무렇게나 선반 위에 쌓여 있었다.

66　　　①

☐ allege v. 강력히 주장하다, 단언하다(=declare)　☐ admonish v. 꾸짖다, 책망하다　☐ accentuate v. 강조하다　☐ allot v. 할당하다, 분배하다

제인(Jane)은 에반젤린(Evangeline)이 그녀의 아들을 찾는 데 평생을 바쳤다고 단언했다.

67　　　①

☐ delinquent a. 직무 태만의; 비행을 저지른; 체납의(=remiss)　☐ puzzling a. 곤혹스럽게 하는, 헷갈리게 하는　☐ callow a. 깃털이 나지 않은; 경험이 없는, 미숙한　☐ submissive a. 복종하는, 순종하는

무관심이나 나태함으로 인해 투표하지 않은 시민들은 시민으로서의 의무를 이행하는 데 있어 태만한 것이다.

68　　　①

☐ sluggish a. 게으른, 나태한; 동작이 느린(=slow)　☐ weak a. 약한, 무력한　☐ quick a. 신속한, 빠른　☐ swift a. 신속한, 빠른

노화되어가는 내 면역계는 의심할 여지없이 예전보다 더 느리다.

69　　　①

☐ kinetic a. 운동(학상)의; 활동적인, 동적인　☐ undulate v. 물결치다, 파동 치다; 기복 치다, 굽이치다(=surge)　☐ induce v. 야기하다, 일으키다, 유발하다　☐ smother v. 숨 막히게 하다, 질식시키다; 억누르다　☐ sneak v. 살금살금 들어오다; 몰래 하다

우리는 그 제목이 없는 움직이는 조각물을 보기 위해 여기에 왔었는데, 그 조각물은 우리가 건물에 들어설 때 우리가 일으킨 공기의 흐름으로 물결쳤다.

70　　　①

☐ undergo v. ~을 받다, 겪다, 경험하다　☐ undaunted a. 불굴의, 겁 내지 않는(=fearless)　☐ wavering a. 흔들리는; 주저하는　☐ disoriented a. 혼란에 빠진, 방향 감각을 잃은　☐ intimidated a. 위축된, 위협을 느낀

사나운 폭풍우 때문에 큰 인명 손실이 있었지만, 그 탐사대는 여전히 겁내지 않았다.

71　　　④

☐ sentient a. 지각 있는, 감각 있는(=conscious)　☐ senile a. 노쇠한, 나이가 많은　☐ melancholy a. 우울한, 음침한; 슬픈　☐ vulnerable a. 상처 입기 쉬운, 취약한

나는 나의 실존을 자각하게 된 첫 순간을 아주 생생히 기억할 수 있다. 처음으로 나는 인지할 수 있는 세계에 내가 지각력이 있는 한 인간이라는 사실을 깨달았던 것이다.

72　　　①

☐ counterfeit a. 모조의, 가짜의(=spurious); 허울만의, 겉치레의　☐ genuine a. 진짜의; 저자 친필의; 진심에서 우러난　☐ precarious a. 불확실한, 믿을 수 없는, 불안정한　☐ enigmatic a. 수수께끼 같은, 불가해한, 정체 모를

조나단 거쉬(Jonathan Gash)의 추리소설의 주인공인 "러브조이(Lovejoy)"는 가짜 골동품을 진짜와 구별하는 법에 대해 독자에게 충고해주는 골동품 상인이다.

73 ②

☐ insist v. 주장하다, 고집하다 ☐ oath n. 맹세 ☐ take an oath 선서하다, 서약하다 ☐ fidelity n. 충성, 충절, 충실(=loyalty) ☐ protection n. 보호 ☐ diligence n. 근면, 부지런함 ☐ hostility n. 적의, 적개심

그들은 국가에 대한 충성을 맹세할 것을 주장했다.

74 ④

☐ plastic a. 형태를 만들기가 쉬운, 가소성이 좋은; 유연한(=malleable) ☐ neuron n. 신경단위, 뉴런 ☐ synapse n. 시냅스(신경 세포의 자극 전달부) ☐ adapt v. (환경 등에) 순응하다 ☐ phenomenon n. 현상 ☐ medium n. 매개물, 매체 ☐ end up with 결국 ~와 함께 하다, ~을 가지게 되다 ☐ original a. 고유의; 독창적인 ☐ vulnerable a. 약점이 있는; (유혹·설득 따위에) 약한 ☐ transparent a. 투명한; 명백한; 명료한

우리는 인간의 뇌가 매우 유연해서 상황이 변함에 따라 뉴런과 시냅스도 변한다는 사실을 알고 있다. 우리가 새로운 매체의 사용을 비롯한 새로운 문화 현상에 적응할 때, 우리는 결국 다른 뇌를 갖게 된다.

75 ②

☐ convinced a. 확신하는 ☐ sincerity n. 성실, 성의 ☐ integrity n. 성실, 정직 ☐ utmost a. 최대한도의, 최고도의, 극도의 ☐ felicity n. 더없는 행복(=bliss) ☐ pursuit n. 추적; 추격; 추구 ☐ cradle n. 요람; 발상지

나는 성실, 성의, 정직이 인생의 행복에 있어 가장 중요한 것이란 확신을 점차 갖게 되었다.

76 ②

☐ ingredient n. 성분, 원료, 재료; 구성 요소(=element) ☐ tenet n. 견해; 주의; 신조 ☐ disposition n. 성향; 배열; 처분 ☐ antecedent n. 전례; 선행자; 선조

감정을 통제할 수 있는 능력은 효과적인 통솔력의 필수적인 요소이다.

77 ②

☐ brilliant a. 찬란하게 빛나는; 훌륭한, 화려한 ☐ coherent a. 일관성 있는, 논리 정연한(=logical) ☐ confusing a. 혼란스러운 ☐ irritating a. 화나게 하는, 짜증나는, 귀찮은; 자극하는 ☐ tedious a. 지루한, 지겨운

우리는 그의 환영사가 훌륭할 것이라 기대했으나 그것은 논리적이지 조차 못 한 것이었다.

78 ④

☐ holocaust n. 대학살, 몰살(=genocide) ☐ operation n. 운영, 경영; 실시, 시행; 수술 ☐ carnival n. 축제, 제전 ☐ suicide n. 자살, 자해

나미로브(Namirov)의 대다수의 인구가 집단 학살 중에 실종되었다.

79 ④

☐ vehement a. 격렬한, 맹렬한; 열심인(=passionate) ☐ concealed a. 숨겨진 ☐ disarmed a. 무장 해제된 ☐ displeased a. 화난, 불쾌한

그 성마른 테니스 선수는 선심에 대한 강렬한 반감을 드러낸 것으로 알려졌다.

80 ①

☐ craftsman n. 장인(匠人) ☐ entrepreneur n. 실업가, 기업가, 사업주 ☐ plethora n. 과다, 과잉(=lot) ☐ handmade a. 손으로 만든 ☐ bit n. 작은 조각; 소량, 조금 ☐ set n. 세트, 한 벌 ☐ bundle n. 묶음, 꾸러미

예술가, 장인, 기업가들은 수많은 수제품과 서비스를 제공하고 있다.

81 ④

☐ accentuate v. 강조하다, 역설하다(=emphasize) ☐ weaken v. 약화시키다; 묽게 하다 ☐ appease v. 달래다; 진정시키다 ☐ mitigate v. 완화하다

이와 같은 법들은 단지 불평등을 강조하는 데 도움이 될 뿐이다.

82 ④

☐ thoughtful a. 생각이 깊은 ☐ discreet a. 사려있는, 신중한, 예의바른(=prudent) ☐ intelligent a. 총명한, 똑똑한 ☐ violent a. 폭력적인, 난폭한 ☐ wealthy a. 부유한; 풍부한

그는 매우 사려 깊고 신중하며 협조적이어서 동료들은 그와 함께 일하는 것을 큰 즐거움으로 여겼다.

83 ④

☐ culprit n. 죄인, 범죄자; (문제의) 원인 ☐ proportional a. 비례의; 균형이 잡힌, 조화된 ☐ delegate n. 대표자, 대리인 ☐ gaffe n. 과실, 실수(=mistake) ☐ flip-flop n. (소신, 태도, 방침 등의) 급변, 전환 ☐ advantage n. 유리, 이익; 장점 ☐ costume n. 복장, 의상; 차림새 ☐ manner n. 방법, 방식; 태도

분석가들은 몇몇 원인들을 지적하고 있는데, 비례대표제도, 그의 실수, 그의 경솔한 언행, 그의 메시지, 심지어는 그의 신념도 여기에 포함된다.

84 ②

☐ neglect n. 태만; 소홀; 무시; 방치 ☐ prevalent a. 일반적으로 행하여
지는, 널리 퍼진(=widespread) ☐ maltreatment n. 거칠게 다룸, 학대
☐ preferred a. 선취권 있는, 우선의; 선호되는 ☐ unfavourable a.
좋지 않은, 불리한, 순조롭지 않은 ☐ suitable a. 적당한, 상당한, 어울리
는, 알맞은

방치는 가장 일반적으로 행하여지는 아동학대의 형태이다.

85 ①

☐ foible n. 약점, 결점, 단점(=defect) ☐ asset n. (pl.) 자산, 재산
☐ riddle n. 수수께끼; 난제 ☐ hardship n. (pl.) 고난, 고초

패티(Patti)의 결점 중 하나는 사람보다 개를 더 좋아하는 성향이었다.

86 ①

☐ undiscriminating a. 식별하지 않는, 무차별한 ☐ analogous to
~과 비슷한, 유사한(=similar to) ☐ sink v. 가라앉히다, 침몰시키다
☐ due to ~때문에 ☐ related to ~과 관계있는 ☐ superior to ~보다
우수한

요즈음 예술계로 흘러가는 무차별적인 투자 자본의 홍수가 1970년대
초에 보르도 와인 산업을 거의 와해시켰던 것과 유사한 위기를 만들어낼
수도 있다.

87 ③

☐ palpable a. 쉽게 자각할 수 있는; 뚜렷한, 명백한(=discernible) ☐
negligible a. 무시해도 좋은; 하찮은 ☐ fuzzy a. 흐릿한, 어렴풋한
☐ damaging a. 손상[피해, 훼손, 악영향]을 주는, 해로운

미국과 유럽 사이의 신뢰감 상실이 올해 정상 회담에서 특히 명백했는
데, 이 정상회담은 전통적으로 북대서양조약기구(NATO) 동맹국들끼
리 상호 안도감을 보여주는 자리이다.

88 ①

☐ pristine a. 완전 새 것 같은, 아주 깨끗한; 자연 그대로의 ☐ abut
v. (나라, 장소 따위가 다른 곳과) 경계를 접하다, 이웃하다(=adjoin) ☐
abolish v. 폐지하다, 철폐하다 ☐ bestow v. 주다, 수여하다, 부여하다
☐ render v. ~이 되게 하다; (보답으로서) 주다

베레나 오웬(Verena Owen)의 네 아들은 깨끗한 호수에서 잡은 물고기
를 먹는데, 그 호수는 시온(Zion)에서 북쪽으로 2마일 떨어져 있는 레이
크 카운티(Lake County)에 있는 그들의 집과 인접해 있다.

89 ④

☐ implore v. 애원하다, 간청하다(=beg) ☐ insist v. 주장하다 ☐
suggest v. 암시하다, 비추다 ☐ shout v. 외치다, 소리[고함]치다

제인(Jane)은 밀러(Miller)에게 10일 안에 거기에 당도해주길 간청
했다.

90 ②

☐ striking a. 눈에 띄는, 두드러진, 현저한 ☐ coerce v. 강요하다
(=compel by pressure); 구속하다, 억압하다 ☐ assent n. 동의, 찬성;
인정 ☐ bring about by persuasion 설득해서 ~을 하다 ☐ coax v.
감언으로 설득하다, 어르다 ☐ restrain by force 힘으로 제지하다

수필은 역사가 길지만, 이러한 사실보다 더 두드러진 것이 있으니, 그것
은 수필이 가진 힘이다. 내가 말하는 "힘"이란 정확히 폭력이 항상 하는
바를 할 수 있는 능력, 곧 동의를 강요하는 것이다.

91 ②

☐ lethargic a. 혼수(상태)의; 둔감한(=apathetic) ☐ hypersensitive
a. 지나치게 민감한, 과민한 ☐ arrogant a. 거만한, 오만한 ☐ rigid
a. 굳은, 단단한; 완고한

무기력한 파트너와 함께 일하는 것을 좋아하는 사람은 아무도 없다.

92 ④

☐ facetious a. 익살맞은, 우스운(=humorous) ☐ selectman n. 도시
행정 위원 ☐ petulant a. 화를 잘 내는, 성마른 ☐ lugubrious a.
슬퍼하는, 침울한 ☐ illogical a. 비논리적인, 불합리한

우리 도시의 쓰레기를 달로 보내는 것에 관한 우리의 제안은 우스운 것
이었지만, 행정 위원장은 그 제안을 진지하게 받아들였다.

93 ④

☐ whodunnit n. 탐정[추리] 소설[영화, 극], 스릴러 ☐ colloquial a.
구어체의; 구어의, 일상 회화의(=conversational) ☐ detective story
탐정 소설 ☐ appealing a. 애원적인; 마음을 끄는, 매력적인 ☐ literal
a. 글자대로의; 정확한, 엄밀한 ☐ mythological a. 신화의, 신화적인;
지어낸 이야기의

추리소설은 탐정 소설의 구어적 표현이다.

94 ③

☐ eccentric a. 별난, 괴벽스러운, 기이한(=peculiar) ☐ unfair a. 불공
정한; 부당한 ☐ conventional a. 전통적인, 인습적인; 틀에 박힌 ☐
sociable a. 사교적인, 붙임성 있는

그 연구소는 존 백(John Baek)이라 불리는 유별나지만 훌륭한 한 과학자에 의해 운영되었다.

95 ③

☐ impending a. 임박한, 곧 일어날 듯한(=imminent) ☐ grueling a. 기진맥진 하게 만드는, 대단히 힘든 ☐ Tour de France 투르 드 프랑스 (매년 프랑스에서 개최되는 국제 장거리 자전거 경주) ☐ seminal a. (앞으로 전개될 일에) 중대한, 영향력이 큰 ☐ resilient a. 탄력 있는; 회복력 있는 ☐ exemplary a. 전형적인, 모범적인

전문 사이클 선수들은 대단히 힘든 투르 드 프랑스 경주를 위해 그날 하루를 임박한 출발을 앞두고 막바지 준비를 했다.

96 ④

☐ callow a. 아직 깃털이 나지 않은; 미숙한(=immature) ☐ tycoon n. (재계의) 거물 ☐ composed a. (마음이) 가라앉은, 침착한 ☐ ugly a. 추한, 못생긴; 비열한 ☐ tough a. 강인한; 튼튼한 ☐ handsome a. 풍채 좋은, 잘생긴

미숙한 그의 외모에도 불구하고, 지난주 독일의 그 십대 거물은 대단히 차분하고 자신만만해 보였다.

97 ④

☐ document v. 문서화하다 (상세히) 보도하다 ☐ embrace v. (신청 따위를) 받아들이다; (주의·신앙 따위를) 채택하다(=espouse) ☐ backsliding n. 퇴보, 타락 ☐ retreat n. 퇴각, 퇴거 ☐ uphold v. 지지하다; 떠받치다 ☐ petrify v. 돌같이 굳게 하다; 깜짝 놀라게 하다 ☐ circumscribe v. 제한[억제]하다; ~의 주위에 선을 긋다 ☐ obviate v. 제거[배제]하다

시카고 포스트의 크리스토퍼 허버트(Christopher Herbert)는 어떻게 공화당원들이 "민주주의의 퇴보"를, 즉 한 전문가의 표현으로는 "민주주의적 규범에 대한 지지 철회"를, 채택할 가능성이 민주당원들보다 훨씬 더 높았는지를 보여주는 연구를 문서화했다.

98 ④

☐ beat v. (게임, 시합에서) 이기다 ☐ opponent n. 적수, 반대자, 대항자(=adversary) ☐ amateur n. 아마추어, 비전문가 ☐ professional n. (지적) 직업인, 전문가; 직업[프로] 선수 ☐ descendant n. 자손, 후예

그 권투선수는 불리한 상황에서도 상대를 이겼다.

99 ④

☐ tentative a. 잠정적인, 임시의(=temporary) ☐ keynote n. 주안점, 기조 ☐ tenable a. 방어될 수 있는; (특정 기간 동안) 유지되는 ☐

conclusive a. 결정적인, 확실한 ☐ putative a. 추정되는

이 시점에서 회의의 세부 프로그램은 잠정적이지만, 세 차례의 기조연설이 있을 것이라고는 확실히 발표되었다.

100 ③.

☐ make allowance for ~을 참작하다, 감안하다(=take into account) ☐ give way to ~에 지다, 양보하다 ☐ put up with ~을 참다, 참고 견디다 ☐ take care of ~을 돌보다; 주의하다

당신은 그가 겪은 최근의 불행을 참작해야 한다.

01 ①	02 ①	03 ①	04 ①	05 ④	06 ④	07 ②	08 ④	09 ①	10 ①
11 ②	12 ③	13 ①	14 ②	15 ②	16 ③	17 ③	18 ③	19 ②	20 ④
21 ④	22 ④	23 ③	24 ②	25 ④	26 ③	27 ③	28 ①	29 ①	30 ③
31 ③	32 ④	33 ③	34 ④	35 ④	36 ③	37 ①	38 ②	39 ③	40 ①
41 ④	42 ①	43 ①	44 ③	45 ④	46 ②	47 ③	48 ①	49 ③	50 ③
51 ②	52 ②	53 ④	54 ④	55 ③	56 ①	57 ②	58 ①	59 ②	60 ①
61 ①	62 ②	63 ④	64 ①	65 ④	66 ④	67 ②	68 ①	69 ①	70 ④
71 ②	72 ④	73 ③	74 ②	75 ④	76 ①	77 ①	78 ④	79 ②	80 ①
81 ①	82 ①	83 ③	84 ③	85 ②	86 ④	87 ③	88 ①	89 ③	90 ②
91 ③	92 ④	93 ③	94 ④	95 ③	96 ②	97 ③	98 ②	99 ④	100 ①

01 　　　　　　　　　　　　　　　　　①

☐ outgoing a. 외향적[사교적]인 ☐ demeanor n. 처신, 태도 ☐ humble a. 겸손한(=modest) ☐ attentive a. 주의를 기울이는 ☐ patient a. 인내심이 강한 ☐ devout a. 독실한

그의 사교적인 태도에도 불구하고, 밀른(Milne)은 40년 이상의 세월을 기부 활동에 바쳐온 것에 대해 이야기 할 때 겸손해진다.

02 　　　　　　　　　　　　　　　　　①

☐ terse a. (문체, 표현 등이) 간결한, 간명한(=concise) ☐ authentic a. 진짜인, 정확한 ☐ expedient a. 편리한, 적당한 ☐ logical a. 논리적인, 타당한

어제 발표된 간결한 성명을 통해, 그 회사는 공장 세 곳을 폐쇄할 것이라고 발표했다.

03 　　　　　　　　　　　　　　　　　①

☐ reference n. 참고서; 참조문헌 ☐ alert a. 방심 않는, 정신을 바짝 차린(=watchful) ☐ laboratory n. 실험실, 연구소 ☐ opportunistic a. 기회주의의; 편의주의적인 ☐ selective a. 신중히 선택하는, 선별적인 ☐ adventurous a. 모험적인; 위험한

참고 문헌이 실험 프로그램에 적합한 것으로 여겨지면, 연구원은 그 문헌자료가 일단 실험실에 받아들여지고 나서 취급되는 방식에 대단히 주의를 기울여야 한다.

04 　　　　　　　　　　　　　　　　　①

☐ sober a. 술 취하지 않은, 맑은 정신의; 침착한, 진지한(=serious) ☐ painful a. 아픈, 괴로운; 애처로운 ☐ mysterious a. 신비한, 불가사

의한; 원인 불명의 ☐ ambiguous a. 애매한, 모호한, 불명료한

그 판사는 매우 진지한 표정을 짓고 있었다.

05 　　　　　　　　　　　　　　　　　④

☐ hub n. 중심, 중추(=center) ☐ high point 중대한 시점, 최고의 시기 ☐ summit n. 정상, 꼭대기, 절정; 극치 ☐ path n. 길, 작은 길, 보도; 통로

리틀 록(Little Rock)은 아칸소 주를 가로지르고 있는 연방 주간 고속도로의 중심지이다.

06 　　　　　　　　　　　　　　　　　④

☐ circumscribe v. 경계선을 긋다; 한계를 정하다(=restrict) ☐ divert v. 전환하다, 딴 데로 돌리다 ☐ uphold v. 지지하다; 받치다 ☐ bypass v. 우회하다, 회피하다

사체를 처리하는 과정들이 결국 어느 정도 법에 의해 제한되고 있다.

07 　　　　　　　　　　　　　　　　　②

☐ opportune a. 형편이 좋은; 시기적절한(=right) ☐ ask a favor of ~에게 부탁을 하다 ☐ wrong a. 그릇된, 부정의 ☐ miserable a. 불쌍한, 가련한, 초라한 ☐ happy a. 행운의, 운 좋은, 경사스러운

그녀에게 부탁을 할 적절한 순간을 포착했다.

08 ④

☐ decipher v. (암호를) 해독하다, 풀다(=decode) ☐ declare v. 선언하다; 단언하다; (세관에) 신고하다 ☐ devise v. 궁리하다, 고안하다, 상상하다 ☐ decide v. 결정하다; 해결하다

과학자들은 점차적으로 유기체의 세포 속에서 발견된 유전자 구조를 해독해내고 있다.

09 ①

☐ incipient a. 시작의, 초기의, 발단의(=initial) ☐ recession n. 일시적 불경기, 경기 후퇴 ☐ final a. 마지막의, 결정적인 ☐ ultimate a. 궁극적인, 최후의 ☐ insufficient a. 불충분한, 부족한; 부적당한

회복의 초기 조짐들에도 불구하고, 경제는 더욱 극심한 불황에 빠졌다.

10 ①

☐ indict v. 기소하다, 고발하다(=charge) ☐ acquit v. 석방하다, 무죄로 하다 ☐ condone v. 용서하다, 너그럽게 봐주다 ☐ sentence v. 판결을 내리다, 형을 선고하다

대배심에서 그 용의자를 기소하면, 그는 재판에 회부될 것이다.

11 ②

☐ maladroit a. 솜씨 없는, 서투른(=clumsy) ☐ take it 믿다, 생각하다 ☐ occupy v. ~의 마음[주의]을 끌다 ☐ smart a. 날렵한; 재치 있는 ☐ generous a. 아끼지 않는; 관대한, 아량 있는 ☐ sympathetic a. 동정적인, 인정 있는; 마음에 맞는

지난밤 파티 중에 내가 너를 배웅해주겠다고 이야기한 것이 얼마나 서툴 렀는지! 그의 표정으로 보아, 너의 남자친구는 네가 딴 남자에게 마음을 뺏긴 것으로 생각했던 것 같아.

12 ③

☐ indigenous a. 토착의, 지역 고유의(=aboriginal); 타고난, 고유한 ☐ invincible a. 정복할 수 없는, 무적의; 극복할 수 없는 ☐ cardinal a. 기본적인, 주요한 ☐ congenial a. 같은 성질의, 마음이 맞는, 마음에 드는

태권도는 한국에서 발전해온 토착 스포츠 중의 하나이다.

13 ①

☐ expel v. 면직시키다, 내쫓다 ☐ exile v. 추방[유배]하다 ☐ liquidate v. (빚을) 청산하다; 정리하다; 숙청하다, 죽이다(=kill) ☐ free v. 자유롭게 하다, 해방하다; 구하다, 석방하다 ☐ punish v. 벌하다; 응징하다; 혼내주다 ☐ prison v. 감금하다, 투옥하다

그의 지지자들은 모두 면직되거나 추방되거나 숙청되었다.

14 ②

☐ thrift n. 검약, 검소 ☐ miserly a. 인색한, 욕심 많은, 쩨쩨한(=stingy) ☐ connotation n. 함축, 내포 ☐ misfiring a. 불발이 되는, 실패하는 ☐ ominous a. 심상치 않은, 불길한; 전조의 ☐ generous a. 이끼지 않는, 후한

국가의 위기로 저축을 장려하던 시기가 있었다. 그러나 오늘날 절약은 부정적이고, 인색한 의미를 내포하고 있다.

15 ②

☐ public appearance 공개석상의 출연 ☐ obsessively ad. 병적으로, 과도하게 ☐ eclectic a. 취사선택하는; 절충적인(=selective) ☐ occult a. 불가사의한, 초자연적인; 비밀의 ☐ imaginative a. 상상의, 가공의 ☐ vivacious a. 쾌활한, 활발한

9년 후, 자신의 현역 인생의 나머지를 녹음실에서 보내고자 그는 공개석 상에 모습을 드러내는 것을 포기했는데, 대개 밤 시간에 여러 음악에서 선별하여 작업하는 일에 몰두했다.

16 ③

☐ impugn v. 이의를 제기하다; 비난하다, 공격하다(=challenge) ☐ perish v. 멸망시키다, 죽게 하다 ☐ disconcert v. 당황하게 하다; 교란시키다 ☐ implement v. 이행하다, 시행하다

내가 바라는 것은 은행의 명예가 어떻게든 비난받지 않는 것뿐이다.

17 ③

☐ ogle v. ~에게 곁눈질하다, 추파를 던지다(=leer) ☐ grill v. (석쇠에) 굽다; 엄하게 심문하다 ☐ doff v. (경의를 표하며) 모자를 벗다, 들어올리다 ☐ pretermit v. 간과하다, 무시하다; 불문에 붙이다

그가 자신에게 너무 심하게 추파를 던져서 그 여자는 화가 났다.

18 ③

☐ present v. 참석하다; 제공하다; ~를 보여주다 ☐ idyllic a. 전원시(풍)의, 목가적인(=arcadian) ☐ assume v. 추정하다; ~인 체하다; 취하다 ☐ associate v. 연상하다, 결부 짓다 ☐ lucrative a. 수지맞는, 이득이 되는 ☐ exasperating a. 분통이 터지는, 화가 나는 ☐ occidental a. 서양(인)의, 서구의

그 그림은 종종 아름다움, 풍요, 그리고 목가적인 장소나 생활, 로맨스나 통속성의 모습, 다시 말해 관람객으로서 우리가 바라거나 연관되고 싶어 하는 것들의 모습을 보여주는 그림이다.

19 ②

☐ inculcate v. 가르치다, 심어 주다(=impart) ☐ improvise v. 즉석에서 짓다, 임시변통으로 마련하다 ☐ implicate v. 관련[연루]시키다 ☐ immunize v. 면역력을 갖게 하다

학생들에게 필요할 분석적인 작문 기술을 가르치기 위해 전국 글쓰기 대회가 만들어졌다.

20 ④

☐ virtuosity n. 예술상의 묘기, 기교 ☐ preserve n. 보존식품; 영역, 분야(=domain) ☐ confine v. 제한하다; 감금하다 ☐ portraiture n. 인물묘사; 초상화 ☐ landscape n. 풍경, 경치; 풍경화 ☐ still-life n. 정물화 ☐ dispersion n. 분산, 확산 ☐ propriety n. 적절성; (pl.) 예의범절 ☐ association n. 협회, 조합; 연합, 합동

시간이 흐름에 따라, 창조적인 기교는 점점 더 남성의 영역이 되었다. 예를 들어, 그림의 경우, 여성들은 초상화, 풍경화, 정물화 등과 같은 특정 장르의 범주에 국한되는 경향을 띠게 되었으며, 대개 예술가로서보다는 아마추어 애호가로서 전시회에 출품했다.

21 ④

☐ venomous a. 독이 있는 ☐ peptide n. 펩티드 ☐ toxin n. 독소 ☐ redoubtable a. 가공할, 무서운(=formidable) ☐ efficacious a. 효과 있는, 유효한 ☐ implicit a. 암시적인 ☐ reproducible a. 재생[재현] 가능한, 복사할 수 있는

진화의 과정에서 독이 있는 동물은 포식동물에 대한 가공할 방어무기인 펩티드 독소를 생산해왔다.

22 ④

☐ germane a. 밀접한 관계가 있는; 알맞은, 적절한(=pertinent) ☐ incompatible a. 맞지 않는, 공존할 수 없는 ☐ extraneous a. 외부로부터의, 밖의; 무관계한, 연고 없는 ☐ incongruous a. 일치하지 않는, 어울리지 않는, 부조리한

그것은 흥미 있는 요점이지만, 우리 토론에는 적절치 않다.

23 ③

☐ complacent a. 자기만족의(=self-satisfied) ☐ vengeance n. 복수, 앙갚음 ☐ with a vengeance 심하게, 맹렬히 ☐ condescending a. 거들먹거리는, 잘난 체하는 ☐ exasperated a. 몹시 화가 난, 격분한 ☐ nonchalant a. 무관심한; 차분한, 태연한

시민들이 점점 자족하는 마음이 되고 기온이 떨어지자, 그 전세계적인 역병이 되돌아와 맹위를 떨쳤다.

24 ②

☐ abundant a. 풍부한, 많은(=plentiful) ☐ pitiful a. 측은한, 가련한 ☐ ponderous a. 크고 무거운, 육중한 ☐ punctual a. 시간을 엄수하는

개체 수가 이미 한 자리로 줄어든 종보다 개체 수가 많은 종의 건강과 서식지를 보호하는 편이 훨씬 더 쉽고 돈도 적게 든다.

25 ④

☐ maudlin a. 눈물을 잘 흘리는, 감상적인(=mawkish) ☐ violent a. 폭력적인, 난폭한 ☐ taciturn a. 말없는, 무언의 ☐ boisterous a. (비·바람 따위가) 몹시 사나운, 거친; 시끄러운

나는 그가 술에 취하면 감상적으로 변하는 습성이 있다는 것을 몰랐다.

26 ③

☐ craggy a. 우악스럽게 생긴 ☐ rubbery a. 탄성이 있는; 강인한 ☐ sardonic a. 냉소적인, 비꼬는(=sneering) ☐ grin n. 웃음, 미소 ☐ lustful a. 호색적인, 탐욕스러운 ☐ glamorous a. 화려한, 매력이 넘치는 ☐ annoying a. 성가신, 귀찮은, 짜증스러운

그는 키가 컸고, 가끔은 얼굴을 찡그려 냉소적 미소를 드러내는 험악하며 강인한 얼굴을 한 사내였다.

27 ③

☐ blanched a. 희어진, 바랜; 표백된(=whitened) ☐ shatter v. 산산이 부수다, 분쇄하다 ☐ prominent a. 현저한, 두드러진; 저명한, 걸출한; 돌출한 ☐ inexplicable a. 불가해한, 설명할 수 없는, 납득이 안 가는

그녀는 가끔 사막의 풍경을 그렸는데, 전경에는 롱혼(뿔이 긴 소)의 하얀 두개골을 그리곤 했다.

28 ①

☐ disclose v. 밝히다, 드러내다, 발표하다 ☐ ubiquitous a. 어디에나 있는, 아주 흔한(=common) ☐ data breach 데이터 유출 ☐ famous a. 유명한, 이름난 ☐ notorious a. 악명 높은 ☐ powerful a. 영향력 있는, 유력한

새로운 규정에 따르면, 또한 기업들은 이제 일반적인 데이터 유출 사고를 72시간 이내에 발표해야 할 것이다.

29 ①

☐ annihilate v. 전멸시키다, 멸망시키다(=decimate) ☐ condone v. 용서하다, 너그럽게 봐주다 ☐ castigate v. 처벌하다, 징계하다; 혹평하다 ☐ prevaricate v. 얼버무려 넘기다, 발뺌하다; 속이다

사람들은 진공 요동을 어느 때에 함께 나타나서, 떨어지고, 합쳐져서 서로를 완전히 없애버리는 여러 쌍의 입자들이라고 생각할 수 있다.

30 ①

☐ perjury n. 거짓 맹세, 위증(죄), 서약을 깨뜨리기(=lying under oath) ☐ imprisonment 종신형, 무기 징역 ☐ aid a criminal 범죄자를 돕다 ☐ destroy v. 파괴하다, 부수다, 분쇄하다; 해치다 ☐ threaten the jury 배심원단을 위협하다

엄숙한 법정 심리에서 위증을 할 경우 종신형에 처해질 수도 있다.

31 ③

☐ denounce v. 공공연히 비난하다, 탄핵하다 ☐ charlatan n. 허풍선이; 사기꾼(=deceiver) ☐ idolater n. 우상 숭배자; 이교도 ☐ receiver n. 수신기; 수취인 ☐ celebrity n. 명성; 유명인 ☐ offender n. 범죄자, 위반자

그 연구소에서 만든 출판물들은 라플라스(Laplace)를 현대판 사기꾼이며 '뉴턴숭배자'라고 비난했다.

32 ①

☐ review n. 재검토, 반성, 비평 ☐ appraise v. 평가하다(=evaluate) ☐ performance n. 성취, 성과 ☐ commend v. 칭찬하다; 권하다 ☐ underrate v. 과소평가하다 ☐ publicize v. 선전하다

반성의 일환으로 사원들은 자신의 업무성과를 평가해보라는 요구를 받을 것이다.

33 ③

☐ identical a. 아주 동일한; 같은(=same) ☐ hidden a. 숨은, 숨겨진 ☐ dark a. 어두운, 암흑의, 거무스름한 ☐ unknown a. 알려지지 않은, 미지의; 알 수 없는

나는 그것을 두었던 곳과 똑같은 곳에서 그것을 찾았다.

34 ②

☐ qualified a. 자격 있는; 제한된, 한정된(=limited) ☐ belittled a. 과소평가된 ☐ completed a. 작성한, 완성된 ☐ reproved a. 비난받는

제한된 수의 학생들만이 마틴(Martin) 교수의 고전 수업을 들을 수 있다.

35 ④

☐ colonial a. 식민지의 ☐ postcolonial a. 식민지 독립 후의 ☐ identity n. 정체성 ☐ plague v. 성가시게 하다, 애태우다, 괴롭히다 (=disturb) ☐ deter v. 단념시키다, 제지하다 ☐ flourish v. 번영하다, 융성하다 ☐ change v. 바꾸다, 변경하다, 고치다

홍콩은 동양인가 아니면 서양인가? 중국인가 아니면 영국인가? 전통적인가 아니면 현대적인가? 식민지인가 아니면 식민지에서 독립했는가? 홍콩이라는 지역은 (이런) 정체성 문제들로 계속해서 시달리고 있다.

36 ③

☐ dispense with ~없이 지내다, 때우다(=do without) ☐ do away with ~을 없애다, 폐지하다 ☐ do for ~에게 도움이 되다; ~을 해치우다 ☐ do with ~을 처리하다, 다루다; ~으로 해나가다

우리는 너무 많은 날 동안 자지 않고서는 견딜 수가 없다.

37 ①

☐ harness v. (말 따위에) 견인줄을 채우다, 동력화하다, 이용하다 (=exploit) ☐ pupil n. (특히 어린) 학생 ☐ static a. 고정된[고정적인] ☐ restrict v. 제한하다 ☐ contract v. 계약하다; 질병에 걸리다 ☐ welcome v. 환영하다

인쇄된 교과서는 빠르게 전자책으로 대체되고 있는데, 전자책은 휴대용 기기의 대화형 기능을 활용하고 간단한 스와이프와 손가락 탭 동작을 통해 학생들을 고정된 페이지 너머로 안내한다.

38 ②

☐ paralyze v. 마비시키다; 무력하게 하다(=disable) ☐ despise v. 경멸하다, 멸시하다 ☐ displace v. 대신하다, 바꾸어놓다 ☐ degrade v. 강등시키다, 떨어뜨리다

택시기사들이 공무를 마비시켰다.

39 ③

☐ tedious a. 지루한, 따분한, 싫증나는(=prosaic) ☐ disorganized a. 무질서한; 엉터리의; 부주의한 ☐ instructive a. 교훈적인, 본받을 점이 많은, 계발적인 ☐ exhilarating a. 기분을 돋우어주는, 유쾌하게 하는; 상쾌한

그의 가장 최근 영화는 무척 지루했다.

40 ①

☐ urgent a. 긴급한, 촉박한(=important) ☐ confidential a. 기밀의, 은밀한 ☐ unpredictable a. 예상할 수 없는 ☐ dangerous a. 위험한

우편물 하나가 다급한 것이라서 내가 전화 걸기 전에 먼저 처리해야 한다.

41 ④

☐ impede v. 방해하다, 지연시키다(=hinder) ☐ utilize v. 이용하다, 활용하다 ☐ render v. ~하게 하다; 주다; 표현하다 ☐ infuse v. 붓다; 주입하다, 고취하다

심지어 그는 경고를 받은 이후에도 계속해서 그들의 진행을 방해하고 있다.

42 ①

☐ feeble a. 연약한, 힘없는; 희미한, 가냘픈(=weak) ☐ contraction n. 수축, 수렴 ☐ jellyfish n. 해파리 ☐ buoy v. 뜨다, 떠오르다(up) ☐ rhythmic a. 율동적인; 억양이 있는 ☐ deliberate a. 신중한, 생각이 깊은, 계획적인 ☐ automatic a. 자동의, 자동적인

약한 수축을 통해 해파리는 몸을 앞으로 나아가며 주위의 물에 의해 뜨게 된다.

43 ①

☐ sanguine a. 낙관적인, 자신감이 넘치는 ☐ somber a. 어두침침한, 흐린, 우울한(=gloomy) ☐ optimistic a. 낙관적인 ☐ wholesome a. 건강에 좋은, 건전한, 유익한 ☐ ignoble a. 비열한, 야비한

이처럼 중요한 때에 낙관적인 태도는 전선에서 우리에게 들려오는 우울한 소식에 의해 정당화되지 못한다.

44 ③

☐ uncompleted a. 미완성의 ☐ artery n. 동맥 ☐ inchoate a. 방금 시작한, 초기의(=incipient) ☐ probe n. 조사, 정밀 조사 ☐ afflict v. 괴롭히다, 피해를 입히다 ☐ threatening a. 협박하는, 위협적인 ☐ haphazard a. 우연한; 되는 대로의 ☐ tricky a. 까다로운; 교활한

미완성 프로젝트들이 나이지리아의 동맥을 따라 있는 것처럼, 초기의 탐사와 조사가 그 시스템을 괴롭힌다.

45 ④

☐ lassitude n. 무기력, 나태(=lethargy) ☐ attachment n. 애착; 접착; 구속 ☐ reaction n. 반응; 반작용 ☐ ecstasy n. 무아경, 황홀 ☐ conviction n. 확신, 신념

만일 신이 카이사르(Caesar)가 달리 행동하는 것에 대해 어떤 생각을 갖고 있다면, 카이사르는 신의 생각에 접근할 수 있다. 비록 그가 무기력이나 시간 부족이나 자신의 분별력에 대한 애착으로 인해 아마도 그 접근을 이용하려고 하지 않겠지만.

46 ②

☐ inequality n. 불평등, 불균등 ☐ blasphemy n. 신성 모독 ☐ sanctity n. 존엄성, 신성함(=divinity) ☐ privilege v. 특권[특전, 특혜]을 주다 ☐ peripheral a. 주변적인 ☐ spirit n. 정신 ☐ vanity n. 덧없음, 무상 ☐ modesty n. 겸손, 조심성

사회주의자들에 따르면, 불평등은 인류의 신성함에 대한 최악의 신성 모독인데, 인간의 보편적인 본질보다 인간의 지엽적인 자질을 우선하기 때문이다.

47 ③

☐ disingenuous a. (사람·언동 등이) 부정직한, 불성실한; 솔직하지 않은(=deceitful) ☐ bellicose a. 호전적인 ☐ deliberate a. 고의적인; 신중한 ☐ distinguished a. 현저한; 출중한

그 광고 표적 소비자들은 엄청난 할인이나 자동차 구입 대출 이자율 인하 같은 거창한 약속을 하는 솔직하지 않은 자동차 판매 광고에 익숙해졌다.

48 ①

☐ depose v. (특히 통치자를 권좌에서) 물러나게 하다, 퇴위시키다 ☐ replace v. 대신[대체]하다 ☐ pliant a. 고분고분한, 유순한(=biddable) ☐ successor n. 후임자, 계승자 ☐ dexterous a. 손재주가 있는, 솜씨 좋은 ☐ brawny a. 근육이 발달한; 건강한 ☐ cerebral a. 뇌의; 지적인

그는 폐위되었고 좀 더 유순한 후임자가 그를 대신하였다.

49 ③

☐ size up ~에 대한 판단을 내리다 ☐ accomplishment n. 업적, 공적 ☐ deleterious a. 해로운, 유해한(=pernicious) ☐ everlasting a. 영원한, 변치 않는 ☐ irreversible a. 되돌릴 수 없는 ☐ vigilant a. 바짝 경계하는, 방심하지 않는

일부 사용자들에게는 사이버스(Cyberse)가 친구들과 연결을 유지하기 위한 긍정적 방법이지만, 성취도를 비교함으로써 자신을 판단하기 위해 그것을 사용하는 다른 사람들은 해로운 영향을 입을 수도 있다.

50 ③

☐ permeate v. 스며들다; 충만하다, 퍼지다(=spread into) ☐ hold sway over ~을 지배하다, 마음대로 하다 ☐ shed light on ~을 비추다; 밝히다, 해명하다 ☐ shape up (좋은 방향으로) 되어가다, 전개되다

식민지 시대에 종교의 영향력이 생활 전반에 스며들었다.

51 ②

☐ dejectedly ad. 기가 죽어, 맥없이, 낙담하여(=sadly) ☐ cheerfully ad. 기분 좋게, 쾌활하게, 기꺼이 ☐ hopefully ad. 희망을 가지고; 잘만 되면 ☐ inquiringly ad. 호기심 많아; 미심쩍어 하는 듯이

그녀는 잠을 잘 만한 배를 찾을 수 없었다. "여기에는 배가 한 척도 없어요."라고 그녀는 낙심하여 말했다.

52 ②

☐ censure v. 비난하다, 책망하다; 혹평하다(=blame) ☐ indiscreet a. 무분별한, 지각없는 ☐ praise v. 칭찬하다, 찬미하다 ☐ realize v. 실현하다; 실감하다; 깨닫다 ☐ welcome v. 환영하다, 기꺼이 맞이하다

그 학생은 분별없는 자신의 행동 때문에 비난받았다.

53 ④

☐ outmoded a. 유행에 뒤떨어진, 구식의(=old-fashioned) ☐ narrow a. 폭이 좁은; 여유가 없는; 한정된 ☐ reinforced concrete 철근 콘크리트 ☐ illegal a. 불법의, 위법의

미국의 다섯 다리 중 한 개는 구식이다.

54 ②

☐ posthumous a. 유복자로 태어난; 저자의 사후(死後)에 출판된; 사후의(=postmortem) ☐ prim a. 깐깐한, 꼼꼼한; 새침 떠는 ☐ primal a. 제일의, 최초의; 원시의; 주요한 ☐ posthaste ad. 급행으로, 황급히

많은 예술가들과 작가들이 생전에 무시당해오다 사후(死後)에야 명성을 얻었다.

55 ③

☐ immutable a. 변경할 수 없는, 불변의, 변치 않는(=unalterable) ☐ indefinable a. 정의를 내릴 수 없는; 막연한 ☐ intangible a. 만져서 알 수 없는, 무형의 ☐ uncountable a. 무수한, 셀 수 없는

고등학교의 성공은 일련의 변하지 않는 특성들에 의해서라기보다는 오히려 교육자들이 만들고 통제하는 교육 여건에 의해서 결정된다.

56 ①

☐ modify v. 바꾸다, 개조하다 ☐ emission control 배기가스 차단 ☐ aspirate v. (가스 따위를) 빨아내다; 빨아들이다 ☐ belch v. 내뿜다 n. 분출 ☐ sooty a. 그을음이 묻는, 거무튀튀한 ☐ exhaust n. 배기가스 ☐ egregious a. 악명 높은, 지독한, 터무니없는, 가증스러운(=heinous) ☐ assiduous a. 근면 성실한, 부지런한 ☐ salacious a. 외설스러운, 음탕한 ☐ crustaceous a. 딱지를 가진; 갑각류의

자동차 소유자들은 배기가스 차단 장치를 개조하여 엔진에 공기를 적게 공급하곤 했는데, 이렇게 하는 경우 시커먼 배기가스를 엄청나게 내뿜으며 자동차의 출력을 증가시킬 수 있었다. 이러한 악질적인 운전 법규 위반 행위는 반드시 근절되어야 한다.

57 ②

☐ indignation n. 분개, 분노(=anger) ☐ pity n. 불쌍히 여김, 동정 ☐ disappointment n. 실망, 기대에 어긋남 ☐ sympathy n. 동정, 헤아림, 호의

그녀는 광부들이 처해 있는 근무 여건에 분개했다.

58 ③

☐ mumble v. 중얼[웅얼]거리다 ☐ prayer n. 기도 문구, 기도문 ☐ deity n. 신; 신적 존재(=god) ☐ nature n. 자연, 천지 만물; 성질, 본질 ☐ king n. 왕, 군주; 거물 ☐ ghost n. 유령, 망령, 원혼

터널 안으로 향하면서, 그는 산과 산속의 모든 금을 다스리는 신에게 중얼중얼 기도를 한다.

59 ②

☐ shield v. 보호하다, 수호하다(=protect); 가리다, 숨기다 ☐ make free ~를 석방하다, 방면하다 ☐ conserve v. 절약하다; 보존하다; 보호하다 ☐ involve v. 수반[포함]하다; 관련[연루]시키다

부모가 그의 자녀들을 모든 위험으로부터 보호하기란 불가능하다.

60 ①

☐ marvel n. 경이, 불가사의, 놀랄만한 일; 놀라운 것[사람](=wonder) ☐ of one's time 당시의, 그 시절의 ☐ dispute n. 논쟁 ☐ frustration n. 좌절, 실패 ☐ model n. 모형, 본, 모범

이리(Erie) 운하가 건설됐을 때, 그것은 당시의 공학 기술의 경이였다.

61 ①

☐ well-meaning a. 선의의, 악의 없는, 호의에서 우러난 ☐ pacify v. 달래다, 진정시키다; 가라앉히다(=calm) ☐ delta n. 삼각주, 델타 ☐ unrest n. (사회, 정치적인) 불안, 불만 ☐ give up v. 포기하다, 그만두다 ☐ develop v. 발달시키다, 개발하다 ☐ patrol v. 순찰[순회]하다

삼각주 지역을 진정시키기 위한 다양한 호의적 계획들에도 불구하고, 정부는 그 지역의 동요를 막는 데 실패했다.

62 ②

☐ overcome v. 극복하다, 압도하다 ☐ fatigue n. 피로 ☐ dullness n. 단조로움, 지루함(=drudgery) ☐ dossil n. 붕대, (상처를 두르는) 린트 ☐ duarchy n. 이두(二頭) 정치 ☐ drollness n. 우스움, 익살맞음

그 작업의 단조로움으로 그녀는 겨우 두시간만에 피로에 압도당했다.

63 ④

☐ Mediterranean a. 지중해의; 지중해성(性) 기후의 ☐ despotic a. 전제의, 독재적인(=tyrannical) ☐ gentile a. 비(非)유대인의; 이방인의 ☐ democratic a. 민주주의(국가)의, 민주적인 ☐ tribal a. 부족의

지금으로부터 3천 년 전에, 지중해 세계의 한 작은 지역에서, 모두 독재적이었던 초기의 건국 전통들과의 결별이 일어났다.

64 ③

☐ taint v. 오염시키다, 더럽히다(=stain) ☐ imprisonment n. 투옥, 감금; 구속 ☐ fraud n. 사기, 협잡; 사기꾼 ☐ upgrade v. 승격시키다, 질을 높이다 ☐ affect v. 악영향을 미치다; 감동시키다 ☐ end v. 끝내다, 종료하다

두 아들이 사기죄로 구속되면서 김(Kim)의 정치 경력 또한 오명을 얻었다.

65 ④

☐ abound v. 풍부하다, 가득하다(=proliferate) ☐ die out 멸종되다; 차차 소멸하다 ☐ occur v. 일어나다, 생기다 ☐ bounce back 되튀다; (건강, 경기) 회복하다

그녀의 죽음의 원인에 관한 소문이 무성하다.

66 ④

☐ disguise v. 변장하다, 위장시키다; 감추다, 숨기다(=hide) ☐ obtain v. 얻다, 획득하다 ☐ include v. 포함하다, 넣다 ☐ show v. 보여주다, 제시하다; 전시하다

당신은 매우 매력적인 사람이다. 그리고 당신은 당신이 숨기려고 애쓰는 내적인 아름다움도 지니고 있다.

67 ③

☐ whimsical a. 변덕스러운; 묘한, 별난(=capricious) ☐ amicable a. 우호적인, 친화적인, 평화적인, 유쾌한 ☐ enthusiastic a. 열렬한; 열중한 ☐ hilarious a. 유쾌한; 웃음을 자아내는, 재미있는

이 여자는 거의 또는 전혀 이유가 없다고 생각될 때에도 매우 변덕스럽다.

68 ①

☐ tactless a. 재치 없는, 분별없는(=thoughtless) ☐ preaching n. 설교 ☐ cathedral n. 대성당 ☐ disfavor n. 탐탁찮게 여김, 냉대, 싫어함 ☐ delicate a. 섬세한, 고운; 섬약한 ☐ diplomatic a. 외교의, 외교적 수완이 있는 ☐ ruthless a. 잔인한, 가차 없는

성공회 사제이자 런던 성 바오로 성당의 주임신부였던 그는 분별없는 설교 때문에 엘리자베스(Elizabeth) 1세의 미움을 사게 되었다.

69 ①

☐ acquaint v. 숙지시키다, 익히 알게 하다, 알리다(=familiarize) ☐ under discussion 심의[토의]중인 ☐ explain v. 설명하다, 밝히다 ☐ classify v. 분류하다, 등급으로 나누다 ☐ acquire v. 취득하다, 얻다

이런 종류의 책을 쓸 때, 나의 주된 목적은 독자들에게 논의 중인 저자들과 시대들에 대한 일반적으로 인정되는 견해를 숙지시키기 위한 것이었다.

70 ④

☐ apathetic a. 냉담한, 무관심한(=indifferent) ☐ lame a. 절름발이의; 불완전한 ☐ futile a. 무익한, 하찮은 ☐ shrewd a. 예민한, 날카로운

우리가 일상생활로 바쁠 때 환경에 대해 무관심해지기 쉽다.

71 ②

☐ embargo n. 출항 금지, 억류; 봉쇄(=ban) ☐ diction n. 용어 선택, 어법, 말씨 ☐ emblem n. 상징, 표상; 전형, 귀감 ☐ compass n. 나침반; 한계, 범위

의회는 외제차에 대한 통상 금지를 고려했다.

72 ④

☐ impetuous a. 격렬한; 성급한, 충동적인(=impulsive) ☐ illustrious a. 뛰어난, 저명한 ☐ impolite a. 무례한, 실례되는 ☐ immune a. 면역성의; 면제된

존(John)은 너무 성급해서 결정을 내리는 데 몇 초도 걸리지 않았다.

73 ③

☐ laudatory a. 칭찬의, 찬미하는(=complimentary) ☐ conclusive a. 결정적인, 확실한, 단호한 ☐ impartial a. 치우치지 않은, 편견이 없는; 공평한 ☐ disparaging a. 얕보는; 험담하는, 비난하는

그 연극은 대부분 호평을 받았다.

74 ②

☐ hand down ~을 물려주다, 남기다(=bequeath) ☐ from generation to generation 대대로(이어져서) ☐ rebuke v. 비난하다, 꾸짖다, 징계하다; 억제하다 ☐ preserve v. 보전하다, 유지하다, 보존하다 ☐ collect v. 모으다, 수집하다, 모이다

반지는 대대로 물려져 내려왔다.

75 ④

☐ refuge n. 피난(처) ☐ lackluster a. 흐릿한; 활기 없는(=dull) ☐ time-tested a. 장기간의 사용[경험]으로 보증이 된

취업시장이 활기가 없을 때 대학원을 피난처로 삼는 것은 오랜 세월에 걸쳐 유효성이 증명된 전략이다.

76 ①

☐ adapt v. 적응시키다, 익숙해지다(=adjust) ☐ adapt oneself to ~에 순응하다, 익숙해지다 ☐ admonish v. 훈계하다, 타이르다, 질책하다 ☐ advocate v. 옹호하다, 변호하다, 주장하다 ☐ attribute v. (~의 원인을) ~에 귀착시키다

밤에 일하는 사람들은 낮 시간동안 잠을 자는 일에 익숙해져야 한다.

77 ①

☐ stealthy a. 비밀의, 남의 눈을 피하는(=surreptitious) ☐ table scrap 식사에서 사람이 먹고 남은 음식 ☐ baleful a. 재앙의, 해로운 ☐ raucous a. 목이 쉰, 쉰 목소리의 ☐ benevolent a. 자애로운

나의 개는 내가 관심을 다른 곳에 두고 있을 때 식탁에 남은 음식을 내 눈을 피해 몰래 먹는 버릇이 있다.

78 ④

☐ ravage v. 약탈[파괴]하다; 황폐하게 하다(=destroy) ☐ forestry n. 임업 ☐ power plant 발전소 ☐ reduce v. 줄이다; 축소하다 ☐ change v. 바꾸다, 변경하다 ☐ increase v. 늘리다, 증가시키다

많은 국가의 황폐화된 농촌 경제는 임업, 운송, 그리고 발전시설 운영 분야에서 수만 개의 새로운 일자리를 창출함으로써 부양될 것이다.

79 ②

☐ throe n. 심한 고통, 고민; 진통(=agony) ☐ in the throes of 한창 ~을 하는 중에 ☐ war n. 전쟁, 싸움, 교전상태 ☐ fight n. 싸움, 전투 ☐ enmity n. 증오, 적의; 불화

혁명이 한창일 때 국가는 외부의 간섭을 받아들이지 않을 것이다.

80 ①

☐ far from 결코 ~이 아닌 ☐ a bolt from the blue 마른하늘에 날벼락, 청천벽력 ☐ commission n. 위원회 ☐ foresee v. 예견하다 ☐ in general terms 개괄적으로, 일상적인 말로 ☐ glitch n. 작은 기술상의 문제, 결함(=problem) ☐ stitch n. (바느질, 자수의) 한 땀 ☐ signal n. 신호; 징조 ☐ glossary n. (특수한 주제, 분야 등에 관한) 용어[어휘]사전

9·11 테러공격은 (상세히는 아니어도) 적어도 개괄적으로는 예견되었으며, 오판, 실수, 작은 기술상의 문제, 백악관 내부의 몇 가지만 아니었다면 충분히 막을 수 있었을지도 모른다는 사실을 그 위원회가 마른하늘에 날벼락처럼 증명한 것이 아니라, 지난 19개월 동안 (지속적으로) 증명하였다.

81 ①

☐ falsification n. 위조; 반증 ☐ distinguish v. 구별하다, 식별[분간]하다(=differentiate) ☐ persuade v. 설득하다 ☐ exempt v. 면제하다 ☐ prevent v. 막다, 방해하다

그 철학자는 과학적 이론과 비과학적 이론을 구분하는 방법으로 반증원리를 도입했다.

82 ①

☐ commotion n. 소동, 동요, 폭동(=agitation) ☐ grimace n. 찌푸린 얼굴, 우거지상 ☐ petulance n. 심술 사나움, 무례한 태도 ☐ sonority n. 울려 퍼짐; 반향(反響)

갑자기 비가 내리기 시작했다. 새들은 더욱 소란을 피웠고, 갈팡질팡 어지러이 머리 위를 빙빙 날아다니고 있었다.

83 ③

☐ emerge v. 출현하다 ☐ periodically ad. 주기적으로(=regularly) ☐ infect v. 감염시키다 ☐ suddenly ad. 갑자기 ☐ widely ad. 널리; 크게, 대단히 ☐ eternally ad. 영원히

그때 이후로 바이러스가 아프리카의 여러 나라에 주기적으로 출현하여 사람들을 감염시켰다.

84 ③

☐ arrogance n. 오만, 거만 ☐ alienate v. 멀리하다, 소원하게 하다(=distance) ☐ compliment v. 칭찬하다; 축하하다 ☐ perish v. 사라지다, 멸망하다 ☐ endear v. 사랑받게 하다

그 작가의 오만함은 출판업자를 포함한 모든 사람으로부터 그를 멀어지게 했다.

85 ②

□ candid a. 정직한, 솔직한, 거리낌 없는, 노골적인(=forthright) □ austere a. 엄(격)한, 준엄한; 꾸미지 않은, 간소한 □ nonpareil a. 비할 데 없는, 둘도 없는 □ rhetorical a. 수사적인; 미사여구의

잘못을 저지른 후에, 그녀는 솔직하게 해명했다.

86 ④

□ middle-of-the-road a. 중도의, 온건한(=moderate) □ stance n. 입장, 태도 □ backward a. 뒤쪽의; 거꾸로의; 뒤떨어진 □ extreme a. 극도의, 극심한; 극단적인 □ futuristic a. 미래의; 선진적인

민주당은 교육 문제에 대해 온건한 입장을 취했다.

87 ③

□ farmyard n. 농장 구내, 농가의 마당 □ cacophony n. 불협화음; 소음(=discordant sound) □ harmonious a. 조화된 □ agreeable a. 기분 좋은, 유쾌한 □ unpleasant a. 불쾌한, 기분 나쁜

농가 마당에 들어서자 동물들이 내는 불협화음이 우리를 맞이했다.

88 ①

□ confide v. 신임하다, 신뢰하다(=believe); 비밀을 털어놓다 □ affront v. 모욕하다, 무례한 언동을 하다 □ protract v. 오래 끌다, 길게 하다, 연장하다 □ upbraid v. 비판하다, 비난하다

그녀는 그녀의 가장 친한 친구를 믿기 망설였다.

89 ③

□ emanate v. (냄새·빛·소리·열 따위가) 방사[발산]하다; (생각·명령 등이) 나오다(=emerge) □ tactical a. 전술적인 □ divine a. 신성(神性)의; 신성한 □ proclamation n. 선언, 포고, 발표 □ dwindle v. 줄어들다, 축소되다 □ eulogize v. 칭찬하다, 칭송하다 □ deteriorate v. (질·가치가) 떨어지다, 악화하다

딕스(Dix)와 리(Lea)의 그림에서, 전쟁의 의미는 전술적인 작전행동이나 신성한 포고로부터 나오지 않는다.

90 ②

□ beautifully ad. 굉장히 □ airy a. 바람이 잘 통하는; 환상적인, 우아한 □ oppressive a. 억압적인, 포악한; 답답한(=cramped) □ relieving a. (고통을) 경감하는; (긴장을) 풀어주는 □ burdensome a. 부담스러운, 힘든; 번거로운 □ balmy a. 향기로운, 은은한

우리의 새로 만든 현대식 트라이베카(Tribeca) 사무실은 굉장히 통풍이 잘됐지만, 몹시 답답했다.

91 ③

□ complicated v. 복잡하게 하다, 뒤얽히게 만들다(=entangle) □ straighten out 바로 잡다, 바르게 하다 □ disentangle v. (엉킨 것을) 풀다, (혼란에서) 빠져나오다 □ simplify v. 단순화[간소화]하다, 간단하게 하다

이러한 새 법규들이 조세 체계를 더욱 복잡하게 만들었다.

92 ④

□ legislation n. 법률, 제정법; 법률의 제정, 입법 행위 □ enact v. 제정하다, 법제화하다(=legislate) □ aftermath n. (전쟁, 사고 등의) 여파, 영향, 후유증 □ high-profile a. 세간의 이목을 끄는 □ child abuse 아동학대 □ waive v. 포기하다, 철회하다 □ dramatize v. 각색하다; 과장되게 표현하다 □ carry out ~을 수행하다, 실시하다

그 법은 작년에 많은 관심을 끌었던 두 건의 아동학대 사건의 여파로 제정되었다.

93 ③

□ nonpartisan a. 당파에 속하지 않는, 무소속의; 공정한(=just) □ economical a. 경제적인, 실속 있는; 검약한 □ party-spirited a. 당파심이 강한 □ prejudiced a. 편견을 가진, 편파적인

세금 징수 기관은 공정해야 한다.

94 ④

□ yen n. 열망(=longing) □ futility n. 무익, 쓸모없음 □ relief n. 안도, 안심 □ outrage n. 격분, 격노

그녀는 해안에 부서지는 파도를 보자 모험과 탐험에 대한 열망이 그녀를 압도했다.

95 ③

□ brag v. 자랑하다, 자만하다(=boast) □ lie v. 눕다; 기대다, 의지하다; 거짓말하다 □ criticize v. 비평하다, 비판하다 □ secretive a. 숨기는; 비밀주의의, 잠자코 있는

존(John)은 그의 아름다운 아내를 자랑한다.

96 ②

□ nebulous a. 흐릿한, 모호한, 불명료한(=ambiguous) □ sole proprietorship 개인영업, 개인기업 □ pliable a. 휘기 쉬운, 유연한; 유순한 □ invincible a. 정복할 수 없는, 무적의 □ swift a. 빠른, 신속한

은행과 투자자들은 흔히 개인기업의 더 불분명한 구조보다 주식회사 구조를 선호한다.

97 ③

☐ reciprocal a. 상호의; 호혜적인; 보답의(=mutual) ☐ concession n. 면허, 특허; 이권 ☐ tariff n. 관세 ☐ functional a. 기능의, 작용의; 직무(상)의 ☐ enthusiastic a. 열심인; 열광적인, 열렬한 ☐ graduated a. 등급이 있는; 단계적으로 배열한; 눈금을 표시한

무역 협정에서 관세를 정할 때 일반적으로 국가들은 상호 특권을 체결한다.

98 ②

☐ abnormal a. 비정상적인, 이상한, 예외적인(=unusual) ☐ substance n. 물질; 본질, 실체 ☐ upset v. 뒤엎다; 전복시키다; 완전히 어지럽히다 ☐ flawless a. 흠 없는, 완전한, 완벽한 ☐ typical a. 전형적인, 대표적인; 상징적인 ☐ symbolic a. 상징적인, 상징하는

어떤 비정상적인 인간의 행동은 뇌의 화학적 균형을 교란시키는 물질을 섭취함으로써 야기될지도 모른다.

99 ④

☐ generic a. 포괄적인, 일반적인; 총칭의(=general) ☐ specific a. 특유한, 일정한, 명확한 ☐ technical a. 기술적인, 전문적인 ☐ scientific a. 과학의; 정확한

소프트웨어는 컴퓨터를 통제하는 일련의 프로그램을 지칭하는 일반적인 용어이다.

100 ①

☐ sanguine a. 명랑한, 자신감이 넘치는; 혈색이 좋은(=buoyant) ☐ pessimistic a. 비관적인, 염세적인 ☐ improvising a. 즉흥적인 ☐ stressful a. 긴장이 많은, 스트레스가 많은

그는 쾌활한 성격을 가지고 있다.

MVP 16-20 ACTUAL TEST

01 ②	02 ①	03 ④	04 ④	05 ①	06 ③	07 ③	08 ②	09 ①	10 ④
11 ③	12 ④	13 ②	14 ②	15 ③	16 ②	17 ①	18 ②	19 ④	20 ①
21 ①	22 ②	23 ①	24 ④	25 ①	26 ③	27 ②	28 ②	29 ①	30 ①
31 ④	32 ②	33 ④	34 ①	35 ④	36 ④	37 ②	38 ④	39 ②	40 ④
41 ③	42 ②	43 ①	44 ②	45 ③	46 ④	47 ②	48 ③	49 ②	50 ②
51 ④	52 ④	53 ①	54 ①	55 ①	56 ③	57 ②	58 ④	59 ②	60 ④
61 ①	62 ③	63 ③	64 ①	65 ④	66 ③	67 ③	68 ④	69 ②	70 ④
71 ①	72 ①	73 ③	74 ①	75 ④	76 ④	77 ③	78 ①	79 ③	80 ①
81 ③	82 ③	83 ①	84 ③	85 ②	86 ④	87 ②	88 ④	89 ①	90 ②
91 ①	92 ②	93 ③	94 ④	95 ②	96 ①	97 ③	98 ④	99 ①	100 ④

01 ②

☐ acquit v. 무죄를 선고하다, 석방하다(=absolve) ☐ disregard v. 무시하다, 경시하다 ☐ upbraid v. 비난하다, 비판하다 ☐ condemn v. 비난하다; 유죄를 선고하다

판사는 다른 사람들에게는 무죄를 선고한 반면, 몇몇에게는 유죄를 선고했다.

02 ①

☐ pollutant n. 오염물질, 오염원 ☐ accelerate v. 가속하다, 촉진하다(=facilitate) ☐ devastate v. 황폐시키다; 철저하게 파괴하다; 압도하다 ☐ decelerate v. 속도를 줄이다, 감속하다 ☐ fluctuate v. 변동시키다, 동요시키다

호수로 흘러드는 오염물질은 자연의 노화과정을 급속하게 가속화시킬 수 있다.

03 ④

☐ detached a. 분리된, 떨어진(=loose); 초연한; 공평한 ☐ damaged a. 손해[피해]를 입은, 하자가 생긴 ☐ fixed a. 고정된; 확고한 ☐ fastened a. 단단히 고정된, 묶인

트레일러는 그것을 끌고 가던 트럭에서 분리됐다.

04 ④

☐ interact v. 상호 작용하다, 서로 영향을 주다(=mingle) ☐ agree v. 동의하다, 승낙하다, 응하다 ☐ identify v. 확인하다; 인지하다; 동일시하다 ☐ compete v. 겨루다, 경쟁하다; 필적하다

벨로(Bellow)의 등장인물들은 자아를 갖고 사회와 상호 작용한다.

05 ①

☐ frolic v. 장난치며 놀다, 시시덕거리다, 뛰놀다(=play) ☐ practice v. 실행하다; 연습하다 ☐ walk v. 걷다; 산책하다 ☐ ride v. 타다; 승마하다

그들은 30분 동안 장난쳤다.

06 ③

☐ taunt n. 비웃음, 조롱(=mockery) ☐ compliment n. 칭찬의 말, 찬사 ☐ indifference n. 무관심, 냉담 ☐ prejudice n. 편견, 선입관

지단(Zidane)은 알제리 출신이라는 이유로 그의 선수 생활 내내 조롱을 당했다.

07 ③

☐ proponent n. 지지자(=advocate) ☐ underlie v. ~의 근저를 이루다 ☐ initiator n. 창시자 ☐ commentator n. 주석자; 시사 해설자 ☐ specialist n. 전문가, 전문의(醫)

독서에 대한 부호기반 접근법의 지지자들에 따르면, 독서는 독서의 밑바탕을 이루는 기초 (학습) 능력을 제공함으로써 가르쳐져야 한다.

08 ②

☐ belated a. 늦은, 뒤늦은(=tardy); 구식의 ☐ fission n. (원자의) 핵분열(=nuclear fission) ☐ beloved a. 사랑하는, 귀여운 ☐ related a. 관계가 있는, 관련된 ☐ premature a. 조숙한; 시기상조의, 너무 이른

뒤늦게 밝혀진 우라늄 분열을 참조하여 이러한 종류의 설명은 더 자세해질 수 있다.

09   ①

☐ tantamount a. 동등한, 상당하는(=equivalent) ☐ impeachment n. 비난; 탄핵, 고발 ☐ tenable a. 공격에 견딜 수 있는; 유지[방어]할 수 있는 ☐ revealing a. 감춰진 부분을 밝히는; 뜻이 깊은 ☐ generous a. 관대한; 풍부한

민주당원들은 그 트윗이 범죄행위에 해당하며 탄핵 가능 항목에 추가될 수 있음을 시사했다.

10   ④

☐ have a stake in ~에 이해관계가 있다 ☐ emergence n. 출현, 발생; 등장(=appearance) ☐ acceptance n. 받아들임, 수락, 승인 ☐ joining n. 접합, 연결 ☐ status n. 상태; 지위, 자격 ☐ appearance n. 출현, 출석; 외양

모든 시민들은 미국이 자유세계의 지도자로서 등장하는 데 이해관계를 가진다.

11   ③

☐ bureaucracy n. 관료제도, 관료 정치 ☐ be geared to (계획, 요구 등에) 맞추어져 있다, ~에 조정되어 있다(=be oriented to) ☐ be provided with ~을 공급받다 ☐ be resistant to ~에 저항하다 ☐ be equipped with ~을 갖추고 있다

관료제도는 그 구조와 기능의 본연의 특성 때문에 안정성과 완만한 변화에 맞춰져 있다.

12   ④

☐ polytheism n. 다신론, 다신교 ☐ virile a. 사나이의, 남성의; 생식력 있는 ☐ fecund a. 다산의; 비옥한; 풍성한(=prolific) ☐ benedictory a. 축복의 ☐ sacred a. 신성한 ☐ reciprocal a. 상호의

다신교에서 신들은 일반적으로 생식력 있고 다산의 상징인 남자 또는 여자로 묘사된다.

13   ②

☐ priceless a. 값을 매길 수 없는, 대단히 귀중한 ☐ painstaking a. 공들인(=thorough) ☐ exuberant a. 열광적인, 열의가 넘치는 ☐ vivacious a. 명랑한, 쾌활한 ☐ impeccable a. 결점 없는, 나무랄 데 없는

그들의 고된 노력이 없었다면, 많은 귀중한 예술품이 영원히 사라졌을 것이다.

14   ②

☐ mandatory a. 의무적인, 강제적인(=compulsory) ☐ grim a. 암울한, 암담한 ☐ modified a. 완화된; 수정된 ☐ exemplary a. 모범적인; 본보기가 되는 ☐ mundane a. 현세의, 세속적인

의무적인 청력 테스트와 인터넷으로 상황이 조금 개선되었지만, 때때로 암담할 수도 있다.

15   ③

☐ aggressive a. 침략적인; 적극적인(=active) ☐ containment n. 봉쇄, 억제; 포함 ☐ minimal a. 최소의, 극소의 ☐ prompt a. 즉석의; 신속한, 기민한 ☐ severe a. 엄한, 엄격한; 심한, 맹렬한

현재 사업 여건은 우리 측의 적극적인 경비 지출 억제 조치를 필요로 한다.

16   ②

☐ decimate v. 대량으로 죽이다; 심하게 훼손하다, 약화시키다(=greatly decrease) ☐ recover slowly 천천히 회복하다 ☐ reduce little by little 조금씩 줄이다 ☐ make up for the loss 손실을 메우다

엘링턴(Ellington) 공작은 암에 시달린 이후로 기력이 많이 쇠퇴했다.

17   ①

☐ skeptical a. 의심 많은, 회의적인(=doubtful) ☐ authentic a. 진정한, 믿을 만한, 확실한, 진짜의 ☐ universal a. 보편적인, 전반적인; 일반적인 ☐ psychological a. 심리적인; 심리학의

심리학자 숀 브라이언트(Shawn Bryant)는 회의적인 입장에서 외계인과의 접촉에 대한 몇몇 보고는 강력한 전자기장에서 비롯된 것이라고 보고 있다.

18   ②

☐ embark on ~에 착수하다, 시작하다(=start out on) ☐ take a trip to ~로 여행하다 ☐ improve upon ~을 개선하다 ☐ have an opinion about ~에 대한 견해를 갖다

그녀는 위스콘신(Wisconsin) 주에서 신문 기자로 일하여 그녀 경력의 첫발을 내디뎠다.

19   ④

☐ stoic n. 금욕주의자 ☐ adversity n. 역경, 불운(=difficulty) ☐ chance n. 기회, 가능성 ☐ failure n. 실패, 불이행 ☐ opposition n. 반대, 대립

그는 금욕주의자다. 고통이나 슬픔을 불평 없이 견디며, 역경에도 불굴의 용기로 대처한다.

20 ①

□ phantom n. 환상; 망상 □ neurologist n. 신경학자 □ persistent a. 지속적인, 끈질긴(=enduring) □ pernicious a. 유해한, 파괴적인 □ perplexed a. 당황한, 난처한, 골치 아픈 □ perilous a. 위험한, 위기에 처한

'망상'은 신경학자들이 사용하는 뜻으로 보자면, (신체의 일부를) 상실한 이후 수개월 내지 수년 동안 지속해서 나타나는, 신체의 일부 중 보통은 팔다리의 이미지나 기억이다.

21 ①

□ bed-ridden a. 병상에 누워있는, 침대에서 못 일어나는 □ pallid a. 핼쑥한, 창백한; 활기 없는(=pale) □ grotesque a. 기괴한, 기이한 □ distorted a. 일그러진, 비틀어진 □ paltry a. 얼마 되지 않는; 하찮은

그녀는 반년간 병상에 누워있었으며, 마침내 대중 앞에 나왔을 때, 창백한 얼굴로 인해 유령 같은 모습이었다.

22 ②

□ intervene v. 사이에 들다, 끼어들다; 방해하다, 개입하다(=intrude) □ intertwine v. 서로 얽히게 하다, 서로 엮다 □ disappear v. 사라지다, 안 보이게 되다 □ percolate v. 스며들다; 서서히 퍼지다

톰은 해변에 가려고 계획했으나, 태풍이 방해했다.

23 ①

□ colossal a. 거대한; 엄청난, 어마어마한(=gigantic) □ somber a. 어둠침침한, 흐린; 음침한, 우울한 □ dignified a. 위엄 있는, 품위 있는, 고귀한 □ inspiring a. 영감을 주는; 용기를 주는

워싱턴 D.C.의 링컨 기념관에 있는 거대한 에이브러햄 링컨 상(像)을 제작한 사람은 다니엘 체스터 프렌치(Daniel Chester French)였다.

24 ④

□ ire n. 분노, 노여움(=anger) □ discomfort n. 불쾌, 불안 □ praise n. 칭찬, 찬양 □ disappointment n. 실망, 기대에 어긋남

가장 많은 분노를 불러일으킨 것은 그 박물관의 첫 번째 전시회인데, 그 전시회는 사람들 마음속의 현실을 반영하지 못한다.

25 ①

□ implicit a. 함축적인, 암시적인(=tacit) □ definite a. 뚜렷한, 명확한 □ concrete a. 유형의, 구체적인 □ inevitable a. 피할 수 없는, 필연적인, 당연한

존슨(Johnson)의 진술에는 미국이 개입한다는 은연중의 위협이 포함되어 있었다.

26 ③

□ border n. 테두리; 경계 □ arbitrary a. 임의의, 멋대로의(=random) □ separate v. 갈라서 떼어놓다, 분리하다 □ discontinuous a. 끊어진, 계속되지 않는 □ whimsical a. 마음이 잘 변하는, 변덕스러운 □ tyrannical a. 폭군 같은; 전제적인 □ absolute a. 절대적인; 순전한

사진 이미지가 지배하는 세계에서는, 영상(映像)의 모든 경계가 임의적인 것처럼 보인다. 어떤 것이든 다른 어느 것으로부터도 분리되어 단절되도록 만들 수 있다.

27 ②

□ saunter v. 산보하다, 어슬렁거리다; 빈둥거리다(=stroll) □ come together 화합하다, 단결하다; 동시에 발생하다 □ enter v. 들어가다; 넣다 □ retire v. 물러가다, 칩거하다; 은퇴하다

12시 50분에 그가 사건의 현장을 거닐었을 때는 아무런 이상이 없었다.

28 ②

□ recapitulate v. 요약하다, 개괄하다(=summarize) □ reveal v. 드러내다; 밝히다; 폭로하다 □ exemplify v. 예증[실증]하다; ~의 예가 되다 □ augment v. ~를 늘리다, 증대시키다

'경제'는 『월든(Walden)』의 첫 장의 제목이고, 그 용어에 대한 소로(Thoreau)의 정의는 숲에서의 생활로부터 자신이 습득했던 교훈을 요약한다.

29 ②

□ sapient a. 지혜로운, 현명한; 박식한(=smart) □ digression n. 지엽으로 흐름, 여담 □ pious a. 신앙심이 깊은; 경건한, 종교적인 □ noisy a. 떠들썩한, 시끄러운 □ assured a. 보증된, 확실한, 확신이 있는

학생들은 그 교수의 정규 강의보다도 지혜로운 여담을 더 즐겨들었다.

30 ①

□ vaguely ad. 어렴풋이, 애매하게(=equivocally) □ demonstrably ad. 논증할 수 있도록; 명백히 □ loudly ad. 큰 소리로; 소리 높게, 떠들썩하게 □ contentedly ad. 만족스럽게; 기꺼이

나는 그의 의도를 이해할 수 없다. 그는 너무 모호하게 말한다.

31   ④

☐ parochial a. (교회) 교구의; 지방적인, 편협한(=narrow-minded) ☐ hostile a. 적대적인; 냉담한 ☐ naive a. 순진한, 남을 쉽게 믿는 ☐ unenergetic a. 기운이 없는

그 신참은 비록 높은 급료를 받았지만, 직장 사람들의 편협한 태도가 몹시 불만족스러웠다.

32   ②

☐ aberrant a. 정도를 벗어난; 비정상의(=deviant) ☐ fastidious a. 까다로운; 괴팍스러운 ☐ impulsive a. 충동적인, 감정에 끌리는 ☐ rebellious a. 반역하는, 반항적인

우리는 술과 마약이 탈선에 영향을 미치는 중요한 요인이라는 것을 알고 있다.

33   ④

☐ viable a. 실행 가능한, 실용적인(=practicable) ☐ credible a. 신뢰할 수 있는 ☐ decisive a. 결정적인, 중대한 ☐ forcible a. 강제적인; 강력한

정부는 그 광산들이 실행(가동) 가능하게 될 수 있다는 것을 보여줄 수 있는 한, 그 광산들이 계속 운영하도록 허용하기로 동의했다.

34   ①

☐ underpinning n. 받침; 토대, 기반(=foundation) ☐ probability n. 가망; 개연성; 확률 ☐ understanding n. 이해; 깨달음 ☐ contemplation n. 묵상; 숙고, 명상

현대 경제학의 주된 경향은 경제학 자체의 방법을 조사하지 않은 채로 두고, 경제학의 역사적, 경험적, 사회적 토대에 아무런 문제도 제기하지 않고 두는 것이다.

35   ②

☐ be free of ~이 없다 ☐ tumult n. 소란, 소동 ☐ trauma n. 정신적 충격 ☐ tranquility n. 고요, 평온(=quietude) ☐ prosperity n. 번영, 번성 ☐ sheer a. 순전한 ☐ equity n. 자기 자본; 공평, 공정 ☐ maturity n. 성숙함, 원숙함 ☐ sincerity n. 성실, 정직

우리 역사상 이제껏 소란과 정신적 충격이 없었던 해는 없었다. 따라서 우리나라가 평온과 번영을 누린 때가 있었다는 생각은 순전히 환상이다.

36   ④

☐ obliterate v. (글자를) 지우다, 말소하다; 흔적을 없애다(=efface) ☐ distort v. 비틀다; 왜곡하다 ☐ block v. 막다; 방해하다, 차단하다 ☐ freeze v. 얼다, 동결하다

눈이 너무 많이 와서 고속도로의 흔적을 없앴다.

37   ②

☐ subsidy n. 보조금(=financial aid) ☐ incentive n. 장려[우대]책 ☐ graft n. 접목, 접붙이기; 이식 ☐ settlement n. 합의, 해결

유럽의 농부들은 농가 보조금 삭감에 대한 대규모 시위를 준비 중이다.

38   ④

☐ genuine a. 진짜의, 진품의; 성실한, 진심의(=real) ☐ imitation n. 모방, 흉내; 모조(품) ☐ inexpensive a. 값싼, 비용이 많이 들지 않는 ☐ artificial a. 인공의; 인위적인, 부자연스러운

그 상인은 그 사파이어가 진품임을 확인했다.

39   ②

☐ elucidate v. (문제 등을) 밝히다, 명료하게 하다, 설명하다(=clarify) ☐ contend v. 논쟁하다, 주장하다 ☐ condense v. 응축하다; (사상·문장 따위를) 요약하다; 간결하게 하다 ☐ imply v. 함축하다, 의미하다

존 배스(John Bath)씨는 이 문제가 더 이상의 조사 없이도 해결될 수 있음을 밝혔다.

40   ④

☐ be sure to V 반드시 ~하다 ☐ keep track of 기억하다 ☐ connection n. (pl.) 유력한 친지[친척], 연고, 연줄 ☐ be flattered 우쭐해하다, 기뻐하다(=feel pleased) ☐ get angry 화내다 ☐ feel betrayed 배신감을 느끼다 ☐ get frightened 겁을 먹다

반드시 사전조사를 하도록 해라. 이름, 얼굴, 연줄 그리고 중요한 날짜를 기억해라. 사람들은 당신이 그들에 대한 것들을 기억해 줄 때 기뻐한다.

41   ③

☐ universal basic income 보편적 기본소득(정부가 자격 요건 없이 개인에게 반복적으로 지급하는 재정적 지원) ☐ naive a. 순진한; 순박한(=ingenuous) ☐ utopian a. 이상적인 ☐ enviable a. 부러운, 샘나는 ☐ inevitable a. 불가피한, 필연적인 ☐ versatile a. 다재다능한

많은 사람들은 보편적 기본소득의 개념이 절대로 실현되지 않을 순진하고 유토피아적인 이상이라고 비판한다.

42
②

□ total eclipse 개기일식 □ eerie a. 섬뜩한, 기괴한, 무시무시한
(=spooky) □ twilight n. (해진 뒤, 해뜨기 전의) 어스름, 해질녘, 황혼,
여명 □ ghostly a. 유령의; 그림자 같은, 희미한 □ corona n. 코로나;
(해, 달의 둘레의) 광환(光環) □ awesome a. 굉장한; 아주 멋진; 엄청난
□ cloudy a. 흐린; 구름이 많은 □ elusive a. 이해하기 어려운; 도피하는

개기일식이 일어나면 달이 태양표면 전체를 가리게 되는데, 이것은 개
기일식 과정을 지켜보고 있는 사람들에게 무시무시한 어스름을 가져오
며 유령 같은 태양의 코로나를 드러낸다.

43
①

□ quaint a. 기묘한, 이상한; 예스러운 멋이 있는(=old-fashioned) □
elegant a. 기품 있는, 품위 있는, 우아한 □ outstanding a. 걸출한,
현저한; 미결제의 □ rural a. 시골의, 지방의, 시골풍의

전기가 들어옴으로 인해, 시골집의 예스러운 멋과 낭만이 사라져갈 것
이다.

44
②

□ ex-convict n. 전과자 □ devote oneself to ~에 헌신하다, 몰두하다
□ community service 사회봉사활동 □ atone v. 속죄하다, 보상하다,
갚다(=make amends) □ misdeed n. 비행, 악행, 범죄 □ cover up
~을 완전히 덮다[가리다]; 숨기다[은폐하다] □ have concern 관심이
있다, 관련이 있다 □ show consideration 동정[참작]을 보이다

그 전과자는 자신이 저지른 과거의 악행을 속죄하기 위해 사회봉사에
헌신했다.

45
③

□ decry v. 공공연히 비난하다, 중상하다(=disparage) □ delete v.
삭제하다, 지우다, 소거하다 □ deceive v. 속이다, 기만하다, 현혹시키다,
사기 치다 □ delude v. 속이다, 착각하게 하다

상대방의 노력을 헐뜯어서 너의 위상을 높이려고 하지 마라.

46
④

□ dissension n. 의견 차이, 불일치(=strong disagreement); 불화, 알력
□ wild applaud 마구 박수치다 □ great curiosity 큰 호기심 □
shared fear 공통된 두려움

나의 제안이 우리 조직의 신입 회원들 사이에 그런 불화를 일으킬 것이
라고는 결코 생각하지 못했다.

47
②

□ inactive a. 활발치 못한, 활동하지 않는; 비활성의(=inert) □
obsolete a. 쓸모없이 못 쓰게 된, 폐물이 된 □ acute a. 날카로운,
뾰족한; 민감한 □ effective a. 유효한, 효력이 있는, 효과적인

네온은 다른 원소들과 쉽게 혼합되지 않는 원소이다. 이러한 특성 때문
에 네온은 불활성 원소라 불린다.

48
③

□ salvation n. 구원, 구조; 구세주 □ heinous a. 가증스러운, 극악[흉
악]한(=atrocious) □ hazardous a. 모험적인, 위험한; 운에 맡기는
□ heedless a. 부주의한, 조심성 없는 □ hindmost a. 제일 뒤쪽의

이러한 행위를 하도록 내몰린 사람은 누구든지 그만두는 것이 그들의
구원을 위해 더 나은 것이기 때문에 그만두어야 한다. 이보다 더 잔악한
범죄는 없다.

49
②

□ affliction n. 고통, 고뇌(=anguish) □ utility n. 유용성, 실용 □
feature n. 특징, 특색; 이목구비 □ capability n. 능력, 역량

제인(Jane)은 그런 난폭한 행동을 예상하지 못했기 때문에, 존(John)의
행동은 제인에게 고통을 안겨 주었다.

50
②

□ rebuke v. 질책하다, 꾸짖다(=admonish) □ pupil n. 학생; 제자
□ assignment n. 과제, 숙제; 임무 □ regard v. ~을 …으로 여기다[평
가하다] □ compliment v. 칭찬하다, 찬사를 말하다 □ refine v. 정제
하다, 제련하다; 개선하다

그 선생님은 숙제를 하지 않은 것에 대하여 계속해서 그 학생을 야단
쳤다.

51
④

□ scrupulous a. 빈틈없는; 양심적인(=meticulous) □ unrelenting
a. 용서[가차] 없는, 엄한, 무자비한 □ obsessive a. 사로잡혀 있는, 강박
적인 □ escalating a. 단계적으로 확대[증대, 강화, 상승]하는

자신의 업무에 세심한 주의를 기울인 덕분에 그는 회사에서 승진할 수
있었다.

52
④

□ inadvertent a. (사람·성격 등이) 부주의한, 우발적인, 고의가 아닌
(=unintended) □ tolerant a. 관대한, 아량 있는 □ negligible a.
하찮은, 무시해도 좋은 □ inevitable a. 피할 수 없는; 필연의

그 신문의 실수는 우발적인 것이었다. 편집자가 희생자의 이름을 포함하려한 게 아니었기 때문이다.

53 ①

□ humbly ad. 겸허하게 □ liable a. 책임을 져야 할, 의무가 있는 (=answerable) □ understandable a. 납득할 수 있는, 당연한 □ inevitable a. 불가피한, 필연적인 □ consentable a. 동의할 수 있는

따라서 나는 이제 내 나름의 생각을 겸허히 제시할 것인데, 나는 이러한 내 생각이 최소한의 반대에도 책임이 없기를(최소한의 반대도 낳지 않기를) 희망한다.

54 ①

□ penalize v. (법·규칙을 어긴 데 대해) 처벌하다[벌을 주다] □ concoct v. (이야기 따위를) 조작하다(=make up) □ get a flat tire 타이어가 펑크나다 □ show off 자랑하다, 뽐내다 □ pick on (제물로서) 골라내다; ~을 비난하다 □ come by 획득하다, 얻다

연습에 빠진 것에 대해 처벌 받는 것을 피하기 위해, 그 축구선수는 타이어에 펑크가 났다는 이야기를 지어냈다.

55 ①

□ kernel n. 핵심, 요점; 가장 중요한 부분(=core) □ format n. 판형, 체재; 전체 구성 □ channel n. 해협; 수로; 경로 □ hospitality n. 친절, 환대

그 메시지의 핵심은 평화가 어느 누구에게도 이익이나 불이익의 근원이 되어서는 안 된다는 것이다.

56 ③

□ unanimous a. 만장일치의, 이의 없는(=accordant) □ wanton a. 방자한, 방종한; 이유가 없는 □ effective a. 유효한, 효과적인; 감동적인 □ tenable a. (이론 등이) 주장할 수 있는, 지지할 수 있는

위원회의 의원들은 특정 사항을 만장일치로 합의했다.

57 ②

□ decline v. 거절하다(=refuse); 기울다 □ prearrangement n. 사전 협의[조정], 예정 □ accept v. 받아들이다; 수락하다 □ consider v. 숙고하다, 고찰하다; 고려하다 □ apply v. 적용하다, 응용하다; 지원하다

나는 너의 파티 초대를 사양해야 하는데 선약이 있기 때문이다.

58 ④

□ charge v. 부담시키다; 비난하다, 고발하다(=blame) □ illusion n. 착각; 환상, 망상 □ arrogance n. 오만, 거만 □ claim v. 요구하다, 청구하다; 주장하다 □ propose v. 제안하다; 신청하다 □ demand v. 요구하다, 요청하다 □ suppose v. 가정하다, 상상하다; 추측하다

사람들은 종종 수학 지식이 확실성에 대한 환상과 그 결과로 발생하는 오만함을 초래한다고 비난한다.

59 ②

□ odd a. 이상한, 특이한(=peculiar) □ aesthetic n. 미적 특질, 미학(적 특질) □ splendid a. 정말 좋은[멋진], 훌륭한 □ paltry a. 보잘것없는; 시시한 □ sketchy a. 대충의, 개략적인

우아한 장식으로 둘러싸인 가운데, 방의 전체적인 미적인 특질과 안 어울리는 듯한 이상한 그림이 걸려 있었다.

60 ④

□ summit meeting 정상 회담 □ bring about ~을 가져오다, 불러일으키다 □ reconciliation n. 화해, 조정(=pacification) □ antagonistic a. 적대적인; 대립하는 □ modesty n. 겸손, 겸허 □ competition n. 경쟁; 시합 □ frugality n. 절약, 검소

그 정상 회담은 이전에는 서로 적대적이었던 진영들 사이에 화해를 가져다줄 것이다.

61 ①

□ uproot v. 뿌리째 뽑다; (악습 등을) 근절하다(=eradicate) □ caste system 계급제, 신분제 □ pervasive a. 만연하는 □ entangle v. 얽히게 하다; (함정, 곤란 따위에) 빠뜨리다 □ adorn v. 장식하다, 꾸미다 □ nourish v. 자양분을 주다; 육성하다, 조성하다

우리는 사회에 가장 널리 퍼져있는 권력구조인 성(性) 차별적 시스템을 근절시켜야 한다.

62 ③

□ upstanding a. 강직한, 정직한 □ moral a. 도덕적인, 윤리의 □ cantankerous a. 성미가 고약한, 심술궂은(=grumpy) □ greedy a. 욕심 많은, 탐욕스러운 □ reckless a. 무모한, 난폭한 □ self-indulgent a. 방종한, 제멋대로의

미키 마우스(Mickey Mouse)가 아이들에게 친근하게 받아들여지다 보니 미키 마우스는 항상 정직하고 도덕적이며, 성미 고약한 도널드 덕 (Donald Duck)은 항상 곤경에 빠져야 했다.

63 ③

☐ devote v. (노력 등을) 쓰다, 바치다, 기울이다 ☐ facilitate v. 촉진하다 ☐ accumulate v. 모으다; 쌓아올리다(=hoard) ☐ exhaust v. 다 써버리다; 고갈시키다 ☐ scatter v. 흩뿌리다; 낭비하다 ☐ disperse v. 흩뜨리다; 퍼뜨리다

원시인들은 생산을 촉진하는 데 특정 종류의 물건들을 사용하며, 때로는 이러한 특별한 목적을 위해 이 물건들을 미리 모아둔다.

64 ①

☐ as for ~에 대해서 말하자면 ☐ perfunctory a. 형식적인, 겉치레의 (=superficial) ☐ substantive a. 실질적인, 현실의; 상당한 ☐ hostile a. 적의를 가진, 적대적인 ☐ spontaneous a. 자발적인; 임의의, 무의식적인 ☐ calculated a. 고의의, 계산된, 계획적인

두 국가의 정상들에 대해서 말하자면, 실질적인 회담을 여는 것이 가장 좋겠지만, 베이징에서 형식적인 악수를 하는 것조차도 꽤 가치 있는 것이 될 것이다.

65 ④

☐ extroverted a. 외향적인, 사교적인 ☐ affable a. 상냥한, 붙임성 있는, 친절한(=friendly) ☐ wary a. 주의 깊은, 신중한 ☐ reserved a. 수줍어하는, 내성적인 ☐ mean a. 비열한; 인색한 ☐ aggressive a. 침략적인, 호전적인; 적극적인 ☐ prudent a. 신중한, 조심성 있는; 분별 있는

때때로 당신은 외향적이고, 붙임성 있고, 또 사교적이지만, 다른 때에는 신중하고 내성적이다.

66 ③

☐ pat ~ on the back ~를 칭찬하다, 격려하다 ☐ enact v. 법령화하다, 법제화하다 ☐ comprehensive a. 포괄적인; 범위가 넓은; 이해력이 빠른 ☐ overhaul n. 철저한 조사, 정밀 검사 ☐ struggling a. 노력하는, 분투하는; (생활고와) 싸우는 ☐ rapacious a. 강탈하는; 욕심 많은, 탐욕스러운(=greedy for money) ☐ giving unwillingly 마지못해 주는 ☐ ready to give ~할 준비가 된 ☐ difficult to deal with 다루기 어려운

캘리포니아의 정치인들은 생활고에 시달리는 집주인들을 탐욕스러운 은행가들로부터 보호하게 될 미국 최초의 주택담보 포괄 검토법을 제정한 것에 대해 스스로를 칭찬하고 있다.

67 ③

☐ plaintive a. 애처로운, 슬픈 듯한, 구슬픈(=melancholy) ☐ healthy a. 건강한, 건장한, 튼튼한 ☐ noisy a. 떠들썩한, 시끄러운 ☐ pleasant a. 즐거운, 유쾌한; 호감이 가는

그 음악은 매우 구슬픈 분위기를 가지고 있다.

68 ②

☐ meditative a. 명상적인, 심사숙고하는(=thoughtful) ☐ gleeful a. 매우 기뻐하는, 즐거운 ☐ desperate a. 자포자기의; 필사적인 ☐ stern a. 엄격한, 단호한; 엄숙한

오늘 밤 너는 생각에 잠긴 것처럼 보인다.

69 ②

☐ tenuous a. 미약한, 빈약한(=flimsy) ☐ spurious a. 가짜의, 위조의 ☐ recalcitrant a. 반항하는, 저항하는, 반대하는 ☐ gauche a. 어색한; 눈치 없는; 서투른

일부 의원들은 그 법안에 반대하는 다소 근거가 약한 주장을 했다.

70 ④

☐ lamentable a. 슬픈, 유감스러운, 한탄스러운(=sad) ☐ respectable a. 존경받는, 존경할 만한; 훌륭한 ☐ accountable a. 책임 있는; 설명할 수 있는 ☐ surprising a. 놀랄만한, 의외의; 눈부신; 불시의

통탄할 일은 외모가 여성 대부분이 추구하도록 장려되는 유일한 형태의 힘이라는 것이다.

71 ①

☐ rhetoric n. 수사(修辭); 수사학; 웅변술; 미사여구 ☐ persuasively ad. 설득력 있게 ☐ malicious a. 악의 있는, 심술궂은(=spiteful) ☐ irritable a. 성미가 급한; 애를 태우는 ☐ contrived a. 인위적인, 부자연스러운 ☐ assiduous a. 끈기 있는, 근면한

수사법(修辭法)은 언어를 설득력 있게 사용하는 기술이다. 그렇다고 해서 수사법이 항상 악의적인 동기에서 사용된다는 말은 아니다.

72 ①

☐ condense v. 응축하다, 압축하다, 농축하다; 요약하다(=abbreviate) ☐ expand v. 넓히다, 팽창시키다, 크게 하다 ☐ continue v. 계속하다, 지속하다, 존속시키다 ☐ postpone v. 미루다, 연기하다

그 연사는 청중들이 질문할 수 있도록 발표를 간략하게 해 달라는 요청을 받았다.

73 ③

☐ tender v. 부드럽게 하다; 제공하다, 제안하다, 신청하다(=offer) ☐ soft a. 부드러운, 연한; 온화한 ☐ regret v. 후회하다; 유감으로 생각하다; 가엾게 생각하다 ☐ deny v. 부인하다, 부정하다; 거절하다

메이필드(Mayfiel) 씨는 마지못해 나에게 사과했다.

74
①

☐ recount v. 자세히 얘기하다(=describe), 하나하나 열거하다 ☐ incur v. (해를) 입다, 당하다 ☐ dispossess v. 빼앗다 ☐ record v. 기록하다 ☐ relieve v. 경감하다, 덜다

팔레스타인 사람들은 그들의 땅을 빼앗긴 후 여러 해 동안 당한 고통을 스토리텔링을 통해 이야기해왔다.

75
④

☐ deluge n. 대홍수, 범람; 쇄도(=flood) ☐ place a burden on ~에게 짐을 지우다, ~에게 부담이 되다 ☐ chaos n. 혼돈, 무질서 ☐ dagger n. 단도, 단검, 비수 ☐ oasis n. 오아시스; 위안이 되는 장소

최근 발생한 정보의 홍수는 정부에게 부담을 안겨 주었다.

76
④

☐ distill v. ~을 증류하여 […으로] 변하게 하다 ☐ free-floating a. 자유로운 입장에 있는 ☐ bigotry n. 심한 편견(=intolerance) ☐ lethal a. 치명적인 ☐ brew n. (여러 생각사건들의) 혼합[조합] ☐ exertion n. 노력, 분투 ☐ volition n. 자유 의지 ☐ perspective n. 관점, 시각

많은 대학들이 미국 사회의 막연한 편협함을 위험한 조합으로 변하게 하는 것처럼 보인다.

77
③

☐ assuredly ad. 확실히(=certainly) ☐ spread v. 확산시키다 ☐ allegedly ad. 주장[소문]에 따르면 ☐ particularly ad. 특히, 특별히 ☐ ultimately ad. 궁극적[최종적]으로

중국의 노력은 확실히 전 세계에 영향력을 확산시키려는 더 큰 계획의 일부였다.

78
①

☐ upscale a. 평균 이상의, 부유층(의)(=high-end) ☐ tacky a. 끈적끈적한; 초라한, 볼품없는 ☐ reasonable a. 합리적인; 정당한 ☐ upbeat a. 오름세의; 낙관적인

보다 값싼 대체상품의 압박에 직면해 있는 고소득층 대상 기업은 스타벅스 뿐만이 아니다.

79
③

☐ omniscient a. 전지의, 모든 것을 다 아는, 박식한(=all-knowing) ☐ optimistic a. 낙관적인, 낙천적인 ☐ credulous a. (남을) 쉽사리 믿는, 속아 넘어가기 쉬운 ☐ philosophical a. 철학의; 이성적인

내가 모든 것을 다 아는 체하는 것은 아니지만, 이 사실에 관해서는 확신하고 있다.

80
①

☐ semi-conductor n. 반도체 ☐ scrap v. 해체하다; 쓰레기로 버리다, 폐기하다(=discard) ☐ preferential a. 우선권[특혜]을 주는 ☐ regime n. 정권; 제도 ☐ collectivize v. 집단농장화하다; 공영화하다 ☐ implement v. 도구를 주다; 필요한 권한을 주다; 이행하다 ☐ modify v. 수정하다, 변경하다; 조절하다; 수식하다

미국과 특혜 조세제도 폐지협정이 체결됨에 따라, 중국은 지방에 위치한 반도체 기업을 육성하는 강경책을 준비 중이다.

81
③

☐ desolate a. 황량한; 쓸쓸한; 사람이 살지 않는(=empty) ☐ noisy a. 떠들썩한, 시끄러운 ☐ busy a. 바쁜, 분주한; 번화한 ☐ queer a. 기묘한; 수상한

수 마일을 가도 주위는 쓸쓸하고 황량한 숲뿐이었다.

82
③

☐ impelling a. 재촉하는; 추진시키는(=motivating) ☐ deterrent a. 단념시키는, 제지하는, 못하게 하는 ☐ organize v. 조직하다, 편성하다, 구성하다 ☐ encroach v. (서서히) 침입하다, 잠식하다

지적 호기심은 과학에서 하나의 추진력으로 작용한다.

83
①

☐ depict v. (그림으로) 그리다 ☐ deftly ad. 솜씨 좋게, 능숙하게 (=skillfully) ☐ superficial a. 표면(상)의, 피상적인 ☐ gaiety n. 명랑 (한 기분); 화려함 ☐ prudently ad. 사려 깊게, 분별 있게; 신중하게 ☐ occasionally ad. 이따금, 가끔; 임시로 ☐ humorously ad. 익살맞게; 변덕스럽게

소설가 어니스트 헤밍웨이(Ernest Hemingway)는 1920년대에 표면적으로 드러난 화려함 밑에 깔려 있는 인간의 비참함을 멋지게 묘사했다.

84
③

☐ jaundiced a. 황달에 걸린; 비뚤어진, 편견을 가진(=prejudiced) ☐ pessimistic a. 비관적인, 염세적인 ☐ cynical a. 냉소적인; 부정적인 ☐ optimistic a. 낙관적인, 낙천적인

당신은 왜 항상 모든 것에 대해 그렇게 편견에 사로잡힌 태도를 보입니까?

85 ②

□ disposition n. 기질, 성향(=temperament) □ be responsible for ~의 원인이 되다 □ affluence n. 풍족, 부유 □ dominance n. 우월, 우세 □ background n. 배경, 배후사정

많은 사람들은 톰의 성향이 이러한 좋은 결과의 원인이 되었다고 생각한다.

86 ④

□ plunge v. 거꾸러지다, 찔러 넣다 □ sift v. 체로 치다, 거르다, 선별하다(=put something through a sieve) □ bent a. 구부러진, 휜 □ bill n. (새의) 부리 □ pull something out ~을 떼어내다 □ change in position or direction 위치나 방향을 바꾸다 □ move forwards or downwards 앞 또는 뒤로 움직이다

홍학은 특이한 방법으로 먹이를 잡아먹는다. 고개를 물 아래에 담그고 구부러진 부리의 가장자리에 있는 고운 머리카락 같은 '빗'으로 진흙을 걸러낸다.

87 ②

□ emulate v. 흉내 내다, 모방하다(=imitate) □ sibling n. 형제자매 □ pay attention to ~에 주목하다 □ quarrel with 싸우다, 언쟁하다; 불평하다 □ admire v. 칭찬하다; 감탄하다 □ entertain v. 즐겁게 하다; 대접[환대]하다

어린아이들은 반드시 손위 형제나 자매를 흉내 낸다. 그래서 형제들은 누가 그들을 보고 있는지에 대하여 주의해야 한다.

88 ②

□ defy v. 무시하다, 얕보다; 반항하다(=disobey) □ flutter v. (깃발 등이) 펄럭이다, 나부끼다 □ manipulate v. 교묘하게 다루다, 조종하다 □ solicit v. 간청하다, 탄원하다

그 주인은 종업원들은 말할 것도 없고, 손님들도 무시하기로 작정한 듯이 보였다.

89 ②

□ mess up (~을) 엉망으로 만들다[다 망치다] □ effrontery n. 뻔뻔스러움, 몰염치(=audacity) □ allegiance n. 충성 □ discretion n. 판단[선택]의 자유; 사려분별 □ vacillation n. 동요; 우유부단

그녀는 모든 것을 엉망으로 만들었지만 아무 일도 없었던 것처럼 행동하는 뻔뻔함이 있다.

90 ②

□ gauge v. (크기, 치수를) 재다, 측정하다(=measure); 평가하다, 판단하다 □ demonstrate v. 논증하다, 증명하다, 설명하다 □ distort v. 찡그리다; 곡해하다, 왜곡하다 □ imitate v. 모방하다, 흉내 내다; 본받다

그들은 모든 종류의 주제에 관해 질문함으로써 그의 전반적인 능력을 측정하려 하고 있다.

91 ①

□ hand down 내리다, 공표하다 □ prison sentence 징역형 □ affluent a. 부유한 □ falsify v. (문서를) 위조[변조, 조작]하다(=forge) □ attest v. 증명[입증]하다 □ allocate v. 할당하다 □ shred v. 갈기갈기 찢다, 조각조각으로 끊다

서류를 위조해 자녀를 국제학교에 부정 입학시킨 부유층 학부모에게 법원이 징역형을 선고했다.

92 ②

□ empirical a. 경험적인, 실험상의(=experimental) □ inventive a. 발명의; 창의력이 풍부한, 독창적인 □ absolute a. 절대적인; 완전한 □ convertible a. 바꿀 수 있는, 개조할 수 있는

그는 경험적인 증거를 통해서 자신의 처음 생각이 틀렸다는 판단이 내려지면 자신의 생각을 기꺼이 바꾸려고 했다.

93 ③

□ conglomerate n. 복합 기업; 집합체(=coalition) □ fluctuation n. 변동; 동요

시애틀의 인구는 서로 다른 인종 및 문화적인 배경의 사람들의 집합체이다.

94 ④

□ bestial a. 짐승의, 야만적인(=brutal) □ ostentatious a. 과시하는 □ prosaic a. 평범한; 따분한 □ furtive a. 은밀한, 엉큼한

이 소설은 문명사회가 무너졌을 때 드러나는 인간의 야만적인 본성을 다루고 있다.

95 ②

□ quarter n. 숙소, 거처 □ ramshackle a. 금방이라도 무너질[주저앉을] 듯한 □ tenement n. 다세대 주택 □ mold n. 곰팡이 □ pillage v. 약탈[강탈]하다(=harry) □ waive v. (권리, 요구 등을) 포기하다 □ pummel v. 강타하다 □ mince v. (고기를) 갈다, 다지다

그들이 사는 숙소는 아크(Ark)라고 하는 금방이라도 무너질 듯한 다세대 주택으로, 벽은 곰팡이로 퍼렇고 계단 난간은 장작을 쓰기 위한 용도로 약탈됐다.

96 ①

☐ salient a. 현저한, 두드러진(=noticeable) ☐ ugly a. 추한; 불쾌한 ☐ strange a. 이상한; 색다른 ☐ attractive a. 마음을 끄는, 매력적인

각진 턱은 조(Joe)의 두드러진 특징 중 하나이다.

97 ③

☐ assert v. 단언하다, 주장하다 ☐ legislative a. 입법의, 입법부의 ☐ gainsay v. 부정하다, 반대하다(=oppose) ☐ prerogative a. 특권의, 특권이 있는 ☐ fritter v. 조금씩 허비하다, 낭비하다 ☐ bolster v. 지지하다, 보강하다 ☐ intrude v. 밀고 들어가다; 끼어들다, 개입하다

저는 입법권이 특권을 부정한다는 점을 강력히 주장하는 바입니다.

98 ④

☐ be forced to ~하도록 강요받다 ☐ skimp v. 절약하다, 아끼다(=economize) ☐ last v. 계속하다; 지속하다; (얼마 동안) 쓰일 만하다 ☐ bluff v. ~에게 허세부리다, (허세 부려) 속이다 ☐ consume v. 소비하다, 다 써 버리다 ☐ squander v. 낭비하다, 함부로 쓰다

그들은 제한된 공급물자로 겨울을 나기 위하여 생필품을 아주 절약해야만 했다.

99 ①

☐ think twice 망설이다 ☐ duplicate v. 사본하다, 복사하다 ☐ pirate v. 저작권을 침해하다, 불법 복제하다 ☐ legitimate a. 합법의, 적법의(=licensed) ☐ fancy a. 공상의; 고급의 ☐ up-to-date a. 최신의; 현대적인 ☐ equivalent a. 동등한, 같은

많은 개인용 컴퓨터 사용자들은 친구를 위해 그들이 좋아하는 소프트웨어 프로그램을 복사하는 것에 대해 거의 망설이지 않았다. 현재 점점 더 많은 수의 기업과 학교들이 이와 같은 행동을 하고 있다. 그들은 직원들이 회사에서 사용하는 모든 컴퓨터의 프로그램을 구입하는 것보다 소프트웨어를 복사하는 것을 허용하며 심지어 장려하기까지 한다. 일부 업계의 추산에 따르면, 합법적으로 구매된 소프트웨어 하나에 네 개꼴로 불법 복제가 이루어진다고 한다.

100 ④

☐ photovoltaic cell 광전지, 태양전지 ☐ wind turbine 풍력 발전용 터빈, 풍력 터빈 ☐ peripheral a. 주변적인, 지엽적인; 외면의 ☐ account for (부분, 비율을) 차지하다 ☐ far-fetched a. 믿기지 않는,

설득력 없는, 억지스러운(=unrealistic) ☐ (it's) about time (too) 진즉에 그랬어야 했다 ☐ logical a. 논리적인 ☐ misleading a. 호도하는, 오해의 소지가 있는 ☐ premature a. 너무 이른, 시기상조의

광전지와 풍력 터빈이 개발되고 거의 150년이 지난 지금에도, 그것들은 여전히 세계 전기의 불과 7%만을 발생시키고 있다. 그러나 놀라운 일이 일어나고 있다. 그것들은 10여 년 전만 해도 에너지 시스템의 주변적인 부분이었지만 지금은 다른 어떤 에너지원보다 빠르게 성장하고 있으며, 비용이 줄어들면서 화석 연료에 대해 경쟁력을 얻어가고 있다. 연구자들은 재생에너지가 향후 20년 동안 전 세계 에너지 공급 증가의 절반을 차지할 것으로 기대하고 있다. 세계가 깨끗하고, 무한하며, 값싼 에너지원의 시대에 접어들고 있다고 생각하는 것은 더 이상 억지스러운 생각이 아니다. 진즉에 그랬어야 했다.

01 ②	**02** ③	**03** ④	**04** ①	**05** ③	**06** ③	**07** ③	**08** ①	**09** ③	**10** ①
11 ①	**12** ②	**13** ②	**14** ④	**15** ①	**16** ①	**17** ①	**18** ②	**19** ①	**20** ④
21 ④	**22** ②	**23** ①	**24** ②	**25** ①	**26** ④	**27** ②	**28** ③	**29** ③	**30** ①
31 ①	**32** ②	**33** ③	**34** ②	**35** ③	**36** ③	**37** ②	**38** ①	**39** ①	**40** ②
41 ①	**42** ②	**43** ④	**44** ②	**45** ④	**46** ①	**47** ③	**48** ①	**49** ③	**50** ①
51 ③	**52** ②	**53** ②	**54** ④	**55** ③	**56** ②	**57** ④	**58** ③	**59** ③	**60** ①
61 ③	**62** ①	**63** ②	**64** ④	**65** ①	**66** ①	**67** ③	**68** ②	**69** ①	**70** ③
71 ①	**72** ④	**73** ④	**74** ①	**75** ①	**76** ②	**77** ④	**78** ③	**79** ④	**80** ②
81 ③	**82** ①	**83** ②	**84** ④	**85** ①	**86** ②	**87** ②	**88** ④	**89** ②	**90** ①
91 ①	**92** ②	**93** ③	**94** ①	**95** ①	**96** ①	**97** ③	**98** ③	**99** ④	**100** ②

01 ②

☐ expel v. 내쫓다, 제명하다, 방출하다(=banish) ☐ welcome v. 환영하다, 기꺼이 맞이하다 ☐ afflict v. 괴롭히다, 피해를 입히다, 시달리게 하다 ☐ revenge v. 원수를 갚다, 복수하다

그는 그 공동체로부터 추방되었다.

02 ③

☐ uncertainty n. 불확실성 ☐ confused a. 혼란스러운; 당황한 ☐ testy a. 성미 급한, 성 잘 내는; 퉁명스러운(=irritable) ☐ despondent a. 기가 죽은, 의기소침한; 낙담한 ☐ placid a. 평온한, 조용한, 차분한 ☐ perplexed a. 난처한, 어찌할 바를 모르는, 당황한

그 불확실성은 모든 이를 혼란스럽고 짜증나게 했다.

03 ④

☐ tangible a. 실체적인; 확실한, 명백한(=palpable) ☐ integral a. 완전한, 완전체의; 필수의 ☐ conventional a. 전통적인; 관습적인; 진부한 ☐ expensive a. 값비싼; 사치스러운

이 자료들로부터, 뇌는 실제 세계에 있는 유형(有形)의 사물을 모방하는 모델을 만들어낸다.

04 ①

☐ uncharted a. 지도에 없는; 미지의(=unknown) ☐ pilgrim n. 순례자, 성지 참배인 ☐ convict n. 죄수, 기결수 ☐ remold v. 고쳐 만들다, 개조하다 ☐ from scratch 처음부터; 무에서부터 ☐ unconsecrated a. 신에게 바치지 않은 ☐ extraordinary a. 비상한, 비범한; 현저한, 훌륭한 ☐ unanimous a. 만장일치의, 합의의

미국은 새로운 이들, 바로 여러분들의 고향이다. 순례자, 죄수, 개츠비들이 아무것도 없는 상태에서 스스로를 개조하기 위해 찾아 나선 미지의 땅이다.

05 ③

☐ jar n. 항아리, 단지, 병 ☐ potable a. 마시기에 적합한(=drinkable) ☐ portable a. 들고 다닐 수 있는; 휴대용의 ☐ transferable a. 옮길 수 있는; 양도할 수 있는 ☐ volatile a. 불안정한, 변하기 쉬운

그 항아리에 든 물은 마실 수 있다.

06 ③

☐ constructed a. 구성된, 고안된, 만들어낸(=artificial) ☐ useful a. 유용한, 유익한 ☐ substitute a. 대리의, 대용의 ☐ surrealistic a. 초현실주의의

에스페란토는 1887년에 L. L. 자멘호프(L. L. Zamenhof)라는 사람이 발명한 언어이다. 에스페란토는 자연적으로 생겨난 것이 아니기 때문에 인공언어라고 불린다.

07 ③

☐ unwonted a. 이례적인, 드문, 특이한(=unusual) ☐ urgent a. 긴급한, 절박한 ☐ imperious a. 전제적인; 오만한; 긴급한 ☐ ancillary a. 보조의, 부수적인

동물들의 특이한 행동은 농부들에게 폭풍우가 임박했음을 암시했다.

08 ①

☐ mawkish a. 유난히 감상적인(=maudlin) ☐ overwrought a. 잔뜩 긴장한; 지나치게 공들인 ☐ venial a. 용서할 수 있는, 경미한 ☐ parsimonious a. 인색한, 검약하는 ☐ torrid a. 타는 듯이 뜨거운; 작열하는, 건조한

그 영화에 대한 비평가의 평은 감상적이고 지나치게 공들인 것 같다.

09 ③

☐ setback n. 방해, 좌절, 패배(=letdown) ☐ up and running 완전히 제대로 작동[운영]되는 ☐ breakthrough n. 난관 돌파; 획기적인 발전 ☐ breakaway n. 탈퇴; 탈피 ☐ turnover n. 방향 전환; 전복

그 회사는 마침내 사업을 본궤도에 올려놓기 전에 수많은 좌절을 경험했다.

10 ②

☐ go forward (일이) 진전되다, 진척되다 ☐ straddle the fence 확실한 태도를 취하지[보이지] 않다, 관망하다(=show an indecisive attitude) ☐ regain v. 되찾다, 회복하다 ☐ confidence n. 신용, 신뢰; 자신감 ☐ impartial a. 공평한, 편견 없는 ☐ verdict n. 평결; 판단, 의견 ☐ arbitrary a. 임의의, 멋대로의; 독단적인 ☐ decision n. 결심, 결의; 결정

그는 일을 추진하는 대신에 친숙한 삶과 마음 깊은 곳에 자신이 해야 했던 삶 사이에서 확실한 태도를 취하지 않았다.

11 ①

☐ soliloquy n. 독백(=monologue) ☐ psychiatry n. 정신의학, 정신병학 ☐ obsession n. 집착, 강박 관념, 망상 ☐ isolation n. 고립, 소외 ☐ silence n. 고요; 침묵

독백은 19세기 말과 20세기 초 유럽 정신의학에서 활발하게 논의되었던 것 같다.

12 ②

☐ larceny n. 절도(죄), 도둑질(=theft) ☐ faith n. 신념; 확신; 신앙 ☐ murder n. 살인; 살인사건 ☐ fraud n. 사기; 사기꾼

빌(Bill)은 절도 전과가 10건 있었기 때문에 무죄가 아니라는 배심원의 평결이 내려졌다.

13 ②

☐ encounter v. 만나다; 부닥치다(=meet); 충돌하다 ☐ attract v. 끌어당기다; 유인하다 ☐ guide v. 안내하다, 인도하다; 지도하다 ☐

invite v. 초대하다, 초청하다

(고객을 대하는) 태도 훈련은 젊은 층의 고객을 만나게 될 모든 사람들에게 필수적이다.

14 ④

☐ salacious a. (이야기, 그림 등이) 외설스러운, 음란한 ☐ scintillate v. (재치, 기지가) 번득이다, 넘치다; 반짝반짝 빛나다(=give off sparks) ☐ group with a cause 대의명분을 가지고 불러 모으다 ☐ help settle differences 차이를 해결하는 데 도움이 되다 ☐ seize by prior right 선취권을 이용해 장악하다

재치를 발휘하지 않고 그 장면들을 외설스럽고 1인칭적인 관점으로 다루고 묘사할 이유는 거의 없다.

15 ①

☐ callous a. 무감각한; 냉담[무정]한(=unsympathetic) ☐ tender a. 부드러운; 예민한, 민감한 ☐ eerie a. 무시무시한, 섬뜩한 ☐ rapturous a. 황홀해하는, 열광적인

그 오페라의 제목은 음악 속에 표현된 냉정한 세계관을 반영한다.

16 ①

☐ incessant a. 끊임없는, 그칠 새 없는(=constant) ☐ cost-cutting n. 경비[비용] 절감 ☐ immediate a. 즉석의, 즉시의 ☐ plausible a. 이치에 맞는, 그럴듯한 ☐ austere a. 엄격한; 금욕적인

항공사들은 끊임없는 비용 절감을 정당화하기 위해서 형편이 어렵다고 우는 소리를 즐겨 내지만, 작년에 전 세계의 항공사들은 350억 달러의 수익을 냈다.

17 ①

☐ bolster v. 지지하다, 보강하다; (사람을) 기운 나게 하다(=boost) ☐ impede v. 방해하다, 지연시키다 ☐ mitigate v. 누그러뜨리다, 완화하다 ☐ extenuate v. (범죄·결점을) 가벼이 보다, 경감하다

그는 이웃의 용기를 북돋아주려는 그 어떤 시도도 하지 않고 있다.

18 ②

☐ carnivore n. 육식 동물 ☐ agile a. 민첩한, 재빠른(=nimble) ☐ claw n. 발톱 ☐ acute a. 날카로운, 예민한 ☐ astute a. 기민한, 약삭빠른 ☐ arduous a. 고된, 힘든 ☐ nefarious a. 사악한; 버릇없는

전형적인 육식 동물은 날카로운 이빨과 발톱, 예리한 청각과 시력, 그리고 잘 발달된 후각을 가진 민첩한 달리기 선수이다.

19 ①

☐ **excitement** n. 흥분 ☐ **mingle** v. 섞이다(=mix) ☐ **apprehension** n. 우려, 불안 ☐ **max** v. 최대한으로 쓰다; 한계에 이르다 ☐ **coax** v. 구슬리다, 달래다, 속이다 ☐ **coat** v. 웃옷으로 덮다, 웃옷을 입히다

새로운 일을 시작하는 흥분은 항상 일종의 두려움과 혼재되어 있다.

20 ④

☐ **elastic** a. 탄력 있는, 신축성 있는; 융통성 있는(=flexible) ☐ **disastrous** a. 비참한, 피해가 막대한; 대실패의 ☐ **entangled** a. 걸려든, 연루된 ☐ **set** a. 위치한, 자리한; 계획된, 정해진

이번 주 나의 시간표는 상당히 유연하다.

21 ④

☐ **deplore** v. 한탄하며 슬퍼하다, 애통해하다(=lament) ☐ **take off** 벗다; 이륙하다; 중단하다 ☐ **appreciate** v. 평가하다, 감정하다; 진가를 인정하다 ☐ **avenge** v. 복수하다, 앙갚음하다 ☐ **divulge** v. (비밀을) 알려주다, 누설하다

만약에 인기 있는 어떤 프로그램이 정치적 압력으로 인해 중단된다면, 우리는 그것을 매우 개탄할 것이다.

22 ②

☐ **sojourn** n. 머무름, 거류, 체류(=brief stay) ☐ **exploration** n. 실지답사, 탐험 ☐ **research tour** 학술 여행 ☐ **performance** n. 실행, 수행, 성취; 공연

아시아에 체류하는 동안 그는 아시아의 고유 풍습에 관해 많은 것을 배웠다.

23 ①

☐ **be loath** 싫어하다, 질색하다(=dislike) ☐ **relinquish** v. 포기하다, 그만두다 ☐ **prestige** n. 명성, 신망 ☐ **agree** v. 동의하다, 응하다; 합치하다 ☐ **long** v. 간절히 바라다, 열망하다; 동경하다 ☐ **bother** v. 괴롭히다, 심히 걱정하다

전쟁 동안 우리를 지배할 수 있는 지위와 권력을 획득한 사람들은 이미 얻은 명성을 포기하기를 싫어했다.

24 ②

☐ **endorse** v. 배서하다, 써넣다; 보증하다(=sign) ☐ **destroy** v. 파괴하다, 부수다, 분쇄하다 ☐ **fold** v. 접다; 구부리다; 싸다 ☐ **deposit** v. 두다; 맡기다, 예금하다

수표를 받자 존(John)은 수표에 이서하고 그것을 은행으로 가져갔다.

25 ①

☐ **extemporaneous** a. (연설 등이) 즉석의, 준비 없이 하는, 즉흥적인 (=impromptu) ☐ **interesting** a. 재미있는, 흥미로운 ☐ **inadvertent** a. 부주의한; 고의가 아닌 ☐ **inveterate** a. 뿌리 깊은, 만성의; 상습적인

에벌리(Eberly)는 자신의 의도를 즉석에서 설명하기 시작했다. 준비 없이 전달하면서도 그는 꽤 자세한 해명의 말을 전달했다.

26 ④

☐ **literal** a. 글자 그대로의, 사실인, 과장 없는(=unexaggerated) ☐ **literary** a. 문학의, 문학적인 ☐ **coin** v. 만들어내다; 주조하다 ☐ **imaginative** a. 상상력이 풍부한

그는 과장 없이 진실만을 이야기하고 있었다.

27 ②

☐ **feasible** a. 실행할 수 있는, 실현 가능한(=executable) ☐ **balloon** n. 고무풍선; 기구(氣球) ☐ **amateur-made** a. 비전문가가 만든 ☐ **spacecraft** n. 우주선, 우주 비행체 ☐ **atmosphere** n. 대기, 대기권 ☐ **impractical** a. 실제[실용]적이 아닌; 실행 불가능한 ☐ **inexpensive** a. 비용이 들지 않는, 값싼 ☐ **expensive** a. 돈이 드는, 값비싼

기구(氣球)를 만들어 우주로 보내는 것은 실행 가능하지만, 비전문가가 만든 어떠한 우주 비행선도 지구 대기권의 경계선에 도달하지 못했다.

28 ③

☐ **perspicacious** a. 선견지명이 있는, 통찰력이 있는(=discerning) ☐ **cultivate** v. 기르다, 숙련하다, 닦다 ☐ **greedy** a. 욕심 많은, 탐욕스러운 ☐ **rewarding** a. 가치가 있는; 수익이 많이 나는 ☐ **courageous** a. 용감한, 담력 있는

그는 선견지명이 있는 투자가로서의 명성을 수십 년 동안 조심스럽게 쌓아왔다.

29 ③

☐ **intrude** v. 참견하다, 방해하다, 개입하다(=trespass) ☐ **preserve** v. 보호하다, 보존하다 ☐ **contain** v. 담고 있다, 포함하다 ☐ **negotiate** v. 협상하다, 교섭하다

나의 이웃집 나무의 뿌리가 내 집 땅을 침범하기 시작했다.

30 ①

☐ **obsolete** a. 쓸모없이 된; 쇠퇴한, 진부한, 시대에 뒤진(=outdated) ☐ **absolute** a. 완전한, 완벽한 ☐ **meritorious** a. 공적 있는, 가치 있는; 칭찬할만한 ☐ **variable** a. 변하기 쉬운, 변덕스러운

일부 젊은이들은 이처럼 빠르게 변하는 시대에는 자기 나라의 전통적 가치가 시대에 뒤진 것이라고 생각한다.

제1세계 국가들[부유한 선진국들]은 적극적으로, 그러나 때로는 무의식적으로, 다양한 정책과 계획을 통해 의존 상태를 영속시킨다.

31 ①

☐ exhilarating a. 신나는, 기분을 북돋우는(=exciting) ☐ sense of mission 사명감 ☐ unheard-of a. 전례가 없는, 전대미문의 ☐ collaboration n. 협력, 합작, 공동 연구 ☐ exhaustive a. 철저한, 완전한; 소모시키는 ☐ gloomy a. 어두운; 우울한, 침울한 ☐ grim a. 엄격한; 험상궂은

그래서 전례 없는 협력을 통해 인터넷의 탁월함을 제시하는 이런 유쾌한 사명감이 있었다.

32 ②

☐ dehydrate v. 탈수하다, 수분을 빼다, 건조시키다(=dry) ☐ package v. 꾸리다, 포장하다

많은 채소들은 나중에 쓰기 위해 탈수시켜 포장하는 것이 쉽다.

33 ③

☐ tolerate v. 관대히 다루다, 묵인하다; 견디다, 참다(=put up with) ☐ show v. 보이다, 제시하다 ☐ encourage v. 격려하다, 고무하다; 권하다; 장려하다 ☐ recognize v. 알아보다, 알아내다; 인지하다

그 교사는 자신의 반에서의 어떠한 무례한 행위도 참지 못했다. 결과적으로 모든 아이들은 얌전히 굴었다.

34 ②

☐ accustomed a. 익숙한, 익숙해져 있는 ☐ athlete n. 운동선수, 선수 ☐ gloat v. (자신의 성공에) 흡족해 하다; (남의 실패를) 고소해 하다 ☐ whine v. 애처로운 소리로 울다, 흐느껴 울다; 푸념하다, 투덜대다 ☐ dreary a. 황량한; 따분한; 서글픈(=lamentable) ☐ blithe a. 즐거운, 유쾌한, 쾌활한 ☐ agreeable a. 기분 좋은, 유쾌한 ☐ gallant a. 용감한; 당당한, 훌륭한

미국인들은 그들의 스포츠 영웅들이 보여주는 저열한 스포츠맨십에 익숙해졌다. 하드 코트, 클레이 코트, 엔드 존, 베이스에서 선수들은 그들의 크고 작은 승리에 대해 흡족해하고, 불운이 닥칠 때는 투덜댄다. 오랜 스포츠팬에게 그것은 통탄할 만한 사건이다.

35 ③

☐ perpetuate v. 영구화하다, 영속시키다(=maintain) ☐ dependency n. 속국, 보호령; 의존(상태) ☐ initiative n. 발의, 계획, 주도권 ☐ abdicate v. (권리 등을) 버리다, 포기하다 ☐ expand v. 넓히다, 확장하다 ☐ terminate v. 끝내다, 종료하다

36 ③

☐ garner v. 모으다, 축적하다(=hoard) ☐ emasculate v. 거세하다; 무기력하게 하다 ☐ restore v. 회복시키다, 복구[재건]하다 ☐ mitigate v. 누그러뜨리다, 완화시키다

미국의 문화적 유산을 고려해볼 때, 미국 언론으로부터 어느 정도의 양이 모아질 수 있을 것이다.

37 ②

☐ take precautions ~을 경계하다, 조심하다; 예방책을 강구하다(=take measures to avoid possible dangers) ☐ avoid going out in the sun 양지에 나가기를 꺼리다 ☐ practice beforehand 미리 연습하다 ☐ take every chance 모든 기회를 이용하다

여름의 열기와 습도는 여러분이 운동을 못 하게 하는 것이 아니다. 여러분은 단지 조심할 필요가 있다.

38 ①

☐ titanic a. 거대한, 강력한(=tremendous); 힘 센 ☐ batter v. ~을 강타하다; ~을 때려 부수다 ☐ stormy a. 폭풍우의, 폭풍의; 날씨가 험악한 ☐ sudden a. 돌연한, 갑작스러운, 불시의, 별안간의 ☐ unexpected a. 예기치 않은, 의외의, 뜻밖의, 돌연한

거대한 파도가 작은 보트를 강타해서 그 보트는 바위 쪽으로 밀려갔다.

39 ①

☐ bleak a. 황폐한, 쓸쓸한; 냉혹한(=desolate) ☐ withdrawal n. 철수, 철퇴 ☐ bucolic a. 목가적인; 전원생활의 ☐ bleary a. 눈이 흐린; 어렴풋한 ☐ drastic a. 격렬한, 맹렬한; 과감한, 철저한

미국 국방부의 우울한 경과 보고서는 미군이 아프가니스탄에서 보다 신속하게 철수해야 하는 타당한 이유들을 제시하고 있다.

40 ②

☐ audacious a. 대담한, 담대한, 겁이 없는(=bold) ☐ embrace v. 맞이하다, 환영하다; 받아들이다 ☐ special a. 특별한, 각별한 ☐ minor a. 사소한, 중요하지 않은 ☐ annual a. 연례의, 연간의

이것은 확실히 대담한 목표였다. 수년 내에, 그것은 제1세계(부유한 선진국들)와 또한 많은 제3세계 국가들에 의해 보편적으로 수용되었다.

41 ①

☐ faction n. 당파, 파벌, 분파(=sect) ☐ removal n. 이동, 이전; 제거, 철거; 해임 ☐ treaty n. 조약 ☐ insect n. 곤충 ☐ bisect v. 양분하다, 이등분하다 ☐ dissect v. 절개하다; 해부하다

1833년 한 소규모 당파는 이전 협정에 서명하는 것에 동의했는데, 그것이 뉴 에코타 조약이다.

42 ②

☐ copious a. 풍부한, 많은(=abundant) ☐ conditional a. 조건부의 ☐ imitative a. 모방적인 ☐ frugal a. 검소한, 절약하는

유럽중앙은행은 인플레이션에 대한 완화된 견해를 확인하고 수년간의 초완화 정책에서 벗어나는 일이 더딜 것임을 시사하면서 2022년에 많은 지원을 약속했다.

43 ④

☐ infallible a. 전혀 틀림이 없는, 의심할 여지없는; (절대로) 확실한(=inerrant) ☐ strict a. 엄격한, 엄한; 정밀한 ☐ effete a. 활력을 잃은, 지친; 맥 빠진 ☐ hellish a. 지옥의, 지옥과 같은; 섬뜩한

그 디자이너는 색상에 대한 절대적인 안목을 가지고 있다.

44 ②

☐ concentration n. 집결, 집중; 농축, 농도(=density) ☐ greenhouse gas 온실 가스 ☐ retain v. 보류하다, 보유하다 ☐ application n. 적용, 응용; 신청 ☐ focus n. 초점; 집중점 ☐ emission n. 방사, 발산

만약 대기 중 온실가스의 농도가 증가하면 아마도 더 많은 열을 보유하게 될 것이다.

45 ④

☐ enigmatic a. 수수께끼 같은, 불가사의한, 알기 어려운(=puzzling) ☐ enlightening a. 계몽적인, 밝혀주는 ☐ disturbing a. 불안하게 하는; 교란시키는 ☐ entertaining a. 재미있는, 유쾌한

그 교수의 강의는 그리스 시(詩)에 대한 알기 어려운 언급으로 가득 차 있었다.

46 ①

☐ grasp n. 붙잡음; 통제, 지배; 이해(=comprehension) ☐ beyond one's grasp 손이 닿지 않는 곳에; 이해할 수 없는 ☐ imitation n. 모방, 흉내 ☐ concentration n. 집중, 전념 ☐ imagination n. 상상력, 공상

그것은 정말 내가 이해할 수 없는 문제이다.

47 ③

☐ diminish v. 줄어들다, 감소하다(=decrease) ☐ swell v. 부풀다; 증가하다 ☐ increase v. 늘다, 증가하다 ☐ thrive v. 번영하다, 번성하다; 성공하다

남극대륙에 있는 펭귄의 수가 감소하고 있다.

48 ①

☐ national interest(s) 국가 이익, 국익(國益) ☐ compatible a. 양립할 수 있는, 모순이 없는(=congruous) ☐ ethical a. 도덕상의, 윤리적인 ☐ ruinous a. 황폐한, 몰락한; 폐허의 ☐ neglectful a. 태만한, 소홀한 ☐ competitive a. 경쟁의, 경쟁적인

외교 정책은 우리나라의 국익을 증진시키는 것과 관련된 것으로, 그 절차는 윤리적인 고려사항들과 항상 양립하지 않는다.

49 ③

☐ demurely ad. 얌전하게, 예절바르게; 점잔빼며(=modestly) ☐ banister n. (계단의) 난간 ☐ majestically ad. 당당하게, 위엄 있게 ☐ joyfully ad. 기뻐서, 기쁜 듯이 ☐ patiently ad. 끈기 있게, 참을성 있게

그녀는 한 손으로 난간을 잡고 다른 한 손에 가운을 잡고 가능한 한 얌전하게 걸어갔다.

50 ①

☐ venal a. 돈으로 움직이는, 매수되기 쉬운, 타락한(=bribable) ☐ needy a. 가난한, 생활이 딱한 ☐ violent a. 격렬한, 맹렬한; 광포한, 폭력적인 ☐ greedy a. 욕심 많은, 탐욕스러운; 갈망하는

원래는 모든 비용을 충당하기에 충분한 자금이 있었는데 뇌물을 좋아하는 관리들이 대부분의 돈을 횡령했다.

51 ③

☐ rejuvenate v. 젊어지게 하다; 활력을 되찾게 하다(=make look young again) ☐ slim v. 살을 빼려 하다, 날씬해지려 하다 ☐ subjugate v. 정복하다, 복종시키다, 종속시키다 ☐ make comfortable 편안하게 하다

엄청난 체중 감량으로 그녀는 다시 젊어 보였다.

52   ②

☐ bellicose a. 호전적인, 싸우기 좋아하는(=pugnacious) ☐ chafe v. 짜증나게 하다, 노하게 하다 ☐ acquaintance n. 지식; 아는 사람, 지인 ☐ capricious a. 변덕스러운, 마음이 변하기 쉬운 ☐ conscientious a. 양심적인, 성실한 ☐ turbid a. 흐린, 혼탁한

그의 호전적인 성격은 동료와 지인들을 짜증이 나게 만들었다.

53   ②

☐ pathetic a. 감상적인; 애처로운, 비참한(=pitiable) ☐ maintain v. 지속[유지]하다 ☐ droll a. 우스운, 익살스러운 ☐ tepid a. 미지근한; 열의가 없는 ☐ indiscreet a. 무분별한, 지각없는

그 장애인이 중심을 잡으려 애쓰는 것을 지켜보는 것은 애처로운 일이었다.

54   ③

☐ eminent a. 저명한; 뛰어난, 훌륭한, 탁월한(=famous and admired) ☐ strong but easily broken 튼튼하지만 쉽게 부서지는 ☐ bold and wicked 과감하고 장난기 있는 ☐ proud and capricious 거만하고 변덕스러운

지능 검사가 실제로 개인의 지능을 측정한다는 사실은 몇몇 저명한 심리학자들에 의해 의문을 제기 받고 있다.

55   ③

☐ indulgence n. 탐닉, 방자, 방종(=luxury) ☐ frugality n. 절약, 검소 ☐ discipline n. 훈련; 수양; 자제 ☐ complaint n. 불평, 불평거리

"즐거운 삶"으로 잘못 불리고 있는 방종의 삶은 행복을 불쌍하게 흉내 내고 있는 것이다.

56   ②

☐ wane v. 시들다, 감소하다; 쇠약해지다(=dwindle) ☐ suspend v. 매달다; 보류하다, 중단하다 ☐ plunge v. 곤두박질치다, 급락하다 ☐ kindle v. 불붙이다; 태우다; 밝게 하다

이것이 그 작가의 열네 번째 책이다. 그리고 그의 창의력이 쇠퇴했다는 것이 명백하다.

57   ④

☐ devout a. 독실한, 경건한, 신앙심이 깊은; 열렬한(=pious) ☐ stout a. 단단한, 억센, 튼튼한; 살찐 ☐ resolute a. 굳게 결심한, 굳은, 단호한 ☐ frugal a. 검약한, 소박한

김(Kim) 박사는 신앙심이 깊은 사람으로 유명하다.

58   ③

☐ salute n. 인사, 경례(=greeting) ☐ information n. 정보 ☐ ceremony n. 의식 ☐ privilege n. 특권, 특전

파도가 높은 바다를 지나가는 배들은 깃발을 한 차례 내렸다 올림으로써 서로 인사를 나눈다.

59   ③

☐ petrify v. (동·식물 등을) 석화(石化)하다; 깜짝 놀라게 하다(=terrify) ☐ transcendental a. 선험적인, 초월적인 ☐ exhilarating a. 명랑하게 하는, 기운 나게 하는 ☐ impressionable a. 인상적인; 민감한

공중 폭격으로 목숨이 극히 위험할 동안 가구 밑에 숨는 것은 무서운 경험이다.

60   ①

☐ demented a. 미친, 정신 이상인(=insane) ☐ insoluble a. 풀 수 없는, 설명할 수 없는 ☐ irrelevant a. 무관한, 상관없는 ☐ incessant a. 끊임없는, 쉴 새 없는

누구든 이것을 한 사람은 미친 사람일 것이다. 그 어떤 정상인 사람도 이런 식으로 행동하지는 않을 것이다.

61   ③

☐ archaeologist n. 고고학자 ☐ baffle v. 난처하게 하다, 당황하게 하다(=puzzle) ☐ implication n. 내포, 함축, 암시 ☐ placate v. 달래다, 위로하다 ☐ elevate v. 높이다, 향상시키다 ☐ alleviate v. 완화하다, 경감하다

그 고고학자들은 그 발견물이 암시하는 바에 대해 당혹스러워했다.

62   ①

☐ touchy a. 성미가 까다로운; 과민한(=sensitive) ☐ distinctive a. 독특한, 특이한, 구별이 분명한 ☐ delighted a. 아주 기뻐하는, 즐거워하는 ☐ sentimental a. 감정적인, 감정에 의거한, 감상적인

사생활을 논하는 것에 대해 민감한 사람이라면 결혼 생활이 어떤지 묻는 것은 좋지 않다.

63   ②

☐ apology n. 사죄, 사과; 변명 ☐ appease v. 달래다, 진정시키다(=placate) ☐ rage n. 격노, 분노 ☐ slight v. 경멸하다, 무시하다 ☐ entrench v. 참호로 에워싸다 ☐ obviate v. 없애다, 제거하다; 미연에 방지하다 ☐ modify v. 수정하다, 변경하다

본인이 직접 하는 사과만이 멸시당했던 것에 대한 그의 분노를 가라앉힐 것이다.

64 ③

☐ affecting a. 감동시키는; 가련한, 애처로운(=moving) ☐ stand around 우두커니 서 있다 ☐ grave n. 무덤 ☐ interesting a. 흥미 있는, 재미있는 ☐ loving a. 애정 어린, 다정한 ☐ approving a. 찬성의, 만족한

감동적인 영화 장면들 중 하나는 군인들이 큰 무덤가에 둘러 서 있는 장면이다.

65 ③

☐ palliate v. (병·고통 따위를) 누그러지게 하다, 일시적으로 완화하다 (=mitigate) ☐ reiterate v. 반복하다, 되풀이하다 ☐ exude v. 스며나오게 하다; 발산하다 ☐ neglect v. 방치하다

오늘날 파킨슨병의 진행 과정에 효과적으로 작용하는 약은 없지만 증상을 일시적으로 완화시키는 약들은 있다.

66 ①

☐ licentious a. 방탕한; 음탕한(=promiscuous) ☐ listless a. 열의 없는, 무관심한, 냉담한 ☐ docile a. 가르치기 쉬운; 유순한 ☐ edifying a. 교훈이 되는, 유익한, 계몽적인

로라(Laura)의 미소에는 뭔가 음탕한 면이 있었다. 그래서 그녀가 베벌리 고등학교에 모습을 드러냈을 때 십 대 남학생들을 둔 엄마들은 걱정스러운 마음이 들었다.

67 ①

☐ sophisticated a. 정교한, 세련된; 복잡한(=complex) ☐ sedentary a. 활동성이 없는, 몸을 많이 움직이지 않는 ☐ desultory a. 산만한, 단편적인; 일관성이 없는 ☐ timorous a. 마음이 약한, 소심한, 겁 많은

위기를 관리하고 정교한 소프트웨어를 이용함으로써, 스탠더(Stander)는 불경기에서 벗어나 훨씬 더 강해졌다.

68 ②

☐ perturb v. 교란하다, 혼란하게 하다(=bother) ☐ arouse v. 불러일으키다, 깨우다, 자극하다 ☐ relieve v. 위로하다; 경감하다, 덜다 ☐ liberate v. 자유롭게 하다, 해방하다, 석방하다

나를 성가시게 하는 것은 요즘 잡지 기사들이 너무 짧아졌다는 것이다.

69 ①

☐ relish v. 즐기다, 좋아하다; 맛있게 먹다, 맛보다(=savor) ☐ arrest v. 체포[구속]하다 ☐ inveigh v. 통렬히 비난하다, 독설을 퍼붓다 ☐ mind v. 상관하다, 개의하다 ☐ defer v. 연기하다, 지연되다

그녀의 아들이 체포됐다고 그녀에게 말하는 것이 즐겁지가 않다.

70 ③

☐ portend v. 전조가 되다, 미리 알리다(=herald) ☐ defy v. 도전하다; 문제 삼지 않다 ☐ belie v. 잘못 전하다, 속이다 ☐ implement v. 도구를 주다; 이행하다; 필요한 권한을 주다

오바마(Obama)의 선거는 변화를 미리 알려주는데, 이 변화의 중대성은 젊은 세대가 성년이 될 때야 여실히 나타날 것이다.

71 ①

☐ impatient a. 조급한; 안달하는, 몹시 ~하고 싶어 하는(=eager) ☐ tolerant a. 관대한, 아량이 있는; 내성이 있는 ☐ stoic a. 금욕의, 냉정한 ☐ enduring a. 참을성 있는; 영속하는

당신은 지금 변화를 갈구하고 있고 이제 그렇게 행동해야 할 시간이다.

72 ④

☐ sustainable a. (환경 파괴 없이) 지속 가능한; 유지할 수 있는 (=continuous) ☐ suspend v. 유예[중단]하다, 연기하다 ☐ reliable a. 의지가 되는, 믿음직한; 확실한 ☐ alternative a. 대체 가능한, 대안이 되는

석유는 지속 가능한 에너지원이 아니기 때문에 점점 더 많은 기업체들이 석유에 대한 의존도를 낮추기 시작하고 있다.

73 ④

☐ get the idea that ~이라고 믿다, 생각하다 ☐ commensurate with ~에 비례하는, 상응하는(=proportional to) ☐ sensuous a. (심미적으로) 감각적인 ☐ composer n. 작곡가 ☐ completed with ~이 완비된 ☐ related to ~와 관련 있는 ☐ applied to ~에 적용되는

음악의 가치가 음악의 감각적인 매력에 비례한다거나 가장 아름답게 들리는 음악이 가장 위대한 작곡가에 의해 만들어진다고는 생각하지 마라.

74 ①

☐ fatuous a. 얼빠진, 어리석은, 우둔한(=inane) ☐ avarice n. 탐욕, 허욕(虛慾) ☐ pretentious a. 자만하는; 건방진 ☐ impetuous a. (바람, 속도 따위가) 격렬한, 맹렬한; 열렬한

당신이 형편이 되지 않는 고급 승용차를 고집하는 것은 어리석은 짓이다.

75 ①

☐ oblivious a. 의식하지 못하는; 잘 잊어버리는(=unaware) ☐ obtrusion n. (의견 등의) 강요, 강제 ☐ sick a. 병든, 앓는; 싫증이 나서 ☐ familiar a. 잘 알려진, 낯익은 ☐ conscious a. 의식하고 있는, 깨닫고 있는

우리 몸에는 우리가 그것을 망각하도록 하는 무엇인가가 존재하며 고통은 우리 몸을 의식 상태로 몰아넣는 것이다.

76 ②

☐ projectile n. 발사체 ☐ deflect v. 비껴가다, 빗나가다(=deviate); 편향하다 ☐ reflect v. 반사하다, 되튀기다; 반영하다 ☐ float v. 뜨다; 떠돌다, 표류하다 ☐ collide v. 충돌하다; 일치하지 않다, 상충되다

코리올리의 힘(지구의 자전으로 비행 중의 물체에 작용되는 편향(偏向)의 힘)은 지구상의 모든 움직이고 있는 발사체를 직선에서 휘어지게 한다.

77 ④

☐ alternate v. 번갈아 일어나다; 교체하다(=interchange) ☐ depict v. 그리다, 묘사하다 ☐ prevent v. 막다; 예방하다 ☐ interest v. 흥미를 일으키다, 관심 갖게 하다

그 아이를 보호하는 일은 그 아버지와 어머니가 번갈아가며 해야 했다.

78 ③

☐ yearn v. 동경하다(=hanker) ☐ simper v. 히쭉히쭉 웃다, 선웃음치다 ☐ search v. 수색하다, 뒤지다 ☐ ensue v. 뒤따르다

그 노인은 자신이 동경해왔던 대형 여객기 조종 경력을 다시 시작한다.

79 ④

☐ conducive a. 도움이 되는(=helpful) ☐ connected a. 관계가 있는; 일관된 ☐ proportionate a. 비례하는 ☐ adaptable a. 순응할 수 있는

그는 이스라엘의 거대한 석유 천연가스 유전 개발은 개발 비용에 도움이 되는 시장을 찾아내는 것에 달려있다고 말했다.

80 ②

☐ savvy a. 소식에 밝은, 정통해 있는(=knowledgeable) ☐ improving

a. 개량하는, 유익한, 도움이 되는 ☐ weak a. 약한, 무력한, 박약한 ☐ pompous a. 거만한, 건방진, 젠체하는; 과장한

오늘날의 여성들은 교육을 잘 받고 자부심이 강한 데다 과학기술을 잘 이해하고 있어, 계속해서 그들을 매우 필요로 하는 노동시장에 진출하고 있다.

81 ③

☐ settler n. 정착민 ☐ enamored a. 매혹된. 홀딱 반한, 사랑에 빠진(=captivated) ☐ surfeited a. 과음한; 몰두한 ☐ transpired a. 발산된 ☐ envisioned a. 가시적인, 구상중인

영국 이주민인 존 롤프(John Rolfe)는 인디언 공주 포카혼타스(Pocahontas)에게 매혹되어 그녀와 결혼했다.

82 ①

☐ verdict n. (배심원의) 평결; 판단, 결정(=decision) ☐ argument n. 논의; 논거; 논법 ☐ testimony n. 증언, 증거, 증명; 고증 ☐ volition n. 의지, 의지력; 결의, 결단력

그 피고인은 배심원단이 올바른 평결을 했다고 생각했다.

83 ②

☐ resurrection n. 소생; 재기, 부활; 부흥(=revival) ☐ abandonment n. 포기; 유기 ☐ abolishment n. 파기, 폐기; 무효화 ☐ revolution n. 혁명; 변혁; 회전

신임 회장은 수십 명의 임원진을 해고함으로써, 회사의 소생을 가능케 했다.

84 ④

☐ currency n. 통화; 지폐 ☐ champion v. ~을 옹호하다 ☐ solidarity n. 결속, 단결(=unification) ☐ expose v. 드러나다, 노출시키다 ☐ impetus n. 자극(제), 추동력 ☐ discord n. 불화, 불일치; 불협화음 ☐ identity n. 신원, 신분; 독자성 ☐ revenue n. 소득, 수입; 세입 ☐ expertise n. 전문적 기술[지식]

유럽을 단결시킨 원천으로 지지받던 그 화폐는 불협화음을 일으키는 자극제임이 밝혀졌다.

85 ①

☐ plaintiff n. 원고 ☐ count as ~으로 간주되다 ☐ bona fide a. 진실된, 진짜의(=authentic) ☐ epistemically ad. 인식에 관하여 ☐ conduct n. 행동 ☐ omnipotent a. 전능한 ☐ immaculate a. 티하나 없이 깔끔한 ☐ benedictory a. 축복의

원고의 법칙은 완전히 인식에 관해 행위를 인도할 수 있으므로 진짜 권위 있는 법칙으로 간주될 수 있다.

86 ②

☐ appreciate v. 진가를 알아보다[인정하다]; 높이 평가하다(=value) ☐ undermine v. 밑을 파다; 몰래 손상시키다 ☐ regard v. 여기다, 간주하다 ☐ overlook v. 내려다보다; 대충 보다, 간과하다

이런 힘든 경험이 그녀로 하여금 삶을 좀 더 가치 있게 여기도록 하는 데 도움을 주었다.

87 ②

☐ seasoned a. 경험 많은, 노련한(=experienced) ☐ sizzling a. 지글지글 소리 내는; 몹시 더운[뜨거운] ☐ tractable a. 유순한, 온순한; 다루기 쉬운 ☐ tempered a. 조절된, 완화된

드래곤스에서 거의 20시즌을 보낸 피트 웹스터(Pete Webster)는 팀에서 가장 노련한 선수들 중 한 명으로, 젊은 선수들에게 풍부한 노하우를 전수할 수 있었다.

88 ④

☐ abominable a. 지긋지긋한, 혐오스러운, 끔찍한(=horrible) ☐ at large (범인 따위가) 자유로운, 잡히지 않은 ☐ miserable a. 비참한, 불쌍한 ☐ minor a. 중요하지 않은 ☐ famous a. 유명한

유감스럽게도 이러한 끔찍한 범죄의 범인 대부분이 아직도 잡히지 않고 있다.

89 ②

☐ gallant a. 씩씩한, 용감한; 당당한(=brave) ☐ pertinent a. 타당한, 적절한; 요령 있는 ☐ obedient a. 순종하는, 유순한, 고분고분한 ☐ courtly a. 궁정의; 예절 바른; 정중한

그 장교는 용감한 태도로 적을 대했다.

90 ③

☐ substitute n. 대리, 대리인; 대체물(=proxy) ☐ estimate n. 추정(치), 추산; 견적서 ☐ analogue n. 유사물, 유사체 ☐ standard n. 표준, 기준

연구자들이 모기의 몸집 크기를 대신하는 것으로서 날개 길이를 측정했을 때, 그들은 습한 기후에서 그 곤충이 더 크게 자란다는 것을 발견했다.

91 ①

☐ unfold v. 펼치다; (생각을) 털어놓다, 나타내다(=reveal) ☐ instruct v. 가르치다, 교육하다; 지시하다, 명령하다 ☐ conceal v. 숨기다, 비밀로 하다 ☐ teach v. 가르치다; 훈련하다

인생에서의 경험에 따르면 그 책은 그에게 새로운 의미들을 보여줄 것이다.

92 ②

☐ vigorously ad. 활발하게, 강력하게(=strongly) ☐ corruption n. 부패, 타락, 퇴폐 ☐ expectedly ad. 예상한 바와 같이 ☐ timidly ad. 겁 많게; 소극적으로 ☐ vaguely ad. 막연하게, 애매하게

그 주지사는 그 부패 스캔들에 대해 사전에 알고 있었음을 강력히 부인했다.

93 ③

☐ fluctuate v. 오르내리다, 변동하다(=vary) ☐ lessen v. 줄다, 작아지다 ☐ dwindle v. 작아지다, 축소하다 ☐ increase v. 늘리다, 증대하다

유네스코 통계연구소(UIS)의 정보에 따르면, 영화 제작은 많은 나라에서 수시로 변하지만, 인도만이 2005년에서 2011년까지 제작된 영화 수에 있어서 꾸준한 증가 추세를 보였다.

94 ①

☐ legislature n. 입법부, 입법기관 ☐ appropriate v. (어떤 목적에) 충당하다; (정부가 어떤 금액을) 예산에 계상(計上)하다; (의회가) ~의 지출을 승인하다; 횡령하다 ☐ charitable a. 자비로운, 자선의 ☐ allocate v. 할당하다, 배분하다(=allot) ☐ recognize v. 인지하다; 인정하다 ☐ spend v. 소비하다 ☐ request v. 요청[요구, 신청]하다

의회가 자선기금의 용도로 지출을 승인한 돈은 아직 배분되지 않았다.

95 ①

☐ depression n. 우울증 ☐ undermine v. 몰래 손상시키다 ☐ persistent a. 끊임없이 지속되는 ☐ mood disorder 기분 장애 ☐ myriad a. 무수히 많은(=countless) ☐ tackle v. (문제 등을) 다루다 ☐ fleeting a. 일시적인, 잠깐 동안의 ☐ hallmark n. (전형적인) 특징 ☐ diagnosis n. 진단 ☐ crucial a. 중대한, 결정적인 ☐ flawless a. 흠[티] 하나 없는, 나무랄 데 없는 ☐ emotional a. 감정적인

우울증은 삶의 질을 손상시킬 수 있고, 특히 극심하거나 만성적인 경우 신체장애의 원인이 될 수도 있다. 일반적으로 어느 한 해에, 성인남녀 15명 중 한 명꼴로 우울증을 경험하거나 최소 한번은 심각한 우울증을 겪을 것으로 추정된다. 이 기분장애는 일상적인 활동 및 업무를 다루는 능력에서부터 대인관계에 이르기까지 한 사람의 인생의 무수히 많은 측면에 영향을 미칠 수 있다. 슬픔이 일시적으로 잠깐 지속되는 것이 아니라

기분이 우울하거나 가라앉는 것과 같은 기분 장애의 전형적인 특징들과 흥미나 즐거움의 상실이 최소 2주간 지속되어야 우울증 진단이 내려지게 된다.

96   ①

☐ serf n. 농노, 노예 ☐ equality n. 평등, 균등 ☐ servant n. 하인, 종 ☐ ordinance n. 법령, 조례 ☐ uproar n. 대소동, 소란(=hubbub) ☐ emancipate v. 해방하다, 석방하다 ☐ humbug n. 사기, 속임수; 사기꾼 ☐ hobble v. 다리를 절다, 절뚝거리다 ☐ hokum n. 엉터리, 허튼소리

1820년대 중반에 이미 노동에서 '자유시장'을 만들려는 대영제국의 시도들이 노예와 농노에 의존하는 식민지의 계층관계에 폭발적인 영향을 끼쳤다. 새로운 규정들은 대우 기준들을 보장했고 '주인'과 '종'에게 법 앞에서의 평등을 확립했다. 노동시장에서 코이산의 이동성을 보장했던 1828년의 조례 50은 소동을 일으켰다. 1834년 노예들은 결국 해방되었다.

97   ③

☐ acquired a. 취득한, 획득한; 후천적인 ☐ associated a. 연합된, 관련된 ☐ in contrast to ~와 대비하여, ~와 현저히 달라서 ☐ congenital a. 타고난, 선천적인(=innate) ☐ coronary artery 관상동맥 ☐ rheumatic a. 류머티즘의, 류머티즘에 의한 ☐ pulmonary a. 폐의, 폐에 관한 ☐ vessel n. 관, 도관; 혈관 ☐ aorta n. 대동맥 heart valve 심장판막 ☐ acute a. 격심한; (질병이) 급성의 ☐ contagious a. 전염되는, 전염성의 ☐ senile a. 나이 많은, 노쇠한

후천성 심장병은 심장과 그것에 연결돼 있는 혈관에 영향을 미치는 질환으로, 일생 동안 발병할 수 있어서 태어나는 순간 존재하는 선천성 심장병과 대조를 이룬다. 후천성 심장병에는 관상동맥 질환, 류마티스성 심장질환, 폐혈관 및 대동맥 질환, 심장판막 질환 등이 있다.

98   ③

☐ affirm v. 단언하다; 긍정하다 ☐ negate v. 부정하다, 부인하다; 취소하다 ☐ capitalize on 이용하다, 기회로 삼다(=take advantage of) ☐ ambiguous a. 애매모호한, 분명치 않은 ☐ marginal a. 가장자리의, 주변적인, 변경의; 중요하지 않은 ☐ deal with 다루다, 처리하다 ☐ draw on ~에 가까워지다; (근원을) ~에 의존하다 ☐ object to ~에 반대하다, 이의를 제기하다

자신들을 흑인들과 비교하는 것을 부정하여 자신들이 백인임을 주장하려 하는 과정에서, 남부의 유태인들은 종종 남부 사회에서 자신들의 지위가 완전히 주변적이라기보다는 모호한 위치에 있었다는 사실을 이용했다.

99   ④

☐ oblige v. 의무적으로 하게 하다, 도움이나 친절을 베풀다 ☐ felicity n. 더할 나위없는 행복(=happiness) ☐ not so much A as B A라기보다는 B ☐ affliction n. 고통, 고뇌 ☐ resolution n. 결의; 해결; 해상도 ☐ performance n. 공연; 연주회

당신의 친절을 받은 사람보다 당신에게 한 번 친절을 베푼 사람이 당신에게 또 한 번의 친절을 베풀 준비가 더 잘 되어있다. 인간의 행복은 좀처럼 일어나지 않는 큰 행운에 의해서보다는 매일매일 일어나는 작은 좋은 일들에 의해서 발생된다.

100   ②

☐ shoulder v. (책임, 비용 등을) 짊어지다, 떠맡다 ☐ leave behind 두고 가다, (기록, 흔적을) 남기다 ☐ concrete a. 구체적인, 유형의; 현실의 ☐ generosity n. 관대함, 너그러움 ☐ philanthropy n. 박애, 자선(=charity) ☐ genial a. 상냥한, 다정한 ☐ audacity n. 뻔뻔스러움, 대담 ☐ publicity n. 널리 알려짐; 광고, 선전 ☐ purity n. 깨끗함, 청결; 순도

아서 페어베언(Arthur Fairbairn) 경은 우아하게, 끊임없이, 그리고 성공적으로 책임을 짊어질 만큼 위대한 사람이었고, 귀족적인 태도로 좋은 일을 하는 상냥한 마음을 지녔으면서 검소한 사람으로 기억될 뿐만 아니라 관대함과 자선의 구체적인 실례를 남겼다.

01 ①	02 ①	03 ④	04 ③	05 ②	06 ②	07 ①	08 ①	09 ③	10 ①
11 ②	12 ①	13 ③	14 ②	15 ①	16 ①	17 ③	18 ②	19 ②	20 ①
21 ③	22 ④	23 ②	24 ②	25 ②	26 ③	27 ②	28 ③	29 ②	30 ③
31 ③	32 ①	33 ③	34 ③	35 ③	36 ①	37 ④	38 ②	39 ①	40 ④
41 ②	42 ①	43 ①	44 ②	45 ③	46 ①	47 ④	48 ②	49 ④	50 ④
51 ②	52 ③	53 ②	54 ①	55 ②	56 ③	57 ①	58 ④	59 ②	60 ④
61 ③	62 ③	63 ②	64 ③	65 ④	66 ④	67 ①	68 ③	69 ④	70 ②
71 ②	72 ②	73 ④	74 ②	75 ①	76 ②	77 ①	78 ③	79 ④	80 ④
81 ③	82 ①	83 ①	84 ④	85 ③	86 ③	87 ①	88 ①	89 ④	90 ③
91 ①	92 ①	93 ②	94 ③	95 ④	96 ④	97 ④	98 ①	99 ②	100 ②

01 ①

□ concede v. 인정하다, 시인하다; 승인하다(=admit) □ fear v. 두려워하다, 무서워하다, 근심하다 □ announce v. 알리다, 고지하다, 공표하다 □ doubt v. 의심하다; 염려하다

나는 그것이 실패했음을 시인했다.

02 ①

□ labyrinth n. 미궁; 미로; 뒤얽혀 복잡한 것(=maze) □ exterior n. 외부, 외면, 표면 □ fragrance n. 향기, 방향; 향기로움 □ fluency n. 유창, 능변; 거침없음

톰(Tom)과 베티(Betty)는 비밀 동굴의 미로에서 길을 잃었다.

03 ④

□ dormant a. 휴지 상태의; 잠자는(=sleeping) □ sedative a. 진정시키는, 누그러뜨리는 □ potential a. 가능성이 있는, 잠재적인 □ confidential a. 비밀의, 기밀의

그 프로젝트는 우리가 후원자를 찾을 때까지 2년 동안 휴면상태에 있었다.

04 ③

□ hardship n. 고난, 고초; 곤란, 곤경(=adversity) □ war n. 전쟁; 무력 충돌; 싸움 □ possession n. 소유; 소유물, 재산 □ competition n. 경쟁; 경기, 시합

인류의 역사는 고난의 역사이다.

05 ②

□ peripheral a. 중요하지 않은, 지엽적인; 주변부의(=marginal) □ secondary a. 부차적인; 종속적인 □ superficial a. 피상적인; 표면적인 □ insignificant a. 사소한, 하찮은

정부는 대도시의 주변 외곽 지역에 도시 개발을 추진할 준비가 되어 있다.

06 ②

□ dyadic a. 두 개의, 한 쌍의 □ triangulate v. 삼각형으로 하다[분할하다] □ rapport n. 관계, 접촉, 협조(=relation) □ image n. 상; 형태, 모습 □ reference n. 참조, 조회; 언급 □ memory n. 기억, 상기

그 장면에서 아버지의 등장으로 인해 어머니와 아이 사이의 한 쌍의 가상의 관계가 삼각관계가 되기 때문에, 그의 요점을 오이디푸스 콤플렉스 관점에서 해석하는 것은 어렵지 않다.

07 ①

□ salutary a. 건전한; 유익한, 이로운(=useful) □ hygienic a. 위생(상)의, 보건상의; 위생학의 □ dubious a. 의심스러운, 수상한; 결정하기 어려운; 반신반의의 □ enforce v. 실시하다, 집행하다; 강요하다

처벌은 그 소년에게 유익한 영향을 미쳤는데 그가 모범생이 되었기 때문이었다.

08 ①

□ disparity n. 상이, 부동, 불균형, 불일치(=inequality) □ separation n. 분리, 분할; 구분 □ unrest n. 불안, 불온 (상태), 근심 □ pessimism n. 비관(주의), 염세론

우리나라에는 경제적인 불균형이 존재한다.

09 ③

□ compromise n. 타협(안) □ chamber n. 방, 실 □ obviate v. 미연에 방지하다, 제거하다(=preclude) □ repeal v. 폐지하다, 철회하다 □ verify v. 확인하다, 입증하다 □ stunt v. 발육을 방해하다

판사실에서 성사된 타협안은 오래 끌고 많은 비용이 드는 소송의 필요성을 없애줄 것이다.

10 ①

□ renowned a. 유명한, 명성 있는(=famed) □ admired a. 존경받는 □ envy v. 부러워하다; 질투하다 □ slight v. 경시하다, 무시하다

그 마을은 깨끗한 거리와 친절함으로 유명하다.

11 ②

□ cramp v. 막다, 방해하다, 제한하다(=hinder) □ detour v. 둘러가다, 우회하다 □ motivate v. 동기를 주다, 자극하다 □ discord v. 일치하지 않다; 사이가 나쁘다

보다 엄격한 공해방지법은 경제 성장을 방해할지도 모른다.

12 ①

□ harass v. 애를 먹이다, 괴롭히다(=bully) □ gossip v. 잡담하다; 수군거리다 □ chat v. 잡담하다, 담화하다 □ beat v. 치다, 때리다; 두드리다

그녀는 그 괴롭힘에 대해 아무 말도 하지 않았다.

13 ③

□ enthrall v. 노예로 만들다; 마음을 사로잡다, 매혹시키다(=captivate) □ shock v. 충격을 주다, 깜짝 놀라게 하다 □ stimulate v. 자극하다, 활발하게 하다; 북돋우다 □ terrify v. 겁나게 하다, 놀래다; 위협하여 ~시키다

청중들은 오케스트라가 연주하는 음악의 완전한 아름다움에 넋을 빼앗겼다.

14 ②

□ manipulate v. 잘 다루다, 조작하다(=handle); 속이다 □ serve v. 섬기다, 봉사하다; 소용이 되다, 이바지하다 □ relieve v. 안도케 하다; (긴장 등을) 풀게 하다; 구원하다; 구제하다 □ grasp v. 붙잡다, 움켜잡다; 터득하다, 파악하다 □ tease v. 괴롭히다, 집적거리다, 희롱하다

스포츠가 시민들로 하여금 그들의 문제점들과 분쟁에 대해 잊어버리게 하는 능력을 지닌 것처럼, 또한 스포츠는 대중들을 조종하거나 정치적 명분을 따르도록 하기 위한 하나의 도구로 이용될 수 있다.

15 ①

□ repercussion n. 되튀기, 반동; 영향, 반향(=strong impact) □ symbolic meaning 상징적인 의미 □ violent protest 격렬한 항의 □ faint echo 희미한 반향

아무도 가격 동결이 미칠 불행한 영향을 예상하지 못했다.

16 ①

□ attribute v. (원인, 결과) ~에 귀착시키다, ~의 탓으로 하다(=ascribe) □ contribute v. 기부하다, 기증하다; 기여하다 □ insinuate v. 둘러서 말하다, 암시하다 □ construe v. 해석하다; 추론하다

우리는 그녀의 성공을 근면과 열정 덕이라고 여긴다.

17 ③

□ merge v. 합병하다; 융합시키다(=combine) □ start v. 출발하다, 떠나다; 시작하다 □ change v. 바꾸다, 고치다; 교환하다 □ succeed v. 성공하다, 출세하다; 계속되다

두 기업체는 1년 전 합병한 이래로 매우 강력해졌다.

18 ②

□ inevitable a. 불가피한; 필연적인, 당연한(=certain) □ strange a. 낯선, 이상한, 기묘한 □ inconsistent a. 일치되지 않는, 조화되지 않는; 모순된 □ proper a. 적절한, 타당한

1861년 남부의 주들이 북부의 여러 주에서 탈퇴하는 것은 당연한 것처럼 보였다.

19 ②

□ concise a. 간결한, 간명한(=brief) □ verbose a. 말이 많은, 장황한 □ rational a. 이성적인 □ coherent a. 일관성 있는 □ erudite a. 박식한

간결하게 하는 것은 장황하게 하는 것보다 훨씬 더 힘들다. 그래서 이것은 노력을 필요로 할 것이다.

20 ①

□ phantom n. 환상; 망상 □ neurologist n. 신경학자 □ persistent a. 지속적인, 끈질긴(=enduring) □ pernicious a. 유해한, 파괴적인

□ perplexed a. 당황한, 난처한, 골치 아픈 □ perilous a. 위험한, 위기에 처한

'망상'은 신경학자들이 사용하는 뜻으로 보자면, (신체의 일부를) 상실한 이후 수개월 내지 수년 동안 지속해서 나타나는, 신체의 일부 중 보통은 팔다리의 이미지나 기억이다.

21 ③

□ adorn v. 꾸미다, 장식하다(=embellish) □ decorative a. 장식용의, 장식적인 □ element n. 요소, 성분 □ column n. 기둥, 원주 □ carving n. 조각; 조각물 □ swaddle v. 가늘고 긴 포대기로 감싸다 □ dangle v. ~을 매달다; 자랑삼아 보이다 □ drape v. 주름을 잡아 예쁘게 덮다[꾸미다]

바로크 시대에 유럽의 교회들은 조각으로 덮여 있는 뒤틀린 기둥과 같은 풍부한 장식적 요소들로 꾸며져 있었다.

22 ④

□ fictitious a. 허구의, 지어낸(=invented) □ forwarding n. 추진, 촉진 □ secret a. 비밀의, 남몰래 하는 □ private a. 사유의, (특정) 개인 소유의

그녀는 신청서에 지어낸 주소를 썼다.

23 ②

□ unearth v. 발굴하다, 파내다; 발견하다(=discover) □ bury v. 묻다; (흙 따위로) 덮다; 매장하다 □ pay attention to ~에 유의하다 □ look over ~을 대충 훑어보다; 일일이 조사하다

그때까지 누구도 흙 속에 묻힌 공룡의 뼈를 발굴한 적이 없었다.

24 ②

□ projecting a. 돌출한, 튀어나온(=protruding) □ rotating a. 회전하는; 순환하는 □ vibrating a. 진동하는, 떨리는 □ contracting a. 수축성 있는; 계약의

개구리와 두꺼비의 혀는 주둥이 앞부분에 고정되어 있어 얼마간 떨어진 곳에서 내밀기가 쉽고 이는 벌레를 잡는 데 크게 도움이 된다.

25 ②

□ salvage v. 구출하다; 인양하다; (폐품 등을) 이용하다(=recover) □ worn-out a. 써서 낡은, 닳아 진; 케케묵은, 진부한 □ modify v. 변경하다, 수정하다 □ dirty v. 더럽히다 □ soften v. 부드럽게 하다; 완화시키다

재생고무는 닳은 타이어, 오래된 튜브, 그리고 그 밖의 폐기된 고무 제품에서 회수된다.

26 ③

□ unassuming a. 젠체하지 않는, 겸손한(=modest) □ demeanor n. 태도, 표정; 품행 □ fragile a. 망가지기 쉬운, 무른; 허약한 □ nimble a. 재빠른, 민첩한 □ thrifty a. 검소한, 절약하는

그 배우가 너무나도 겸손한 태도를 보였기 때문에 사람들은 행사에서 그를 거의 알아채지 못했다.

27 ②

□ scathing a. 냉혹한, 가차 없는, 통렬한(=ruthless) □ candid a. 정직한, 솔직한; 노골적인 □ generous a. 관대한, 후한; 푸짐한 □ skeptical a. 의심 많은, 회의적인; 믿지 않는

엘리트를 후원하는 사람의 편에서는 자신들이 성공하도록 허용하지 않은 사람들에 대해서는 아마 약간 더 비판적인 경향이 있다.

28 ③

□ assault v. 급습[강습]하다; 폭행하다, 공격하다(=assail) □ retaliate v. 보복하다, 앙갚음 하다, 응수하다; 악으로 갚다 □ reasonable a. 도리에 맞는; 온당한, 적당한; 합당한 □ endorse v. 배서[서명]하다; 보증하다 □ divulge v. (비밀을) 누설하다, 밝히다; 폭로하다 □ curtail v. 짧게 줄이다, 생략하다, 단축하다

만약 내가 육체적으로 공격받는다면, 그에 온당한 폭력으로 보복하는 것이 허락될 것이다.

29 ②

□ imperceptible a. 감지할 수 없는, 알아차릴 수 없을 만큼의, 미세한(=unnoticeable) □ naught a. 파멸한, 망한; 무익한 □ strange a. 이상한, 야릇한, 기묘한 □ unattractive a. 남의 눈을 끌지 않는, 아름답지 못한

아침과 저녁에 나뭇잎이 푸르른 정도의 차이는 거의 알아차릴 수 없을 정도이다.

30 ③

□ compulsively ad. 강제적으로, 억지로, 마지못해(=irresistibly) □ constantly ad. 변함없이, 항상, 끊임없이 □ always ad. 늘, 언제나, 항상 □ invariably ad. 변함없이, 언제나

강박감에 사로잡힌 듯이 새로운 것을 추구하는 사람들은 오래되고 평범한 것에 만족하는 사람들보다 약물을 남용하는 경향이 있다.

31 ③

☐ tenor n. 방침, 진로; 성격, 성질(=nature) ☐ result n. 결과, 성과, 결말 ☐ intonation n. 억양; 음조, 어조 ☐ punctuation n. 구두점; 구두(법)

과학(학문)에 대한 중대한 기여는 다음 세대들에 의해 제기된 문제들의 성격을 변화시키는 것들이다.

32 ①

☐ turn up 파 뒤집다, 발굴하다, 조사하다 ☐ preoccupied a. 몰두한, 여념이 없는, 정신이 팔린(=absorbed) ☐ measure v. 측정하다[재다]; 판단하다 ☐ passage n. (시간의) 흐름[경과] ☐ excluded a. 제외되는 ☐ provided a. 준비된 ☐ convicted a. 유죄로 결정된

기록과 유물을 발굴하는 어디에서나, 우리는 모든 문화권에서 일부 사람들이 시간의 흐름을 측정하는 데 몰두하고 있었다는 것을 대개 발견한다.

33 ④

☐ temperance n. 절제, 조심, 자제(=restraint) ☐ humility n. 겸손, 겸양; 비하 ☐ stigma n. 치욕, 오명, 불명예 ☐ spontaneity n. 자발성, 자발적 행동; 무의식

새로운 코칭스태프는 시즌 중에는 절제할 것을 그 축구팀에 요구했다.

34 ③

☐ high-powered a. 영향력이 큰; 혈기[원기] 왕성한 ☐ hauteur n. 거만(한 태도), 오만(=arrogance) ☐ assistant n. 조수, 보조원 ☐ partiality n. 편파, 편애 ☐ tenacity n. 고집; 끈기 ☐ continence n. 절제, 극기

큰 영향력이 있는 최고경영자는 새로 고용된 비서에게 거만한 태도를 보일지도 모른다.

35 ③

☐ contritely ad. 회개하면서, 죄를 깊이 뉘우치면서(=repentantly) ☐ smoothly ad. 매끄럽게, 원활하게, 유창하게 ☐ repeatedly ad. 되풀이하여, 여러 차례 ☐ tiredly ad. 피곤하여, 싫증나서

"다시는 그런 일이 없을 겁니다."라고 그녀는 뉘우치며 약속했다.

36 ①

☐ portent n. 조짐, 전조(=presage) ☐ tremor n. 소동; 전율, 떨림 ☐ upheaval n. 격변, 동란 ☐ plethora n. 과잉, 과다, 과도

오늘 아침 우리가 들었던 멀리서 우르릉거리는 소리는 오늘 오후에 우리 지역을 강타한 폭풍의 전조였다.

37 ④

☐ automaton n. 자동 장치[기계]; 자동인형; 기계적으로 행동하는 사람[동물] ☐ mechanical a. 기계상의, 기계에 의한; 기계 장치의 ☐ self-operating a. 자동의; 자동적인 ☐ actuate v. 작용하다; 작동시키다; 행동시키다(=set in motion) ☐ timed a. 시한의; 정기의 ☐ construct v. 세우다, 건설하다, 건조하다 ☐ clean up 청소하다, 깨끗이 하다

자동 장치란 한번 작동되기만 하면 자동적으로 움직이는 기계적인 장치를 말한다.

38 ①

☐ jeopardy n. 위험; 위험성(=danger) ☐ put ~ in jeopardy ~을 위험에 빠뜨리다 ☐ range n. 범위, 한계 ☐ review n. 재검토; 복습 ☐ perspective n. 전망

예산 감축으로 인해 그 나라 일자리의 10%가 위태롭게 되었다.

39 ①

☐ disclaim v. (권리 등을) 포기하다; (관계, 책임 등을) 부인하다, 거부하다(=repudiate) ☐ liability n. 책임 있음, 책임; 부담, 의무 ☐ arrogate v. 사칭하다; (권리를) 침해하다 ☐ predicate v. 단정[단언]하다; (어떤 근거에) 입각시키다 ☐ incriminate v. (남에게) 죄를 씌우다; 연루시키다

이러한 경우에 저희는 아무런 책임을 지지 않음을 양해해 주십시오.

40 ④

☐ infidelity n. 신을 믿지 않음, 불신앙; 배신(=unfaithfulness) ☐ charity n. 자애, 자비, 박애, 자선 ☐ torpedo n. 어뢰(魚雷), 수뢰 ☐ disaster n. 천재, 재해, 재난, 참사

모든 배우자의 50퍼센트 이상이 부정(不貞)의 피해자라고 보고된다.

41 ②

☐ communicable a. 전염성의; 전달되는(=contagious) ☐ adjustable a. 조절할 수 있는; 적응할 수 있는 ☐ dangerous a. 위험한, 위태로운 ☐ incurable a. 치료할 수 없는, 불치의

쓰나미로 인해 죽는 사람만큼이나 많은 사람들이 전염병으로 죽을 가능성이 확실히 있다.

42   ①

☐ horrid a. 무서운 ☐ prospect n. 예상, 기대; (종종 pl.) (장래의) 가망 ☐ bleak a. 황폐한; 암담한 ☐ torpid a. 마비된; 무기력한(=inert) ☐ epoch n. 시대; 신기원 ☐ dark a. 어두운; 은밀한 ☐ spectacular a. 장관을 이루는; 극적인 ☐ fantastic a. 환상적인, 기상천외의

TV가 우리 앞에 열어 보이는 무시무시한 전망은 말하는 사람이 없고 책 읽는 사람이 없어 암담하고 무기력한 시대가 앞에 놓여있을지 모른다는 것을 암시한다.

43   ①

☐ indolent a. 나태한, 게으른, 무활동의(=lazy) ☐ industrious a. 근면한, 부지런한, 열심인 ☐ impudent a. 뻔뻔스러운, 철면피의, 염치없는 ☐ vigilant a. 자지 않고 지키는, 부단히 경계하고 있는

나의 삼촌은 게을렀기 때문에 세 곳의 직장에서 해고되었다. 그는 제시간에 출근하기는 하지만, 일은 거의 하지 않고 일찍 퇴근한다.

44   ②

☐ redeem v. 벌충하다, 상쇄하다; 상품으로 바꾸다(=exchange) ☐ revise v. 개정하다, 교정하다 ☐ save v. 지키다, 수호하다 ☐ buy v. 사다, 구입하다

많은 주부들은 녹색 도장을 모으곤 했다. 그들은 이 도장을 모든 종류의 물품과 바꾸었다.

45   ③

☐ fathom v. 추측하다, 간파하다, 이해하다(=understand) ☐ trust v. 신뢰하다, 신임하다, 의지하다 ☐ apply v. 적용하다, 응용하다 ☐ question v. 질문하다, 묻다; 조사하다

어린아이로서는 특히 신변 안전의 문제에 있어 부모님의 지혜를 충분히 이해하기가 어려울 것이다.

46   ①

☐ hinder v. 방해하다, 저지하다, 훼방하다(=retard) ☐ mask v. 가면을 씌우다; 감추다, 가리다 ☐ reverse v. 거꾸로 하다, 반대로 하다; 뒤집다; 전환하다 ☐ monitor v. 감시하다, 관리하다

과다한 칼슘 섭취는 아이들의 성장을 방해할 수 있다.

47   ④

☐ vulgar a. 상스러운, 저속한, 천박한(=indecent) ☐ holistic a. 전체론의; 전신용의 ☐ substantial a. 상당한; 실재하는 ☐ remarkable a. 주목할 만한, 현저한

TV는 독서를 대신하는 저속한 대안이 되므로 독서의 가치를 증가시켜 놓았다.

48   ②

☐ depiction n. 묘사, 서술(=description) ☐ object n. 물건, 대상 ☐ sculpture n. 조각 ☐ canvas n. 도화지 ☐ chalk n. 분필 ☐ alteration n. 변화, 개조; 수정 ☐ imitation n. 모조품; 모방 ☐ symbol n. 상징, 부호

어떤 사람들에게 미술은 어떤 대상을 묘사하는 것으로, 예를 들면 사람을 소재로 한 그림이나 조각이다. (그러나) 다른 이들에게 미술은 아무 것도 그려지지 않은 도화지나 (아무것도 쓰지 않은) 분필 한 자루일지도 모른다.

49   ④

☐ be remembered for ~으로 기억되다, 유명하다 ☐ inspirational a. 영감을 주는 ☐ determination n. 투지; 결심; 결단(력) ☐ overcome v. 이기다; 압도하다, 정복하다; 극복하다 ☐ courage n. 용기, 담력 ☐ segregation n. 분리, 격리; 인종 차별(=discrimination) ☐ racism n. 민족적 우월감; 인종적 차별, 인종적 편견 ☐ disturbance n. 소란, 소동, 불안, 혼란; 방해, 장애(물) ☐ restriction n. 제한, 규제, 제약, 구속 ☐ interruption n. 중단, 방해; 중절, 중지

오늘날, 윌마 루돌프(Wilma Rudolph)는 신체적 장애를 극복한 그녀의 고무적인 의지와, 차별과 인종주의를 넘어선 용기로 유명하다.

50   ④

☐ choking n. 숨 막힘 ☐ obstruct v. 막다, 차단하다; 방해하다(=block) ☐ restructure v. 재구성하다; 개혁하다 ☐ debauch v. 타락시키다; 더럽히다 ☐ vent v. (감정 등에) 배출구를 주다; (감정 등을) 터뜨리다, 발산하다

폐로 공기가 유입되는 것이 차단될 때 질식이 발생한다.

51   ②

☐ enforce v. 시행하다, 실시하다, 집행하다(=carry out) ☐ overlook v. 간과하다; 내려다보다; 감독하다 ☐ give up 포기하다, 단념하다, 체념하다 ☐ alternate v. 교체하다; 번갈아 하다

시민을 보호하고 법을 집행하는 것이 경찰의 의무이다.

52   ③

☐ arrogant a. 거만한, 오만한(=imperious) ☐ judicious a. 사려 분별이 있는, 현명한, 판단이 적절한 ☐ perceptive a. 지각력이 있는; 민감한 ☐ adamant a. 단호한, 확고한

어리석을 정도로 거만했던 나는 지적 능력과 업적을 기준으로 사람의 가치를 판단하곤 했다.

53 ②

☐ **amid** prep. ~의 한복판에, ~이 한창일 때 ☐ **fury** n. 격노, 격분; 격심함 ☐ **levity** n. 경솔, 경박; 변덕; 가벼움, 우스움(=amusement) ☐ **solemnity** n. 장엄, 엄숙, 근엄함 ☐ **firmness** n. 견고, 견실; 확고부동 ☐ **gloom** n. 어둠, 암울함; 우울, 침울

전운(戰雲)과 전화(戰禍)의 시기에 리베라(Rivera)는 우리 모두에게 순간의 오락과 희망의 이유를 제공해 주었다.

54 ①

☐ **physical punishment** 체벌 ☐ **provoke** v. 유발하다; ~을 화나게 하다 ☐ **resentment** n. 분함, 억울함, 분개; 원한, 적의(=indignation) ☐ **rejection** n. 거절; 배제 ☐ **demonstration** n. 시위, 데모 ☐ **impropriety** n. 부적당; 잘못

가벼운 체벌조차도 분노를 유발시켜 계속해서 잘못된 행동을 하게 될 수 있다.

55 ②

☐ **berserk** a. 광포한, 난폭한(=violent) ☐ **overbearing** a. 거만한, 오만한 ☐ **perturbed** a. 혼란된, 어지러워진 ☐ **stagnant** a. 정체된; 불경기의, 부진한

서방 국가의 지도자들과 러시아의 지도자들이 광포해지면 그것이 전 세계에 재난을 초래할 수도 있을 것이다.

56 ②

☐ **fertile** a. 비옥한, 기름진; 다산의(=productive) ☐ **flamboyant** a. 현란한, 화려한 ☐ **imminent** a. 절박한, 급박한, 긴급한 ☐ **hostile** a. 적의 있는; 적대하는; 반대하는

저마다 독특한 문화적 주체성을 갖고 있다고 생각하는 공동체들의 정치적 통합은 민족주의자들의 반발이 나타날 비옥한 토양을 제공한다.

57 ①

☐ **modest** a. 겸손한, 신중한 ☐ **bore** v. 지루하게 만들다 ☐ **petty** a. 사소한, 하찮은(=insignificant) ☐ **accomplishment** n. 성취, 완성; 업적 ☐ **personal** a. 개인적인 ☐ **stingy** a. 인색한 ☐ **magnificent** a. 장려한, 웅장한

우리는 겸손해야 하며 우리의 하찮은 성과에 대한 이야기로 다른 사람들을 지루하게 만들기에는 인생이 너무 짧다는 것을 기억해야 한다.

58 ④

☐ **helm** n. 키(자루), 타륜; 조타 장치; 지도적 지위, 지배(=controlling position) ☐ **committee** n. 위원회; 위원 ☐ **stock market** 증권거래소 시장; 증권 매매 ☐ **cabin** n. 오두막, 선실, 객실

콜트 텔레콤 그룹은 그 회사의 최고 경영 간부인 피터 매닝(Peter Manning)을 최고경영자 자리에 임명함으로써 5개월간에 걸친 새로운 최고경영자 물색을 끝냈다.

59 ②

☐ **trace** n. 발자국; 자국, 자취, 흔적(=indication) ☐ **smell** n. 후각; 냄새, 향기 ☐ **color** n. 빛깔, 색, 명암 ☐ **spread** n. 퍼짐; 폭, 넓이, 뻗음; 보급, 전파

화학자가 분석한 그 커피에는 독극물의 흔적이 없었다.

60 ④

☐ **abridge** v. 단축하다, 생략하다; 축소하다(=curtail) ☐ **diversify** v. 다양화하다, 다채롭게 하다 ☐ **dictate** v. 구술하다; 명령하다, 지시하다 ☐ **increase** v. 늘리다, 증가시키다

프로그램은 시장이 이용할 수 있는 선택의 범위를 줄이는 것이 아니라 늘리도록 설계되어야 한다.

61 ③

☐ **occlude** v. 막다, 폐색(閉塞)하다(=block) ☐ **ruptured** a. 파열된 ☐ **artery** n. 동맥 ☐ **remove** v. 치우다; 제거하다 ☐ **conduct** v. (특정한 활동을) 하다 ☐ **transplant** v. 이식하다

심각한 부상을 입은 환자를 치료할 때 의사는 과도한 출혈을 막기 위해 파열된 동맥을 막아야 할 수도 있다.

62 ③

☐ **mend** n. 개선, 차도(=recovery) ☐ **repair** n. 수리, 보수 ☐ **change** n. 변화, 변경 ☐ **correction** n. 정정, 수정

시위에서 중상을 입었던 이라크 전쟁 참전 용사 스콧 올슨(Scott Olsen)은 지금 병세가 호전되어서 다음 주 시위에 다시 참석할 것이다.

63 ②

☐ **dearth** n. 부족, 결핍; 기근(=deficiency) ☐ **contamination** n. 오염, 더러움 ☐ **equilibrium** n. 평형상태, 균형 ☐ **abundance** n. 풍부, 많음

비가 부족하면 몇 년 안에 사막이 생길 수 있다.

64 ③

☐ Teaism n. 다도(茶道) ☐ cult n. (특정한) 의식 ☐ adoration n. 숭배, 동경 ☐ sordid a. 추악한, 몹시 지저분한; 부도덕한(=filthy) ☐ rigorous a. 엄격한, 철저한 ☐ defiant a. 반항적인, 도전적인 ☐ impudent a. 뻔뻔스러운, 철면피의

다도(茶道)는 일상생활의 비도덕적인 사실들 가운데 미(美)를 동경하는 것에 바탕을 둔 의식이다.

65 ④

☐ indigenous a. 토착의, 원산의; 고유의(=native) ☐ hard-working a. 근면한, 열심히 일하는, 몸을 아끼지 않는 ☐ advanced a. 앞으로 나아간, 진보한, 나아간 ☐ poor a. 가난한, 불쌍한, 부족한

그 마을 주민의 거의 3분의 2가 토착 문명의 후예들이다.

66 ④

☐ surpass v. 뛰어넘다, 능가하다(=excel) ☐ recession n. 경기 후퇴, 불경기 ☐ prosper v. 번영[번창, 번성]하다 ☐ undermine v. 해치다, 저해하다 ☐ lose v. 잃다; 상실하다, 분실하다 ☐ suppress v. 억누르다, 진압하다

중국과 인도는, 연간 자동차 판매 대수가 1,320만 대와 1,230만 대로 불경기 동안에 처음으로 미국을 능가했고, 중산층이 번영함에 따라 계속해서 가장 크게 성장하는 시장이 될 것이다.

67 ①

☐ engross v. 집중시키다, 열중시키다(=attract) ☐ suspend v. (매)달다, 걸다; 중지하다 ☐ bewilder v. 당황하게 하다, 어리둥절하게 하다 ☐ ignore v. 무시하다, 묵살하다

그들의 토론은 그의 관심을 집중시켰다.

68 ①

☐ ensue v. 계속해서 일어나다, 뒤이어 일어나다; 결과로서 일어나다 (=result) ☐ join in ~에 참여하다, 참가하다 ☐ begin v. 시작하다, 착수하다 ☐ fall down 쓰러지다, 엎드리다; 병들어 눕다; 실패하다

"어떤 결과가 일어나더라도 난 진실을 말할 거야."라고 그 여주인공은 스스로 다짐했다.

69 ④

☐ groan n. 신음소리, 끙끙거리는 소리; 불평하는 소리 ☐ disquieting a. 불안하게 하는, 걱정하게 하는(=uneasy) ☐ discontented a. 불만족한, 불만스러워 하는, 불평스러운 ☐ disparate a. 본질적으로 다른 ☐

☐ dissemble v. 속이다, 감추다

주말에 시험이 있을 것이라는 걱정스러운 소식을 접했을 때 학급 전체에 불평하는 소리가 흘렀다.

70 ②

☐ incumbent a. 현직의, 재임 중인; 의무로서 지워지는(=obligatory) ☐ accountable a. 책임이 있는, 해명할 의무가 있는 ☐ irresponsible a. 무책임한, 신뢰할 수 없는 ☐ disadvantageous a. 불리한, 불편한 ☐ commandable a. 명령할 수 있는

고위직에 있거나 고위직을 얻고자 하는 사람들이 일리노이주의 유권자들에게 전적으로 책임을 지는 것이 의무이다.

71 ②

☐ violation n. 위반; 방해, 침해 ☐ apparent a. 명백한; 겉치레의 ☐ extra-judicial a. 재판 외의, 사법 절차에 의하지 않는 ☐ detention n. 구류, 구금, 유치 ☐ deem v. 생각하다, 간주하다(=consider) ☐ prejudice v. ~에 편견을 갖게 하다; 손상시키다 ☐ premise v. 전제로 말하다, 가정하다 ☐ presuppose v. 미리 가정하다; 전제로 하다

가장 최근에 있었던 협정 위반은 본토 지도자들에 대해 비판적인 것으로 여겨지는 홍콩 출판업자 5명을 명백히 재판 없이 구금한 것이다.

72 ②

☐ retreat v. 물러가다, 후퇴하다; 퇴각하다; 은퇴하다(=recede) ☐ adverse a. 역(逆)의, 거스르는; 적자의 ☐ deteriorate v. 나쁘게 하다, 열등하게 하다 ☐ augment v. 증가하다, 늘리다 ☐ increase v. 늘다, 증대하다 ☐ stagnate v. (액체가) 흐르지 않다; 썩다; 침체되다

악화되고 있는 해외 상황의 불리한 영향으로 인해 한국의 경제 성장은 2000년에 9%로 예상되었던 것에서 올해 5.7%로 후퇴할 것이다.

73 ④

☐ doleful a. 슬픈, 쓸쓸한(=dirgeful) ☐ stressful a. 긴장이[스트레스가] 많은 ☐ gleeful a. 매우 기뻐하는; 즐거운 ☐ wasteful a. 낭비하는; 사치스런

외로운 조랑말의 슬픈 눈을 들여다본 그 소녀는 그 조랑말을 몹시 집으로 데려가고 싶었다.

74 ②

☐ algebra n. 대수학(代數學) ☐ off-hand ad. 준비 없이, 즉시로, 당장 (=at once) ☐ at all 전혀, 조금도 ☐ by and by 머지않아, 가까운 장래에 ☐ on and off 단속적으로, 이따금씩

나는 그에게 어려운 대수 문제를 하나 제시했는데 그는 그것을 즉석에서 풀어냈다.

75 ①

☐ construe v. 해석하다, ~의 뜻으로 파악[이해]하다(=understand) ☐ criticize v. 비평하다, 비판하다 ☐ laugh at 비웃다 ☐ report v. 보고하다

윈스턴(Winston)은 자신의 논평이 인종차별적으로 이해될 수 있다는 것을 인정했다.

76 ②

☐ meticulous a. 세심한, 꼼꼼한(=thorough) ☐ solar cycle n. 태양활동 주기 ☐ terrestrial a. 지구의 ☐ enigmatic a. 수수께끼 같은, 불가사의한 ☐ cursory a. 피상적인, 겉핥기의 ☐ prolonged a. 오래 계속되는, 장기적인 ☐ scientific a. 과학의; 체계적인

한 세기 동안 세심하게 조사한 후에도, 태양활동 주기와 지구 기상의 관계는 여전히 수수께끼로 남아있다.

77 ①

☐ seclude v. 은둔하다, 고립시키다(=isolate) ☐ abstain v. 삼가다, 그만두다 ☐ refrain v. 그만두다, 삼가다

그는 명백히 정부가 젊은이들로부터 우리를 떼어놓을 계획을 만들어왔다고 말했다.

78 ③

☐ carnivore n. 육식 동물(=predator) ☐ prey n. 먹이; 희생자 ☐ reptile n. 파충류 ☐ amphibian n. 양서류

세렝게티의 대이동 기간 동안 큰 무리의 육식 동물들은 2백만 마리가 넘는 대형 초식 동물들을 따라간다.

79 ④

☐ conspicuous a. 눈에 잘 띄는, 뚜렷한; 두드러진(=prominent) ☐ modest a. 겸손한, 정숙한 ☐ humble a. 겸손한; 비천한, 보잘것없는 ☐ subtle a. 미묘한, 난해한; 엷은

경제적인 희생이 불가피한 이들 산업 국가 가운데 가장 두드러진 국가들은 동유럽 국가들이다.

80 ④

☐ preponderance n. (무게, 힘에 있어서의) 우세; 다수(=majority)

☐ portent n. 전조, 징후, 조짐 ☐ milieu n. (사회적, 문화적) 환경 ☐ predilection n. 편애; 매우 좋아함

2천 3백만 명의 공무원들 대다수는 국민에게 직접 봉사하고 있다.

81 ③

☐ ample a. 충분한, 풍부한(=sufficient) ☐ rare a. 드문, 진기한, 희박한 ☐ scanty a. 부족한, 불충분한 ☐ inadequate a. 부적당한, 불충분한

이로 인해 그녀는 하루에 세 끼 식사를 준비할 수 있는 충분한 시간을 갖게 된다.

82 ①

☐ deadly ad. 극도로, 지독히(=extremely) ☐ quietly ad. 조용히, 고요히 ☐ secretly ad. 비밀로, 몰래 ☐ mildly ad. 온화하게, 부드럽게

그녀는 그가 농담을 하고 있다고 생각했지만 그는 매우 진지했다.

83 ①

☐ confront v. 직면하다, 맞서다; 대면하다(=face) ☐ optimism n. 낙천[낙관]주의; 희망적 관측 ☐ avoid v. 피하다, 회피하다 ☐ evade v. 피하다, 모면하다; 회피하다 ☐ conclude v. 끝내다, 결말짓다

우리는 우리나라의 미래에 낙관적으로 대처해야 한다.

84 ④

☐ armistice n. 휴전; 정전; 휴전협정(=cease-fire agreement) ☐ arms deal 무기 거래 ☐ military justice 군사재판 ☐ military court 군사법정

전투는 휴전협정이 조인될 때까지 여전히 계속되었다.

85 ③

☐ serene a. 고요한, 잔잔한(=calm) ☐ romantic a. 낭만적인; 몽상적인; 허구의 ☐ hot a. 뜨거운, 열이 있는; 열렬한 ☐ exciting a. 흥분시키는, 자극적인

그 소녀가 바닷가를 걷던 때는 고요한 여름밤이었다.

86 ③

☐ penitent a. (잘못을) 뉘우치는, 후회[참회]하는(=apologetic) ☐ victim n. 희생, 희생자 ☐ pardon n. 용서, 허용; (죄인에 대한) 사면 ☐ artificial a. 인공의, 인위적인 ☐ natural a. 자연의; 타고난 ☐ generic a. 일반적인, 포괄적인

그 살인자가 죄를 뉘우치지 않는다고 주장하면서, 희생자의 가족은 그의 사면이 거부되어야 한다고 생각했다.

87 ①

☐ **perfidy** n. 불성실, 배반(=betrayal) ☐ **audacity** n. 대담(성), 담대함 ☐ **recklessness** n. 무모함, 부주의함 ☐ **agitation** n. 불안, 동요

말로우(Marlow)는 폭풍이 오기 전 그들의 집을 포기하기를 거부했는데, 그의 행동은 일종의 배신으로 간주된다.

88 ①

☐ **commission** n. 의뢰, 주문; 수수료 ☐ **secular** a. 세속의; 현세의; 비종교적인(=worldly) ☐ **patron** n. 보호자, 후원자 ☐ **spiritual** a. 정신적인; 숭고한; 종교상의 ☐ **religious** a. 종교의, 종교적인 ☐ **seductive** a. 유혹적인, 매력적인

그 피렌체 조각가는 교회와 세속 후원자로부터 오는 많은 자금을 가지고 있었다.

89 ④

☐ **congruent** a. 일치하는; 적절한(=corresponding) ☐ **incomparable** a. 비교할 수 없는; 견줄 데 없는 ☐ **dissimilar** a. 비슷하지 않은, 다른 ☐ **indecent** a. 버릇없는, 꼴사나운; 외설한

그 두 연극에 나타난 일치된 주제를 알아보는 것은 쉬운 일이다.

90 ③

☐ **disrupt** v. 붕괴시키다, 분열시키다; 혼란시키다(=upset) ☐ **prolong** v. 늘이다, 길게 하다; 연장하다 ☐ **tantalize** v. 감질나게 하다, 애타게 하다 ☐ **demarcate** v. 경계를 정하다; 한정하다, 구분하다

많은 산업 분야에서 결근과 지각은 생산성을 해치며, 일이 전문화되어 있기 때문에 통상적인 공장 업무를 마비시킨다.

91 ①

☐ **Miranda rights** 미란다 권리(묵비권·변호인 접견권 등 피의자의 권리) ☐ **arrest** n. 체포, 검거 ☐ **confuse** v. 혼동하다 ☐ **undercover** a. 비밀리에 하는, 첩보 활동[위장 근무]의 ☐ **inept** a. 솜씨 없는, 서투른(=clumsy) ☐ **auspicious** a. 길조의, 상서로운 ☐ **recluse** a. 속세를 떠난, 은둔[은퇴]한 ☐ **merciless** a. 무자비한, 인정사정없는

일부 경찰관들은 범인을 체포할 때 범인에게 미란다 권리를 읽어 주는 것을 잊어버리고, 은밀히 숨겨야할 자신의 정체를 잘못하여 드러내며, 심지어 미숙한 업무처리로 직장에서 해고당하기도 한다.

92 ①

☐ **makeshift** a. 임시변통의, 일시적인(=temporary) ☐ **urgent** a. 긴급한, 매우 위급한; 재촉하는 ☐ **ignoble** a. 성품이 저열한, 비열한; 비천한 ☐ **outrageous** a. 난폭한, 사악한; 무법의

이것은 우리가 해야 할 것을 결정할 때까지 일시적인 계획이다.

93 ②

☐ **subside** v. 가라앉다, 진정되다(=diminish) ☐ **disapprove** v. 반대하다, 비난하다 ☐ **subtract** v. 빼다, 공제(控除)하다 ☐ **dispel** v. (걱정 등을) 떨쳐버리다

경찰은 그 폭력사태가 곧 가라앉기를 바라고 있다.

94 ③

☐ **infamous** a. 악명 높은, 악랄한(=notorious) ☐ **trivial** a. 사소한, 하찮은; 평범한 ☐ **captivating** a. 매혹적인, 매력적인 ☐ **terrific** a. 빼어난, 대단한; 무시무시한

알 카포네(Al Capone)는 악명 높은 갱이었다.

95 ④

☐ **discharge** v. 석방[방면]하다(=release) ☐ **on oath** 선서를 하고 ☐ **be of good behaviour** (재소자가) 선행을 하다 ☐ **humiliate** v. 욕보이다, 창피를 주다 ☐ **criticize** v. 비평[비판]하다 ☐ **evaluate** v. 평가하다

그녀는 선행을 하겠다는 선서를 하고 조건부로 석방되었다.

96 ④

☐ **tantrum** n. 울화, 짜증, 화(=temper) ☐ **hatred** n. 증오, 원한 ☐ **fabrication** n. 꾸밈, 날조, 거짓 ☐ **apathy** n. 냉담, 무관심 ☐ **mischief** n. 장난, 짓궂음 ☐ **brutality** n. 잔인, 무자비

스크루지(Scrooge)가 울화를 터뜨림에도 불구하고 크리스마스에 대한 그의 증오는 꾸며낸 것이라는 것을 우리는 곧 알게 된다.

97 ④

☐ **wan** a. 핏기 없는; 병약한; 창백한 ☐ **cadaverous** a. 송장 같은(=corpse-like); 창백한; 수척한 ☐ **vinegar** n. 식초 ☐ **fragility** n. 부서지기 쉬움, 여림, 허약 ☐ **dangerous** a. 위험한, 위태로운; 위독한 ☐ **charming** a. 매력적인, 아름다운; 호감이 가는 ☐ **plump** a. 포동포동한, 토실토실한; 충분한

유럽의 낭만주의 시대에 남성들은 병약하고 죽은 사람처럼 창백한 모습의 여성들을 좋아했다. 때때로 여성들은 창백해 보이고 관심을 끌기 위

해 식초를 마시거나 밤새도록 뜬눈으로 지새웠다. 연약하게 보이는 것이 가장 중요했기 때문이다.

98
①

☐ incorrigible a. 교정할 수 없는, 구제할 수 없는; 다루기 힘든 (=consummate) ☐ liar n. 거짓말쟁이 ☐ screwed a. 나사로 된, 나사 모양의; 비뚤어진 ☐ rigid a. 단단한, 딱딱한; 완고한 ☐ close a. 가까운; 빽빽한, 밀집한

그는 어쩔 도리가 없는 거짓말쟁이지만 대단한 매력을 지니고 있다.

99
②

☐ dispute n. 논쟁, 말다툼 ☐ vehemently ad. 격렬하게, 맹렬하게 ☐ remonstrate v. 이의를 말하다, 항의하다(=say or plead in protest) ☐ reconciliation n. 화해, 조화 ☐ find fault with ~의 흠을 찾다, 비난[탓]하다 ☐ treat roughly or cruelly 거칠게 혹은 잔인하게 다루다 ☐ keep down or hold back 억압하거나 억제하다

새 집의 위치를 놓고 다툰 지 이틀 만에 그녀가 집으로 돌아왔을 때, 남편은 버스 노선 변경에 대해 격렬하게 이의를 제기하는 전화통화를 하고 있었다. 그녀는 휴대전화를 꺼내 남편이 어느 가엾은 공무원에게 항의하는 것을 몰래 녹음했다. 그녀는 그것이 너무나도 재미있어서 자신의 블로그에 올렸고, 이로 인해 마침내 두 사람은 화해하게 되었다.

100
②

☐ addictive a. 습관성의, 중독성의(=habit-forming) ☐ present in tobacco products 담배제품에 존재하는 ☐ harmful to health 건강에 해로운 ☐ remains in our body for a long time 우리 몸에 오랫동안 남은 것

담배 회사들은 니코틴이 중독성이 있긴 하지만 모든 식물에도 니코틴이 들어 있다고 했다. 이 이야기를 듣고 (투나잇 쇼의 진행자인) 제이 르노(Jay Leno)는 "어째서 비 오는 날 사무실 밖에서 가지를 먹으며 서 있는 사람들을 볼 수가 없죠?"라며 익살을 떨었다.

MVP 31-35 ACTUAL TEST

01 ①	02 ①	03 ④	04 ①	05 ④	06 ④	07 ①	08 ①	09 ④	10 ①
11 ③	12 ①	13 ①	14 ③	15 ①	16 ①	17 ①	18 ①	19 ③	20 ②
21 ④	22 ③	23 ②	24 ①	25 ①	26 ③	27 ②	28 ②	29 ①	30 ②
31 ②	32 ①	33 ①	34 ①	35 ①	36 ③	37 ①	38 ③	39 ④	40 ③
41 ①	42 ①	43 ①	44 ④	45 ④	46 ④	47 ①	48 ②	49 ④	50 ②
51 ②	52 ④	53 ②	54 ①	55 ③	56 ②	57 ③	58 ④	59 ①	60 ①
61 ③	62 ①	63 ①	64 ①	65 ①	66 ①	67 ①	68 ①	69 ①	70 ①
71 ③	72 ①	73 ②	74 ①	75 ②	76 ②	77 ④	78 ①	79 ②	80 ①
81 ③	82 ②	83 ②	84 ①	85 ②	86 ②	87 ②	88 ②	89 ④	90 ②
91 ③	92 ④	93 ②	94 ①	95 ③	96 ④	97 ②	98 ③	99 ④	100 ①

01   ①

☐ visage n. 얼굴, 용모; 외관(=look) ☐ apparel n. 의복 ☐ conduct n. 행위, 품행 ☐ knack n. 요령, 재주; 버릇

그녀의 용모는 자수성가한 여성의 모습이었다.

02   ①

☐ lend oneself to ~에 도움이 되다, ~에 적합하다 ☐ pithy a. (표현 등이) 힘찬, 함축성 있는; 간결한(=laconic) ☐ jejune a. 너무 단순한, 고지식한 ☐ erratic a. 괴짜의, 이상한, 엉뚱한 ☐ opulent a. 부유한; 풍부한

물리학은 간결하게 소개하기에 적합하지 않다.

03   ④

☐ undergo v. ~을 받다, 당하다; 겪다, 경험하다(=experience) ☐ thorough a. 철저한, 충분한, 완전한 ☐ confide v. 신임하다, 신뢰하다 ☐ exasperate v. 노하게 하다, 격앙시키다; 악화시키다 ☐ unearth v. 발굴하다, 파내다; 발견하다

그녀는 병원에서 정밀 검진을 받았다.

04   ①

☐ bead n. 구슬, 염주알 ☐ ward off ~을 피하다, 막다(=avert) ☐ conduce v. 도움이 되다, 이바지하다, 공헌하다 ☐ anticipate v. 예상하다, 기대하다 ☐ resume v. 재개하다, 다시 시작하다

악(惡)을 막아내는 데 서로 다른 종류의 염주가 사용된다.

05   ④

☐ crude a. 천연 그대로의, 가공하지 않은; 조잡한(=rough) ☐ painted a. 그린, 색칠한; 꾸며진 ☐ resilient a. 되튀는; 곧 원기를 회복하는; 쾌활한 ☐ unseasoned a. 양념하지 않은; 미숙한, 미경험의

초기의 통나무집은 튼튼한 건물이긴 했지만 조잡했다.

06   ④

☐ vainglorious a. 자만심이 강한; 허영심이 강한(=haughty) ☐ invalid a. 타당하지 않은, 실효성이 없는; 박약한 ☐ polished a. 광택이 나는, 문질러 닦은; 세련된 ☐ outrageous a. 난폭한, 포학한, 잔인무도한; 무법한

그녀는 자만심이 강한 사람이었다.

07   ①

☐ penurious a. 몹시 아끼는, 인색한; 빈곤한(=stingy) ☐ shrewd a. 예민한, 날카로운, 영리한 ☐ flippant a. 건방진, 무례한 ☐ truculent a. 반항적인, 약간 공격적인

그 가족의 인색한 기질로 인해 그들은 삶의 작은 기쁨마저 누리기 어려웠다.

08   ①

☐ ignominious a. 불명예스러운, 수치스러운; 비열한(=disgraceful) ☐ pitiless a. 무자비한, 몰인정한, 냉혹한 ☐ honorable a. 명예로운; 존경할 만한 ☐ dangerous a. 위험한, 위태로운

내 성격의 불균형을 엄한 훈련을 통해 조화시키려는 노력은 나를 거의 똑같은 불명예스러운 결과로 이끌었다.

09 ④

☐ utterly ad. 아주, 완전히(=completely) ☐ hardly ad. 거의 ~아니다, 조금도 ~아니다 ☐ finally ad. 최후의; 마침내; 최종적으로 ☐ rapidly ad. 빠르게, 재빨리, 신속히

많은 의사와 간호사들은 그 약의 효과에 대해 전적으로 확신했다.

10 ①

☐ boundary n. 경계; 한계, 범위, 영역 ☐ barrier n. 장벽, 장애물; 울타리 ☐ retard v. 속력을 늦추다, 지체시키다(=defer) ☐ diffusion n. 전파, 유포; 만연 ☐ replenish v. 다시 채우다, 보충하다 ☐ facilitate v. 손쉽게 하다; 촉진하다 ☐ blur v. 희미하게 하다, 흐리게 하다

정치적 경계는 생각 혹은 지식의 확산에 대해 장벽의 역할을 하여, 문화의 전파를 지체시킬 수 있다.

11 ③

☐ mind-boggling a. 대단히 놀라운; 믿기 어려운(=incredible) ☐ spontaneous a. 자발적인; 즉흥적인 ☐ sophisticated a. 세련된; 정교한, 복잡한 ☐ poignant a. 통렬한; 신랄한

이 놀라운 생각을 이해하기 위해 우주에 떠 있는 블랙홀을 생각해보라.

12 ①

☐ solemn a. 엄숙한, 중대한(=serious) ☐ pledge n. 약속, 맹세 ☐ root out 뿌리째 뽑다, 근절시키다 ☐ suitable a. 적당한, 상당한 ☐ fitful a. 단속적인; 일정치 않은 ☐ ruthless a. 무자비한, 가차 없는

정부는 공무원들의 부정부패를 근절하겠다는 확고한 의지를 표명했다.

13 ①

☐ remiss a. 태만한, 부주의한; 무기력한(=negligent) ☐ scrupulous a. 빈틈없는, 면밀한, 꼼꼼한; 양심적인 ☐ attentive a. 주의 깊은, 세심한; 마음 쓰는 ☐ careful a. 주의 깊은, 조심스러운; 신중한, 꼼꼼한

그의 마음속에 골치 아픈 문제가 너무나 많았기 때문에 그는 자신의 의무를 수행하는 데 소홀했다.

14 ③

☐ omnipotent a. 전능한, 무엇이든 할 수 있는(=almighty) ☐ means of life 삶의 방법 ☐ aggrandizement n. 확대, 강화 ☐ ultimate

target 궁극적인 목표

과학이 무엇이든지 할 수 있게 되었다는 것은 대단히 위험한 생각이다.

15 ①

☐ cash v. 수표를 현금으로 바꾸다 ☐ notice n. 통지 ☐ raze v. 없애다, 무너뜨리다(=demolish) ☐ rent v. 임차하다; 임대하다 ☐ purchase v. 구입하다 ☐ enlarge v. 크게 하다, 확대하다, 증대하다

4월 급료수표를 현금으로 바꾸고 하루가 지난 후 우리는 이사해야 한다는 통지를 받았다. 집을 철거할 계획이었다.

16 ①

☐ real estate 부동산 ☐ expensive a. 값비싼 ☐ resident n. 거주자, 거류민 ☐ offset v. 상쇄하다, 벌충하다(=overweigh) ☐ fault line 단층선 ☐ outlive v. ~보다 더 오래 살다 ☐ hazard v. 위태롭게 하다 n. 위험(요소) ☐ underscore v. 강조하다, 뒷받침하다

캘리포니아의 부동산은 세계에서 가장 비싼 부동산에 속한다. 캘리포니아 주에 살고 있는 수백만 명의 주민들은 서부 해안에서 사는 데서 오는 즐거움이 단층선을 따라 사는 위험을 상쇄한다고 생각을 정했다.

17 ①

☐ spore n. (균류(菌類)·식물의) 포자(胞子); 종자, 씨 ☐ blight n. 마름병, 병충해 ☐ fungus n. 버섯, 균류 ☐ water-borne a. 수계감염(水系感染)의, 물로 전파(傳播)되는 ☐ germinate v. 싹트다, 발아하다; 자라기 시작하다, 커지다(=grow) ☐ moisture n. 습기, 수분 ☐ decay v. 썩다, 부패하다 ☐ infect v. 감염되다, 오염되다 ☐ recover v. 회복하다

마름병 진균의 포자는 물로 전파된다. 그것은 움직일 때 수영을 하며, 따라서 잘 자라나기 위해서는 소량의 수분이 필요하다.

18 ①

☐ bully v. (약자를) 괴롭히다, 왕따시키다 ☐ subordinate n. 하급자, 부하 ☐ sheer a. 얇은; 순전한, 완전한(=pure) ☐ exercise v. (권력을) 발동하다, 행사하다 ☐ decent a. 좋은, 버젓한, 알맞은, 예의 바른 ☐ scanty a. 희박한, 적은, 부족한 ☐ transparent a. 투명한; 명쾌한

흔히 매니저들은 권한을 행사하는 순전한 기쁨을 위해 부하 직원들을 괴롭혔다.

19 ③

☐ amaze v. ~을 놀라게 하다 ☐ breathtaking a. (너무 아름답거나 놀라워서) 숨이 막히는 ☐ landscape n. 풍경, 경치; 전망(=scenery) ☐ venue n. 행위의 현장; 개최지 ☐ geography n. 지리, 지형; 지리학 ☐ vignette n. 우아한 문예 소품, 삽화

그들은 숨이 막힐 것 같은 경치에 깜짝 놀랐다.

그렇게 좁은 장소에서 자동차를 조종하는 것은 어려운 일이었다.

20 ②

☐ esoteric a. 비밀의; 난해한 ☐ please v. 만족시키다 ☐ bewilder v. 당황하게 하다, 어리둥절하게 하다(=puzzle) ☐ terrify v. 무섭게 하다 ☐ fascinate v. 마음을 사로잡다 ☐ bruise v. (감정을) 상하게 하다

비평가들을 만족시키지만, 대중들을 당황하게 하는 난해한 영화들이 항상 있었다.

21 ④

☐ impulse n. 추진력; 충격; 충동(=desire) ☐ board v. (탈것에) 올라타다 ☐ cost v. (귀중한 것을) 희생시키다, 잃게 하다 ☐ trickery n. 속임수, 사기 ☐ soot n. 그을음, 매연 ☐ allowance n. 수당, 급여액

아서(Arthur)는 움직이고 있는 기차에 타려다 거의 목숨을 잃을 뻔했다.

22 ③

☐ cognizant a. 인식하고 있는, 알고 있는(=aware of) ☐ legally responsible 법적으로 책임이 있는 ☐ very careful 매우 조심하는 ☐ careless about ~에 무관심한

판사는 그 소송 사건에 대해 자기는 알지 못한다고 말했다.

23 ②

☐ executive n. (기업이나 조직의) 간부, 경영진 ☐ accomplishment n. 성취, 달성; 업적(=achievement) ☐ duty n. 의무, 임무 ☐ accumulation n. 축적, 누적 ☐ imposition n. 부과(물), 과세

그가 회사의 중역이었을 때 첫 번째 업적은 더 나은 근로환경을 조성한 것이었다.

24 ③

☐ undependable a. 신뢰할 수 없는, 의지할 수 없는(=irresponsible) ☐ grave a. 중요한, 심각한 ☐ crumpled a. 뒤틀린; 쭈글쭈글한; 주름살 투성이의 ☐ shamble v. 비틀비틀 걷다

자신이 버는 것보다 더 많은 돈을 쓰는 사람들은 돈에 관해 신뢰할 수 없는 사람들이라고 한다.

25 ①

☐ maneuver v. 연습시키다; 조종하다(=manipulate) ☐ fare v. 가다, 여행하다 ☐ shake v. 흔들다; 진동시키다 ☐ chop v. 자르다; 잘게 썰다

26 ③

☐ recede v. 물러나다, 몸을 빼다, 움츠리다(=withdraw) ☐ renovate v. 새롭게 하다, 혁신하다, 개선하다 ☐ rearrange v. 재정리하다, 재배열 하다 ☐ withstand v. 저항하다, 잘 견디다, 버티다

과거의 위협들은 사라지거나 물러났지만, 이제 새로운 위협이 나타나고 있다.

27 ②

☐ laissez-faire a. 자유방임주의의(=permissive) ☐ interventional a. 개입의, 조정의 ☐ disrupted a. 붕괴된, 분열된 ☐ anarchic a. 무정부의, 무질서의

권위주의 방식은 긴급 상황에서 더 효과적인 것처럼 보이고, 민주주의 방식은 대부분의 상황에 가장 효과적이며, 자유방임 방식은 보통 비효과적이다.

28 ②

☐ impecunious a. 돈이 없는, 가난한(=penniless) ☐ transitory a. 일시적인 ☐ imminent a. 절박한, 일촉즉발의 ☐ affluent a. 풍부한; 부유한

그는 잘못된 투자로 인해 자신이 하룻밤 사이에 무일푼이 되었다는 것을 알게 되었다.

29 ①

☐ deride v. 조롱하다, 조소하다, 비웃다(=ridicule) ☐ delegate n. 대표(자) ☐ mimic n. 모방자, 흉내쟁이 ☐ designate v. 가리키다, 지시하다; 지명하다 ☐ name v. 이름을 붙이다, 이름 짓다, 명명하다 ☐ degenerate v. 나빠지다, 퇴보하다, 퇴화하다

국제고래잡이위원회의 5일간의 회담 기간 동안 일본은 고래잡이에 반대하는 국가의 대표자들을 '그린피스를 흉내 내는 사람들'이라며 비웃었다.

30 ②

☐ reveal v. 보여주다, 드러내다 ☐ reiterate v. 반복하다, 되풀이하다 (=repeat) ☐ meritocracy n. 능력주의 사회, 실력 사회 ☐ withdraw v. 철수하다; 철회하다 ☐ emphasize v. 강조하다; 역설하다 ☐ publish v. 출판하다

제퍼슨(Jefferson)이 능력주의에 관한 자신의 생각을 되풀이해 말했음을 역사 기록들이 보여주고 있다.

31 ②

☐ tease out ~을 빗다; (정보 따위를) 기어이 얻어내다(=uncover) ☐ validate v. 정당함을 입증하다, 확인하다 ☐ manipulate v. 교묘하게 다루다; 조작하다 ☐ distort v. 찡그리다; 왜곡하다

과학자들은 후이겐스(Huygens)가 남겨놓은 자료에서 보다 귀중한 과학적 지식을 알아낼 필요가 있으면 언제라도 그럴 것이다.

32 ①

☐ relish n. (큰) 즐거움, 기쁨 ☐ insignificant a. 하찮은, 무의미한 (=trivial) ☐ geology n. 지질학 ☐ cosmos n. 우주 ☐ uncivilized a. 미개한, 야만의 ☐ unfathomable a. 이해할 수 없는, 불가해한 ☐ short-sighted a. 근시의; 근시안적인

많은 과학자들은 지질학과 우주의 시간 척도와 비교될 때 우리 인간이 얼마나 하찮은가에 대해 흥미 있게 이야기한다.

33 ①

☐ impair v. 약화시키다, 해치다(=undermine) ☐ enhance v. 높이다, 강화하다, 올리다 ☐ influence v. 영향을 끼치다; 좌우하다 ☐ restore v. 복구하다, 재건하다; 회복시키다

독감약이 자동차를 포함한 여러 기계류를 작동하는 능력을 손상시킨다는 사실은 널리 알려져 있지 않다.

34 ①

☐ suicide n. 자살 ☐ relentlessly ad. 냉혹하게, 가차 없이; 끊임없이 (=incessantly) ☐ bully v. (약한 자를) 괴롭히다, 왕따시키다; 위협하다 ☐ accurately ad. 정확하게; 빈틈없이 ☐ moderately ad. 적당하게, 알맞게 ☐ whimsically ad. 변덕스럽게, 즉흥적으로

그는 학교에서 끊임없이 왕따를 당한 끝에 자살을 시도했다.

35 ①

☐ fascinate v. 황홀케 하다, 매혹시키다, 반하게 하다(=attract) ☐ inform v. 알리다, 통지하다, 기별하다 ☐ improve v. 개량하다, 개선하다; 이용하다 ☐ fashion v. 모양 짓다, 형성하다, 만들다

인터넷이 새 천년의 지구촌의 가치관을 형성하는 데 특히 중요하기 때문에, 많은 사람들은 여전히 인터넷에 매혹되어 있다.

36 ③

☐ accuse v. 고발[비난]하다, 혐의를 제기하다 ☐ plagiarism n. 표절 ☐ outright ad. 철저하게, 완전히; 즉시 ☐ slanderous a. 헐뜯는, 중상하는, 명예를 훼손하는(=defamatory) ☐ infelicitous a. 불행한, 불운한

☐ parsimonious a. 인색한, 극도로 아끼는 ☐ untrustworthy a. 신뢰할 수 없는

표절 혐의를 받고 있는 최고경영자는 명예훼손 혐의를 즉각 부인했다.

37 ①

☐ antioxidant n. 노화방지제, 산화방지제 ☐ indispensable a. 필수적인, 없어서는 안 되는(=vital) ☐ counter v. 대항하다; ~에 대응하다 ☐ potential a. 잠재적인 ☐ chemical n. 화학물질 ☐ free radical 유리기 ☐ indigenous a. 고유한, 토종의, 토착의 ☐ unperturbed a. 동요하지 않는, 침착한 ☐ superfluous a. 과잉의, 불필요한

비타민 A, C, 그리고 E 같은 산화방지제는 유리기로 알려진 화학물질의 잠재적인 해로움에 대항하는 데 있어 필수적이다.

38 ③

☐ temporarily ad. 일시적으로, 임시로 ☐ avert v. (타격, 위험을) 피하다, 막다(=avoid) ☐ disaster n. 재난, 재해 ☐ pension n. 연금 ☐ divert v. 전환하다, 딴 데로 돌리다; 전용[유용]하다 ☐ induce v. 권유하다, 설득하여 ~하게 하다; 야기하다

회사는 직원 연금에서 각각 십 달러를 빼돌려 일시적으로 대참사를 막아냈다.

39 ②

☐ imposing a. 인상적인; 당당한(=massive) ☐ trifling a. 하찮은, 사소한; 약간의 ☐ bewildering a. 당혹케 하는, 갈피를 못 잡게 하는 ☐ notorious a. (나쁜 의미로) 소문난, 유명한

겉보기에 그녀는 매력적이기보다는 당당했다.

40 ③

☐ qualm n. (행동에 대한) 불안한 마음; 양심의 가책(=compunction) ☐ rifle n. 라이플총, 소총 ☐ sight n. (총 등의) 가늠쇠[자], 조준기 ☐ aplomb n. 침착, 태연자약; (마음의) 평정 ☐ indulgence n. 탐닉; 방종; 관대 ☐ equilibrium n. 평형상태, 균형; (마음의) 평정

그 영화 속의 크라이스트 카일(Christ Kyle)은 자신의 소총 가늠쇠 안에 들어온 그녀를 죽이는 데 있어서 양심의 가책을 전혀 느끼지 않았다.

41 ①

☐ ethnicity n. 민족성 ☐ placate v. 달래다, 회유하다(=pacify) ☐ specify v. 명시하다 ☐ duplicate v. 복제하다, 사본을 만들다 ☐ implicate v. 관련시키다

마블은 중국의 검열관과 관객들을 달래기 위해서 한 등장인물의 민족 출신을 티베트인에서 켈트인으로 바꾸었다.

42 ①

□ bursary n. (대학의) 회계과 (사무실); (대학의) 장학금 □ bestow v. 주다, 수여[부여]하다(=confer) □ annually ad. 해마다, 매년 □ schedule v. 일정[시간 계획]을 잡다, 예정하다 □ palliate v. 누그러지게 하다, 일시적으로 완화하다 □ repudiate v. 거부하다, 부인하다; 의절하다

입학시험에서 최고 점수를 받은 학생에게 매년 장학금이 수여된다.

43 ①

□ identify v. 확인하다, 증명하다, 식별하다(=recognize) □ chemical n. 화학 제품[약품] □ fetal a. 태아(fetus)의 □ regenerative a. 재생시키는; 개조하는 □ intensify v. 심화시키다, 강화하다 □ standardize v. 표준화하다; 규격에 맞추다 □ exemplify v. 예증하다, 예시하다

과학자들은 태아 세포에 재생력을 가져다주는 화학물질을 알아낼 수 있었다.

44 ④

□ infectious a. 전염하는; (영향이) 옮기 쉬운(=contagious) □ thundering a. 큰 소리를 내는; 굉장한, 엄청난 □ mischievous a. 유해한; 장난기 있는, 장난을 좋아하는 □ hearty a. 진심 어린, 마음이 따뜻한

그의 웃음은 전염성이 있다. 왜냐하면 그가 웃기 시작하면, 모든 사람이 웃기 시작하기 때문이다.

45 ④

□ unjustified a. 정당하지 않은 □ calumny n. 중상, 비방(=slander) □ phrase n. 구절, 관용구 □ credo n. 신조 □ vestige n. 자취, 흔적

그녀는 전혀 정당화될 수 없는 연속된 비방의 희생자였다.

46 ④

□ accessory n. 공범, 종범(=accomplice) □ answerable a. 책임이 있는; 대답할 수 있는 □ misogynist n. 여자를 싫어하는 사람 □ misanthrope n. 사람을 싫어하는 사람, 염세가 □ humanitarian n. 인도주의자

남편이 떠나지 않겠다면, 당신이 떠나라. 당신이 이제 사후(事後) 종범자이다. 당신도 책임이 있다. 당신과 아이들은 가지고 있는 모든 것을 잃을 수도 있다.

47 ①

□ Space X 스페이스 엑스(로켓과 우주선의 개발 및 발사를 통해 우주 수송을 맡아 하는 미국 기업) □ restore v. 회복하다, 복구하다, 수리하다(=refurbish) □ routinely ad. 일상적으로 □ replace v. 대신하다, 대체하다 □ allocate v. 할당하다, 배분하다 □ reciprocate v. 교환하다; 보답하다

만약 스페이스 엑스(Space X)가 1단계 로켓을 복구하여 재사용하는 일을 일상적으로 할 수 있다면, 우주선 발사 비용을 현저하게 줄일 수 있을 것이다.

48 ②

□ exempt a. 면제된; 면세의; 면역의(=excluded) □ loan n. 대여, 대출; 대출금 □ serve in the military 군복무를 하다 □ depressed a. 의기소침한, 우울한; 궁핍한, 빈곤한; 불황의 □ isolated a. 외떨어진, 외딴; 고립된 □ agonized a. 괴로워하는, 고뇌하는

올해부터, 저소득 가정 학생들은 학자금 대출에 대한 이자를 군복무를 하는 동안은 면제받게 될 것이라고 국방부가 어제 발표했다.

49 ④

□ autopsy n. (사체) 부검, 검시 □ pending a. 미결[미정]인, 계류 중인(=undecided) □ release v. 발표하다 □ determined a. 결심한 □ anticipated a. 예상되는

관계자들은 그의 사인이 알려지지 않았으며, 부검 결과가 아직 나오지 않았다고 말한다.

50 ②

□ submit v. 복종하다, 굴복하다 □ amiable a. 붙임성 있는; 상냥한(=agreeable) □ servile a. 노예의; 비굴한 □ shrewd a. 예민한, 날카로운; 영리한 □ wretched a. 비참한, 불행한; 비열한

나는 굴복해서 상냥한 노예의 삶을 살 수도 있었으나 그것은 불가능했다.

51 ②

□ contend v. (강력히) 주장하다(=claim) □ rote a. 기계적으로 암기한, 기계적인 □ repetition n. 되풀이, 반복 □ mimicking n. 흉내 내기, 모사(模寫) □ report v. 보고하다, 전하다 □ conform v. (사회의 관습 따위에) 적합[순응]시키다; 따르게 하다 □ counter v. 반대하다, 논박하다; 대응하다

아이들이 기계적인 학습을 매우 잘하고, 의미 없는 반복과 모방을 잘 활용한다고 주장하는 것은 옳지 않다.

52   ④

☐ languidly ad. 노곤하게; 기력이 모자라서; 활기 없이(=feebly) ☐ incessantly ad. 끊임없이, 계속적으로 ☐ hilariously ad. 즐겁게, 유쾌하게 ☐ aggressively ad. 공격적으로, 정력적으로

힘없이 나뭇잎을 뜯어 먹고 있는 기린 두세 마리와 흘끗 본 몇 마리 안 되는 영양들이 우리가 마지막으로 봤던 사냥감이었다.

53   ②

☐ absurd a. 불합리한, 부조리한(=foolish) ☐ serious a. 진지한; 진정의; 중대한 ☐ strange a. 이상한, 낯선, 생소한 ☐ pleasant a. 즐거운, 기분 좋은

분별 있는 사람도 때때로 어리석은 일을 저지른다.

54   ①

☐ unknown n. 미지의 것(들)[세계], 미지수 ☐ taxing a. 부담을 주는; 힘드는(=burdensome) ☐ terrifying a. 무섭게 하는, 놀라게 하는; 무서운 ☐ soluble a. 가용성의; 해결[해답]할 수 있는 ☐ stagnant a. 고여있는, 침체된

코로나바이러스 유행병이 종식된 후에 사회가 어떻게 될 것인지에 대한 미지수는 큰 부담을 주고 있다.

55   ③

☐ obediently ad. 고분고분하게, 공손하게(=dutifully) ☐ skillfully ad. 능숙하게; 교묘하게 ☐ safely ad. 안전하게, 무사히 ☐ currently ad. 일반적으로, 널리; 현재

연안 경비대의 책무 중 하나는 모든 배들이 번잡한 항구에서 운항 규칙을 충실히 준수하는지 확인하는 것이다.

56   ②

☐ drought n. 가뭄, 한발 ☐ soil erosion 토양 침식 ☐ spawn v. 산란하다; 대량 생산하다; (소문을) 낳다, 야기하다(=generate) ☐ follow v. ~을 쫓다, 동행하다; 계속하다 ☐ indicate v. 가리키다, 지적하다, 보이다 ☐ intensify v. 강렬하게 하다; 증강하다

가뭄과 토양 침식이 1930년대 대평원 전역에 걸쳐 모래 강풍을 크게 일으켰다.

57   ③

☐ willing a. 열렬한, 적극적인 ☐ storyteller n. 이야기 작가; (특히 아동도서관 등의) 이야기 해주는 사람 ☐ an hour or so 한 두 시간 ☐ ensconce v. 감추다; (몸을) 편안히 앉게 하다(=settle) ☐ enforce

v. 시행하다, 집행하다 ☐ dazzle v. 눈부시게 하다; 현혹시키다 ☐ eclipse v. ~을 무색하게 만들다

심지어 기꺼이 이야기를 들려주려는 사람을 구할 수 있을 때조차도, 하루 한 시간 정도의 시간은 대부분의 아이들이 다른 사람들의 상상 속에 자리 잡고 보내는 시간보다 더 많은 시간이었다.

58   ④

☐ meager a. 메마른; 빈약한, 야윈; 불충분한(=scanty) ☐ generosity n. 관대, 관용; 아까워하지 않음 ☐ good a. 좋은; 훌륭한; 고급의 ☐ mediocre a. 보통의, 평범한 ☐ sympathetic a. 동정적인, 인정 있는

그의 봉급은 얼마 되지 않았지만, 그것이 그의 큰 씀씀이에 부정적인 영향을 미치진 못했다.

59   ①

☐ elapse v. (시간이) 경과하다, 지나다(=go by) ☐ be wasted 버려지다 ☐ be saved 구조되다 ☐ be lonesome 외롭다, 쓸쓸하다

그녀가 떠나간 후 3개월이 흘렀다.

60   ①

☐ embryonic a. 초기의; 배아(胚芽)의, 태아의 ☐ outright ad. 철저하게, 완전히(=utterly) ☐ harshly ad. 사납게, 모질게 ☐ zealously ad. 열광적으로, 열성적으로 ☐ dejectedly ad. 기가 죽어, 낙담하여

연구원들은 지카(Zika) 바이러스가 뇌를 형성하는 데 도움을 주는 배아 세포를 침범하여 그중 일부를 완전히 죽일 수 있다는 사실을 발견했다.

61   ③

☐ water table 빗물막이, 도로 옆의 배수구; 지하수면 ☐ saturation n. 침투, 침윤(浸潤); 포화, 포화상태(=soaking) ☐ freezing n. 결빙, 냉동 ☐ humidity n. 습기, 습도 ☐ dryness n. 건조, 건조 상태

지하수면에는 포화대(飽和帶)라고 불리는 수위가 있다.

62   ①

☐ weirdly ad. 기묘하게도, 불가사의하게도 ☐ somnolent a. 졸리는, 나른하게 만드는(=languid) ☐ portentously ad. 불길하게; 경이적으로 ☐ prime v. (특정 목적·작업을 위해) 준비시키다; 미리 가르쳐 놓다, 미리 알려 주다 ☐ elliptical a. 타원형의; 생략된 ☐ ecstatic a. 열중한, 황홀한 ☐ shifty a. 책략이[재치가] 풍부한, 잘 둘러대는

위험에 대해, 회교 사원이 불타고 거리에 피가 낭자한 사태에 대해 불길한 느낌을 우리에게 미리 알려주는 내용임을 감안하면, 그의 소설은 기이할 정도로 나른하다.

63 ①

☐ imaginary a. 가상의 ☐ comical a. 우스운 ☐ peremptory a. 오만한, 위압적인, 독단적인(=dictatorial) ☐ discredit v. 불신케 하다, 신용을 해치다 ☐ cause n. 대의, 주장 ☐ capricious a. 변덕스러운 ☐ indecisive a. 우유부단한 ☐ eccentric a. 괴상한

가상의 위험을 익살스럽고 독단적인 방식으로 집중해서 다룸으로써 그는 공화당의 대의를 불신받게 했다.

64 ①

☐ track v. ~을 추적하다, 뒤를 쫓다(=follow) ☐ paw n. (발톱 있는 동물의) 발 ☐ classify v. 분류하다, 구분하다 ☐ catch v. 붙들다, 붙잡다; 잡아내다 ☐ train v. 훈련하다, 양성하다

비 온 뒤에 동물을 추적하는 일은 더 쉬울지도 모른다. 왜냐하면 젖은 땅 위에 동물의 발바닥이 찍힌 자국이 나타나기 때문이다.

65 ①

☐ odds n. 가망, 가능성, 확률 ☐ accidentally ad. 우연히, 뜻하지 않게 ☐ conversation n. 대화, 회화 ☐ device n. 장치, 설비 ☐ confirmation n. 확정, 확증(=authorization) ☐ advice n. 조언, 충고 ☐ connection n. 연결, 결합 ☐ privacy n. 사생활, 사적[개인적] 자유

가정용 (인공지능) 비서가 뜻하지 않게 대화를 녹음할 가능성은 낮으며, 그 장치는 제3자에게 정보를 보내기 전에 확인을 요청해야 한다.

66 ④

☐ exhaustively ad. 남김없이, 속속들이, 철저하게(=thoroughly) ☐ tiredly ad. 피로하여, 지쳐서; 싫증 난, 물린 ☐ enthusiastically ad. 열광적으로, 열중하여, 매우 열심히 ☐ descriptively ad. 서술적으로, 설명적으로

조이스(Joyce)는 『율리시즈(Ulysses)』에서 우리의 삶에 대한 참여가 어떠한지, 또는 우리가 매순간 살아갈 때 그것이 우리에게 어떻게 보이는가를 언어로 표현할 수 있는 한 철저하고, 정밀하고, 정확하게 표현하려 했다.

67 ①

☐ definition n. 정의; 설명 ☐ phenomenology n. 현상학 ☐ assert v. 단언하다; 주장하다 ☐ negligible a. 무시해도 좋은, 하찮은 ☐ paramount a. 탁월한; 가장 중요한(=preponderant) ☐ mephitic a. 악취 있는, 독기 있는; 유독한 ☐ craven a. 비겁한, 겁 많은 ☐ arcuated a. 아치형의

메를로 퐁티(Merleau-Ponty)는 현상학에 대한 그의 정의에서 "육체는 무시할 수 있는 것이 아니라, 가장 중요한 것이다."라고 주장한다.

68 ④

☐ bemoan v. 슬퍼하다, 애도하다(=bewail) ☐ masculinity n. 남자다움, 남성미 ☐ resist v. 저항하다; 참다, 견디다 ☐ venerate v. 존경하다, 공경하다 ☐ bewilder v. 당황하게 하다

미국에서 이전의 경제위기들은 남자들이 일자리를 잃게 만들었으며, 우리는 그로 인해 남자다움이 타격을 입은 것을 애석하게 여겨 왔다.

69 ③

☐ appropriate v. (공공물을) 사용하다, 착복하다, 횡령하다(=steal) ☐ donate v. 기부하다, 기증하다 ☐ save v. 구하다; 저축하다 ☐ borrow v. 빌리다

그 장관이 많은 액수의 정부기금을 횡령해 온 것이 발각되었다.

70 ①

☐ headstrong a. 완고한, 고집 센, 억지 쓰는(=stubborn) ☐ rash a. 분별없는, 경솔한, 성급한 ☐ snobbish a. 속물의, 신사인 체하는 ☐ intellectual a. 지적인, 지능적인, 총명한

메리 윌셔(Mary Wilcher)의 가족은 고집스러운 기질로 악명 높다.

71 ③

☐ presidential a. 대통령의 ☐ tenure n. 보유, 유지; 보유권; 재임 기간, 임기(=term) ☐ block v. 막다, 방해하다 ☐ dictatorship n. 독재(권), 절대권 ☐ approval n. 승인, 찬성 ☐ statement n. 성명; 성명서; 진술 ☐ legacy n. 유산; 유증(遺贈)

현행 대통령 5년 단임제는 독재를 막기 위한 것이었다.

72 ①

☐ abolish v. (법률·제도·습관 따위를) 폐지[철폐]하다(=abrogate) ☐ surrogate v. ~의 대리로 임명하다; 대용하다 ☐ subjugate v. 정복하다, 복종시키다 ☐ congregate v. 모으다, 집합시키다

지금은 미국에서 엄마가 된다는 것이 의미하는 바에 대해 우리가 가지고 있는 생각을 철폐하고 정책적인 차원에서 그것을 재정립할 때다.

73 ②

☐ unequivocal a. 명백한, 분명한 ☐ eyewitness n. 목격자 ☐ controvertible a. 논쟁의 여지가 있는, 논쟁할 만한(=ambiguous) ☐ lucid a. 명쾌한, 명료한 ☐ infallible a. 틀림없는, 절대 확실한 ☐ theoretical a. 이론(상)의

증인들이 제공한 분명한 설명들과는 다르게, 비행 기록 장치에서 얻은 증거는 오히려 논쟁의 여지가 있었고 이로 인해 추락 사고를 설명하는 서로 다른 여러 이론들이 생겨났다.

74 ①

☐ informal a. 비격식적인, 비공식의, 약식의(=casual) ☐ professional a. 직업의, 전문적인 ☐ atmosphere n. 분위기 ☐ conventional a. 전통적인, 인습적인 ☐ official a. 공무의, 직무의; 공식의 ☐ illegal a. 불법의, 위법의

그들은 친절하고 비격식적이지만 전문적인 분위기에서 새로운 기술을 배울 기회를 제공한다.

75 ②

☐ graze v. 풀을 뜯어먹다; 방목하다 ☐ meadow n. 풀밭, 목초지 ☐ bucolic a. 목가적인; 시골풍의(=rustic) ☐ splendor n. 현저함, 훌륭함 ☐ craven a. 겁 많은, 비겁한 ☐ servile a. 노예의; 노예근성의, 비굴한 ☐ querulous a. 투덜거리는, 불평이 많은; 성마른

가을 단풍이 변하는 것, 오래된 돌담, 원경, 푸른 목장에서 풀을 뜯어 먹고 있는 말은 전원생활의 멋진 광경의 예이다.

76 ②

☐ lavish a. 아끼지 않는; 사치스러운(=prodigal) ☐ frugal a. 검약한, 소박한 ☐ hygienic a. 위생적인; 위생에 좋은 ☐ abstinent a. 금욕적인

혼자 있기 좋아하는 페일리(Paley)는 직원들과 관계가 소원하고 그의 자녀들에게 냉담했으며 개인적인 생활양식에 있어서는 사치스러웠다.

77 ④

☐ repellent a. (사람에게) 혐오감을 주는, 불쾌한(=unpleasant) ☐ reserved a. 보류된, 따로 치워둔; 예약의; 수줍어하는 ☐ insincere a. 불성실한, 언행 불일치의, 위선적인 ☐ aggressive a. 침략적인, 공세의; 싸우기 좋아하는; 진취적인

그 납치범의 행동들은 너무나 혐오스러워서 그녀에게 어떤 동정심도 얻기 어려웠다.

78 ③

☐ spacious a. 넓은; (지식 따위가) 광범위한(=roomy) ☐ comfortable a. 기분 좋은, 편한, 위안의 ☐ luxurious a. 사치스러운, 호사스러운; 쾌락을 추구하는 ☐ quiet a. 조용한, 고요한, 소리 없는

학장의 널찍한 새 집무실은 대학 캠퍼스를 내려다보는 위치에 있었다.

79 ②

☐ exhaust v. 고갈시키다, 다 써버리다 ☐ installment n. 할부; 납입금 ☐ annuity n. 연금(=pension) ☐ debt n. 빚, 부채; 은혜 ☐ lease n. 임대차 계약; 임대차 계약서 ☐ investment n. 투자, 출자

그때 이미 그는 자신의 어머니에게조차 당회분의 연금을 지급할 수 없을 정도로 자금을 다 써버렸다.

80 ①

☐ depreciate v. 가치가 떨어지다(=devalue) ☐ denote v. 조짐을 보여주다; 의미하다 ☐ assess v. 평가하다 ☐ exalt v. 높이다; 칭찬하다

당신이 차를 몰고 나가자마자, 당신의 새 차는 이미 수천 달러의 가치가 하락했다.

81 ③

☐ perverse a. 심술궂은; 잘못된(=contrary) ☐ kind a. 친절한, 상냥한 ☐ generous a. 관대한 ☐ interesting a. 흥미 있는, 재미있는

팀(Tim)이 창가 좌석을 고집하는 것은 심술이다. 아주 높은 곳에서 아래를 내려다보면 그는 비행기 멀미를 하니까 말이다.

82 ②

☐ sticky-fingered a. 손버릇이 나쁜, 도벽이 있는 ☐ finagler n. 속임수를 쓰는 사람, 사기꾼(=swindler) ☐ peddler n. 행상인, 마약 판매인 ☐ wanderer n. 유랑자, 방랑자 ☐ gambler n. 도박꾼, 노름꾼

코카인 중독자와 손버릇이 나쁜 사기꾼들은 지역사회의 최선의 이익에 해가 된다.

83 ②

☐ indelible a. 잊을[지울] 수 없는(=unforgettable) ☐ incomparable a. 비교할 수 없는; 비길 데 없는 ☐ impressionable a. 쉽게 외부의 영향을 받는 ☐ indistinguishable a. 분간할 수 없는

메리 타일러 무어(Mary Tyler Moore)는 잊을 수 없는 두 개의 시트콤 배역으로 가장 기억에 남아 있는데, 그 배역은 바로 "딕 반 다이크 쇼(The Dick Van Dyke Show)"에서의 로라 페트리(Laura Petrie) 역과 "메리 타일러 무어 쇼(The Mary Tyler Moore Show)"에서의 메리 리처즈(Mary Richards) 역이었다.

84 ①

☐ distinguished a. 두드러진, 현저한; 저명한, 훌륭한(=eminent) ☐ inventive a. 창의력이 풍부한, 독창적인 ☐ dynamic a. 동력의, 동적인, 활동적인 ☐ enthusiastic a. 열렬한, 열광적인

탐 존슨(Tom Johnson)은 비평가이자 작가로서 모두 뛰어났다.

85 ②

☐ decree v. 명하다; 포고하다(=order) ☐ cease v. 그치다, 멎다, 중지하다 ☐ resolve v. 결심하다; 해결하다

서기 394년 로마의 황제 테오도시우스(Theodosius) 1세는 올림픽 경기 개최를 중단할 것을 포고했다.

86 ②

☐ vogue n. 유행; 인기, 호평(=popularity) ☐ voice n. 목소리, 음성 ☐ sound n. 소리, 음, 음향 ☐ tempo n. 속도, 빠르기

컨트리 음악의 최근 유행은 주로 테네시 주에서 시작되었다.

87 ②

☐ archaeologist n. 고고학자 ☐ remains n. 잔존물; 유물, 유적; 유해 ☐ material n. 재료; 자료; 도구, 용구(用具) ☐ deduce v. (결론·진리 등을) 연역하다, 추론하다(=infer) ☐ prehistoric a. 선사시대의 ☐ reduce v. (양·액수·정도 따위를) 줄이다; 축소하다 ☐ produce v. 산출하다; 생산하다 ☐ report v. 보고하다; 전하다, 말하다

고고학자들은 과거 인간의 삶과 물질들의 물질적 유물을 연구하여 선사시대 사람들이 어떻게 살았는지 추론한다.

88 ②

☐ castigate v. 징계하다, 벌주다; 혹평하다(=rebuke) ☐ aspirate v. (가스, 먼지 등을) 빨아들이다, 흡입하다 ☐ culminate v. 절정에 이르다, 최고조에 달하다 ☐ alleviate v. 덜다, 완화하다, 경감하다

그는 관용을 권력자의 '지적인 자선 행위'라고 혹평하는 것 같다.

89 ④

☐ reimburse v. (빚을) 갚다, 상환하다; 변상하다(=refund) ☐ withhold v. 억누르다, 억제하다, 말리다 ☐ reduce v. 줄이다; 축소하다, 한정하다 ☐ wane v. (달이) 이지러지다, 작아지다, 쇠약해지다

음료수를 구입한 사람이 회사로부터 환불받았다는 내용이 경비보고서에 나타날 것이다.

90 ②

☐ whirlpool n. 소용돌이 ☐ consign v. 건네주다, 인도하다; 위탁하다, 위임하다(=commit) ☐ oblivion n. (완전 파괴되어) 흔적도 없이 사라짐 ☐ compare v. 비교하다, 견주다; 비유하다 ☐ compile v. 엮다, 편집하다; 수집하다 ☐ conserve v. 보존하다, 유지하다; 절약하다

18세기 후반 이래로 그 생각은 상상할 수 없을 정도로 강력한 우주의 소용돌이가 우주의 물질들을 빨아들여 흔적도 없이 없애버리는 모습을 연상시키며 천문학자들을 매료시키고 있다.

91 ③

☐ pernicious a. 유해한, 유독한; 파괴적인(=harmful) ☐ costly a. 값이 비싼, 비용이 많이 드는 ☐ disgusting a. 구역질나는, 정떨어지는, 지겨운 ☐ healthful a. 건강에 좋은, 위생적인

그런 위험한 행위를 함으로써 그는 감옥에 갔다.

92 ④

☐ extreme a. 극도의, 극심한; 과격한 ☐ seriousness n. 진지함; 중대함 ☐ desertification n. 사막화 ☐ tremendous a. 거대한, 엄청난; 지독한, 무서운(=enormous) ☐ reverse v. 거꾸로 하다; 뒤집다; 역전시키다 ☐ augmented a. 증가된; <음악> 증음된 ☐ unacceptable a. 받아들이기 어려운, 용인할 수 없는 ☐ inadequate a. 부적당한, 부적절한, 무능한

사막화가 극히 심각한 것은 그 과정을 되돌리거나 심지어 지연시키는 것조차도 대단히 어려울 뿐만 아니라, 영향을 받는 땅이 대단히 넓고 또 영향을 받는 사람의 수가 엄청나게 많기 때문이다.

93 ②

☐ ooze v. 스며나오다, 새어나오다(=exude); 누설되다 ☐ stain n. 더럼, 얼룩; 오점 ☐ absolve v. 용서하다; 면제하다 ☐ absorb v. 흡수하다, 열중케 하다 ☐ consume v. 다 써버리다; 소비하다

붉은색 액체가 옷에 스며들어 커다랗고 둥근 얼룩이 생겼다.

94 ①

☐ Antarctica n. 남극 대륙(=the Antarctic Continent) ☐ inhospitable a. 살기에 부적당한; (기후가) 혹독한 ☐ living things 생명체 ☐ teeming a. 풍부한, 우글우글한(=crowded) ☐ magnificent a. 장려한, 웅장한; 훌륭한 ☐ enormous a. 막대한, 거대한 ☐ colossal a. 거대한, 엄청난

남극대륙의 지표면은 대부분의 생명체가 살기에 적당하지 않지만, 남극대륙 주위의 바다는 살아있는 생물들로 가득하다.

95 ③

☐ swiftly ad. 신속히, 즉각(=quickly) ☐ welding n. 용접 (기술) ☐ universally ad. 보편적으로, 널리; 도처에 ☐ sweetly ad. 달게, 맛있게; 제대로, 순조롭게 ☐ usefully ad. 유용하게, 유익하게

레이저 응용법은 수술, 용접, 금속 절단과 소리와 비디오를 녹화하는 것과 같은 분야에서 빠르게 증가했다.

96   ④

☐ tackle v. (일, 문제 따위를) 다루다, 착수하다(=undertake) ☐ complicate v. 복잡하게 하다, 뒤얽히게 하다 ☐ correct v. 정정하다, 고치다, 바로잡다 ☐ analyze v. 분석하다, 분해하다

나는 존재하는가? 나는 실재하는가? 내가 보고 만지는 것은 실재하는가? 인간들은 삶의 의미에 관한 질문을 제기한다는 점에서 동물들과 다르다. 사람들은 항상 새로운 문제들을 만난다. 그 문제들이 사소하든 중대하든 간에, 자아와 세계 사이의 관계를 이해하는 것이 바로 사람이 문제들을 해결하는 토대가 된다.

97   ②

☐ intravenous a. 정맥주사의 ☐ as such 따라서 ☐ serve to do (특정한) 결과를 낳다 ☐ inflame v. 불붙이다; 부채질하다 ☐ stigma n. 낙인, 오명 ☐ amplify v. 증폭시키다 ☐ entrenched a. 깊게 뿌리박힌(=established) ☐ homophobia n. 동성애 공포증 ☐ racism n. 인종차별 (주의) ☐ contempt n. 경멸 ☐ eschew v. 피하다, 삼가다 ☐ encroach v. 침범하다 ☐ endanger v. ~을 위험에 빠뜨리다

특히 초기에는 남성 동성애자, 아이티(Haiti)인, 그리고 정맥주사 마약 사용자라는 세 집단이 에이즈(후천성 면역 결핍증)에 주로 걸렸다. 그래서 에이즈는 이 세 집단에 대한 기존의 낙인을 더욱 강화시켰고, 이미 깊게 뿌리박힌 동성애 공포증, 인종차별주의, 그리고 마약 중독자에 대한 경멸을 증폭시키는 결과를 낳았다.

98   ③

☐ deliberately ad. 신중히; 고의적으로(=intentionally) ☐ remove v. 제거하다; 치우다; 벗다 ☐ respectable a. 존경[존중]할만한, 훌륭한; 신분[지위, 명성]이 있는 ☐ optional a. 임의의, 선택의 ☐ obligatory a. 의무로서 해야 할, 의무적인 ☐ seriously ad. 진지하게; 심각하게 ☐ carefully ad. 주의 깊게; 면밀히, 신중히 ☐ reluctantly ad. 마지못해, 싫어하며

1922년에 이집트의 저명한 페미니스트 후다 샤아라위(Hoda Shaarawi)가 의도적으로 베일을 벗기 전에는, 모든 훌륭한 중산층, 상류층 여성들이 공공장소에서 베일을 썼다. 그러나 1935년에는 이미, 베일은 이집트에서 선택적인 것이 되어있었다. 반면에, 아라비아 반도에서는 베일이 지금까지도 의무적인 것으로 남아있다.

99   ④

☐ irrespective of ~와 상관없이, ~와 관계없이 ☐ emit v. (빛, 열, 소리 따위를) 내다, 발하다, 방출하다 ☐ absorb v. 흡수하다, 빨아들이다 ☐ atmosphere n. 대기; 공기; 분위기 ☐ consequence n. 결과, 결말; 중요성 ☐ uniform a. 한결 같은, 균일한 ☐ adverse a. 불리한; 해로운;

불운[불행]한 ☐ unilateral a. 일방적인; 한쪽에만 제한된(=one-sided) ☐ unauthorized a. 월권의; 공인[승인]되지 않은 ☐ zero-sum a. (게임, 관계 등이) 쌍방 득실(得失)의 차가 없는 ☐ conventional a. 전통적인, 인습적인, 관습적인

기후변화가 전 지구적인 성격을 갖는 것은 지구에서 온실가스는 배출되는 곳과 관계없이 대기 중으로 급속히 흡수되어 지구의 이곳저곳으로 확산된다는 사실에서 비롯된다. 그러나 그로 인해 초래되는 전 지구적 기후변화의 결과는 결코 획일적이지 않을 것으로 예상되어서, 몇몇 국가는 다른 국가들에 비해 나쁜 영향을 훨씬 더 크게 받을 것으로 보인다. 그뿐만 아니라, 어느 한 국가의 일방적인 조치로는 이러한 상황에 의미 있는 변화를 가져올 수 없다. 따라서 그 문제를 해결하기 위해서는 개선을 위한 국제적 차원에서의 합치된 협력이 반드시 필요하다.

100   ①

☐ watchword n. (정당의) 표어, 슬로건; 암호(=words that sum up attitude to a particular subject) ☐ statements or principles that are generally accepted to be true 일반적으로 사실로 받아들여지는 주장 또는 원칙 ☐ units of language that can be represented in writing or speech 글이나 담화에서 표현되는 언어의 단위 ☐ words that you must know in order to be allowed to enter a place 어떤 장소에 들어가기 위해서 반드시 알아야 하는 단어

열정, 공감, 참여는 그 축제의 슬로건이었다.

MVP 36-40 ACTUAL TEST

01 ①	02 ①	03 ①	04 ③	05 ①	06 ④	07 ④	08 ①	09 ②	10 ④
11 ④	12 ①	13 ④	14 ③	15 ③	16 ③	17 ④	18 ①	19 ②	20 ③
21 ③	22 ③	23 ①	24 ①	25 ①	26 ③	27 ①	28 ④	29 ③	30 ①
31 ③	32 ②	33 ①	34 ③	35 ①	36 ①	37 ②	38 ①	39 ①	40 ④
41 ②	42 ④	43 ③	44 ④	45 ④	46 ④	47 ①	48 ②	49 ③	50 ④
51 ②	52 ①	53 ②	54 ④	55 ②	56 ②	57 ②	58 ②	59 ②	60 ③
61 ④	62 ③	63 ②	64 ①	65 ③	66 ②	67 ②	68 ④	69 ④	70 ①
71 ②	72 ③	73 ④	74 ①	75 ③	76 ③	77 ①	78 ①	79 ②	80 ②
81 ②	82 ①	83 ①	84 ②	85 ④	86 ③	87 ②	88 ①	89 ①	90 ②
91 ①	92 ①	93 ①	94 ③	95 ④	96 ②	97 ②	98 ①	99 ②	100 ①

01   ①

☐ ajar a. (문이) 조금 열린(=slightly open) ☐ widely open 활짝 열린 ☐ unlocked a. 잠겨 있지 않은 ☐ unfixed a. 고정되지 않은; 분명치 않은

그녀는 고양이가 들어올 수 있도록 문을 조금 열어두었다.

02   ①

☐ bone china n. 본차이나(뼛가루를 섞어 만든 고급 도자기류) ☐ durable a. 영속성 있는; 오래 견디는, 튼튼한(=sturdy) ☐ impeccable a. 죄를 범하지 않은, 과실 없는; 결점 없는 ☐ elastic a. 탄력 있는, 신축성 있는; 휘기 쉬운 ☐ brittle a. 부서지기 쉬운, 무른

품질 좋은 본차이나는 튼튼하고 내구성이 강하기 때문에, 매우 실용적이다.

03   ①

☐ infinitesimal a. 극소의, 극미의; 무한소의(=minute) ☐ prescribed a. 규정된, 미리 정해진 ☐ limited a. 한정된, 유한의, 좁은 ☐ restricted a. 한정된, 제한된

극소량의 코발트는 생활에 꼭 필요한 금속 가운데 하나이다.

04   ③

☐ take the brunt of ~의 가장 큰 타격을 받다 ☐ collapse n. 무너짐, 와해; 붕괴(=breakdown) ☐ construction n. 건설, 건축; 구조 ☐ intrusion n. 강요; 침입; 침해 ☐ change n. 변화, 변경

중산층은 통화와 주식 시장의 붕괴에 가장 큰 타격을 받아왔다.

05   ①

☐ blithe a. 즐거운, 쾌활한; 태평스런; 경솔한, 분별없는(=careless) ☐ coming a. 다가오는; 다음의 ☐ defensive a. 방어적인; 수비의; 변호의 ☐ discreet a. 신중한; 예의 바른; 조심스러운 ☐ ungrounded a. 근거 없는, 이유 없는, 사실무근의

그는 다가오고 있는 허리케인에 대해 분별없는 발언을 했다.

06   ④

☐ palatial a. 궁전의[같은]; 호화로운, 광대한(=grand) ☐ attractive a. 매력적인, 멋진 ☐ comfortable a. 편안한, 쾌적한 ☐ friendly a. 친절한, 상냥한

톰은 이 집이 유명 인사들의 호화로운 집이라고 말한다.

07   ④

☐ plot n. (극, 소설 따위의) 줄거리 ☐ predictable a. 예측 가능한; 새로운 게 없는 ☐ mediocre a. 보통의, 평범한(=undistinguished) ☐ potent a. 강력한, 유력한 ☐ peculiar a. 독특한, 고유의 ☐ impressive a. 인상적인, 감동을 주는

그 영화의 줄거리는 예상할 수 있으며, 연기도 평범하다.

08   ①

☐ emblem n. 상징(=symbol) ☐ falsehood n. 허위; 거짓말 ☐ disgrace n. 불명예, 망신 ☐ boast n. 자랑(거리)

진짜 존재하던 날조된 것이던, 네시(Nessie)는 오랫동안 스코틀랜드의 상징이었다.

09　②

☐ layoff n. 일시 해고; 강제 휴업(=redundancy) ☐ bankruptcy n. 파산, 도산(倒産); 파탄 ☐ innovation n. (기술) 혁신, 일신, 쇄신 ☐ advance n. 진전, 진출; 승급

방위 산업에서는 갑작스러운 해고가 흔한 일이다.

10　④

☐ obfuscate v. 어둡게 하다, 흐리게 하다, 혼란케 하다(=obscure) ☐ detonate v. (폭약을) 폭발시키다, 폭파시키다 ☐ illumine v. 조명하다, 밝게 하다, 비추다 ☐ elucidate v. 밝히다, 명료하게 하다

무관한 주장을 오래 끌어서 쟁점을 흐리지 마시오.

11　④

☐ revelation n. 폭로 ☐ enhance v. (가치를) 높이다, 향상시키다 (=improve) ☐ increase v. 증가시키다, 늘리다 ☐ influence v. 영향을 미치다 ☐ develop v. 개발하다, 성장하다

최근의 폭로는 확실히 그녀의 이미지를 개선시키지 못할 것이다.

12　①

☐ postponement n. 연기(=delay) ☐ rain check 우천 교환권; 후일의 약속[요구] ☐ cancellation n. 취소, 말소; 해제 ☐ vengeance n. 복수, 앙갚음

비 때문에 경기가 연기되었다.

13　④

☐ unflagging a. 불요불굴의, 지칠 줄 모르는(=indefatigable) ☐ brave a. 용감한; 훌륭한; 멋진 ☐ unified a. 통일된, 통합한 ☐ hurried a. 매우 급한; 허둥대는, 소홀한

구조대의 지칠 줄 모르는 노력 때문에, 몇 시간 후에 아이들이 발견되었다.

14　③

☐ emblem n. 상징, 표상 ☐ tableware n. 식탁용 식기류 ☐ denote v. 의미[뜻]하다, 나타내다(=indicate) ☐ surface v. 표면화시키다, 드러내다 ☐ treasure v. 소중히 하다 ☐ retail v. 이야기하다

그 식기 바닥의 작은 금색 상징은 품질과 우수성을 나타낸다.

15　③

☐ implement v. (약속 따위를) 이행[실행]하다(=put into action) ☐ humane a. 자비로운, 인도적인 ☐ alternative n. 대안, 다른 방도 ☐ make up 만들다; 편성하다; 화장하다 ☐ stand for 대표하다; 상징하다 ☐ ask for 요구하다

우리는 학생들이 인도적인 대안을 선택할 수 있도록 하는 정책을 시행할 계획이다.

16　③

☐ dread n. 두려움; 우려, 걱정(=fear) ☐ boredom n. 지루함, 따분함 ☐ admiration n. 감탄, 존경 ☐ native n. 토착민, 현지인; 토종

매슬로우(Maslow)가 보인 태도의 부분적인 이유는 그의 친구들과 그의 누나들 간의 언쟁이 더 심해질까 두려워서이다.

17　④

☐ acoustic a. 청각의, 소리의; 음향의(=auditory) ☐ sensory a. 감각 (상)의 ☐ tactile a. 촉각의, 촉감의 ☐ visible a. 눈에 보이는

어떤 음향 문제들은 부적절한 설계나 건축의 한계로부터 초래된다. 만약 큰 울림을 피하려면 소리 파장이 집중되지 않도록 해야 한다.

18　①

☐ bent n. 좋아함, 기호; 성향, 소질(=disposition) ☐ credulity n. (남을) 쉽사리 믿음, 고지식함 ☐ abhorrence n. 혐오, 증오; 질색인 것 ☐ undeviating a. 정도를 벗어나지 않는, 일관된 ☐ curiosity n. 호기심; 진기함

우리는 모두 고지식함, 즉 다른 사람들이 말하는 것을 쉽게 믿는 선천적 기질을 가지고 이 세상에 태어난다.

19　②

☐ amaze v. 몹시 놀라다 ☐ infinite a. 무한한, 무궁한, 끝없는; 막대한 (=numerous) ☐ assortment n. 구분, 분류, 유별; 잡다한 것의 모임 ☐ erudite a. 박학[박식]한, 학식 있는 ☐ exclusive a. 배타적인, 독점적인 ☐ adroit a. 교묘한, 손재주가 있는; 재치 있는

우리는 아주 작은 상점에 매우 많은 종류의 과일과 채소가 있는 듯 보여서 몹시 놀랐다.

20　③

☐ perplex v. 당황하게 하다, 난처하게 하다(=puzzle) ☐ discover v. 발견하다; 알다, 깨닫다 ☐ call v. 부르다, 외치다, 불러내다 ☐ dub v. (새 이름을) 주다, 붙이다, ~이라고 부르다

자신이 살던 시대에도 독특했지만, 공룡의 운명은 한 세기 이상이나 과학자들을 혼란스럽게 했다.

21 ③

□ validate v. 정당성을 입증하다, 실증하다(=justify) □ refute v. 논박하다, 반박하다 □ challenge v. 도전하다; ~에 이의를 제기하다 □ neutralize v. 중립화하다; 무효로 하다

저자의 분석과 과학적 증거는 개인이 만족하기 위해 동일한 양의 여가시간을 필요로 하지는 않는다는 입장을 입증한다.

22 ③

□ versatile a. 다재다능한; 다용도의(=many-sided) □ creative a. 창조적인 □ energetic a. 정력적인, 활기에 찬 □ long-lasting a. 오래가는, 장기간에 걸친

그는 대단한 예술가는 아닐지 모르지만 대단히 다재다능한 사람이다.

23 ①

□ barracuda n. 창꼬치(이빨이 날카롭고 공격적인 꼬치고기과의 물고기) □ ferocious a. 사나운, 잔인한, 흉포한(=savage) □ predator n. 포식자, 포식 동물 □ indistinct a. 희미한, 흐릿한 □ flagrant a. 명백한; 극악한, 악명 높은 □ lavish a. 아끼지 않는, 후한; 낭비벽이 있는, 사치스러운

창꼬치는 사나운 포식자로서 때때로 열대 해역의 호랑이라고 불린다.

24 ①

□ screen v. 가리다, 감싸다; 선발하다, 가려내다(=filter) □ block v. 막다, 방해하다 □ investigate v. 조사하다, 연구하다, 심사하다 □ show v. 보이다; 제시하다; 지시하다; 나타내다

대기업에서는 회사를 위해 일하고 싶어 하는 모든 사람들을 면접할 수는 없어서 가장 우수한 지원자들을 선발하기 위해 종종 컴퓨터로 먼저 이력서를 심사한다.

25 ①

□ encapsulate v. 캡슐로 싸다; 보호하다; 요약하다(=condense) □ feature v. 특징을 이루다, 특색으로 삼다 □ reduce v. 줄이다, 감소시키다, 축소하다 □ locate v. 정하다; (위치를) 알아내다

톰(Tom)은 500페이지의 보고서를 이해하기 쉽게 25페이지짜리 요약본으로 요약했다.

26 ③

□ condemn v. 비난하다, 힐난하다, 나무라다 □ abuse v. 남용하다, 악용하다(=misuse); 학대하다 □ demystify v. 알기 쉽게 설명하다 □ preserve v. 보호하다, 지키다, 보존하다 □ denounce v. 비난하다; 탄핵하다; 고발하다

민주주의 국가에서 언론의 자유를 제한하려는 어떠한 노력도 응당 비난받는다. 그러나 이 자유는 쉽게 악용될 수 있다.

27 ①

□ aptitude n. 재능, 수완 □ amass v. 쌓다, 모으다, 축적하다 (=accumulate) □ deplete v. 감소시키다, 고갈시키다 □ bequeath v. 물려주다, 유증하다 □ donate v. 기부하다, 기증하다

카렌(Karen)의 사업 수완은 그녀가 30세가 되기 전에 약간의 재산을 모을 수 있게 해주었다.

28 ④

□ impervious a. 통하지 않는, 스며들게 하지 않는(=resistant); 무감동한 □ antagonistic a. 적대적인, 반대하는 □ precarious a. 불확실한, 믿을 수 없는; 위험한 □ peripatetic a. 걸어 돌아다니는, 순회하는

비가 스며들지 않았기 때문에, 텐트는 폭풍우가 치는 동안 훌륭한 피난처가 되었다.

29 ③

□ elementary school 초등학교 □ relieve v. 경감하다, 덜다, 완화하다(=allay) □ crowd v. 붐비다 □ induce v. 유도하다, 야기하다, 유발하다 □ reinforce v. 강화하다 □ intensify v. 격렬하게 하다; 강화하다

새로 개교하는 두 초등학교는 플로리다 팜비치카운티의 (학급) 과밀을 덜어줄 것이다.

30 ①

□ preferable a. 더 좋은; 선호되는 □ caprice n. 갑작스러운 변화, 변덕(=whim) □ unpredictable a. 예측할 수 없는 □ prestige n. 위신, 명성 □ blessing n. 축복; 승인, 허락 □ introspection n. 내성(內省), 자기 성찰

부유하지만 너무나 예측할 수 없는 왕의 변덕 속에 사는 것보다 가난하지만 자기 운명의 주인이 되는 것이 더 좋다.

31 ③

□ immigration n. 이주, 입국; 이민 □ heat up ~을 뜨겁게 하다; 격화되다 □ pit v. 겨루게 하다, 경쟁시키다 □ advocate n. 옹호자, 지지자

(=proponent) ☐ adversary n. 적, 상대 ☐ rebel n. 반역자, 모반자 ☐ priest n. 성직자, 사제

불법 이민자들의 합법화를 옹호하는 자들과 더욱 강력한 반이민 조치들을 지지하는 자들 사이에 격돌이 벌어지면서 이민논쟁이 대서양 양쪽(미국과 유럽)에서 가열되고 있다.

32 ②

☐ be involved in ~에 관련되다 ☐ wanton a. 제멋대로의, 무자비한; 방종한(=unruly) ☐ innocent a. 결백한, 무죄인, 무고한 ☐ deliberate a. 고의의, 의도적인, 계획적인 ☐ illegal a. 불법의, 위법의 ☐ intentional a. 고의의, 의도적인 ☐ stubborn a. 완고한, 고집 센

강도들은 제멋대로 무고한 사람을 때리고 고의적으로 은행 건물을 파괴한 혐의를 받고 있었다.

33 ①

☐ out of stock 품절[매진]된(=unavailable) ☐ overpriced a. 너무 비싼, (제 가치보다) 값이 비싸게 매겨진 ☐ not for sale 비매품 ☐ the wrong size 잘못된 치수

죄송하지만 그 품목들은 일시적으로 품절되었습니다.

34 ④

☐ fickle a. 변하기 쉬운, 변덕스러운(=capricious) ☐ measurably ad. 분명하게 ☐ drought n. 가뭄; 고갈 ☐ scanty a. 부족한, 모자란 ☐ perpetual a. 영원한, 영속하는 ☐ voracious a. 게걸스레 먹는; 탐욕스러운

비가 너무 변덕스럽게 내리고, 날이 상당히 더워지고, 가뭄이 더 자주 발생해서, 그들의 땅에서 충분한 식량을 재배할 수 없었기 때문에, 서아프리카의 남성과 소년들은 고향을 떠나야 한다.

35 ①

☐ alienate v. 소외시키다, 이간하다 ☐ unsettle v. (사람을) 불안하게 만들다 ☐ clamorous a. 떠들썩한, 시끄러운(=noisy) ☐ high-rise a. 고층건물의 ☐ flash n. (감정 등이) 갑자기 떠오름 ☐ panic n. 공황, 공포 ☐ glamourous a. 화려한, 매력이 넘치는 ☐ cumbersome a. 크고 무거운 ☐ skeletal a. 해골 같은

도쿄의 떠들썩한 고층건물의 낯선 풍경에 소외되고 불안해진 샬럿(Charlotte)은 문득 자신의 인생에 대해 공포감을 경험한다.

36 ①

☐ encompass v. 포함하다, 망라하다(=cover) ☐ manufacturing n. 제조, 생산 ☐ distribution n. 배급, 유통 ☐ retailing n. 소매 ☐

promotion n. 판매촉진, 선전 ☐ apparel n. 의류, 의복 ☐ encounter v. 만나다, 마주치다 ☐ compare v. 비교하다, 견주다 ☐ spur v. 박차를 가하다; 자극하다

그 산업은 모든 종류의 의류에 대한 기획, 제조, 유통, 마케팅, 소매, 광고, 그리고 판촉활동을 망라한다.

37 ②

☐ moody a. 침울한, 시무룩한(=depressed) ☐ romantic a. 낭만적인, 연애 소설적인; 신비적인 ☐ foolish a. 미련한, 바보 같은 ☐ numb a. 감각을 잃은, 마비된; 무감각한, 둔한

집안일이 잘 되어가지 않아서 그는 늘 시무룩하다.

38 ③

☐ fanciful a. 공상에 잠기는; 비현실적인, 공상의, 가공의 ☐ delude v. 속이다, 착각하게 하다, 현혹하다(=fool) ☐ vindicate v. ~의 정당성을 입증하다 ☐ acquit v. 무죄로 하다, 방면하다, 석방하다 ☐ execute v. 실행하다, 수행하다; 집행하다

화가의 비현실적인 꿈이 그 자신과 그의 가족을 현혹시켰다.

39 ①

☐ a far cry from ~와는 크게 다른 ☐ halcyon a. 화려한, 번영의, 풍요로운(=prosperous) ☐ turbulent a. 사나운; 소란스러운; 광포한 ☐ impoverished a. 가난해진; 허약해진, 빈약한 ☐ embryonic a. 배아의; 미발달의; 초기의

그의 사업이 1990년대 초의 번영기로 되돌아가기란 아직 요원하다.

40 ③

☐ launch v. 시작[착수]하다(=commence) ☐ initiative n. 발단; 새로운 계획 ☐ tackle v. (일, 문제 따위에) 달려들다 ☐ counterfeit a. 모조의; 가짜의 ☐ substandard a. 표준 이하[미달]의; 규격 미달의 ☐ modify v. 수정[변경]하다 ☐ announce v. 고지[발표]하다 ☐ examine v. 검사하다, 조사하다

세계보건기구(WHO)는 가짜로 제조되고 규격이 미달된 약물이 증가하는 문제를 해결하기 위해 새로운 계획에 착수했다.

41 ②

☐ ambiguous a. 애매한, 모호한, 분명치 않은(=uncertain) ☐ angry a. 성난, 노한; 험악한 ☐ clear a. 맑은, 투명한; 분명한 ☐ humorous a. 유머러스한, 익살스러운

아버지가 우리에게 모호한 대답을 한 것이 오늘 벌써 세 번째다.

42　④

☐ make the point that ~라고 주장하다　☐ unprecedented a. 전례 없는　☐ extent n. 정도, 크기, 규모(=degree)　☐ explicit a. 노골적인　☐ critique n. 비판　☐ quality n. 품질; 특성, 속성　☐ extant a. 현존하는, 잔존하는　☐ extra n. 여분의 것, 특별한 것

힙합음악을 소비하는 백인들에 관한 그의 토론은 백인 젊은이들이 '백인' 사회에 대한 노골적인 비판에 전례 없는 수준으로 귀 기울이고 있다는 주장을 하고 있다.

43　③

☐ concur with 일치하다, 동의하다(=agree with)　☐ occur v. 생기다, 발생하다　☐ dispute v. 논쟁하다, 말다툼하다　☐ recur v. 재발하다

그 회사의 어떤 누구도 존슨(Johnson)에게 동의하는 것 같지 않았다.

44　④

☐ convict v. 유죄를 선언하다, 유죄를 입증하다　☐ thief n. 도둑　counterfeiter n. 위조자, 화폐위조자　☐ death penalty 사형　☐ deterrent n. 억제하는 것, 억제책(=hindrance)　☐ beacon n. 횃불; 등대　☐ amphibian n. 양서류 동물　☐ eminence n. 높음, 고귀함; 명성

유죄판결을 받은 절도범들과 화폐위조범들은 종종 사형을 선고받았는데, 이는 다른 범죄자들을 억제하는 대책으로 여겨졌다.

45　④

☐ sentence v. 선고하다, 판결하다, 형에 처하다(=condemn)　☐ plead v. 탄원하다, 간청하다　☐ leniency n. 관대, 관용　☐ nominate v. 지명하다; 임명하다　☐ investigate v. 연구하다; 조사하다　☐ arrest v. 체포하다; 저지하다

그가 실형 선고를 받을 때가 되었을 때, 그의 아버지는 선처를 바랐다.

46　④

☐ obituary a. 사망의, 사망기록의, 죽은(=dead)　☐ outlandish a. 이국풍의; 기이한, 이상한　☐ difficult a. 어려운, 힘이 드는　☐ cheap a. 값이 싼, 돈이 적게 드는

"죽은 아이디어들은 이제 그만!"이라고 그녀가 말했다.

47　①

☐ decry v. 비난하다, 헐뜯다　☐ indiscriminate a. 무차별의, 닥치는 대로의, 분별없는(=haphazard)　☐ pesticide n. 살충제, 농약　☐ innovative a. 혁신적인, 창조적인　☐ unpleasant a. 불쾌한, 기분 나쁜,

싫은　☐ indispensable a. 불가결의, 없어서는 안 될, 절대 필요한

『고요한 봄(Silent Spring)』이라는 소설에서, 레이첼 카슨(Rachel Carson)은 살충제의 무분별한 사용을 강력히 비난했다.

48　②

☐ adopt v. 채용하다, 채택하다, 차용하다(=employ)　☐ expedite v. 촉진시키다, 추진하다　☐ manipulate v. 교묘하게 다루다, 조종하다　☐ abandon v. 버리다; 그만두다

그 위원회의 위원들은 그 일을 성공리에 완수하기 위해 두 가지 전략 중 어느 것을 채택할지 결정하지 못했다.

49　③

☐ dated a. 시대에 뒤진, 구식의(=old-fashioned)　☐ damaged a. 손상을 입은, 파손된　☐ monotonous a. 단조로운; 변화 없는, 지루한　☐ poorly designed 잘못 설계된

아마존 닷컴(Amazon.com)을 통해 나로부터 책을 구입한 고객은 그 책에 관해 "너무 구식이다"는 불평과 함께 좋지 않은 평점을 매겼다.

50　④

☐ achievement n. 성취, 달성, 업적　☐ pompous a. 점잔 빼는, 거만한; 과시하는(=arrogant)　☐ tolerant a. 관대한, 아량 있는　☐ variant a. 다른, 상이한, 어긋난　☐ compliant a. 유순한, 고분고분한

그녀는 자신의 공로에 관해 거만하게 들리지 않게 이야기 하는 것이 힘들다는 것을 알게 되었다.

51　②

☐ tailor-made a. (특정한 개인, 목적을 위한) 맞춤의, 안성맞춤의(=custom-built)　☐ off-the-peg a. 기성복의　☐ off-the-rack a. (옷이) 기성품인　☐ ready-made a. 이미 만들어져 나오는; 기성품의　☐ incomparable a. 견줄 데 없는, 비교가 되지 않는

도덕은 정말로 존재해야 한다. 그러나 그것은 기성복 같은 것이 아닌, 개인의 독특한 개성에 맞춰진 것이어야 한다.

52　①

☐ salacious a. 외설스러운(=obscene)　☐ incorrigible a. 다루기 힘든, 제멋대로 구는; 고질적인　☐ scathing a. (비판이) 가차 없는, 냉혹한　☐ malicious a. 악의 있는, 심술궂은

그것은 대중매체에서 보편적으로 외설적이라는 취급을 당하는 주제이다.

53 ②

☐ rehabilitate v. 원상태로 되돌리다, 복원하다(=restore) ☐ concoct v. 조작하다, 날조하다 ☐ compensate v. 보상하다, 배상하다 ☐ imagine v. 상상하다, 가정하다

행정부는 관세를 철폐하는 과감한 조치를 취함으로써 이미지를 되살릴 수 있을 것이다.

54 ④

☐ obtrude v. 강요하다, 억지 쓰다; 불쑥 내밀다(=emerge) ☐ vanish v. 사라지다, 자취를 감추다, 희미해지다 ☐ relinquish v. 포기하다, 양도하다; 그만두다; 버리다 ☐ suffer v. 경험하다, 입다, 받다; 견디다

불안은 정신의 무의식적인 단계에서 나타나는 내적 자극에 반응하여 생겨난다.

55 ②

☐ composition n. 구성; 작문 ☐ legible a. 읽기 쉬운, 읽을 수 있는 (=comprehensible) ☐ conclusive a. 결정적인, 확실한, 단호한 ☐ audible a. 들리는, 들을 수 있는 ☐ valiant a. 용감한, 씩씩한; 훌륭한

존(John)의 작문은 형편없게 구성되어 있었지만 적어도 알아볼 수는 있었다.

56 ②

☐ separate a. 서로 다른, 별개의 ☐ restrain v. 억제하다, 누르다; 제지하다(=curb) ☐ unified a. 통일된 ☐ release v. 자유롭게 하다, 해방하다, 풀어주다 ☐ distract v. 흐트러뜨리다; 전환시키다 ☐ promote v. 승진시키다; 촉진하다

비록 캐나다는 19세기 말엽에 형성되었지만, 여러 별개의 정치적, 경제적, 지리적 세력들이 20세기 내내 지속되어 통일된 교육 발전을 저해했다.

57 ②

☐ indifferent a. 냉담한, 무관심한(=apathetic) ☐ outcome n. 결과 ☐ bother v. 괴롭히다, 귀찮게 하다; 일부러 ~하다, ~하려 애쓰다 ☐ amenable a. 순종하는, (도리를) 따르는 ☐ congenial a. 같은 성질의, 마음이 맞는 ☐ cogent a. 설득력 있는, 적절한

대중들은 그 야구 경기의 결과에 너무도 무관심했기 때문에 다음날 신문 기사에서 그것에 관해 굳이 읽어보려 하는 사람조차 거의 없었다.

58 ②

☐ pursuit n. 추구 ☐ thwart v. ~을 방해하다, ~을 훼방 놓다(=impede)

☐ compel v. 강제하다, 억지로 ~하게 시키다 ☐ spawn v. 낳다, 야기하다 ☐ augment v. 늘리다, 증대시키다

행복을 방해하는 것은 바로 그 행복의 추구이다.

59 ③

☐ surprisingly ad. 놀랄 만큼; 의외로; 놀랍게도 ☐ averse a. 싫어하는, 반대하는(=hostile) ☐ surrender v. 내어주다, 양도하다; 항복하다 ☐ sovereignty n. 주권, 통치권 ☐ restive a. 고집이 센; 다루기 힘든, 난폭한; 말을 안 듣는, 반항적인 ☐ determined a. 결연한, 단호한; 굳게 결심한 ☐ obedient a. 순종하는, 유순한, 고분고분한, 말을 잘 듣는 ☐ agreeable a. 기분 좋은; 선뜻 동의하는; 알맞은

주권을 양도하는 것에 반대하는 사람들이 최근에 점차적으로 단호해지는 것은 놀랄 일이 아니다.

60 ③

☐ endow v. ~에게 (재능·특징 등을) 부여하다 ☐ inalienable a. 양도할 수 없는(=nontransferable) ☐ irreverent a. 불손한, 불경한 ☐ discriminatory a. 차별적인 ☐ statutory a. 법에 명시된, 법으로 정한

인간은 누구나 행복을 추구할 양도할 수 없는 권리를 부여받고 태어났다.

61 ④

☐ poisoning n. 중독, 독살 ☐ induce v. 권유하다; 야기하다, 유발하다 (=cause) ☐ vomiting n. 구토 ☐ control v. 지배하다; 통제하다, 관리하다, 감독하다 ☐ lessen v. 줄이다, 적게 하다, 작게 하다 ☐ stop v. 멈추다; 중지하다, 그만두게 하다

어떤 유형의 중독에서는, 토하도록 유도하기 위해 즉시 다량의 비눗물이나 소금물을 주도록 하라.

62 ③

☐ hazy a. 흐릿한, 모호한(=nebulous) ☐ recall v. 기억해 내다, 상기하다 ☐ scanty a. 부족한, 불충분한 ☐ impetuous a. 성급한, 충동적인 ☐ surreal a. 아주 이상한, 비현실적인

시간이 흐르면서 구체적인 진술을 떠올리는 데 애를 먹었기 때문에 그 목격자의 진술은 약간 모호했다.

63 ②

☐ prestigious a. 명성 있는, 유명한; 존경 받는, 유명한(=reputable) ☐ repugnant a. 비위에 거슬리는, 혐오스러운 ☐ susceptive a. 민감한, 감수성이 예민한 ☐ presumptuous a. 뻔뻔스러운, 건방진

그것은 나라에서 가장 명성 있는 학교 중 하나다.

64
①

□ unduly ad. 과도하게, 심하게(=excessively) □ apprehensive a. 염려하는, 걱정하는 □ locality n. 위치, 장소, 소재(所在) □ impinge on ~에 영향을 주다; 침해하다 □ tellingly ad. 유효하게; 재미있게 □ flagrantly ad. 극악무도하게, 악명 높게 □ forthrightly ad. 똑바로, 곧바로, 즉시

그들이 기후변화에 대해 과도하게 우려하는 것은 아닐지 모르지만, 그들은 온실 효과에 대해, 그리고 세계 전체와 자신들이 살고 있는 지역의 상태가 자신들의 삶에 어떻게 영향을 미치는지에 대해 알고 있다.

65
③

□ ratify v. 비준하다, 재가하다, 승인하다(=approve) □ treaty n. 조약, 협정 □ deny v. 부인하다, 부정하다; 거절하다 □ purge v. 제거하다, 숙청하다 □ elucidate v. 명료하게 하다, 밝히다; 해명하다

우리는 그 공화국들이 조약을 비준하길 바란다.

66
②

□ lustrous a. 광택 있는, 빛나는 □ ductile a. 연성(延性)의; 유연한; 유순한(=pliable) □ versatile a. 다재다능한; 다용도의 □ serviceable a. 쓸모 있는, 유용한; 실용적인 □ shiny a. 빛나는, 청명한

순은은 거의 백색이고 광택이 있고 부드러우며, 매우 잘 휜다.

67
④

□ stock a. 표준의, 평범한 □ remedy n. 치료, 치료약; 구제책 □ malingerer n. 꾀병을 부리는 사람(=shirker) □ placebo n. 위약(僞藥) □ trooper n. 기병(騎兵), 낙하산병 □ mercenary n. (외국인) 용병, 고용된 사람

헤이콕(Haycock) 박사는 염화암모늄과 설탕의 혼합물을 처방했는데, 이것은 꾀병을 부리는 군인들에 대한 표준 치료약이었다.

68
④

□ hit-or-miss a. 되는 대로의, 소홀히 하는, 부주의한(=careless) □ lucrative a. 수익성이 좋은, 이익이 되는, 수지맞는 □ attentive a. 주의하는, 신경을 쓰는 □ targeted a. 표적이 된, 목표로 정해진

교수는 우리의 연구가 질적인 면을 소홀히 했다고 비판했다.

69
④

□ loom v. 어렴풋이 나타나다; 불쑥 나타나다(=emerge) □ shake v. 흔들다, 잡아 흔들다 □ collapse v. 붕괴되다, 무너지다 □ explode v. 폭발하다, 파열하다

등산가들은 그들 앞에 산의 정상이 나타난 것을 보고 놀랐다.

70
①

□ reckless a. 분별없는, 무모한 □ derivative a. 유도된; 끌어낸; 파생적인(=unoriginal) □ detach v. 떼어내다; 분리하다 □ disingenuous a. 솔직하지 않은; 부정직한 □ foreign a. 외국의; 외국풍의; 타지방의 □ speculative a. 사색적인; 투기적인

세계 시장에서 실물 경제와 동떨어진 복잡한 파생상품들이 무분별하게 유통되어 세계 금융 시장을 위기에 빠뜨렸다.

71
②

□ high-profile a. 세간의 이목을 끄는, 눈에 띄는(=renowned) □ ardent a. 열렬한, 열심인, 정열적인 □ stern a. 엄중한, 근엄한 □ sophisticated a. 세련된, 교양 있는

아마도 크레아틴 보충제를 지지하는 사람들 중에서 가장 세간의 이목을 끄는 사람은 프로야구선수인 마크 맥과이어(Mark McGuire)일 것이다.

72
③

□ hamper v. 방해하다, 훼방하다(=obstruct) □ intensify v. 강화하다, 증강하다 □ endow v. 기부하다 □ occupy v. 차지하다

관심이 주말에 참석할 파티에 집중되어 있었기 때문에, 맨디(Mandy)는 수학 시험을 치르는 것이 방해를 받았다.

73
④

□ critical a. 비판적인; 결정적인, 중대한(=crucial) □ ambiguous a. 애매한, 모호한 □ surprising a. 놀라운, 의외의; 불시의 □ conditional a. 조건부의, 잠정적인

그는 중대한 실수를 범하여 시험에 떨어졌다.

74
①

□ inevitable a. 피할[면할] 수 없는, 부득이한, 필연적인 □ pent-up a. 갇힌; 억압된, 울적한 □ erupt v. 분출하다, 폭발하다; 쏟아져 나오다(=go off) □ violence n. 폭력, 난폭; 격노; 격렬(함) □ come off 벗어나다, 떠나다, 실행되다, 실현되다 □ bring into ~와 접촉시키다 □ come about 일어나다, 생기다

울적한 감정이 폭력으로 분출되는 것은 필연적인 것이었다.

75 ③

☐ dubious a. 수상쩍은, 의심스러운; 모호한, 애매한(=doubtful) ☐ delightful a. 매우 기쁜, 즐거운, 쾌적한 ☐ creditable a. 명예가 되는; 칭찬할 만한, 훌륭한 ☐ trustful a. 믿는, 신뢰하는

대중들은 주지사의 세금감면 계획에 대해 매우 반신반의한다.

76 ③

☐ reckless a. 분별없는, 무모한; 염두에 두지 않는(=irresponsible) ☐ unnecessary a. 불필요한, 쓸데없는, 무용의; 무익한 ☐ limited a. 한정된; 좁은, 얼마 안 되는; 편협한 ☐ continuous a. 연속적인, 끊이지 않는, 부단한

제약을 두지 않고 무분별하게 살충제를 사용함으로써 얼마나 많은 피해를 입었는지가 입증되었다.

77 ①

☐ recount v. 자세히 말하다, 이야기하다; 열거하다 ☐ perseverance n. 인내(력), 참을성(=endurance) ☐ skill n. 수완, 솜씨 ☐ generosity n. 관용, 너그러움 ☐ disturbance n. 소란, 방해

남극 탐험에 관한 역사는 인내와 고난에 관한 많은 이야기들을 차례차례 열거해준다.

78 ①

☐ perpetual a. 영속적인; 부단한, 끊임없는 ☐ obstacle n. 장애물, 방해물 ☐ uncouth a. 거친, 세련되지 않은(=crude) ☐ noble a. 귀족의, 고귀한; 고상한 ☐ undaunted a. 굽히지 않는, 대담한 ☐ laudable a. 칭찬할만한

톰(Tom)의 똑똑한 사촌은 그의 조잡한 야망의 행로에서 끊임없이 방해물이 됐었다.

79 ②

☐ fancy v. 공상하다, 상상하다; 생각하다(=imagine) ☐ everything from A to Z 하나에서 열까지 모두 ☐ like v. 좋아하다 ☐ trust v. 신뢰하다; 의지하다 ☐ declare v. 선언하다, 발표하다; 밝히다

너는 나를 미쳤다고 생각한다. 미친 사람들은 아무것도 모른다. 하지만, 나는 하나에서 열까지 모든 것을 다 알고 있다.

80 ②

☐ maxim n. 격언, 금언; 좌우명(=principle) ☐ commander n. 지휘관 ☐ subordinate n. 부하, 하급자 ☐ police n. 경찰, 경찰관 ☐ tradition n. 전통, 관례 ☐ service n. 봉사; 업무

부하가 하는 것이나 하지 못한 것이나 모든 것에 대한 책임은 지휘관에게 있다는 군사상의 원칙이 있다.

81 ②

☐ unique a. 유일(무이)한, 하나밖에 없는; 특별한, 독특한(=peerless) ☐ proven a. 증명된, 입증된 ☐ understated a. 억제된, 절제된 ☐ understandable a. 이해할 수 있는, 알 만한

업튼 비올 싱클레어(Upton Beall Sinclair)는 자신의 소설에서 사회 역사를 재창출해내는 남다른 재주를 보여주었다.

82 ①

☐ gauche a. 솜씨가 서투른, 미숙한, 세련되지 못한(=awkward) ☐ sophisticated a. 재치 있는, 고도로 세련된 ☐ brave a. 용감한, 두려워하지 않는 ☐ painful a. 아픈, 괴로운

다른 사람들의 면전에서 누구나 다 겪는 일반적인 고통의 깃발을 흔드는 (고통을 드러내는) 것은 세련되지 못한 일이다.

83 ①

☐ saturnine a. 음침한, 음울한; 무뚝뚝한(=sullen) ☐ patrician n. 귀족 ☐ plaintive a. 구슬픈, 애처로운 ☐ everyman n. 보통사람; 15세기 영국 도덕극의 제목 및 주인공 ☐ falter v. 비틀거리다; 말을 더듬다 ☐ dissident a. 의견을 달리하는; 반체제의 ☐ sinistral a. 왼쪽의, 좌측의 ☐ foolhardy a. 무모한, 터무니없는

그 연극에서, 휴스턴(Huston)이 맡은 무뚝뚝한 귀족과 제이콥(Jacob)이 맡은 애처로운 평민의 연기는 절대 불안정하지 않았다.

84 ②

☐ vagary n. 별난 생각[행동], 기행; 변덕(=caprice) ☐ good manners 예의범절 ☐ up to date fashion 최신 유행하는 패션 ☐ attitude n. 태도, 마음가짐, 자세, 몸가짐

빨간 드레스만 입겠다는 그녀의 결심은 순전히 괴팍스러운 변덕일 뿐이었다.

85 ④

☐ obtuseness n. 무딤, 둔감함(=callousness) ☐ acuity n. (감각의) 예민함; (바늘 따위의) 예리함 ☐ enmity n. 증오, 적의 ☐ enthusiasm n. 열중, 열광

이러한 둔감함의 많은 부분은 정부의 간섭이 전혀 없는 '자유방임주의' 경제 원칙에 대한 19세기 중반 영국 정치인들의 광신적인 믿음에서 비롯되었다.

86 ③

☐ unsavory a. 불쾌한, 재미없는(=unpleasant) ☐ diverse a. 다양한, 여러 가지의 ☐ confusing a. 혼란스러운 ☐ predictable a. 예측할 수 있는, 예언할 수 없는

나는 그의 이야기의 내용과 접근 방법이 불쾌하다고 생각한다.

87 ②

☐ intermediate a. 중간의; 중급의(=average) ☐ meridian a. 정오의; 전성기의, 정점의 ☐ advanced a. 전진한; 진보적인 ☐ introductory a. 소개의, 서론의, 예비의; 입문의

이 소설은 중급 수준의 영어 실력을 가진 학생들에게는 너무 어렵다.

88 ①

☐ tenet n. 주의, 교리, 원리(=principle) ☐ benefit n. 이익, 이득 ☐ privilege n. 특권, 특전, 특별 취급 ☐ strength n. 힘, 세기; 체력

미개발지의 보호는 수십 년간 미국 환경 운동의 근본 원리였다.

89 ①

☐ intimacy n. 친교, 친밀함(=friendliness) ☐ currency n. (화폐의) 통용, 통화, 화폐; 세상의 평판 ☐ identity n. 일치, 동일성; 개성, 독자성 ☐ hinge on ~여하에 달려 있다, ~에 따라 정해지다 ☐ hired-gun n. 청부살인업자; 난국 타개책[사업 추진]을 위해 고용된 사람 ☐ airbrush v. 에어브러시로 착색하다; (사진을) 에어브러시로 수정하다 ☐ photo shoot (유명인, 패션모델 등에 대한) 사진 촬영 ☐ popularity n. 인기; 대중성, 통속성 ☐ resemblance n. 닮음, 비슷함, 유사함 ☐ similarity n. 유사점, 닮은 점

아티스트의 정체성과 이미지가 돈이 되면 뭐든지 하는 히트곡 가수들, 에어브러시로 수정된 사진, 소셜미디어의 게시물에 좌우되는 때에, 친밀감이 있다는 것은 매우 귀중한 평판이다.

90 ②

☐ evident a. 분명한 ☐ heredity n. 유전(적 특징)(=genetics) ☐ account for 설명하다, 처리하다 ☐ archetype n. 원형(原型); 전형 ☐ milieu n. 주위, 환경 ☐ constitution n. 구성, 구조, 조직

유전만으로나 경험만으로는 개인의 차이를 설명할 수 없다는 것이 이제 명확하다.

91 ①

☐ joyous a. 즐거운, 기쁜 ☐ daybreak n. 새벽 ☐ captivity n. 속박, 감금(=imprisonment) ☐ captivation n. 매혹, 매력 ☐ capturing

n. 포로로 잡기 ☐ capacity n. 용량; 수용력

그것은 그들의 오랜 속박의 밤을 끝내는 즐거운 새벽으로 다가왔다.

92 ①

☐ pandemic a. 전국적[세계적]으로 유행하는(=widespread) ☐ locally spread 지역적으로 퍼진 ☐ quickly spread 빠르게 퍼진 ☐ aerially spread 공기중에 퍼진

공식적으로 기록된 전 세계적으로 유행한 가장 끔찍한 독감은 많은 사람들을 사망케 한 악명 높은 스페인 독감으로 인해 발생된 것이었다.

93 ①

☐ canary in a coal mine 아직 다가오지 않은 위험을 알려주는 경고 ☐ a false report 허위 보고, 유언비어(=canard) ☐ ascription n. 탓으로 함, 기인시킴 ☐ recapitulation n. 요점의 되풀이; 요약 ☐ dispatch n. 파견, 특파, 발송

오늘날 성과가 저조한 펀드들이 속담에 나오는 위험을 알려주는 경고라는 생각은 유언비어인 것 같다.

94 ③

☐ reparation n. 보상, 배상(=quittance) ☐ restraint n. 제지, 금지 ☐ extortion n. 강요; 강탈 ☐ disadvantage n. 불리, 불이익; 손해

패전국은 승리한 군대가 저지른 파괴에 대해서 배상을 요구했다.

95 ④

☐ deter v. 단념시키다; 저지[억지]하다(=prevent) ☐ repay v. (~에게 돈을) 갚다; 보답하다; 보복하다 ☐ criticize v. 비평하다, 비판하다 ☐ anticipate v. 예상하다, 예감하다

어제 이스라엘의 안보 내각은 팔레스타인의 새로운 공격을 막기 위한 여러 조치들을 결정했다.

96 ②

☐ familiarity with ~와 친숙함 ☐ irrational a. 불합리한; 이성이 없는, ☐ ingrained a. 깊이 스며든, 뿌리 깊은(=embedded) ☐ overmaster v. ~을 압도하다; 이기다 ☐ infringe v. 범하다, 위반하다; 침해하다 ☐ intimidated a. 겁먹은, 위축된 ☐ encountered a. 봉착한, 직면한

내가 늑대과에 대해 매우 잘 알고 있음에도 불구하고, 이 상황은 불합리하지만 뿌리 깊은 편견들이 이성과 경험을 완전히 압도하는 상황이었다.

97   ②

☐ ascribe v. (원인·기원 등을) ~에 돌리다, (성질·특징을) ~에 속하는 것으로 생각하다(=attribute) ☐ prescribe v. 처방을 내리다; 규정하다, 지시하다 ☐ conscript v. 징집하다 ☐ contribute v. 기부하다; ~의 한 원인이 되다

그 벽돌이 역사적으로 유명한 건축물인 하드리아누스 방벽(Hadrian's Wall)에 속하는 것이라고 역사학자가 말했을 때, 동료들 중 그의 말을 믿는 사람은 아무도 없었다.

98   ①

☐ comply with 순응하다, 지키다, 준수하다(=obey) ☐ presume v. 추정하다, 상상하다, 가정하다 ☐ improve v. 개량하다, 개선하다; 향상시키다 ☐ agree v. 의견이 맞다, 동의하다

만약 당신이 유치원을 운영하려고 한다면, 당국이 정해놓은 규정을 따라야만 한다.

99   ②

☐ caliber n. 직경; 도량, 재간; 능력, 품질(=quality) ☐ quantity n. 양, 수량 ☐ motivation n. 자극, 동기부여; 열의 ☐ background n. 배경, 바탕

우리의 등급은 우리 전교생의 역량과 우리 교직원들의 헌신, 그리고 우리의 교육 프로그램의 장점을 확고히 나타내는 것이며, 우리 학생들에게 보다 양질의 교육을 제공하려는 우리의 지속적인 헌신을 보여주는 것이다.

100   ①

☐ quilt n. 누비이불 ☐ functional a. 기능의, 기능본위의 ☐ elaborate a. 공들인, 정교한 ☐ parsimonious a. 인색한, 지극히 검소한(=frugal) ☐ scrap n. 작은 조각; 토막 ☐ notorious a. 유명한, 악명 높은 ☐ capricious a. 변덕스러운 ☐ rancorous a. 원한을 품은

가장 초기의 누비이불은 비교적 단순한 디자인으로 만들어졌으며, 정교한 예술적 표현의 수단이라기보다는 기능에 중점을 두고 제작되었다. 매우 검소한 여성들은 대단히 값비싼 재료 조각들을 재활용하여 누비이불을 만들고 수선했다.

MVP 41-45 ACTUAL TEST

01 ②	02 ④	03 ②	04 ②	05 ④	06 ②	07 ①	08 ④	09 ①	10 ③
11 ④	12 ②	13 ③	14 ④	15 ②	16 ①	17 ②	18 ②	19 ①	20 ③
21 ③	22 ②	23 ④	24 ①	25 ③	26 ④	27 ③	28 ④	29 ①	30 ④
31 ④	32 ①	33 ④	34 ①	35 ③	36 ④	37 ④	38 ④	39 ②	40 ③
41 ①	42 ①	43 ③	44 ②	45 ①	46 ③	47 ①	48 ④	49 ②	50 ④
51 ①	52 ①	53 ④	54 ①	55 ②	56 ③	57 ③	58 ②	59 ②	60 ②
61 ③	62 ③	63 ①	64 ③	65 ①	66 ①	67 ①	68 ②	69 ①	70 ①
71 ③	72 ②	73 ①	74 ③	75 ②	76 ②	77 ①	78 ①	79 ②	80 ①
81 ①	82 ③	83 ④	84 ④	85 ②	86 ③	87 ④	88 ④	89 ③	90 ②
91 ①	92 ④	93 ②	94 ①	95 ①	96 ②	97 ④	98 ④	99 ③	100 ④

01   ②

☐ despise v. 경멸하다, 멸시하다, 얕보다(=look down upon) ☐ put up 올리다, 게시하다; (집 등을) 짓다 ☐ keep off 막다, 가까이 못 오게 하다 ☐ get out of ~에서 나오다; (책임, 임무를) 회피하다

그녀는 그가 가난하다는 이유만으로 그를 멸시했다.

02   ④

☐ squander v. 낭비[허비]하다 ☐ patrimony n. 세습 재산; 유전, 전승 (=inheritance) ☐ saving n. (pl.) 저축한 돈, 저금, 예금 ☐ plethora n. 과다, 과잉 ☐ dividend n. 배당(금)

그 남자는 그가 물려받은 재산을 빠르게 낭비했다.

03   ②

☐ jocose a. 우스꽝스러운, 익살맞은(=facetious) ☐ venomous a. 독이 있는, 악의에 찬, 원한을 품은 ☐ intuitive a. 직관에 의한, 직관력 있는 ☐ sober a. 술 취하지 않은; 절제하는; 침착한, 얌전한

그 외판원은 아주 익살맞은 사람이었다.

04   ②

☐ acquire v. 취득하다, 얻다(=obtain) ☐ inquire v. 묻다, 문의하다 ☐ sell v. 팔다; 장사하다 ☐ give up 포기하다, 단념하다

그 회사는 최근에 지분의 5%를 추가로 취득했다.

05   ④

☐ of one's own accord 자발적으로, 자진하여; 저절로(=voluntarily) ☐ enthusiastically ad. 열심히, 열광적으로, 열렬하게 ☐ unwillingly ad. 마지못해서, 본의 아니게 ☐ unhesitatingly ad. 서슴없이, 재빠르게

그는 자발적으로 그 계획에 동의했다.

06   ②

☐ applause n. 박수갈채, 칭찬 ☐ fawning a. 알랑거리는, 아첨하는, 아양 부리는(=flattering) ☐ cater to ~에 영합하다 ☐ denounce v. 비난하다 ☐ consider v. 숙고하다 ☐ summon v. 소환하다, 호출하다

그는 당신이 그에 관해 아첨하고 그의 욕망에 영합하기보다는 그의 업적에 대해 칭찬하는 것을 듣고 싶어 할 것이다.

07   ①

☐ forswear v. 맹세코 그만두다(=abandon) ☐ corporal punishment 체벌 ☐ rote learning 암기 학습 ☐ reform v. 개혁하다 ☐ inflict v. 입히다, 가하다 ☐ endure v. 견디다, 인내하다

그녀는 체벌을 하지 않고 암기 학습보다 창의력을 장려하는 선생님들을 선발했다.

08   ④

☐ negligent a. 태만한, 무관심한; 부주의한(=forgetful) ☐ unpleasant a. 불쾌한, 기분 나쁜, 싫은 ☐ ambitious a. 대망을 품은, 야심 있는 ☐ careful a. 주의 깊은, 신중한; 꼼꼼한

너는 그렇게 소홀히 해놓고 정말 칭찬받을 거라고 생각하느냐?

09   ①

☐ interject v. (말 따위를) 불쑥 끼워 넣다, 던져 넣다, 사이에 끼우다 (=interpolate) ☐ interrupt v. 가로막다; 중단하다, 방해하다 interpret v. 해석하다, 설명하다; 통역하다 ☐ interest v. 흥미를 일으키게 하다

그녀는 오랫동안 말이 없다가 회의가 끝날 때쯤 불쑥 몇 마디 의견을 말했다.

10   ③

☐ convert v. ~을 변환[전환, 변화]시키다; 개종시키다(=change) ☐ transmit v. 보내다; 전하다, 알리다 ☐ represent v. 나타내다, 의미하다; 대표하다 ☐ manufacture v. 제조하다, 제작하다

청각에서 귀의 기능은 음파를 신경자극으로 전환하는 것이다.

11   ④

☐ strive for ~을 얻으려고 노력하다 ☐ derail v. 탈선하다; (계획 따위를) 실패하게 하다(=thwart) ☐ sustainable a. 지속 가능한 ☐ alleviate v. 완화하다, 경감하다 ☐ rationalize v. 합리화하다 ☐ evaluate v. 평가하다, 감정하다

최대 이익을 얻으려고 노력하는 것 또한 지속 가능한 개발을 좌절시킬 수 있다.

12   ②

☐ yearn for 동경하다 ☐ solitude n. 고독; 외로움(=isolation) ☐ strain v. 한계에 이르게 하다, 무리를 주다 ☐ amity n. 우호, 친선 ☐ indolence n. 게으름, 나태 ☐ vanity n. 자만심, 허영심

혼자만의 도피 공간을 원하는 수백만 명의 독신들은 유럽의 도시 주택 시장을 한계에 이르게 하고 있다.

13   ③

☐ contemporary a. 동시대의; 현대의, 당대의 ☐ criticism n. 비평, 비판 ☐ assert v. 단언하다, 역설하다; 강력히 주장하다 ☐ misreading n. 오독(誤讀) ☐ elicit v. (진리·사실 따위를 논리적으로) 이끌어 내다 (=draw) ☐ ban v. 금지하다 ☐ counter v. 반대하다; 거스르다 ☐ grill v. 불에 굽다; 엄하게 심문하다

일부 현대 비평 이론에서는 신뢰할 수 있는 유일한 텍스트(글) 읽기가 오독(誤讀)이며 텍스트(글)의 유일한 존재는 그것이 이끌어내는 일련의 반응들에 의해 주어진다고 주장한다.

14   ④

☐ peanut gallery n. (극장의) 최상층 뒷좌석; 요금이 싼 좌석 ☐ lanky a. 마르고 키 큰, 호리호리한(=lean) ☐ brunette n. 흑갈색 머리의 백인 여성 ☐ swaddle v. (포대기 등으로 단단히) 싸다, 두르다 ☐ pantsuit n. (여성용 슬랙스와 재킷이 한 벌이 된) 슈트 ☐ lope v. 성큼성큼 달리다; 껑충껑충 뛰다 ☐ plump a. 통통한, 포동포동한 ☐ beautiful a. 아름다운, 멋진 ☐ dainty a. 고상한; (기호가) 까다로운

라벤더 슈트, 장갑, 카우보이 모자로 온몸을 둘러싼 삐쩍 마른 흑갈색 머리의 백인 여성인 미스 로데오 아메리카(Miss Rodeo America)가 공연장을 가로질러 성큼성큼 달려간 바로 그때 우리는 맨 뒤 좌석으로 올라갔다.

15   ②

☐ compensate v. ~을 보상하다, 벌충하다(=make up for) ☐ make the best of ~을 최대한 이용하다 ☐ make up with ~와 화해하다 ☐ be punished for ~으로 인해 처벌받다

잃어버린 시간을 벌충하기 위해 너는 서둘러야 할 것이다.

16   ①

☐ feign v. 가장하다, ~인 체하다(=pretend) ☐ convincing a. 설득력 있는, 납득이 가게 하는 ☐ boost v. 후원하다; 촉진하다; 증가시키다 ☐ dodge v. 잽싸게 피하다; 교묘하게 둘러대다 ☐ surrender v. 양도하다; 굴복하다

그녀는 최선을 다했지만, 기분 좋은 체하는 그녀의 노력이 설득력 없다는 것을 알았다.

17   ②

☐ arsenal n. 병기고, 비축 ☐ shore up 지지하다, 버티다(=buttress) ☐ regime n. 정권; 제도, 체제 ☐ discontent n. 불만, 불평 ☐ impoverished a. 가난한 ☐ undermine v. 저해하다, 약화시키다 ☐ maneuver v. 기동시키다 ☐ publicize v. 홍보하다

그는 가난한 대중들 사이에 불만이 날로 증가하고 있음에도 불구하고 그의 나라의 핵무기가 정권을 지탱시켜줄 것이라고 믿는다.

18   ②

☐ mock v. 조롱하다, 비웃다(=ridicule) ☐ mob v. 떼를 지어 습격하다; 쇄도하다 ☐ strike v. 치다, 때리다 ☐ help v. 돕다, 거들다, 원조하다

나쁜 아이들은 눈먼 여자 옆을 지나갈 때 그녀를 놀렸다.

19 ①

☐ by rote 기계적으로, 외워서 ☐ reckon v. 생각하다, 여겨지다 ☐ tiresome a. 성가신, 짜증스러운(=annoying) ☐ clumsy a. 어설픈, 서투른 ☐ trivial a. 사소한, 하찮은 ☐ plausible a. 타당한 것 같은, 이치에 맞는

암기식 학습이 때때로 아무리 필요하더라도 성가신 일로 여겨지는 것은 당연하다.

20 ③

☐ process v. 가공하다; 처리하다, 정리하다(=work on) ☐ try v. 노력하다, 해보다; 시도하다 ☐ provide v. 주다, 공급하다, 지급하다 ☐ raise v. 올리다, 일으키다; 세우다; 높이다

그 시(市)가 신청서 처리를 늦게 하여 많은 노인들이 주택 공급 혜택을 받지 못하고 있다.

21 ③

☐ perpetrate v. (나쁜 짓, 죄를) 행하다, 범하다, 저지르다(=commit) ☐ stop v. 멈추다, 중단하다 ☐ view v. 바라보다; 조사하다 ☐ interfere with ~을 방해하다, 지장을 주다

그 도둑들은 사무실 빌딩에서 강도질을 저지르려 하고 있었다.

22 ②

☐ establish v. 설립하다, 창립하다; 제정하다(=found) ☐ authorize v. 권한을 주다; 위임하다 ☐ construct v. 건설하다, 세우다, 조립하다 ☐ understand v. 이해하다, 알아듣다

뉴욕에 설립된 콜롬비아 대학은 1636년에 설립된 하버드 대학과 함께 미국에서 가장 오래된 대학 중 하나이다.

23 ④

☐ enlighten v. 계몽하다, 교화하다; 가르치다(=instruct) ☐ despise v. 경멸하다, 멸시하다 ☐ simulate v. ~한 체[척]하다, 가장하다 ☐ surpass v. ~을 능가하다, 뛰어나다

교육은 무지한 사람들을 계몽하기 위한 도구로 널리 인정받아왔다.

24 ①

☐ desist v. 그만두다, 단념하다(=cease) ☐ inflate v. 부풀게 하다; 팽창하다 ☐ standardize v. 표준에 맞추다; 표준화하다, 획일화하다 ☐ express v. 표현하다, 표명하다; 나타내다

법원은 그에게 이웃을 괴롭히는 것을 그만두라고 명령했다.

25 ③

☐ sanction n. 재가, 인가; 시인, 찬성(=approval) ☐ opinion n. 의견, 견해; 판단 ☐ coercion n. 강제; 위압; 압제 정치 ☐ insistence n. 주장, 강조, 고집; 강요

모든 사회에서 법적인 결혼은 대개 결혼에 대한 집단의 인정을 나타내는 어떤 종류의 의식에 의해서 행해진다.

26 ④

☐ impute v. ~에게 돌리다, 탓으로 하다, 전가하다(=ascribe) ☐ notify v. 통지하다, 통보하다 ☐ proclaim v. 선언하다, 공포하다 ☐ ascertain v. 확인하다, 조사하다, 알아내다

우리는 친절한 사람들에게 불순한 동기가 있다고 봐서는 안 된다.

27 ③

☐ psychoanalysis n. 정신분석, 정신분석학 ☐ hypothesis n. 가설, 가정; 억측(=assumption) ☐ origin n. 기원, 발단 ☐ paranoia n. 편집병(偏執病), 망상증; (근거 없는) 심한 공포 ☐ unconscious a. 무의식의; 모르는, 깨닫지 못하는 ☐ hyperbole n. 과장, 과장어구 ☐ argument n. 논의 ☐ confluence n. (강 따위의) 합류점; (사람 따위의) 집합, 군중

시그먼트 프로이트(S. Freud)의 정신분석은 어른들의 편집증의 기원을 어린 시절에 무의식이 억압됐던 경험에서 찾을 수 있을지도 모른다는 가설에서 시작한다.

28 ④

☐ sepulchral a. 무덤 같은, 음울한; (음성이) 음침한(=dismal) ☐ husky a. 약간 쉰 듯한 ☐ fierce a. 사나운, 험악한 ☐ inaudible a. 들리지 않는, 알아들을 수 없는

그녀가 응접실을 나서자마자 드러커(Drukker) 부인은 테이블에 기대어 마컴(Markham)을 향해 음산한 목소리로 소곤거렸다.

29 ①

☐ snatch v. 잡아[낚아]채다, 움켜잡다 ☐ defiantly ad. 반항적으로, 도전적으로(=boldly) ☐ daintily ad. 우아하게; 섬세하게; 까다롭게 ☐ hastily ad. 급히, 서둘러서 ☐ precisely ad. 바로, 꼭, 정확히

단 5초가 남아있는 상황에서, 그 농구 스타는 볼을 가로채서 그것을 바스켓에 과감히 집어넣었다.

30 ④

☐ carving n. 조각(술) ☐ commitment n. 실행, 수행; 공약, 서약 ☐ medium n. 수단, 방편; 매개물(=material) ☐ aesthetic a. 미(美)의,

미학의; 심미안이 있는 ☐ component n. 구성 요소, 성분 ☐ aspect n. 양상, 외관; 관점; 용모 ☐ subject n. 주제; 학과, 과목; 대상

직접 조각하는 것의 중요한 일면은 예술가가 매체(재료)의 매력적인 미적 특성과 질감 특성을 드러나게 작업하면서 그 매체의 성질을 나타내 보이려 애쓴다는 것이다.

31   ④

☐ densely ad. 조밀하게, 빽빽하게, 짙게(=heavily) ☐ sloppily ad. 단정치 못하게; 적당히 얼버무려 ☐ sparsely ad. 드문드문, 성기게 ☐ improperly ad. 부적당하게; 온당치 못하게

인구 밀도가 높은 지역은 사람들이 살기가 힘들다.

32   ①

☐ incisive a. (사물 인식 능력이) 예리한, 날카로운(=sharp) ☐ derelict a. 버려진 ☐ empirical a. 경험에 의거한, 실증적인 ☐ incessant a. 끊임없는

그 사회복지사의 날카로운 관찰로 그 소녀의 문제점이 분명하게 드러났다.

33   ④

☐ aggrieved a. 권리를 침해당한, 학대받은(=mistreated) ☐ laid-off a. 일시 해고된 ☐ retire v. 은퇴하다, 퇴직하다; 철수하다 ☐ mourn v. 애도하다, 슬퍼하다

배심원단은 권리를 침해당한 그 회사의 전 직원들에게 천만 달러를 배상하도록 했다.

34   ①

☐ hapless a. 불운한, 불행한(=unlucky) ☐ patient a. 인내심이 강한, 끈기 있는 ☐ weak a. 약한, 무력한 ☐ apparent a. 명백한; (눈에) 또렷한

참가자 가운데 약 60%가 그들이 불행한 피해자에게 잠재적으로 치명적인 충격이 될 거라고 생각한 것을 전달할 준비가 돼 있었다.

35   ③

☐ sever v. 절단하다, 끊다, 자르다, 분리하다(=dissolve) ☐ improve v. 개량하다, 개선하다; 이용하다 ☐ proclaim v. 포고하다, 선언하다 ☐ embellish v. 아름답게 꾸미다; 윤색하다

존 애덤스(John Adams)는 영국 왕과의 개인적인 유대관계를 끊으려고 했다.

36   ④

☐ mission-critical a. (조직의) 임무 수행에 필수적인 ☐ call for ~을 필요로 하다 ☐ acumen n. (일에 대한) 감각, 통찰력(=insight) ☐ eminence n. 명성 ☐ ethics n. 도덕, 윤리 ☐ activity n. 활동; 활기, 활발

미국에서 (조직의) 임무 수행에 필수적인 업무의 대부분은 정치적인 통찰력보다 리더십과 인격을 요구한다.

37   ④

☐ breakthrough n. 돌파, 돌파구; 큰 발전(=advance) ☐ panacea n. 만병통치약 ☐ device n. 장치, 고안품; 고안, 방책 ☐ sample n. 견본, 샘플, 시료

의사들은 유방암 치료에 있어 수술 대신에 약물을 사용하여 큰 발전을 이루어냈다고 믿고 있다.

38   ④

☐ adamant a. 요지부동의, 단호한(=unyielding) ☐ flexible a. 융통성 있는; 구부릴 수 있는 ☐ indecisive a. 결단성 없는, 우유부단한 ☐ pessimistic a. 비관적인, 염세적인

그는 나의 있는 그대로의 모습과 꾸며야 할 모습에 대해 매우 단호했다.

39   ②

☐ flatboat n. 평저선(平底船) (주로 얕은 물에 씀) ☐ transport v. 수송하다, 운반하다(=ferry) ☐ load v. (짐을) 싣다, 적재하다 ☐ pursue v. 쫓다, 추격하다; 추구하다 ☐ inspect v. 면밀하게 살피다, 검사하다

평저선(平底船)들은 미국과 캐나다 사이의 오대호에서 자동차를 수송한다.

40   ③

☐ coarse a. (사람·태도 등이) 야비한, 천한; 상스러운(=uncouth) ☐ vulgar a. 저속한, 상스러운 ☐ unimportant a. 중요하지 않은, 하찮은 ☐ unrealistic a. 비현실적인 ☐ unguarded a. 부주의한, 방심한

그녀는 일용직 노동자들의 웃음과 시끌벅적한 게임을 추잡하고 상당히 천박하다고 생각했다.

41   ①

☐ nettle v. 초조하게 하다, 화나게 하다(=vex) ☐ endue v. (능력, 재능 등을) 부여하다, 주다 ☐ palpate v. ~을 만져보다; <의학> 촉진(觸診)하다 ☐ ascertain v. 확인하다; 확정하다

찰스(Charles)는 빈정거리는 발언으로 의장을 짜증나게 했다.

42 ①

☐ abuse v. 남용하다; 학대하다 ☐ undermine v. 밑을 파헤치다; 손상시키다(=damage) ☐ resource n. 자원, 자산 ☐ indifference n. 무관심, 냉담 ☐ back v. 후원하다, 지지하다; 뒷받침하다 ☐ reward v. 보상[보답]하다 ☐ delay v. 연기하다

중소기업들이 대형 거래처들의 횡포에 피해 받지 않도록 보호하려는 노력이 자원 부족과 관료들의 무관심에 의해 손상되고 있다.

43 ③

☐ parking fine 주차 위반 벌금 ☐ impound v. 압수하다, 몰수하다(=confiscate) ☐ confine v. 제한하다, 국한시키다 ☐ reproach v. 비난하다, 책망하다 ☐ lubricate v. 윤활유를 바르다

내가 지난해에 주차위반 벌금을 전혀 내지 않아서, 이제 당국에서는 내 차를 압수하려 하고 있다.

44 ②

☐ compassion n. 동정(심), 연민(=sympathy) ☐ condolence n. 애도; 애도의 말 ☐ composure n. 평정, 침착 ☐ digression n. 지엽으로 흐름, 탈선

기사에 의하면 달라이 라마(Dalai Lama)는 2008년 1월 18일 인도 아마다바드 인도 경영대학원(IIM-A)에서 윤리와 상업에 대해 연설하면서 다른 사람들을 대하는 데 동정심을 강조했다.

45 ①

☐ remarkable a. 주목할 만한, 현저한, 남다른 ☐ save prep. ~을 제외하고, ~이외에 ☐ blazing a. 불타는; 대단한 ☐ chagrin n. 원통함, 분함, 유감(=embarrassment) ☐ discontent n. 불만, 불평 ☐ feature n. 용모; 특징, 특색 ☐ pride n. 자랑, 자존심; 자만심 ☐ satisfaction n. 만족(감); (욕구 등의) 충족 distraction n. 마음의 혼란; 기분전환, 오락

그 사람에게 주목할 만한 점은 단지 불타는 듯한 붉은 머리카락과 얼굴 이목구비에 나타난 극도의 유감과 불만의 표정이었다.

46 ③

☐ urban a. 도시의, 도회지에 사는; 도시풍의(=of a town or city) ☐ lacking self-confidence 자신감이 부족한 ☐ in the lowest position 가장 낮은 위치에 ☐ ready to quarrel or attack 싸우거나 공격할 준비가 된

많은 도시의 흑인들은 여전히 우울하리만치 형편없는 환경에서 산다.

47 ①

☐ enmity n. 증오, 적의(=repugnance) ☐ empathy n. 감정이입 ☐ sympathy n. 동정; 호의, 찬성 ☐ antipodes n. 대척지; 정반대의 사물

민주주의를 찬미하는 사람들은 전체주의에 대해 반감을 가지고 있다.

48 ②

☐ incursion n. (갑작스러운) 침입, 침략; 습격(=assault) ☐ assistance n. 원조, 보조 ☐ withdrawal n. 물러남, 퇴출; 철수 ☐ reconstruction n. 재건, 복구, 부흥

세계 200개 나라의 역사를 연구하면서, 그는 영국의 침략을 겪지 않았던 나라들을 찾으려고 했다.

49 ②

☐ pertinent a. 타당한, 적절한(=apt) ☐ obliging a. 도와주는, 친절한 ☐ veracious a. 진실을 말하는, 정직한 ☐ illusory a. (실제가 아니라) 환상에 불과한

적절한 질문은 어떻게 일을 올바르게 하느냐가 아니라 해야 할 올바른 일을 어떻게 찾느냐이다.

50 ④

☐ recant v. (신앙, 주장을) 바꾸다, 취소하다, 철회하다(=withdraw) ☐ criticize v. 비평하다, 비판하다, 비난하다 ☐ reinforce v. 강화하다, 보강하다 ☐ repeat v. 되풀이하다, 반복하다

두 선수에 대한 강간죄 고소가 취하되자 그 사건의 보도 내용에 대한 의문점들이 제기되었다.

51 ①

☐ belabor v. 장황하게 말하다(=elaborate) ☐ summarize v. 요약하다, 간략하게 말하다 ☐ put off 미루다, 연기하다 ☐ refrain v. 그만두다, 삼가다

그 강연자는 자신의 강연에서 모든 사항들을 장황하게 말했기 때문에, 기진맥진한 청중들은 그가 말해야 했던 모든 것에 흥미를 잃었다.

52 ①

☐ disband v. 해체하다, 해산하다(=dissolve) ☐ banter v. 희롱하다, 농담하다 ☐ inspect v. 조사하다, 검사하다 ☐ convene v. 소집하다; 소환하다

외국에서 들리는 소문에 따르면 그 지도자는 대통령 직접 통치를 선언하고 의회를 해산할지도 모른다고 한다.

53   ④

☐ berate v. 질책하다, 호되게 꾸짖다(=chide) ☐ evolutionist n. 진화론자 ☐ overindulgence n. 탐닉; 지나친 방임 ☐ advocate v. 옹호하다, 지지하다 ☐ adore v. 존경하다, 숭배하다 ☐ charm v. 매혹하다, 마음을 빼앗다

아이러니하게도, 전문적인 과학자들은 라마르크(Lamarck)와 체임버스(Chambers) 같은 초기 진화론자들이 상상력에 지나치게 빠져 있었다고 몹시 비난했다.

54   ①

☐ visible a. 눈에 보이는, 볼 수 있는; 명백한(=discernible) ☐ descend v. 내리다, 내려가다; 경사지다; 아래로 내리 뻗다 ☐ coincident a. 일치하는, 부합하는; 동시에 일어나는 ☐ grotesque a. 괴상한, 괴기한; 우스꽝스러운 ☐ gallant a. 용감한, 씩씩한

앞에 있는 차들은 보이지 않았다. 그 차들이 도로에까지 드리운 짙은 구름 때문에 숨겨져 있었기 때문이다.

55   ②

☐ terrain n. 지대, 지역; 영역, 분야 ☐ dean n. 학장 ☐ preside v. 통할하다, 주재하다 ☐ din n. 소음, 시끄러운 소리(=noise) ☐ place n. 장소, 곳; 공간 ☐ rule n. 규칙, 규정 ☐ start n. 출발; 선발(권), 우선(권)

학장인 존 왓슨(John Watson)만큼 구내식당의 문화적, 인종적인 분포 구성을 잘 아는 사람은 거의 없는데, 그는 점심시간 때의 소란을 처리한다.

56   ③

☐ uncanny a. 초인적인, 엄청난; 신비스러운(=extraordinary) ☐ beautiful a. 아름다운, 고운, 예쁜 ☐ intelligent a. 지적인, 지성을 갖춘, 지능이 있는 ☐ natural a. 자연의, 타고난, 자연스러운

그는 사람의 영적인 영역을 꿰뚫어 보는 초인적인 힘을 지닌 작가이다.

57   ③

☐ disturbing a. 불안하게 하는, 충격적인, 불온한 ☐ morose a. 시무룩한, 뚱한(=dour) ☐ self-pity n. 자기 연민 ☐ egoistic a. 이기적인 ☐ solitary a. 고독한, 외로운 ☐ impulsive a. 충동적인

대통령이 음주하는 것 중 가장 불안하게 보이는 사진은 리처드 닉슨(Richard Nixon)이 보여주는데, 그는 시무룩한 자기 연민에 빠지는 경향이 있는 사람이다.

58   ②

☐ complaisant a. 공손한, 순종적인, 고분고분한(=submissive) ☐ sluggish a. 둔한, 느린, 부진한 ☐ belligerent a. 호전적인, 도발적인 ☐ truthful a. 진실의, 정직한

그 기사는 고분고분한 태도로 왕의 명령에 복종했다.

59   ②

☐ meanness n. 하찮음; 비열, 쩨쩨함 ☐ generosity n. 관대, 관용, 아량 ☐ prudence n. 신중, 세심, 사려분별 ☐ boldness n. 대담함(=audacity) ☐ timidity n. 겁 많음, 소심, 수줍음 ☐ admiration n. 감탄, 존경 ☐ seclusion n. 격리; 은퇴, 은둔 ☐ cleanness n. 깨끗함, 청결; 결백

야비함과 관대함, 신중함과 대담성, 담력과 소심함, 연약함과 강함, 이 모든 점을 사람들은 본성에 따라 카드놀이에서 보여준다.

60   ②

☐ cement v. 시멘트로 바르다[굳게 하다]; 단단히 연결하다, 견고하게 하다(=consolidate) ☐ alliance n. 동맹, 연합 ☐ delegate v. 위임하다, 선정하다 ☐ scrutinize v. 세심히 살피다, 면밀히 조사하다 ☐ renounce v. 포기[단념]하다

그 대통령의 방문은 두 나라의 동맹을 강화시키기 위한 것이었다.

61   ③

☐ reconnoiter v. 답사하다; 정찰하다(=scout) ☐ retain v. 유지[보유]하다 ☐ subside v. 가라앉다, 진정되다 ☐ allocate v. 할당하다

소규모의 군인들이 공격을 감행하기 전 그 지역을 정찰했다.

62   ③

☐ homogenized a. 동질화된, 균질화한(=identical) ☐ artificial a. 인위적인, 인공의 ☐ new-fashioned a. 신식의, 새로운 유행의 ☐ mechanical a. 기계적인; 기계에 의한

세계는 점점 더 동질화되어가고 옛 문화들은 사라져가기 때문에 몇몇 사람들은 그들의 과거에 대한 지식을 유지하려고 노력한다.

63   ①

☐ mutual trust 상호 신뢰 ☐ pivotal a. 중심이 되는, 중추적인(=crucial) ☐ alliance n. 동맹, 연합 ☐ elementary a. 초보의; 기본적인 ☐ perspicuous a. (언어·문제 등이) 명쾌한, 명료한 ☐ vulnerable a. 취약한, 연약한

그의 발언은 동맹에서 가장 중추적인 요소인 상호 신뢰를 완전히 뒤흔들어 놓는다.

64 ③

☐ ambassador n. 대사 ☐ innocuous a. 무해한, 위험하지 않은; 악의 없는(=harmless) ☐ diplomatic a. 외교의, 외교상의 ☐ dispute n. 토론; 논쟁 ☐ vague a. 희미한; 모호한, 애매한 ☐ gracious a. 친절한, 정중한; 우아한 ☐ incompetent a. 무능한, 쓸모없는; 부적당한

그 대사의 발언은 대체로 악의 없는 내용이었지만, 그것은 양국 간에 외교적 논쟁을 불러일으켰다.

65 ①

☐ sabotage n. 태업; 공장 설비의 파괴, 생산 방해(=subversion) ☐ heinousness n. 가증스러움, 극악함 ☐ subterfuge n. 구실, 핑계; 속임수 ☐ infiltration n. 침입, 침투, 스며듦

전시에는 직접적인 폭력뿐만 아니라 파괴 행위에 대한 예방조치를 취해야 한다.

66 ③

☐ drought n. 가뭄 ☐ harbinger n. 선구자; 전조(前兆)(=precursor) ☐ mishap n. 불운한 일, 재난 ☐ hoax n. 짓궂은 장난; 날조 ☐ repercussion n. 영향, 반향

캘리포니아 주의 가뭄은 인구와 산업이 성장하는 세계 어디에서나 발생할 수 있는 일들의 전조이다.

67 ①

☐ meek a. 순한, 온순한; 패기 없는(=humble) ☐ aggressive a. 공격적인, 침략적인, 적극적인 ☐ endearing a. 사람의 마음을 끄는, 사랑스러운 ☐ patient a. 인내심 있는, 끈기 있는, 느긋한

그는 너무 온순한 사람이기 때문에 그 부탁에 '아니오(No)'라고 말할 수 없었다.

68 ②

☐ reclusive a. 세상을 버린; 은둔한; 쓸쓸한, 적막한(=hermitic) ☐ anonymous a. 작자[저자] 불명의 ☐ ardent a. 열렬한, 열정적인 ☐ pretentious a. 자부하는, 자만하는

은둔 생활을 하는 작가는 실내에서 너무 많은 시간을 보내면 창백해질 수 있을 것이다.

69 ②

☐ elusive a. (교묘히) 피하는, 잘 잡히지 않는; 파악하기 어려운(=tricky) ☐ tremendous a. 엄청난; 굉장한, 대단한 ☐ insignificant a. 무의미한, 하찮은, 사소한 ☐ scarce a. 부족한, 희귀한

호주에서 발견되는 전갈에는 세 종류가 있는데, 가장 치명적인 것이 가장 잡기 어렵다.

70 ④

☐ gratitude n. 감사, 감사하는 마음, 사의(=appreciation) ☐ asset n. 자산; 재산 ☐ contribution n. 기부, 공헌, 기여 ☐ scarcity n. 부족, 결핍; 기근

그는 병원에서 그러한 훌륭한 보살핌을 받은 것에 대하여 많은 기부금을 내는 것으로 감사의 마음을 표시했다.

71 ③

☐ tender a. 상냥한, 다정한 ☐ affectionate a. 애정이 깊은; 다정한 ☐ petulant a. 성마른, 화를 잘 내는(=peevish) ☐ judgemental a. 비판을 잘하는 ☐ decided a. 결정적인; 단호한; 명확한 ☐ steadfast a. 확고부동한, 고정된; 불변의 ☐ predictable a. 예언할 수 있는, 예상할 수 있는

상냥하고 다정하다가도 화를 잘 내고 비판을 해대는 연인은 사랑과 헌신의 감정뿐만 아니라 좌절과 분노의 감정도 불러일으킨다.

72 ②

☐ exheredate v. 상속권을 박탈하다 ☐ rage n. 격렬한 분노, 격노(=fury) ☐ qualification n. 자격; 단서; 조건 ☐ eternity n. 영원, 영겁 ☐ impulse n. 충동

자신의 딸이 그 사내와 결혼하자 그는 화가 나서 딸의 상속권을 박탈했다.

73 ①

☐ impregnable a. 난공불락의, 견고한; 확고한(=unconquerable) ☐ implicit a. 은연중의, 함축적인, 암시적인 ☐ fragile a. 망가지기 쉬운, 허약한 ☐ phenomenal a. 놀라운, 경이적인, 굉장한

계속해서 군대는 헛되이 그 요새를 공격했지만, 그 요새가 난공불락이라는 결론에 이르렀다.

74 ③

☐ conglomeration n. 모임; 복합체(=combination) ☐ organization n. 단체, 조직; 조직화된 것 ☐ symmetry n. 좌우대칭, 균형 ☐ illustration n. 삽화, 도해; 설명

미국의 재즈는 미국과 아프리카의 민속 음악, 유럽의 고전 음악, 그리고 기독교의 찬송가와 같은 다양한 자료에서 차용된 소리들의 복합체이다.

75 ②

☐ servile a. 노예의; 노예 근성의; 비굴한(=fawning) ☐ preposterous a. 말도 안 되는, 터무니없는 ☐ prodigal a. 낭비하는 ☐ reticent a. 말을 잘 안 하는, 말이 없는

비굴한 사람들은 생계를 꾸리기 위해 권위에 복종함으로써 그들 자신을 낮추는 경향이 있다.

76 ②

☐ placid a. 고요한; 침착한(=tranquil) ☐ perturbed a. 교란된; 불안한 ☐ frozen a. 얼어버린, 동결된 ☐ clean a. 깨끗한, 청결한

고요한 호수의 잔잔한 표면이 주변의 산들을 비추어주었다.

77 ①

☐ wary of ~를 조심[경계]하는(=cautious of) ☐ intervention n. 개입, 간섭 ☐ familiar with ~에 익숙한 ☐ insensitive to ~에 둔감한 ☐ displeased with ~에 불쾌한

사람들은 이집트인들이 특히 군사개입을 경계할 것으로 예상했을지도 모른다.

78 ①

☐ fight back 싸워서 저지하다, 저항[반격]하다 ☐ retreat v. 물러가다, 퇴각하다, 후퇴하다 ☐ complete v. 완료하다, 완성하다, 끝마치다 ☐ objective n. 목적, 목표(=mission) ☐ invasion n. 침입, 침공, 침략; 침범 ☐ conquest n. 정복, 극복 ☐ conflict n. 투쟁, 전투, 싸움, 분쟁

그들은 저항을 받고 퇴각하였지만, 그들의 목적을 가까스로 완수했다.

79 ②

☐ maim v. 불구로 만들다(=disable) ☐ kill v. 죽이다, 살해하다 ☐ cure v. 낫게 하다, 치유하다 ☐ disrupt v. 방해하다, 지장을 주다

과학 지식은 인간의 건강 회복을 도울 수 있지만, 인간을 불구로 만드는 데 사용될 수도 있다.

80 ①

☐ malign a. 해로운, 악의 있는; 악성의(=evil) ☐ benign a. 인자한, 친절한; 상서로운, 길조의 ☐ flattering a. 아첨하는; 알랑거리는 ☐ exaggerated a. 과장된, 떠벌린

이것이 그의 연설이 온갖 악평을 면할 수 없게 만든다.

81 ①

☐ onset n. 개시, 시작(=beginning) ☐ dramatic a. 극적인, 인상적인 ☐ timeless a. 영원한; 시대를 초월한 ☐ decline n. 감소, 하락 ☐ transformation n. 변화, 변환 ☐ expansion n. 확장, 팽창

갑작스러운 인터넷 문화의 시작은 인간이 된다는 것이 무엇을 의미하는지에 관한 영원한 질문에 있어서 매우 극적인 전환점이다.

82 ③

☐ spoil v. 망치다, 버려 놓다 ☐ pamper v. 지나치게 소중히[애지중지] 하다(=coddle) ☐ discipline v. 징계하다, 훈육하다 ☐ overlook v. 못 보고 넘어가다, 간과하다 ☐ scold v. 야단치다, 꾸짖다

부모가 자녀들을 지나치게 애지중지하면 아이들은 버릇이 없어진다.

83 ④

☐ ruin v. 망치다, 엉망으로 만들다(=vilify) ☐ candidate n. 후보자 ☐ spread rumors 헛소문을 퍼뜨리다 ☐ induce v. 설득하다; 초래하다 ☐ transact v. 거래하다 ☐ transcribe v. 베끼다, 복사[등사]하다

그 후보의 정적들은 그의 과거에 대해 헛소문을 퍼뜨림으로써 그의 명성을 망치려 했다.

84 ④

☐ decisiveness n. 결정적임, 단호함 ☐ even-handed a. 공평무사한, 공명정대한(=impartial) ☐ devotee n. 헌신적인 추종자, 열성적인 애호가 ☐ detractor n. 중상자, 명예 훼손자 ☐ ambidextrous a. 양손잡이의 ☐ participatory a. 참여의 ☐ pretentious a. 가식적인

그의 결단력과 공명정대한 접근방식이 비방하는 사람들보다 훨씬 더 많은 지지자를 그가 얻게 했다.

85 ②

☐ adverse a. 거스르는, 반대의; 불리한(=unfavorable) ☐ authentic a. 진정한, 진짜의; 믿을 만한 ☐ averse a. 싫어하는, 반대하는 ☐ apparent a. 또렷한, 명백한; 외관의, 겉모양의

비행기는 기상 악화 때문에 지연되었다.

86 ③

☐ feckless a. 연약한, 무기력한(=ineffective) ☐ operant a. 움직이는, 작동하는 ☐ dexterous a. 솜씨 좋은, 교묘한, 능란한 ☐ inexpensive a. 비용이 들지 않는, 값싼

화이트삭스는 놀라우리만치 부진한 양키스와의 시합 후 거칠 것 없이 순항하면서 그리고 맹렬하지만 결국 무기력한 클리블랜드 인디언스의 추격을 받아 가면서 우승을 향해 바짝 다가가고 있다.

87 ④

☐ replace v. 되돌리다; 대신하다, 대체하다 ☐ launch v. (사업 등을) 시작하다; (공격을) 가하다, 개시하다 ☐ lethal a. 죽음을 가져오는, 치명적인(=deadly) ☐ crackdown n. (갑작스러운) 타격; 강경 조처; (경찰의) 단속, 탄압 ☐ irritable a. 성미가 급한, 성마른 ☐ legal a. 법률의; 합법적인, 적법한 ☐ lawful a. 합법의, 적법한

모하메드 무르시(Mohamed Morsi)를 대신하여 들어선 군사정부는 그의 이슬람교 지지자들과 그 외 다른 정적(政敵)들에 대해 치명적인 탄압을 가했다.

88 ④

☐ sallow a. 창백한, 혈색이 나쁜(=pasty) ☐ high forehead 넓은 이마 ☐ deep-set a. (눈이) 움푹 들어간 ☐ bereft a. 빼앗긴, 잃은 ☐ indiscreet a. 무분별한, 지각 없는 ☐ unassuming a. 겸손한

그는 대머리에 작고 움푹 들어간 눈에 다소 혈색이 안 좋았다.

89 ③

☐ restless a. 침착하지 못한, 불안한(=uneasy) ☐ slack v. 완화하다; 느슨해지다 ☐ languid a. 힘없는[느릿느릿한], 나른한 ☐ exuberant a. 활기[생동감] 넘치는

면접 대기실에서 내 차례를 기다리고 있으니 마음이 불안해서 다리가 계속 떨렸다.

90 ②

☐ menial a. 하인의, 낮은, 비천한; 비굴한(=lowly) ☐ significant a. 중요한, 소중한; 의미 있는 ☐ rough a. 거친; 다듬어지지 않은; 대강의 ☐ remedial a. 치료의, 교정의

많은 이민자들은 미국에 처음 도착했을 때 허드렛일에 종사하도록 강요받았다.

91 ①

☐ perpetual a. 영구의, 영속하는; 끊임없는(=continual) ☐ practical a. 실제의; 실용적인 ☐ credible a. 믿을[신뢰할] 수 있는, 확실한 ☐ ingenuous a. 솔직한, 성실한; 순진한, 꾸밈없는

끊임없는 유혹이 없다면 인간의 정신은 절대 단련되고 강화되지 못할 것이다.

92 ④

☐ perceive v. 지각하다, 인지하다; 이해하다(=understand) ☐ affect v. 영향을 미치다, 작용하다 ☐ betray v. 배반하다; 누설하다 ☐ grumble v. 불평하다, 투덜거리다

그 학생들은 곤충들이 세상을 어떻게 인지하는지를 연구하려고 한다.

93 ②

☐ soggy a. 축축한, 눅눅한(=soaked) ☐ impetuous a. 격렬한, 맹렬한 ☐ desiccated a. 건조된; 무기력한, 생기를 잃은 ☐ limpid a. 맑은, 투명한; 명쾌한

폭풍이 부는 동안 창문이 열려 있었고, 내 책상 위에 있는 종이들이 흠뻑 젖은 상태로 어지럽혀있었다.

94 ①

☐ lenient a. 너그러운; 인자한, 관대한(=generous) ☐ ridiculous a. 웃기는; 터무니없는 ☐ harsh a. 거친; 가혹한, 냉혹한 ☐ unexpectant a. 기대하지 않는

많은 사람들은 그 무례한 학생에 대한 처벌이 너무 관대했다고 생각했다.

95 ①

☐ facility n. 시설; 능력(=ability) ☐ convenience n. 편리, 편의 ☐ imagination n. 상상력, 상상, 창의력 ☐ ease n. 쉬움, 용이함

연관이 전혀 없는 것들을 관련지어 생각하는 능력으로 인해 천재들은 다른 사람들이 놓친 것들을 볼 수 있다.

96 ②

☐ dexterous a. 손재주가 있는, 솜씨 좋은; 민첩한, 빈틈없는(=nimble) ☐ sluggish a. 게으른, 나태한; 느린, 굼뜬 ☐ wary a. 조심성 있는; 신중한 ☐ inept a. 부적당한, 부적절한; 서투른; 무능한

그 마술사는 너무 재빨라서 그가 묘기를 부릴 때 우리는 그 동작을 (눈으로) 따라갈 수 없었다.

97 ④

☐ in full accord 만장일치의(=unanimous) ☐ approval n. 승인; 인가, 재가 ☐ dissertation n. 학위 논문 ☐ indecisive a. 우유부단한, 결단력이 없는 ☐ shrewd a. 영리한; 빈틈없는 ☐ vulnerable a. 비난 받기 쉬운, 약점이 있는

학사학위 심의위원회는 그들의 학위 논문 승인에 있어서 반드시 만장일치가 되어야 한다.

98 ④

☐ confine v. 한정하다, 제한하다; 가두다(=restrict) ☐ professed a. 공언한, 공공연한; 자칭의 ☐ beggar n. 거지; 가난뱅이 ☐ expand v. 넓히다; 확장하다 ☐ entitle v. 칭하다; 권리를 주다 ☐ incline v. ~의 경향이 생기다; 기울다

그의 의도는 자칭 걸인들의 자녀들만을 부양하는 것에 국한된 것이 전혀 아니다.

99 ③

☐ indomitable a. 굴하지 않는, 불굴의(=invincible) ☐ confront v. (문제나 곤란한 상황에) 맞서다, 직면하다 ☐ racial segregation 인종차별 ☐ inequity n. 불공평 ☐ ingenuous a. 솔직한, 꾸밈없는; 순진한, 천진난만한 ☐ invidious a. 비위에 거슬리는, 불쾌한 ☐ ingenious a. 교묘한, 독창적인, 정교한

매리 트래버스(Mary Travers)는 카리스마가 강하고, 굴하지 않고, 아름답기로 유명했는데, 그 이유는 그녀가 사람들을 고무시켜 인종차별에 대항하고, 베트남에서 부도덕한 전쟁을 중지하고, 남녀 사이의 많은 역사적인 불평등을 바로잡도록 했기 때문이다.

100 ④

☐ straightforward a. 솔직한 ☐ impenetrable a. 꿰뚫을 수 없는; 헤아릴 수 없는, 불가해한(=incomprehensible) ☐ threaten v. 위협하다; (재해·위험 따위의) 징후를 보이다 ☐ profound a. 심오한, 심원한 ☐ assumption n. 가정, 억측; 가설 ☐ debonair a. 쾌활한; 명랑한 ☐ irksome a. 넌더리나는; 지루한 ☐ congenital a. 타고난, 선천적인

"흑인들은 남자답게 대우받기를 원한다." 이것은 단 7개의 단어로 이루어진 매우 솔직한 말이다. 칸트, 헤겔, 셰익스피어, 마르크스, 프로이트, 그리고 성경을 통달한 사람들은 이 말을 전혀 이해할 수 없다. 그 생각은 심오하고 거의 의식하지 못하는 가정들을 위협하는 것으로 보인다.

01 ③	02 ④	03 ①	04 ③	05 ③	06 ②	07 ①	08 ③	09 ③	10 ②
11 ④	12 ②	13 ③	14 ①	15 ①	16 ②	17 ②	18 ①	19 ③	20 ②
21 ②	22 ②	23 ③	24 ②	25 ①	26 ④	27 ④	28 ①	29 ②	30 ②
31 ③	32 ③	33 ③	34 ④	35 ④	36 ④	37 ②	38 ①	39 ②	40 ①
41 ①	42 ③	43 ③	44 ③	45 ③	46 ④	47 ①	48 ①	49 ②	50 ②
51 ④	52 ④	53 ③	54 ④	55 ①	56 ①	57 ①	58 ①	59 ④	60 ④
61 ①	62 ③	63 ③	64 ①	65 ②	66 ③	67 ①	68 ④	69 ④	70 ④
71 ②	72 ①	73 ③	74 ②	75 ④	76 ④	77 ①	78 ②	79 ①	80 ①
81 ①	82 ③	83 ③	84 ①	85 ④	86 ②	87 ③	88 ④	89 ④	90 ③
91 ②	92 ②	93 ④	94 ①	95 ④	96 ③	97 ④	98 ①	99 ④	100 ③

01 ③

☐ lewd a. 추잡한; 외설스러운; 호색의(=obscene) ☐ prim a. 꼼꼼한, 까다로운; (특히 여자가) 새침 떠는 ☐ decent a. 버젓한, 알맞은; 예의 바른 ☐ vigorous a. 정력적인, 강건한, 원기 왕성한

그 영화는 일부 사람들로부터 외설적이라고 간주되었다.

02 ④

☐ hatred n. 증오[혐오](감)(=contempt) ☐ eagerness n. 열의, 열심 ☐ obsession n. 강박관념, 망상 ☐ charm n. 매력

그가 잔뜩 증오에 찬 눈길로 나를 보았다.

03 ①

☐ empower v. ~에게 권한을 부여하다, 자격을 부여하다(=authorize) ☐ negotiate v. 협상[협의]하다 ☐ order v. 명령하다; 주문하다; 배열하다 ☐ motivate v. 동기를 주다, 자극하다, 유발하다 ☐ forbid v. 금하다, 허락하지 않다; 방해하다

주(州) 정부는 그에게 그 계약을 협상할 권한을 부여했다.

04 ③

☐ manifest v. 명백히 하다, 명시하다; 표명하다(=show) ☐ deny v. 부인하다, 부정하다; 거절하다 ☐ hide v. 숨기다; 가리다; 감추다 ☐ emphasize v. 강조하다; 역설하다

왕은 호탕한 웃음으로 자신의 기쁨을 드러냈다.

05 ③

☐ smack v. 세게 때리다, 탁 소리가 나게 치다(=bash) ☐ tear v. 찢다, 째다, 잡아 뜯다 ☐ slant v. 비스듬히 하다; 기울이다 ☐ slash v. 베다; 내리쳐 베다; 짓이기다

그녀는 자기 책을 탁자 위에 찰싹 소리를 내며 내려놓았다.

06 ②

☐ petroleum n. 석유 ☐ embargo n. 금수(禁輸) 조치, 통상 금지령 ☐ ration v. 배급하다, 할당하다(=allot) ☐ locate v. ~의 위치를 …에 정하다; 위치를 찾아내다, 장소를 알아내다 ☐ dole v. 베풀다, 조금씩 나누어주다 ☐ confiscate v. ~을 압수하다, 몰수하다

최근 석유 금수 기간 동안 자동차 연료를 배급해야만 했다.

07 ①

☐ antics n. 익살스러운 짓, 우스꽝스러운 행동 ☐ attract v. 끌다, 끌어당기다; 매혹하다(=engross) ☐ bore v. (구멍, 터널을) 뚫다, 도려내다 ☐ turn off 잠그다, 멎게 하다; ~을 끄다 ☐ turn up 갑자기 일어나다; 나타나다

그 원숭이의 기괴한 행동은 많은 군중의 마음을 끄는 듯했다.

08 ③

☐ ponder v. 숙고하다, 깊이 생각하다; 신중히 고려하다(=think about) ☐ deny v. 부인하다, 부정하다; 거절하다 ☐ justify v. 옳다고 하다, 정당화하다 ☐ cherish v. 소중히 하다, 귀여워하다

종교는 자신들의 기원(起源)에 대해 깊이 생각하려는 사람들의 필요로부터 생겨났다.

09 ③

☐ caudate a. 꼬리가 있는; 꼬리 모양을 한　☐ amphibian n. 양서류　☐ newt n. 영원(蠑螈), 도롱뇽　☐ stubby a. 그루터기 같은; 땅딸막한, 짧고 굵직한(=thick and short)　☐ long and thin 길고 얇은　☐ undeveloped a. 발달하지 못한, 미발달의; 미개발의　☐ powerful a. 강한, 강력한; 유력한, 우세한

도롱뇽과 같은 꼬리가 있는 양서류들은 대개 긴 꼬리와 땅딸막한 다리가 있다.

10 ②

☐ shift to 옮기다, 이동하다, 변경하다(=convert to)　☐ exaggerate v. 과장하다; 지나치게 강조하다　☐ imitate v. 모방하다, 따르다; 모조하다　☐ refuse to work with ~와 함께 일하는 것을 거부하다

한때 추상음악 작곡가였던 아론 코플랜드(Aaron Copland)는 나중에 더 많은 사람들이 이해할 수 있는 유형으로 음악을 바꾸었다.

11 ④

☐ tarry v. 지체하다, 꾸물거리다(=delay)　☐ officiate v. 식을 집행하다; 직무를 수행하다　☐ wane v. 줄어들다, 작아지다; 쇠약해지다　☐ skitter v. 잽싸게 달리다, 경쾌하게 나아가다

자기가 한 행동의 끔찍한 결과에 직면하고 싶지 않아서 제인(Jane)은 위원회 앞에 나오기 전 최대한 꾸물거렸다.

12 ②

☐ entail v. 수반하다; 들게 하다(=involve)　☐ advocate v. 옹호하다; 주장하다　☐ exaggerate v. 과장하다, 지나치게 강조하다　☐ announce v. 알리다, 고지하다, 공표하다

배우와 청중 간에 직접적인 상호 작용을 수반하는 연극이 배우들에게 특별한 어려움을 주는 것은 아니다.

13 ③

☐ scholarly a. 학술적인, 전문적인　☐ recondite a. 심원한, 알기 어려운, 난해한(=abstruse)　☐ contradictory a. 모순된, 양립하지 않는　☐ obscure a. 분명치 않은, 흐릿한; 애매한　☐ provocative a. 자극하는; 성나게 하는

그 학술지는 너무 난해해서 전혀 이해할 수 없을 정도였다.

14 ①

☐ kinetic a. 운동의; 활동적인(=active)　☐ introspective a. 자기 성찰적인　☐ auditory a. 귀의, 청각의　☐ visual a. 시각의, 눈에 보이는

활동적인 학습자는 주로 행동함으로써 배운다. 이러한 사람은 지시나 명령을 받지 않고 개별적으로 과업을 수행하는 것을 선호한다.

15 ①

☐ acclaim v. 칭송하다, 갈채를 보내다(=applaud)　☐ understand v. 이해하다, 알아듣다　☐ reflect v. 반사하다; 반영하다　☐ criticize v. 비평하다, 비판하다

그 저자의 신간은 주요 평론가 모두로부터 갈채를 받았다.

16 ②

☐ graceful a. 우아한; 단아한　☐ awkwardly ad. 어색하게, 서투르게(=clumsily)　☐ joyfully ad. 즐겁게, 기뻐하며　☐ smoothly ad. 매끈하게; 부드럽게, 순조롭게　☐ tactfully ad. 재치 있게; 솜씨 좋게

그녀는 우아했고 결코 서툴게 행동하지 않았다.

17 ②

☐ toxic a. 유독한; 치명적인(=poisonous)　☐ textual a. 본문의; 원문의; 원문대로의　☐ useful a. 쓸모 있는, 유용한, 유익한, 편리한　☐ harmless a. 해가 없는, 무해한, 악의 없는

이 화학약품들은 사람의 목숨에 유해하다고 알려져 왔다.

18 ③

☐ haggle with ~와 논쟁하다, 입씨름하다(=argue with)　☐ suffer from ~으로 고통받다　☐ support v. 받치다; 유지하다; 부양하다; 지지하다　☐ get the help from ~으로부터 도움을 얻다

그의 어머니가 암으로 죽어가는 동안 의료회사들과 논쟁하는 것을 지켜보는 것에 대한 그의 말이 그의 연설 중에서 더 진정으로 감동적인 부분 중 하나라고 나는 항상 생각했다.

19 ③

☐ abortive a. 실패의, 무산된(=unsuccessful)　☐ immature a. 미숙한, 미완성의　☐ imperfect a. 불완전한, 미완성의　☐ experimental a. 실험의, 실험적인

그 시도는 완전히 실패였다.

20 ②

☐ incredible a. 신용할 수 없는, 믿어지지 않는(=unbelievable)　☐ incredulous a. 의심 많은, 쉽사리 믿지 않는, 회의적인　☐ uncertain a. 불확실한, 모호한　☐ undoubtful a. 의심할 여지가 없는

샐리(Sally)를 만난 이후 지금까지 톰(Tom)이 얼마나 많이 변해왔는지 믿어지지 않는다.

21   ②

☐ unflinching a. 움츠리지 않는, 굽히지 않는(=resolute) ☐ stand up for ~을 옹호하다, 지지하다 ☐ imperative n. 필요(성), 의무 ☐ pompous a. 당당한, 화려한, 호화스러운 ☐ formidable a. 무서운, 겁나는 ☐ incessant a. 그칠 새 없는, 부단한

그 정치가는 사회적 가치문제를 도덕적 의무뿐 아니라 정치적 의무로서 옹호하는 데 굽히지 않는다.

22   ②

☐ faculty n. 능력, 재능(=capacity); (대학의) 학부 ☐ aptitude n. 적성, 소질; 경향 ☐ intelligence n. 지능, 이해력, 사고력 ☐ professor n. 교수; 교사; 선생, 스승

우리가 우리의 언어 능력을 행사할 때 우리는 본성을 실현하는 것일 뿐이다. 이는 결과적으로 우리가 옳음과 그름, 선과 악, 정의와 불의에 대하여 다른 사람들과 협의할 것을 요구한다.

23   ③

☐ protagonist n. 주인공 ☐ paragon n. 모범, 전형(=exemplar) ☐ purity n. 순수 ☐ paradox n. 역설 ☐ advocate n. 옹호자

그 소설에서 주인공은 순수와 완벽의 전형으로 묘사되고 있다.

24   ②

☐ conduct v. 행동하다; 안내하다; 지도하다(=perform) ☐ discuss v. 토론하다, 토의하다, 논의하다 ☐ debate v. 토론하다, 논의하다; 숙고하다 ☐ start v. 시작하다, 착수하다

실험은 대개 실험실의 통제된 상황 아래서 행해진다.

25   ①

☐ scourge n. 재앙, 골칫거리(=chastisement) ☐ pockmarked a. 곰보자국이 있는, 마맛자국이 있는 ☐ estimated a. 평가상의, 견적의 ☐ amputee n. (손발의) 절단수술을 받은 사람 ☐ vicissitude n. 변화, 변천 ☐ upheaval n. 대변동, 격변 ☐ turmoil n. 소란, 혼란

이 재앙이 가져온 인명피해는 캄보디아를 찾아오는 누구에게나 분명하게 드러난다. 상처가 깊이 패여 있는 그 나라는 절단수술을 받은 사람이 40,000명에 이르는 것으로 추정되고 있다.

26   ④

☐ senator n. 상원의원 ☐ means n. 재산, 재력(=affordability) ☐ beyond one's means 분수에 넘치는; 자기 형편 이상으로 생활하는 ☐ intention n. 의향, 의지; 목적, 의도 ☐ device n. 고안; 계획; 장치 ☐ lowliness n. 초라함, 보잘 것 없음

포요트(Foyot)는 프랑스 상원의원들이 식사를 하는 레스토랑인데, 내 형편에는 너무나도 과분한 곳이었기 때문에 나는 그곳에 가볼 생각조차 해본 적이 없었다.

27   ④

☐ frequent v. 자주 가다, ~에 늘 드나들다(=visit) ☐ found v. 설립하다, 창설하다 ☐ favor v. 호의를 보이다, 베풀다 ☐ support v. 지원하다, 후원하다; 부양하다

그 당시 가장 영향력 있는 예술가들 중 몇몇이 그 미술관에 자주 출입했었다.

28   ①

☐ fallow a. 미개간의; 사용하지 않는(=unexploited) ☐ productive a. 생산적인, 생산력을 가진 ☐ multifarious a. 가지각색의, 잡다한 ☐ unvaried a. 변화 없는; 단조로운

또한 민간 농민들이 미사용 정부 토지를 사용해서 그 이익들을 갖도록 허용하기 위해 실험들이 진행 중이다.

29   ②

☐ levy v. 할당하다, 부과하다, 징수하다(=impose) ☐ predict v. 예언하다 ☐ repulse v. 격퇴하다; 논박하다 ☐ supplicate v. 탄원하다

아무리 대단한 노력을 하더라도, 실패하는 사람들에게는 비난과 책임이 가해질 것이다.

30   ②

☐ obstinate a. 완고한, 억지 센 ☐ recusant n. 반항[저항]하는 사람(=dissident) ☐ by no means 결코 ~이 아닌 ☐ oath n. 맹세, 서약 ☐ bandit n. 산적, 노상강도 ☐ vagabond n. 부랑자, 방랑자 ☐ sophist n. 궤변가

그는 완고하게 저항하는 사람이며 결코 맹세를 하지 않을 것이다.

31   ③

☐ paltry a. (금액 등이) 얼마 안 되는; 하찮은(=meager) ☐ solvent a. 지불 능력이 있는; 용해하는 ☐ significant a. 중요한; 의미가 있는 ☐ replete a. 가득한, 충분한

그 노동자는 주급으로 쥐꼬리만 한 임금을 받아서 자신의 가족을 부양하기에 빠듯했다.

32 ③

☐ thoroughly ad. 대단히; 완전히 ☐ dismay v. 당황케 하다, 놀라게 하다; 실망[낙담]시키다(=disappoint) ☐ disrupt v. 혼란시키다, 분열시키다 ☐ disavow v. 부정하다, 부인하다 ☐ disable v. 무능하게 하다; 불구로 만들다

시장은 자신의 새로운 사업계획에 대한 대중의 지지 부족에 대단히 실망했다.

33 ③

☐ appalling a. 소름 끼치는, 무시무시한(=dreadful) ☐ desolation n. 쓸쓸함, 외로움 ☐ accepting a. 쾌히 받아들이는; 솔직한 ☐ asymmetric a. 어울리지 않는; 비대칭의 ☐ crazy a. 미친, 미치광이의

그러나 여하튼 나는 그 지독한 고독을 결코 이해하지 못했다.

34 ④

☐ claim n. 요구; 주장; (상품 등의) 선전 문구 ☐ exaggerated a. 과장된, 부풀린, 지나친(=overestimated) ☐ abridged a. 요약[축약]된 ☐ inconstant a. 변하기 쉬운, 일정하지 않은 ☐ unreliable a. 신뢰할 수 없는

의사들은 다이어트 (제품) 판촉자들의 체중 감량 선전 문구가 매우 과장된 것이라고 한다.

35 ④

☐ give vent to 표출하다, 발산하다(=express) ☐ masquerade v. 가장하다, ~인 체하다 ☐ extinguish v. 끄다; 소멸하다; 무효화하다 ☐ suppress v. 억압하다, 진압하다

테레사(Theresa)는 심지어 공공장소에서도 짜증을 자주 내곤 했다. 그녀는 자신의 화를 억누를 줄 알아야 할 필요가 있다.

36 ④

☐ obsession n. 강박관념, 망상, 집념; 집착(=fixation) ☐ sequence n. 연달아 일어남; 연속; 결과, 결론; 순서, 차례 ☐ promulgation n. 공포, 선포; 공표; 보급, 선전 ☐ interpellation n. 질문, 설명 요구

그녀는 매일 (신문의) 부고란을 읽는 강박관념을 갖고 있었다.

37 ②

☐ puzzling a. 당혹하게 하는, 어리둥절하게 하는(=perplexing) ☐ penetrating a. 꿰뚫는; 통찰력이 있는; 예리한, 예민한 ☐ strange a. 이상한, 야릇한; 낯선, 생소한 ☐ attractive a. 마음을 끄는; 매력적인

"사과는 왜 올라가지 않고 떨어지는가?" 많은 어린이들은 이 질문을 당혹스러운 것으로 생각한다.

38 ①

☐ redundant a. 여분의, 과잉의, 남아도는(=superfluous) ☐ plausible a. (이유·구실 따위가) 그럴 듯한, 정말 같은 ☐ sarcastic a. 빈정거리는, 비꼬는 ☐ liable a. 책임이 있는

그 식당의 서빙 직원들은 새로운 서빙 로봇의 도입으로 남아돌게 되었다.

39 ②

☐ sneer v. 냉소하다, 조소하다; 비웃다, 비꼬다(=show contempt by means of a derisive smile) ☐ primitiveness n. 원시성; 미개한 상태, 낙후한 상태 ☐ pay no attention to ~에 유의하지 않다 ☐ decide that something is not worth considering 고려할 가치가 없다고 판단하다 ☐ think something is more important than it really is 어떤 것을 실제 가치보다 더 중요하게 여기다

박식한 오늘날의 마케팅 담당자나 사업가들은 생산 중심의 접근법을 원시적이라고 비웃기 쉽다.

40 ①

☐ incidentally ad. 우연히; 덧붙여 말하면(=additionally) ☐ separate a. 분리된; 따로따로의 ☐ distinct a. 별개의, 다른 ☐ consequently ad. 따라서, 그 결과로서 ☐ likewise ad. 똑같이, 마찬가지로 ☐ on the contrary 이에 반해, 도리어

덧붙여 말하자면, 일부 아메리카 원주민들은 여전히 서로 분리된 개별 인디언 종족들의 구성원들인데, 각 종족은 고유의 언어, 문화, 전통, 그리고 심지어는 정부도 가지고 있다.

41 ①

☐ howl v. 윙윙거리다, 울부짖다, 조롱하다 ☐ mob n. 군중; 폭도 ☐ renounce v. (권리 등을 정식으로) 포기하다, 단념하다(=abjure) ☐ blanch v. (얼굴이) 핼쑥해지다; 표백하다 ☐ prognosticate v. 예언하다, 예측하다 ☐ decussate v. X자형으로 교차하다

조롱하는 군중들에 맞서, 그는 종교도 직책도 포기하기를 거부했다.

42 ③

☐ pass away 죽다, 돌아가시다 ☐ solace n. 위안, 위로(=consolation) ☐ wealth n. 부(富), 재산 ☐ esteem n. 존중, 존경 ☐ solitude n. 고독; 외로움

오랜 암 투병 끝에 할머니께서 돌아가셨을 때, 제니퍼(Jennifer)는 할머니와 함께 지낸 시간을 추억하며 위안을 찾았다.

43 ③

☐ temerity n. 무분별, 무모함, 만용(=audacity) ☐ ignorance n. 무지, 무식 ☐ distress n. 비탄, 괴로움 ☐ affectivity n. 감정, 정서 상태

교양 있는 현대인이 어떻게 한 인종 집단이 반드시 다른 인종 집단보다 지적으로 뛰어나다고 뻔뻔하게 주장할 수 있는지 이해하기 어렵다.

44 ③

☐ corrosive a. 부식성의(=caustic) ☐ provocative a. 도발적인, 성나게 하는 ☐ psychoactive a. 정신에 작용하는 ☐ lethal a. 치명적인

이 약은 부식성이 있어서 약을 복용하는 사람들은 목에 염증이 생기는 것을 막기 위한 조치를 취해야 한다.

45 ③

☐ vanish v. 사라지다, 없어지다(=disappear) ☐ glacier n. 빙하 ☐ freeze v. 얼다, 결빙하다 ☐ activate v. 활성화하다 ☐ impact v. 영향을 끼치다

다음 20~30년 내에 아프리카와 남아메리카에 있는 대부분의 빙하는 완전히 사라질 것이다.

46 ④

☐ bouncer n. 거대한 사람; 경비원 ☐ eject v. 쫓아내다, 축출하다; 퇴거시키다(=banish) ☐ fistfight n. 주먹다짐, 주먹 싸움 ☐ modify v. 변경하다; 조절하다; 수식하다 ☐ criticize v. 비난하다, 비판하다, 평론하다 ☐ beat v. 치다, 두드리다; 때리다

주먹다짐을 하려는 사람들을 쫓아내기 위해 경비원은 제때 도착했다.

47 ①

☐ posterity n. 자손, 후세, 후대(=descendant) ☐ neighbor n. 이웃, 이웃집 사람; 동료, 동포 ☐ fortune n. 운, 우연; 운명; 재산 ☐ youth n. 젊음, 원기; 청춘기; 청년

그들은 후대를 위해 희귀한 책을 아주 많이 보존했다.

48 ①

☐ antagonistic a. 적대적인, 반대의, 상반되는, 대립하는(=opposed) ☐ ignorant a. 무지한, 무식한 ☐ charitable a. 자비로운; 관대한; 자선의 ☐ curious a. 호기심 있는, 알고 싶어 하는

그녀는 교회 신도들에게 다소 적대적이다.

49 ②

☐ unruliness n. 고분고분하지 않음, 제어하기 어려움 ☐ diffuse v. 흩뜨리다, 발산하다; 유포하다 ☐ constitution n. 구성; 헌법; 체질, 체격; 성격 ☐ waive v. 포기하다, 철회하다; 보류하다(=put aside) ☐ pursue v. 뒤쫓다; 추구하다 ☐ fluctuate v. 변동시키다, 동요시키다 ☐ spread v. 펴다, 펼치다

제멋대로 하는 정신이 우리들 사이에 퍼져 나갔으며, 그 영향 하에, 문화의 차이와 성격의 차이는 문제 되지 않고 보류되었다.

50 ②

☐ embroider v. 수를 놓다; (이야기를) 윤색하다[꾸미다](=embellish) ☐ disclose v. 밝히다, 드러내다 ☐ reiterate v. 반복하다, 되풀이하다 ☐ clarify v. 분명히 말하다

선착장에 앉아 있는 한 어부가 오늘 아침 그가 거의 잡을 뻔했던 38인치 줄무늬 배스에 대해 당신에게 말한다면, 그는 사실을 과장해서 말하는 법을 찾았을지도 모른다.

51 ④

☐ verbose a. 말이 많은, 다변의, 장황한(=wordy) ☐ obtuse a. 우둔한, 둔감한 ☐ nefarious a. 범죄의; 비도덕적인 ☐ intractable a. 고집센, 제어할 수 없는

이 글은 장황하다. 그래서 우리는 이 글을 수정할 필요가 있다.

52 ④

☐ malevolent a. 악의 있는, 심술궂은(=wicked) ☐ glittering a. 반짝이는, 빛나는; 성공적인 ☐ violent a. 격렬한, 맹렬한; 광포한 ☐ friendly a. 친한, 우호적인; 마음에 드는 ☐ scary a. 무서운, 두려운; 잘 놀라는, 겁 많은

그의 시선은 심술궂어 보였고, 입은 다물고 있었지만 눈은 밝게 빛나고 있었다.

53 ③

☐ perspicuous a. 명료한, 명쾌한(=clear) ☐ eliminate v. 제거하다, 배제하다 ☐ misinterpretation n. 오해; 오역 ☐ muddied a. 진흙투성

이가 된 □ twisted a. 비뚤어진, 뒤틀린 □ confusing a. 혼란시키는, 당황하게 하는

그녀의 명쾌한 논평은 모든 오해의 가능성을 없앴다.

54 ③

□ humidity n. 습기 □ stagnant a. 고여 있는, 정지된(=static) □ endemic n. 풍토병 □ epidemic n. 전염병, 유행병 □ mobile a. 움직이기 쉬운, 가동성의 □ warm a. 따뜻한, 따스한 □ tepid a. 미지근한, 열의 없는

중국 전통에서 습기와 고인 물은 풍토병과 전염병의 근원으로 간주된다.

55 ①

□ spill the beans 비밀을 누설하다(=let the cat out of the bag) □ make a big deal 유난을 떨다 □ do in one's shoes ~의 입장이 되어보다 □ observe v. 지키다, 준수하다

제인(Jane)을 위해 깜짝 파티를 계획하는 중입니다. 절대 비밀을 누설하면 안 됩니다.

56 ①

□ discard v. 버리다, 폐기하다(=dispose of) □ disregard v. 무시하다, 경시하다 □ disseminate v. (씨를) 흩뿌리다; 널리 퍼뜨리다, 선전하다 □ dissolve v. 녹이다, 용해시키다; (모임을) 해산시키다

이 스펀지를 뜨거운 물에 10내지 20분 더 담그고, 그런 다음 그 물을 버려야 한다.

57 ①

□ sedentary a. 앉아 있는, 몸을 많이 움직이지 않는(=immobile) □ quiet a. 조용한, 고요한 □ serene a. 고요한, 잔잔한 □ surreptitious a. 비밀의, 은밀한

나쁜 식습관, 운동 부족, 그리고 앉아 있는 생활 방식으로 인해 전체 인구가 비만이 되어가고 있다.

58 ④

□ penetrate v. 관통하다, 꿰뚫다(=pass through); 스며들다, 침투하다 □ substance n. 물질; 물체; 본질 □ light up 밝게 하다, 밝아지다; 명랑해지다, 명랑하게 하다 □ identify v. 신원을 확인하다, 동일시하다 □ repair v. 수리하다, 수선하다; 되찾다, 회복하다

레이저빔은 심지어 가장 딱딱한 물체를 뚫는 데도 이용된다.

59 ①

□ faction n. 당파, 파벌 □ uniformity n. 균일성, 일치(=consensus) □ shortage n. 부족, 결핍; 결점 □ constancy n. 불변성; 지조, 절개 □ diversity n. 다양성, 포괄성

그 분야에 존재하는 너무나 많은 파벌을 고려하면, 애나 프로이드(Anna Freud)가 의견의 일치를 기대하는 것은 비현실적이었다.

60 ④

□ reluctant a. 마음 내키지 않는, 꺼리는, 마지못해 하는(=hesitant) □ indifferent a. 무관심한, 냉담한, 대수롭지 않은 □ interested a. 흥미 있는; 이해관계가 있는 □ impatient a. 참을 수 없는, 성마른

학생들은 처음에는 젊은 교사의 말을 잘 듣지 않으려 했다.

61 ①

□ innumerable a. 무수한, 셀 수 없이 많은(=too many to be counted) □ less valuable 덜 귀중한 □ uproarious a. 떠드는, 시끄러운, 떠들썩한 □ trustworthy a. 신뢰할 수 있는, 믿을 수 있는

마그네슘은 경금속을 원하는 많은 나라에서 무수히 많은 용도로 사용되고 있다.

62 ③

□ extinction n. 멸종, 절멸; 단절(=extermination) □ class n. (동식물 분류상의) 강(綱) □ subsidence n. 함몰; 가라앉음, 침전; 침전물 □ augmentation n. 증가, 증대; 증가율 □ propagation n. (동식물의) 번식, 증식; 선전, 보급

동물의 한 강(綱) 전체의 멸종을 목격하는 것은 드문 일이다.

63 ③

□ platitude n. 평범한 의견, 상투어; 평범(=banality) □ empirical a. 경험적인 □ dogmatism n. 독단주의; 독단론 □ gloss over ~에 대해 얼버무리고 넘어가다 □ plethora n. 과다, 과잉 □ glitch n. 사소한 결함; 작은 기술상의 문제 □ trapping n. 덫 놓기; 개입 중단

중요한 문제들을 진지하게 논의하지 않고 아무렇게나 얼버무림으로써 우리에게는 경험적으로 되는 것, 미묘한 차이를 띠게 되는 것, 독단주의를 피하는 것 등에 관한 진부한 말들만 남게 된다.

64 ①

□ sincere a. 진정한, 진심 어린 □ commitment n. 약속(한 일); 의무, 책무 □ redress v. 바로잡다, 시정하다 □ entice v. 꾀다, 유도[유인]하다(=lure) □ appease v. 달래다, 요구를 들어주다 □ defile v. (신성하

거나 중요한 것을) 더럽히다 ☐ undermine v. 약화시키다

진정한 사과는 경제 상황을 바로잡기 위한 정부의 노력을 알리는 신호가 되고 생산 투자를 유도할 수 있을지도 모른다.

65 ②

☐ considerate a. 사려 깊은, 신중한(=thoughtful) ☐ considerable a. 상당한, 많은 ☐ peevish a. 짜증을 잘 내는 ☐ dominant a. 우세한, 지배적인

많은 사람들이 그들 중 잭슨(Jackson)을 가장 사려 깊은 사람이라고 생각한다.

66 ③

☐ volunteer n. 자원 봉사자 ☐ sign up 참가하다, 가입하다; 계약하다 ☐ solicit v. ~에게 간청하다, 부탁하다(=entreat) ☐ fund-rating n. 자금조달, 모금 ☐ offer v. ~을 권하다, 제공하다 ☐ accuse v. 고발하다, 고소하다 ☐ inquire v. 묻다, 문의하다

오바마를 위한 개별 모금 웹페이지를 호스팅하여 친구와 가족들에게 (모금을) 부탁하기로 자원한 사람들이 그들을 포함해 9,500명이었다.

67 ①

☐ delicate a. 섬세한; 연약한; 민감한(=fragile) ☐ expansive a. 팽창력이 있는; 광대한; 포괄적인 ☐ complex a. 복잡한; 어려운; 합성의 ☐ unusual a. 보통이 아닌, 드문; 별난

숲은 취약한 체계여서 만일 교란시키면 영구히 파괴될 수 있다.

68 ④

☐ resist v. 저항하다, 반대하다 ☐ restriction n. 제한, 규제, 제약, 구속 ☐ impediment n. 방해(물), 장애(=hindrance) ☐ priority n. 우선 사항, 우선; 우선권 ☐ measure n. 수단, 방책 ☐ stimulant n. 격려, 자극[격려]이 되는 것

인도는 환경 규제를 경제 성장에 대한 장애물로서 오랫동안 거부해왔다.

69 ③

☐ seal v. 봉인하다; 증명하다, 보증하다(=endorse) ☐ attach v. 붙이다, 달다, 첨부하다 ☐ write v. 글씨를 쓰다; 저술하다 ☐ issue v. 공포하다; 발행하다

영국 신사의 약속은 피로서 보증된 수표와 같다.

70 ④

☐ quandary n. 곤혹; 진퇴양난; 곤경, 궁지(=plight) ☐ insolvency n. 채무 초과, 파산 ☐ delusion n. 미혹, 기만; 혹함 ☐ collocation n. 병치; 배열; (문장 중의) 말의 배치; <언어> 연어(連語)

정부는 많은 사람들과 함께 무엇을 해야 할지에 관해 곤경에 빠져 있는 듯하다.

71 ②

☐ libel n. 명예 훼손(죄), 비방, 모욕(=slander) ☐ ferocity n. 사나움, 잔인성; 만행 ☐ propensity n. 경향, 성질, 버릇 ☐ arson n. 방화; 방화죄

신문에 나온 보도 내용에 화가 난 그녀는 명예훼손으로 고소했다.

72 ①

☐ caprice n. 변덕; (태도, 행동의) 갑작스러운 변화 ☐ baneful a. 유해한, 해독을 끼치는(=baleful) ☐ lachrymose a. 눈물 잘 흘리는; 애절한 ☐ rattling a. 덜거덕거리는; 활기찬 ☐ redoubtable a. 가공할, 경외할 만한

그의 이론적 변덕이 바이런(Byron)의 이탈리아 연극에 해로운 영향을 미쳤던 것이 분명하다.

73 ①

☐ choppy a. 물결 이는, 파도 치는 ☐ bring halt to 정지시키다, 멈추게 하다(=discontinue) ☐ skim v. (액체 위에 뜬 기름기 등을) 걷어 내다 ☐ reinforce v. 강화하다, 보강하다 ☐ consolidate v. 통합하다; 강화하다 ☐ fatigue v. 피곤하게 하다; 약화시키다

파도가 거칠게 이는 바다로 인해 미시시피 해안 주변에서 기름을 걷어내려는 노력이 중단되었다.

74 ②

☐ deceive v. 속이다, 기만하다(=take in) ☐ obesity n. 비만 ☐ diabetes n. 당뇨병 ☐ heart disease 심장병 ☐ put off 연기하다 ☐ back up 도와주다 ☐ turn down 거절하다

코카콜라는 지난 몇 년 동안 설탕이 든 탄산음료와 비만, 당뇨, 심장병과 같은 질환의 연관성에 대해 대중을 속이려고 했다.

75 ④

☐ immune a. (특정 질병에) 면역성이 있는; ~의 영향을 받지 않는 (=unsusceptible) ☐ insidious a. 교활한, 음험한; (질병) 잠행성의 ☐ immanent a. 내재하는 ☐ endangered a. (동식물이) 멸종위기에 처한

그러나 그 대륙도 극단주의 세력의 공격에 전혀 영향을 받지 않는 것이
아니다.

76 ④

□ incarcerate v. 투옥[감금]하다(=put in prison) □ exonerate v.
(죄·과실을) 범하다, 저지르다 □ put on probation 보호관찰 아래에
두다 □ fine v. ~에게 벌금을 부과하다

상원은 좀도둑질이나 경범죄와 같은 사소한 범죄를 저지른 사람들을 투
옥하는 법안을 승인했다.

77 ①

□ deceptive a. 속이는, 현혹시키는; 믿을 수 없는(=misleading) □
conducive a. 도움이 되는, 이바지하는 □ reasonable a. 도리에 맞는,
논리적인; 적당한 □ lucrative a. 이익이 있는, 유리한, 수지맞는

낮은 가격은 (소비자를) 현혹시킨다. 구매가 완료되기 전에 많은 수수료
가 더해진다.

78 ②

□ concentrate on ~에 집중하다 □ distract v. (마음·주의를) 흐트러뜨
리다, 딴 곳으로 돌리다(=divert) □ daunt v. 겁먹게[기죽게] 하다 □
disclose v. 밝히다, 드러내다 □ devour v. 게걸스레 먹다

일부 사람들은 인터넷이 다른 일들에 정신이 산만해지지 않고 어떤 하나
의 일에만 집중하기를 더 어렵게 만든 것이 아닌가 하고 궁금히 여긴다.

79 ①

□ fatal a. 죽음을 초래하는, 치명적인 □ underscore v. 강조하다
(=emphasize); 뒷받침하다; 예고하다 □ eliminate v. 제거하다, 배제하
다; 몰아내다 □ ignore v. 무시하다, 묵살하다 □ undermine v. 밑을
파다; 훼손시키다

오늘날 치명적인 총기 난사로 인해 보다 엄격한 총기 규제법에 대한 필
요성이 강조되고 있다.

80 ①

□ defuse v. 제거하다; 진정시키다, ~의 긴장을 완화하다(=calm) □
racial tension 인종 간의 긴장[갈등] □ ignite v. 불을 붙이다, 점화하다;
흥분시키다 □ aggravate v. 악화시키다, 가중시키다 □ disconnect
v. 분리하다, 떼어놓다

지역 경찰은 그 지역 내의 인종갈등을 완화시키기 위해 애쓰고 있다.

81 ①

□ pejorative a. 가치를 떨어뜨리는; 경멸적인(=critical) □ imply v.
함축[암시]하다; 의미하다 □ manipulation n. 교묘하게 다루기; 조작,
속임수 □ mystification n. 신비화; 속임수 □ permeable a. 투과할
수 있는, 침투성 있는 □ lucid a. 맑은, 투명한; 명료한 □ ludicrous
a. 익살맞은, 우스운

전통을 창출하는 것에 들어 있는 경멸적인 의미는 조작과 속임수가 개입
되었음을 암시하는 것이며, 따라서 그것을 전통이 보편적으로 가진 특
징으로 간주해서는 안 된다.

82 ③

□ participation n. 관여, 참여, 참가 □ military operation 군사작전
□ sparse a. 부족한, 빈약한(=scanty) □ affluent a. 풍부한; 유복한
□ effeminate a. (남자가) 사내답지 못한, 연약한 □ loathsome a.
싫은; 불쾌한

여성들의 참여가 이렇게 늘어난 부분적인 이유는 많은 군사작전에서 기
술적 진보가 순전히 육체적인 측면의 힘을 대체하여, 여성들로 하여금
여성들의 참여가 극히 적은 일자리에서 새로운 역할을 수행하도록 해주
었다는 점이다.

83 ③

□ dilute v. 희석하다, 묽게 하다(=weaken) □ delete v. 삭제하다,
지우다 □ soak v. 적시다, 담그다 □ fortify v. 강화하다, 요새화하다;
확증하다

오렌지 주스가 너무 달아서, 엘렌(Ellen)은 물로 그것을 희석했다.

84 ①

□ patriotic a. 애국적인 □ get on the bandwagon 유행[시류]에 편승
하다 □ graphic a. 눈앞에 보는 것 같은, 생생한(=vivid) □ atrocity
n. 끔찍한 짓, (전시의) 잔혹행위 □ enrollment n. 등록; 입학 □
deprecated a. (기분이) 우울한 □ drawn a. 무승부의; (얼굴이) 일그러
진 □ speechless a. (충격 등으로) 말문이 막힌

할리우드가 애국주의 물결에 편승해 2차 세계대전의 군대를 다룬 다큐
멘터리 영화 <우리가 싸워야 하는 이유>를 제작했을 때, 적군의 잔혹행
위에 대한 생생한 묘사가 실제로는 관객 입장을 감소시킨다는 것을 알게
되었다.

85 ④

□ appoint v. 임명하다, 지명하다(=designate) □ ambassador n. 대
사; 사절, 특사 □ acquit v. 무죄로 하다, 방면하다, 석방하다 □
promote v. 촉진하다; 승진시키다, 진급시키다 □ condemn v. 비난하
다, 책망하다

대통령은 대사를 임명할 권리를 가지고 있다.

86 ②
☐ falter v. 발에 걸려 넘어지다; 머뭇거리다, 움찔하다; 말을 더듬다 (=stammer) ☐ exclaim v. 외치다, 고함을 지르다 ☐ scream v. 소리치다, 날카로운 비명을 지르다 ☐ yell v. 고함치다, 소리 지르다, 외치다

"무슨 일 있니?"라고 그가 더듬거리며 말했다.

87 ③
☐ obliquely ad. 비스듬히; 완곡하게, 간접적으로(=indirectly) ☐ powerfully ad. 강력하게, 유력하게; 많이, 매우 ☐ elaborately ad. 공들여, 애써서; 정교하게 ☐ uncompromisingly ad. 타협하지 않고; 단호히; 강경히

로버트 하이든(Robert Hayden)의 시는 주제를 간접적으로 표현한다.

88 ④
☐ convince v. 확신[납득]시키다; 설득하다(=induce) ☐ abandon v. 버리다; 그만두다, 포기하다 ☐ dominate v. 지배하다, 위압하다; 억누르다 ☐ nibble v. 조금씩 물어뜯다, 갉아먹다 ☐ ridicule v. 비웃다, 조소하다, 조롱하다

그는 잃어버린 아이를 찾을 거라는 희망을 버리도록 우리를 설득할 수 없었다.

89 ④
☐ ardent a. 열렬한, 열정적인(=enthusiastic) ☐ apathetic a. 무관심한; 냉담한 ☐ flabby a. 축 늘어진, 무기력한 ☐ diligent a. 부지런한

일 중독자들은 대개 하던 일을 그만두지 않는 것을 선호한다. 그들은 팔십대, 구십대에도 여전히 일에 열정적이다.

90 ③
☐ demolish v. 헐다, 파괴하다; 폐지하다(=destroy) ☐ rebuild v. 재건하다, 다시 짓다, 개축하다 ☐ move v. 움직이다, 이동시키다; 감동시키다 ☐ remodel v. 개작하다, 개조하다

지난해 초에 학교 건물의 토대가 너무 불안정해서 학교의 일부를 헐어야만 했다.

91 ②
☐ prop up ~을 떠받치다, 지지하다; 보강하다(=support) ☐ realize v. 실현하다, 현실화하다; 실감하다 ☐ repudiate v. 거부하다, 부인하다,

받아들이지 않다 ☐ cultivate v. 갈다, 경작하다; 재배하다; 신장하다

그 과학자들은 가설을 뒷받침할 만한 증거를 찾느라 바쁘다.

92 ②
☐ agony n. (정신 또는 육체의) 고통, 고뇌(=suffering) ☐ boredom n. 지루함 ☐ drawback n. 결점, 약점 ☐ spirit n. 정신, 영혼, 마음

마라톤은 고통을 견뎌내고 어떻게든 한발 한발 계속 앞으로 내딛는 힘을 키우는 것이다.

93 ④
☐ integral a. 필수적인, 절대 필요한(=essential) ☐ digestion n. 소화 ☐ immune a. 면역의 ☐ trivial a. 사소한, 하찮은 ☐ furtive a. 은밀한, 엉큼한 ☐ virulent a. 악성의, 치명적인; 매서운

박테리아는 건강한 삶의 필수적인 부분이다. 대부분의 박테리아는 소화, 비타민 형성, 면역체계 형성, 그리고 우리의 건강 유지에 도움을 준다.

94 ①
☐ collateral a. 부수적인, 이차적인(=additional) ☐ complimentary a. 칭찬의; 무료의 ☐ major a. 주요한, 중요한 ☐ reciprocal a. 상호의, 호혜적인

정부 산업 전략의 부수적인 목표는 고용을 늘리는 것이다.

95 ④
☐ bicker v. 말다툼하다, 언쟁하다(=argue) ☐ hug v. 꼭 껴안다; 품다 ☐ joke v. 농담하다, 조롱하다 ☐ refer v. 언급하다; 조회하다; 가리키다

브라운(Brown)과 그의 아내는 항상 언쟁을 한다.

96 ③
☐ point-blank ad. 정면으로, 노골적으로(=directly) ☐ angrily ad. 화가 나서, 격분하여 ☐ indifferently ad. 무관심하게 ☐ politely ad. 예의 바르게

이제 막 운전을 배우기 시작한 그녀는 차와 전화 없이 지낼 생각을 하니 참을 수 없었다. 그래서 그녀는 참여하는 것을 노골적으로 거절했다.

97 ④
☐ enervated a. 활력을 잃은, 무기력한(=tired) ☐ depressed a. 의기소침한, 우울한 ☐ lethargic a. 무기력한, 활발하지 못한 ☐ energized

a. 열정적인 ☐ refreshed a. (기분이) 상쾌한 ☐ unsatisfied a. 만족[충족]하지 않은

따뜻한 바람은 많은 사람들을 무기력하고 우울한 느낌을 갖도록 한다. 그 때문에 이곳 사람들은 이 기간 동안 무기력해진다.

98 ①

☐ hectic a. 매우 바쁜, 분주한(=hasty) ☐ burning a. 불타는, 강렬한, 격심한 ☐ terrific a. 굉장한, 빼어난, 엄청난 ☐ formidable a. 무서운, 만만찮은

가족 심리학자인 제리 위코프(Jerry Wyckoff)는 생활의 분주한 속도 때문에 (아직도) 자녀에 대한 체벌이 남아 있는 것이라고 말했다. "우리는 다소 전략이 뒤처지고 있습니다."라고 그는 말했다. "사람들은 좌절하고, 시간은 많지 않아서 바로 지금 결과를 원합니다."

99 ④

☐ obsolescence n. 퇴화, 노후화(=wane) ☐ mankind n. 인류 ☐ onset n. (불쾌한 일의) 시작 ☐ grind n. (시간이 오래 걸리는) 고된 일 ☐ lull n. (소란 사이의) 잠잠한 시기, 소강상태

컴퓨터의 설계에 컴퓨터를 사용함에 따라, 변화의 속도가 너무나 빨라져서 하드웨어와 소프트웨어는 약 5년마다 노후화되었다. 컴퓨터보다 더 많이 혹은 더 빨리 인류의 생산성을 증가시켰던 다른 기술은 여태까지 전혀 없었다.

100 ③

☐ galactic a. 은하계의, 성운의 ☐ core n. 핵심; 중심, 중심부 ☐ fertile a. 비옥한, 기름진; 다산의 ☐ congregate v. 모이다; 집합하다 (=gather) ☐ element n. 요소, 성분; 원소 ☐ plentiful a. 많은, 충분한, 풍부한 ☐ halfway ad. 도중에, 중간에 ☐ possess v. 소유하다, 가지고 있다 ☐ orbit v. 궤도에 진입하다, 궤도를 그리며 돌다 ☐ planet n. 행성 ☐ disperse v. 흩어지다, 헤어지다 ☐ expand v. 퍼지다, 넓어지다 ☐ revolve v. 회전하다, 선회하다; 공전하다

블랙홀 주위가 격렬함에도 불구하고, 은하계의 중심은 다산(多産)의 곳이다. 별들이 은하계의 중심에 모여 있어서, 별들이 만들어내는 생명을 부여하는 중(重)원소들이 거기에 가장 풍부하다. 블랙홀과 은하계 가장자리 사이 중간에 위치한 우리 태양 가까이 있는 신생한 별들조차도 궤도를 도는 가스 먼지 원반들을 갖고 있으며 이 원반들은 충분히 오랫동안 생존해서 행성을 탄생시킬 수 있다.

MVP 51-55 ACTUAL TEST

01 ④	02 ②	03 ①	04 ①	05 ④	06 ③	07 ④	08 ②	09 ①	10 ③
11 ③	12 ②	13 ②	14 ①	15 ①	16 ③	17 ④	18 ②	19 ②	20 ④
21 ④	22 ④	23 ④	24 ②	25 ③	26 ①	27 ①	28 ②	29 ④	30 ①
31 ③	32 ②	33 ②	34 ②	35 ②	36 ④	37 ②	38 ③	39 ②	40 ②
41 ④	42 ②	43 ③	44 ①	45 ②	46 ④	47 ②	48 ①	49 ②	50 ①
51 ②	52 ②	53 ①	54 ①	55 ③	56 ④	57 ③	58 ②	59 ④	60 ③
61 ③	62 ②	63 ④	64 ①	65 ①	66 ②	67 ③	68 ②	69 ①	70 ②
71 ②	72 ④	73 ①	74 ①	75 ②	76 ③	77 ③	78 ④	79 ③	80 ③
81 ③	82 ①	83 ④	84 ①	85 ②	86 ③	87 ②	88 ②	89 ①	90 ③
91 ④	92 ①	93 ③	94 ①	95 ②	96 ④	97 ③	98 ④	99 ①	100 ②

01   ④

☐ incentive n. 장려금, 우대조치; 동기(=motive) ☐ request n. 요구, 요망, 요청 ☐ instinct n. 본능; 직관, 직감 ☐ desire n. 의욕, 추진력; 돌진

우리는 여러 가지 동기에 의해 움직인다.

02   ②

☐ anonymous a. 익명의, 작자 불명의(=unsigned) ☐ friendly a. 친한, 우호적인; 친절한 ☐ hostile a. 적의 있는; 적대하는 ☐ congratulatory a. 축하의, 경축의

그 교수는 익명의 편지 한 통을 받았다.

03   ①

☐ humid a. 습기 있는, 눅눅한(=damp) ☐ hot a. 뜨거운, 더운; 열렬한 ☐ cold a. 추운, 찬, 냉정한 ☐ warm a. 따뜻한; 열렬한

금속들은 습기가 많은 지역에선 아주 빠르게 부식한다.

04   ①

☐ dwell on ~을 깊이 생각하다, 숙고하다(=contemplate) ☐ reside v. 거주하다; 존재하다 ☐ speak v. 말을 하다; 연설을 하다 ☐ enter v. 들어가다; 참가하다

우리는 그 불쾌한 주제를 깊이 생각하고 싶지 않다.

05   ④

☐ species n. (생물 분류상의) 종(種) ☐ evolve v. (서서히) 발전하다; 진화하다 ☐ adapted a. 개조된, 개작된 ☐ thrive v. 번영하다, 번성하다(=flourish) ☐ offspring n. (사람, 동물의) 자식, 새끼; 자손; 결과 ☐ surpass v. 능가하다, 뛰어나다 ☐ survive v. 살아남다, ~보다 오래 살다 ☐ develop v. 발달[발전]시키다; 개발하다

종(種)은 진화하며, 환경에 가장 잘 적응한 종이 번영하고 더 많은 자손을 남긴다.

06   ③

☐ contrary a. 반대의, 상반되는(=opposite) ☐ pertinent a. 타당한, 적절한; 관련 있는 ☐ similar a. 유사한, 비슷한 ☐ relevant a. 관련된, 적절한

그가 한 일은 그가 말했던 것과 정반대되는 것이었다.

07   ④

☐ resolve v. 용해하다; 분해하다; 해결하다; 결심하다(=determine) ☐ hesitate v. 주저하다, 망설이다, 머뭇거리다 ☐ offer v. 권하다, 제공하다; 제안하다 ☐ refuse v. 거절하다, 거부하다, 물리치다

그는 즉시 행동에 옮기기로 결심했다.

08   ②

☐ melt away 녹아 없어지다; 서서히 사라지다(=disappear) ☐ solve v. 풀다, 해석하다; 해결하다 ☐ increase v. 늘리다, 증대하다; 증진시키다 ☐ incite v. 자극하다, 격려하다, 고무하다

당신의 불안감은 일단 의사의 진찰을 받고 나면 틀림없이 사라질 것이다.

09 ①

☐ perk n. 편익, 수입; 특전(=perquisite) ☐ blunder n. (어리석은) 실수 ☐ prevision n. 선견, 예지, 선견지명 ☐ amercement n. (자유재량의) 벌금형; 벌금

학생이 됨으로써 얻게 되는 특전은 항공요금이 싸다는 것이다.

10 ③

☐ heedless a. 부주의한, 조심성 없는, 무관심한(=inattentive) ☐ wary a. 경계하는, 주의 깊은, 신중한 ☐ meticulous a. 꼼꼼한, 세심한 ☐ dauntless a. 겁없는, 불굴의

등산로의 경고에도 아랑곳하지 않고 젊은 등산객은 숲속으로 더 깊이 들어갔다.

11 ③

☐ capitalize on ~을 활용하다 ☐ rebellious a. 반항적인 ☐ allure n. 매력, 매혹(=charm) ☐ faction n. 파벌 ☐ exclusivity n. 고급스러움 ☐ vivacity n. 생기, 활기

기업들은 종종 하위문화의 반항적인 매력을 이용하려고 할 것이다.

12 ②

☐ steep in ~에 담그다, 배어들게 하다; 몰두하게 하다(=permeate) ☐ incline v. 내키게 하다; ~으로 향하게 하다 ☐ obsess v. 사로잡다, 귀신이 붙다; 괴롭히다 ☐ indebt v. 빚을 지게 하다, 은혜를 입히다

일본은 과거의 전통과 상징이 배어 있는 문화를 지닌 사회이다.

13 ②

☐ intoxicating a. 취하게 하는; 도취[열중]케 하는(=captivating) ☐ drunken a. 술이 취한; (행동 등이) 취중의 ☐ intimidating a. 위협적인, 겁을 주는 ☐ poisonous a. 유독한, 독성이 있는

내가 전에 그 이야기를 몇 차례 들은 적이 있었음에도 불구하고, 그녀의 목소리는 매혹적이었다.

14 ①

☐ invaluable tip 매우 귀중한 팁[비결, 조언](=important hint) ☐ haggle v. (조건·값 등에 대해) 옥신각신하다, 흥정을 하다 ☐ unworthy help 적절하지 않은 도움 ☐ unnecessary content 불필요한 내용

☐ profitable bargain 유리한 흥정

"자동차 구매자 가이드"에는 가장 좋은 가격을 얻어내기 위해 흥정하는 법에 관한 귀중한 팁을 비롯해서 자동차 구매에 대해 알아야 할 모든 것들이 들어 있다.

15 ①

☐ impartial a. 치우치지 않은, 공평한(=indifferent) ☐ useless a. 소용없는, 쓸모없는 ☐ skillful a. 숙련된, 솜씨 좋은, 능숙한 ☐ ideal a. 이상적인, 가장 알맞은

과학자는 투르게네프(Turgenev)의 시에 나오는 자연만큼 공평하다.

16 ③

☐ layman n. 속인(俗人), 평신도; 아마추어, 비전문가(=non-specialist) ☐ jargon n. 특수 용어, 전문어 ☐ expert n. 숙련가, 전문가 ☐ mentor n. 조언자, 믿을 만한 의논 상대 ☐ misanthrope n. 인간을 싫어하는 사람, 염세가

그 외과의사는 비전문가적인 관점에서 그 과정을 설명하려고 애썼지만, 너무 많은 의학 용어를 사용했기 때문에 나는 그가 무슨 말을 하고 있는지 알 수 없었다.

17 ④

☐ crafty a. 교활한, 간교한, (나쁜) 꾀가 많은(=cunning) ☐ artistic a. 예술적인, 미술적인 ☐ humanistic a. 인문학의; 인도주의적인 ☐ capable a. 유능한, 능력 있는

모든 문화에 있어서 다른 동물들은 지능이 떨어지는 것으로 여겨지는 반면 하나 혹은 두 종류의 동물이 꾀가 많은 동물로 간주된다.

18 ②

☐ obeisance n. 공경, 숭배; 존경(=reverence) ☐ interpretation n. 해석, 설명 ☐ rapture n. 기쁨, 환희 ☐ deviance n. 일탈

그는 부자와 권력자들에게 무비판적으로 경외하는 것에 대해 신문을 공격했다.

19 ②

☐ searing a. 무더운, 타는 듯한(=parching) ☐ harangue v. 열변을 토하다, 장광설을 늘어놓다 ☐ inescapability n. 달아날 수 없음, 불가피함 ☐ relentless a. 가차 없는, 잔인한, 혹독한 ☐ autocritique n. (특히 정치적) 자기비판 ☐ sealing a. 봉인하는, 밀봉하는 ☐ sorrowful a. 슬픈, 비탄에 잠긴 ☐ frigid a. 추운, 혹한의; 냉담한, 냉랭한

당연히, 많은 사람들은 이 일을 원하지 않을 것이다. 그 일에는 타는 듯한 고독, 단 한 문장이 될 이야기를 장황하게 나타내는 훈련, 그리고 피할 수 없는 냉혹한 자기비판 등이 수반되기 때문이다.

20 ④

☐ extirpate v. 제거하다, 없애다(=uproot) ☐ subsidize v. 보조금을 주다 ☐ deprecate v. 반대[비난]하다 ☐ ameliorate v. 개선하다

히틀러(Hitler)는 천주교인과 유대인이 모든 악의 근원이었다고 생각했기 때문에 가톨릭교를 없애고 싶어 했다.

21 ④

☐ rebut v. 반박하다, 논박하다(=disprove) ☐ spur v. 박차를 가하다; 자극하다 ☐ vacate v. 비우다; 사임하다; 무효로 하다 ☐ grieve v. 몹시 슬프게 하다, 비탄케 하다

그는 연설의 대부분을 그의 외교 정책에 대한 비판을 반박하는 데 할애했다.

22 ④

☐ convoluted a. 대단히 난해한[복잡한](=intricate) ☐ circuitous a. 에두르는, 간접적인 ☐ subtle a. 미묘한 ☐ crafty a. 술수가 뛰어난, 교활한

루드 골드버그 장치는 아주 단순한 일을 아주 간접적이고 복잡한 방식으로 수행한다.

23 ④

☐ venomous a. 독이 있는; 악의에 찬, 원한을 품은(=spiteful) ☐ affectionate a. 애정 깊은, 사랑에 넘친, 다정한 ☐ complementary a. 보충하는; 서로 보완하는 ☐ flattering a. 아첨하는; 알랑거리는; 비위 맞추는

그는 이름을 밝히지 않고서 악의에 찬 말을 해대는 전화에 무척이나 놀랐다.

24 ②

☐ distance oneself from ~으로부터 거리를 두다 ☐ fiasco n. 큰 실수, 대실패(=debacle) ☐ alliance n. 동맹, 연합 ☐ withdrawal n. 철회, 취소, 철수 ☐ liberation n. 해방

유럽의 지도자들은 철수하기로 한 결정을 대체적으로 지지함에도 불구하고 아프가니스탄에서의 실패로부터 거리를 두려고 하고 있다.

25 ③

☐ persecute v. 박해하다, 학대하다; 괴롭히다(=wrong) ☐ pamper v. 만족시키다; 하고 싶은 대로 하게 하다 ☐ accommodate v. 수용하다; 적응시키다 ☐ indulge v. (취미, 욕망 등에) 빠지다, 탐닉하다

그의 최근 영화는 게이로 살면서 괴롭힘을 당한 경험에 관한 것이다.

26 ①

☐ recoup v. (손실 등을) 되찾다, 벌충하다, 메우다(=get back) ☐ well-timed a. 시의적절한 ☐ explain away 잘 설명[해명]하다, 교묘히 변명하여 발뺌하다 ☐ pay off (빚을) 전부 갚다 ☐ look into 조사하다

그 투자자는 나중에 몇 번 적시에 투자함으로써 이전의 손실을 메웠다.

27 ①

☐ dark-money n. 출처를 밝히지 않고 선거운동에 쓰인 돈 ☐ negative a. 부정적인, 네거티브의(선거 전략이 자기주장을 펴기보다 상대후보를 공격하는) ☐ deceptive a. 기만적인, 현혹시키는 ☐ disclose v. 밝히다, 드러내다(=reveal) ☐ discover v. 발견하다, 찾다 ☐ disqualify v. 자격을 박탈하다, 실격시키다 ☐ repudiate v. 거절하다; 부인하다

불법선거자금이 사용된 광고 10개 중 거의 9개는 네거티브 광고이며, 애넌버그 공공정책센터에 의한 분석에 따르면, 이런 광고의 26%가 기만적인 것인데, 이는 기부자의 신원을 밝히는 단체들에 의한 광고보다 약간 높은 수치이다.

28 ③

☐ premonition n. (특히 불길한) 예감(=foreboding) ☐ hindsight n. 뒤늦은 깨달음 ☐ sign n. 징후, 조짐 ☐ peroration n. (강연·논설 따위의) 결론, (힘을 준) 맺음말

그녀는 그 날 그녀의 고양이가 어떻게든 다칠 거라는 예감이 들었다.

29 ④

☐ irreparable a. 수선[회복]할 수 없는, 돌이킬 수 없는(=irretrievable) ☐ irreproachable a. 나무랄[흠잡을] 데 없는 ☐ irrecognizable a. 인식[분간]할 수 없는 ☐ irresistible a. 억누를[저항할] 수 없는

사람들은 의심할 여지없이 어린 시절을 잊어버리고, 그것은 아무리 사람들이 가볍게 받아들인다 할지라도 돌이킬 수 없는 손실이다.

30 ①

☐ quench v. (갈증)을 풀다, ~을 만족시키다(=satiate) ☐ absorb v. 흡수하다, 받아들이다 ☐ savor v. 맛을 내다; ~의 기미를 보이다 ☐ curb v. 억제하다, 제어하다

그 탐험가는 갈증을 해소하기 위해 개울가에 멈추어 섰다가 성난 곰을 보고 무서워서 달아났다.

31 ③

☐ coax v. 감언으로 설득하다, 구슬리다(=blandish) ☐ haggle v. 실랑이를 벌이다, 흥정하다 ☐ direct v. 지시하다, 명령하다 ☐ render v. 만들다, ~이 되게 하다

그는 자기 친구를 좋은 말로 설득해 자기 회사 제품을 구매하게 했다.

32 ②

☐ ethno-racial a. 민족-인종적인 ☐ transition n. 변천 ☐ betoken v. 나타내다, 의미하다(=signify) ☐ upheaval n. 대격변 ☐ declare v. 선언하다 ☐ ascribe v. ~에 돌리다 ☐ aggrandize v. 확장하다

많은 미국인의 마음에서 이러한 민족-인종적인 변천은 정치·문화·사회적인 대변화를 의미한다.

33 ②

☐ prosecute v. 기소하다, 공소하다; 수행하다; 경영하다 ☐ obscene a. 외설한, 음란한, 추잡한, 음탕한(=salacious) ☐ indecent a. 외설적인; 노출이 심한 ☐ chaste a. 순결한; 순수한, 담백한 ☐ arrogant a. 오만한, 거만한 ☐ despicable a. 비열한, 야비한

『헤럴드(The Herald)』지는 외설적이고 음란한 광고를 게재한 이유로 기소 당했다.

34 ②

☐ indefatigable a. 지칠 줄 모르는, 끈질긴(=tireless) ☐ rousing a. 감동적인; 열렬한 ☐ decisive a. 단호한, 확고한 ☐ sociable a. 사교적인, 친목적인 ☐ persuasive a. 설득력 있는 ☐ reasonable a. 분별 있는, 이치를 아는

그는 지칠 줄 모르는 연구가였고, 감동을 주는 대중 연설가였으며, 결단력 있는 행정가였다.

35 ②

☐ pliable a. 휘기 쉬운, 유연한; 유순한, 온순한(=plastic) ☐ movable a. 움직일 수 있는; 가동성의 ☐ unadaptable a. 적응[적합]할 수 없는, 융통성 없는 ☐ inflexible a. 구부러지지 않는; 강직한, 완고한

각 장치의 끝부분은 일반적인 크기의 부드럽고 잘 휘는 물질로 만들어졌다.

36 ④

☐ sap v. 약화시키다, 차츰 무너뜨리다(=gradually weaken) ☐ jeopardize v. 위태롭게 하다, 위태로운 경지에 빠뜨리다 ☐ challenge v. 도전하다 ☐ stir up 잘 젓다, 흔들다; 일으키다; 선동하다

분석가들은 일본의 경기 침체가 투자자들의 신뢰를 서서히 약화시켰다고 말한다.

37 ②

☐ repentant a. 뉘우치는, 회개하는(=penitent) ☐ marginalized a. 사회적으로 소외된 ☐ elusive a. 붙잡기[파악하기] 어려운; 이해하기 어려운 ☐ sagacious a. 현명한 ☐ adamant a. 요지부동의, 단호한

백인 정치 지도자들이 진정으로 회개한다면 우리 사회에서 흑인과 사회적으로 소외된 다른 사람들의 말에 귀를 기울일 것이다.

38 ③

☐ harrowing a. 비참한, 마음 아픈(=distressing) ☐ frustrating a. 불만스러운, 좌절감을 주는 ☐ irritating a. 초조하게 하는, 화나게 하는; 귀찮은 ☐ aggravating a. 악화하는; 화나는

이야기가 마음 아픈 것들이어서, 종종 참여자들 자신과 초대된 관객들의 눈물을 자아내고 있다.

39 ②

☐ contaminate v. 오염시키다, 더럽히다(=spoil) ☐ carcinogen n. 발암(發癌)(성) 물질 ☐ preserve v. 보호하다, 지키다 ☐ reheat v. 다시 데우다 ☐ keep v. 지키다, 유지하다

한 신문기사는 발암 물질의 일종인 다이옥신 때문에 전자레인지 속에서 플라스틱을 가열하는 것은 음식에 나쁜 영향을 미칠 수 있다는 우려를 일으켰다.

40 ②

☐ retentive a. 보유하는; 기억력이 좋은(=recollective) ☐ absurd a. 불합리한 ☐ distinct a. 별개의; 뚜렷한 ☐ infinite a. 무한한

비록 그는 정규 교육을 받지 못했지만, 그는 놀랄 만큼 뛰어난 기억력과 배움에 대한 열정을 가지고 있었다.

41 ④

☐ doctrine n. 교의, 교리 ☐ pervasive a. 널리 퍼져 있는, 어디에나 있는(=permeating) ☐ contemporary n. 동시대의 사람; 현대인 ☐ petrify v. 겁에 질리게 만들다, 석화시키다 ☐ pejorative a. 가치를 떨어뜨리는; 경멸적인 ☐ pernicious a. 유해한, 유독한, 악성의

그 소설가는 여기에서 근면의 교의를 표현하고 있는데, 그 교의는 그의 동시대인들에게 영감을 준 널리 퍼져 있던 개념이다.

42 ②

□ jovial a. 명랑한, 즐거운, 유쾌한(=cheerful) □ station v. 배치하다, 주둔시키다 □ behave oneself 예절 바르게 행동하다 □ serene a. 고요한, 평화로운 □ deliberate a. 고의의, 의도적인 □ monotonous a. 단조로운, 변함없는

그 현장은 차분하고 유쾌해 보였고, 근처에 배치된 경찰은 방문객들이 대체로 예의 바르게 행동하고 있다고 말했다.

43 ③

□ cloying a. 싫증나게 하는, 넌더리나는; 지나치게 감상적인(=mawkish) □ nugatory a. 하찮은, 쓸모없는 □ phlegmatic a. 침착한, 냉정한 □ obstreperous a. 시끄러운, 떠들썩한

그 식당의 서비스는 정중했지만, 지나치게 감상적일 정도는 아니었다.

44 ①

□ throng n. 군중, 인파; 다수, 가득 참(=crowd) □ sad-colored a. 칙칙한, 어두운 □ steeple-crowned a. (모자 등이) 꼭대기가 높고 뾰족한 □ edifice n. (크고 인상적인) 건물; 조직 □ member n. (단체 따위의) 일원; 회원 □ number n. 수; 수량 □ row n. 열, 줄, 횡렬

우중충한 색의 옷에다 높고 뾰족한 회색 모자를 쓴, 턱수염을 기른 많은 남자들이 한 목조 건물 앞에 모여 있었다.

45 ③

□ usher v. 안내하다, 인도하다; 선도하다(=guide) □ announce v. 알리다, 발표하다, 공표하다 □ push v. 밀다; 밀어 나아가게 하다 □ force v. 강요하다, 억지로 ~시키다

그는 기다리고 있는 차로 안내되어, 차로 두 시간 동안 바이에른의 교외로 갔다.

46 ④

□ vicinity n. 가까움, 근접; 부근(=proximity) □ distance n. 거리, 간격; 원거리 □ end n. 끝, 종지; 최후 □ rear n. 뒤, 배면; 맨 뒤

식료잡화점이 너의 집 근처에 있다.

47 ②

□ enclose v. 에워싸다, 둘러싸다(=encompass) □ empower v. ~에게 권능을 부여하다, ~할 수 있도록 하다, ~할 자격을 주다 □ encumber v. 방해하다, 폐를 끼치다, 막다 □ obligate v. 의무를 지우다; 강요하다

이 교재는 기말시험에서 좋은 점수를 얻기 위해 네가 익혀야 할 정보들을 포함하고 있다.

48 ①

□ vulnerable a. 취약한; 비난받기 쉬운, 상처를 입기 쉬운(=weak) □ strong a. 힘 센, 강한, 튼튼한 □ resistive a. 저항하는, 저항력 있는 □ formidable a. 무서운; 굉장히 많은

호텔과 식당들은 불경기에 극도로 취약하다.

49 ②

□ housekeeper n. 주부; 가정부 □ into the bargain 게다가(=as well) □ at a discount 할인하여 □ for a nominal wage 명목상의 임금으로

게다가 새 가정부는 훌륭한 요리사로 밝혀졌다.

50 ①

□ vaunted a. 과시되고 있는, 자랑의 □ emancipation n. 해방, 벗어남 (=liberation) □ enthusiasm n. 열광; 열정, 열의 □ infringement n. 위반; 침해 □ mantra n. 만트라, 진언

미국이 자랑하는 직장에서의 해방은 세상에 잘 알려져 있다.

51 ②

□ disdain n. 경멸(감), 업신여김, 무시(=scorn) □ comrade n. 동료, 동지, 전우 □ flee v. 달아나다, 도망하다 □ respect n. 존경, 경의 □ ambivalence n. <심리> 양면 가치, 모순, 동요 □ authority n. 권위, 위신

그 병사는 첫 총격이 있은 후에 전투에서 도망쳤기 때문에 그의 전우들에게 멸시를 받았다.

52 ②

□ sinister a. 불길한; 사악한, 악의를 품은(=suspicious) □ indigenous a. 고유한, 타고난 □ conspicuous a. 잘 보이는, 두드러진 □ unknown a. 알려지지 않은, 미지의, 알 수 없는

덤불 뒤를 걷고 있던 다소 수상쩍은 사람이 한 명 있었다.

53 ①

☐ rectify v. 시정하다, 조정하다; 교정하다; 수정하다(=correct) ☐ qualify v. 자격을 주다; 제한하다 ☐ integrate v. 통합하다; 적분하다; 조정하다 ☐ disdain v. 경멸하다, 멸시하다

50년 후에 그는 그의 배반 행위를 바로 잡을 방법이 없다는 것을 알았으며, 그들도 또한 그걸 알았다.

54 ①

☐ dismal a. 암울한, 음울한(=depressing) ☐ attested a. 증명된, 입증된 ☐ undeniable a. 부인할 수 없는, 명백한 ☐ complicated a. 복잡한, 까다로운

슬프게도 존(John)에게는 너무 늦었지만, 이런 암울한 사실에도 불구하고 희망은 있다.

55 ③

☐ impulsivity n. 충동성 ☐ augur v. 점치다, 예언하다; 징조를 나타내다(=herald) ☐ delinquency n. 의무 불이행, 직무 태만; (청소년의) 비행 ☐ augment v. 늘리다, 증가시키다 ☐ formulate v. 명확히 말하다; 공식화하다 ☐ mask v. 감추다, 가장하다

남자 아이들의 경우, 유년기의 충동이 청소년 비행이나 폭력의 높은 위험성을 예고하는 것일지도 모른다.

56 ④

☐ automatic a. 자동의, 기계적인; 무의식적인, 습관적인 ☐ integral a. 없어서는 안 될, 절대 필요한; 구성 요소로서의 ☐ component n. 구성 요소, 성분(=part) ☐ grow up 성장하다, 장성하다 ☐ reminder n. 생각나게 하는 것; 기념품 ☐ decision n. 결정, 해결; 결심 ☐ result n. 결과, 결말, 성과, 귀착

아이들에게 놀이는 성장을 위한 필연적이며 없어서는 안 되는 요소이다.

57 ③

☐ compulsory a. 강제적인, 의무적인, 필수의(=mandatory) ☐ harsh a. 거친; 가혹한 ☐ diversified a. 변화 많은, 다양한 ☐ complicated a. 복잡한, 까다로운; 뒤얽힌

1850년 이후 미국의 여러 주(州)들이 의무적인 학교 출석 법안을 통과시키기 시작했다.

58 ②

☐ autonomous a. 자치권이 있는; 자율의, 자주적인(=independent)

☐ supportive a. 지탱하는; 지지하는; 유지하는 ☐ resistant a. 저항하는; 저력력 있는 ☐ interfering a. 간섭하기 좋아하는

미국 원주민들은 여러 가지 면에서 독립적으로 간주되기 때문에 수많은 미국 주 법률들의 적용 대상이 아니다.

59 ④

☐ drought n. 가뭄, 한발 ☐ devastate v. 황폐시키다; 철저하게 파괴하다 ☐ cattle n. 소, 가축 ☐ ranch n. 목장, 방목장 ☐ swath n. 한 번 낫질한 넓이, 베어낸 한 구획; 길게 줄지은 열, 넓은 길 ☐ arable a. 경작에 알맞은, 개간할 수 있는(=tillable) ☐ abominable a. 지긋지긋한, 혐오스러운, 꺼림칙한 ☐ barren a. 불모의, 메마른 ☐ sterile a. 메마른, 불모의

호주의 현재 가뭄이 아직 역사상 가장 긴 가뭄은 아니지만, 가장 더운 가뭄인 까닭에 전국의 소와 목장과 양 농장과 넓은 경작지를 황폐화시켰다.

60 ③

☐ homosexuality n. 동성애 ☐ deviance n. 이상 (행동), 일탈 ☐ in some cases 경우에 따라서는, 어쩌면 ☐ prosecute v. 해내다, 수행하다; 속행하다; 기소하다, 공소(公訴)하다(=indict) ☐ restrain v. 구속하다, 검거하다; 억제하다, 누르다; 제지하다 ☐ offend v. 성나게 하다, 감정을 상하게 하다; (법을) 위반하다, 어기다 ☐ affront v. 모욕하다; 과감하게 맞서다

지난 세기 동안, 동성애는 종종 심각한 형태의 일탈로 여겨졌고 몇몇 경우에는 법에 의해 기소되어 처벌받았다.

61 ③

☐ refute v. 반박하다; 이의를 제기하다(=disprove) ☐ extenuate v. 경감하다; 변명하다 ☐ fight v. 싸우다, 전투하다; 노력하다 ☐ avoid v. 피하다; 무효로 하다

그 결백한 사람은 혐의 사실에 반박했다.

62 ②

☐ dramatically ad. 극적으로, 눈부시게 ☐ keep pace with ~와 보조를 맞추다, ~에 뒤지지 않도록 하다 ☐ surge n. 급증, 급등(=sharp growth) ☐ menacing behavior 위협적인 행동 ☐ mysterious decrease 이해하기 힘든 감소 ☐ urge to race 질주하고 싶은 충동

많은 국가에서 도로 위의 차량 수가 급격히 증가하고 있는데, 도로는 종종 이와 같은 운전자의 갑작스러운 급증과 보조를 맞추지 못해 왔다.

63   ④

☐ appreciably ad. 분명히, 상당히(=noticeably) ☐ abundantly ad. 풍부하게, 충분히 ☐ immeasurably ad. 헤아릴 수 없을 정도로 ☐ unendingly ad. 무한히, 끝없이

지난 몇 년 동안, 이 지역에서는 겨울 몇 달 동안 기온이 통상적인 겨울 기온보다 현저히 낮았다.

64   ③

☐ confound v. 어리둥절[당혹]하게 만들다(=baffle) ☐ disseminate v. (정보·지식 등을) 퍼뜨리다[전파하다] ☐ deduce v. 추론[추정]하다, 연역하다 ☐ demean v. 품위를 손상시키다, 위신을 떨어뜨리다

갑작스러운 주가 하락에 경제 전문가들이 어리둥절해하고 있다.

65   ①

☐ redress v. 바로잡다, 시정하다(=correct) ☐ revalue v. (통화를) 평가 절상하다 ☐ defy v. 도전하다 ☐ assess v. 평가하다 ☐ justify v. 옳음[타당함]을 보여 주다

현 지도부는 통화를 평가 절상함으로써 심각한 경제 상황을 바로잡고자 노력했지만, 그것은 상황을 악화시켰을 뿐이다.

66   ③

☐ spare v. 할애하다; 모면하게[겪지 않아도 되게] 하다 ☐ liability n. 책임, 의무, 부담(=burden) ☐ relegate v. ~을 내쫓다; (일 따위를) ~에게 이관하다; 맡기다 ☐ recrudescence n. 재발, 도짐; 재연 ☐ palimpsest n. 씌어 있던 글자를 지우고 그 위에 다시 쓴 양피지 ☐ impunity n. 형벌을 받지 않음, 무사함

미 의회 의원 해밀턴(Hamilton)은 항복문서에 서명하는 일을 그의 정치 고문들에게 맡겼으므로 그것에 대한 책임은 면했다.

67   ③

☐ hidebound a. 완고한, 편협한(=intolerant) ☐ innocuous a. 악의 없는, 무해한 ☐ indolent a. 게으른, 나태한 ☐ indifferent a. 무관심한

예를 들어, 일반적으로 두 데이터 포인트를 연결하는 선이 그 선의 이전 구획과 연속적이라고 가정하지만, 이는 편협한 현실이 아니라 가정이다.

68   ②

☐ smallpox n. 천연두 ☐ dreaded a. 두려운, 무서운 ☐ fatal a. 치명적인, 파멸적인; 운명의(=mortal) ☐ anxious a. 걱정하는, 근심하는; 갈망하는 ☐ acute a. 예리한; 격렬한 ☐ sharp a. 날카로운, 예리한

천연두는 아주 최근까지 무서우면서도 종종 치명적인 질병이었다.

69   ①

☐ stern a. 엄격한, 단호한; 가차 없는 ☐ consent v. 동의하다, 승낙하다, 찬성하다(=agree) ☐ assemble v. 모으다, 집합시키다, 소집하다 ☐ convene v. 소집하다; 소환하다 ☐ refrain v. 그만두다, 삼가다, 참다

그 엄격한 아버지에겐 딸의 결혼에 동의하지 않을 합당한 이유가 있었다.

70   ②

☐ immigrant n. (외국으로부터의) 이민, 이주자 ☐ advent n. 도래, 출현(=appearance) ☐ newcomer n. 새로 온 사람 ☐ recruit v. (신병·신입 회원·사원 등을) 모집하다 ☐ outdate v. ~을 진부하게[시대에 뒤지게]하다 ☐ retrogression n. 후퇴, 퇴보, 역행 ☐ retardation n. 지연, 지체; 방해

과거에 새로운 이민자들은 종종 쉽게 일자리를 얻을 수 있었다. 이제 새로운 기술의 출현으로 인해 새 이민자들은 채용되기 위해 더 많은 교육을 받아야 한다.

71   ②

☐ plume himself on ~을 자랑하다, 뽐내다(=pride oneself on) ☐ feel lucky 예감이 좋다 ☐ doubt v. 의문을 가지다 ☐ hardly believe 좀처럼 믿지 않다

그는 자신이 회사에서 빠르게 승진한 것에 대해 자랑한다.

72   ④

☐ statesman n. 정치가 ☐ sensible a. 분별 있는, 양식(良識)을 갖춘, 지각 있는 ☐ opponent n. 적, 상대 ☐ fervent a. 열심인, 열렬한(=passionate) ☐ voracious a. 게걸스럽게 먹는; 탐욕스러운 ☐ acute a. 빈틈없는, 명민한 ☐ ferocious a. 사나운, 잔인한; 모진

다른 지각 있는 사람들과 마찬가지로, 훌륭한 정치가는 항상 그의 열렬한 지지자들에게서보다 그의 적들에게서 더 많은 것을 배운다.

73   ①

☐ plight n. 곤경, 궁지(=hardship) ☐ salvation n. 구조, 구출, 구제 ☐ whim n. 잘 변하는 마음, 일시적인 생각 ☐ anger n. 노염, 성, 화 ☐ curse n. 저주; 악담, 욕설; 저주

한때 작은 섬 국가에서 민주주의의 희망이었던 아리스티드(Aristide)는 최근에 사람들의 구세주가 아니라 그들을 곤경에 빠뜨리는 원인으로 간주되고 있다.

74 ①

☐ manifest a. (보거나 이해하기에) 분명한 ☐ latent a. 숨어 있는, 보이지 않는, 잠재적인(=dormant) ☐ exposed a. 드러나 있는; 노출된 ☐ impose v. 도입[시행]하다, 부과하다 ☐ fake a. 가짜의, 거짓된

명백한 꿈과 잠재된 꿈을 구별할 필요가 있다.

75 ②

☐ genial a. 정다운, 친절한; 온화한(=friendly) ☐ lyric a. 서정시의, 서정적인 ☐ utterance n. (말로) 표현함, 발언 ☐ delicate a. 섬세한, 예민한 ☐ religious a. 종교상의, 종교적인 ☐ insistent a. 고집 세우는, 강요하는

시인은 온화한 사회적 행위를 열정적인 서정적 표현으로 바꾼다.

76 ③

☐ irrational a. 비이성[비논리]적인; 분별이 없는 ☐ excitement n. 흥분; 동요 ☐ anemic a. 빈혈의; 무기력한, 허약한(=feeble) ☐ abnormal a. 보통과 다른, 정상이 아닌; 변칙의 ☐ pathological a. 병리학적인, 병적인 ☐ irregular a. 불규칙적인, 변칙적인

세계 지도자들은 오늘의 무기력한 경제보다는 내일의 분별없는 동요에 갑자기 더 관심이 있는 것 같다.

77 ③

☐ ingenious a. 독창적인, 재간이 많은(=original) ☐ genuine a. 진짜의, 진품의 ☐ influential a. 영향력 있는 ☐ indifferent a. 무관심한; 중요치 않은

그녀는 그 문제에 대한 독창적인 해결책을 생각해냈다.

78 ④

☐ fare n. 음식, 식사(=diet) ☐ fee n. 수수료, 요금 ☐ rate n. 비율; 가격, 시세 ☐ charge n. 책임, 의무; 요금

많은 가족들은 더 다양한 음식을 얻기 위해 이전에는 구할 수 없었던 과일, 채소와 유제품을 이용할 수 있었다.

79 ③

☐ astronomer n. 천문학자 ☐ detect v. 발견하다; 탐지하다 ☐ emit v. (빛·열·냄새·소리 따위를) 내다, 방출하다(=release) ☐ radiation n. 방사선; 복사에너지 ☐ interstellar a. 별과 별 사이의, 항성(恒性)간의 ☐ expand v. 확장하다, 팽창시키다 ☐ condense v. 응축하다, 압축하다 ☐ exhaust v. 다 써버리다, 고갈시키다

천문학자들은 블랙홀을 탐지하는 데 어려움을 겪는데, 이는 블랙홀이 전자 방사선을 전혀 방출하지 않기 때문이다. 따라서 블랙홀의 존재 여부는 그러한 방사선의 부재에 의해서나 부근에 있는 성간(星間) 물질 구름으로부터 블랙홀을 향해 물질이 끌어당겨지는 것에 의해 추론된다.

80 ③

☐ meddlesome a. 지겹게 참견하는(=officious) ☐ dearly ad. 극진히 ☐ assiduous a. 근면한 ☐ instructive a. 유익한, 교육적인, 교훈적인 ☐ official a. 공식의, 공인된; 공무의

스미스(Smith) 부인은 그녀의 사촌 일에 지겹게 참견하지만 그녀의 사촌을 매우 사랑한다.

81 ③

☐ antipathy n. (강한) 반감, 혐오 ☐ dispute v. 논쟁하다, 논의하다(=altercate) ☐ argumentative a. 논쟁적인, 논쟁을 좋아하는 ☐ assent v. 동의하다, 찬성하다 ☐ discourse v. 이야기하다, 말하다; 연설하다 ☐ repute v. ~라고 평하다, 여기다, 생각하다, 간주하다

그는 논쟁을 극도로 싫어했기 때문에 친구와의 논쟁적인 토론을 피했다.

82 ①

☐ smear v. 중상[비방]하다(=slander) ☐ squash v. 억누르다, 진압하다 ☐ elevate v. 향상시키다, 고상하게 하다; 기분을 돋우다 ☐ muzzle v. (사람들에게 의견 표현을 못하도록) 재갈을 물리다

그 이야기는 야당 대표를 비방하려는 시도였다.

83 ④

☐ delegate v. 특파하다, 파견하다; 위임하다(=assign) ☐ demand v. 요구하다, 요청하다; 필요로 하다 ☐ align v. 정렬하다; 제휴하다 ☐ share v. 분배하다, 나누다; 공유하다

의장으로서, 당신은 위원회의 각 위원들에게 책임을 위임해야 할 것이다.

84 ①

☐ undertake v. 떠맡다, 착수하다(=wage) ☐ head v. (어떤 지점으로) 향하다, 전진하다; 지휘하다 ☐ compute v. 계산하다; 평가[어림]하다 ☐ haunt v. 자주 가다, 노상 다니다; 출몰하다

1775년부터 1776년까지 미국인들은 캐나다에서 영국에 대항하여 군사행동을 벌였으나 무위에 그쳤다.

85
②

☐ outlaw v. 불법이라고 선언하다, 금지하다 ☐ onerous a. 부담되는, 매우 힘든(=demanding) ☐ toil v. 수고하다, 고생하다, 애써 일하다 ☐ scatter v. ~에 흩뜨려 놓다, 산재(散在)시키다 ☐ liberal a. 진보적인; 관대한 ☐ profuse a. 풍부한, 많은, 다량의 ☐ extravagant a. 낭비하는

가장 힘든 형태의 아동 노동을 의회가 불법화하고 59년이 지났지만, 미성년 노동자들은 미국 전역에 산재해 있는 들판과 공장에서 여전히 힘들게 일하고 있다.

86
③

☐ address v. (문제를) 역점을 두어 다루다 ☐ body shame 외모를 기준으로 평가하다, 상대방의 외모를 조롱하다 ☐ impose v. (의무·세금·벌 따위를) 지우다, 부과하다 ☐ ban n. 금지 ☐ unsolicited a. 청하지 않은, 요구받지 않은 ☐ derogatory a. (명예·품격·가치 등을) 손상하는 (=disparaging) ☐ arrogant a. 거만한, 오만한 ☐ provocative a. 화나게 하는; 자극적인, 선동적인 ☐ conclusive a. 결정적인, 단호한

그 회사가 최근 들어 강하게 추진한 것은 "누군가의 외모, 체형, 체격, 건강에 대해 원치 않는 모욕적인 발언을 하는 것"을 금지함으로써 외모를 조롱하는 문제를 해결하는 것이다.

87
②

☐ reject v. 거절하다; (이식된 장기, 조직에) 거부 반응을 나타내다 ☐ obstacle n. 방해(물), 장애(물)(=impediment) ☐ factor n. 요인, 요소 ☐ occurrence n. 발생, 일어남; 사건, 일어난 일 ☐ phenomenon n. 현상; 사건

이질적인 것에 거부 반응을 나타내는 인체의 성향은 성공적인 조직 이식의 주요 걸림돌이다.

88
②

☐ scanty a. 부족한; 빈약한; 인색한(=meager) ☐ theoretical a. 이론의, 이론상의 ☐ indeterminate a. 불확실한, 불확정한; 막연한 ☐ implicit a. 은연중의, 함축적인, 암시적인, 암묵의

적어도 세계 언어 중 3분의 2에 대한 우리의 지식은 여전히 빈약하다.

89
①

☐ conduct v. (열, 전기, 소리 등을) 전도하다 ☐ muffler n. (내연 기관의) 소음기(消音器) ☐ baffle n. (기류, 음향, 유체 등의) 조절[차폐]장치, 방해판 ☐ soak up ~을 빨아들이다, 흡수하다(=absorb) ☐ echo v. 메아리치다, 울리다 ☐ deflect v. 빗나가게 하다; 편향하다 ☐ release v. 풀어놓다; 방출하다; 해방하다; 면제하다

자동차 소음기는 배기가스를 배플이라 불리는 일련의 방해 장치로 보내어 소음을 흡수한다.

90
③

☐ sincere a. 성실한, 진실의 ☐ credence n. 신용, 신임(=confidence) ☐ statement n. 성명, 진술 ☐ invocation n. 기도, 기원; 탄원, 청원 ☐ nonchalance n. 무관심, 냉담, 태연 ☐ misgiving n. 걱정; 의혹; 불안, 염려

그 정치가는 매우 진실해 보여서 누구도 그의 말을 믿을 수밖에 없었다.

91
④

☐ summon v. 소환하다, 호출하다 ☐ interrogation n. 질문, 심문 ☐ allegation n. 주장, 진술 ☐ embezzle v. 횡령하다, 착복하다 (=divert fraudulently) ☐ inadvertently invest 부주의하게 투자하다 ☐ take as a bribe 뇌물로 받다 ☐ illegally confiscate 불법적으로 압수하다

막대한 회사 자금을 횡령했다는 혐의에 대해 심문을 받기 위해 SK그룹 회장이 소환될 것이다.

92
①

☐ impotent a. 무력한, 무기력한; 허약한(=powerless) ☐ aristocrat n. 귀족 ☐ chivalry n. 기사도; 정중한 태도 ☐ bring somebody/something to life ~에 활기[생기]를 불어넣다 ☐ dictatorial a. 독재자의; 오만한 ☐ impartial a. 공평한, 편견 없는 ☐ tainted a. 더럽혀진, 썩은; 부패한

그 당시에는 평소엔 기사도를 들먹거리면서도 실제로 행하진 않은 무기력한 귀족들이 있었다.

93
③

☐ hallmark n. (현저한) 특징, 특질(=distinguishing characteristic) ☐ reason for success 성공의 이유 ☐ guiding light 본보기, 모범 ☐ mark of excellence 일류 상표

제퍼슨(Jefferson)의 삶의 특징은 자신감이었다.

94
①

☐ disentangle v. (엉킨 것을) 풀다, (혼란에서) 풀어내다(=unravel) ☐ coordinate v. 통합하다; 조정하다, 조화시키다 ☐ abolish v. 폐지하다, 철폐하다 ☐ underrate v. 과소평가하다, 깔보다

과거에 종교는 사회에 직면한 복잡한 문제들을 해결하는 데 매우 중요했다.

95   ②

☐ exploit v. 이용하다; 활용하다; 착취하다   ☐ theatrical a. 연극조의, 과장된   ☐ spectacle n. 광경, 모습, 상황   ☐ sweep v. (장소를) 휩쓸다; (장소·사람을) 열광시키다   ☐ opulent a. 부유한; 풍부한(=rich)   ☐ excessive a. 과도한, 지나친   ☐ unfamiliar a. 낯선, 익숙지 않은   ☐ mysterious a. 신비의, 불가사의한

한스 마카르트(Hans Makart)는 극적 광경(스펙터클)의 잠재력을 활용했고 그의 관객들을 풍부한 판타지의 세계로 몰아넣었다.

96   ④

☐ commence v. 시작하다, 착수하다(=start)   ☐ agree v. 동의하다, 찬성하다   ☐ plan v. 계획하다, 입안하다   ☐ decide v. 결정하다

선거 후에 정부는 새 고속도로 건설에 착수했다.

97   ③

☐ enrapture v. ~에 넋을 잃게 하다, 황홀하게 만들다, 도취시키다 (=enchant)   ☐ resuscitate v. 소생시키다; 부흥하다   ☐ mollify v. 달래다, 진정시키다   ☐ convince v. 확신시키다, 납득시키다

관중들은 그 젊은 독주자의 연주에 넋을 잃었다.

98   ④

☐ structural integrity 구조적 일체성, 구조적 무결성   ☐ compromise v. 타협하다; (명예·평판·신용 따위를) 더럽히다; 위태롭게 하다(=impair)   ☐ measure v. 재다, 측정하다   ☐ shatter v. 산산이 부서지다, 산산조각 나다   ☐ harass v. 괴롭히다, 애먹이다

지진에 의해 구조적 일체성이 훼손된 그 댐에 대해 보수 작업이 즉시 시작되었다.

99   ①

☐ royalist a. 왕당파의, 왕정주의자의   ☐ the Continent (영국과 구별하여) 유럽 대륙   ☐ leave behind (처자, 재산 등을) 버리다   ☐ valiantly ad. 용감히, 의연하게(=dauntlessly)   ☐ ceaselessly ad. 끊임없이, 잇따라   ☐ languidly ad. 활기 없이, 노곤하게   ☐ surreptitiously ad. 몰래; 부정하게

유럽 대륙으로 도망친 (영국의) 많은 왕당파는 의연하게 싸운 아내와 가족을 뒤에 버려두고 갔다.

100   ②

☐ leap to a conclusion 성급한 결론을 내리다   ☐ facile a. 손쉬운, 용이한(=effortless)   ☐ virile a. 남자다운, 남성적인; 씩씩한, 힘찬, 강건

한 ☐ convincing a. 설득력 있는   ☐ vote-catching a. 인기 영합의

'초포식자'시대처럼 일부 정치인들은 쉽게 성급한 결론을 내리고 쉬운 목표인 유색인종의 젊은이들에게 그것을 꺼내들고 있다.

MVP 56-60 ACTUAL TEST

01 ④	02 ③	03 ②	04 ③	05 ④	06 ①	07 ①	08 ③	09 ②	10 ④
11 ③	12 ①	13 ①	14 ①	15 ③	16 ④	17 ①	18 ③	19 ③	20 ②
21 ③	22 ①	23 ③	24 ③	25 ④	26 ①	27 ④	28 ①	29 ②	30 ④
31 ④	32 ②	33 ④	34 ④	35 ①	36 ②	37 ①	38 ④	39 ④	40 ④
41 ③	42 ④	43 ③	44 ②	45 ①	46 ④	47 ④	48 ①	49 ④	50 ①
51 ②	52 ③	53 ②	54 ①	55 ③	56 ②	57 ①	58 ④	59 ④	60 ③
61 ①	62 ②	63 ③	64 ①	65 ①	66 ②	67 ④	68 ②	69 ①	70 ②
71 ①	72 ③	73 ④	74 ③	75 ①	76 ①	77 ①	78 ③	79 ②	80 ②
81 ③	82 ②	83 ③	84 ③	85 ②	86 ③	87 ③	88 ③	89 ③	90 ①
91 ④	92 ④	93 ②	94 ④	95 ④	96 ①	97 ②	98 ④	99 ④	100 ②

01 ④

☐ unsuitably ad. 부적절하게, 어울리지 않게(=inappropriately) ☐ illogically ad. 비논리적으로, 조리에 맞지 않게 ☐ unrealistically ad. 비현실적으로; 비사실적으로 ☐ indiscreetly ad. 무분별하게, 지각없이

유성은 항성(恒星)이 전혀 아니기 때문에 어울리지 않는 이름이 붙여진다.

02 ③

☐ at random 무작위로, 임의로(=aimlessly) ☐ on purpose 의도적으로, 고의로 ☐ painstakingly ad. 힘들여, 공들여 ☐ to the point 적절한, 간단명료한

그는 무작위로 많은 질문을 했다.

03 ②

☐ temperamental a. 기분의; 신경질적인, 감정적인(=emotional) ☐ understanding a. 사려 분별이 있는, 이해가 빠른 ☐ confident a. 확신하는; 자신 있는; 대담한 ☐ hardworking a. 근면한, 열심히 일하는

내 동생은 좋은 직장에 취직한 후부터 점점 더 쉽게 성을 낸다.

04 ③

☐ havoc n. 큰 황폐, 큰 파괴; 대혼란(=destruction) ☐ wind n. 바람; 숨, 호흡 ☐ treatment n. 취급; 대우; 치료(법) ☐ immersion n. 열중, 몰두

허리케인은 그 섬을 황폐화시켰다.

05 ④

☐ obliged a. 고맙게 여기는, 감사하는(=thankful) ☐ polite a. 공손한, 예의 바른 ☐ opposed a. 반대의, 적대하는, 대항하는 ☐ accepted a. 일반적으로 인정된, 용인된

이웃이 베푼 모든 도움에 대해 감사한다고 존(John)은 말했다.

06 ①

☐ relinquish v. 그만두다, 버리다, 포기하다(=abandon) ☐ regret v. 후회하다; 유감스럽게 생각하다 ☐ secure v. (힘들게) 얻어 내다 ☐ pursue v. 추구하다

그녀는 올해 유럽에 갈 모든 희망을 포기했다.

07 ①

☐ attest v. 증명하다, 증언하다, 명백히 하다, 인증하다(=confirm) ☐ impeach v. 탄핵하다, 고발하다 ☐ protrude v. 내밀다, 튀어나오게 하다 ☐ stipulate v. 규정하다, 명기(明記)하다, 명문화하다

그 젊은이의 능력은 그의 빠른 승진으로 증명되었다.

08 ③

☐ credit analysis 신용분석 ☐ assess v. (가치·양을) 평가하다, 사정하다(=appraise) ☐ facilitate v. 돕다, 조장하다, 촉진하다 ☐ contract v. 계약하다; 친교를 맺다; 병에 걸리다 ☐ deteriorate v. 악화되다; 타락하다

모든 단계에서, 투자자는 회사의 부채 상환 능력을 평가하기 위해 신용분석을 할 것이다.

09 ②

☐ undomesticated a. 길들여지지 않은; 가정적이 아닌(=feral) ☐ pet v. (동물아이를 다정하게) 어루만지다, 쓰다듬다 ☐ fatuous a. 어리석은, 얼빠진 ☐ prodigal a. 낭비하는; 방탕한 ☐ preposterous a. 터무니없는, 가당찮은

길들지 않은 그 고양이는 우리가 쓰다듬는 것을 허락하지 않을 것이다.

10 ④

☐ moderate a. 보통의; 알맞은, 적당한(=reasonable) ☐ skillful a. 숙련된, 솜씨 좋은 ☐ honest a. 정직한; 솔직한 ☐ passionate a. 열정적인, 열렬한

팀의 코치나 조직의 지도자는 열정을 보여주는 데 있어서 항상 적절한 수준을 유지해야 한다.

11 ③

☐ drag v. (힘들여) 끌다[끌고 가다]; (원치 않는 곳에) 가게하다 ☐ listless a. 열의 없는, 무관심한; 생기 없는(=unconcerned) ☐ neurotic a. 신경증의, 신경과민의 ☐ pointless a. 무딘; 무의미한, 적절하지 못한 ☐ repulsive a. 불쾌한; (태도 등이) 쌀쌀맞은

그 어린아이들은 너무 많은 박물관에 끌려다녀서 그들이 공룡 전시장에 도착했을 때, 그들의 반응은 몹시 무관심했다.

12 ①

☐ designate v. 명시하다, 가리키다; 지명하다, 선정하다(=appoint) ☐ discharge v. 짐을 부리다; 해방하다; 해고하다 ☐ delude v. 속이다, 현혹하다; 속여서 ~하게 하다 ☐ collect v. 모으다, 수집하다; 징수하다

파티에서 휘터커(Whitaker) 씨는 맥주보다는 위스키를 마셨기 때문에, 그의 친구들은 그를 안전하게 귀가시켜줄 운전사를 정했다.

13 ①

☐ engender v. 생기게 하다, 발생케 하다(=beget) ☐ beguile v. 현혹시키다, 속이다, 기만하다 ☐ embroider v. 수를 놓다; 윤색하다, 과장하다 ☐ enlighten v. 계몽하다, 교화하다; 가르치다

동정은 흔히 사랑을 낳는다.

14 ①

☐ feature v. ~의 특징을 그리다; ~의 특색을 이루다 ☐ endemic a. 풍토성의, 한 지방 특유의(=indigenous) ☐ be eager to ~을 하고 싶어하다 ☐ point out 지적[언급]하다 ☐ tropical a. 열대(지방)의, 열대성의 ☐ significant a. 중요한, 중대한 ☐ giant a. 거대한; 엄청난

자연탐사 여행은 몇 가지 토착 식물을 특색으로 삼고 있었으며, 안내자는 그 점을 지적하는 데 열심이었다.

15 ③

☐ flamboyant a. 화려한, 현란한(=showy) ☐ somber a. 어두침침한, 거무스름한 ☐ subdued a. 가라앉은, 좀 우울한 ☐ petulant a. 성마른, 화를 잘 내는

이 부츠에는 일반적인 잉글랜드 여성들에게는 어울리지 않는 현란한 요소가 있다.

16 ④

☐ console v. 위로하다, 달래다(=soothe) ☐ let out (울음소리, 신음소리 등을) 내다 ☐ frantic a. 정신없는, 이성을 잃은 ☐ seduce v. 부추기다; 유혹하다 ☐ persuade v. 설득하다 ☐ repress v. 억누르다

그녀는 이성을 잃은 듯이 울고 있는 사람들을 달래려고 노력했지만, 잠시 후에 모든 것이 침묵에 빠졌다.

17 ①

☐ redound v. (신용, 이익 등을) 늘리다, 높이다(=contribute) ☐ credit n. 신용; 신망 ☐ overflow v. 넘치다 ☐ subtract v. 빼다, 덜다, 공제하다 ☐ deprive v. 빼앗다, 허용하지[주지] 않다

정치가들이 이러한 진전에 반응을 보인다면 모든 것이 그들의 신용을 높일 것이다.

18 ③

☐ regain v. 되찾다, 회복하다 ☐ affection n. 애정 ☐ bumptious a. 자만하는, 거만한(=arrogant) ☐ abandon v. 버리다 ☐ in pursuit of ~을 쫓아서 ☐ affluent a. 풍부한, 유복한 ☐ indecisive a. 우유부단한 ☐ cunning a. 교활한 ☐ brutal a. 잔인한, 야만적인

주아나(Juana)는 더 유복한 도나 이네스(Dona Ines)를 쫓아 그녀를 버리는 그녀의 거만한 연인 돈 질(Don Gil)의 사랑을 되찾지 못한다.

19 ③

☐ verisimilitude n. 신빙성, 정말[진실] 같음(=authenticity) ☐ abyss n. 심연(深淵); 나락 ☐ similarity n. 유사점, 닮은 점 ☐ vicissitude n. 변화, 변천; (인생의) 부침(浮沈)

고전 오페라는 인간 감정의 진실성이 아니라 화려함, 호기심, 운명 등을 다룬다.

20 ②

☐ polish v. ~을 닦다, 광을 내다(=burnish) ☐ statue n. 조각상 ☐ misguided a. 잘못 판단한 ☐ direction n. 지시, 명령 ☐ offer v. 제공하다, 권하다 ☐ capture v. 붙잡다, 획득하다 ☐ picture v. 묘사하다; 표시하다

톰(Tom)은 상관의 잘못된 지시로 말미암아 온종일 그 조각상을 윤이 나도록 닦았다.

21 ③

☐ upbeat a. 긍정적인, 낙관적인(=optimistic) ☐ preeminent a. 걸출한, 뛰어난 ☐ belligerent a. 적대적인, 공격적인 ☐ laid-back a. 느긋한, 태평스러운 ☐ obsequious a. 아부하는

그의 긍정적인 태도와 뛰어난 일 처리 능력은 우리 모두에게 자극이 되었다.

22 ①

☐ cook up ~을 꾸며[지어]내다 ☐ stand by ~을 변함없이 지지하다; ~을 고수하다 ☐ assertion n. 단언, 단정; 주장(=claim) ☐ excuse n. 변명, 해명 ☐ suspicion n. 혐의, 용의, 의심 ☐ brag n. 허풍, 자랑

물론 그것은 작가가 무대 위의 대리 자아를 위해 마련한 근사한 엔딩에 미치지 못했다. 그리고 그는 자신의 온라인상에서의 데이트 경험이 대부분 끔찍했었다는 주장을 지지한다.

23 ③

☐ bridle n. 굴레 v. 언짢게 하다(=offend) ☐ relieve v. 경감[완화]시키다; 안도시키다 ☐ surprise v. (깜짝) 놀라게 하다 ☐ sadden v. 슬프게 하다

내가 머무른다는 소식에 그녀가 언짢아한다는 것을 나는 알았다.

24 ③

☐ limpid a. 투명한; 애매모호하지 않은, 명쾌한(=lucid) ☐ lofty a. 매우 높은; 고상한 ☐ literary a. 문학의, 문학적인 ☐ lukewarm a. 미지근한; 열의가 없는, 냉담한

그 작가는 명쾌한 문체로 글을 썼다.

25 ④

☐ incorporate v. 통합시키다; 합병하다(=integrate) ☐ provision n. 조항, 규정; 공급 ☐ degenerate v. 나빠지다, 퇴보하다; 타락하다 ☐ puncture v. 펑크 내다; 망쳐놓다 ☐ flirt v. 장난삼아 연애하다, 시시덕거리다; 장난삼아 해보다

의회는 몇 개의 새로운 조항들을 세금 법안에 통합시킬 계획이다.

26 ①

☐ regurgitate v. ~을 토하다, 게우다; 되풀이하다, 반복하다(=repeat) ☐ dull v. 약해지다, 누그러지다 ☐ manipulate v. 다루다, 조작하다 ☐ distort v. 왜곡하다 ☐ obliterate v. 지우다, 없애다

학생들이 위키피디아와 같은 웹사이트에서 찾은 사실과 수치를 그대로 되풀이하도록 하는 것은 그들의 비판적 사고를 무디게 할 뿐이다.

27 ④

☐ peer n. 동료; (사회적·법적으로) 동등한 사람(=colleague) ☐ collage n. 콜라주 (기법) ☐ conductor n. 지휘자, 안내원, 승무원 ☐ college n. 대학, 단과 대학

새로운 연구는 로봇이 권위자가 아니라 동료로 제시될 때 더 설득력이 있다는 것을 보여준다.

28 ①

☐ gaudy a. 번쩍번쩍 빛나는, 화려한(=showy) ☐ enormous a. 거대한, 막대한 ☐ antiquated a. 낡은, 구식의, 노후한 ☐ simple a. 단순한, 간단한

샌프란시스코에 있는 19세기 빅토리아 양식의 화려한 가옥들 가운데 상당수는 1906년에 발생한 지진으로 인해 잃게 되었다.

29 ②

☐ mutual a. 서로의, 상호의(=reciprocal) ☐ burdensome a. 무거운 짐이 되는; 번거로운 ☐ dithery a. 주저하는, 떨리는 ☐ generous a. 관대한

러시아 측 동역자들과 함께 일하는 사람들은 수년에 걸친 협업으로 인해 강한 유대관계와 상호 존중이 생겨났다고 말한다.

30 ④

☐ suspicious a. 의심스러운, 미심쩍은 ☐ uneasy a. 불안한, 우려되는(=anxious) ☐ decisively ad. 결정적으로; 단호히 ☐ adamant a. 요지부동의, 단호한 ☐ indifferent a. 무관심한, 냉담한 ☐ united a. 연합한, 협력한, 단결한

지나치게 강력한 대통령은 미덥지 않지만, 그럼에도 미국 국민들은 대통령이 단호하게 행동하지 못할 때는 불안해한다.

31 ④

□ shun v. 비키다, 피하다(=avoid) □ thrive on ~을 잘 해내다 □ lack v. 모자라다, 결핍하다 □ demand v. 요구하다, 청구하다; 필요로 하다

과격 단체는 판에 박힌 정책을 피해왔다.

32 ②

□ remedy n. 치료, 의료; 구제책 □ indigence n. 극심한 곤궁, 극빈 (=poverty) □ forthright a. 똑바른; 솔직한 □ appeal n. 호소; 간청; 매력 □ hardship n. 고난, 고초 □ industry n. 공업, 산업; 근면 □ anguish n. 고통, 괴로움, 번민

소득이 빈곤에 대한 구제책이라는 생각에는 어떤 솔직한 매력이 있다.

33 ④

□ forerunner n. 선구자, 선조(=ancestor); 전조 □ player n. 선수, 경기자 □ dictator n. 독재자, 지배자 □ transformer n. 변화시키는 사람; 변압기

19세기의 Western Baseball League는 오늘날 메이저리그의 전신이었다.

34 ③

□ traduce v. 비방[중상]하다(=malign) □ titillate v. 기분 좋게 자극하다, ~의 흥을 돋우다 □ quell v. 진압[평정]하다 □ embrace v. 받아들이다, 아우르다

역사를 통해서 여성들은 비방을 당하고 침묵을 요구받았다. 이제는 이제 우리의 이야기를 우리의 언어로 말할 때이다.

35 ①

□ against all (the) odds 강한 저항[곤란]을 무릅쓰고 □ tenaciously ad. 끈질기게, 집요하게(=doggedly) □ indefinitely ad. 막연히; 무기한으로 □ perfunctorily ad. 건성으로, 형식적으로 □ waveringly ad. 흔들리면서; 갈팡질팡하여

오랜 세월 동안, 여성들은 온갖 역경을 무릅쓰고서 투표권을 얻기 위해 끈질기게 싸웠다.

36 ②

□ startling a. 놀라운, 깜짝 놀라게 하는(=surprising) □ statistic n. 통계치 □ segment n. 단편, 조각, 구분 □ emerging a. 최근 생겨난, 최근에 만들어진 □ pessimistic a. 비관적인, 염세적인 □ shining a. 빛나는, 반짝이는

세계 인구 가운데 노년층이 가장 빨리 늘어나고 있다는 것은 깜짝 놀랄 만한 통계수치이다.

37 ①

□ inherent a. 고유의, 타고난(=inborn) □ superficial a. 표면상의; 피상적인 □ inhuman a. 몰인정한, 냉혹한; 비인간적인 □ intelligent a. 지적인; 총명한

아마도 어떤 사람들은 동물도 단지 우리보다 더 적기는 하지만 얼마간의 내재적 가치를 갖고 있다고 말할 것이다.

38 ④

□ remedy v. 고치다, 치료하다; 개선하다, 바로잡다(=correct) □ understand v. 이해하다, 알아듣다 □ identify v. 확인하다, 식별하다 □ utilize v. 활용하다, 이용하다, 소용되게 하다

기술의 몇 가지 부정적인 측면은 바로잡기 매우 어렵다.

39 ④

□ annul v. 무효로 하다, 취소하다, 폐기하다(=nullify) □ support v. 지지[옹호, 재청]하다 □ avert v. (~에서) 돌리다, 비키다, 외면하다; (위험 등을) 피하다 □ abominate v. 혐오하다, 증오하다

이 새로운 계약은 두 회사 간 이전 합의를 무효로 만들 것이다.

40 ④

□ relegate v. 격하[좌천]시키다(=demote) □ besiege v. 포위하다, 에워싸다 □ terrify v. 무섭게[겁먹게] 하다 □ integrate v. 통합시키다

만약 한국에서 그가 흑인 혼혈인으로서 자랐더라면 2등 시민으로 전락했을 가능성이 높다.

41 ③

□ unbridled a. 억제되지 않은, 방종한(=unrestrained) □ crafty a. 간사한, 교활한 □ involuntary a. 본의 아닌, 마음이 내키지 않는; 무심결의 □ lucrative a. 수익성이 좋은, 유리한

토니 아담스(Tony Adams)가 케빈 키건(Kevin Keegan)의 축구를 향한 억제할 수 없는 열정을 처음 발견한 것은 약 10년 전이었다.

42 ④

□ eliminate v. 제거하다, 삭제하다; 무시하다(=exclude) □ yell v. 고함치다, 소리 지르다, 외치다 □ recognize v. 알아보다; 인지하다; 인정하다 □ study v. 공부하다, 연구하다 □ experiment v. 실험하다

조사원들은 인터뷰가 진행되는 동안 집에서 소리를 지른 적이 한 번도 없다고 이야기한 사람들을 제외시켰다.

43 ②

☐ odds n. 가망, 공산, 가능성(=likelihood) ☐ horrendous a. 대단히 충격적인, 참혹한 ☐ catastrophe n. 참사, 재앙 ☐ endeavor n. 노력; 시도, 진력 ☐ provocation n. 도발, 자극 ☐ apathy n. 무관심, 냉담

우리는 가장 끔찍한 재앙을 막을 가능성을 높이기 위해 우리가 생각하는 것보다 훨씬 더 많은 것을 할 수 있다.

44 ②

☐ retort v. 보복하다, 응수하다(=respond) ☐ humiliated a. 수치를 느낀 ☐ ignore v. 무시하다 ☐ denounce v. 공공연히 비난[공격]하다

어린 인도 소녀들은 아무리 수치스러운 느낌이 든다고 할지라도 응수하지 말라고 그들에게 교육하는 부모들에 의해 길러진다.

45 ①

☐ buoyancy n. 부력; 회복력(=resilience) ☐ breach n. 위반 ☐ potential n. 가능성, 잠재력 ☐ depression n. 우울증; 불경기, 불황

작년이었더라면 우리는 지금 우리가 마주하고 있는 경제적 회복력을 갖고서 매우 기뻐했을 것이다.

46 ④

☐ ferret out ~을 캐내다, 찾아내다, 발견하다(=search for) ☐ chime in 맞장구치다, 찬성하다 ☐ write up ~을 완전히 작성하다, 기록하다 ☐ refer to ~을 나타내다, 관련 있다

그들은 지난 시즌에 해럴드(Harold)를 연출가로 뽑았고, 그는 그가 생각하기에 단원들이 공연하기 좋아할 만한 몇 가지 대본들을 찾아냈다.

47 ④

☐ commonwealth n. (the C-) 영국 연방, 영연방 ☐ marvelous a. 불가사의한, 놀라운 ☐ testimony n. 증거, 증명(=proof) ☐ injustice n. 부정, 불의 ☐ exam n. 시험 ☐ accusation n. 고발, 고소 ☐ phenomenon n. 현상, 사건

영연방은 어떻게 불법 행위와 억압이 협력과 조화로 바뀔 수 있는지를 보여주는 놀라운 증거라고 일부 역사가들은 주장한다.

48 ①

☐ undoubtedly ad. 의심할 여지없이, 틀림없이, 확실히 ☐ convict

v. 유죄를 입증하다, 유죄를 선고하다(=condemn) ☐ culprit n. 범죄자, 죄인, 범인 ☐ larceny n. 절도(죄), 도둑질 ☐ extend v. 뻗다, 내밀다; 연장하다 ☐ scorch v. 태우다, 그슬리다 ☐ supplant v. 대신 들어앉다, 탈취하다; 대신하다

배심원단은 틀림없이 그 범인에게 중(重) 절도죄에 대해 유죄판결을 내릴 것이다.

49 ④

☐ decisive a. 결정적인, 과단성 있는(=resolute) ☐ nimble a. 재빠른, 민첩한 ☐ unilateral a. 일방적인, 단독의 ☐ vigilant a. 바짝 경계하는, 조금도 방심하지 않는

멕시코는 유행성 독감을 발견하고 확산을 막는 데 있어서 신속하고 과단성 있는 조치를 취하지 못한 듯 보인다.

50 ①

☐ conquer v. 정복하다, 공략하다(=vanquish) ☐ forfeit v. 몰수당하다; 상실하다 ☐ transcend v. 초월하다, ~을 능가하다 ☐ refute v. 논박하다, 반박하다

10년이라는 기간 동안 나폴레옹(Napoleon)은 대부분의 발트해 국가들과 스페인을 정복했다.

51 ②

☐ wartime a. 전시의 ☐ clear-eyed a. 총명한, 통찰력 있는; 현실적인 ☐ eloquent a. 웅변[연설]을 잘 하는, 유창한(=fluent) ☐ orator n. 연설가, 웅변가 ☐ calm a. 침착한, 차분한 ☐ rational a. 합리적인, 이성적인 ☐ candid a. 정직한, 솔직한

윈스턴 처칠(Winston Churchill)은 전시의 지도자이자, 통찰력 있는 역사학자이자, 유창한 웅변가로 잘 알려져 있다.

52 ③

☐ come to a head (종기가) 곪아 터질 지경이 되다; 때가 무르익다; 위기에 처하다; 막바지에 이르다 ☐ fructose n. 과당(果糖) ☐ obesity n. 비만 ☐ epidemic n. 유행병, 전염병 ☐ unwavering a. 동요하지 않는; 확고한(=steadfast) ☐ fluctuating a. 변동하는; 동요하는 ☐ partial a. 불공평한, 편파적인 ☐ unprecedented a. 전례 없는

고과당(高果糖) 옥수수 시럽의 위기와 긴급한 비만 대유행에서의 역할은 2004년에 정점에 이른 후 지금까지 식품업계의 확고한 부인에 직면해왔다.

53 ④

☐ eclipse v. ~의 명성·중요성 따위를 가리다; 능가하다(=surpass) ☐

expose v. 노출시키다; (환경 따위에) 접하게 하다; 폭로하다 □ hamper v. 방해하다; ~의 방해[장애]가 되다 □ muster v. (검열·점호에) 소집하다, 모으다

영화 "포레스트 검프"의 명성은 그 영화의 원작 소설의 명성을 쉽게 뛰어넘었다.

54 ①
□ maul v. 상처를 내다; 거칠게 다루다(=beat); 혹평하다 □ cuddle v. 꼭 껴안다, 부둥키다 □ throw v. (내)던지다, 팽개치다; 내동댕이치다 □ trap v. 덫을 놓다, 궁지로 몰다

우리는 사람들이 서로 상대방을 거칠게 다루지 못하게 해야 한다.

55 ③
□ diverse a. 여러 가지의, 다양한(=different) □ common a. 공통의, 공동의; 일반의 □ stubborn a. 완고한; 단단한 □ concentrated a. 집중된; 응집된, 응축된

다양한 관심을 가진 사람은 많은 주제들에 관해 말할 수 있다.

56 ②
□ negate v. 부인하다, 부정하다; 무효로 하다, 효력이 없게 만들다(=repudiate) □ validate v. 정당성을 입증하다, 실증하다, 확인하다; 비준하다 □ accredit v. 믿다, 신용하다, 신임하다; (어떤 일을) ~의 공적으로 돌리다 □ acquaint v. 익히 알게 하다, 알리다; 소개하다

그 나라는 자국민을 석방시키기 위해 납치범들에게 어떠한 몸값도 지불하지 않았다고 공개적으로 부인해 왔다.

57 ①
□ encumber v. 방해하다, 폐끼치다, 훼방 놓다, 지장을 주다(=hamper) □ pamper v. 소중히 보살피다 □ contemplate v. 고려하다, 심사숙고하다 □ modify v. 수정하다

그 작가들은 이전에 그들이 했던 일의 중압감에 방해받지 않았다.

58 ④
□ strained a. 긴장한, 부자연스러운(=not natural) □ direct a. 똑바른; 직접의; 솔직한 □ not familiar 익숙지 않은, 낯선 □ opposite a. 마주 보고 있는, 맞은편의; 역의, 정반대의

예술 작품은 그 자체에 검증 기준을 내포하고 있어서, 부자연스러운 개념들은 이미지로 전환되어야 하는 검증 기준에 부합되지 못한다.

59 ④
□ dispute n. 분쟁, 분규 □ arbitrate v. 중재재판에 부치다, 중재하다(=mediate) □ comply with 응하다, 따르다 □ determine v. 결심하다, 결정하다 □ engage v. 약속하다, 계약하다; 고용하다 □ avoid v. 피하다, 방지하다

판사는 분쟁이 중재되어야 하며 우리가 그것에 따라야 한다고 분명하게 말했다.

60 ③
□ treaty n. 조약, 협정, 맹약 □ rupture n. 파열, 터짐; 결렬, 단절; 불화(=crack) □ fan n. 부채; 환풍기 □ lore n. (전승적) 지식; 민간 전승 □ crank n. 크랭크; 묘한 현상; 기인, 괴짜

임박한 조약에 대한 의견 불일치로 인해 양국 간의 관계가 틀어졌다.

61 ①
□ fabrication n. 제작; 구조물; 꾸며낸 것(=invention) □ mystery n. 신비, 비밀 □ failure n. 실패, 실수; 낙제 □ sensation n. 감각, 느낌, 기분

그의 동료들은 그의 최근 실험이 날조된 것이라고 주장하지 않았는가?

62 ②
□ asset n. 자산, 재산(=property); 장점, 이점 □ exhibition n. 전람, 공개, 전시 □ attribute n. 속성, 특성, 특질 □ obligation n. 의무, 책무, 책임

네가 가진 가장 소중한 자산은 신용이라는 것을 잊지 말아야 한다.

63 ③
□ radical a. 급진적인, 과격한 □ trait n. (성격, 습관의) 특징, 특색, 특질(=tendency) □ blow n. 강타; 타격 □ trade n. 매매, 상업, 장사, 거래, 무역 □ hostility n. 적의, 적대 행위, 전쟁 행위 □ sycophant n. 아첨꾼, 추종자

그들 모두가 공유하고 있는 이데올로기의 특징인 급진적이고 과격한 반서구주의의 대의는 심한 타격을 입을 것이다.

64 ①
□ board n. 이사회, 위원회 □ obvious a. 명백한, 명료한(=manifest) □ flaw n. 결함, 결점 □ candidate n. 후보자, 지원자 □ tremendous a. 굉장한, 엄청난 □ resplendent a. 빛나는, 눈부신 □ critical a. 비판적인; 위기의 □ composite a. 혼성의, 합성의

위원회가 후보자로서의 그녀의 명백한 결점을 무시해버릴 수 있다면,

그들은 그녀가 그 역할을 할 엄청난 잠재력을 갖고 있다는 것을 알게 될 것이다.

65 ④

☐ descent n. 하강; 하락, 몰락; 출신, 혈통(=lineage) ☐ character n. 특성; 인격, 성격 ☐ temperament n. 기질, 성질 ☐ alliance n. 동맹; 협력

아메리카 원주민은 인디언 혈통의 아메리카 사람들을 지칭한다.

66 ②

☐ tempt v. ~할 생각이 나게 하다 ☐ jump to a conclusion 성급히 결론을 내리다(=draw a rash conclusion) ☐ build v. 만들다, 확립하다 ☐ fail to ~하지 못하다, 실패하다

많은 문제가 있는 상황에서는, 빠른 해결책을 내기 위해 성급히 결론을 내리고 싶은 생각이 나게 마련이다.

67 ④

☐ viable a. 실행 가능한, 실용적인; 성장할 수 있는 ☐ congested a. 혼잡한, 정체된(=jammed) ☐ subsonic a. 음속 이하의 ☐ meddling a. 참견하는, 간섭하는 ☐ free a. 자유로운

헬리콥터는 종종 혼잡한 육상 교통에 대해 경쟁력 있는 대체수단을 제공한다.

68 ②

☐ nefarious a. 못된, 사악한; 부정(不正)한, 무도한(=iniquitous) ☐ stolid a. 둔감한, 신경이 무딘 ☐ boorish a. (사람이나 행동이) 상스러운, 천박한 ☐ churlish a. 막된, 무례한

실질적이거나 인지된 사악한 행동이 있었다 하더라도, 그만두기로 한 나의 결정은 결코 세련된 것은 아니었다.

69 ①

☐ misgiving n. (pl.) 불안, 의심, 걱정, 염려(=distrust) ☐ mischief n. 해악, 악영향; 손해 ☐ misconception n. 오해, 착각, 그릇된 생각 ☐ disenchantment n. 각성, 눈뜸

핵에너지를 반대하는 사람들은 그 안전성에 대해 깊은 의혹을 가지고 있다.

70 ③

☐ judicial a. 사법의, 재판의(=legal); 공정한 ☐ fractional a. 단편의

☐ official a. 공식의, 공무상의; 공인의 ☐ exact a. 정확한; 엄격한; 정밀한

사법당국에 따르면 그는 가중폭행죄로 기소되었다.

71 ①

☐ pledge v. 서약하다, 굳게 약속하다(=make a solemn promise of) ☐ make a serious request for ~을 간청하다 ☐ recommend in a good will 선의로 조언하다 ☐ provide a suitable solution for ~에 대한 알맞은 해결책을 제시하다

우리는 시대가 무엇을 요구하든지 그들을 도울 최상의 제의에 엄숙히 서약한다.

72 ③

☐ jettison v. (긴급 시 부담스러운 짐을) 버리다(=discard) ☐ defend v. 방어하다, 옹호하다 ☐ revise v. 개정하다, 수정하다, 교정하다 ☐ assert v. 단언하다

미국과 영국처럼 양당 체제에서는 우파가 집권하지만, 우파를 정의했던 가치를 버림으로써만 집권한다.

73 ④

☐ pore over ~을 자세히 조사하다, 보다(=give close attention to) ☐ change v. 바꾸다, 갈다; 교환하다 ☐ overlook v. 바라보다, 내려다보다; 눈감아주다 ☐ recapitulate v. 요점을 되풀이하여 말하다

미국 중재자들과 함께 협상을 벌이고 있는 이스라엘과 팔레스타인의 협상 당사자들은 헤브론에 대한 난해한 협정을 또다시 지연시키면서 협정서 초안 작성에 신중을 기했다.

74 ③

☐ obnoxious a. 밉살스러운, 불쾌한, 싫은(=disagreeable) ☐ fugitive n. 도망자, 탈주자 ☐ lustrous a. 광택 있는, 번쩍이는, 빛나는; 저명한 ☐ anomalous a. 변칙의, 파격의, 이례의; 이상한 ☐ hypocritical a. 위선의; 위선(자)적인

그들은 비위에 거슬리는 어떤 망명자를 희생시킴으로써 황제의 보호를 기꺼이 얻어냈다.

75 ①

☐ grief-stricken a. 비탄에 빠진, 슬픔에 젖은 ☐ pusillanimous a. 겁 많은, 소심한(=cowardly) ☐ treacherous a. 기만적인, 신뢰할 수 없는 ☐ political a. 정치적인 ☐ immoral a. 비도덕적인, 부도덕한

시장이 큰 슬픔에 잠긴 가족과의 만남을 거절한 것은 매우 소심한 행동이었다.

76 ①

☐ portable a. 들고 다닐 수 있는, 휴대용의(=movable) ☐ relievable a. 구제할 수 있는; 경감할 수 있는 ☐ vivid a. 생생한, 눈에 보이는 듯한 ☐ elastic a. 탄력 있는, 탄성의

판매원은 그 소형 TV가 휴대가 가능한 것으로 선전했다.

77 ①

☐ repeal v. 폐지하다(=abolish) ☐ immunity n. (책임의) 면제 ☐ post v. 게시하다 ☐ enact v. (법을) 제정하다 ☐ revise v. 수정하다 ☐ oppose v. 반대하다

우리는 소셜미디어 사이트들에게 그들의 사용자들이 게시하는 모든 것에 대해 책임을 면제해주는 그 법을 폐지해야 한다.

78 ③

☐ hit the ceiling 격노하다, 화가 나서 길길이 날뛰다 ☐ detain v. 붙들어두다; 억류하다, 구금하다(=imprison) ☐ disorderly a. 무질서한, 난잡한 ☐ charge v. 고발하다, 고소하다 ☐ murder v. 살해[살인]하다 ☐ imprison v. 투옥하다, 감금하다 ☐ torment v. 괴롭히다, 고문하다

대니(Danny)의 아버지는 아들이 풍기문란 행위로 경찰에 구금되었다는 소식을 전해 듣고는 격노했다.

79 ②

☐ creditable a. 명예가 되는; 칭찬할 만한, 훌륭한(=laudable) ☐ rendition n. 번역; 연출, 연주; 공연 ☐ concerto n. 콘체르토, 협주곡 ☐ nonsensical a. 무의미한; 터무니없는, 시시한 ☐ calamitous a. 불행한, 비참한 ☐ inadvertent a. 고의가 아닌, 우연의; 의도하지 않은

그 바이올린 연주자는 훌륭한 협주곡 연주를 해냈다.

80 ②

☐ grief n. 큰 슬픔, 비탄 ☐ abate v. 감소하다; 누그러지다 ☐ rend v. ~을 째다, 찢다(=tear); (마음을) 산란케 하다 ☐ fill v. 채우다 ☐ pack v. 싸다, 채우다 ☐ remind v. 상기시키다, 생각나게 하다

잠시 동안 누그러졌던 그의 슬픔이 다시 일어나 더 맹렬한 기세로 그의 마음을 찢어 놓는다.

81 ③

☐ querulous a. 불평하는, 짜증내는(=whining) ☐ sanguine a. 낙관적인, 자신감이 넘치는 ☐ avaricious a. 탐욕스러운, 욕심 많은 ☐ servile a. 노예의; 비굴한

자신들의 시험이 너무 가혹하게 채점되었다고 믿는 학생들의 불만에 찬 목소리는 학교 건물 반대편에서까지도 들을 수 있었다.

82 ②

☐ crave v. 간청하다; 열망하다(=desire) ☐ eat v. 먹다, 식사하다 ☐ prepare v. 준비하다, 대비하다 ☐ look for ~을 찾다; 기다리다

외국에 사는 동안 때때로 사람들은 고국의 특식을 그리워한다.

83 ③

☐ apply for 지원하다, 신청하다 ☐ issue v. 내다, 발하다, 발포하다; 발행하다 ☐ gratis ad. 무료로(=for free) ☐ in confidence 비밀로, 극비로 ☐ at random 무작위로, 임의로, 닥치는 대로 ☐ for credit 신용으로

인도 시민들은 관광 비자를 신청해야 하지만 이 비자는 무료로 발급된다.

84 ③

☐ transitory a. 일시적인, 덧없는(=fleeting) ☐ transcendental a. 선험적인 ☐ deceptive a. 현혹시키는, 거짓의 ☐ translucent a. 반투명의; 명백한

스코틀랜드의 겨울은 다른 나라에 비해 더 길고 어둡기 때문에 비록 일시적이나마 독하고 따뜻한 술이 빛과 휴식을 제공한다.

85 ②

☐ in tatters 너덜너덜 해어진, 다 망가진 ☐ might n. 힘, 세력 ☐ spearhead v. 선두에 서다, 이끌어나가다(=lead) ☐ endanger v. 위험에 빠뜨리다, 위태롭게 하다 ☐ slow down 느긋해지다; (속도, 진행을) 늦추다; 쇠해지다 ☐ speed up 속도를 빠르게 하다, 가속하다

세계 경제 국가들 중 너무 많은 국가가 파탄 상태에 있는 가운데, 중국과 인도가 서로 힘을 합한다면 향후 몇십 년 동안 세계 경제 성장을 이끌어 갈 수 있을 것이다.

86 ③

☐ ambush v. 매복하다; 매복하여 습격하다(=attack by surprise) ☐ hide from sight 시야에서 가리다 ☐ spy on from afar 멀리 떨어져 정찰하다 ☐ shadow on sight 시야에 그림자를 드리우다

우리는 그가 훈련 도중 다치거나 캠프로 가거나 돌아오는 여행길에서 매복한 테러리스트들에게 습격을 받을까봐 걱정했다.

87 ③

☐ talkie n. 발성영화(=talking picture) ☐ patron n. 보호자, 후원자; 단골, 고객(=customer) ☐ owner n. 임자, 소유(권)자 ☐ actor n. 배우 ☐ critic n. 비평가, 평론가, 감정가, 흠 잡는 사람

'발성영화'가 소개되고 2년 후에 1929년까지 미국의 극장에서는 매주 1억 명의 관람객을 끌어모았다.

88 ③

☐ expedite v. (계획 따위를) 진척시키다, 촉진하다; (일을) 신속히 처리하다(=hasten) ☐ certify v. 증명하다, 보증하다; 공인하다 ☐ prompt v. 자극하다; 격려하다, 고무하다 ☐ impose v. 부과하다; 강요하다

입국심사를 신속하게 진행하기 위해, 창구에 오시기 전에 입국신고서를 작성해 주십시오.

89 ③

☐ bypass v. 회피하다, 무시하다 ☐ place the onus on ~에게 책임을 물리다 ☐ onus n. 부담; 책임, 의무(=liability) ☐ favor n. 호의, 친절 ☐ menace n. 위협 ☐ nuisance n. 골칫거리

비판자들은 이 법이 범죄자들에게 그들의 상황 변화를 보고할 책임을 지우기 때문에 회피하기 너무 쉽다고 말한다.

90 ①

☐ sloth n. 마음이 내키지 않음; 게으름(=indolence) ☐ ill-restrained a. 절제되지 않은 ☐ fondness n. 좋아함; 기호, 취미 ☐ illness n. 병; 불쾌 ☐ inhibition n. 금지; 억제 ☐ industry n. 공업, 산업; 근면

나는 사서가 되길 꿈꿨다. 게을러지고 여행에 완전히 빠져버리는 바람에 다른 길을 가게 됐다.

91 ④

☐ stumble upon 넘어지다, 비틀거리다; 실수하다; 우연히 마주치다 (=discover by accident) ☐ be aware of ~을 알아채고 있다, 알고 있다 ☐ be intrigued by ~에 흥미를 느끼다 ☐ learn by experimentation 실험을 통해 배우다

3,000년 이전에, 고대인들은 몇몇 곰팡이들이 질병을 치료할 수 있다는 사실을 우연히 발견했다.

92 ④

☐ eyebrow n. 눈썹 ☐ oddly ad. 기묘하게; 이상하게 ☐ menacing a. 위협적인, 협박을 가하는(=threatening) ☐ sturdy a. 강건한, 튼튼한 ☐ gloomy a. 우울한, 비관적인 ☐ friendly a. 친한, 우호적인

강한 인상을 주는 짙은 눈썹은 그의 얼굴에 이상하리만치 위협적인 표정을 띠게 한다.

93 ②

☐ enmesh v. 그물로 잡다; (곤란 따위에) 빠뜨리다, 말려들게 하다 (=entangle) ☐ encroach v. 침입하다, 잠식하다 ☐ embitter v. 쓰라리게 하다, (감정 등을) 몹시 상하게 하다 ☐ enlighten v. 계몽하다, 계발하다; 가르치다

미군은 유혈이 낭자한 콜롬비아 내전에 더 깊이 말려들고 있다.

94 ④

☐ reasoning n. 추론 ☐ needlessly repetitive 불필요하게 반복적인 (=tautological) ☐ hark v. 주의 깊게 듣다, 경청하다 ☐ pathological a. 병적인, 걷잡을 수 없는 ☐ adnominal a. 명사를 수식하는 ☐ dolose a. 범의(犯意) 있는

그의 추론은 동일한 생각에 귀 기울이고 있다는 점에서 불필요하게 반복적인 것으로 드러났다.

95 ④

☐ stem from ~에서 생겨나다, 기인하다 ☐ elimination n. 제거, 배제 ☐ irrelevant a. 무관한, 상관없는(=trivial) ☐ complex a. 복잡한, 얽히고설킨 ☐ confusing a. 혼란스러운 ☐ specific a. 구체적인, 명확한

경제 모형의 힘은 관계없는 세부사항들을 제거하는 것에서 비롯되는데, 이것은 경제학자로 하여금 그가 이해하려고 시도하는 경제 상황의 근본적인 특징에 집중할 수 있도록 해준다.

96 ①

☐ circumspect a. 신중한, 주의 깊은(=cautious) ☐ devious a. 우회하는, 에두르는; (방법 등이) 상도를 벗어난 ☐ genuine a. 진짜의; 진심에서 우러난 ☐ industrious a. 근면한, 부지런한

대통령은 그들의 조언에 크게 의존해야 할 것을 알고 있었기 때문에 보좌관들을 선임하는 데 신중했다.

97 ②

☐ mystic n. 신비주의자 ☐ speculate v. 여러 가지로 생각하다; 추측하다; 사색하다 ☐ intrigue v. 흥미를[관심을] 갖게 하다; (흥미·호기심을)

끌다(=fascinate) ☐ **nether** a. 아래의; 지하의, 지옥의 ☐ **tantalizingly** ad. 감질나게, 애타게 ☐ **grasp** n. 붙잡음; 통제; 이해, 납득 ☐ **elude** v. 교묘히 피하다, 회피하다 ☐ **beleaguer** v. 포위[공격]하다; 괴롭히다 ☐ **dumbfound** v. (너무 놀라서) 말을 못하게 만들다 ☐ **nonpluss** v. 어찌할 바를 모르게 하다

신비주의자들은 오랫동안 다른 세계가 존재할 가능성에 대해 여러 가지로 생각해 왔다. 그들은 아무도 탐험한 적이 없는 이 지하 세계들이 감질나게 가까이 있지만 단지 우리가 신체적으로 붙잡을 수 없어 감각적으로 느낄 수 없는 것일지도 모를 가능성에 흥미를 가져 왔다.

98   ④

☐ **queue** v. 줄을 서서 기다리다 ☐ **balloting** n. 투표, 추첨 ☐ **farce** n. 소극(笑劇), 익살극; 웃음거리(=comedy) ☐ **oust** v. 내쫓다, 쫓아내다, 퇴거시키다 ☐ **reform** n. 개정, 개혁, 개선 ☐ **coup** n. 대성공; 쿠데타 ☐ **process** n. 과정, 공정, 처리, 방법

2011년 11월 28일에 시작된 선거를 위해 투표소 밖에서 참을성 있게 줄 서 있던 많은 이집트인들은 그들이 역사를 만들고 있다는 것을 알고 있었다. 그들은 사람들의 기억 속에서 최초로 결과를 미리 알지 못한 채 투표하라고 요청받았는데, 이것은 축출된 호스니 무바라크(Hosni Mubarak) 대통령 정권에 의해 행해졌던 선거 코미디와는 행복한 대조를 이루고 있다.

99   ④

☐ **offended** a. 기분이 상한, 불쾌한 ☐ **officious** a. 참견하기 좋아하는, 주제넘게 나서는(=meddlesome) ☐ **unwanted** a. 원치 않는 ☐ **dos and don'ts** 따라야 할 행동수칙 ☐ **judicious** a. 신중한, 현명한 ☐ **convivial** a. 쾌활한, 명랑한 ☐ **courteous** a. 예의바른, 정중한

나는 은행 서비스를 기다리는 중에 웬 낯선 사람이 사적인 질문을 하면서 참견하려 했을 때 불쾌했다. 그녀는 내 직업에 대해 원치 않는 조언을 계속했고 심지어 내 결혼에 대해 이런저런 행동수칙 따위를 늘어놓으면서 조언하려고까지 했다.

100   ②

☐ **follow suit** 선례를 따르다(=do the same as another has done) ☐ **cutback** n. 삭감, 축소; 중지 ☐ **argue against other suggestions** 다른 제안들에 대해 반대하다 ☐ **not have the right quality** 적절한 품질을 갖추지 못하다 ☐ **carry out legal actions** 사법조치를 취하다

5천만 달러의 적자에 직면한 컬럼비아 대학교는 26개 인문·자연과학 학과의 학과장들이 급료 삭감이 지나치게 가혹하면 그만두겠다고 위협했음에도 아마도 선례를 따를 것이다.

MVP

Vol.1 워크북

APPENDIX

[01-25] 다음의 대화들 중 흐름이 가장 적절하지 <u>않은</u> 것을 고르시오.

01 ① A: Is there a pretty good chance that you'll finish on time?
B: Yes, it is as sure as death.
② A: Do you think she will admit to her mistake?
B: I doubt it. She's as proud as a peacock.
③ A: Is there any chance he'll change his mind?
B: No way. He's as dry as a bone.
④ A: Have you seen the new baby? How is she?
B: She's as cute as a button.

02 ① A: Can we go to the movies?
B: I wish I could, but I can't swing it today.
② A: Can we move up the meeting?
B: That's a good idea. I want to meet them later.
③ A: Out of the blue, he opened up a business on a shoestring.
B: That's a feather in his cap.
④ A: I'm racking my brain to find a way to keep my head above water.
B: I didn't know you were hard up.

03 ① A: Brian, is this camera what you've been looking for?
B: Cool. It's just the job!
② A: Oh, It's already 12:35. I have another appointment at 12:40.
B: Must dash. Break a leg.
③ A: Shawn, I need your help this time. Can you give me a hand?
B: In your dreams. Do you mind me asking?
④ A: All tech stocks will reach all time high!
B: I can't get my head round it. What's your ground?

04 ① A: He is a good seller in the fish market, isn't he?

   B: Yes, he often throws a red herring.

② A: Jackson gives me the creeps.

   B: You bet! He always sleepwalks around at night.

③ A: I don't know why he spent so much time doing nothing last week.

   B: Probably, he lost his bearings.

④ A: I think he is always punctual at work.

   B: Yes, his word is as good as his bond.

05 ① A: What's wrong with Joe?

   B: He is feeling bad because his boss jumped all over him this morning.

② A: Can you lend me a hand?

   B: I need to do my homework now. I'll help you when I finish.

③ A: Do you know these drinks are on the house?

   B: Don't worry. I'll pay the earth for them.

④ A: You should not spill the beans.

   B: You bet! My lips are sealed.

06 ① A: Sorry to hear that you are left high and dry.

   B: Yeah. I'm not going to let this destroy me. I will make the best of it.

② A: Can't you stay some more days?

   B: No, I don't want to wear out my welcome.

③ A: I can't seem to be able to finish writing this thesis.

   B: Just take the bull by the horns and go for it.

④ A: Man, I'm up a tree today.

   B: I will let you do the honors.

07 ① A: Hey, Ryan. Can you do me a favor?

   B: I have a lot on my plate. But what is it?

② A: Can you join us to play the games tonight?

   B: Sure, I'm so glad to know that you guys are totally screwed.

③ A: Maggie, you can earn a fortune if you invest your money in this sector at the stock market.

   B: Let's not be naive here. Money doesn't grow on trees.

④ A: Ma'am. You're speeding at 150 miles here at Transnational Highway 1.

   B: Could you please let it aside, sir?

08 ① A: I wonder how she came up with such a peculiar idea!

B: I think some of her ideas are often off the wall.

② A: He skived off as he does everyday.

B: Yes, he always wants to help clean up.

③ A: He scoffed a dish of noodle at lunch time.

B: Probably, he didn't eat breakfast this morning.

④ A: I faffed around in the library.

B: Did you find the book you wanted?

09 ① A: I can't understand why so many people think that Sam and Jack are a lot alike.

B: I don't see it either. Actually, I think that they are poles apart.

② A: Sorry to hear that your friend left you high and dry.

B: Yeah. I'm not going to let this destroy me. I'm going to make the best of it.

③ A: My sister got so angry with me, but I guess I had it coming.

B: Yes, I'll be bitter if I were you.

④ A: Come in. Have a seat and take the load off.

B: Thanks. I've been on my feet all day long.

10 ① A: You don't know how hard it is to run a restaurant in the city.

B: I've been there. You don't need to spell it out.

② A: How does a nice hot chocolate sound?

B: Wow, I think that would hit the spot.

③ A: Is that the right answer?

B: No, now you're getting colder.

④ A: I always see eye to eye with him.

B: Oh, he's really hard to work with.

11 ① A: He seems to take out on me for the result.

B: Right, he really appreciates for your efforts.

② A: She doesn't have it in her to do the job.

B: I agree. She needs more experiences to carry out such a task.

③ A: I hate watching monster movies late at night.

B: Me, too. They give me the creeps.

④ A: Why did you listen to the lecture without taking it in?

B: Because I am keen on it.

12

  ① A: Marry is teed off again.

      B: She always flips out when her friend comes to visit without any notice.

  ② A: He had it coming to him.

      B: You are telling me. He has to know better.

  ③ A: Donald is a fair-weather friend to me.

      B: Yeah, he is really a friend in need.

  ④ A: I'm so glad that you come to my support when I need you.

      B: When the chips are down we all need someone to lean on.

13

  ① A: He talks like he knows music, but he's still a greenhorn.

      B: Right, he is a rank amateur.

  ② A: Can you put me up for the night?

      B: Of course, you can come sleep over.

  ③ A: Let's call it quits for the day.

      B: Ok, we can tie up the loose ends on Monday.

  ④ A: The film laid an egg at the box office.

      B: Wow, I heard it drew audiences totaling a million people.

14

  ① A: Drive it to the last minute.

      B: No, I will give it up.

  ② A: I will let myself loose this time.

      B: Right, you need patience.

  ③ A: Put your cards on the table.

      B: But I am afraid you will be angry.

  ④ A: Jim earned his fame for his novel.

      B: It's a just a flash in the pan.

15

  ① A: Did she get well today?

      B: She blew hot and cold.

  ② A: Surely we need a break.

      B: Let up for a while and have some coffee.

  ③ A: He keeps making a nuisance of himself.

      B: Right, he is a black sheep.

  ④ A: We can't be late for work again!

      B: Ok, let's not drag our feet.

16 ① A: I don't like your idea, Ryan. It's too radical.

B: Oh, come on! Don't thumb your nose at it without giving it a fair shake.

② A: Are you coming to play tennis with us?

B: Sure, I'm completely snowed under.

③ A: I am really excited for the new movie.

B: I know. Many movie-goers are just chomping at the bit to see it.

④ A: There were plenty of new faces that showed up in the meeting last night.

B: I think they heard through the grapevine that the event was worth attending.

17 ① A: How did Mike do in the race?

B: He turned the tables and in the end he won the race.

② A: Hi, Jenny! How have you been doing?

B: I've just moved to a new place and everything is still at sixes and sevens.

③ A: Tom was right. This movie is just horrible!

B: I can't agree more. Tom has to eat his words.

④ A: I can't seem to shake off this cold. I've been flat on my back for a week.

B: Don't rush back to work. We know you're under the weather.

18 ① A: You look tired today, David. What happened?

B: I was under the gun to impress my girlfriend's father.

② A: Where did the traveling circus go?

B: They're constantly on the move.

③ A: Did you bring the picnic cloth to sit on?

B: Oops, I totally forgot. I guess we'll have to rough it this time.

④ A: Our sponsors have pledged one dollar for every mile we run in this marathon.

B: You had better sit on the sidelines.

19 ① A: Isn't it funny to see that Vince always goes by the book?

B: Right. He definitely gives it a big charge.

② A: Have you found a good mechanic for your car?

B: I have given it to a new mechanic for repair. Hope he delivers the goods.

③ A: I tried calling you all morning yesterday. Who were you talking with?

B: Betty and I were just chewing the fat.

④ A: Grandpa is always in the pink. He still goes mountain-climbing.

B: No wonder he looks fit as a fiddle.

20 ① A: Good job, Neil. You didn't look worried at all.

B: Well, when it was my turn to speak, I really had my heart in my mouth.

② A: Can't John see he'll never get anywhere if he goes on like this?

B: Yes. If he's serious about going to college, he really will have to pull his socks up.

③ A: Ah ha! You've found a girlfriend at last, haven't you?

B: Yes. Now, you've no need to worry about me. At the moment, you promise the moon.

④ A: This dish is so delicious! Where did you get its recipe?

B: I hunted high and low across the Internet looking for it.

21 ① A: I can't find my new diamond necklace!

B: Not to worry! We'll go through this house with a fine tooth comb.

② A: The rumor is that Mr. Kim is head over heels with Miss Park.

B: That's good. They need to get on the bandwagon.

③ A: Isn't Julie a fantastic cook?

B: Yes, indeed. When she cooks, it's a four-course meal. She does nothing by halves!

④ A: I heard the news that Bob's firm has gone to bankruptcy.

B: Don't worry about Bob. He always lands on his feet.

22 ① A: Are you coming to the party?

B: Only an act of God could keep me away.

② A: I think what you did was to rub salt in his wound.

B: I know. I fear that I made him feel even worse about the matter.

③ A: Just put your John Hancock on the dotted line.

B: Give me a break. Let me sleep on it and get back to you later.

④ A: When I saw that big truck bearing down on me, I thought my number was up.

B: You have really made your bed!

23 ① A: Did you eat dinner yet?

B: Yes, I bought a pig in a poke.

② A: I heard that Bob and Jen got a good price when they sold their house.

B: Yes, they did. Now they're really sitting pretty.

③ A: I have no idea who will win the race. All jockeys are playing at their best.

B: I guess the race will go down to the wire.

④ A: I had to fire Mike today. He never completed his work in time.

B: Some people just can't cut the mustard.

24 ① A: I bet he will get the best records at the final exam.

　　　B: If it happens, I will eat my hat.

　　② A: I lost a huge amount of money at the deal.

　　　B: You got what you bargained for.

　　③ A: I spent a wonderful holiday on the beach. Moreover, I ran into an old friend whom I hadn't seen in years.

　　　B: It is an icing on the cake.

　　④ A: He does not want to join our fund raising for a charity.

　　　B: Every dog has his day.

25 ① A: Ten years ago, I could have been paid twice as much as for the job I've taken now.

　　　B: The fish that got away.

　　② A: I wanted to reprimand him hard, but, instead, I tried to remain calm and nice to him.

　　　B: A soft answer turns away wrath.

　　③ A: My car brings out troubles quite frequently.

　　　B: Turning green with envy.

　　④ A: I am looking for my car key, still I don't see it.

　　　B: It is on the table. If it were a snake, it would bite you.

01 ③	**02** ②	**03** ③	**04** ①	**05** ③	**06** ④	**07** ②	**08** ②	**09** ③	**10** ④
11 ①	**12** ③	**13** ④	**14** ②	**15** ①	**16** ②	**17** ③	**18** ④	**19** ①	**20** ③
21 ②	**22** ④	**23** ①	**24** ④	**25** ③					

01 ③

③ 'as dry as a bone'은 '아주 말랐다'는 의미로 그가 마음을 바꿀 가능성이 없냐는 질문에 부적절한 답변이다. No way라고 했으므로 '고집이 세다'는 표현의 'as stubborn as a mule'이 대화의 흐름상 적절하다.

☐ on time 제시간에 ☐ as sure as death 확실히, 틀림없이 ☐ as proud as a peacock 건방진, 의기양양한, 거만한 ☐ as dry as a bone (뼈처럼) 바싹 마른, 앙상한 ☐ as cute as a button (여성·어린아이 등이) 귀여운

① A: 제시간에 끝낼 가능성이 꽤 큰가요?
   B: 네, 죽음만큼이나(아주) 확실합니다.
② A: 그녀가 자신의 실수를 인정할 것 같나요?
   B: 아닐걸요. 그녀는 정말 거만해요.
③ A: 그가 마음을 바꿀 가능성은 없나요?
   B: 말도 안 돼요. 그는 정말 메말랐어요.
④ A: 새로 태어난 아기를 보셨나요? 어때요?
   B: 정말 귀엽네요.

02 ②

② A가 말한 move up the meeting은 '회의를 앞당기다'의 의미이므로, B가 말하는 '나중에 만나고 싶어요'라는 말과 어울리지 않는다.

☐ swing it 어떤 일을 잘 해내다 ☐ move up the meeting 회의를 앞당기다 ☐ out of the blue 느닷없이 ☐ on a shoestring 적은 돈으로 ☐ a feather in one's cap 특별한 자랑거리 ☐ rack one's brain 머리를 짜서 생각하다, 생각해내려 애쓰다 ☐ keep one's head above water 빚 안 지고 살아가다 ☐ hard up 재정적으로 힘든

① A: 영화 보러 갈까요?
   B: 그러고 싶지만, 오늘은 그럴 수 없네요.
② A: 회의를 앞당길 수 있나요?
   B: 좋은 생각이네요. 그들을 나중에 만나고 싶어요.
③ A: 그는 갑자기 빈손으로 사업을 시작했습니다.
   B: 그게 정말 자랑이죠.
④ A: 어떻게든 적자를 면할 방법을 찾으려고 머리를 싸매고 노력하고 있습니다.
   B: 그렇게 힘든 줄 몰랐어요.

03 ③

③ A가 B에게 도움을 요청했는데, B가 꿈을 깨라(어림도 없다)고 답을 한 다음에, A에게 "뭐 좀 물어봐도 되니?"라고 질문을 하고 있으므로 대화의 흐름이 어색하다.

☐ cool ad. 좋아, 그래 ☐ just the job (특정 상황에 필요한) 바로 그것 ☐ dash v. (급히) 서둘러 가다 ☐ break a leg 행운을 빌다 ☐ give someone a hand ~을 돕다 ☐ in your dreams 꿈같은 얘기로군(가망 없는 꿈을 꾸고 있다는 뜻) ☐ stock n. 주식 ☐ all time 역대 ☐ get one's head round something ~을 이해하다

① A: 브라이언, 이 카메라가 네가 찾던 거니?
   B: 그래. 바로 그거야!
② A: 아, 벌써 12시 35분이야. 12시 40분에 약속이 또 하나 있는데.
   B: 서둘러 가야겠구나. 행운을 빈다.
③ A: 션, 이번에는 네 도움이 필요해. 좀 도와줄래?
   B: 꿈 깨. 내가 뭐 좀 물어봐도 되니?
④ A: 기술 관련주가 역대 최고로 오를걸!
   B: 이해할 수가 없네. 왜 그렇게 생각해?

04 ①

① 그가 수산시장에서 물건을 잘 판매하는 사람이냐는 질문에 B가 Yes 라고 답을 했으므로 그가 물건을 잘 판다는 내용이 적절하다. 그런데, 그가 종종 주의를 딴 데로 돌린다고 했으므로 대화의 흐름이 어색하다.

☐ throw a red herring 주의를 딴 데로 돌리다 ☐ give somebody the creeps 소름끼치게 하다 ☐ sleepwalk v. 몽유병 증세를 보이다 ☐ lose one's bearings 방향을 잃다, 어찌할 바를 모르다 ☐ punctual a. 시간을 엄수하는 ☐ as good as one's bond 반드시 약속을 지키는

① A: 그는 수산시장에서 판매를 잘 하지?
   B: 그래. 그는 종종 주의를 딴 데로 돌려.
② A: 잭슨을 보면 난 소름끼쳐.
   B: 맞아! 늘 밤에 몽유병 환자처럼 돌아다니잖아.
③ A: 그 사람은 지난주에 그렇게도 많은 시간을 보내면서 왜 아무것도 하지 않았는지 모르겠어.
   B: 아마, 어찌할 바를 몰랐을 거야.
④ A: 그는 항상 회사에서 시간을 엄수해.
   B: 맞아, 그의 말은 보증수표나 마찬가지야.

05 ③

③ A가 이 술이 무료라는 것을 알고 있냐는 질문을 했으므로, 그 술은 무료임을 알 수 있다. 그런데 B가 자신이 술값을 계산하겠다고 답했으므로 어색하다.

☐ jump all over someone ~을 비난하다 ☐ lend someone a hand 도움을 주다 ☐ on the house 무료의 ☐ pay the earth for ~의 값을

지불하다 □ spill the beans 무심코 비밀을 누설하다 □ you bet 물론이지 □ lips are sealed 비밀을 굳게 지키다

① A: 조에게 무슨 일 있니?
　 B: 상사가 오늘 아침 그를 야단쳐서 기분이 안 좋아.
② A: 나 좀 도와줄 수 있어?
　 B: 지금 숙제해야 해. 끝내고 도와줄게.
③ A: 이 술이 무료라는 것 알고 있어?
　 B: 걱정 마. 내가 낼게.
④ A: 비밀을 누설해선 안 돼.
　 B: 물론이지! 비밀 꼭 지킬 거야.

06　　　　　　　　　　　　　　　　　④

④ A가 힘든 상황에 있다고 했으므로, B는 기운 내라는 정도의 말을 해야 하는데, 주인 노릇을 하게 해줄게라는 대답은 어색하다.

□ high and dry (사람이) 먹고 살 길이 막막한, 고립무원의 □ make the best of ~을 극복하다, ~을 최대한 활용하다 □ wear out one's welcome 너무 오래 머물러 미움 사다 □ thesis n. 논문 □ take the bull by the horn 문제에 정면으로 맞서다 □ up a (gum) tree 진퇴양난[곤경]에 빠져 □ do the honors 공식적인 일을 맡아 하다, 주인 노릇하다

① A: 형편이 어려워졌다니 유감이다.
　 B: 그래. 이대로 무너지지는 않을 거야. 꼭 이겨낼 거야.
② A: 며칠 더 있다 가면 안 돼?
　 B: 아니야. 너무 오래 있어서 눈총 받고 싶지 않아.
③ A: 이 논문을 다 못 쓸 것 같아.
　 B: 문제를 회피하지 말고 정면으로 맞서 봐.
④ A: 이봐, 나 오늘 힘들어.
　 B: 주인 노릇 하게 해줄게.

07　　　　　　　　　　　　　　　　　②

②에서 A가 게임을 같이 하자고 B에게 물어봤는데, B가 너희들이 완전히 망해서 기분이 좋다고 했으므로 대화의 흐름상 부적절하다.

□ have a lot on one's plate 해야 할 일이 산더미처럼 있다 □ screwed a. 망가진, 엉망이 된 □ stock market 주식 시장 □ naive a. 순진한 □ grow on trees 쉽게 손에 들어오다[생기다] □ let it aside 그냥 내버려두다, 더 이상 언급하지 않다

① A: 이봐, 라이언. 내 부탁 하나 들어줄래?
　 B: 나도 할 일이 많아. 하지만 뭔데?
② A: 오늘밤에 게임을 하려는데 너도 같이 할래?
　 B: 물론. 너희들이 완전히 망해서 난 너무 기뻐.
③ A: 매기, 주식 시장에서 이 부문에 돈을 투자하면 큰돈을 벌 수 있어.
　 B: 순진하게 굴지 말자. 돈은 그렇게 쉽게 생기지 않아.
④ A: 부인, 부인은 트랜스내셔널 1번 고속도로에서 150마일로 달리셔서 속도위반을 하셨어요.
　 B: 경관님, 제발 좀 넘어가 주실 수 없을까요?

08　　　　　　　　　　　　　　　　　②

② 그가 오늘도 수업에 빠졌다는 A의 말에 B가 Yes라고 대답했으므로

이에 상응하는 말이 이어져야 하는데, B는 그가 청소를 돕기 원한다는 동문서답을 하므로 ②가 대화의 흐름상 부적절하다.

□ come up with ~을 생각해내다 □ peculiar a. 이상한, 특이한, 기이한 □ off the wall 특이한 □ skive off 뺑소니치다; (수업에) 빠지다 □ scoff v. 게걸스레 먹다 □ faff around v. 정신없이 돌아다니다

① A: 어떻게 그녀가 그렇게 특이한 아이디어를 생각해냈는지 모르겠어!
　 B: 내 생각에도 그녀의 몇몇 아이디어는 종종 정말 특이해.
② A: 그는 늘 그렇듯 오늘도 수업에 빠졌어.
　 B: 그래. 그는 항상 청소를 돕고 싶어 해.
③ A: 그는 점심식사 때 국수를 게걸스레 먹더군.
　 B: 아마도 오늘 아침밥을 걸렀을 거야.
④ A: 도서관에서 정신없이 돌아다녔어.
　 B: 보고 싶은 책은 찾았어?

09　　　　　　　　　　　　　　　　　③

③에서 A가 자신의 행위로 인해 누나에게 혼나는 것이 '자업자득이다, 인과응보다'라는 식으로 말하였는데 B가 그 말에 대해 '그래, 나라면 억울할 것 같다'고 말하는 것은 자연스럽지 않다.

□ poles apart 전혀 다른, 정반대인 □ high and dry 먹고 살길이 막막한, 속수무책으로 버려진, 빈털터리의 □ make the best of ~을 최대한 이용하다, (역경·불리한 조건 따위)를 어떻게든 견뎌내다 □ have it coming (자업자득으로) 당연한 응보를 받다 □ bitter a. 억울해하는, 몹시 분한 □ take the load off 짐[부담]을 내려놓다

① A: 많은 이들이 샘과 책이 많이 닮았다고들 하는데, 나는 이해가 안 돼.
　 B: 나도 마찬가지야. 오히려 그 두 사람은 완전히 다른걸.
② A: 친구가 너를 빈털터리로 만들었다니 유감이야.
　 B: 그래. 나는 이걸로 망가지진 않겠어. 어떻게든 견뎌낼 거야.
③ A: 누나가 내게 아주 화를 냈지만 그건 나의 자업자득인 것 같아.
　 B: 그러게, 내가 너라면 정말 분할 거야.
④ A: 들어와요. 자리에 앉고 짐을 좀 내려놓아요.
　 B: 감사합니다. 오늘 하루 종일 걸었거든요.

10　　　　　　　　　　　　　　　　　④

④에서 A가 '그 사람과 의견이 항상 일치한다'고 했는데, B가 '그 사람과 함께 일하기 힘들다'고 응답하는 것은 자연스럽지 않다.

□ spell out 상세히 설명하다 □ hit the spot 딱 그것이다 □ you're getting colder 정답으로부터 점점 더 멀어지고 있다 □ see eye to eye with ~와 견해가 완전히 일치하다

① A: 그 도시에서 레스토랑을 운영하는 게 얼마나 어려운지 당신은 모를 겁니다.
　 B: 저도 거기 가봤거든요. 자세히 설명 안 하셔도 압니다.
② A: 맛있는 핫 초콜릿 한 잔 어때요?
　 B: 오, 딱 좋겠는데요.
③ A: 이거 정답이야?
　 B: 아니, 점점 더 멀어지고 있어.
④ A: 나는 항상 그와 의견이 완전히 일치해.
　 B: 오, 그는 정말 함께 일하기 정말 힘들어.

11
① A가 '그가 나에게 화풀이를 한다'고 하는데 B가 '너의 노력에 고마워서 그렇다'라고 한다면, 이는 전혀 엉뚱한 대답이라고 할 수 있다.

□ take out on ~에게 화풀이를 하다 □ have it in one to V ~할 능력[역량]이 있다 □ give ~ the creeps ~를 소름 끼치게 하다 □ take ~ in ~을 받아들이다, 이해하다 □ keen on ~에 관심이 많은

① A: 그는 그 결과에 대해 내게 화풀이를 하는 것 같아.
　 B: 맞아, 그는 너의 노력에 정말 고마워하지.
② A: 그녀는 그 일을 감당할 능력이 없어.
　 B: 나도 동의해. 그녀가 그런 업무를 수행하려면 더 많은 경험이 필요해.
③ A: 나는 한밤중에 괴물 영화를 보는 건 싫어.
　 B: 나도 마찬가지야. 그런 영화는 소름 끼쳐.
④ A: 너는 이해하지도 못하면서 왜 그 강의를 들었던 거니?
　 B: 나는 그것에 대해 관심이 많거든.

12
③에서 A가 말하는 '좋을 때만 친구(곤경에 처하면 등을 돌리는 친구)'와 B가 말하는 '어려울 때 친구(진정한 친구)'는 반대되는 개념이므로, 한 사람의 태도를 표현하는 말로서는 서로 모순된다.

□ teed off 짜증이 난, 화가 난 □ flip out 벌컥 화를 내다 □ have it coming to ~가 (인과응보로 안 좋은 일을) 당하다, 그런 일을 당해 마땅하다 □ You're telling me! 내 말이 바로 그 말이에요(전적으로 동의해요)! □ know better 어리석지 않다 □ fair-weather a. 날씨가 좋을 때만의, 유리할 때만의 □ the chips are down 상황이 불리해지다, 힘든 상황이 닥치다

① A: 매리가 또 짜증을 내.
　 B: 그녀는 친구가 아무 연락도 없이 찾아오면 늘 화를 내.
② A: 그는 마땅히 당해야 할 일을 당했어.
　 B: 내 말이 바로 그 말이야. 그는 좀 더 지각 있게 굴어야 해.
③ A: 도널드(Donald)는 나에게 좋을 때만 친구야.
　 B: 그래, 그는 정말 어려울 때의 친구지.
④ A: 내가 너를 원할 때 나를 돕기 위해 와줘서 정말 기뻐.
　 B: 우리는 모두 어려울 때 의지할 사람이 필요하잖아.

13
④에서 A는 그 영화가 흥행에 실패했다고 말했는데, B는 이에 대해 놀라움을 표현한 뒤 백만 명의 관객을 모았다고 했으므로, A와 B가 그 영화의 흥행에 대해 서로 다른 이야기를 하고 있다. 따라서 ④가 대화의 흐름상 적절하지 않다.

□ greenhorn n. 미숙한 사람, 초심자, 풋내기 □ rank a. (특정한 상태 등을 강조하여) 순전한 □ put somebody up for the night ~를 하룻밤 묵게 하다 □ sleep over (남의 집에) 묵다 □ call it quits (일 등을) 일단락 짓다, (오늘은) 이만 하기로 하다 □ tie up the loose ends 결말을 짓다, 매듭짓다, 끝마무리하다 □ lay an egg (익살·흥행 따위가) 완전히 실패하다

① A: 그는 음악을 알고 있는 것처럼 말하지만, 그는 여전히 풋내기야.
　 B: 맞아, 그는 순전히 아마추어야.
② A: 하룻밤 재워줄 수 있나요?
　 B: 물론이죠, 저희 집에 와서 주무셔도 됩니다.
③ A: 오늘은 이만하기로 하자.
　 B: 좋아, 월요일에 마무리 지을 수 있을 거야.
④ A: 그 영화는 흥행에 완전히 실패했어.
　 B: 굉장한데, 그 영화가 총 백만 명의 관람객을 모았다고 들었어.

14
②에서 A가 이번에는 내 생각대로 할 거라고 했는데, B는 이에 대한 대답으로 Right라고 했다. 따라서 Right 다음에는 A의 의견에 동조하는 말이 필요한데, 참을성이 필요하다고 했으므로 ②가 대화의 흐름상 적절하지 않다.

□ drive it to the last minute 마지막까지 질질 끌다 □ let oneself loose 거리낌 없이 말하다, 자기 생각대로 하다 □ put your cards on the table 생각을 정직하게 말하다, 속내를 털어놓다 □ a flash in the pan 반짝[일시적인] 성공

① A: 끝까지 물고 늘어져라.
　 B: 아니, 포기할거야.
② A: 이번에는 내 생각대로 할 거야.
　 B: 맞아, 너는 인내심이 필요해.
③ A: 솔직하게 말해봐.
　 B: 하지만 나는 네가 화낼까봐 걱정돼.
④ A: 짐은 그의 소설로 명성을 얻었어.
　 B: 그것은 일시적인 성공일 뿐이야.

15
①의 대화문에서 get well은 '병이 나아지다, 쾌유하다'는 의미이다. 그런데 blow hot and cold는 '변덕이 심하다'는 의미이므로, '그녀의 상태가 좀 나아졌는가?'하고 묻는 물음에 어울리지 않는 대답이다.

□ get well 병이 나아지다 □ blow hot and cold 이랬다저랬다 하다, 변덕이 심하다 □ let up 느슨해지다 □ make a nuisance of oneself 다른 사람들을 성가시게 하다, 폐를 끼치다 □ black sheep 골칫덩어리, 말썽꾼 □ drag one's feet 꾸물거리다

① A: 오늘은 그녀가 좀 나아졌습니까?
　 B: 그녀는 변덕이 심했어요.
② A: 정말로 우리는 휴식이 필요해요.
　 B: 잠깐 일을 멈추고 커피나 좀 마십시다.
③ A: 그는 계속 다른 사람들에게 폐를 끼치고 있어요.
　 B: 맞아요, 정말 골칫덩어리죠.
④ A: 오늘 또 직장에 지각할 순 없어요.
　 B: 물론이죠, 꾸물거리지 맙시다.

16
② 테니스를 치러 가자는 제안에 대해 '그래요(Sure)'라고 한 후에, '일이 너무 많아 쩔쩔매고 있다'고 말하는 것은 흐름이 적절하지 않다.

□ thumb one's nose at ~에 대해 비웃다 □ a fair shake 공평한 기회, 공정한 조처 □ be snowed under (많은 일에) 파묻히다, 쩔쩔매다 □ chomp at the bit 안달하다, 빨리하고 싶어 못 견디다 □ hear through the grapevine 소문으로 소식을 듣다

① A: 라이언, 난 네 생각이 마음에 들지 않아. 너무 급진적이야.
   B: 아, 왜 그래? 공평한 기회조차 주지 않고 비웃지는 마.
② A: 우리랑 테니스 치러 가지 않을래요?
   B: 그래요, 일이 너무 많아 쩔쩔매고 있어요.
③ A: 그 새 영화 너무 기대돼.
   B: 맞아. 많은 영화팬들이 그 영화를 보고 싶어 안달이야.
④ A: 어제 밤 모임에 많은 새로운 얼굴들이 등장했는데.
   B: 그 행사가 와볼만 하다는 소문을 들었었나봐.

17   ③

"Tom의 말이 옳았다."라는 표현에서 Tom이 일찍이 이 영화가 좋지 않다고 경고했음을 짐작할 수 있다. Tom의 견해와 A의 말에 동의한 뒤에 다시 "Tom은 자신의 말을 취소해야 한다."라고 말하는 것은 대화의 흐름상 적절하지 않다.

□ turn the table 형세를 역전시키고 우위를 차지하다 □ at[to] six(es) and seven(s) 난잡하게, 혼란하게 □ I can't agree more 전적으로 동의해(= I fully agree) □ eat one's words 먼저 한 말을 취소하다, 자신의 잘못을 인정하다 □ flat on one's back (병 따위로) 누워 있기만 하는 □ rush back to 시급히 ~에 돌아가다 □ under the weather 몸이 안 좋은

① A: 그 경주에서 마이크는 어땠니?
   B: 그는 형세를 역전시키고 결국 경주에서 이겼어.
② A: 안녕, 제니! 그동안 어떻게 지냈니?
   B: 얼마 전에 새로 이사를 와서 모든 것이 혼란스러워.
③ A: 톰이 옳았어. 이 영화는 정말 최악이야!
   B: 네 말에 전적으로 동의해. 톰이 자기 말을 취소해야 돼.
④ A: 이번 감기가 떨어지질 않아요. 일주일째 꼼짝 못 하고 있어요.
   B: 너무 서둘러 다시 출근하려 하지 마세요. 당신이 몸이 안 좋다는 것을 우리는 잘 알고 있어요.

18   ④

마라톤 대회 후원사에서 기금을 지원하겠다는 말에 대한 응답으로는 '잘 된 일이다'와 같은 표현이 적절하지, '수수방관하는 것이 더 낫다'는 말은 바람직한 표현이 아니다.

□ under the gun 스트레스를 많이 받는 □ rough it 잠시 불편한 생활을 하다 □ sit on the sidelines 방관하다

① A: 데이비드, 너 오늘 피곤해 보인다. 무슨 일 있었니?
   B: 여자 친구 아버지에게 좋은 인상을 주느라고 스트레스를 많이 받았어.
② A: 그 순회 서커스단은 어디로 떠났습니까?
   B: 그들은 항상 이리저리 이동합니다.
③ A: 깔고 앉는 야외용 돗자리 가져왔니?
   B: 맙소사, 완전히 잊어버렸어. 이번에는 잠시 불편하게 지내야 하겠다.

④ A: 우리가 참가하는 마라톤 대회의 후원사에서 1마일당 1달러씩 지불하겠다고 약속했어.
   B: 너는 방관하는 것이 더 좋겠다.

19   ①

①에 쓰인 go by the book은 '원리원칙대로 하다'는 의미이므로, '책에 대해 값을 높게 책정하고 있다'고 한 대답은 자연스럽지 않다.

□ go by the book 원리원칙대로 하다, 규칙대로 하다 □ deliver the goods 제 할 일을 하다, 기대에 부응하다 □ chew the fat 오래 담소를 나누다, 수다 떨다 □ in the pink 기력이 왕성한, 매우 건강한 □ (as) fit as a fiddle (신체가) 아주 팽팽한[탄탄한]

① A: 빈스(Vince)가 항상 원리원칙대로 하는 것을 알고 보니 재밌지 않니?
   B: 그러게 말이야. 빈스는 분명히 그것에 많은 요금을 책정하고 있어.
② A: 네 차를 고쳐 줄 뛰어난 정비사를 찾았니?
   B: 새 정비사에게 수리를 맡겼어. 그가 제대로 고쳐주길 바라고 있어.
③ A: 어제 아침 내내 너한테 전화했었어. 누구랑 통화하고 있었니?
   B: 베티(Betty)랑 수다 떨고 있었어.
④ A: 할아버지는 언제나 기력이 왕성하셔서 아직도 등산을 가셔.
   B: 건강해 보이시는 게 당연하구나.

20   ③

③의 promise the moon이라는 표현은 '(하늘의 달도 따다 준다며) 지키지 못할 약속을 하다, 얼토당토않은 약속을 하다'라는 의미이다. 불필요한 자리에 들어가서 의미전달을 그르치고 있다.

□ have one's heart in one's mouth[throat] 몹시 놀라다 □ pull up one's socks 정신을 차리고 새로 시작하다 □ promise the moon 엉터리 약속을 하다 □ hunt high and low 이곳저곳을 찾아다니다

① A: 잘 했어, 닐. 넌 전혀 당황하지 않는데.
   B: 웬걸, 내가 말할 차례가 되자, 거의 정신이 다 나갔지.
② A: 계속 이런 식이면 아무데도 갈 수 없다는 걸 존(John)은 알지 못할까?
   B: 그러게요. 만약 그가 대학진학에 대해 진지하게 생각한다면, 그는 정신 바짝 차려야 할 거에요.
③ A: 아하! 너 드디어 여자 친구를 찾았구나, 그렇지 않니?
   B: 그래. 이제 더 이상 나를 걱정할 필요는 없어. 지금 넌 엉터리 약속을 하고 있어.
④ A: 이 음식 정말 맛있는데요! 어디서 그 요리법을 구하셨어요?
   B: 그걸 찾으려고 인터넷 여기저기를 다 뒤져봤지요.

21   ②

'미스터 김이 미스 박에게 푹 빠져 있다'는 말에 대해 '시류에 편승하거나 유행을 쫓아가다'라고 이야기하는 것은 동문서답으로 볼 수 있다.

□ go over with a fine tooth comb 면밀히 조사하다, 철저히 수사하다 □ be head over heels 푹 빠져 있다 □ get on the bandwagon 시류에 편승하다 □ by halves 불완전하게 □ land on one's feet 궁지에서 벗어나다

① A: 새로 산 다이아몬드 목걸이를 도저히 못 찾겠어!
　　B: 걱정하지 마! 우리가 집을 샅샅이 찾아볼게.
② A: 소문에 의하면 미스터 김이 미스 박에게 푹 빠져 있다는데.
　　B: 좋은 일이지, 그들도 시류에 편승해야지.
③ A: 줄리는 정말 요리를 잘하죠?
　　B: 예, 정말 그래요. 그녀가 요리를 하면, 최고급 정찬이 되죠. 그녀는 무엇이든 철저하게 합니다!
④ A: 밥의 회사가 파산했다는 소식을 들었어.
　　B: 밥에 대해서는 걱정하지 마. 그는 항상 궁지에서 벗어나거든.

22
④

트럭에 치일 뻔한 아찔한 상황에 대해 이야기하고 있으므로 이에 대한 대답으로는 다치지 않았는지 묻는 등의 염려하는 표현이 와야 적절하다.

☐ an act of God 천재지변, 불가항력 ☐ rub salt in[into] somebody's wound 사태를 더욱 악화시키다, 불난 집에 부채질하다 ☐ John Hancock (누구의) 자필 서명 ☐ give me a break 그만 좀 해; 좀 봐줘 ☐ sleep on (하룻밤 자며) 심사숙고하다 ☐ get back 대답하다, 답장을 주다 ☐ bear down ~을 향해 돌진하다 ☐ one's number is up 곤경에 빠지다; 운이 다하다 ☐ make one's (own) bed (구어) 불행을 자초하다

① A: 그 파티에 갈거니?
　　B: 천재지변이 나면 몰라도 꼭 갈 거야.
② A: 내 생각엔 너의 행동이 그의 기분을 더 악화시킨 것 같아.
　　B: 그래. 내가 그 문제에 대해 그의 기분을 더 나빠지게 한 것 같아 걱정돼.
③ A: 점선 위에 당신의 자필 서명을 하세요.
　　B: 좀 봐줘요. 좀 더 생각해보고 답변을 드릴게요.
④ A: 커다란 트럭이 내게 돌진하는 것을 보면서, 내 운이 다했다고 생각했죠.
　　B: 불행을 자초하신 거군요!

23
①

①의 대화에서 저녁식사를 했는지 묻고 있는데 식사와는 전혀 관계없는 물건을 산 것에 대해 답하고 있으므로 대화의 흐름이 적절하지 않다.

☐ buy a pig in a poke 잘 모르고 물건을 사다 ☐ be sitting pretty 유리한 입장에 있다; 안락한 생활을 하고 있다, 쾌적한 상태에 있다 ☐ jockey n. 〈경마〉 기수; 운전자 ☐ play at one's best 최선을 다하다 ☐ down to the wire 끝까지(결승선까지) ☐ cut the mustard 기대만큼 성과를 올리다

① A: 벌써 저녁식사 하셨나요?
　　B: 예, 나는 잘 모르고 물건을 샀어요.
② A: 밥과 젠이 그들의 주택을 팔았을 때 좋은 가격을 받았다고 들었어요.
　　B: 예, 그들은 그랬죠. 이제 그들은 정말로 안락한 생활을 하고 있죠.
③ A: 누가 경주에서 이길지 모르겠어요. 모든 기수들이 최선을 다하고 있어요.
　　B: 제 생각에는 경주는 끝까지 가봐야 알 것 같아요.
④ A: 나는 오늘 마이크(Mike)를 해고해야 했어. 그는 결코 업무를 제시간에 끝낸 적이 없어.
　　B: 기대만큼 성과를 올리지 못하는 사람들이 있어.

24
④

④에서 A가 "그는 우리가 벌이고 있는 자선모금 활동에 참여 하길 원치 않는다"고 했는데, B는 "쥐구멍에도 볕들 날이 오겠지(고생을 하는 사람도 좋은 때를 만날 적이 있다)"라고 동문서답하고 있다.

☐ eat one's hat 도저히 그럴 리가 없다; 손에 장을 지지다 ☐ get what one bargained for 자업자득이다 ☐ the icing on the cake 금상첨화 ☐ Every dog has his day. 쥐구멍에도 볕들 날 있다.

① A: 나는 그가 기말시험에서 최고의 성적을 낼 거라고 확신해요.
　　B: 그런 일이 일어난다면, 내가 손에 장을 지지겠어요.
② A: 저는 그 거래에서 큰돈을 잃었어요.
　　B: 자업자득이에요.
③ A: 그 해변에서 즐거운 휴가를 보냈어. 더구나, 여러 해 동안 못 봤던 오랜 친구도 우연히 만났지.
　　B: 금상첨화였겠네.
④ A: 그는 우리가 벌이고 있는 자선모금 활동에 참여 하길 원치 않아.
　　B: 쥐구멍에도 볕들 날이 오겠지.

25
③

자동차 고장이 너무 빈번하게 발생한다는 문제를 말하고 있기 때문에 이에 대한 대답으로는 어떤 해결책을 제시하는 대답이나 유감을 나타내는 대답이 적절하다.

☐ the fish that got away 애석하게도 놓친 것 ☐ A soft answer turns away wrath. 부드러운 말이 분노를 누른다.(웃는 낯에 침 뱉으랴.) ☐ If it were a snake, it would bite you. 뱀이었으면 하마터면 물릴 뻔했다.(물건을 한참 동안 찾지 못하다가 바로 옆에 있는 것을 발견하고서 쓰는 말임. 미국 남부 지방에 뱀이 많아서 생긴 표현임.)

① A: 지금 내가 하고 있는 일에 대해, 10년 전에 두 배는 더 받을 수 있었을 텐데 그러지 못 했어.
　　B: 안 됐지만, 이미 지나간 일이야.
② A: 나는 그를 심하게 질책하고 싶었는데 흥분을 가라앉히고 점잖게 대하려고 했어.
　　B: 부드러운 말은 (상대방의) 화를 누그러뜨리는 법이지.
③ A: 내 차는 고장이 너무 잦아.
　　B: 부러워 죽겠다.
④ A: 자동차 키를 찾고 있는데, 아직도 못 찾겠어.
　　B: 테이블 위에 있잖아. 바로 코앞에 있는데, 뱀이었으면 벌써 물렸겠다.

Memo